# Manufacturing Organization
# and Management

PRENTICE-HALL INTERNATIONAL, INC., *London*
PRENTICE-HALL OF AUSTRALIA, PTY. LTD., *Sydney*
PRENTICE-HALL OF CANADA, LTD., *Toronto*
PRENTICE-HALL OF INDIA (PRIVATE) LTD., *New Delhi*
PRENTICE-HALL OF JAPAN, INC., *Tokyo*

# Manufacturing Organization and Management

**Second Edition**

Harold T. Amrine

*Professor and Head*
*School of Industrial Engineering*
*Purdue University*

John A. Ritchey

*Professor of Industrial Engineering*
*Purdue University*

Oliver S. Hulley

*Manager-Manufacturing Education Service*
*General Electric Company*

PRENTICE-HALL, INC., *Englewood Cliffs, New Jersey*

Current Printing (last digit):
10  9  8  7  6  5  4  3  2  1

Library of Congress Catalog Card Number 66-19881
*Printed in the United States of America*
55578C

# Preface

The purpose of this book is to acquaint the person inexperienced in the field of management with the principles and functions of manufacturing management. Because the material is presented in a non-technical manner, it is suitable for both engineers and non-engineers. It is also well-suited for undergraduate courses as well as graduate-student instruction when the graduate student has had little contact with the areas concerned.

Primary emphasis is placed on functions that usually are controlled by the manager of manufacturing. However, the areas of marketing, finance, and personnel are amply included to show the interrelationship between these areas and overall management problems. Chapters dealing with these related areas have been grouped together in a separate section, making it easier for an instructor to include or exclude them in his course as he sees fit. Other chapters have been regrouped for this edition in order to provide a more logical arrangement of material in terms of modern manufacturing theory and practice.

Many new developments have taken place since the first edition of this book was published. Because of these changes, much new material has been added on automation, operations research, value engineering, PERT, work sampling, maintenance engineering, reliability, and other recent developments. Although the book is somewhat longer than the previous edition, we offer it as a condensed version of the principles of manufacturing management, including the philosophy and practices of management generally.

Case problems and discussion questions appear at the end of most chapters and can serve as a sound basis for discussing the principles of manufacturing management as discussed in the given chapter. Instructors may wish to introduce additional questions or problems of their own, in particular some problems requiring quantitative solutions. The basis for quantitative problems has been provided in many cases, although we have not emphasized the quantitative aspects of management.

Our appreciation is extended to the many companies, publishers, and individuals who have furnished illustrations and other materials for this book. We are also deeply indebted to our many colleagues at Purdue University and elsewhere who have offered constructive criticism and suggestions for improvement. To fail to mention by name the many persons who have assisted in the production of this revised edition is in no way to minimize our gratitude for their efforts. Although we have made liberal use of the suggestions and comments of our friends and colleagues, we bear full responsibility for the results.

H.T.A.

J.A.R.

O.S.H.

*West Lafayette, Indiana*

# Contents

# Manufacturing Organization
# and Management

# Manufacturing Management—
# Past, Present, and Future

# CHAPTER ONE

# Productivity and
# Manufacturing Management

Recent years have led to many changes in the composition of world society. There has been rapid economic expansion, reasonably stable employment, an upsurge in nationalism, rapid rise in world population, industrialization of backward nations, and a general world-wide demand for higher standards of living. All of this has led to much attention being focused on productivity. To get some idea of the stress being placed on this topic, one need but pick up his daily newspaper or newsmagazine and read about the goals being established or achievements claimed.

One of the inevitable goals of manufacturing management is increased productivity. Since many of the functions that we shall be discussing in this book have a direct bearing on productivity, it seems only fitting that we devote part of this introductory chapter to an overview of this subject. At the outset, let us distinguish between *production* and *productivity*. Production is the output of the productive forces, whereas productivity is a measure of the output resulting from a given input—such as the number of radios assembled by a crew in one hour.

## Productivity in the United States

For many years, the United States has been looked to as the acme of high productivity. It has been singled out as symbolizing the ultimate in industrial attainment, and many people have visited the United States in an effort to study its manufacturing and distribution methods with a view to introducing these into their nations. What has the United States done to deserve this attention? What are its accomplishments? A review of the latest economic figures would reveal that the per capita output (converted to a dollars per person basis) in the United States would be about 30 per cent higher than the next highest country (Canada). If the productivity of labor in manufacturing in the United States can be assumed to be about 100 per cent, then that of the next highest country would be only about 80 per cent. If we wished to compare the purchasing power of employees, we would find that it requires fewer minutes of work in the United States to earn the price of a loaf of bread, a pair of shoes, or a new car than anywhere else in the world.

Although the United States has been looked to as having great knowledge about productivity, it is interesting to note that our experts on the subject aren't in complete agreement as to exactly what it means or how to measure it. There has been a tendency to use the figures on production per man-hour, put out by the Bureau of Labor Statistics, as an indication of productivity levels, but these are somewhat deficient because they are based on census figures and are always several years late for corrective action. Then again, output per man-hour tells only half the story because it measures productivity solely in terms of labor, whereas capital in the form of machines and physical facilities also plays an important role. Thus, productivity becomes very complex and really designates the balance between all factors of production that will give the greatest ouput for the smallest effort, or input.

Despite our inability to measure productivity accurately, there is one thing that appears to be agreed upon, and that is that increased productivity in the long run is never achieved by increased worker effort. The real growth in productivity can come about only through capital investment in newer and better machines, equipment, and facilities. In addition, as Peter Drucker points out, "At least as important but unexplored is the increase in productivity achieved by replacing manual labor, whether skilled or unskilled, by educated, analytical, theoretical personnel—the replacement of 'labor' by managers, technicians, and professionals; the substitution of 'planning' for 'working.' Obviously, this substitution must take place before capital equipment is installed to replace men's animal energy; for someone must plan and design the equipment—a conceptual, theoretical and analytical task."[1]

Studies, such as that performed by Stanford Research Institute,[2] disclose that the productivity differential between the United States and Western Europe is not solely a matter of capital investment. In many cases their

---

[1]Peter Drucker, *The Practice of Management* (New York: Harper and Sons Company, 1955), p. 34.

[2]Drucker, *ibid.*, p. 34.

companies are as well-equipped as ours, and yet productivity is as much as two-thirds below that of their United States counterparts. The only explanation is the smaller proportion of managers and technicians they use and the poor organization structure of European industry. Many United States companies are spending almost as much on managerial, technical, and professional personnel as on direct labor. And as the complexity of manufacturing increases there is every reason to believe that this trend will continue.

Before getting further into some of the factors that may have influenced productivity in the United States, let us dwell for a few moments on the social and economic background of industry in the United States.

## Social and Economic Background of American Industry

Because of her early democratic philosophy, the United States developed as a "classless" society composed of a "melting pot" of people. People from many foreign countries brought with them their own customs and ideas and made their unique contributions to a conglomerate society. Newcomers and their descendents became aware that in the United States the opportunity to succeed and to be judged on the basis of accomplishments was the ideal. Thus, the country's growth was built on the achievements of men such as Henry Ford, Andrew Carnegie, and many others. Those who have been successful in business have been looked to with great respect in America and came to be considered the "cream" of American society.

In 1890, at about the time the United States was changing from being principally an agricultural nation, the Sherman Antitrust Act was passed. This law was designed to protect against monopolies by declaring that any combination in restraint of trade among the states was illegal. The rigid enforcement of this national policy prevented price-fixing, the formation of cartels, and other practices common in some European countries. Because of the limitations imposed by this law, the managers of the businesses in the United States accepted the concept of true competition and concentrated their attention on ways in which they could increase their volume of business. The spirit of competition has continued unabated, and *competition* is the keynote among American businessmen. Many people consider competition to be the most important single factor leading to the development of the United States as a great industrial nation.

The United States, as a result of its early immigration policy, has been blessed with an ever increasing population. The result of this ever increasing population has been to provide an adequate supply of labor and a large internal market that has been conducive to mass production. A large population is not synonymous with high production or national prosperity, however, as is evidenced by India. Rather, it is the combination of a large and growing population, high real wages, and a desire for material goods that has led to mass production in the United States.

Many trade-union advocates argue that the strong unions that developed in the United States have had significant influence on the level of productivity attained. They contend that the continuous pressure put on management for higher wages, shorter working hours, pension plans, and other benefits has forced management to reduce costs and to operate businesses efficiently. There may be a considerable element of truth in this assertion, but at the same time, there has been a tendency for certain unions to resort to restrictive practices and to slow progress. Despite this, however, the unions undoubtedly have contributed markedly in other and more constructive ways. For example, as Kerr has pointed out, "The great necessity for and contribution of unions is their participation in rule-making. This participation is one of the greatest guarantees of order and stability in industrial society where interdependence and complexity make order and stability primary requirements. This is an almost overwhelming consideration when evaluating the impact of nonrevolutionary unionism and is the primary contribution of unionism to the long-term productivity of society broadly viewed."[3]

Not one of the least significant factors contributing to the industrial development in the United States has been our educational system, founded on the philosophy that it is the right of everyone to have an education. This has led to a system of higher education capable of producing the great numbers of engineers, scientists, accountants, and others possessing the necessary skills that have been in increasing demand by American industry.

There are many other factors that have influenced the growth of industry in the United States. Among these are: the influence of installment buying and its tremendous impact on the purchasing power of the nation, and the great emphasis placed on market research.

## Industrial Management in the United States

Clark Kerr has stated: "Management is a national resource—worthy of investment just as is capital; and an improvement in managerial performance can be related closely to productivity—although not as directly as capital investment."[4] Further, he has pointed out that, "The managerial

---

[3]Clark Kerr, "Productivity and Labor Relations," as reported in *Productivity and Progress* (Sydney: Angus and Robertson, 1957).
[4]Kerr, *Ibid.*

force in the United States per firm is approximately twice as large as in comparable firms in Great Britain and Western Europe and the ratio is even greater when comparison is made with less developed economies. Particular attention is directed towards specialized staff personnel and towards the selection, training, and motivation of foremen. Managerial personnel is recruited widely with relatively little attention to family and none to class origin."

The basic functions of management are to plan, organize, staff, direct, and control the activities of a business in accordance with its objectives. In other words, the job of management is to *manage*. The managers of most companies have proven to be particularly adept at fulfilling this responsibility. Much of this ability may stem from the source of personnel for managerial positions. Companies have been relying more and more on university graduates to fill managerial positions, from the foreman level on up.

At the outset, the university graduates are usually given intensive on-the-job training, which may include shop and classroom-type training. Their progress is closely watched, and they are advanced as rapidly as possible—they are schooled under intense competitive pressure, and the emphasis is on ability and accomplishment, not age. As a result of such grooming, and the assigning of responsibility as rapidly as a man is capable of assuming it, many men reach major executive positions prior to the age of thirty-five or forty.

There are a number of general practices that *able* American management has adhered to. Among these are the following: (1) they have maintained balanced emphasis on all phases of business activity and have tried to develop each function as a complement to the others; (2) they have demonstrated a willingness to take business risks and have evidenced a galloping dissatisfaction with the "status quo"; (3) they have been willing to open their doors and to share information with others; (4) they have recognized the need for expert advice and have been quick to employ staff specialists or to employ outside consultants; (5) they have recognized the need for aids in "decision-making" and have established operations research groups, industrial engineering departments, computer facilities, and so forth; (6) they have recognized that there is no need to manufacture a product if it can't be sold, and they have put great stress on market research, advertising, and sales promotion—and on sound methods of distribution; (7) they have endeavored to establish a sound organization structure, for they have recognized that organization is the principal factor determining the productivity of labor, assuming capital and natural resources to be constant; (8) they have recognized that organizations must be built around "people" and not "things," that the foreman is the "key manager," and that strong emphasis must be placed on supervisory leadership; and (9) they have stressed the need for continuous training and cooperation with educational institutions.

Although the previous discussion points out some of the factors contributing to the effectiveness of industrial management in the United States, there are many different schools of thought as to how management should be taught and practiced. A number of different approaches to its study have been set forth by the different proponents. These are discussed in some detail in Chapter 26. The many different schools of thought on the practice of management are indicative of the great attention being paid to the subject, and at the same time they clearly indicate the need for continuing research.

In the remainder of this chapter, let us give consideration to some of the more specific characteristics of modern manufacturing.

## Characteristics of Modern Manufacturing

Modern manufacturing has a number of characteristics that make for increasing success year after year. Many of these will be explained throughout this book, but a few deserve mention at this point, for they are basic to most manufacturing activity.

One of the first characteristics of manufacturing today is that of *specialization*. Some manufacturers concentrate on producing a single item, and others restrict production to a line of related products. The result of such specialization is usually lowered cost of production and improved quality. Specialization also means the division of work or effort, and this operates both at the worker level and at the management level. At the worker level there are those who work in trades requiring a great deal of skill, such as machinists, tool and die makers, and welders; such craftsmen become highly skilled specialists. Other workers do special semi-skilled or unskilled jobs. Both skilled and unskilled specialists keep our mass-production assembly lines going day after day. Although such specialization has elements of monotony and inflexibility, it does result in volume production at low cost.

Specialization of effort also operates at the management level. Management effort, generally, is divided into various special functions such as engineering, sales, and finance—the more so as a business grows in size and complexity. Within any one specialized function there will probably be further specialization or subspecialization. Engineering, for example, will have its specialists in electrical, industrial, and mechanical work. The efficiency of the engineer will probably increase as the scope of his assigned responsibility is narrowed.

A second manufacturing characteristic today is *mechanization*. The Industrial Revolution was the application of the mechanization idea. Early inventions in spinning and weaving made machine operations of what had until then been handwork. Eli Whitney's system of interchangeable manufacture made possible the mass-production industries we now take for granted. Today, mechanization has been carried so far that we no longer consider it simply a manufacturing characteristic. The use of machines has become a part of our way of life, whether we are mowing the lawn or operating a factory.

Although man has for many years been able to transfer his manual skill to machines, it has only been recently that he has been able to transfer a certain amount of intelligence to machines. In other words, some machines today can do much of their work without the aid of human thinking during the process. This has led to the extensive use of numerical control, to automation of an advanced variety, and to dreams of a completely automatic factory.

Whether or not there is an identifiable distinction between automation and mechanization is open to question, and this question is pursued at some length in Chapter 6. At this point it should be sufficient to say that the definition of automation varies considerably, depending upon the person doing the defining. Some say it results when machines are developed to "think" for themselves as implied above. This usually involves the use of a feedback or closed-loop control system. The principle is much the same as that employed by the thermostat in one's living room, which regulates the operation of a furnace to control the temperature in the room.

Another concept of automation is the introduction of transfer mechanisms between machines already automatic. There is nothing new about automatic machines, for they have been in existence for a good many years; however, until relatively recently, parts or materials had to be transferred from one machine to the next by hand. The introduction of the automatic transfer device makes it possible for automobile engine blocks, for example, to have operations performed on them through a whole series of automatic machines and never be touched by human hands.

Both of these concepts have been called automation. Whether or not either concept is truly automation is not our concern at the moment. It seems obvious regardless of the term used—mechanization or automation—that a characteristic of modern management is the ever increasing use of mechanical power to replace muscle power. There is every reason to believe the trend will continue so long as it is able to increase productivity.

A third characteristic of modern manufacturing management is the increasing *use of industrial engineering*.[5] By elimination of waste and ineffi-

---

[5]According to the American Institute of Industrial Engineers: "Industrial engineering is concerned with the design, improvement, and installation of integrated systems of men, materials, and equipment. It draws upon specialized knowledge and skills in the mathematical, physical, and social sciences together with the principles and methods of engineering analysis and design to specify, predict, and evaluate the results to be obtained from such systems."

ciency, industrial engineering has made significant contributions to increasing production and reducing costs. Principles and techniques of industrial engineering (to be discussed throughout this book) have been found to apply to every phase of the business, whether it be factory, office, or sales room. The result has been a growing field with increasing influence and status in the management of business and industry.

A fourth characteristic of modern manufacturing is the increasing use of *computers and data processing equipment.* Perhaps no other recent development has had more impact on American industry than the widespread usage of the digital computer. It has made possible the handling of enormous amounts of data and the solving of complex mathematical problems at fantastic rates of speed. The range of application of computers and data processing equipment has been extended almost as rapidly as new equipment and techniques of application have been developed, and includes: computations for scientific research, control of manufacturing processes, production and inventory control, quality control, maintenance control, processing of payrolls, keeping of accounts, and many others. The computer promises to be an increasingly valuable aid to production management through its ability to provide speedy answers to mathematical problems involving models, to eliminate much unnecessary clerical work, and to control various kinds of manufacturing processes.

The fifth characteristic is the *use of the scientific method.* In abbreviated form the steps of this method are:

1. Clearly state the problem.
2. Gather all facts pertaining to the problem.
3. Analyze the facts.
4. From analysis, synthesize principles to be followed.
5. Arrive at solution to problem.
6. Test solution to prove or disprove its adequacy.

This method has application in the solution of any problem whether it be essentially in engineering or in management. In solving engineering problems we use it almost automatically. But solutions to engineering problems are usually quantitative, and management problems, on the other hand, often do not lend themselves to quantitative answers. And so, management problems are subject to solutions based on judgment or opinion. In recent years industrial engineering, operations research, and management sciences have developed to the point where quantitative answers are often available even for management problems.

The sixth and last characteristic to be discussed here is the *use of operations research* as an aid in decision-making. Operations research, like automation, is another popular term and one that is difficult to define. The general approach to problem solving by use of operations research is little different from that of the scientific method just discussed. The principal difference is that operations research places particular emphasis on reducing the available facts to quantitative terms that permit use of mathematical models or other scientific formulas in determining the relationships between cause and effect. Simply stated, operations research is a quantitative objective approach to the problems of management.

This method of solving broad operational problems had its beginning during World War II when teams of scientists in both Great Britain and the United States were asked by the armed forces to aid in the solution of very difficult strategical and tactical problems. Being schooled in the physical sciences, these scientists applied this methodology to the operational problems presented to them. Their successes were outstanding and included increasing the efficiency of anti-submarine warfare and the determination of the optimum size of a bomber fleet.

This wartime experience with operations research demonstrated three principles that have been and are of particular importance to manufacturing management. The first is that operational problems frequently can be reduced to quantitative terms that lend themselves to mathematical manipulation. Second, it is not necessary for a scientist to have had a lifelong association with management problems in order for him to make a contribution to the solution of those problems. It is not unusual for chemists or biologists to make outstanding contributions to managerial problems by using the operations research approach. Third, there is value in the cooperation of scientists from different disciplines working together as teams toward the solution of problems. To some, this principle is so important that they claim there is no operations research unless teams are utilized. It seems true that there is more cross-fertilization of ideas from a team approach, and that such an approach usually results in more successful operations research.

Many improvements of industrial operations have resulted from the use of operations research and application of the above principles. Detailed discussions of these improvements are beyond the scope of this book, but the following list will give some appreciation of the range of operations research work to date:

1. Establishing the most desirable quantities to purchase.
2. Planning production schedules for minimum cost.
3. Loading machines for maximum utilization.
4. Determining the most favorable preventive maintenance budget.
5. Minimizing waiting time between operations.
6. Scheduling flow of material to minimize handling costs.
7. Minimizing freight costs by proper location of warehouses.

The foregoing list is not complete, for new applications are being discovered every day. This is not to imply, however, that operations research is a panacea for all the problems of management. First, there are limitations in the application of this technique, and second, operations research doesn't pretend to make decisions for the industrial manager. Instead, it simply provides factual and quantitative information that will *assist* the manager in making his decision. Better decisions should result, since they are made by well-informed management.

## QUESTIONS

1. Does "automation" have a meaning appreciably different from "mechanization"?

2. Discuss the likelihood that productivity both on the farm and in the factory will become so high that the average person will need to work only 20 hours a week.

3. The eight richest countries with one-tenth of the world's population possess over 50 per cent of the world's wealth. What impact may increased production and productivity in the underdeveloped nations have on manufacturing in the United States?

4. Define the management functions of planning, organizing, directing, and controlling in terms of some business or organization with which you are familiar.

5. In addition to the factors discussed in this chapter, what other factors have had influence on the attainment of a high level of industrial productivity in the United States?

6. Increasingly, the managers of American companies are college or university graduates. What are the long-range implications of this as a company policy?

7. Can specialization of effort in manufacturing be carried too far? If so, what are the consequences?

8. Apply the scientific method to a simple problem in your everyday life and report on the results.

9. In the long run, what effect may the increasing use of computers and data processing equipment have on employment levels?

# CHAPTER TWO

# Background of
# Manufacturing Management

Until the development of the factory system and the general concept of manufacturing, there was no such thing as management as we know it. It is true that people operated businesses of one kind or another, but for the most part these people were owners of the business and did not regard themselves as managers as well. The development and use of the management concept probably occurred for three reasons. The first has already been mentioned, namely, the development of the factory system of production. The second essentially stems from the first, namely, the development of the large corporation with many owners and the necessity to hire people to operate the business. The third reason stems from the work of many of the pioneers of scientific management who were able to demonstrate the value, from a performance and profit point of view, of some of the techniques they were developing. For the most part, the early developments were applied in manufacturing concerns, but later, and particularly today, we see these management concepts having great application in all types of businesses including banks, department stores, farms, insurance companies, and many others.

The student of management or of manufacturing management should have some knowledge of the background of the field he is studying, and with that knowledge he should be in a better position to contribute further to its growth and application in the world of business and industry.

## Management Prior to 1800

Evidence of the development and use of management principles in antiquity is meager, but nevertheless it is present. The Babylonians made use of the minimum-wage rate principle in about 1950 B.C., and the Chinese applied the principle of division of labor about 1644 B.C. The Egyptians as far back as 1300 B.C. recognized the importance of organization and administration in the bureaucratic states. The Greeks have left us little evidence of their having insight into the principles of management, but the existence of their various councils, popular courts, and boards indicate an appreciation of the managerial function. Socrates discusses the advantages of specialization of labor in connection with the development of an ideal city in Plato's *Republic*. Finally, the Bible tells us that Moses "chose able men out of all Israel, and made them heads over the people, rulers of thousands, rulers of hundreds, rulers of fifty, and rulers of ten."

Advancing to English industry in recent centuries, we find considerable evidence of the recognition of the principles of management in relation to doing work. Standard practice instructions, employee welfare plans, and recognition of the principle of overhead charges were in use in various industries in Great Britain between 1600 and 1800. In 1776, Adam Smith, a British economist, published his *Wealth of Nations,* in which he discredited the economic policies of the past and promoted the overthrow of practices that had come down from earlier times but were unsuited to modern society. Smith dealt with such subjects as capital, freedom of trade, rent, wages, and profit, but his premise was that the annual labor of a nation is the source from which it derives its supply of the necessities and conveniences of life. He developed the concept that improvement in the productivity of labor depends largely upon its division and upon the wages paid to labor.

Adam Smith wrote during the period of time in Great Britain when the Industrial Revolution was taking place. In a certain sense, Adam Smith provided some theoretical concepts that, when coupled with the practical problems forced upon industry by the Industrial Revolution, provided the basis for modern manufacturing management.

## The Industrial Revolution

The beginnings of modern industry can be accurately dated and placed. The series of events that brought into being the factory system are referred to as the Industrial Revolution and occurred largely in England from 1770 to the early 1800's. These events are generally referred to as the great inventions, and these inventions brought the machine age to all civilized people.

At the time, they revolutionized the character of industrial England, and somewhat later, the industrial life of the United States.

The great inventions are eight in number, with six of them having been conceived in England, one in France, and one in the United States. Most of them have to do with the spinning of yarn and the weaving of cloth. This is logical from the point of view that cloth was the principal export commodity of England at the time and was in short supply owing to the considerable expansion of England's colonial empire and its commercial trade. The inventions are listed in their chronological order as follows:

*Hargreaves' Spinning Jenny.* In 1764, James Hargreaves invented a spinning machine capable of spinning eight threads of yarn at one time in contrast to the usual single thread on the spinning wheel. His invention was not patented until 1770—the date usually associated with it.

*Arkwright's Water Frame.* Richard Arkwright, a barber, established in 1771 the first of numerous successful mills employing his patented spinning machine driven by water power; hence its name, "water frame." Arkwright's interest in the mills themselves gained him a reputation as a promoter of efficiency and developer of the factory system.

*Crompton's Mule.* Samuel Crompton's invention in 1779 superseded both of the previous inventions. It was called the "mule" and combined the principles of the "jenny" and "water frame" and can be thought of as a hybrid mechanical offspring. This invention produced an enormous increase of production and did away with hand spinning.

*Cartwright's Power Loom.* The three previous inventions increased enormously the capacity to spin raw fibers into yarn, and the next need was for a machine to weave the yarn into cloth. In 1785 Edmund Cartwright, a clergyman, patented the "power loom," a machine for weaving. It was not adopted by industry to any great extent until 1811, but the basic principle had been developed, and machine weaving became the chief factor in destroying the ancient system of domestic manufacture or manufacture in the home.

*Watt's Steam Engine.* Clearly, the new spinning and weaving machinery could not revolutionize industry of themselves, for power was needed to drive them, and the water power in use was insufficient and not always available. James Watt patented his steam engine in 1769, but nearly ten years passed before he was able to build a large operating machine, and it was not until 1785 that the steam engine was introduced into a factory for spinning cotton. Its advantages over water power as a prime mover were immediately apparent, and manufacturers rushed to adopt it.

*Berthollet's Chlorine Bleaching Discovery.* The next bottleneck in the industry turned out to be bleaching capacity. Until this time, bleaching had been accomplished by wetting the cloth with a mild alkali and spreading it in large fields where it would be exposed to the action of sunlight. The process itself was a very slow one—let alone the limitations of inconstant sunlight—so that it took at least six months for the weavers to get their "gray goods" bleached. In 1785 a French chemist, Claude Louis Berthollet, discovered the bleaching power of chlorine. The chemical bleaching agent whitened cloth in a few hours and worked as well on dull days as on sunlit days. The original process was handicapped by the hazardous fumes of the chlorine gas, but in 1798 Charles Tennant discovered the process of making bleaching powder from chlorine and lime, which eliminated this problem.

*Maudslay's Screw-Cutting Lathe.* Early machines were made largely of wood, and it was evident that metal machinery for manufacturing would be limited in application unless there were means available to build such machinery and keep it in repair. Henry Maudslay, in 1797, developed the combination of a slide rest, change gears, and power-driven lead screw, which is a distinguishing feature of all machine tools even today. Maudslay's lathe made possible machines with which to build other machines and was therefore extremely important in the development and continuation of the Industrial Revolution.

*Interchangeable Manufacture.* The eighth great invention of the Industrial Revolution was neither a machine nor a process but a system of interchangeable manufacture, meaning that the parts of any assembly can be produced to so close a tolerance that they can be selected at random and assembled into a component. An American, Eli Whitney, is given credit for first establishing such an interchangeable system of manufacture in 1798, in carrying out a contract for ten thousand muskets. Simeon North did the same thing in 1799 on a contract for five hundred pistols. Interchangeable manufacture is commonplace to us today, but its origin and development played an extremely important role in the growth of mass-production techniques.

## Charles Babbage

Although the practice of manufacturing management began and spread during the Industrial Revolution, it was the work of Charles Babbage that began to reveal the science of manufacturing management. His book, *On the Economy of Machinery in Manufactures* (1832), clearly indicates that he was much in advance of his time and that he influenced later manufacturing management thinking. Much of his work has application today; so a study of Babbage is of more than historical interest.

Charles Babbage (1792–1871) was a professor of mathematics at Cambridge University and spent a considerable portion of his life, his private fortune, and a grant from the British government in an attempt to build an analytical calculating machine. He never successfully completed the machine; however, he provided all the specifications necessary to build an effective automatic computer.

Babbage's problems in constructing his computer were centered around the difficulty of getting its various parts produced with sufficient accuracy to allow the computer to operate. He spent ten years visiting workshops and factories, both in England and on the Continent, in an attempt to search out means of producing his various required parts. These years offered him a unique opportunity to observe and study the various problems introduced by the developments of the Industrial Revolution and the growth of the factory. His book relates his experiences and indicates his main thoughts on the subject. Following is a brief summary of some of his main ideas:

First, Babbage took the concept of labor developed by Adam Smith and extended it, indicating that Smith had not gone far enough in his analysis. Babbage showed that the division of labor made it possible to hire workers with precisely the skills required for the various parts of the total job to be done, and that these specialized workers could be paid salaries commensurate with the skills they brought. This, he believed, would have the effect of lowering the total cost of a manufactured article. Babbage was interested in the establishment of proper costs of manufacture, and in controlling these costs he gave attention to the problem of depreciation and obsolescence and discussed the relationship between fixed costs and volume.

Babbage also recognized the existence of management problems as distinct from the various techniques used in manufacturing. He thought that scientific methods should be applied to the management of an enterprise and even suggested a list of questions to be answered in making a systematic survey of the enterprise. He advocated an organizational pattern very similar to our line and staff type of organization today.

Babbage was also greatly interested in the problems of production and human relations. His interest in timesaving methods can be compared to that of Taylor or Gilbreth a generation or so later in the United States. He was aware of the time-study practice and of the difficulty in obtaining correct measurements, in view of the fact that workers under observation tend to be self-conscious. Control of waste and of the use of by-products also received his attention. He treated the problem of human relations at length and showed concern for the unfortunate opinion among workmen that their own interest and that of their employers were at variance. He said that the consequences of this frame of mind would be neglect, lack of participation, and possibly even sabotage.

Finally, Babbage indicated an interest and knowledge of advertising, selling, and the development of new products. He advised the manufacturer to reduce his unit price as much as possible in order to increase his market, and to expect his profit from the volume of goods sold rather than from a wide margin of profit on each unit.

## Management Beginnings in America

The Industrial Revolution in Great Britain came to the United States in 1790 in the building of the Slater Cotton Mill at Pawtucket, Rhode Island. The principles and practice of manufacture of this mill made possible the growth of the factory system in the United States. The bringing together in one location of relatively large concentrations of men and raw materials created problems of management that had never been faced before. No one knew how such efforts should be organized, directed, or controlled. Businessmen applied their efforts more directly to problems of machines, material, and equipment, rather than to management activity as such. Workers received little attention as individuals, and management as a process involving people was largely disregarded.

It was not until after the Civil War that the basic ideas of management began to take shape in ways useful to businessmen. The ideas of Babbage had not penetrated our mind (nor England's mind either, to any great extent), and it remained for Frederick Taylor to develop the basic concepts in America, and to lead the crusade toward their adoption by business and industry.

Before turning to Taylor's work, one significant development needs to be noted. At the annual meeting of the American Society of Mechanical Engineers in 1886, Henry R. Towne, president of Yale and Towne Company, presented a paper titled, "The Engineer as an Economist." Towne pleaded for the recognition of management as a field distinct from the various techniques employed in industry and expressed the belief that shop management was of equal importance to engineering in the successful conduct of industrial establishments. At the same meeting, Henry C. Metcalfe, a captain in the U.S. Army Ordnance Department, presented a paper titled, "The Shop Order System of Accounts." In his paper, Metcalfe suggested a plan of organization based on the fundamental division of work between the shop and the office. Frederick Taylor was present at the meeting and participated in the discussion that followed the presentation of both papers. In particular, he mentioned that at the Midvale Steel Company during the past ten years he had been organizing a system similar to that of Mr. Metcalfe.

## Frederick W. Taylor

Frederick Taylor was born in 1856 and studied in France, Germany, and Italy during his youth. Impaired eyesight kept him from entering college.

Instead, he served as an apprentice in a small pump works in Philadelphia. Later, after his eyesight had improved, he earned an M.E. degree at Stevens Institute. He was employed by the Midvale Steel Company from 1878 to 1889, beginning as a laborer, then progressing to clerk, machinist, gang boss, foreman, chief draftsman, and finally chief engineer; he achieved the latter position after taking his degree. He served as a consulting engineer after 1889, and one of his best-known assignments was with the Bethlehem Steel Company between 1898 and 1901. In addition to his consulting, he developed various new processes of manufacturing, taking out about a hundred patents. He retired from practice in 1901, and until his death in 1915, he devoted all of his time and effort to the cause of "scientific management."

Taylor's best-known papers are "A Piece Rate System," published in 1895; "Shop Management," published in 1903; and "On the Art of Cutting Metals," published in 1906. He later condensed his thinking and experience in a book, *The Principles of Scientific Management*, published in 1911.

Taylor is properly called "the father of scientific management." Although his basic approach followed the lead of Babbage and Towne, he was the first to advocate a science of management—or a science of doing work—the same as there was a science in other fields. Taylor had had experience in the shop, and he knew the conditions there; so he attacked the problem from the bottom up, focusing his attention upon the worker, his wages, and the methods by which wages were determined (see Chapter 8).

To overcome the problems he had observed, Taylor believed that management should accept some special responsibilities for planning, directing, and organizing work. Furthermore, he felt it essential to separate the planning of work from its execution, so that each individual would be able to work at his highest level of efficiency and could be compensated accordingly. Under this concept, management would have four new duties: first, management must develop a science for each element of a man's work, which would replace the old rule-of-thumb method; second, management should scientifically select and train, teach, and develop the workman, whereas in the past the workman chose his own work and trained himself as best he could. Third, management must heartily cooperate with employees so as to insure that all the work be done in accordance with the principles of science that have been developed. Fourth, although in the past the workers were doing almost all the work and also had the greater part of the responsibility, in the future management should assume the greater part of the responsibility and the work, for which they are better fitted than the workmen.

Taylor's charge to management was to have far-reaching effect on modern manufacturing. Perhaps even today we could benefit by a closer study of his basic principles. One of the more significant aspects of his influence was the "mental revolution," which he insisted was the essence of scientific management. Perhaps Taylor was guilty of overstating his case, and using the word "science" somewhat loosely. He succeeded, however, in demonstrating that the philosophies, attitudes, and processes of the managers of his times were grossly inadequate. Through his efforts, rule-of-thumb methods were replaced by measurement and experimentation, and, in fact, this process continues even today.

## Other Management Pioneers

Taylor had many contemporaries and associates who carried forward his ideas and who developed many divergent views. Of particular significance was the work of Henry L. Gantt, the Gilbreths, and Harrington Emerson. These people did much to extend scientific management thinking beyond the factory where Taylor did most of his work.

*Henry L. Gantt.* Gantt worked with Taylor at Midvale Steel and generally held the same views that Taylor did, except that Gantt gave more attention to the man who was performing the work than to just the work itself. He appears to have had a better understanding than Taylor of worker psychology and recognized the importance of morale and the use of non-financial rewards to promote morale.

In 1902 Gantt opened an office as a scientific management consultant and concentrated on the establishment of bonus systems, although he was also responsible for the reorganization of many plants. He is widely known, even today, for his development of the "Gantt Chart," which is a technique for graphically representing work to be done and work already accomplished (see Chapter 14). This chart evolved from his work for the United States government during World War I.

*Frank and Lillian Gilbreth.* Frank Gilbreth was a successful contractor who became interested in work methods while working earlier as a bricklaying apprentice. Subsequently he developed many improvements in the methods of bricklaying and in other construction trades. His new concepts of work planning and of training workers in the correct methods of work not only increased productivity but contributed to the health and safety of the workers.

Frank Gilbreth's tremendous energy and capacity for organization resulted in the development of motion study and its inclusion as a basic part of scientific management. He and his wife, Lillian, were responsible for the introduction of various special charts and the use of motion pictures to help analyze, study, and improve jobs (see Chapter 9). They were both interested in the employee as an individual and placed considerable emphasis upon the psychological factors in management. Upon the untimely death of Frank in 1924, Mrs. Gilbreth carried on their work alone.

*Harrington Emerson.* Emerson got into scientific management work after having had experience as a teacher of modern languages and in banking and real-estate operations. He later started his own consulting firm and did special economic and engineering research work for the Burlington Railroad. In addition, he carried out the reorganization of the Atchison, Topeka, and Santa Fe Railroad. His background and interest in the railroads qualified him to serve as an expert witness in the I.C.C. wage hearings of 1910 and 1911. He testified that if all American railroads improved their management as much as the Santa Fe had done, the total savings would be more than a million dollars a day.

Although Emerson worked at the same time as Taylor, their methods of operation were different. Taylor was quite precise with his work and was interested in the determination of basic data. Emerson, on the other hand, was much more flexible in his approach and attempted to apply the ideas of scientific management to a broader range of organization. Emerson was particularly interested in efficiency and wrote extensively on the subject. He further emphasized the importance of correct organization in efforts to achieve high productivity.

## QUESTIONS

1. To what extent can Frederick Taylor be considered the father of an Industrial Management Revolution in this country?

2. Why wasn't Charles Babbage's work in management recognized much earlier?

3. In the years to come, will the current age of automation be considered a "second" Industrial Revolution?

4. Explain the difference between Babbage and Adam Smith in their approach to the division of labor.

5. Select a name from among the following and investigate his contribution to the scientific management movement: Frederick A. Halsey, Harry Hopf, Henry S. Dennison, Carl Barth, and James Rowan.

6. Why didn't the factory system get started before the Industrial Revolution?

7. Check the management principles of Henri Fayol as stated in Chapter 26 and then compare Fayol's approach to management with that of Frederick Taylor.

8. Henry Towne's paper, "The Engineer as an Economist," was presented before the A.S.M.E. in 1886. Discuss the need for an engineer to be an economist today.

9. Compare and contrast "interchangeable manufacture" with "duplicate manufacture."

10. On what basis was the word "scientific" attached to the work of the various management pioneers?

# Manufacturing
# Systems Design

# CHAPTER THREE

# Organization
# and Planning
# for Manufacturing

This section of the book, comprised of Chapters 3 through 10, is concerned with the design of manufacturing systems. For the most part these chapters deal with the various physical facilities that make up a manufacturing system. The selection and arrangement of such physical facilities is extremely important, from both the points of view of materials handling and job design. Following the discussion of these topics in this section, we will review in the next section various types of control that are exercised in the operation of a manufacturing system.

Before turning to the design of manufacturing systems, however, it is desirable to consider the problem of organization and its relationship to manufacturing. No human group activity is ever really successful unless it is "organized." Only rarely do people achieve satisfactory results without first having organized their thoughts or organized their method of approach before tackling a problem or task. It is with this thought in mind that we take up the subject of organization of a manufacturing concern before getting into either its design or its control. The effort of every person in a manufacturing concern must be related to the common purpose and to the efforts of all other persons in the enterprise. Proper organization and planning attempts to accomplish this essential coordination.

## Organization in Manufacturing

Although we are speaking largely of the manufacturing concern, it should be obvious that the points made under the heading of organization and planning apply to the non-manufacturing firm as well. Banks, hospitals, department stores, and railroads are examples of other types of enterprises, and though the functions performed in these enterprises may be considerably different from those in many manufacturing establishments, the need to coordinate and organize their functions is universal.

**Need for good organization.** Irrespective of automation, a manufacturing organization is an association of individuals working together to obtain the goals of an enterprise. When two or more individuals cooperate in a work effort, one of them must direct the actitivities of the group, or else they will work as individuals at cross-purposes with each other. Direction from one source is therefore essential for the coordination and success of any group effort.

It has been clearly demonstrated that every member of a manufacturing organization performs better on his job when he knows clearly what his job is, who his boss is, what the organization structure is, what his own authority is, what he should do in case of an emergency when his boss is not present, and how and to whom to report essential information. These factors are essential to a good organization and apply to all members of an organization whether they be managers, supervisors, machine operators, or laborers. All will do better work if they understand their roles in the organization, both individually and collectively.

Good organization does not eliminate the need to hire good people or to train them properly after hiring them. It will never be possible to design an organization and describe the jobs in that organization in such a manner that good judgment on the part of the people comprising that organization will not be required. Nonetheless, good organization should tend to reduce the number of management problems which arise, minimize effort involved, reduce organizational friction, promote effective teamwork, and keep operating costs at a minimum.

**Objectives of organization.** The overall objective of manufacturing organization is to develop teamwork that functions as a single instrument for low cost production. In other words, the manufacturing organization should prove the concept that the whole is greater than the sum of its parts.

Divisional and departmental activities in an enterprise are set up to obtain efficient and maximum performance. It is expected that their managers will control operating results, conserve and coordinate human effort, and optimize costs and profits. From top to bottom each member of the organization must be motivated to maximize the results in his own job, coordinate his efforts with other departments, and generally develop the necessary team spirit. Without mutual understanding and cooperation the organization whole could easily turn out to be less than the sum of its parts.

**Organization design.** The preceding discussion of organization, its need, and its objectives, may seem reasonable enough, but we must finally get to the point of actually designing the organization to meet the requirements specified. However, prior to the design of the organization itself, there must be a thorough understanding of the goals of that organization and the nature of the business to be conducted. This is covered more completely in Chapter 26, "Management Requirements," but at this point we must keep in mind the influence that certain goals may have on the nature of the organization itself. Manufacturing requirements must be analyzed to determine the various types of production facilities and departments needed. The sales objectives, the types of customers to be served, the line of products to be offered, and the goals in regard to employment, payrolls, and employee standards of living may influence the organization design. These are only a few of the items dealing with business objectives that need to be thoroughly considered.

Once these goals and objectives for the business have been formulated, the next step is to determine what functions are necessary in order to achieve these goals. For a manufacturing organization typical functions include the following: production, distribution, finance, procurement, personnel and employee relations, engineering and research, control, and general offices. These categories are obviously functional and in any particular case would undoubtedly be broken down into various subdepartments. For example, a control function might be divided between production control, quality control, and inventory control. The problem of the individual organization designer is to determine which functions for this particular business are important enough to warrant at least one person assigned to that function

The next step in organization design is to group or relate the various functions that have been specified. The principle of *span of control* (see later discussion) tells us that there is a limit to the number of subordinates who should report to one person; so it is necessary for us to plan for different levels in our organization. Therefore, if certain functions seem logically to relate to each other, they might possibly be grouped together and report to one man who in turn would report to a higher level. The three control functions referred to earlier could logically be grouped together in this manner. After grouping and relating all of the previously specified functions, we can see a pyramid developing, as is typical of most organization charts.

Our next step in organization design is to design or describe the various jobs that will later have to be filled. We have previously identified functions that would be of sufficient importance to warrant at least one job, but conceivably some functions, in particular those dealing with actual production departments, would require many more persons. This step, then, requires the close examination of each previously identified function and the outline of the various positions that will be required. A job description for each position should be prepared that outlines the general duties and responsibilities of the incumbent, as well as the background, education, and experience deemed desirable of the person placed on that job.

Our final step in organization design is that of filling all of the jobs that have just been specified and described. If this is a new organization, obviously an extensive recruiting program would be necessary to find persons of the necessary skills to fill the jobs described. In a going organization, people presently on the payroll must be utilized, and so the task becomes one of matching job requirements with the personal qualifications of the people available. In either case, it is highly probable that job designs must be modified somewhat in order to make use of the personal qualifications available. Or an extensive training program may be necessary in order to upgrade or otherwise qualify people for the jobs that have been designed.

Two points need to be especially emphasized about this approach to organization design. One is that this is admittedly an ideal approach. Many will say that it is so ideal that it has absolutely no practical application. This may be true in some cases. However, the procedure can be defended on the grounds that it is better to set up a tailor-made organization to fit the particular needs of the company than to allow an organization to grow and develop according to the accident of who happens to be around at the time. In other words, in practically all other aspects of modern manufacturing management we do not allow things to develop by chance; so why should we make an exception of organization?

The second point to be emphasized in regard to organization design is its great need for flexibility. The procedure discussed is not something to be done once and then left standing throughout eternity without further review or change. Flexibility is one of the most important characteristics of good organization. The objectives, policies, and procedures of the company should be constantly under review and updated as conditions and experience dictate. These changes in turn should cause the organization to be examined and modified accordingly. New jobs may be created from time to time. Other jobs may be eliminated and still others combined or rearranged in any way it is believed will lead to more effective operation of a department or the company as a whole. Further flexibility must be built into the organization design in order to provide for the development of people and their eventual promotion within the organization. Some jobs can be used mainly as training positions, and others may have their content modified from time to time in order to allow for the qualifications and/or the development of the incumbent. In summary, then, at any one time there should be an ideal organization toward which the company is moving in its procurement and training of personnel. However, as time passes, the concept of flexibility in the organization design must be adopted in order to meet the changing requirements of the company.

**Organization charts.** The result of an organization design is usually an organization chart that shows the formal relationships among functions and the people responsible for those functions. An example of such a chart for a medium sized company is shown in Figure 3-1. Some companies do not make use of organization charts, feeling that they might induce a certain structural rigidity. These companies feel that loosely defined relationships among people in the organization will provide an incentive for those people to expand their spheres of interest and activity for the ultimate good of the business. In other words, they feel that organization charts effectively place strait jackets on aggressive, energetic executives.

It is not our purpose to settle the argument as to the usefulness of organization charts. Instead let it be emphasized that organization is not an end in itself but simply a means to an end. So the organization should not be considered an eternal arrangement, but rather a picture of the organization structure at one particular moment. If a strait jacket is then imposed, it will not be done by the organization chart, but by the executives using the chart. The chart can and should be changed as often as necessary, and in a company of any size and complexity it can be a very useful tool of coordination regardless of the frequency of changes.

Figure 3-1 shows an organization chart in the pure and simple form; that is, only the basic structure of departments and functions is displayed. Sometimes more information is desired, in which case the names of men in charge and perhaps the number of people they supervise will be included. Duties and requirements of a job may also be shown, but these are usually placed in the organization manual, which will be discussed later.

The advantages and uses of the organization chart are appreciable. First, they do show the lines of direct authority and thereby serve as a quick check on who is responsible for the various functions. Charts also show up weaknesses in an organization, such as more than one person being assigned the same work, or certain work never having been assigned to anyone. The chart can serve as a training device and as a guide in planning for expansion. It can be used to alert the public about work relationships within the company as well as to remind employees about who supervises whom.

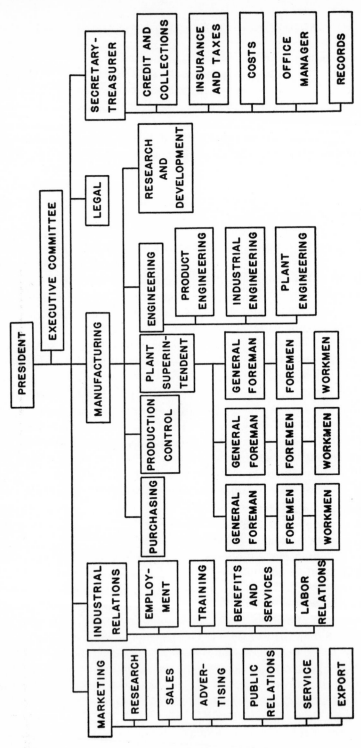

Figure 3-1. Organization chart of a medium-sized company.

## Organization Principles

Volumes have been written about principles of organization, all of which are designed to assist in the development of an organization structure able to carry out its basic objectives. In this section we shall review a few of the more common principles and show their application to the organization design.

### Span of Control

Span of control, or span of management, as it is often referred to, is one of the more widely known organization principles. Specifically, the term refers to the number of persons that report to any one supervisor or executive. A favorite point of discussion revolves around the number of subordinates who should report to any one supervisor, and various writers have concluded that the ideal span is between about four and eight. Studies in actual practice, however, indicate that in many organizations there is a much greater span than this. It is fairly common to have as many as twelve subordinates reporting to one person, and surveys have shown the number to vary from one to twenty-four.

The important point about the span-of-control principle is not so much the use of any "magic" number of subordinates, but the realization that each supervisor undoubtedly has a limitation in the number of subordinates that he can adequately supervise. The number will vary considerably from person to person and from situation to situation. Below are some of the factors to be considered in working out the proper span of control.

1. *Level in the organization.* Generally speaking, executives at the top of an organization will have fewer people reporting to them than will foremen supervisors at the bottom of the managerial hierarchy.

2. *Type of problems encountered.* This factor will probably correlate closely with level in the organization, for the more difficult policy-type decisions usually rest at the top of the organization, whereas the carrying out of routine procedures is done at the lower levels. However, there are exceptions to this at both the higher and lower levels; so the factor needs separate identity. Subordinates carrying out routine work regardless of the level will require less supervision than do subordinates carrying out work that requires many policy decisions and coordination with the work of others. This means that narrower spans would probably exist in maintenance and research departments, and wider spans would be suitable for assembly-line work or routine clerical operations.

3. *Abilities of the persons involved.* For reasons not always clearly under-

stood, some supervisors can handle the work of more subordinates than other supervisors and do so without undue strain on themselves or reducing the efficiency of the organization. Likewise, a group of highly skilled and qualified subordinates will require less supervision, and in such a case the span could be broadened. The necessity to train subordinates in new procedures will almost always reduce the desirable span.

4. *Willingness of the supervisor to delegate authority.* Some supervisors find it extremely difficult to delegate authority and may even go to the extent of checking every action taken by every subordinate. For such individuals the span of control is necessarily limited. Hopefully, however, supervisors can be trained to delegate more duties and authority to their subordinates, and in fact, some companies force their supervisors to delegate more of their work through the simple expedient of assigning them more work than they can possibly get done by their usual methods of close supervision.

## Organization Levels

In applying the span-of-control principle to an organization design it is easy to see that many levels will be or could be created, since the narrower the span of control, the more levels will be necessary to accomplish the same amount of work. Generally speaking, however, a large number of organizational levels between the chief executive and the lowest-level worker seems to be undesirable from a communication point of view. Information that must travel through a number of different levels in an organization in order to reach its destination almost invariably becomes distorted, if not lost. This fact is easily demonstrated by playing the parlor game in which a message is repeated from person to person around the room by whispering. The last person to receive the message states it out loud, and usually the stated message has little or no accuracy in relation to the message that was started around the room in the first place. Although such misunderstandings may be fun in the parlor, they can be catastrophic in a manufacturing organization and for this reason many companies make it a point to keep the number of levels in the organization as few as possible, perhaps no more than four, between the chief executive and the lowest level of supervisor.

Clearly, if one attempted to impose a specific number for a span of control and another specific number for organization levels, a bind could easily result in the design of the organization. The only answer to this dilemma, within the scope of this volume, is to point out the factors mentioned above in regard to span of control, and to remind the reader that principles such as these are only guidelines to be modified as necessary to meet the situation at hand.

### Subdividing Activities

The various activities and functions necessary to carry out the objectives of a manufacturing enterprise must be broken down and grouped in some manner for efficient operation and coordination. Departments and heads of departments should be assigned a homogeneous group of functions or activities, and hopefully this might be composed of one primary function together with the related secondary functions. Following are some of the common bases for subdividing activities:

**Function.** The most common basis for subdividing activities is by function, such as manufacturing, engineering, and sales. This is perhaps the most basic breakdown of activities, for it allows the company to take advantage of specialists in each of the various fields. The other bases for subdividing activities have more to do with subdividing within one of these functions.

**Process.** To subdivide manufacturing activities by process is quite natural. Such processes as plating, refining, distilling, bleaching, or machining all lend themselves to subdivision as separate and distinct activities.

**Equipment.** Subdividing by equipment follows very closely that by process. "Equipment" refers to such items as punch presses, drill presses, milling machines, and machine tools in general. Such classes of equipment often provide a basis for separating activities, and the idea is not an exclusive one with the factory. Offices often have their typing or calculating departments, thereby indicating a subdivision by equipment.

**Location.** Activities may be segregated simply on the basis of where they are physically located. This may at times mean some strange combinations, but such combinations may make possible a much more efficient organization and smoother operation.

**Product.** Many times activities are separated according to the product. One department may make TV cabinets while a second department makes end tables. One group in the engineering department may work on pumps and a second group on nozzles. The same could be true for functions such as sales, purchasing, or advertising.

**Classes of customers.** A sales department can divide its activities according to the classes of customers it serves. One sales group may service the retail trade and another the wholesale trade. Or, in advertising, one group may handle advertising in the popular media such as television, radio, and the popular magazines, while another group might handle advertising in trade magazines and other specialized media.

In speaking of these various bases for subdividing industrial activities it is not implied that all would be used in every company or that no other bases exist. It is important that an organization be set up to accomplish the goal or mission of the enterprise in the most efficient manner. In setting up the organization for any particular industrial situation, one must select the bases for subdivision that will give the best results for that situation. The criterion that groups of people should comprise a workable, homogeneous, and separate field of activity should be applied. In many types of business the pattern of organization may be well established, but one must remember that although these established patterns have worked well in the past, it is still possible that a more efficient pattern may be found in the future.

### Responsibility and Authority

Often the owner-manager of a business will be willing to delegate the *responsibility* for a particular activity but will retain the *authority* for himself. For example, a man may be given the responsibility for rate setting in a company, but unless he is given the authority to control and direct the means of rate setting, he cannot be effective. He may see opportunities to improve the handling of this important function but be powerless to install the improvements without first receiving authority from his superior. It is like being responsible for guiding a boat down the river but not being able to reach the rudder.

The idea behind this principle works the other way too. Many people in management are constantly seeking more authority. Such additional authority makes them feel important. But if a person seeks and is given additional authority, is he willing to accept the responsibility that should go along with it? He might want the authority to control and set rates, but he might hesitate to accept responsibility in case they turn out all wrong. In such a case he might be tempted to point his finger at the boss, at the union, or at almost anyone to demonstrate that he wasn't responsible. Glory is fine but blame is for someone else!

Obviously, responsibility and authority must go together if effective work is to be performed. It is equally important that each person in the organization know and understand the extent or limits of his responsibility and authority. A supervisor who doesn't understand where his responsibility starts or stops lives in fear of going either too far or not far enough. The definition of limits of responsibility and authority is one of the purposes of the organization manual, which will be discussed more in detail later.

### Matching Abilities and Requirements

We have already outlined the ideal approach to organization design, whereby positions are fully worked out and described, and then persons to fill these positions are either recruited or trained. This is called an ideal approach, but it has its practical aspects. Jobs, whether they be management jobs or worker jobs, can be analyzed and a determination made as to the physical, mental, and skill requirements for each. In like manner, employees or potential employees can be evaluated through the process of interviewing, testing, checking references, and determining interests and aptitudes. A scientific approach to both job design and to man-evaluation makes it relatively easy for a company to match the abilities of its employees or prospective employees with the requirements of the various jobs it has available.

Occasionally, when a person leaves the organization it may prove impossible to find another worker who matches exactly the requirements of the open position. In such a case, the job must be modified to make it possible to staff the opening, particularly if time is a factor. This means there will be an exchange of job functions until the person available and the job open do match. The necessity to modify the ideal organization design emphasizes the desirability of flexibility in organizations. However, it should be emphasized that men should be fitted to jobs whenever possible.

## Organization Structures

The basic structure of an industrial organization depends upon the size of the company, the nature of the business, and the complexity of the problems faced. The most common form of organization structure is the line and staff, but there are a number of variations of this basic form.

### Line Organization

The simplest form of organization is the straight line. The significant feature, as the name implies, is that the positions listed on the organization chart are in a vertical line, as can be seen in Figure 3-2. In this organization the president handles all problems that arise, whether they have to do with production, sales, finance, or personnel. He has no "staff" to aid him and so must be a Jack-of-all-trades. Any company that starts small probably starts with a line type of organization. The owner is the general manager, and he may have one or two people working for him. As the business grows he finds he is overburdened with details of hiring, sales, purchasing, and so he needs a line and staff type of organization.

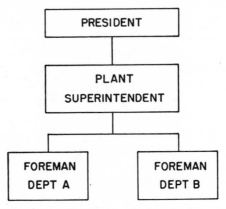

**Figure 3-2.** Line organization chart.

### The Line and Staff Organization

The line and staff type of organization in simplified form is shown in Figure 3-3. One can see that the only difference between this and the line type of organization of Figure 3-2 is the addition of some specialists. In this case the specialists are the chief engineer and the sales manager, who were added in order to relieve the president of some of his burden. Certain responsibilities are shared by the two specialists, but they report to the president, who retains overall responsibility for the operation of the business.

The idea of the addition of staff people can be and has been extended much further than this simple example shows. Figure 3-1 shows an organ-

**Figure 3-3.** Line and staff organization chart.

ization making extensive use of the staff idea. It would be impossible for a company of any size to use a pure line type of organization, for no one man possesses the ability to manage all the various functions that must be performed in a diversified business. It may be possible· in a one-man machine shop, but not in a factory employing several thousand men and women.

It was mentioned earlier that staff people should be given a certain amount of authority and responsibility. The question is: How much? Does a chief engineer make *all* decisions in regard to engineering matters and a sales manager *all* decisions in regard to sales? In a true line and staff organization the answer is "probably not". The staff man only studies a situation and makes recommendations to his superior. The superior makes the decision. Of course, the superior would be foolish to hire a specialist in a field and then never pay any attention to what he recommends. The function of the superior in this case is to coordinate the recommendations of all the specialists who report to him.

It is felt in many cases that the specialist should do more than recommend: he should have full authority over his particular function. This principle is followed in many companies and is called a line and functional staff type of organization. It is a variation of the regular line and staff; the only difference is in the *degree* of authority that is granted the people concerned.

Frederick Taylor first developed the idea of a functional type of organization in his paper entitled "Shop Management," which was presented in 1903. Taylor suggested a pure functional organization. In his arrangement each worker would report to a speed boss, a gang boss, a repair boss, an inspector, a time and cost clerk, an instruction card clerk, a route clerk, and a disciplinarian. Each boss would have full authority over his particular function and would instruct the workmen in that function.

It is doubtful whether this particular type of organization exists in any company, for it has the obvious drawback that each man has too many bosses. Probably too high a premium is placed on coordination and cooperation among the various bosses. However, pure functional organization has the advantage of full and maximum utilization of the specialties of the various bosses. This advantage has led to the broadening of responsibility and authority granted ordinary staff people without disturbing their basic relationships with the line.

### Types of Staff Departments

Staff departments are not all alike and are generally thought to be of four kinds: (1) advisory, (2) control, (3) service, and (4) coordinating. The four categories are not mutually exclusive, and in fact it may turn out that many staff departments have duties and responsibilities that fall into all four categories.

An advisory group has little authority in itself but is expected to serve as a group of specialists in a particular area and advise the decision-making executives as to the best course to follow in any particular instance. Typical advisory groups are legal, public relations, and labor relations.

Control departments include personnel, credit, budgeting, accounting, and auditing, and such departments typically have full authority to see that their particular functions are properly carried out everywhere in the organization.

Service departments are those assigned to carry out certain specific duties such as construction, purchasing, traffic, insurance, maintenance, engineering, and research. These groups seldom advise and seldom have authority; they usually are referred to as "staff" groups since they do not actually work on the product.

Coordinating departments typically give advice, but such advice is usually followed by the line groups so that essentially such departments do turn out to have authority. Typical departments might be order and distribution departments as well as a production planning department.

### Use of Committees

Someone has said that a committee is a group of people who take a week to do what one good man can do in an hour. Despite the number of cases in which this is undoubtedly true, a committee in an organization quite often performs worth-while tasks. If two heads are better than one, the use of a committee will pay off.

A committee is often found on an organization chart at a high level of management. The organization of Figure 3-1 shows a committee at the top level. Such a committee is usually composed of all the various heads of departments or functions and often serves to formulate and direct policy for the entire business. Other committees may exist further down in the organization; some may be standing committees; others may be formed to work on one particular problem, being dissolved once they have arrived at a solution.

The purpose served by forming a committee at any level in the organization may be one or more of the following:

**To coordinate various functions.** A committee to consider new products might be composed of representatives from sales, production, and engineering in order to insure that any new development would meet the requirements of all three groups.

**To secure cooperation of various personnel.** An executive issuing an order cannot always be certain the order will be carried out in the manner he desires. Talking over the proposed order with a committee gives him an opportunity to answer questions about it, and likewise gives the people concerned a chance to air their objections. The usual result of such a session is better understanding all the way around.

**To solve a problem.** This is where the "two heads better than one" idea can demonstrate its effectiveness. An individual faced with a problem may not have the ability to come up with a solution; or perhaps he may become stagnant in his thinking. The stimulation brought about by discussing the problem with others often brings about a solution.

**To train younger executives.** Committee meetings may be called to give the younger executives a keener insight into the operation of the business. Or a young executive may be given an assignment and asked to explain his results to the committee, thereby demonstrating his capabilities. His superiors can appraise his performance and plan his future training.

One other use of a committee should be mentioned in passing. It may rubber-stamp the ideas of the executive who forms it. This, of course, is undesirable and quite wasteful, but committees are often used for this purpose by the executive who is afraid to stand behind his own decisions. He wants others to share the responsibility, so he uses a rubber-stamp committee.

A committee will be more successful if the following requirements are met:

1. There must be a real need for the committee.
2. There should be as few individuals on the committee as possible.
3. The chairman must conduct meetings as efficiently as possible, having the agenda prepared in advance and prohibiting discussions not relating to the matter at hand.
4. Meetings must begin and end on time.
5. Any item that can be more effectively handled by an individual rather than by the committee should not be included on the committee agenda.
6. The duties, responsibility, and authority of the committee should be clearly defined.
7. Committees should be disbanded upon completion of the objectives for which it was formed.

One can see that the factor underlying the above list is the avoidance of wasted time and the cost that goes with it. Committees enjoy a certain degree of unpopularity in many companies because everyone associates wasted or lost time with a committee meeting. This can be to a great extent avoided by following the requirements listed.

## The Informal Organization

The discussion in the preceding paragraphs concerned what might be termed the "formal organization." On paper are set down the precise relationships among the various jobs in the company in terms of a formal organization chart, and the need for such an arrangement has been emphasized. We must return to the facts of organizational life, however, and realize that these jobs are held by people and not by robots. As a result some informal relationships exist that are not shown on any chart.

Superimposed on the formal organization chart of Figure 3-4 is an informal organization that might exist. The informal organization is shown by the dotted lines. Disregarding for the moment the cause of these informal relationships, the effect could be something with which to reckon. Executive 3 has some relationship with Employee 211, which could easily bypass the formal relationship through Employees 2 and 21. In a similar manner Employee 31 has a special relationship with Employee 411 that could mean a disruption of the normal channels. And so on for the rest of the informal relationships shown.

**Figure 3-4.** Informal relationships indicated on top of a formal organization chart.

Such informal relationships come about for a variety of reasons. Some people are natural leaders wherever they are placed in an organization, and other people will go to them for advice regardless of the formal organization structure. Social activities are probably the largest cause of informal relationships, for if Employee 21 and Employee 311 bowl on the same team every Monday night, inevitably there will be created a strong bond between them that no formal organization chart can break. Looking at the darker side of the picture, if Employee 41 takes Employee 42's girl friend away from him, a very special relationship may exist between these two men.

Extreme friendship may create favoritism to the detriment of overall employee relations, and animosity may make for inefficiency and breakdown of respect for superiors. On the other hand, many times these special relationships result in things being done more efficiently. The important point is that special relationships exist in every organization, and they do not necessarily follow the lines shown on the formal organization chart.

As Chester I. Barnard points out in *The Functions of the Executive*,[1] the informal organization does have an important role to play: it serves as a communications channel, and it maintains the feeling of personal integrity and self-respect of those in the organization. Both of these might seem to destroy the formal organization, but instead they probably reinforce it. Formal organizations tend to forget the personality of individuals and emphasize the impersonal aspects of duties and responsibilities. Through informal organization employees can exercise a certain amount of choice and receive reinforcement of personal attitudes, and so they are more willing to go along with the authority imposed by the formal organization.

## Tools of Coordination

Coordination is of prime importance in an organization, for without proper coordination the efforts and the purposes of the people employed by a company are not unified. To achieve coordination, companies make use of certain tools. One of these is the organization chart, which has already been discussed in some detail. Two others are the *organization manual* and the *standard practice instructions*.

### Organization Manual

The organization chart is usually an outline or skeleton of a company's organization, showing only job titles and their relationship to each other. It is the organization manual that provides substance for the chart. The manual will normally outline in detail all the duties and responsibilities that go with each job the chart shows. In addition, some manuals include for each job an outline of relationships with other jobs, the public, other companies, and the government.

Such written information about the positions in an organization helps work to progress much more smoothly. First of all, everyone knows exactly what he is to do and what the scope of his authority is. Secondly, overlap of duties and responsibilities can be avoided, thereby making for a more

---

[1](Cambridge, Mass.: Harvard University Press, 1938), p. 122.

efficient organization. Thirdly, such a manual assists in training, for a new man taking over a job can tell exactly what is required of him; he doesn't depend upon his predecessor to remember all the various aspects of his job.

An organization manual can be useful only if it is kept up to date; and it is this burden of keeping it up to date that causes many companies not to use them or to discard them once they are started. The same can be said of the organization chart. This tendency can be minimized by refraining from making the chart and manual too elaborate to start with and by designing both so that they will be easy to change. Manuals in loose-leaf form can be changed readily. Charts made using some of the special tapes developed for this purpose are equally flexible. The use of such timesaving devices will give the maximum incentive to keep the chart and manual up to date and thereby insure their usefulness.

### Standard Practice Instructions

Although the organization manual outlines who has what responsibilities, it does not say *how* these various operations are to be carried out. This is the purpose of the standard practice instructions.

Such instructions cover a great variety of procedures. Examples might be requisitioning supplies, issuing employee passes, computing vacation pay, and receiving material from a vendor. Standard practice instructions may also include material on how to perform the manufacturing processes, although these instructions are more likely to be in another booklet sometimes called "manufacturing standards."

Of course it is assumed that the method of performing a job as outlined in the standard practice instructions is the best one available. Even more important, perhaps, is that the SPI will insure the use of the *same* method throughout the company. In other words, consistency in performing tasks is achieved. Certainly it would be undesirable, for example, if various departments were computing vacation pay using different formulas. The possibility of such an occurrence is minimized with use of up-to-date standard practice instructions.

The remarks made earlier about keeping the organization manual up to date also apply to the standard practice instructions. Nothing can be more exasperating than to be following a procedure outlined in the SPI and then be told that the procedure is out of date. Unless the booklet can be kept current, it is probably better to have none at all.

When the organization chart, the organization manual, and the standard practice instructions have been prepared, they become tools to facilitate coordination in the enterprise. The organization chart tells who is to perform a function and how that function is geared into the organization. The organization manual explains what the person's responsibilities and duties are. Finally, the standard practice instructions describe how the various tasks are to be performed.

## Organization Planning

We have tried to emphasize the importance of proper organization to successful operation of a manufacturing concern and to give some indication of what makes for proper organization. Two other points have also been emphasized. One is that organization is a dynamic sort of thing. It changes and needs to be changed. It is not something to be worked out on a chart and then filed away. Secondly, organization is given consideration in a business only because such consideration contributes to the good of the business. Organization is not a goal in itself—it *assists* in arriving at the goal. This assistance is felt in some companies to be so important that separate departments of organization have been established. Such departments are charged with the responsibility of organization planning, of continually defining and grouping the separate activities of the enterprise so that each can better contribute to company objectives. Giving this responsibility to a person or department insures that it will not be overlooked. Of course, separate organization departments can be justified only in the fairly large companies; so some companies have made organization planning the responsibility of the industrial engineering department. This has worked out satisfactorily; industrial engineers can seek out improvements in organization as well as improvements in methods, materials handling, or production control.

Basically, the work of organization planning is to establish "ideal" organization and to engineer and plan so as to approach that ideal. We must recognize that the ideal itself won't remain static. Conditions change, objectives change, and management concepts change, but at any one time there should be a common understanding of what organization would be ideal.

Working the company's actual organization toward the ideal is the main task of organization planning. Many factors keep the company from announcing that "tomorrow morning we will start operating using the ideal organization." One of the more important factors is the informal organization, which we have discussed earlier. Informal organizations cannot be overlooked; so it is the job of organization planning to reconcile the informal relationships with the formal ones. Another factor is that there may not be people available who are capable of taking over the responsibilities called for in the ideal organization. Long-range management development programs may be called for to insure a source of competent executives. A third factor is the natural resistance to change possessed by people presently in the organization. Once people get accustomed to associating with a certain group of co-workers, they don't want to change. They can be forced to change, but the consequence may be resentment and inefficiency.

These factors may deter us from making organizational changes in the short run, but they should not deter us in the long run. We can also make changes at certain opportune times. There are always retirements, people quitting for better jobs, or other eventualities that force change. Changes can then be made in the direction of the ideal organization plan. In the course of time a rational plan of organization can be achieved without seriously disturbing the people involved.

We see, then, that organization planning involves the patient changing of an organization structure and accompanying job descriptions toward an ideal or ultimate plan of organization that most effectively meets the requirements of the business.

Some advantages of organization planning are as follows:

1.  Provides for succession. Analyzing the retirement dates of executives will alert the company to the need to groom replacements. Having a plan of replacements for all jobs will minimize the emergency should someone quit or die unexpectedly.

2.  Facilitates promotion from within and the improvement in morale that accompanies the adoption of such a policy. Looking at organization requirements ahead of time makes it feasible to train some good prospect for a top job, rather than depending on bringing someone in from the outside.

3.  All will have a better understanding of what is required on their jobs and consequently will perform better. Organization planning means that each job must be carefully studied as to duties, responsibilities, objectives, limits of authority, and relationships with other parts of the organization. These facts become part of the organization manual and will eliminate any uncertainty in the minds of job incumbents. Friction will be reduced, and executives can spend time on policy matters rather than in settling differences.

4.  Provides a long-range plan for the handling of special problems. In any organization there are certain people who don't fit in. These people and their problems can't be eliminated all at once, but a plan will indicate a more desirable course of action than simply "waiting for something to happen."

5.  Provides for the long-run strength of the business. The strength of any manufacturing enterprise depends upon the dynamics of its organization. By planning its organization a business can be assured of a strong position not only today but also tomorrow.

## QUESTIONS

1.  Does a partnership have any organization problems?
2.  Can a manager delegate *all* of his responsibilities?

3. Explain the principle of responsibility and authority.

4. On what bases are the activities listed on the organization chart in Figure 3-1 divided? How might the other bases for subdividing activities be used on this chart?

5. Explain the development of the informal organization in a company and outline the desirable and undesirable features of such a development.

6. What are the strengths and weaknesses of the line type of organization?

7. What are the strengths and weaknesses of the functional type of organization?

8. Explain how the organization chart, the organization manual, and standard practice instructions are tools of coordination.

9. Would a small company, say of 200 employees, have need for the tools of coordination? Explain.

10. What is an "ideal" organization and how is it useful in organization planning?

## CASE PROBLEMS

### Katz Manufacturing Company

When the Katz Manufacturing Company acquired all the outstanding stock of the Hill Machine Company four years ago, it brought Mr. R. S. Stiner into the organization for the express purpose of managing Hill Machine Co. as a division of Katz Manufacturing Co. Mr. Stiner had been highly recommended for the position and had been very successful with a number of other companies —particularly when assigned overall responsibility for an activity. Managing the Hill Machine Division seemed a responsibility made to order for him.

After four years under Mr. Stiner's direction the Hill Machine Division showed a net return on investment of 5% as compared to 10-23% for the other divisions of the company. All other phases of Hill Machine operations were more than satisfactory.

Mr. Stiner recognized that action must be taken to improve his division profit record, and the action he prescribed was the establishment of an "organization department." The purpose of the department was to study organization, procedures, and manufacturing methods. It would have authority to make investigations throughout the division and recommend changes. All actual changes would be approved by Mr. Stiner. In this way Mr. Stiner felt he could secure closer control over the operations of his division.

*Questions:*

1. Should Mr. Stiner be allowed to set up his "organization department"?
2. Should the department be temporary or permanent? Explain your answer.
3. What advice could you give the person placed in charge of the new department?
4. Would such a department give Mr. Stiner closer control over operations? Explain.

### Pearson Punch Presses, Inc.

The management of Pearson Punch Presses, Inc., consists of seven men: Mr. Eli Pearson heads the company as president, and, reporting directly to him, there are six supervisors who in turn head divisions of the manufacturing operations. The six divisions are machining, casting, small parts, assembly, die shop, and forge shop. Eight types of standard punch press are produced by the company, and each division is thoroughly familiar with the requirements for each of the types. Little difficulty is experienced in coordinating the work of the various divisions.

All sales are handled through manufacturers' agents, and Mr. Pearson himself spends considerable time working with the various agents and promoting sales through them. He also handles the purchasing activity since he maintains outside contacts. Ten clerks in the office handle all paper work connected with sales, purchasing, and payrolls. In addition to the ten clerks there are 145 factory employees.

The division supervisors are called upon to handle a variety of activities. Each operates his division more or less as a separate factory, hiring and firing his own employees, handling grievances, making out purchase requisitions, setting pay rates, inspecting materials and parts, figuring time cards, and maintaining equipment. All supervisors are capable and, although kept busy, they enjoy the broad responsibility and authority granted them by Mr. Pearson.

Through his contacts with other companies Mr. Pearson realizes that the machine tool industry is growing and that his company must grow with it or be left behind. The market for his eight standard presses will probably contract in the future unless he can reduce costs. In addition, new and improved presses with automatic controls must be developed.

Mr. Pearson can see many problems ahead of him in trying to get his company in line with the times. One of these involves his company's organization structure. He has expressed the feeling that "a more modern organization" would be needed before the company could progress very far toward expansion.

*Questions:*

1.  Draw an organization chart of Pearson Punch Presses, Inc., as it now stands.
2.  Draw a recommended organization structure for this company.
3.  Outline and explain the particular points or features of your recommended structure.

# CHAPTER FOUR

# Plant Location
# and Buildings

The many manufacturing establishments that dot our countryside are not something that sprang up overnight but represent the culmination of many man-hours of planning. Countless decisions, such as the products to be made in the plant, the equipment required, the type of structure needed, and the location of the plant, had to be made before the ground could be broken to build the plant. In this chapter and those that follow in Section II, we shall be giving consideration to the various problems associated with the location and design of the physical facilities for manufacturing concerns.

## Plant Location

The immensity of the plant-location problem is attested by the fact that billions of dollars are spent each year on new manufacturing buildings in the United States, not to mention the ever increasing investment in foreign subsidiaries. For each of these plants, someone had to make a decision as to where to put it, and many plants have ended up in somewhat surprising locations. Indeed, the widespread dispersion of our factories has done much to alter the industrial landscape. Thus, among other developments, we find the chemical industry forming a new industrial band running southwest to northeast from Mexico to the Canadian border. We notice the extension of the steel industry from Pennsylvania to Chicago and elsewhere, the departure of much of the textile industry from the New England states, and the widespread location of many plants in the electronic components industry. We have witnessed the development of many industrial districts in metropolitan areas, the establishment of research parks near major universities, and a great movement of industry into small communities and the country.

In those companies operating many plants, each plant must be evaluated on the basis of its economic relationship to the other plants and distribution warehouses. In such circumstances, it is desirable to minimize the total manufacturing-distribution costs. A number of companies have made effective use of mathematical programming to minimize these overall costs.

Three situations require an answer to the question of plant location: (1) a new plant just being started, (2) a new branch of an existing plant, or (3) a new location for an existing plant.

Analysis of the reasons why many companies were started in their present locations will reveal that they were located in the community that was the home of the founder. For example, one of the country's leading fountain pen companies was started in a middle western city because the founder owned a jewelry store in that community; a prominent pharmaceutical company was started in its present location by a former druggist in that city; and a shoe company developed out of a basement shop started in the founder's home. These and countless other examples lead us to believe that, in general, the exact location of an existing industrial plant is probably not too important. On the other hand, locating a new plant or a branch plant in a suitable place is significant because factory organizations tend to be quite immobile and, once established in a community, will tend to remain there. Then too, where a plant is located may have considerable influence on operating costs and profits. For these reasons, the location of a plant necessitates thorough analysis.

### Location Planning

Before a location for a plant is sought, long-range forecasts should be made anticipating the future needs of the company. These should be based upon the company's expansion policy, the anticipated diversification of products, the changing market, the changing source of raw materials, and any other foreseeable influences. Careful attention should be given to all of the economic factors that influence the need for the new plant and the size and location of the plant.

The selection of an appropriate plant location usually results from a three-step process involving: first, the region (e.g., Pacific Coast, New England, Midwest, Southeast, or Southwest) in which the factory should be situated; second the community in which it should be placed; and, finally, the exact site in the city or countryside. The location study is frequently performed by a special committee within the organization, although it is not uncommon to use an outside consulting firm that specializes in location studies. The purpose of the location study is to find an optimum location—one that will result in the greatest advantage to the organization.

The benefits to be gained from the relocation of an existing plant may best be shown by the example illustrated in Figure 4–1. These figures were complied by an office-equipment manufacturer in an eastern city. This company was planning to expand in its existing location but found that big savings could be achieved with a new plant located in any of four sites in the Midwest. Note the significant savings estimated at Site A.

| | Present Factory in East | Site A Midwest | Site B Midwest | Site C Midwest | Site D Midwest |
|---|---|---|---|---|---|
| Labor | $12,106,000 | $10,054,000 | $10,548,000 | $10,934,000 | $11,092,000 |
| Overhead (Including local taxes) | 1,190,000 | 618,000 | 602,000 | 636,000 | 662,000 |
| Freight costs | 507,000 | 432,000 | 366,000 | 360,000 | 338,000 |
| Utilities | 204,000 | 248,000 | 214,000 | 236,000 | 246,000 |
| *Total* | $14,007,000 | $11,352,000 | $11,730,000 | $12,166,000 | $12,338,000 |
| Estimated yearly savings at new plant: | | $ 2,655,000 | $ 2,277,000 | $ 1,841,000 | $ 1,669,000 |
| Savings as per cent of costs at present factory: | | 19.0% | 16.3% | 13.1% | 11.9% |

**Figure 4-1.** Comparison of costs of operating an office-equipment manufacturing plant in an Eastern city and in four sites in the Midwest. (*Source:* U.S. News and World Report, December 21, 1959, p. 87)

### Factors Influencing Location

In a study of plant-location patterns (sponsored by the Rockwell-Standard Corporation[1]), more than 4100 firms that had built new plants, transferred plants, begun business, or expanded were surveyed. The key factors generally contributing to the selection of locations were (1) proximity to good highways, (2) abundant labor supply, (3) availability of suitable land, and (4) proximity to markets. How important each of these factors is, as well as other factors, varies greatly from industry to industry. Other factors, such as an adequate water supply, are of prime importance to many manufacturing processes and would have to be given equal consideration along with

---

[1] The Manufacturing Newsletter, "Why They Choose New Sites," *Factory* (July 1963).

the four factors just mentioned. Figure 4-2 contains a summary of those factors that are commonly considered in selecting the general region, the community, and the exact site.

| Factors | Region | Community | Site |
|---|---|---|---|
| Proximity to good highways | × | × | × |
| Labor supply | × | × | |
| Nearness to market | × | | |
| Nearness to raw materials | × | | |
| Nearness to an existing plant | × | × | |
| Suitable land and land costs | | × | |
| Transportation | × | × | |
| Water supply | × | × | |
| Power supply | × | × | |
| Waste disposal | | × | |
| Taxes | | × | |
| Climate | × | | |
| National defense | × | | |
| Community administration and attitude | | × | |
| Schools, churches, and residential areas | | × | |
| Zoning restrictions | | × | × |
| Space for expansion | | | × |

**Figure 4-2.** Factors commonly considered in locating a plant. Note that some of them are important in selecting both the region and the community.

Since, as is illustrated in Figure 4-2, several of the factors have a bearing on both the region and the community in which the plant is to be located, we shall discuss these without regard to which of the two is under consideration.

**Proximity to good highways.** Among the 4100 firms surveyed by the Rockwell-Standard Corporation, the most frequent factor that prompted the companies to build where they did was the quality of the highway system, particularly its relationship to markets, raw materials, and labor supply. The existence of excellent highways, such as the interstate superhighways, makes the suburbs, small communities, and country as readily accessible as the cities. Then too, the superhighways have a direct bearing on labor supply. In the streetcar era, a factory could draw its workers only from as far away as about six miles. Now the labor supply can come as far as thirty to fifty miles.

**Labor supply.** Obviously, a company can't operate without employees, and the nature of the labor market should be investigated to insure that an adequate supply of qualified employees is available in the area. It is necessary in some organizations that skilled craftsmen be hired to fill many of the positions, and it is desirable to locate the plant in an area where a sufficient number are available. Many factory jobs, however, are of a semi-skilled nature and unskilled persons can soon be taught to perform them.

The level of wages paid the workers in a community is a vital factor for those companies whose labor costs form a high percentage of the manufacturing cost. Also, the productivity level attained by the workers and the history of labor relations in the community are being given increasingly serious consideration. It has been particularly noteworthy in recent years to observe the large number of light industries that have moved into small communities where they could get the advantage of country labor at lower hourly rates and higher productivity. Also, some companies that have experienced labor problems in highly unionized localities have chosen to locate new plants in areas where they can expect harmonious labor relations and high productivity.

**Nearness to market.** The cost of and time required for transporting the product to the customer is a major consideration for many companies. For this reason, it is desirable that the company be located near the center of its market. This is particularly true when the manufacturing process increases the bulk of the products. Examples are the many automobile assembly plants situated in various parts of the country and the regional tire plants built by the major rubber companies.

When locations are chosen for branch plants, the market to be served may be the determining factor. For example, a branch plant of a California shoe company was located in Ohio in order to be nearer the midwestern, eastern and southeastern market for ladies' "play" shoes. Other examples include the many cement, brick, roofing, and gypsum board plants scattered across the United States.

If a plant has already been established in some community, its present location may tend to restrict its market to the area in which it is located. But for those companies producing items such as fountain pens, jewelry, and watches, in which the costs of materials and labor are high, shipping costs are of secondary importance, and the location of the plant with reference to its market is not too important.

**Nearness to raw materials.** Companies using bulky or perishable materials find it desirable to be near a readily available source of their materials. The food industry has this problem with its canning factories, meatpacking plants, and creameries. Other examples include steel mills, sawmills, paper mills, and cement manufacturers. In these industries, the guiding principle is what the economists refer to as "weight losing." If the raw material loses a lot of weight in processing, then the plant should be located near the source of raw materials.

The relative cost of transporting raw materials must be weighed against the cost of shipping the finished product so that the plant, ideally, may be situated in that location where the costs are at a minimum. This is sometimes referred to as "weight balancing" and involves the reaching of a low-cost equilibrium between the costs of shipping raw materials and fuels and that of shipping the product to the market. The two factors of "weight losing" and "weight balancing" govern nearly all plant locations in the extractive industries. The steel industry, a prime example, has tended to locate near the coal supply because this is near the major markets for steel. Thus, the Fairless Works of U.S. Steel was located near Morrisville, Pennsylvania, where it can receive coal from Pennsylvania or West Virginia, and iron ore by ship, and is closer to the New York market than one of its competitors, Bethlehem Steel Company.

A company may find it desirable to be near another plant for which it is manufacturing component parts, shipping crates, or similar items. This reduces the transportation time and cost and facilitates coordination between the two plants.

**Nearness to an existing plant.**    Oftentimes, one of the principal factors in the location of a new branch plant is that of keeping it reasonably close to the parent plant. The National Industrial Conference Board found in a survey of 476 new plant locations that the sites were chosen in 42 per cent of the cases because they were near an existing plant or warehouse. That so high a percentage would select sites for this reason indicates its importance. For many companies it is important that new plants be located in an area where executive supervision and staff consultations will be facilitated. This, of course, conserves the executive's time and allows him to provide closer supervision of those activities under his jurisdiction.

As an example of a company influenced by this factor, a small plastics manufacturer located a new plant in a small town about 75 miles from its main plant and executive offices. As a result of this location, the engineers and executives are able to make frequent automobile trips to the new plant.

In considering nearby communities, caution should be exercised to insure that the plants do not compete in the same labor market.

**Availability of land and land costs.**    The cost of land is usually a minor factor in the choice of a location. However, the availability of an adequate site sometimes presents a problem. In communities that are interested in attracting new industries, land may be offered at a considerably reduced price or at no cost, and this may influence some companies to locate there. However, a company should not be misled into accepting a site that might later prove to be a serious handicap.

**Transportation.**    The company should be located in an area where adequate transportation facilities of the desired type are available. Some companies find it desirable to be located at an ocean port or on one of the inland waterways to take advantage of the lower cost of transporting materials by boat or barge. This is particularly true for bulk materials such as coal, iron ore, and petroleum products. For other companies, access to railroad and/or trucking facilities is adequate.

The costs of shipping the product or bringing in raw materials are significant factors for many companies, and the reduced freight rates available in some areas should be weighed against other operating costs to determine the predominant consideration.

**Water supply.** For those companies requiring large quantities of water in processing their products, the water supply must be given serious attention in choosing a plant location. This was a major consideration in locating a plant of a pharmaceutical company requiring tremendous quantities of water. The underground supply of water is gradually being depleted in many areas and presents a matter of critical importance to the companies already situated there. In some cases, it may force these companies to relocate their plants.

Consideration should be given to any pollution of the water, which might cause processing difficulties. Although most states have antipollution laws, the waste materials dumped into the rivers or streams may create problems for new companies requiring a supply of fresh, pure water.

**Power supply.** Every company has need for electric power, but only to those companies using tremendous quantities is this item of major importance in choosing the plant site. An adequate supply of power at low rates is available in most areas; seldom is it necessary for the company to develop its own power. However, some companies prefer to maintain a power station in a standby condition to take care of any emergencies that may arise.

**Waste disposal.** Companies manufacturing products such as antibiotics, steel, chemicals, and those using radioactive materials are confronted with a waste disposal problem that must be given consideration in locating the plant. Most states and communities have legislation preventing the dumping of untreated industrial waste materials into the streams and rivers or piling it on the land.

**Taxes.** The kinds and amounts of taxes levied by a state or community should be considered in locating a plant. Taxes become one of the operating costs; the kinds of taxes and the basis for fixing them should be thoroughly investigated. As an enticement to get plants to locate there, some states and territories (particularly Puerto Rico) offer companies tax exemptions for a stipulated period of time. This has influenced many companies to locate in these areas.

**Climate.** Seldom does the climate influence the location of a plant. In those companies requiring controlled temperature, humidity, and ventilation, it is possible to install equipment to maintain the required conditions.

Sometimes the personal preferences of the company executives, who will be working in the plant, influence locating a plant in a particular climate.

**National defense.** The location of certain plants that manufacture products important to our national defense is influenced by the government's desire for dispersion of these plants. By and large, however, the government's attempt to get dispersion of industry for security purposes has met with little success. Nevertheless, a considerable amount of industrial dispersion has come about as a result of many logical business decisions.

**Community administration and attitude.** Since all industries have a social responsibility to the communities in which they are located, it is important that the local authorities and the populace of the community be anxious to have the plant located there. Likewise, it is essential that the community be able to provide the necessary municipal services in the way of police and fire protection, maintenance of streets, refuse disposal, and so forth.

**Schools, churches, parks, and residential areas.** Finding the best town for a new plant is not solely an impersonal search for lowest transportation costs, low tax rates, and an adequate water supply, but is also a search for a community in which the employees will have excellent schools, churches, parks, and residential areas available to them. For, as H. C. Stuckerman[2] points out, "Our final decision on a location of the Rockwell Manufacturing Company is made by an unscientific walk around town. We look at the parks to see if the grass is cut, at the schools to see what shape they're in, at the churches and the homes to see if they're painted and well kept. These casual observations reveal as much as all the inducements and welcomes extended." Rockwell finds that a new plant employing 300 people affects roughly 2710 people and that it makes sense to pick a town that will provide the best services and living atmosphere for their employees and their families.

---

[2]"Picking Plant Sites the Unscientific Way," *Factory* (July 1958).

## Local Sites

After the community for a plant has been selected, the problem still exists of selecting the exact site on which the plant is to be built. The final choice of sites will usually result from considering the relative merits of each of the available sites. In weighing these sites against one another, the following questions should be asked about each of the factors that should be considered:

**Transportation facilities:** Is the location easily accessible to the main highways? Are the railroad facilities adequate to insure prompt receipt and shipment of goods? Can a railroad siding be made available?

**Availability of water, electric power, gas, and sewers:** Is water available in sufficient quantities? Is adequate electric power available? Is adequate gas available? Is the sewer system adequate to take care of the plant's needs?

**Zoning restrictions:** Will the zoning restrictions interfere with the company's building plans or operations?

**Soil characteristics:** Are the soil bearing characteristics suitable for supporting the building and equipment? Will the soil provide adequate drainage?

**Drainage:** Will the area drain away all surface water so that the buildings will not become an island in the middle of a flooded area?

**Parking areas:** Is adequate space available to provide for employee- and visitor-parking?

**Space for expansion:** Is sufficient space available to take care of expansion of the plant within the foreseeable future?

**Accessibility by workers:** Can the site be reached by public transportation? Is the road and street network leading to the site adequate to allow speedy entrance and exit of employees during rush periods?

**Cost of land:** Can the site be secured at a reasonable price?

**Existing buildings:** Are existing buildings available that might be suitable for the company's operation, and can they be rented or purchased at reasonable prices?

## Sources of Information

There are a number of excellent sources of information pertaining to plant locations. These include the United States Department of Commerce, state industrial development groups, state employment agencies, railroad promotion departments, and chambers of commerce. Brief information about different states and communities is contained in advertisements sponsored by these agencies in many of the leading magazines and newspapers. Complete facts and figures about the growth of the area, availability of labor, transportation facilities, wage levels, and similar information can be obtained from one or more of these groups.

## Evaluation of Plant Locations

It is very difficult to make a final decision as to the choice for a plant location. One location may have the advantage from the market standpoint, another may be closer to the materials supply, and a third may provide a better labor supply. In attempting to weigh these and other factors against one another, two methods are commonly used. These are *rating plans* and *cost analyses.*

**Rating plan.** In the rating plan, weights are assigned to each of the factors that should be considered. The factor deemed most important is given the highest weight (see Figure 4–3) and each of the other factors a lesser amount. For example, nearness to raw materials might be weighted at 400 points, nearness to market at 300, the labor supply at 275, and the other factors at lesser amounts. The total number of points for each of the alternative locations is determined and is used to assist in making a decision. In most cases this rating should be supplemented with a cost analysis.

| Factor | Maximum Possible Points | City A | City B | City C |
|---|---|---|---|---|
| Nearness to raw materials | 400 | 300 | 250 | 150 |
| Nearness to market | 300 | 150 | 200 | 250 |
| Labor supply | 275 | 150 | 225 | 175 |
| Transportation | 125 | 125 | 100 | 125 |
| Water supply | 200 | 100 | 150 | 175 |
| Power | 200 | 150 | 150 | 100 |
| Waste disposal | 100 | 50 | 75 | 75 |
| Land and construction costs | 70 | 60 | 50 | 50 |
| Climate | 50 | 25 | 40 | 35 |
| Taxes and laws | 40 | 35 | 25 | 40 |
| Local site | 40 | 40 | 30 | 35 |
| Total | 1800 | 1185 | 1295 | 1210 |

**Figure 4-3.** Rating chart for three alternative plant locations.

**Cost analysis.** As an aid in evaluating alternative plant locations, estimates should be made for all costs entering into the operation of the plant in each of the locations. This estimate should cover the initial cost of the physical facilities, the cost of raw materials, the cost of manufacture, and the cost of distribution (see Figure 4–4). After the determination of each of these costs, the unit cost for manufacturing the product in each of the locations can be reckoned and may be used to aid in deciding on the optimum location.

| COST COMPARISON CHART | | | |
|---|---|---|---|
| | | *Location* | |
| *Costs* | *City A* | *City B* | *City C* |
| *Operating Costs per Year:* | | | |
| Transportation Costs: | | | |
| Incoming materials | $  100,000 | $   90,000 | $   85,000 |
| Outgoing materials | 160,000 | 165,000 | 170,000 |
| Labor | 200,000 | 225,000 | 250,000 |
| Utilities: | | | |
| Power | 60,000 | 65,000 | 65,000 |
| Water | 30,000 | 28,000 | 32,000 |
| Fuel | 60,000 | 70,000 | 65,000 |
| Plant overhead: | | | |
| Rent or carrying costs | 60,000 | 55,000 | 64,000 |
| Taxes | 10,000 | 12,000 | 14,000 |
| Insurance | 5,000 | 5,000 | 5,500 |
| Miscellaneous | 5,000 | 8,000 | 8,500 |
| Total | $  690,000 | $  723,000 | $  759,000 |
| *Construction Costs:* | | | |
| Land | $  100,000 | $   50,000 | $   75,000 |
| Building | 1,500,000 | 1,250,000 | 1,600,000 |
| Special requirements | 40,000 | —— | —— |
| Total | $1,640,000 | $1,300,000 | $1,675,000 |

**Figure 4-4.** Cost comparison chart for three alternative plant locations.

## Trends in Plant Location

Pronounced trends are apparent in the location of industrial plants. More and more companies are decentralizing their operations and locating plants in small towns or suburban areas—particularly the large companies that require extensive space for buildings, parking lots, and other facilities. Also, many companies are choosing local sites that are in the country. This allows them to secure ample space and also frees them from paying the higher tax rate usually found in the city.

Often a number of advantages can be gained by locating a plant in a small town. Inexpensive building sites with ample space for expansion are usually available, and the community will probably welcome the increased revenue the company will bring into the area; a friendly atmosphere should prevail. In addition, labor is commonly available at a lower rate than in cities and more harmonious relations with the workers may be possible.

## Plant Buildings

When the company has chosen the community in which it will locate, consideration must be given to providing physical facilities. If the company is small, it may be able to rent or buy an existing building. Seldom, however, will a company requiring extensive space be able to find suitable facilities available for rent or purchase. This necessitates, then, the design and construction of new buildings.

When the construction of additional buildings or new buildings is planned for the relocation of the company, the responsibility for this function is commonly given to the plant-engineering group. This group will work closely with the architect and contractor in designing and constructing the buildings. If the company prefers, it can employ one of the large industrial construction firms, which will handle all the details of planning and constructing the buildings. Figure 4–5 illustrates a factory building built by such an organization.

**Figure 4-5.** Engineering Building, Penn Controls, Inc., Goshen, Indiana. (Design and construction by the Austin Co.)

In planning a building for the manufacturing facilities, a number of factors must be given consideration. These include:

1. Nature of the manufacturing process.
2. Plant layout and space requirements.
3. Lighting, heating, ventilating, and air conditioning.
4. Service facilities.
5. Future expansion.
6. Appearance.

Each of these will be discussed in detail in the sections that follow.

### Nature of Manufacturing Process

One of the chief determinants of the kind of building required will be the type of manufacturing process. The various machines and equipment used in the manufacture of steel plate, glass bottles, rubber tires, metal castings, food products, and other items dictate the type of building to be constructed. A building must allow sufficient floor loading, head space, bay size, and ventilation, as well as providing for the storage and flow of materials and adequate loading docks and railroad sidings.

Some manufacturing processes require considerable ventilation or controlled temperature and humidity. This influenced one company, which manufactures food products requiring a high degree of ventilation, to build a new plant in Texas that has no side walls. The prevailing winds blow through the plant and carry away fumes and dust-laden air. Obviously, this type of building would be unsuited to most manufacturing processes and climates.

### Plant Layout and Space Requirements

All the factors influencing the internal arrangement of a manufacturing plant are discussed in Chapter 10. Suffice it to say at this point that the location of the machines, service centers, and offices, the size of the bays required, and the degree of flexibility desired all will have considerable influence on the kind of building created. Ideally, the optimum plant layout should be determined, and the building should be just a shell around this design. However, a building that may prove to be ideal at the outset may lead to great inflexibility in the future. Thus, most new factory buildings are a compromise between the present ideal and the need to insure the necessary flexibility to meet the future needs.

## Lighting, Heating and Ventilating, and
## Air Conditioning

During recent years, industry has placed less and less reliance on natural light and has made increasing use of artificial illumination. (See Figure 4–6.) One of the greatest changes in the way in which plants are making use of power is through improved lighting. The Illuminating Engineering Society has recommended 100 ft.-c as an accepted level for general office work and 50 ft.-c to 100 ft.-c as an accepted level for most production areas. Many new plants are being designed to meet or to exceed these standards. This has had considerable impact on the power system design. For one thing, the main substation capacities are greater, and the distribution voltages are more frequently mated to optimum lighting economies (i.e., 480/277 volts and no lighting transformers) rather than to convenience levels (240 or 120 volts) as was formerly practiced.

It is quite common in larger plants to provide separate buildings for

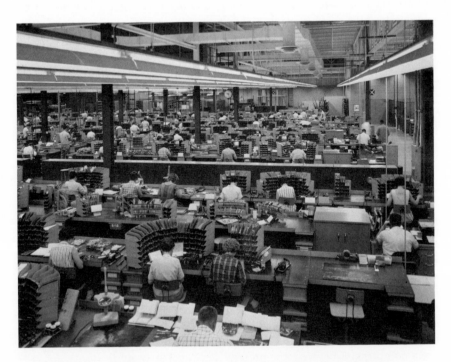

**Figure 4-6.** Interior view of modern factory building. Controlled conditions are maintained throughout this plant. Note the excellent lighting and lack of windows. (Courtesy Collins Radio Co.)

housing high-pressure boilers for heating purposes. The sizes of these will depend on the heating requirements and the need for steam and hot water for production purposes. In several plants built recently, the boilers had the following capacities: 600-hp high pressure (250 psi) at 30,000 lbs. per hour, 465-hp, and a 200-hp Scotch marine boiler for a hot-water heating system at 30-lb. pressure. Whereas larger plants may use boilers for heating purposes, many smaller plants use individual gas-fired infrared heaters.

Most modern plants provide ample ventilation by means of roof ventilators and exhaust fans. In some areas of the plant, these may change the air as often as every three minutes. Although more and more plants are being air conditioned, such installations tend to be limited largely to those requiring controlled conditions, such as in the electronics industry. On the other hand, most of the office facilities are being air conditioned—frequently through the use of combination heating and cooling units.

### Service Facilities

In addition to the heating, ventilating, and air-conditioning facilities, many companies maintain other service facilities, such as the following: fire fighting equipment, incinerators, sewage-treating systems, emergency power equipment, cooling towers, compressed-air equipment, and so forth. Some of these may be housed in separate buildings, the construction of which may be quite different from that of the main plant building.

### Future Expansion

The enormous expansion of industry in recent years has made management aware of the importance of planning for future expansion. Most companies erecting new buildings give consideration to this problem. If widespread expansion is anticipated, this may dictate the type of building to be constructed. Usually, single-story plants can be added onto much easier than multi-story plants, and in many cases a false wall is left in that side of the building to which a new addition is to be connected.

If multi-story buildings are to be enlarged by the erection of additional floors, this must be planned in advance so that the original structure will possess sufficient footings and supporting members to carry the added weight.

### Appearance

Appearance is being given considerable attention in choosing the style of architecture and building materials for modern plants. Modern factories are no longer ugly, smoke-spewing clusters but are rapidly becoming attractive structures in well-landscaped surroundings (see Figure 4–7).

**Figure 4-7.** Exterior view of a modern factory building. (Courtesy Woodward Governor Co.)

### Single- vs. Multi-Story Buildings

In planning factory buildings the advantages of single-story vs. multi-story arrangements must be weighed and that type of building selected that will best meet the needs of the company. The advantages of the single-story building are as follows:

1. Low construction cost per square foot of space.
2. Requires less time to erect.
3. Easy to expand.
4. Will take high-floor loads.
5. Suitable for assembly of heavy or bulky products.
6. Allows high ceilings.
7. No space lost for elevators and stairs.
8. Fewer columns.
9. Easier to handle materials.
10. Allows flexibility in layout.
11. Rest rooms and servicing equipment may be located in overhead trusses.
12. Maximum use of daylight and natural ventilation is possible.

13. Easier to isolate obnoxious or hazardous areas.
14. Easier supervision.

And the advantages of the multi-story building:

1. Requires less land.
2. Allows use of gravity for materials movement.
3. Allows more compact layouts.
4. Allows vertical arrangement of production and storage space.
5. Lower heating cost.
6. Top stories may be used for departments requiring special conditions.

## Shapes of Buildings

Factories are built in a large variety of shapes, although the trend appears to be to make them square or rectangular. The square or the rectangle allows a maximum of floor space with a minimum of wall area and is also conducive to flexibility.

In order to take advantage of natural light and other factors, many buildings have the shape of an L, E, F, H, T, I, or U.

## Construction of Buildings

**Types of construction.** The types of construction used on factory buildings have varied from highly flammable wood frames to fireproof reinforced concrete. Many of the older factory buildings were of the so-called mill-construction type. These buildings consisted of brick load-bearing walls, large wooden supporting members and thick plank floors. Owing to the heavy wood members, the buildings were somewhat fireproof because the pillars would still support the building even after being partially charred.

Many modern single-story factory buildings are being built with concrete, concrete block, or brick curtain walls and columns to support the roof. (See Figure 4–8). The columns are usually structural steel or poured reinforced concrete. The buildings built out of reinforced concrete are usually considered fireproof because all of the members affected by heat are encased in concrete.

In some cases, companies have made use of prefabricated steel buildings to provide additional manufacturing or storage space.

**Walls.** Walls may be constructed of a large variety of materials including:

1. Cement or cinder block.

**Figure 4-8.** Interior view of a steel frame factory building under construction. Note the use of I beams and steel roof deck.

2. Brick.
3. Tile.
4. Concrete.
5. Wood or wood products.
6. Insulated metal panels.
7. Corrugated metal panels.
8. Asbestos cement panels.

A combination of brick and either cement or cinder block is being
extensively used in the construction of modern buildings. Also, windows
comprise an increasing portion of the wall area in those buildings that are
not air conditioned.

**Roofs.** Roofs present a constant problem from the maintenance
standpoint and serious consideration should be given to their construction.
Flat roofs are probably most common; they are frequently insulated by
means of foam-glass blocks and/or cooled by roof ponds or spraying systems. The sawtooth roof is used in some buildings as a means of providing
natural overhead lighting.

The common materials used in the roof include corrugated or ribbed steel (see Figure 4–8) or aluminum, concrete, or lightweight mixtures of concrete and insulating materials. The use of wood is decreasing.

Bitumen and stone, pitch emulsion and stone, neoprene and hypalon synthetic rubbers, metal, and corrugated asbestos transite are commonly used for waterproofing a roof.

**Floors.** Concrete is the material most commonly used for floors. It is cheap and serviceable under almost any kind of manufacturing conditions and traffic, although when subjected to repeated heavy loads it does have a tendency to chip and powder. Other materials in frequent use are wood blocks laid on concrete, grease-resistant asphalt tile, and vinyl-asbestos tile laid on concrete.

### Trends in Building Construction

The trend appears to be to build a single-story plant connected to a single- or multi-story office and located in a spacious area (see Figure 4–9). Plants are being located on large tracts of land to allow space for parking lots and future expansion.

**Figure 4-9.** Aerial view of a modern factory building. (Courtesy Link-Belt Co. Building design and construction by the Austin Co.)

Bay sizes are being increased to as much as 40 feet by 60 feet or more in order to allow unrestricted processing areas and to facilitate flexibility. Increased use is being made of rigid or semi-rigid frames; the size of structural members is thereby reduced and framing problems are simplified. Precast concrete units are being used more widely.

Increased use is being made of the overhead space among the roof supporting members as an area in which to locate service equipment. This space is accessible for installation and maintenance.

For those plants that are completely air conditioned the tendency is to eliminate windows. Extensive use is being made of glass block to enhance the appearance of the building.

Modern plant buildings are being designed to add to the beauty of the community. Through the combination of attractive designs and building materials and beautifully landscaped grounds, factory buildings may become a feature of which the community is proud.

## QUESTIONS

1. Analyze why some company you know of may have located where it did.

2. What factors might be of major importance in determining the location of a fertilizer plant?

3. There has been much criticism of some locations selected for American plants in Europe. What factors should be considered in picking a plant location abroad?

4. A candy company, now located in the New York City area, plans to relocate in a small community of about 5000 persons about 45 miles away. What reasons might this company have for changing its location?

5. In recent years, many dehydrated milk plants have been started throughout the United States. What factors should be given maximum consideration in locating these plants?

6. One large manufacturer prefers not to use more than about 10 to 15 per cent of the available labor supply in any of its many new branch plants. Is this a good policy? Why?

7. Devise a plan for rating plant locations for some company with which you are familiar.

8. Why are so many companies locating their plants in the country rather than in cities?

9. Describe in your own words the typical factory building being constructed today, and comment on how it might be built more cheaply.

10. Some of the new power plants are being designed with no walls around them. What are the advantages and disadvantages of such a plant?

11. Discuss the factors to be considered in deciding what type of factory building would be best for a company.

12. Devise a method for rating the factors discussed in question 11.

13. Since the air conditioning of plants is very expensive, what justification does a company have for doing it?

# CASE PROBLEMS

**Wright Radio Company**

The Wright Radio Company was started in a midwestern city by John Wright in 1935. As a result of the development of an outstanding radio transmitter and excellent management, the company experienced steady growth. During World War II it became the largest industry in the community and employed over 4000 persons.

By 1959 John Wright decided to diversify the company's line of products and to develop several new items in the electronics field. The new products were well engineered and received widespread acceptance in the aircraft and electronics industries. It became obvious that, in order to meet the demand for these, the company must expand its production facilities.

After much consideration Mr. Wright recommended to the board of directors that the company build a new plant in another community. Further, he recommended that the new plant be located on the Pacific Coast so that it would be near the aircraft and electronics companies. Among the sites that were proposed were Seattle, San Francisco, and Los Angeles. Mr. Wright and the board finally decided to locate the plant in one of the Los Angeles suburbs.

*Questions:*

1. What factors should Mr. Wright and the board have considered in selecting the new plant location?
2. Do you consider Los Angeles a good choice? Why?

**Rhinehart Products Company**

Mr. T. J. Rhinehart, President of the Rhinehart Products Company, has developed a new injection molding machine for making small plastic parts. He feels there is a real future for such a machine and would like to begin manufacturing it. However, Rhinehart Products Company, which manufactures plastic wall tile and toilet seats, doesn't possess the necessary space or equipment to manufacture a machine of this type.

During the course of shopping for a suitable building, Mr. Rhinehart learned about a small plant in Illinois that had been used by a furniture manufacturing company that had gone bankrupt. This plant, which is located in a small town of about 1000 population, can be purchased for about $60,000, including the woodworking equipment.

Mr. Rhinehart decided to visit the plant and found it to possess the following features: (1) single-story, concrete-block construction, rectangular shape (40 ft.

$\times$ 250 ft.), (2) woodtruss roof with wood deck, (3) concrete floor, (4) building built three years ago, (5) heat supplied by unit gas heaters in the shop and hot-air furnace in the offices, (6) three offices and a reception room that take up approximately 1200 square feet at the front of the building, (7) located on a railroad siding, (8) adequate truck and railroad docks, and (9) adequate parking space for about 40 cars.

Mr. Rhinehart decided to buy the building and to convert it into a job-lot, metal-working plant for manufacturing plastic molding machines and for producing tools and dies.

*Questions:*
1. Do you think Mr. Rhinehart made a wise decision? Why?
2. Will this building be suitable for the purpose for which he purchased it? Why?
3. What additional information should be considered before buying a building to be used for this purpose?

# CHAPTER FIVE

# Design of
# Manufacturing Processes

The success of an industrial enterprise is to a great degree dependent upon the careful planning of manufacturing processes in advance of the actual production of goods.

Design of manufacturing processes is not restricted to the new concern or the new product. To meet competition, progressive manufacturing organizations are continually reviewing their operations with the objective of increased production of higher quality products at lower manufacturing costs. The introduction of new products, product improvements, and model changes make it mandatory that adequate organization and procedures be provided for the planning of manufacturing methods. Many techniques and procedures are involved, such as methods engineering, plant layout, and others. A close interrelationship of all is prerequisite to optimum results.

## Functional Scope of Process Design

Modern industry employs a definite pattern of activity in the design of manufacturing processes. Generally speaking this activity starts with the receipt of the product specifications and ends with the final plans for the manufacture of the product. In a broad sense this pattern of activity is uniform, regardless of the kind of product or the type of manufacturing involved. The steps are as follows:

1. A careful review of the product design and specifications to make sure that economical manufacture is feasible.

2. Determination of the methods of manufacture that will result in the optimum manufacturing cost.

3. Selection—or development—and procurement of all machines, tools, and other equipment required for the manufacture of the product at the required quality and rate of production.

4. Layout of the production area and auxiliary spaces, and installation of the manufacturing facilities.

5. Planning for and establishing the necessary control of money, materials, machines, and manpower to insure the effective utilization of the manufacturing facility for the economical production of the product.

The above steps may be identified as functions of various recognized activities, such as manufacturing engineering, process engineering, methods engineering, tool engineering. No matter what the group or groups involved are called, the functional scope of process-design activity can be identified as all work that is necessary to arrange the manufacture of the product by the most economical means.

## Organization for Process Design

In a more restricted sense the design of the manufacturing process is the determination of how the product is to be made. Organization for this activity varies. The manufacturing engineering group may report to a manufacturing executive, to the chief product engineer, or to some other function of management. Because specialized knowledge and skill are required, best results are obtained if these manufacturing specialists function as a staff activity; however, in a small manufacturing plant process design may become a part-time responsibility of one or more members of the manufacturing line organization. Generally speaking, manufacturing engineering groups are concerned with methods, machines, tools, equipment, and the layout of the production area.

## Basic Factors Affecting Process Design

There are three basic factors that affect the design of a manufacturing process. A careful study of each factor must be made and pertinent information gathered and evaluated. These basic factors are:

1. The volume or quantity of the product to be manufactured.
2. The required quality of the product.
3. The equipment that is available, or that can be procured, for the manufacture of the product.

## Volume

The volume to be manufactured must always be considered as the volume to be produced within a given period—or as the rate of production. In this manner it can be related to the capacity of the manufacturing equipment under consideration and the best methods selected accordingly.

The anticipated volume should be based also upon a sales forecast. This is of particular importance in the introduction of a new product. Funds should be expended for the improvement of processes only when the forecast indicates such a volume of sales that an appropriate return on the investment can be realized.

Generally speaking, the greater the volume of the product to be produced, the greater is the opportunity to incorporate advanced methods of manufacture into the design of the manufacturing process.

The number of identical units to be produced vitally affects the selection of manufacturing methods. The savings per unit of product, or per component part, when multiplied by the total volume to be produced may be applied to the purchase of more modern equipment. It may justify new and better machine tools or other major items. More often, however, it will justify better auxiliary equipment such as jigs, fixtures, or dies, which will in turn increase the productive capacity of the existing major equipment in the plant.

Methods of manufacture vary widely with the volume to be produced. The production of heavy industrial apparatus and ships involves very few units of product, requires skilled machinists or artisans using general-purpose machines and tools, and assembly is by skilled labor. On the other hand the mass manufacture of washing machines, refrigerators, radios, automobiles, and similar goods is accomplished with a large proportion of automatic machinery—in many cases with a high degree of mechanization or automation—and on a planned assembly line that requires a minimum of skill (see Chapter 6).

**Product explosion and standardization.**    Many concerns are engaged in multi-product operations; that is, they make more than one product or product line. Most products are assembled and can be "exploded"—or broken down—into assemblies, subassemblies, and component parts. Where more than one product is involved there is usually standardization of subassemblies or component parts among the different products.

The process engineer must design processes at all levels of fabrication— that is, for producing assemblies, subassemblies and component parts. When considering the volume to be produced, particularly of component parts, he must plan on the total requirements. Thus, standardization of component parts and product explosion are of primary importance to the process engineer.

**Economic manufacturing lot size.**   A major portion of the activity of the process engineer deals with the individual component parts of the assembled product. For many component parts the productive capacity of the machines used exceeds by far the planned daily use of these parts in assemblies. As a result these parts are produced intermittently, or in "lots." The optimum size of these lots must be determined by the process engineer. This quantity is known as the *economic manufacturing lot size.*

Many factors must be considered in the determination of the economic manufacturing lot size. Numerous formulas or models have been developed for this procedure, and quantitative measures are under constant development and improvement. Essentially, however, the following factors govern:

*Rate of usage.*   Of first importance is the anticipated rate of usage of the part; this rate must be considered together with the time required to produce a replacement lot. Quantities should be so established that at all times stock will be available to the assembly departments. This same principle is used by the materials control function in determining minimum inventory levels.

*Cost to manufacture.*   Next in importance is the cost to manufacture. The larger the lot size, the lower is the cost per unit to set up machines and to prepare the paper work that enters and controls the production of the order. At the same time, the larger the lot size the greater is the working capital investment in material and labor, the greater is the cost of handling and storing the material, and the higher are insurance and tax charges. Smaller manufacturing lot sizes increase unit setups and preparation charges and decrease working capital investment, storage costs, and insurance and tax charges.

For example, if it costs $40 to set up a machine—that is, to mount the tools and get them properly set—and if only ten pieces were to be made, the unit distribution of this cost would be $4. If 1000 pieces were to be produced, setup costs would be only 4 cents per unit. If the cost of making each part on the machine is $3 and the material for the part cost $2, the in-process investment for a lot of ten pieces would be $90—at a cost of $9 for each part. On the other hand, if 1000 parts were made the in-process investment would be $5,040—and the manufacturing cost of each part only $5.04.

*Deterioration or obsolescence.*   Another factor to be considered is the possibility of loss owing to either deterioration or obsolescence of a large stock of parts.

All these factors must be weighed by the process engineer and an economic manufacturing lot size determined that will result in the production of parts at an optimum cost per unit. Availability of productive capacity for such lot sizes must be determined and included in the considerations.

Economic manufacturing lot sizes must be checked periodically as they are subject to revision owing to sales trends and variations in the factors mentioned above.

*Lot size models.* The use of economic lot size models has been in effect for many years, and the literature abounds with the many formulations that have been proposed. One of the problems that arises in the use of mathematical models is the fact that many factors have a bearing on optimum lot sizes, and one can't weigh all of them in a simple formula. On the other hand, a number of the factors that appear in many of the complex formulas that have been developed have so little effect on the final answer that they may be left out. Also, one finds that the unit costs obtained for an economic lot size will vary only slightly for quantities a little above or below the exact economic lot size.

In considering economic manufacturing lot sizes, two opposing sets of costs come into play—the carrying costs per unit and the setup costs per unit. It is evident that the carrying costs per unit will increase as the size of the lot increases; likewise, the setup costs will decrease as the lot size increases. This may be represented mathematically by the classic lot size model:

$$\text{Total cost} = \frac{QI}{2} + \frac{RS}{Q}$$

where the first term defines the carrying cost and the second the setup cost. If this relationship were depicted graphically, the point at which the two curves cross would be the minimum economic lot size ($Q_0$) which is defined by:[1]

$$Q_0 = \sqrt{\frac{2RS}{I}}$$

in which $Q$ = Economic lot size
  $R$ = Annual use of the item in units per year
  $S$ = Setup cost each time a new lot is started
  $I$ = Carrying cost per unit per year

As an example of the use of this model, let us consider the following numbers:

  $R$ = 1000 units per year
  $S$ = $20.00 per setup
  $I$ = $0.20 per piece per year

---

[1]W. Warren Haynes and Joseph L. Massie, *Management Analysis Concepts and Cases* (Englewood Cliffs, N.J.: Prentice-Hall, Inc., 1961), p. 433.

$$Q_0 = \sqrt{\frac{2(1000)(20.00)}{0.20}} = \sqrt{200,000} = 447 \text{ units}$$

A note of caution should be cited about the use of this model. It is a simplified version and may not fit the conditions in many real life situations. For example, it does not take into account variable demand, variable inventory carrying costs, and other factors. Thus, if this model doesn't fit the situation, then a model must be tailored to fit the problem.

The use of lot size models for the many different products that have to be made on a production line can frequently lead to highly unbalanced production in the manufacturing facility. This has led many companies to use computers to do the necessary computations and to provide for the "smoothing" or "leveling" of the total production output.

### Quality of the Product

The required quality of the product has a definite effect on the design of the manufacturing process. When the quality level is determined, it is the responsibility of the product or design engineer to stipulate it in the drawings and specifications. Bills of materials, parts lists, assembly and detail drawings, and engineering releases should give the process engineer a clear understanding of the quality requirements for all assemblies, subassemblies, and component parts. Then, methods and equipment must be selected that assure the production of parts of the required quality at the lowest manufacturing cost.

The dimensional requirements, types of surfaces to be produced, and other characteristics of parts to be manufactured must be matched to the capabilities of different types of machines and methods. The mechanical condition of equipment should be checked carefully to determine whether it will produce parts in accordance with its rated performance. Capability studies have been developed that by the use of applied statistics, will predetermine the quality level for an operation by the machine that has been selected either by the planning or routing group.

Generally speaking, the higher the required quality level of a product, the higher is the cost to manufacture it. Quality problems will be discussed in greater detail in the chapter on quality control (see Chapter 15).

### Equipment

In the majority of situations the process engineer must attempt to design manufacturing processes that are adaptable to and will balance the productive load of available existing equipment. In the case of a new plant and a new product this does not apply; however, this latter condition is the exception rather than the rule in industry.

Adapting methods to types of available equipment is a principal factor when manufacturing in economic lots. At times the number of machines available of a given type or size may influence the design of the process. The process as designed may overload the productive capacity of a certain machine group. In such a case an alternate method may be planned using other types of equipment even though this plan results in an increase in the manufacturing cost. Close liaison must be established with the production control function where current machine loads are maintained.

That only existing types of equipment can be used by the process engineer should not be stipulated. This would stifle any progressive ingenuity on his part. Often new methods may be devised the use of which will justify the purchase of new and more productive equipment. When considering a new machine, its adaptability for use in the manufacture of all parts of the product should be carefully reviewed; the volume of production of one component part might not indicate sufficient savings to warrant the purchase, whereas additional changes in processes of other parts might justify the new equipment and result in an overall reduction in the cost of manufacture.

Process engineers must be constantly alert to new improvements in machine tools and equipment that may be used in the manufacture of the product.

## Types of Manufacturing

Based upon a careful consideration of volume, quality, and equipment, the process engineer can determine the type of manufacturing best suited for any manufacturing situation. The type of manufacturing to be employed is generally determined by the manufacturing process design. For the most part the various types of manufacturing involve either *continuous* or *intermittent* production of goods.

### Continuous Manufacture

Continuous manufacture is the production of goods on a flow basis at a predetermined rate. Flow methods require that the product move constantly —or approach constant movement—from operation to operation without a controlled storage at any point in the process. Continuous manufacture is typical of large food-processing plants and many chemical industries. (See Figure 5-1.)

Continuous manufacture is also characteristic of the assembly-line

**Figure 5-1.** Washing machines being assembled on slat-type conveyor. (Courtesy The Maytag Company).

techniques used by manufacturers of automobiles, radios, refrigerators, and similar products. Usually a constantly moving conveyer is employed, the base frame of the product starting at the head of the line and other component parts or subassemblies being added as the "growing product" moves along, the final finished assembly being taken off the conveyer at the end of the line.

Continuous manufacture may also be employed in the manufacture of component parts, such as a transmission housing. In this situation a "balanced line" of machine tools or operations is planned. For example, the operator of the first machine will take a rough casting from a stock pile and perform the first operation. The partly processed part is then passed on, usually by placing it on some type of conveyer, to the next operator, who performs the next operation. Thus, operation by operation the casting is processed until a completely machined part has been produced (see Figure 5-2).

**Balancing lines.** To be economical each operation in a continuous line must require approximately the same length of time—or else two or more machines working simultaneously be provided for the "slow" operations. The design of a continuous process line to equalize the time required

**Figure 5-2.** Parts being machined on Newton Mills. Since this is the first machining operation on this part, the parts are obtained from the wire basket in the foreground and asided to the carriers on the monorail conveyor at the left. The large tubes leading up from the machines are part of the chip removal system designed to keep the fixtures and tools free of the considerable metal removed from these parts at this operation. (Courtesy The Maytag Company).

at each work station is called *balancing the line*. The balancing of an assembly line involving manual labor is not as difficult as the balancing of a line of machine tools, because once the operation time of a machine is established it becomes fixed. On the other hand, manual labor can be redistributed to gain an effective steady flow by changing the job content for each operator on the line.

Recent advances in line balancing have been made possible through the use of computers. For example, in one company a program was developed for a high-speed computer that enables the machine to determine 1000 complete manpower combinations and then pick the 10 best. The final choice among the 10 is then up to the industrial engineer.

**Mechanization and automation.** Current trends towards mechanization and automation—the "push-button factory"—indicate the future potential of continuous manufacturing in industry. The development of loading, unloading, and transfer devices is resulting in mechanized production lines. Also the further addition of measuring and feedback mechanisms for the full control of the process results in automation. This subject will be discussed in further detail in Chapter 6.

## Intermittent Manufacture

When continuous manufacture is not feasible, either for large or small quantities of product, intermittent manufacture is employed. In this type of manufacture the product is processed in lots rather than on a continuous flow basis. It is a function of the process engineer to determine the economic manufacturing lot size for each component part, subassembly, and assembly.

For example, the economic lot size for the production of a gear to be used on a power lawn mower might be 1500 pieces. In this case 1500 blanks might be cut from steel bar stock and tagged for a specific job number. The 1500 blanks would then travel from work station to work station. At each work station the operation would be completed on all of the 1500 parts before the lot was moved to the next work station.

Ideally, there would be no waiting time as each lot arrived at the next work station. Realistically, this objective is hard to attain. In an intermittent manufacturing plant there are usually one or more lots ahead of each work station awaiting processing. This is one fundamental reason why intermittent manufacturing requires a larger inventory of goods in process than continuous manufacturing.

Intermittent manufacture is particularly adaptable to concerns making product lines, such as several sizes of the same basic design of water pump. In situations such as this it is good practice to standardize component parts for use in many different products or sizes of products. Accumulation of the many product requirements results in optimum economic manufacturing lot sizes.

**Job-Lot Manufacture.** Intermittent manufacture is often referred to as job-lot production when manufacturing to a customer's purchase order or specification. Job-lot production is characteristic of concerns manufacturing large or expensive machines or equipment. A customer may order one, two, or more units of the product; a manufacturing order is entered for that lot only, material is procured, the units produced and shipped. The product may be considered standard so far as the manufacturer is concerned, but units are produced only after they are sold.

Although in some instances repeat orders may be received, the possibility of such is discounted in the design of the manufacturing processes and in the computation of the production costs. On the other hand the special tools, patterns, and dies are usually stored for such a contingency. This practice presents a difficult storage problem for the job-lot manufacturer.

### Mixed Types of Manufacture

Most industries use both continuous and intermittent manufacture in the production of goods. True continuous production of all the component parts of a product—the objective of the automatic factory—is not as common as might be expected. The reason is the difficulty of balancing the unit manufacturing times for all component part requirements. For example, the productive capacity of a plant making a line of electric motors might be such that a year's requirement for a small special pin could be produced on an automatic screw machine in two days. On the other hand, the power presses producing the stampings used in the stators and rotors might have to work to capacity to keep the assembly line supplied with parts. Thus the power presses producing these stampings could be placed in a continuous process line, which in turn would flow into the motor assembly line. To attempt to "tie-in" the production of the special pin on a continuous manufacturing basis is obviously out of the question.

Many factories are classified as continuous manufacturing plants even though they may use both continuous and intermittent manufacturing techniques. This classification is justified by the fact that each plant is designed to utilize its full capacity in the production of assembled products at a planned rate of production.

The real challenge today is to increase the flexibility of mechanized or of automated equipment so that its use is possible for more than one size of part or so that different parts may be processed on the same mechanized line. The successful solution of this problem will result in a greater degree of integration of continuous manufacturing techniques in a normal intermittent manufacturing situation.

## Relation of Process Design to
## Types of Manufacturing

There is a definite relationship between the design of the manufacturing process and the type of manufacture that is adopted. For continuous manufacture the methods and processes must be determined before the line is set up. The manufacturing process is built into the line. Once processing lines are established, any further changes in methods should be held to a minimum owing to the dependency of each operation on all preceding operations. Changes usually require that the line be shut down with the resultant loss of the productive capacity of the entire plant. Changes in the line for improvement of methods are usually held up until a model change is made in the product. For continuous manufacture the design of the manufacturing process must be thorough and accurate.

Although the volume to be produced is not a controlling factor in the selection of the type of manufacturing, continuous manufacturing usually means that the volume of production is large. Large volume usually justifies the use of highly specialized tools and equipment; thus the machine tool may be built to fit the methods. (See Figure 5-3) In this case the methods would control the selection of tools and equipment.

**Figure 5-3.** Special purpose machine used to drill, ream and tap holes simultaneously on two diesel engine blocks. (Courtesy International Harvester Company)

For intermittent production no lines are set up. The process engineer is usually required to adapt the methods and processes to the types of equipment available or to be procured. General-purpose machine tools and equipment are employed, as each machine may be used for varying operations on many different component parts of the product. (See Figure 5-4.) One advantage of intermittent manufacture over continuous manufacture is that changes in methods can be made more readily and seldom will interfere with the overall productive capacity of the plant.

**Figure 5-4.** General purpose machine tool. (Courtesy South Bend Lathe, Inc.)

## The Design of Manufacturing Processes

Although the fundamentals of process engineering are the same for all types of manufacturing and all kinds of products, the procedures and techniques will vary among different industries. The design of manufacturing processes by a large chemical or food-processing plant will involve different procedures and techniques from those used in designing processes for the manufacture of heavy industrial equipment by a job-lot industry. Each, however, will follow the same basic pattern.

None of the steps in the design of a manufacturing process can be eliminated. It is simply a matter of when certain things are done and by whom they are accomplished. What characterizes modern industry is the careful planning of manufacturing methods by technically qualified personnel as opposed to the early attitude of "let the shop make it"—where the final plans for making the part were often left to the operator actually doing the operation.

### Process Design Procedures

A typical industry that presents all phases of process design in a logical order might be a manufacturer of home appliances such as refrigerators, stoves, and washing machines. Such plants usually employ both continuous and intermittent manufacturing techniques and, in the total, are usually planned as continuous manufacturing plants.

To the layman the design of manufacturing processes for such a plant presents a complicated picture. Actually the procedure is simple; it looks complex only because the layman looks at the product as a whole. The process engineer, on the other hand, usually starts with the consideration of a single component part. A basic procedure in this type of plant might be as follows:

1. The product designer and the process engineer work in close co-operation during the design of the part to insure that all possible manufacturing problems are taken into consideration as the component part design is developed. Close cooperation between the process engineer and the product engineer is of major importance to the economical manufacture of a product. Best results can be obtained when these two join forces in the early design stages of the product. Consideration should be given to the detailed design of each component part to insure the best manufacturing methods for the product as a whole. Such a procedure will insure the minimum of design changes that may be required at a later date to accommodate the manufacturing process.

2. Completion of the design of the part makes it possible to proceed with the determination of the three basic factors of volume, quality, and the manufacturing equipment available. In many cases the purchase or development of new and more modern equipment enters the considerations.

3. The next step is the decision to "make or buy." Because of the wide range of the impact of this decision on the plant, the final decision is normally made at an organizational level higher than the process engineer. To date, no universally acceptable quantitative formula has been developed for the solution of this problem. Comparison of the price of the finished part delivered to the plant can be made with the estimated manufacturing or shop cost as determined by the process engineer. Many rather intangible factors, such as maintenance of level of employment, optimum utilization of plant facilities, and trade relations with sources of supply are involved. The decision to make or buy must be considered in all manufacturing situations.

4. Assuming that the part is to be made, the next step is to consider all the work that is necessary to bring the part from the raw material stage to the completely machined or processed part ready for assembly. Whether or not an actual list of the work to be done is prepared will depend to a large extent on the experience of the process engineer. In any event this step will translate the designer's blueprint of the part into a complete understanding of what has to be done by the manufacturing group.

5. The process engineer next groups the work to be done into operations. The basic factors of volume to be produced, the required quality of the product, and the capabilities of the equipment available are carefully considered in this step. Each operation is assigned to the type and size of machine —or work station—that will perform the job most economically. The number

of operations required to complete the part is established at the optimum point that will keep the manufacturing costs at a minimum. Quantitative measurement is somewhat easier in this step than the step of "make or buy." The various techniques of methods engineering and work measurement— including the use of standardized time values—are employed in this phase of manufacturing process design.

A typical part is shown in Figure 5-5; the work involved is listed in

**Figure 5-5.** Drawing of a check valve cap.

Figure 5-6. This particular part can be processed in two operations on a turret lathe (see Figure 5-7) if grouped into operations as shown in Figure 5-8.

a.   Turn $1\frac{15}{16}$ D
b.   Turn 1.745–1.740 D
c.   Turn 1.500–1.490 D
d.   Turn 1.000–0.934 D
e.   Form $2\frac{1}{4}$ R
f.   Shave $2\frac{1}{4}$ R
g.   Thread $1\frac{1}{2}$–12 NF–3
h.   Thread 1–14 NF–3

i.   Chamfer $\frac{1}{16}$ × 45 degrees–1.500 D
j.   Chamfer $\frac{1}{16}$ × 45 degrees–1.000 D
k.   Drill $\frac{27}{64}$ thru
l.   Counterbore $\frac{13}{16}$ × $\frac{5}{8}$ deep
m.   Countersink 90 degrees to $\frac{9}{16}$ D
n.   Tap $\frac{1}{2}$–13 NC–3
o.   Drill $\frac{11}{16}$ × $\frac{1}{2}$ deep
p.   Tap $\frac{3}{4}$—16 NF-3 × $\frac{3}{8}$ full thread

**Figure 5-6.**   List of work to be done on check valve cap P-17567.

6.    The last step in operation analysis is to arrange the operations in the proper sequence for the most economical manufacture.

**Figure 5-7.** Turret lathe. (Courtesy Gisholt Machine Co.)

**Use of process analysis charts.**   The process analysis chart is a useful technique for accumulating and summarizing the work of the process engineer. This technique presents a complete and graphical picture of the process planned for the manufacture of the product. Careful analysis of such charts by experienced process engineers will often indicate opportunities for improvement—or anticipate possible "bottlenecks"—in the manufacturing process.

Process charts and their preparation are covered in the chapter on methods engineering (see Chapter 7).

**Pilot processes.** Many manufacturing process designs, particularly in the chemical industry, are prechecked by the building and operation of a "pilot plant." A pilot plant is a small-scale operation of the total manufacturing plan—either as to the size of the equipment or the productive capacity of the experimental setup. In many cases only parts of the manufacturing process are checked by this technique. In any event the objective of the pilot-plant operation is to verify whether the process design will produce the required results at the anticipated manufacturing costs.

## Process Design Communications and Records

In designing the manufacturing process, the process engineer determines the work methods, the type of machines to be used, and the operation sequence for each component part, subassembly, and final assembly of the product. To be of value to the manufacturing organization this information must be presented in a clearly understandable and systematic manner. Sound communications between the process engineer and the operating departments is most essential. Information must be accurate and up to date all at times.

### Standard Process (Operation) Sheets

To be usable the final design of the manufacturing process must be recorded. The actual forms of these records vary; however, they all carry essentially the same basic information and are prepared for the same purpose. These records have many names: master route sheet, operation sheet, process sheet, process and tooling record, master plan. A typical form is shown in Figure 5-8.

Regardless of the name or type of form used, the information recorded represents a plan for a standard way of making the product. The term most descriptive of this objective is *standard process sheet*.

The importance of clearly stated and complete standard process sheets cannot be overemphasized. A master copy should be maintained in the process engineering department at all times, if possible. The master file of standard process sheets represents the "know-how" in the manufacture of

| STANDARD PROCESS SHEET | | | | | | | |
|---|---|---|---|---|---|---|---|

Material Specs. _1112 CRS_
Purchased Stock Size _1¾" hex. × 16'_
Pcs. Per Pur. Size _107_
Weight _1.35 # per unit_

Part Name _Check Valve Cap_
Usage _Speed Control Valve Assy._
Assy. No. _P8015_
Sub. Assy. No. _P17570_

Part No. _P17567_
Date Issued _____
Date Sup'd. _____
Issued By _T.E.C._

| Oper. No. | Operation Description | Dept. | Machine | Set up | Rate | Tools |
|---|---|---|---|---|---|---|
| 10 | Turn 1.745 D, turn 1.500 D and chamfer; | K | Turret lathe | 1.50 hr | 10/hr | Lot P #210 |
|  | form turn 1.000 D, 2½ R and 1½ D, |  | WS 2 AW |  |  |  |
|  | shave 2½ R; Drill 23/64 thru, c'bore |  | equal |  |  |  |
|  | 13/16 × 5/8 deep, ctsk. 90° to 9/16 D; |  |  |  |  |  |
|  | thread 1½ -12 and tap ½ -13; cutoff. |  |  |  |  |  |
|  |  |  |  |  |  |  |
| 20 | Chamfer 1.000 D; drill 4/8 × ½ deep | K | " | 0.50 hr | 35/hr | Lot P #211 |
|  | tap ¾ -16 × ⅜ full thread; thread |  |  |  |  |  |
|  | 1 -14. |  |  |  |  |  |
|  |  |  |  |  |  |  |
|  |  |  |  |  |  |  |
|  |  |  |  |  |  |  |
|  |  |  |  |  |  |  |
|  |  |  |  |  |  |  |
|  |  |  |  |  |  |  |
|  |  |  |  |  |  |  |
|  |  |  |  |  |  |  |

**Figure 5-8.** Standard process sheet for making a check valve cap.

the product and is probably one of the most valuable assets of the manufacturing concern.

It is emphasized that operation descriptions should be brief, concise and clear, and leave no room for misinterpretation. Also it should be noted that the process engineer selects the *type* of machine or equipment to be used—not a specific machine by its shop number. Selection of machines by shop number restricts the flexibility of the routing function of production control and should be avoided in the design of the manufacturing process. Routing, which determines *where* an operation is to be performed, is discussed more fully in Chapter 14.

### Preparation and Use of Standard Process Sheets

All work done in the processing of a product should be planned and recorded on standard process sheets. As a rule, a standard process sheet is prepared for each process in the plant. (A "process" is all operations that take place on any component part, subassembly, or assembly between controlled storages; or all operations that are performed on a continuous process or assembly line.) On long assembly lines it is common practice to post the operation description at each work station in the line; such descriptions are of a specific job or operation—not of a process. Standard process sheets are not normally prepared for purchased parts that require no work before their use at assembly.

A principal problem in the distribution of standard process sheets is the necessity of keeping them up to date. The trouble that might result from the production of a lot of goods from an obsolete standard process sheet is obvious. It is to avoid this possibility that some plants issue the standard process sheet only with the manufacturing order for the production of a specific quantity of parts. In these cases it is common practice to duplicate the information from the standard process sheet on the route sheet that accompanies the work through the plant. The combination of these forms with the addition of the manufacturing order number constitutes the manufacturing order. These orders are destroyed after the production has been completed. This practice is particularly adaptable to intermittent or job-lot production. Various duplicating systems are available by which the master record of the standard process sheet can be used to duplicate information direct to the route sheet or manufacturing order copies.

Job-lot plants furnish manufacturing orders or route sheets based upon the design of the manufacturing process. The master standard process sheets are then filed so that they may be available if a repeat order is received. In some industries this presents quite a problem. The manufacture of airplanes has been plagued with an almost constant change in product specifications and methods of manufacture. As a result the microfilm recording of manufacturing records has been adopted by many manufacturers.

On the other hand, in a continuous manufacturing industry the use of the standard process sheet in the operating departments may be so limited that it is almost non-existent. This does not mean that the process was not carefully designed. As a matter of fact the manufacturing process was designed into the process and assembly lines—thus requiring much greater care in the planning than in the case of intermittent manufacture. Once the process is designed into the line the operating personnel have little, if any, need for reference to the standard process sheet.

## Improvement of Product Design for Manufacturing

Often the product—or its component parts—is so designed that economical production is not possible. The logical solution is to modify or redesign the product in order to permit manufacture at a lower cost. Another situation that may call for the redesign of a product is the lack of suitable machines or equipment.

In such situations the process engineer has four possible solutions:

1. The part may be purchased from a concern having the proper equipment.

2. The necessary equipment may be procured.

3. Existing equipment may be modified to produce the part.

4. The part may be redesigned so that it can be produced on available equipment.

In many instances the fourth solution will prove the most feasible.

It is not the prerogative of the process engineer arbitrarily to make changes in the design of the product. It is, however, his responsibility to recommend to the product designer such changes as might result in cost reductions. All changes in product design and specifications must originate from the product-engineering group to insure that no change made will materially affect the functional requirements of the product.

## Evaluation of the Design of Manufacturing Processes

The objective in designing the manufacturing process is to insure the production of the product at the optimum cost. A major problem confronting the process engineer is the determining of when this objective has been attained.

Manufacturing methods is a dynamic and changing area of activity. Better tools and equipment are constantly being developed. New materials are being introduced and new uses for old materials discovered. Every process engineer must be alert to changes in the basic factors of volume, product quality level, and equipment available. Any of these changes may affect the design of the manufacturing process.

A basic tenet of the process engineer is that there is always a better way to make the product. Cost-reduction programs sponsored by management are common in industry. Competition makes such policies prerequisite to success in manufacturing.

The use of the staff specialist—the process engineer—contributes to this end. A clearly thought-out plan of manufacturing will uncover possible pitfalls and predict for management the manufacturing cost. This estimate can be translated into anticipated profits. Careful planning insures a complete coverage of all operations in manufacturing a product and of the costs involved.

The improvement of manufacturing plans cannot go on indefinitely to the exclusion of the production of the product. Production schedules must be met. Plant facilities may also limit the extent of the improvements that can be made within the current manufacturing plan. All of these problems are best solved by the cooperative efforts of all functions involved. Any solution, however, should be accepted as only one bench mark in the continuing improvement of the manufacturing process.

Many intangibles must be considered from time to time. Among these are: the cost of larger inventories caused by the leveling of production to prevent labor turnover, the more common problems of overhead distribution, and the value of the customer goodwill that may be lost through late deliveries or poor quality of product. These and many other intangible values enter into the total evaluation of the manufacturing process design.

## QUESTIONS

1. The Welch Manufacturing Company is a new firm being started to manufacture power lawn mowers. What information would be needed to make a decision as to whether or not it should be planned for continuous or intermittent manufacture?

2. (a) Write a standard process sheet for something that you have made.
   (b) How might you change your methods if you were going to make 5000 units?

3. Why does a higher quality level of product usually result in higher manufacturing costs?

4. Select some common object—a cigarette lighter, a pencil sharpener, a pair of pliers—and sketch a new design that you feel would cost less to manufacture.

5. From a trade magazine get an advertisement of a new process or piece of equipment. Discuss the advantages claimed by the manufacturer of the equipment.

6. Discuss the necessity of close cooperation between the product engineer and the process engineer.

7. What is the function of the standard process sheet?

8. Make a list of all factors you can think of that would influence the economic manufacturing lot size. Indicate those that suggest large lots and those that suggest small lots.

9. Explain the meaning and application of "balancing out the line."

10. What is the best measure of success of the work of the process engineer?

## CASE PROBLEMS

### The Dallas Corporation

The Dallas Corporation produces space heating units in a number of types and sizes. Most of the parts for these units are made by the company and stored for later use during assembly of the heaters.

Since many different items are made and stored, the company wishes to be certain to manufacture these items in the most economical lot size. The formula used to make this determination is:

$$\text{Economic lot} = \sqrt{\frac{2 \times \text{quantity used per year} \times \text{total setup cost}}{\text{manufacturing cost per piece} \times \text{interest rate}}}$$

The company recognized that the formula gave only approximate results, but its use was justified because of its simplicity.

Model BY space heater has enjoyed steady sales over the years, and an assembly line operating at a fairly uniform rate of 30 units a day has been set up to produce this heater. This model takes a special nozzle that is not used on any other model. The nozzle is produced on a turret lathe that can be set up for the job at a cost of $15. The combined labor, material, and overhead cost of producing the nozzle once the machine is set up is $2.16 each. The company regularly computes inventory carrying charges at 20% of the average investment in the inventory. The plant operates regularly 5 days a week for 50 weeks of the year.

*Questions:*

1. What is the economic manufacturing lot size of nozzles for Model BY?
2. What other factors might influence the manufacturing lot size?
3. What types of charges are included in the 20% inventory carrying charge?
4. Comment on the suitability of the formula used.

### Standard Motor Company

One of the major problems confronting Standard Motor Company, manufacturers of automobile starters and generators, is that of reducing manufacturing costs. Among the ideas suggested for reducing the cost of materials and machinery is that of making the shafts out of strip steel instead of bar stock. Several shafts of this type were made and subjected to rigorous testing and met all requirements. The senior engineer in charge of motor design recognizes that this change in design would pose many production problems and has scheduled several meetings with representatives of the process engineering department.

After these meetings, Archie Simmons, from process engineering, was given the assignment of checking on the equipment required and problems that might be anticipated in manufacturing shafts in this new manner.

*Questions:*

1. Of what value is a close working relationship between product and process engineers?
2. What kind of information should Archie Simmons seek and from what sources?
3. Under what circumstances can the company justify switching to this new process?
4. If it is decided to install the new process, who will be involved and in what way?

# CHAPTER SIX

# Industrial Equipment

Industrial equipment, or *machines*, is one of the basic necessities for the production of manufactured goods. Such equipment, when operated by men, can transform an empty building into a dynamic plant or factory, ready to convert raw materials into products needed or desired by man. This chapter will be devoted to a discussion of the types of processing equipment (sometimes called "manufacturing equipment") currently used in industry. Materials handling equipment will be discussed in Chapter 9.

## Processing Equipment

*Processing equipment* includes all of the machine tools, auxiliary tooling and equipment, and other manufacturing items that are directly employed in the working, treatment, inspection, or packaging of the workpiece or product. Such items of equipment as turret lathes, sewing machines, inspection devices, chemical tanks, meatcutters, sand molders, and polishing tools fall into this classification.

### Basic Manufacturing Processes

There are hundreds of types of processing equipment in use in today's manufacturing plants. Some means of classifying such equipment is needed to clarify the relationship between machines and the particular process or processes for which they are best suited. One common method of such classification is in terms of the type of work performed on the workpiece while in (or on) the unit of processing equipment. Broaching, turning, coining, drawing, milling, welding, sewing, shearing, mixing, stamping, and mortising are examples of basic manufacturing operations. It should be noted that there may be one or many different machines that can perform any particular basic process. For instance, gear shaping is somewhat limited to a specific type of equipment; drilling, however, can be done on drilling, boring, and tapping machines, as well as on any of the machines in the lathe family.

The basic manufacturing process can be subdivided, in many cases, into more detailed elements of work, and these are sometimes known as *work units*. The work unit is simply the smallest subdivision of processing, and is usually accomplished without intentional interruption. For the basic process of drilling, for instance, the work unit would specify the specific diameter and depth of the hole to be formed. Work-unit names such as coredrill, centerdrill, tapdrill, and drill are applied for specific types of work on the partpiece. It should be noted that one or more work units make up an *operation*, which has been defined as all of the work that is performed on a part at essentially one location, or in one unit of processing equipment.

Some of the basic processes are associated with specific types of partpiece material; for instance, mortising is primarily a woodworking process. Likewise, the associated equipment may be classified by material type as metal working, woodworking, plasticworking, and so on. Thus, processing equipment can be classified to some extent by the particular industries in which used.

### Types of Processing Equipment

Processing equipment may also be classified by the construction and mounting of the unit: fixed power tools and equipment, portable power tools and equipment, portable hand tools and equipment, and auxiliary tools and equipment. *Fixed power tools and equipment* include all of the machines and other power-operated processing units that are floor- or bench-mounted or supported, such as drill presses or wood shapers. *Portable power tools and equipment* are those that can be picked up in the hand or hands for use, such as electric hand drills. *Portable hand tools* include the many types of wrenches, screwdrivers, chisels, measuring rules, and so forth, which are used in the hands and are not power-operated. *Auxiliary tools and equipment* are the cutting tool bits, cutters, press dies, jigs, fixtures, gages, and so forth, which are needed by industry to adapt the basic manufacturing equipment to specific products and processes. Such items as benches, tables, desks, and chairs are usually classified as plant equipment, along with service facilities, dust collectors, lockers, and others.

Processing equipment may also be classified as general purpose or special. *General-purpose equipment* is designed for maximum flexibility, so that many different products and processes can be performed on each unit. The common engine lathe, shaper, wood lathe, and drill press are examples of such equipment; skilled operators are required to set up and use such equipment in order to produce the specific products desired. These machines are adapted to various products and processes by the attachment of auxiliary tooling and equipment, and by the application of operator skills. They are used extensively in intermittent manufacture, where a unit of production equipment may be employed on several different products or operations within a short time. General-purpose equipment is often arranged in the plant in groups or departments of identical or similar machines. The distinct advantage of general-purpose equipment is its adaptability to many products and basic processes.

*Special-purpose equipment*, on the other hand, is designed and is used to produce one or a few specific products, and it does not have the flexibility of the general-purpose unit. Automatic controls are commonly built into these machines to minimize the need for skilled operators and to eliminate so far as is practical the possibilities for human error. Higher production rates and lower unit manufacturing costs are the chief advantages claimed for such equipment. Special-purpose equipment is often arranged in the plant into product lines, permitting direct flow of the product from machine to machine in a nearly straight line and offering much more opportunity for conveyorization of materials. This equipment is commonly designed with integral automatic handling devices and automatic or semi-automatic controls.

## Trends in Machine Design

Because of industrial competition, unit manufacturing cost (the cost to manufacture one complete unit of product) has become increasingly important as a measure of operating success. Consequently, many manufacturers are finding it desirable to concentrate their production facilities on one or a few products that they can make and sell in large quantities, thus permitting the installation of high-production and low-unit-cost manufacturing lines. This type of specialization is a strong incentive for manufacturers to obtain processing equipment that can produce specific products rapidly and accurately. Technological developments in cutting-tool materials, machine construction, and automatic handling and control devices have stepped up the movement toward more specialized equipment. Carbide and ceramic-oxide cutting tools, combined with automatic, high-horsepower machines can work materials at rates considered to be out of all reason only a few years ago.

The majority of machine tools are built by the many manufacturers who specialize in this field. Often, however, companies that require special equipment either make it themselves or contract it out to small job shops. As an example, the General Electric Company has designed, developed, and built the first models of many of the machines used in the lamp industry.

One of the recent trends has been to design equipment incorporating materials handling devices to transfer the product from one work station to another. *Transfer* machines have been developed to move the part, sometimes mounted in a holding fixture, from station to station. Transfer machines lend themselves particularly to drilling, boring, reaming, tapping, end milling, and similar processes. These machines are sequence controlled through the use of limit switches, cams, and time-delay relays. All of the processing work and the movement of the product from the feed end of the machine to the discharge end is done automatically. Transfer machines have been used most commonly on castings and large forgings. Their primary advantage is in automating the production process, eliminating the necessity for heavy manual work, and expediting the manufacture of the product. An 11-station Le Maire Transfer Machine for processing diesel engine cylinder blocks is illustrated in Figure 6-1.

**Figure 6-1.** A transfer machine composed of four individual machines, each with a numerical control system, arranged to operate separately or linked together to function as a complete unit. (Courtesy International Harvester Company)

Another type of machine that incorporates material handling is the rotary indexing machine. This machine is built around a cylindrical base casting topped by a rotary indexing table to which fixtures are attached for holding and positioning the parts. The processing tools are mounted over the rotary table at the index positions. Each part receives a progressive series of work as it indexes from station to station through one complete (or partial) revolution of the table. Illustrated in Figure 6-2 is a Kingsbury machine containing 12 units with 17 spindles, 13 work fixtures, and capable of turning out 227 parts per hour. This machine is used to drill, tap, ream, mill, chamfer, and to insert a bushing into a power steering gear housing.

**Figure 6-2.** A 12-work station rotary indexing machine for machining parts. (Courtesy Kingsbury Machine Tool Corporation)

Rotary indexing machines have also been adapted for assembly work. Figure 6-3 shows a Multra Automatic Assembly Machine designed by Barnes Engineering Company. These 7000-pound machines, with the aid of proper tooling, can assemble a diversity of products, and a change-over from one product to another can be accomplished in a matter of hours.

Another equipment design trend is to *programmed* machines (see Figures 6-4 and 6-5), automatically controlled in operation by punched cards, magnetic or punched tape (see Figure 6-6), or magnetic storage drums or grids. All of these devices permit the storage of information in a "memory" system in a coded form, such that the information can be withdrawn in the sequence needed. The information stored is the work to be performed on the partpiece while it is in the machine. Once the program has been made, the machine will operate to make parts according to the program for as long as desired. Thus, automation is obtained with what is essentially a general purpose machine, since any number of different programs for different

**Figure 6-3.** Rotary indexing machine used for assembling parts. (Courtesy Multra Corporation)

**Figure 6-4.** A six-spindle tape-controlled drill press capable of performing the functions of drilling, boring, tapping, reaming, counterboring, and spotfacing. (Courtesy Collins Radio Company)

parts can be fed to the machine. An example of this type of machine is an electronically controlled milling machine developed by the Servomechanism Laboratory of the Massachusetts Institute of Technology. This machine is operated by controls responding to electrical impulse instructions read from a punched paper tape. The tape is prepared in advance by the use of a computer, working directly from the drawing and specifications for the part to be made.

**Figure 6-5.** A 3-axis numerically controlled machine featuring an automatic tool changer that provides for random selection of tools from the rotary tool storage magazine. (Courtesy Kearney & Trecker Corporation)

There has also been considerable development in tracer-type machines. Such equipment uses a master part or template as a reference for machining successive parts. Tracer lathes and duplicators are the best known examples of this type of equipment. Once the master part or template has been prepared, the machine will reproduce identical parts automatically, or at least semi-automatically, by duplicating the master. This equipment is less costly and perhaps more rugged than the electronically controlled machines. However, there are definite limitations to the design of parts that can be reproduced by tracing.

There is some indication that processing equipment of the future may be designed to make better use of the vertical space in a plant as a means of saving on floor space, for equipment is tending to become larger. Transfer machines may one day move the product up and down as well as back and

**Figure 6-6.** Punched tape being installed in one of the control consoles for the transfer machine illustrated in Figure 6-1. (Courtesy Allen-Bradley Company)

forth. Volume utilization of space may replace present-day linear utilization considerations.

## Mechanization and Automation

For centuries man has been seeking to replace or reduce manual work with tools and other devices that either provide leverage for human effort or supplement man's power with another power source. Automation is the continued effort to mechanize work, by replacing manual activity with machine activity. It is difficult to distinguish between mechanization and automation, since the two terms are used interchangeably throughout industry. However, automation would seem to encompass more than is generally accepted as a definition for mechanization. This distinguishing feature is the inclusion of feedback control in automation, which makes it possible for machines to operate entirely automatically and to correct or adjust for variations from preset conditions or criteria. The use of automation necessitates serious consideration of its far-reaching effects upon the economic and social relationships in the world, since the ultimate aim would appear to be the complete freeing of man from physical work in industry. Obviously, however, automation increases considerably the need for skilled setup men and operators and for maintenance and planning personnel.

One of the first examples of automation was a flour-processing mill constructed by Oliver Evans in Philadelphia in 1784. In this mill, grain was handled entirely by powered conveyors from the receiving bin through to the finished sacks of flour. Another early example was an automatic loom, operated from punched paper cards, which was developed by Joseph Jacquard in Paris in 1801. Of the larger American companies, the A.O. Smith Corporation and the General Electric Company mechanized some of their operations at an early date. The word *automation* dates back to about 1947, when the Ford Motor Company set up a section in one of its plants to design automatic handling equipment for its operations. Since that time, the term has spread widely to represent many different things.

The unit-operations industries, such as the refineries and chemical processing plants, have seen much more development of mechanized handling and automatic control than have the industries that manufacture discrete product units, which often require individualized handling from operation to operation. In the past few years, however, there has been a real push in the development and use of automatic handling and control equipment in these latter industries. As an illustration of this advancing technology, the Kitchens of Sara Lee has built an automated bakery in which a digital computer directs the entire manufacturing operation—from the receiving dock to the shipping platform. The computer will perform such multitudinous operations as: monitor the bulk storage status and use of liquid and dry ingredients; monitor batch blending and mixing operations; compute and monitor oven zone temperatures and speeds of oven conveyors; monitor product change-overs automatically on many different selections of cakes; direct the random storage of palletized products in a holding freezer, direct order picking, and assemble loads of mixed products onto pallets.

Automatic production involves essentially four elements:

**1.   Automatic handling of product between processing units.**   This is accomplished primarily by conveyorization, by the use of power-operated materials handling equipment that provides continuous or intermittent movement of the product or materials on belts, chains, slats, or by oscillation or pneumatic pressure.

**2.   Automatic infeeding of processing units.**   There are many different types of automatic infeeding equipment; however, most of the currently available equipment can be classified into six categories: (1) bar feed mechanisms, (2) mechanical transfer arms, (3) hopper feeders, (4) magazine feeds, (5) dial feeds and indexing tables, and (6) roll grip feeds. All of these devices serve to transfer materials from storage racks, hoppers, stock reels, or directly from conveyors into the processing position in the machine. In some cases, a progression of two or more such mechanisms may be employed. The selection of an infeed unit depends upon the particular machine to be fed, the physical characteristics of the part to be handled, and the production rate desired. Feeding equipment may be built in by the machine tool builder, or it may be added separately by the user.

**3. Automatic control of processing units during the cycle of operation.** Automatic control equipment also comes in many varieties, ranging from the simple cam or tracer attachment to complex electronic systems. An *automatic controller* has been defined by the American Society of Mechanical Engineers as:

> A mechanism which measures the value of a variable quantity or condition and operates to correct or limit deviation of this measured variable from a selected reference. It includes both the measuring and the controlling means.

This definition applies to feedback or closed-loop control providing automatic corrective action for physical changes in the process value or condition under control. However, automatic control is considered by many to include *sequence control,* or the timing of occurrences in an operating cycle through the use of cams, counters, gears, and so forth. Automatic screw machines and transfer machines, for instance, are time- or sequence-controlled—there is no feedback or corrective action involved. Closed-loop or feedback[1] control circuits, which have been used for many years in the unit-operations industries, have only recently begun to be applied to discrete-item equipment.

**4. Automatic discharge of the product from the processing unit.** Removal of the product from a processing unit may be accomplished by conveyor, chute, transfer arm, pneumatic ejectors, or similar devices. This element is usually the least difficult to provide.

Automation of processing equipment offers great promise for the elevation of human work in industry to a level requiring the further development and application of the human mind, while machines perform the physical work.

## Portable Tools

Portable tools cannot be neglected in any consideration of the processing equipment used in industry. These tools, which include both power-operated and non-power equipment, are usually supported in the hand or hands while in use. Such tools as screwdrivers, wrenches, and so on are non-power portable tools; those that have electric or pneumatic motors are power-

---

[1]Feedback control is used today on time-sequencing operations for varying conveyor or indexing speeds, numerically controlled machines, automatic weighing, counting, packaging, inspecting, and so forth.

operated. Electric power tools may be used anywhere in the plant where there is a suitable outlet. But many industrial plants use pneumatic tools because they do not require as much maintenance, have a longer life, and are not as subject to petty theft.

### Auxiliary Tools and Equipment

Machine tools, presses, and certain other types of processing equipment must be adapted with auxiliary tooling before they can be used. Auxiliary tooling includes the cutting tools, press dies, jigs and fixtures, gages, and other auxiliary devices that are used on or with the basic processing units.

*Cutting tools* do the actual work in modifying the workpiece or product. They are mounted onto the machine tool either on an arbor or in a tool holder. During the cutting process, heat is created by the action of the chip rubbing on the face of the tool, and this heat tends to destroy or break down the cutting edge. The suitability of a tool for cutting a particular material, therefore, depends upon the ability of the tool material to retain its hardness at elevated temperatures, as well as on the ratio of the hardness of the tool material to the hardness of the partpiece material.

There are five primary cutting tool materials in use today: carbon steel, high-speed steel, cast alloys, cemented carbides, and ceramic oxides. Diamonds, carborundum, aluminum oxide, and other abrasive materials are also used in grinding wheels and other special cutting tools.

*Press dies* make up another classification of auxiliary tooling. The more common types of dies are (1) cutting dies, (2) forming dies, (3) drawing dies, (4) extrusion dies, and (5) forging dies. Dies are used to adapt power presses to perform specific work units.

*Jigs and fixtures* are the auxiliary tools used to support and locate the workpiece on units of processing equipment. There is a technical distinction between a *jig* and a *fixture*, even though the two terms are often used interchangeably. A fixture is simply a holding device, and the workpiece is positioned to the tools by controls on the machine (see Figure 6-7). A jig, however, not only holds the workpiece but also guides the tools to it. Fixtures are used in milling, planing, shaping, assembly, and similar operations. Jigs are employed in drilling, boring, reaming, and certain welding operations.

*Gages* and other types of inspection equipment make up another classification of tooling. Gages are of two different types; *measurement gages*, which provide a specific reading or value for any measurable characteristic of the workpiece, and *attribute gages*, which only indicate whether a measurable characteristic is within or beyond set limits. A comparator is an example of a measurement gage; a plug gage is an example of the attribute type. Figure 6-8 illustrates these two types of gages.

**Figure 6-7.** Fixtures used on the numerically controlled machine illustrated in Figure 6-5. (Courtesy Kearney & Trecker Corporation)

In the chemical and food-processing industries, as well as others, such items as mixers, molding forms, patterns, and attachments are examples of auxiliary equipment. Certainly sewing-machine attachments in the textile industry fall into this general category.

Economics is an important factor in all tool-selection considerations. The higher cost of more durable materials, closer tolerances, finer workmanship, more rugged construction, must always be weighed costwise against the benefit to be gained. In many cases the expected usage for a tool in terms of number of applications will be a determining factor in tool

**Figure 6-8.** Measurement and attribute gages. (Courtesy B. C. Ames Co. and N. A. Woodworth Co.)

selection. Other factors include the workpiece material, weight, shape, and size. In many cases, the use of commercially available standard tools or tool components will be more economically justifiable than the design and building of special auxiliary tooling and equipment.

**Tool control.** Because so many auxiliary tools are used in an industrial plant, a control system of some type is essential to avoid excessive duplication and loss or misplacement. In such a system of control, each tool is classified according to type and uses and is assigned a tool inventory number. These tools are kept in a crib, or cribs, until needed on the production floor. Tool control promotes standardization of tools, and assures that the tools will be kept in good condition and ready for use when needed.

## Determination of Equipment Requirements

There are many facets to the problem of selecting the best possible equipment for any particular manufacturing enterprise. It has already been indicated that the basic manufacturing processes at least limit the choice of equipment for making a particular product. The process engineer in many manufacturing plants is responsible for indicating the type of equipment to be used for each operation as he develops the routing or sequence of operations for a product. Therefore, he should conscientiously familiarize himself with improvements in equipment and with new processes. He may specify either a specific machine, or (preferably) only a general type of machine—the latter so that there may be some flexibility in scheduling and routing the product to specific machines in the plant. Such flexibility is also desirable for plant-layout and materials-handling considerations.

**Human factors in machine selection.**   An important consideration in the selection of a new unit of equipment for a plant should be the type and degree of operator skill required in relation to the skills presently available within the organization. The ease with which the equipment can be operated and the safety features provided are equally important selection factors. So far as possible machines should be fitted to the plant labor force.

**Standardization of equipment.**   It is also economically desirable to standardize on processing equipment, provided that such standardization does not take from an operation the equipment best suited to meet quantity and quality requirements. Standardization reduces the cost of maintenance; a smaller number of repair parts need to be stocked, and the maintenance crews grow more familiar with the equipment. Standardization may also permit better utilization of equipment, since various product schedules can be superimposed on the available standardized machines. Where specialized equipment is economically desirable, some attempt should be made to standardize at least on service parts within the company.

**Equipment purchase vs. rental.**   For the plant that has been making products and has equipment available, it is logical to use this equipment to the fullest extent before leasing or buying new equipment, so long as a new or different machine is not significantly better. When it is desired to add equipment in the plant, there are three possibilities: (1) the equipment can be purchased new or used, (2) the equipment can be leased or rented, or (3) the equipment can be fabricated within the plant. Since World War II, industrial companies producing defense items have been able to lease some of their needs through the national government. All companies can lease some kinds of equipment through the machine tool builders or through machinery-rental concerns. It is not always desirable for a company to purchase a machine when one is needed. Thorough economic analyses should be conducted by the plant that is considering additional equipment before deciding whether to lease or buy.

## Determination of the Number of Machines Required

The number of pieces of each type of equipment needed to produce a product is contingent upon the quantity of product to be made within any given time period, the number of working hours in the plant within this same time period, the various production rates on the operations to be performed, as well as the setup time for each operation, the number of setups per machine for the time period, the operating efficiency of the plant (i.e., the per cent of effective utilization of equipment), and finally, the scrap loss at each operation. All of these factors must be either known or estimated before a reasonably accurate determination of machine requirements can be made. Since scrap loss is cumulative, it is usually necessary to calculate equipment requirements starting at the last operation to be performed on the product and working backward towards the first operations. To find the requirements for any particular piece of equipment in a process, the total number of hours per month (or other time period) that the equipment is required to produce the desired quantity is divided by the total number of hours per month that the equipment is available, taking plant efficiency into account. Then the total requirements for all operations to be performed on each unit of equipment are considered in terms of the number of setups involved and the time required per setup. In a product-line layout of equipment, where each machine is set up to perform only one operation, the setup time can be neglected, but the problem of line balancing becomes important. For the process-type layout, where machines are commonly used on several different parts and/or operations, setup and scheduling time losses must be carefully considered; however, balancing is not a serious problem.

In balancing the capacities of various machines in a product-line layout, it may be desirable to buy more than enough machines, where the equipment is not too expensive, if this will avoid possible shutdown or restriction of the entire manufacturing line. However, when such equipment is quite expensive, it may be necessary to provide only the minimum number of machines and rely upon overtime or extra shifts to meet production requirements when breakdowns occur.

Machine capacities can thus be stretched by increasing the available hours per month, by decreasing the required hours through an increase in operating efficiencies, or by decreasing scrap losses and setup times.

### Equipment investment

The purchasing of equipment involves capital expenditures, so there are several important economic elements to be considered in deciding what equipment to buy and when to buy it. New equipment is purchased either to meet specific requirements of a process or to improve upon a process as performed on an existing or available unit of equipment. Greater productivity, reduced unit-manufacturing costs, and higher quality are the primary objectives in equipment replacement.

**Equipment replacement policies.** In recent years manufacturing management has given serious consideration to policies for replacement of equipment. There are some who feel that any piece of equipment that is over ten years old is obsolete and should be replaced. To some extent this is certainly true, since many types of industrial equipment are being continually improved upon year after year. The trend towards higher-horsepower machines to use the capabilities of the newer cutting-tool materials is a clear indication of the need for replacing equipment that is not operating as productively as possible. The developments in mechanized equipment, in equipment that will hold tighter tolerances, and in equipment that is better designed from a methods standpoint, are all good reasons for replacing old equipment. The question, of course, is *when* should the replacement be made, and *what* is the best replacement unit.

A well-designed equipment replacement policy must consider all of the comparisons between an existing unit of equipment and its possible replacement or replacements. In order to make a sound economic comparison, all of the factors must be converted into cost considerations. One of the best known of the replacement formulas was developed by the Machinery and Allied Products Institute and is known simply as the MAPI formula.[2] In this formula, the terms *defender* and *challenger* are used to represent, respectively, the presently owned or available equipment and the proposed equipment.

In some cases, there may be two or more challengers to one defender for purposes of selecting the best replacement equipment if replacement is indicated. This MAPI method is a special type of cost analysis in which the defender and the challenger or challengers are compared for a period of *one year* after the assumed replacement of the defender by the challenger. The *operating inferiority* of the defender is compared to the *additional costs* of the challenger. From this comparison, the next year's gain from replacement can be determined, and an estimate can be made of the investment recovery period.

One of the limitations of many replacement policies is that only the particular units of equipment involved are considered, whereas on a plant-wide cost basis the effect of replacement upon other operating costs may be highly significant. Recently modern mathematics, such as is incorporated in linear programming, has been successfully applied to replacement studies. In such a study all of the relative factors are taken into account including the interactions between various costs. Both direct and indirect costs should be considered in any replacement study, since one may be affected by the other. Overhead costs are increasing quite rapidly in many of today's mechanized factories; therefore, machine utilization, materials handling, quality, and other factors are important considerations. As modern industry con-

---

[2]The *MAPI Replacement Manual* can be obtained from the Machinery and Allied Products Institute in Washington, D.C.

tinues towards more highly mechanized and automated plants, the selection and evaluation of new and replacement equipment will be an increasingly important function in industrial management.

**Machine selection decisions.** Any time that a company decides to purchase a new machine or piece of equipment, a decision must be made as to which item to buy. Many factors will influence this decision, including such items as: the initial cost, operating expenses, service policy, delivery dates, and reputation of the manufacturer. Assuming that everything else is equal, the problem tends to become essentially one of economic selection and in picking the machine that minimizes cost.

In endeavoring to make a decision among alternative machines, a problem arises in trying to decide what costs should be included and how they should be determined. These costs will usually include the initial cost of the machine and the costs of operating the machine, such as: direct and indirect labor, direct and indirect materials, power, maintenance, replacement parts, insurance, and interest on invested capital. The service life and expected salvage value at the end of the service life must also be predicted. With this information available two alternative machines may be compared as illustrated in the following example:

|  | Machine A | Machine B |
|---|---|---|
| Initial cost | $10,000 | $15,000 |
| Annual operating cost | 2,000 | 1,500 |
| Expected years of life | 10 | 10 |
| Salvage value | 1,000 | 2,000 |
| Total cost for 10 years | $29,000 | $28,000 |

On the basis of this simple economic analysis, Machine B would be favored.

One of the deficiencies of the foregoing analysis is the failure to take into consideration interest and the time value of money. Interest is an important factor to be taken into account in investment decisions and should be given consideration as a part of the total economic analysis. Thus, the different initial investments in and operating costs of the two machines illustrated in the previous example will influence the interest costs associated with each of them.

Several economic methods are available for evaluating alternative machines, and we shall discuss two of the more common types: the annual cost method and the present worth method. Basic to a discussion of these two methods is some insight into interest and the time value of money. Interest can be considered as rental for use of money. Thus, we are willing to put money into a savings account in a bank in return for which we expect to draw interest at a fixed level (e.g., compounded annually). In return for $100 invested today at 4 per cent interest, we would expect to have $148 credited to our account 10 years hence. By means of this example, it becomes evident that the values of sums of money at different points of time depend upon the interest rate and the time spans.

The value of a future sum of money ($S$) resulting from a present amount ($P$) compounded at a fixed interest rate for a given period may be represented by the formula given below:

$$S = P(1 + i)^n$$

where $i =$ interest rate and $n =$ number of years.

To illustrate the use of this formula, let us assume that we have $10,000 and wish to know how much it will be worth in 10 years at an interest rate of 6 per cent:

$$S = 10,000(1 + .06)^{10} = 10,000(1.791) = \$17,910$$

The factor 1.791 which is $(1.06)^{10}$ may be secured from Table A-3 in Appendix A. As a further illustration, let us assume that we would like to have $10,000 at the end of 10 years. How much must be invested now at 6 per cent interest?

$$P = \frac{S}{(1 + i)^n} = \frac{10,000}{(1 + .06)^{10}} = 10,000(0.5584) = \$5584.00$$

**Annual cost method.** Now let us consider the *annual cost method* of evaluating alternative machines. In essence, this method compares the annual costs (capital recovery plus operating costs) of obtaining a service from two or more machines. The annual cost of capital recovery ($CR$) may be calculated by the following formula[3] (for equal annual costs):

$$CR = (P - L)\left[\frac{i(1 + i)^n}{(1 + i)^n - 1}\right] + Li$$

or
$$CR = (P - L) \text{ (Capital Recovery Factor)} + Li$$
$$= (P - L) \text{ (C.R.F.)} + Li$$

where $P =$ first cost of machine, $n =$ life of study or machine in years, $L =$ salvage value at end of $n$ years, C.R.F. $=$ Capital Recovery Factor (available from tables in Appendix A), $i =$ interest rate or minimum attractive return. The following example illustrates the use of the annual cost method to compare two alternative machines:

|  | *Machine A* | *Machine B* |
|---|---|---|
| Initial cost | $10,000 | $15,000 |
| Annual operating costs | 2,000 | 1,500 |
| Expected years of life | 10 | 10 |
| Salvage value | 1,000 | 2,000 |
| Minimum attractive return = 6 per cent | | |

[3]See H. G. Thuesen and W. J. Fabrycky, *Engineering Economy* (3rd ed.; Englewood Cliffs, N.J.: Prentice-Hall, Inc., 1964),pp. 79, 141.

For Machine A:

$CR$ at $6\% = (\$10,000 - \$1,000)\,(0.13587) + (\$1000)\,(.06)$

$\qquad = 1222.83 + 60.00 = \$1282.83$

The C.R.F. used in this formula may be found in Table A-3, in the Appendix.

Total annual costs $= CR +$ Operating costs

$\qquad\qquad = \$1282.83 + \$2000 = \$3282.83$

For Machine B:

$CR$ at $6\% = (\$15,000 - \$2,000)\,(0.13587) + (\$2000)\,(.06)$

$\qquad = 1766.31 + 120 = \$1886.31$

Total annual costs $= \$1886.31 + \$1500 = \$3386.31$

On the basis of this analysis, Machine A would be favored.

**Present worth method.**  The present worth method consists of reducing all receipts and expenditures for each alternative machine to a present worth basis. One of the important considerations in the use of this method is to make certain that equal services are being compared.

The data used in the example in the previous section will be used to illustrate the present worth method:

For Machine A:

| | | |
|---|---|---:|
| Initial cost | | $10,000.00 |
| P.W. of annual operating costs $=$ | $2000(\text{P.W.F.})_{EP}$ | |
| | $= 2000(7.360)$ | 14,720.00 |
| Total P.W. of disbursements | | $24,720.00 |
| Less: P.W. of salvage values $=$ | $1000(\text{P.W.F.})_{SP}$ | |
| | $1000(0.5584)$ | 558.40 |
| P.W. of net disbursements for | | |
| Machine A for 10 years | | $24,161.60 |

The P.W.F.'s used in these calculations were secured from Table A-3 in the Appendix.

For Machine B:

| | | |
|---|---|---:|
| Initial cost | | $15,000.00 |
| P.W. of annual operating costs $=$ | $1500(\text{P.W.F.})_{EP}$ | |
| | $= 1500(7.360)$ | 11,040.00 |
| Total P.W. of disbursements | | $26,040.00 |
| Less: P.W. of salvage value $=$ | $2000(\text{P.W.F.})_{SP}$ | |
| | $= 2000(0.5584)$ | 1,116.80 |
| P.W. of net disbursements for | | |
| Machine B for 10 years | | $24,923.20 |

On the basis of the present worth analysis, Machine A would be favored. This is the same conclusion as arrived at by the annual cost method and raises the question of which method is preferable. Morris points out that, "When choosing among assets having equal service lives either the present worth principle or the equivalent annual cost principle may be used."[4] On the other hand, the use of annual cost comparisons fits in well with the thinking of many manufacturing managers, and they are better able to interpret the results.

**Depreciation and obsolescence.** The concepts of *depreciation* and *obsolescence* must be examined in order to evaluate various replacement policies that have been developed. Depreciation can be defined as a method for spreading the cost of a long-term asset over the life, or expected years of usage, of the asset. It is an arbitrary figure used to "write off" the financial investment in such assets in terms of yearly operating expense. Factors that enter into the calculation of depreciation are the initial cost of the item, its anticipated life, and its estimated salvage value at the end of the depreciation period.

Any reasonable method that is consistently applied may be used in computing depreciation.[5] The three methods most generally used are the (1) straight line method, (2) the declining balance method, and (3) the sum of the years-digits method. Each of these will be discussed briefly in the sections that follow.

The *straight line method* is the simplest method for computing depreciation. Under this method, the cost of the equipment less its salvage value is generally deducted in equal annual amounts over its period of estimated useful life. The method of calculating this amount may be illustrated by the following example: For an engine lathe that cost $6000, is estimated to have a service life of 8 years, and a salvage value after 8 years of $1200, the annual depreciation would be:

$$D = \frac{\$6000 - \$1200}{8} = \$600 \text{ per year}$$

In the *declining balance method*, the amount of depreciation each year is subtracted from the cost or other basis of the equipment before computing the next year's depreciation—so that the same depreciation rate applies to a smaller or declining balance each year. Thus, a larger depreciation deduction is taken for the first year that the method is used. A gradually smaller

---

[4]W. T. Morris, *The Analysis of Management Decisions* (Homewood, Illinois: Richard D. Irwin, Inc., 1964), p. 58.

[5]See *Tax Guide for Small Business*, U.S. Treasury Department, Internal Revenue Service, Publication No. 334 (1960).

deduction is taken in each succeeding year. Within limits a depreciation rate is used that is greater than the rate that would be used in the straight line method. Under some circumstances a rate may be used that would be twice as great as the rate that would be proper under the straight line method. As an example of the use of this method, assume that a new drill press has been purchased for $2000 and has an estimated life of 10 years. Under the straight line method of depreciation, the rate is 10 per cent per year. Since this machine meets the Internal Revenue Service's requirements, it may be depreciated under the declining balance method at a rate that is twice the straight line method, or 20 per cent. Thus, the allowance for the first year would be 20% of $2000 or $400; for the second year it would be 20% of ($2000 — $400) or $320; for the third year it would be 20% of ($1600 — $320) or $256; and so forth. The salvage value is not deducted from the cost of the equipment in using this method, but the property may not be depreciated below an amount equal to its reasonable salvage value.

As is true of the declining balance method, the *sum of the years-digits method* is based on the assumption that the item of equipment should be depreciated a decreasing amount each year as its age increases. Under this method, a different fraction is applied each year to the cost of the item less its estimated salvage value. The formula for computing the depreciation is based on a fraction whose denominator is equal to the sum of the digits representing the estimated useful life of the equipment; for example, if the estimated useful life is 5 years, the denominator is $1 + 2 + 3 + 4 + 5 = 15$. The numerator of the fraction changes each year to a number that represents the years of useful life remaining at the beginning of the year for which the computation is made. For the first year of a 5-year estimated useful life, the numerator would be 5, the second year, 4; the third year, 3; and so forth. On the basis of this method, a machine costing $6500 and having a salvage value of $500 after a useful life of 5 years, would have a depreciation allowance of 5/15 ($6000) or $2000 for the first year, 4/15 ($6000) or $1600 for the second year, and so forth.

Comparative amounts of depreciation under each of the three methods just discussed are illustrated below (based on a machine with an estimated life of 5 years, a cost of $11,000 and a salvage value of $1000):

Straight Line Method:

| Year | Cost less salvage | Rate | Deduction | Reserve Dec. 31 |
|------|-------------------|------|-----------|-----------------|
| 1 | $10,000 | 20% | $2,000 | $ 2,000 |
| 2 | 10,000 | 20% | 2,000 | 4,000 |
| 3 | 10,000 | 20% | 2,000 | 6,000 |
| 4 | 10,000 | 20% | 2,000 | 8,000 |
| 5 | 10,000 | 20% | 2,000 | 10,000 |

Declining Balance Method:

| Year | Unrecovered cost Jan. 1 | Rate | Deduction | Reserve Dec. 31 |
|------|-------------------------|------|-----------|-----------------|
| 1 | $11,000 | 40% | $4,400 | $ 4,400 |
| 2 | 6,600 | 40% | 2,640 | 7,040 |
| 3 | 3,960 | 40% | 1,584 | 8,624 |
| 4 | 2,376 | 40% | 950 | 9,574 |
| 5 | 1,426 | 40% | 426 | 10,000 |

*Note:* Only $426 is allowed in the 5th year, since the asset must not be depreciated below the $1,000 salvage value.

Sum of Years-Digits Method, General Rule:

| Year | Cost less salvage | Fraction | Deduction | Reserve Dec. 31 |
|------|-------------------|----------|-----------|-----------------|
| 1 | $10,000 | 5/15 | $3,333 | $ 3,333 |
| 2 | 10,000 | 4/15 | 2,667 | 6,000 |
| 3 | 10,000 | 3/15 | 2,000 | 8,000 |
| 4 | 10,000 | 2/15 | 1,333 | 9,333 |
| 5 | 10,000 | 1/15 | 667 | 10,000 |

The amount of depreciation written off each year affects the cost of doing business, which in turn affects the profits. Low depreciations mean high profits and high depreciations mean low profits—so far as the books are concerned. A company wishing to show good earnings records will undoubtedly depreciate its equipment as little as possible. On the other hand, if a company wishes to avoid high income taxes it will try to depreciate its equipment as much as possible. If tax rates stay the same over the years and if the business is fairly stable, it won't matter how fast or slow equipment is depreciated. In the long run a company can only depreciate its assets down to zero dollars.

Depreciation rates and depreciation policies cannot be determined in a completely arbitrary manner. Since depreciation is a cost of doing business, it has an effect on the profits of the business. As profits vary so does the federal income tax paid by the concern. The result is that the Internal Revenue Service takes considerable interest in a company's depreciation policies just in case there is an attempt to "manipulate" the amount of income tax due. In general the Bureau will go along with any reasonable method of depreciation as long as it is consistently applied.

Let us remind ourselves that this discussion on how fast or how slow equipment is depreciated has nothing to do with the performance or maintenance of the equipment. Instead this is only a bookkeeping operation. It should also be pointed out that the depreciation process, which on a company's books shows a depreciation reserve account, does not set aside money with which to buy new equipment as the old wears out. It simply charges off the cost of equipment to each year's operation. The company still has to dig up cash somewhere in order to purchase new equipment.

Obsolescence causes loss in value of equipment, but in this case the loss comes about because of the development and introduction of a new and better machine or process. Our first machine may produce at 100 per cent efficiency and be in first-class condition, but it may be capable of producing at a rate of only ten pieces an hour. I someone comes out with another machine that is capable of producing at a rate of 130 pieces an hour, then our first machine is rendered obsolete in spite of its first-class mechanical condition. And this may have happened during the second year of its life! The first machine certainly can still be operated, but the cost per piece produced will be so much higher than for those produced from the second machine that the product may be priced out of the market.

## QUESTIONS

1. Of concern in equipment selection are *processes*, *operations*, and *work units*. Briefly define these three terms, telling how they differ.

2. What type of equipment would usually be found in a metal-working job shop? List the types of machines, auxiliary tooling, and other processing equipment you would expect to find in such a shop.

3. What technological developments within recent years have contributed to the development of more special purpose equipment in industry?

4. You are a member of a planning group in a manufacturing plant making automotive transmission housings. What type or types of mechanized equipment would you propose for this plant?

5. Describe the operation of a typical "programmed" machine tool.

6. What are the manual elements in production that must be replaced by machine elements in order to have automation? Are there some manual elements that, at least at the present time, cannot be effectively replaced by machines?

7. What are *forming dies* used for in press operations?

8. Is a vernier caliper a *measurement* gage *or* an *attribute* gage? Discuss.

9. How does the "human factor" enter into equipment selection?

10. The "hardening" operation in a certain production line is a "bottleneck" operation. If the cost of additional equipment is prohibitive, how can the capacity of the present hardening equipment be "stretched" when necessary?

11. Under what circumstances would it be advantageous for a company to use the declining balance method of depreciation instead of the straight line method?

12. The purchasing agent of the CFT corporation has contacted two reputable manufacturing companies for quotations on a new lathe. Company X quoted a price of $4500 and estimated annual operating costs of $1000 per year. Company Y quoted a price of $5000 and estimated annual operating costs of

$750. If each machine is estimated to have a useful life of 10 years and a salvage value of $500, determine the best investment if the minimum attractive return is 6 per cent and the CFT corporation utilizes the annual cost method of equipment evaluation.

# CASE PROBLEMS

## Shay-Moore Company

The Shay-Moore Company plans to manufacture four new products in the following quantities: Product A—4000 per month, Product B—800 per month, Product C—1500 per month, and Product D—25,000 per month. Loren Todd, the process engineer, has been asked to determine the machine requirements for manufacturing these products. General-purpose machines are to be used, arranged in departments of like machines.

Loren finds that all of the products require engine lathe processing. Production standards for the operations to be performed in the engine lathe department are as follows: Product A—9 pcs./hour, Product B—15 pcs./hour, Product C—25 pcs./hour, and Product D—60 pcs./hour. As has been the company's practice, he decides to base machine requirements upon the optimum scheduling of products to the machines, and estimates that an overall efficiency of 88%, including down time for setups, can be obtained in the engine lathe department. The plant will operate on a one 8-hour shift, 5 days per week, 50 weeks per year basis—less 6 paid holidays.

*Questions:*

1. Neglecting scrap loss, what is the minimum number of engine lathes required to produce the specified monthly schedules in the lathe department? (Use estimated efficiency and compute requirements to the nearest tenth of a machine. You may assume that all of the engine lathes are interchangeable.)
2. If each product requires a different type of engine lathe, how many machines will be required for each of the four products, if an overall efficiency of 94% can be obtained with specific machines assigned to specific products? (Specify the number of whole machines without decimal remainder.)
3. How many engine lathes would be required to produce the schedule for Product A only, if a scrap loss of 5% is taken into account? (Use 94% efficiency.)
4. Under what circumstances would it be desirable to purchase special-purpose machines to fill orders such as these?

## McClellan Corporation

The McClellan Corporation is studying a vendor's proposal to replace a presently owned turret lathe in the plant with a new automatic lathe. It has been decided to use the MAPI formula in making a replacement study. The new machine is priced at $14,000 and the presently owned turret lathe has an estimated sale value of $2,500.

A comprehensive cost comparison between the two machines for the next year of operation shows a "defender operating inferiority" of $1800. This means that the proposed automatic lathe should save $1800 in operating expenses during the next year if replacement is made. In addition, the capital cost of keeping the present turret lathe for another year is estimated at $700 for decline in salvage value and interest charges. The "defender's adverse minimum" is thus $1800 plus $700, or $2500.

The "challenger's adverse minimum" for the next year is computed at $3400, indicating that replacement at this time cannot be economically justified, since the minimum total cost of owning the proposed automatic lathe would clearly be greater than the minimum total cost of keeping the present owned turret lathe.

*Questions:*

1. How much would it cost the McClellan Corporation during the next year to replace the present turret lathe with the proposed automatic lathe?
2. What factors do you feel must be included in computing the "challenger's adverse minimum"? Explain why each of these factors is important.
3. Should the McClellan Corporation buy the new automatic lathe if the two "adverse minimums" are computed to be equal? What other factors might influence a decision on equipment replacement?
4. If the "defender's adverse minimum" were $5200 in the above replacement study, how many years would be required to recover the investment in the new automatic lathe, based on the next year's gain from replacement? (Express your answer to the nearest tenth of a year.)

# CHAPTER SEVEN

# Methods Engineering

The history of American industry has been one of a never-ending search for more efficient manufacturing methods. The highly competitive nature of business forces management to give constant heed to ways in which production per man-hour can be increased. Methods engineering has contributed immeasurably to the search for better methods, and the effective utilization of this management tool has helped in the accomplishment of these objectives.

Methods engineering is that body of knowledge concerned with the analysis of the methods and the equipment used in performing a job, the design of an optimum method, and the standardization of the proposed method. This field is frequently referred to as "motion study" or "operation analysis." It is closely affiliated with the function of "work measurement" or "time study," which will be discussed in the next chapter.

## Areas of Application

The application of methods engineering may be required in a variety of circumstances. It ranges from the design of a new plant, to the design of a new process, to the improvement of an existing process, or to the improvement of an existing workplace. Wherever work is being done, methods engineering is a desirable function to insure that the work is being done in the easiest, safest, and most productive manner. Following are examples of the attainments of methods engineers in a variety of circumstances:

A pneumatic nut driver saves over 70 per cent of the time needed to install phenolic fuse holders in electronic chassis made by Altec Lansing Corporation, Whittier, California. Also, it tightens fuse nuts to the right degree of tension and eliminates stripping the fine phenolic threads. The women assemblers find powered nut driving less fatiguing than manual tightening.[1]

A new mechanized spray-up conveyor system for Fiberglas-reinforced panels hits costs four ways at Brunswick Corporation, Muskegon, Michigan. It doubles production speed over manual spray-up, halves manpower needs, assures uniform resin distribution, and cuts material waste to a negligible level. The plant-designed system shaped like a race track, is made up of 22 cars attached to a dragline conveyor.[2]

A revolving assembly line linked with a new welding technique has sliced production cost more than 50 per cent at the General Electric Company, Air Conditioning and Heating Division, Trenton, New Jersey. An added benefit was a 90 per cent reduction of down time. Advantages of the new setup are many: it reduces the size of the working area, provides better quality and inventory control, cuts maintenance down time, creates cleaner and less noisy work stations, increases plant capacity, and cuts the number of production steps from six to four.[3]

An automatic printing machine installed at the McClouth Steel Corporation, Detroit, Michigan, marks stainless steel sheets in half the time it originally took. In the old method, four men loaded the sheets into a printer, ran them through, and unloaded them. Now, the Flexograph printer marks four sheets per minute as they travel through it carried by a conveyor. In addition to reducing the marking costs, the new printer also eliminated smudging.[4]

Packages and paper work flow along the same route in receiving operations at Westinghouse's Air Arm Division. On-the-move receiving saves at least two day's time for each shipment. Delays are cut because many conventional receiving steps are eliminated. The time saved and other benefits stem from a change-over from batch handling methods. Now about 350 packages move by belt through the receiving area each day. Paper work is carried along with the packages and is processed beside the belt. It is easy to relate paper work steps and moving packages.[5]

The foregoing examples illustrate the universal need for methods design and the tremendous benefits to be derived from sound applications. Because of the economies that result from continuous methods improvement programs, industry has long considered this one of the best avenues to manufacturing cost reduction.

## Origin of Methods Engineering

Methods engineering grew out of the pioneering developments of the Gilbreths (Frank B. and his wife Lillian M.), who developed many of the tools of "motion study" as a part of formulating a systematic approach to the analysis of work methods. Frank B. Gilbreth first became interested in methods analysis as an outgrowth of his observations of bricklaying. Gil-

---

[1]"Airpower Tightens Nuts Just Right," *Factory*, Vol. 121, No. 1 (January 1964), p. 207.

[2]"Automatic Sprayer Sprays Costs," *Factory*, Vol. 121, No. 1 (January 1964), p. 206.

[3]"Assembly Line Welding Cuts Costs and Downtime," *Factory*, Vol. 122, No. 2 (February 1964), p. 168.

[4]"Printer Pays Off," *Factory*, Vol. 122, No. 2 (February 1964), p. 169.

[5]Edmund Roberts, "On-the-Move Receiving Cuts Costs," *Modern Materials Handling* (December 1962), p. 65.

breth, who in 1885 was employed as an apprentice bricklayer, soon observed that a journeyman bricklayer used one set of motions when laying bricks slowly, another set when working at average speed, and still a different set when working at rapid speed. As a result of his observations, he invented an adjustable scaffold and developed a set of motions that greatly increased the number of bricks that could be laid in a day.

Gilbreth eventually became so engrossed in motion study that he discontinued the successful contracting business he had established in order to concentrate his full attention on the development of motion study. His wife, Lillian Gilbreth, who was a psychologist, proved to be a capable partner in the development of the many motion study techniques credited to them. Prior to his death in 1924, the Gilbreths had developed many of the analysis techniques in common use today. In their quest for the "one best way" the Gilbreths made use of: the process chart, the right- and left-hand operation chart, micromotion study, therbligs, and the chronocylegraph. These will be discussed later in this chapter.

## Organization for Methods Engineering

As indicated previously, methods engineering is a necessary function to insure that the most efficient methods are being used. This activity is most frequently performed by industrial engineers. These engineers may be assigned to a central methods engineering or industrial engineering department or may be assigned on a decentralized basis to specific operating departments. Some multi-plant companies, such as the Procter and Gamble Company, maintain both a central industrial engineering group to work on problems common to many plants and also assign industrial engineers to each plant to work on projects pertinent to only that plant.

It is readily apparent that methods design may be either "before the fact" or "after the fact." That is, it may consist of designing a new process or system not previously used in the organization, or it may consist of the improvement of an existing process or workplace. In attempting to determine how much engineering time and effort can be justified on a methods project, the following factors should be taken into account: (1) the volume of production to be scheduled on the job, (2) the anticipated life of the job, (3) the current investment in machines, tools, and equipment, and (4) the personnel considerations (union requirements, retraining time, and so forth).

As a specialist in methods design, the methods engineer must work with and secure information from many persons. Thus, he comes in close contact with product engineers, quality control engineers, tool engineers, production planning engineers, plant engineers, production supervisors, and many others. On major projects, the methods engineer frequently may serve as chairman of a planning committee composed of such persons as a product engineer, a tool engineer, a quality control engineer, a production supervisor, or others.

## Approach to Methods Design

In order to insure that the optimum method[6] is found, a systematic approach to methods design is far superior to the use of a "hit or miss" method. Stated in its simplest form this approach consists of the following steps:[7]

1. *Analyze the problem.* Identify the problem and then secure all known information about it through the use of appropriate analysis techniques.

2. *Question the present method.* If a present method exists, question the details of the known information to determine the principles violated.

3. *Synthesize a proposed method.* Formulate a proposed method for performing the work, embodying all the principles of sound methods engineering.

4. *Apply the proposed method.* Standardize and apply the new method.

To assist in the first two steps of the procedure outlined above, a number of analysis techniques have been developed, and suitable questions have been prepared in the form of checklists. Several of these analysis techniques and their accompanying questions will be discussed in the sections that follow.

## Tools for Methods Analysis

### Process Chart

In analyzing the movement of a product, man, or paper work, the *flow process chart* is invaluable in providing a graphical representation of the step-by-step sequence that takes place. The A.S.M.E. Standard[8] defines a flow process chart as follows:

---

[6]The search for the best methods is a never-ending one, and the optimum method today will be superseded by a better method in the future.

[7]Examination will reveal this to be a version of the scientific approach discussed in Chapter 1. For a discussion of a more detailed approach, see M. E. Mundel, *Motion and Time Study Principles and Practice* (3rd ed.; Englewood Cliffs, N. J.: Prentice-Hall, Inc., 1960), p. 27.

[8]Committee on Standardization of Therbligs, Process Charts, and Their Symbols, "Operation and Flow Process Charts" (New York: The American Society of Mechanical Engineers, 1947), p. 3.

A flow process chart is a graphic representation of the sequence of all operations, transportations, inspections, delays, and storages occurring during a process or procedure, and includes information considered desirable for analysis such as time required and distance moved.

(a) The material type presents the process in terms of the events which occur to the material.

(b) The man type presents the process in terms of the activities of the man.

To facilitate the charting of a process, it is common practice to make use of symbols such as those illustrated in Figure 7-1.

| Symbol | Name | Activities Represented |
|--------|------|------------------------|
| ◯ | Operation | Modification of object at one workplace. Object may be changed in any of its physical or chemical characteristics, assembled or disassembled, or arranged for another operation, transportation, inspection, or storage. |
| ⇨ | Transportation | Change in location of object from one place to another. |
| ☐ | Inspection | Examination of object to check on quality or quantity characteristics. |
| D | Delay | Retention of object in a location awaiting next activity. No authorization is required to perform the next activity. |
| ▽ | Storage | Retention of object in location in which it is protected against unauthorized removal. |

**Figure 7-1.** Symbols used for process charting.

The use of these symbols is illustrated in Figure 7-2, which shows a flow process chart for the present method of manufacturing a steel collar. Examination of this chart will show that it outlines the various operations, transportations, inspections, delays, and storages that take place on that part as it moves from one stage of completion to another.

The proposed method illustrated in Figure 7-3 resulted from questioning each of the steps in the present method and synthesizing a proposed method. Typical questions that may be raised about each of the steps on a process chart include the following:

1. Can an operation be eliminated?
2. Can an operation be combined with another operation?
3. Can the production sequence be changed?
4. Can an operation or inspection be simplified?
5. Can a movement be eliminated or shortened?
6. Can a delay or storage be eliminated?
7. Can this step be eliminated by redesigning the product or using different material?

## Right- and Left-Hand Operation Chart

The right- and left-hand operation chart provides a suitable means of analyzing man activity when a man is working at essentially one location. This

| FLOW PROCESS CHART | | | NO. 326  PAGE 1 OF 1 |

**SUMMARY**

| | PRESENT | | PROPOSED | | DIFFERENCE | |
|---|---|---|---|---|---|---|
| | NO. | TIME | NO. | TIME | NO. | TIME |
| ○ OPERATIONS | 5 | | | | | |
| ⇨ TRANSPORTATIONS | 4 | | | | | |
| □ INSPECTIONS | 0 | | | | | |
| D DELAYS | 5 | | | | | |
| ▽ STORAGES | 0 | | | | | |
| DISTANCE TRAVELLED | 200 FT. | | FT. | | FT. | |

DEPARTMENT *127*
OPERATION *Machining collar*
ITEM CHARTED *Collar* NO. *RO-352*
CHARTED BY *E. S. T.* DATE _____

| | DETAILS OF (PRESENT/PROPOSED) METHOD | Symbols | DISTANCE IN FEET | QUANTITY | TIME | ANALYSIS WHY? (WHAT? WHERE? WHEN? WHO? HOW?) | NOTES | ACTION |
|---|---|---|---|---|---|---|---|---|
| 1 | In storage rack | ○⇨□▽ | | | | ✓ | Can rack be located nearer saw? | ✓ |
| 2 | Attached to hoist | ○⇨□▽ | | 1 | | ✓ | | ✓ |
| 3 | Moved to saw | ○⇨□▽ | 15 | 1 | | | | |
| 4 | Unloaded from hoist | ○⇨□▽ | | 1 | | ✓ | | ✓ |
| 5 | Cut to length | ○⇨□▽ | | 1 | | | | |
| 6 | Await move man | ○⇨□▽ | | | | | Can conveyor be used? | ✓ |
| 7 | To lathe #16 | ○⇨□▽ | 35 | 36 | | | | |
| 8 | Await lathe operator | ○⇨□▽ | | | | | | ✓ |
| 9 | Face end, turn seat & thr'd | ○⇨□▽ | | 1 | | | | |
| 10 | Await move man | ○⇨□▽ | | | | | | ✓ |
| 11 | To lathe #17 | ○⇨□▽ | 20 | 36 | | | | |
| 12 | Face end & turn shoulder | ○⇨□▽ | | 1 | | | Is shoulder necessary? | ✓ |
| 13 | Await move man | ○⇨□▽ | | | | | | ✓ |
| 14 | To assembly dept. | ○⇨□▽ | 130 | 36 | | | | |
| 15 | | ○⇨□▽ | | | | | | |
| 16 | | ○⇨□▽ | | | | | | |
| 17 | | ○⇨□▽ | | | | | | |
| 18 | | ○⇨□▽ | | | | | | |
| 19 | | ○⇨□▽ | | | | | | |
| 20 | | ○⇨□▽ | | | | | | |
| 21 | | ○⇨□▽ | | | | | | |
| 22 | | ○⇨□▽ | | | | | | |
| 23 | | ○⇨□▽ | | | | | | |
| 24 | | ○⇨□▽ | | | | | | |
| 25 | | ○⇨□▽ | | | | | | |

**Figure 7-2.** Flow process chart for present method of manufacturing a steel collar.

121

| SUMMARY | PRESENT | | PROPOSED | | DIFFERENCE | |
|---|---|---|---|---|---|---|
| | NO. | TIME | NO. | TIME | NO. | TIME |
| ○ OPERATIONS | 5 | | 2 | | 3 | |
| ⇨ TRANSPORTATIONS | 4 | | 3 | | 1 | |
| ☐ INSPECTIONS | 0 | | 0 | | 0 | |
| D DELAYS | 5 | | 4 | | 1 | |
| ▽ STORAGES | 0 | | 0 | | 0 | |
| DISTANCE TRAVELLED | 200 FT. | | 148 FT. | | 52 FT. | |

**FLOW PROCESS CHART** NO. 327  PAGE 1 OF 1

DEPARTMENT 127
OPERATION Machining Collar
ITEM CHARTED Collar      NO. 80-352
CHARTED BY E.S.T.      DATE

DETAILS OF (~~PRESENT~~ PROPOSED) METHOD

| # | Details | Symbols | Distance in feet | Quantity | Time | Analysis Why? | Notes | Action Change |
|---|---|---|---|---|---|---|---|---|
| 1 | In storage rack | ○⇨☐D▽ | | | | | | |
| 2 | To saw | ○⇨☐D▽ | 3 | 1 | | | | |
| 3 | Cut to length | ○⇨☐D▽ | | 1 | | | | |
| 4 | Await move man | ○⇨☐D▽ | | | | | Conveyor uneconomical | |
| 5 | To lathe # 16 | ○⇨☐D▽ | 35 | 36 | | | | |
| 6 | Await lathe operator | ○⇨☐D▽ | | | | | | |
| 7 | Face end, turn seat, & thread | ○⇨☐D▽ | | 1 | | | | |
| 8 | Await move man | ○⇨☐D▽ | | | | | | |
| 9 | To assembly dept. | ○⇨☐D▽ | 110 | 36 | | | | |
| 10 | | ○⇨☐D▽ | | | | | | |
| 11 | | ○⇨☐D▽ | | | | | | |
| 12 | | ○⇨☐D▽ | | | | | | |
| 13 | | ○⇨☐D▽ | | | | | | |
| 14 | | ○⇨☐D▽ | | | | | | |
| 15 | | ○⇨☐D▽ | | | | | | |
| 16 | | ○⇨☐D▽ | | | | | | |
| 17 | | ○⇨☐D▽ | | | | | | |
| 18 | | ○⇨☐D▽ | | | | | | |
| 19 | | ○⇨☐D▽ | | | | | | |
| 20 | | ○⇨☐D▽ | | | | | | |
| 21 | | ○⇨☐D▽ | | | | | | |
| 22 | | ○⇨☐D▽ | | | | | | |
| 23 | | ○⇨☐D▽ | | | | | | |
| 24 | | ○⇨☐D▽ | | | | | | |
| 25 | | ○⇨☐D▽ | | | | | | |

**Figure 7-3.** Flow process chart for proposed method of manufacturing a steel collar.

# OPERATION CHART

PURDUE UNIVERSITY
MOTION & TIME STUDY
LABORATORY

SUMMARY PER _1_ PIECES

| | PRESENT | | PROPOSED | | DIFFERENCE | |
|---|---|---|---|---|---|---|
| | LH | RH | LH | RH | LH | RH |
| OPERATIONS | 2 | 6 | | | | |
| TRANSPORTS | 3 | 6 | | | | |
| HOLDS | 9 | 0 | | | | |
| DELAYS | 0 | 2 | | | | |
| TOTAL | 14 | 14 | | | | |

COMPANY _A.C. Wright Corp._
DEPARTMENT _Assembly_
OPERATION _Assemble ball point pen_
_No. RT45_
OPERATOR _R.O. Jenkins_
CHARTED BY _S.O.J._ DATE _____
PRESENT } METHOD   SHEET _1_ OF _1_
PROPOSED }

| LEFT HAND | OPER. TRANS. HOLD DELAY | | OPER. TRANS. HOLD DELAY | RIGHT HAND |
|---|---|---|---|---|
| To barrel | O⊳∇D | 1 | O⊳∇D | To ink cartridge |
| Grasp " | O⊳∇D | 2 | O⊳∇D | Grasp " " |
| To assembly area | O⊳∇D | 3 | O⊳∇D | To assembly area |
| Hold barrel | O⊳∇D | 4 | O⊳∇D | Insert cartridge in barrel |
| " " | O⊳∇D | 5 | O⊳∇D | To spring |
| " " | O⊳∇D | 6 | O⊳∇D | Grasp " |
| " " | O⊳∇D | 7 | O⊳∇D | To assembly area |
| " " | O⊳∇D | 8 | O⊳∇D | Assemble spring on cart'ge |
| " " | O⊳∇D | 9 | O⊳∇D | To cap |
| " " | O⊳∇D | 10 | O⊳∇D | Grasp cap |
| " " | O⊳∇D | 11 | O⊳∇D | To assembly area |
| " " | O⊳∇D | 12 | O⊳∇D | Assemble cap to barrel |
| To rack | O⊳∇D | 13 | O⊳∇D | Wait for left hand |
| Place in rack | O⊳∇D | 14 | O⊳∇D | " " " " |
| | O⊳∇D | 15 | O⊳∇D | |
| | O⊳∇D | 16 | O⊳∇D | |
| | O⊳∇D | 17 | O⊳∇D | |
| | O⊳∇D | 18 | O⊳∇D | |
| | O⊳∇D | 19 | O⊳∇D | |
| | O⊳∇D | 20 | O⊳∇D | |
| | O⊳∇D | 21 | O⊳∇D | |
| | O⊳∇D | 22 | O⊳∇D | |
| | O⊳∇D | 23 | O⊳∇D | |

Figure 7-4. Operation chart for right and left hand in assembling a ball point pen. (Courtesy Purdue University Motion and Time Study Laboratory.)

type of analysis is particularly suitable for operations involving assembly work and inspection where no machine is involved.

Figure 7-4 illustrates a right- and left-hand operation chart for assembling a ball-point pen. Examination of this chart discloses that the operation is broken down into a series of simultaneous actions (suboperations, transportations, delays, and holds) performed by the two hands. In performing Step 2 (questioning), of the systematic approach, each of the steps on the original method should be questioned by means of a series of questions such as the following:

1. Can a suboperation be eliminated or combined?
2. Can a transportation be eliminated or shortened?
3. Can the sequence of motions be changed to facilitate the operation?
4. Can a delay be eliminated?
5. Can a hold be eliminated through the use of a jig or fixture?

### Multiple Activity Chart

In those operations involving the combination of a man and a machine, a man and several machines, or any combination of men and machines where delays are prevalent, the multiple activity chart provides a convenient technique for analyzing the combined activity. Very often the objectives of this type of analysis are to attain the maximum utilization of a machine, to attain the optimum man-and-machine relationship, or to bring about the best balance of crew activity. For this reason, the time factor is an important consideration and necessitates the use of a graphical representation involving time. Figure 7-5 contains a chart illustrating the present method of performing the operation "drill cleat." Use of this chart is very similar to that of the right- and left-hand operation chart except that the symbols are used in column form in order that the time factor may be represented, and an additional column is used to represent the machine. Where more than one man and one machine are analyzed, it is common practice to use a column to represent each man and each machine.

The formulation of a proposed method will result from a questioning approach and synthesis similar to that used for the right- and left-hand operation chart.

### Micromotion Study

Micromotion study, which was originated by Frank B. Gilbreth, is one of the most exacting forms of work analysis available for job improvement. It is an analysis technique making use of motion pictures taken at a constant and

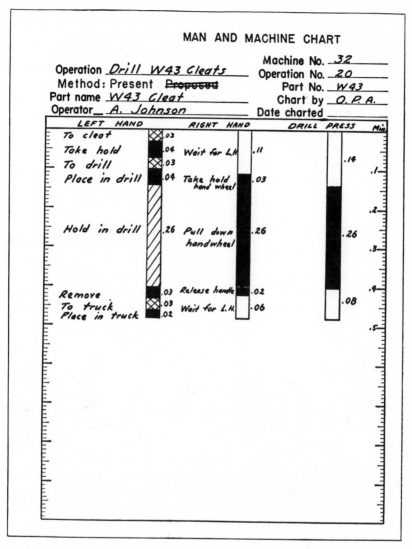

MAN AND MACHINE CHART

Operation _Drill W43 Cleats_    Machine No. _32_
Method: Present  ~~Proposed~~    Operation No. _20_
Part name _W43 Cleat_    Part No. _W43_
Operator_ _A. Johnson_    Chart by _O.P.A._
Date charted _____

| LEFT HAND | | RIGHT HAND | | DRILL PRESS | Min. |
|---|---|---|---|---|---|
| To cleat | .03 | | | | |
| Take hold | .04 | Wait for L.H. | .11 | | .14 |
| To drill | .03 | | | | .1 |
| Place in drill | .04 | Take hold hand wheel | .03 | | |
| | | | | | .2 |
| Hold in drill | .26 | Pull down handwheel | .26 | .26 | .3 |
| | | | | | .4 |
| Remove | .03 | Release handle | .02 | | |
| To truck | .03 | Wait for L.H. | .06 | .08 | .5 |
| Place in truck | .02 | | | | |

Figure 7-5. Man and machine chart for drilling wood cleats. (Adapted from M. E. Mundel, _Motion and Time Study_, 2nd Ed., Englewood Cliffs, N.J.: Prentice-Hall, Inc., 1955.)

known speed. The film becomes a permanent record of both the method being used and the time consumed in doing the work.

Although micromotion study was originally employed primarily for job analysis work, in recent years several new uses have been found for this analysis tool. It may be used for the following purposes: to study the inter-relationships among the members of a work group, to study the relationship between an operator and his machine, to obtain the time for an operation, to establish a permanent record of a job method, and similar activities. Even though micromotion study is a valuable analysis tool, it has not been used extensively in industry, because it is expensive, time-consuming, and frequently meets with union resistance (because of the motion pictures).

Micromotion study provides a valuable technique for making minute analyses of those operations that are short in cycle, contain rapid movements, and involve high production over a long period of time. Thus, it is very useful in analyzing operations such as the sewing of garments, assembling small parts, and similar activities.

The usual procedure for performing micromotion study is to take motion pictures of the operations, analyze the resulting film, and to prepare a *simo* (simultaneous motion cycle) chart from the results of the film analysis. In analyzing the film, very accurate time values (commonly $1/_{2000}$ minute) may be obtained by reading a clock (microchronometer) that appears in each frame of the motion picture. Most persons prefer not to use the clock and instead use a camera driven by a constant-speed motor. This makes possible a constant time interval (such as $1/_{1000}$ minute, $1/_{10}$ minute, 1 second) between adjacent frames of the film (see Figure 7-6).

The film is analyzed by breaking the job cycle down into *therbligs*[9] or

**Figure 7-6.** Motor driven motion-picture camera (Reproduced by permission from M. E. Mundel, *Motion and Time Study*, 2nd ed., Englewood Cliffs, N.J.: Prentice-Hall, Inc., 1960, p. 265.)

---

[9]Therblig (an anagram of GILBRETH) is a term coined by Frank Gilbreth to describe the 17 basic subdivisions of human activity.

basic body motions. Although the 17 therbligs are not the smallest subdivisions into which human activity can be subdivided, they are widely known and used and can be conveniently applied.

Figure 7-7 shows the therbligs with their symbols, colors, and definitions.

| Name of Symbol | Symbol | Color | Activity Represented |
|---|---|---|---|
| Search | Sh | Black | Occurs when hand or eyes are hunting or groping for something. *Example:* Trying to find or pick a part from a pile. |
| Select | St | Gray | Occurs when one object is being picked from among several. *Example:* Locating a particular bolt from among several. |
| Grasp | G | Lake red | Consists of taking hold of an object. *Example:* Closing the fingers around a pencil. |
| Transport empty | TE | Olive green | Refers to moving the empty hand while reaching for something. *Example:* Reaching for a desk pen. |
| Transport loaded | TL | Grass green | Refers to moving an object from one place to another. *Example:* Carrying a desk pen from the holder to the paper. |
| Hold | H | Gold ochre | Refers to the retention of an object in a fixed location. *Example:* Retaining a fountain pen barrel in one hand while assembling the cap to it with the other. |
| Release load | RL | Carmine red | Occurs when the hand lets go of an object. *Example:* Letting go of a desk pen when it is placed in a holder. |
| Position | P | Blue | Consists of aligning or orienting an object preparatory to fitting it into some location. *Example:* Aligning a plug preparatory to inserting it into an electrical outlet. |
| Pre-position | PP | Sky-blue | Consists of locating an object in a predetermined manner and in the correct position for some subsequent motion. *Example:* Lining up a desk pen for insertion into its holder. |
| Inspect | I | Burnt ochre | Examination of an object to determine some quality such as size, shape, or color. *Example:* Visual examination of finish of a desk. |
| Assemble | A | Violet, heavy | Consists of combining one object with another. *Example:* Putting a nut on a bolt. |
| Disassemble | DA | Violet, light | Consists of separating two objects which were combined. *Example:* Removing a nut from a bolt. |

**Figure 7-7** Therblig symbols and definitions. (continued on page 128.)

| | | | |
|---|---|---|---|
| Use | U | Purple | Consists of applying or manipulating a tool, control or device for the purpose for which intended. *Example:* Tightening a bolt with a crescent wrench. |
| Unavoidable delay | UD | Yellow ochre | Refers to a delay by body member which is beyond the control of the operator. *Example:* Right hand pauses during the operation of assembling a mechanical pencil while the left hand asides a completed pencil. |
| Avoidable delay | AD | Lemon yellow | Refers to a delay by body member which is within the control of the operator. *Example:* An operator pauses or deviates from the normal motion pattern. |
| Plan | Pn | Brown | Refers to a delay in a motion pattern while the operator decides how to proceed. *Example:* An operator assembling a complex valve pauses to decide which part should be next. |
| Rest for overcoming fatigue | R | Orange | Occurs when a worker pauses to overcome the fatigue from the previous work. *Example:* An operator pauses to rest after having lifted several heavy castings into a metal truck. |

**Figure 7-7.** Continued.

In analyzing the motion-picture film it is common practice first to record the description on a *film analysis sheet;* from this information, a simo chart may be prepared. Examination of the simo chart illustrated in Figure 7-8 discloses that the simultaneous action of either hand may be determined by reading horizontally across the chart and that the duration of each therblig is illustrated by the time column.

After the simo chart of the operation has been made, the chart should be studied and subjected to question in order to find a better way of doing the work. Every attempt should be made to eliminate those therbligs that are non-productive (hold, avoidable delay, unavoidable delay, plan, rest, select, search), as well as to shorten those that are productive.

### Memomotion Study

Before leaving the general area of micromotion study, let us touch briefly on memomotion study. Memomotion study, which was originated by M. E. Mundel, is a special form of micromotion study in which the motion pictures are taken at slow speeds. Sixty frames per minute and one hundred frames per minute are most common.

Memomotion study has been used frequently to study the flow and handling of materials, crew activities, multi-man-and-machine relationships,

## SIMO-CHART

Method _Original_     Film No. _A-6-CC_
Operation _Assembly_     Operation No. _DT27A_
     Part No. _27_
Part name _Bottle dropper top_     Chart by _Ross_
Operator _Armstrong-157_     Date charted _____

| LEFT HAND DESCRIPTION | Symbol | Time | Total time = 20/100 | Time | Symbol | RIGHT HAND DESCRIPTION | Clock |
|---|---|---|---|---|---|---|---|
| Finished part to tray | TL | 8 | 0 | | | | 120 |
| | RL | 2 | | 20 | TE | To rubber tops | |
| To bakelite cups | TE | 16 | | | UO | | 130 |
| | | | 20 | 10 | G | Rubber tops | 140 |
| Bakelite cup | G | 8 | | | | | |
| To work area | TL | 4 | | 12 | TL | To work area | 150 |
| | P | 2 | 40 | | | | |
| For assembling | N | 18 | | 8 | P | To bakelite | 160 |
| | | | | 6 | A | | 170 |
| For RH to grasp top | P | 2 | 60 | 2 | RL | Rubber tops | |
| | | | | 4 | TE | To top of rubber | |
| For RH to pull rubber top | N | 14 | | 2 | G | Top of rubber | 180 |
| | | | | 8 | A | Pull rubber thru | |
| For glass | P | 4 | | 2 | RL | | 190 |
| | | | 80 | 6 | TE | To glass rods | |
| | | | | 8 | G | Glass rod | 200 |
| For assembly of glass | N | 32 | | 8 | TL | To cup | |
| | | | 100 | 2 | P | | 210 |
| | | | | 10 | A | Insert glass | 220 |
| | | | 110 | 2 | RL | | |
| | | | | | | | 230 |

LH Summary          RH Summary

| | | | | | | |
|---|---|---|---|---|---|---|
| 50.2% | N | 64 | 24 | A | 21.8% | |
| 14.6% | TE | 16 | 20 | TE | 18.2% | |
| 11.0% | TL | 12 | 20 | G | 18.2% | |
| 7.2% | G | 8 | 20 | TL | 18.2% | |
| 7.2% | P | 8 | 10 | P | 9.1% | |
| 1.8% | RL | 2 | 10 | UO | 9.1% | |
| | | | 6 | RL | 5.4% | |

**Figure 7-8.** Simo-chart for assembling dropper bottle tops. (From M. E. Mundel, *Motion and Time Study*, 2nd Ed., Englewood Cliffs, N.J.: Prentice-Hall, Inc., 1955. Reprinted by permission.)

stockroom activities, department store clerks, and a variety of other jobs. It is particularly valuable on long cycle jobs or jobs involving many inter-relationships. In addition to all of the advantages of micromotion study, it can be used at relatively low film cost (about 6 per cent of the film cost at normal camera speeds) and permits rapid visual review of long sequences of activities.

### Principles of Motion Economy

Through the pioneer work of Gilbreth and other investigators, certain rules for motion economy and efficiency have been developed. Some of the most important of these principles are the following:

1. The movements of the two hands should be balanced and the two hands should begin and end their motions simultaneously.

2. The hands should be doing productive work and should not be idle at the same time except during rest periods.

3. Motions of the hands should be made in opposite and symmetrical directions and at the same time.

4. The work should be arranged to permit it to be performed with an easy and natural rhythm.

5. Momentum and ballistic-type movements should be employed wherever possible in order to reduce muscular effort.

6. There should be a definite location for all tools and materials, and they should be located in front of and close to the worker.

7. Bins or other devices should be used to deliver the materials close to the point of use.

8. The workplace should be designed to insure adequate illumination, proper workplace height, and provision for alternate standing and sitting by the operator.

9. Wherever possible, jigs, fixtures, or other mechanical devices should be used to relieve the hands of unnecessary work.

10. Tools should be pre-positioned wherever possible in order to facilitate grasping them.

Through the application of these principles, it is possible greatly to increase the output of manual labor with a minimum of fatigue.

## Work Simplification Programs

In recent years, it has become common practice to conduct *work simplification* or *methods improvement* programs in industry. These programs usually have as their objective the reduction of manufacturing costs through the participation of many persons. For example, in a work simplification program conducted by a large electrical manufacturing company, anticipated annual savings contributed by some 3000 supervisors was estimated to approach $7,500,000.

The concept of work simplification was introduced by Allen H. Mogensen in the 1930's and emphasized worker participation as a means of achieving maximum cost reduction. In the widespread adoption of these programs throughout industry, government agencies, and elsewhere, there has been recognition of the need to acquaint many people with the aims and objectives of methods improvement programs. This orientation should take place at all levels, not only to bring about greater acceptance of methods improvement programs, but also to provide the knowledge of good methods design to all persons who may benefit from such information. Thus, it has been found profitable to present the programs to members of management (including the president of the company), product engineers, process engineers, tool engineers, foremen, group leaders, and key operators. Frequently, the company suggestion system may be incorporated as part of the work simplification program.

It is customary for the methods engineers to conduct a training program as a basis for implementing the work simplification programs. These programs may be given in one continuous session, but more often are limited to a series of two- or three-hour sessions held once or twice each week. In one large company, the course consists of twenty hours and covers the following topics:

1. General economics.
2. Problem-solving approach.
3. Process charts.
4. Operation charts.
5. Multiple-activity charts.
6. Principles of motion economy.

Usually, the participants in the program are asked to apply the principles that they have learned to one or more operations being performed in their respective departments. Through the discussion of these problems, they are able to appreciate the benefits to be derived from a methods improvement program. Also, these people, being closer to their jobs than the methods engineers, can often suggest methods improvements that would escape the trained methods engineer.

Most of the principles that are applied in methods improvement programs have the tendency to reduce the content of a job method. Though this is done to reduce the skills required to do the job, it may result in jobs that are boring and monotonous and lead to little worker satisfaction. Some people are of the opinion that perhaps the industrial engineer has gone too far in reducing the job to its simplest components, and that it has been a serious mistake to have a worker performing a job requiring so little human potential. They[10] suggest that the jobs should be enlarged, and that

---

[10]For a discussion of job enlargement, see R.H. Guest, "Job Enlargement—A Revolution in Job Design," *Personnel Administration* (March–April 1957), p. 11; M. D. Kilbridge, "Do Workers Prefer Larger Jobs?" *Personnel* (September–October 1960), p. 45.

labor effectiveness can be increased and unit cost reduced by having the operator assume greater responsibility for the work he does, especially the quality of his work, and that he should have closer identity with the product he turns out.

There is evidence to show that job enlargement may be both desirable and profitable in some cases, and some general rules pertaining to work design[11] appear to be developing that will aid in sound work methods design.

## Value Analysis

An activity that is closely related to both methods improvement programs and to purchasing and that is being used increasingly in industry and the government is *value analysis.* "Value analysis is an objective study of every item of cost in every component part, subassembly, or piece of equipment. This includes a study of the design, the material and the process in a continual search for other possible materials and new processes."[12] Value analysis involves the evaluation of an item's function and relates its effect on the end product. The purpose of it is to attempt to insure that every element of cost contributes proportionately to the function of the item.

Just as in the work simplification approach, value analysis uses a questioning attitude and asks some key questions:

1. What is it?
2. What does it do?
3. What does it cost?
4. What is it worth?
5. What else will do the job?
6. How much will it cost?

It is obvious from the questions that value analysis is concerned with function, cost, and value. It probably tends to put more emphasis on materials than the traditional methods analysis or work simplification programs. At the same time, it is an important ingredient of a total cost-reduction program.

## Suggestion Systems

An important source of ideas for cost-saving improvements is the suggestion system. The purpose of the suggestion system is to motivate the worker to

---

[11]A. Richard Marks, "A Theory of Job Design and Research Findings," Paper presented to the Congress of the International Association of Applied Psychology (Rome, Italy, April 1958).

[12]Frank J. Johnson, "Value Analysis-Engineering-Function Oriented Cost Reduction," Proceedings Fourteenth Annual Conference, American Institute of Industrial Engineers (Denver, May 1963), p. 144.

present any ideas he may have on ways in which the company can be operated better. As a reward for submitting his suggestion, it is common practice to pay the worker a percentage of the annual savings that will result.

Some companies have found it difficult to administer suggestion systems successfully and have discontinued them. On the other hand, many companies have found them to be an invaluable source of cost-saving ideas and are happy to pay out large sums of money each year in order to encourage the continuance of this stream of potential savings.

## Social and Economic Effects of Methods Study

As was pointed out at the beginning of this chapter, modern industry is constantly searching for better methods. When a business ceases to move forward it will lose ground and may eventually fail. It is for this reason that the major companies have organized industrial engineering departments, work simplification and value analysis programs, suggestion systems, and other methods of achieving reduced costs of manufacturing their products. One of the consequences of these programs has been increased mechanization, which, in turn, has led to the production of more and more goods per man-hour. Among the long-range benefits derived from this increased output have been: higher real wages, an improved standard of living, a shorter work week, and a reduction of the physical rigors of the job.

Besides the long-run effects, there are many short-run effects; these may have a marked effect on the worker and are probably uppermost in his mind. It is obvious that in order to have methods improvement, there must be continuous changes in the status quo. This will invariably lead to worker resistance because it is normal to resist change. And if a worker is "laid off" as a result of methods changes, he, and perhaps his fellow workers, probably will be bitter about the change. In order to avoid this situation some companies have adopted the policy that no employee will be "laid off" as a result of methods changes.

## QUESTIONS

1.  Based upon your observations, how extensively do you think methods design has been applied to industry and to the home?
2.  Why is it desirable to use a systematic procedure in methods design?
3.  Describe some job you have witnessed recently in which the person obviously was using a poor method. How would you suggest improving the method?
4.  If you desired to chart the steps required in lubricating an automobile, which analysis chart would probably be of most value? Why?

5. How do you account for the fact that only a small percentage of companies use suggestion plans?

6. In seeking an improvement, what are some of the questions you might ask about each of the therbligs required in the operation of removing your pen from your pocket and writing your name on a sheet of paper?

7. Why do workers resist change? How might this resistance be reduced?

8. Is job enlargement inconsistent with the goals of a methods improvement program? Why?

9. Is it possible for a company to be using good methods even though it does not have a methods improvement program?

10. Observe a waitress or other person performing a job and chart the activities on a flow process chart.

11. Who should be responsible for and involved in a value analysis program?

## CASE PROBLEMS

### Jacobson Foundry

One of the high production operations in the Jacobson Foundry consists of removing sand cores (8″ × 16″ × 1″) from drier plates (plates on which cores are stacked while in the drier) and then placing them in wood storage boxes (18″ × 18″ × 10″ deep), for moving to the molding department.

In performing this operation, the packer picks up a handful of cores in her left hand and places them one at a time in the box with her right hand. The boxes are flat on the packing table, so the packer is forced to stretch to see inside.

George Winston, one of the methods engineers, has been asked to see what can be done to increase the output on this operation.

*Questions:*

1. How should George Winston proceed in trying to improve the present method used on this operation?

2. What additional information does he need?

3. What analysis technique (chart) will probably prove of greatest value?

4. If you were George Winston, what method would you recommend?

### Illinois Machine Company

The Illinois Machine Company manufactures tremendous quantities of automatic screw machine parts for use in its line of handcraft tools. When the parts are discharged from the machine, they roll down chutes and into a tote box. The length of the drop has caused nicks and scratches on some parts that couldn't take this kind of handling. This has led to an excessive number of rejects.

Arthur Erickson, the foreman, has just completed the company's work simplification training program and has decided to analyze this operation for improvement. As suggested by his instructor, he decides to use a logical procedure in tackling this problem.

*Questions:*

1. Perform each of the steps of the procedure as they might be performed by Arthur Erickson.
2. Suggest ways in which the rejects could be eliminated.

# CHAPTER EIGHT

# Work Measurement

Work measurement (commonly referred to as "time study") is concerned with the determination of the amount of time required to perform a unit of work. For many years, its principal use was for wage-incentive purposes; however, present-day industry finds many uses for work measurement, and it has become one of management's most important tools. Increasingly, it has been used to measure indirect labor (e.g., maintenance workers and materials handlers) and office work.

Work measurement is used to determine the amount of time required by a qualified worker, using a standard method and working at a standard work pace, to perform a specified task. The time required for this task is commonly referred to as the "standard" or "allowed" time.

## Origin of Work Measurement

Frederick W. Taylor is credited with having introduced work measurement or time study, as an essential part of scientific management, in the Midvale Steel Company in 1881. While serving with Midvale as a gang boss and foreman, Taylor was confronted by questions such as: "What is the best way to do the job?" "What equipment should be used?" "What is a fair day's work?" In attempting to answer these questions, he studied each of various jobs for the purpose of finding the best method. He taught the worker how to use the new method, maintained the working conditions so the worker could do the job properly, established a time standard for accomplishing the work, and then paid the worker a premium for doing the work in the prescribed time and manner. "With Taylor, as with the factory manager today, work measurement was a tool to be used in increasing the overall efficiency of the plant, making possible higher wages for labor, and lower prices of the finished products to the consumer."[1]

## Uses of Work Measurement Data

Analysis of the many manufacturing and control functions required in the fabrication of a product will disclose most of them to depend upon time. Without using some unit of time it would be virtually impossible to plan and schedule production, to make cost estimates on new work, to balance production lines, or to control labor costs. If standard or allowed times are to be used, they should, for greatest accuracy, be obtained by a formal system of work measurement.

The standard or allowed time values are usually determined for each of the operations required in the manufacture of a product and are commonly expressed in hours per piece or per 100 pieces. Standard times may be used for any of the following purposes:

1. The balancing of production lines for new models or new products.
2. The balancing of crew activities on those jobs requiring several workers.
3. Planning and scheduling the flow of production through the plant.
4. Making cost estimates on new products or new models.
5. Providing a basis for cost determination.
6. Providing a basis for wage-incentive plans.
7. Establishing supervisory objectives and providing a basis for measuring supervisory efficiency.

It should be obvious from the above list that work measurement is often justified for other than wage-incentive purposes.

## Work Measurement Equipment

Following its introduction by Taylor, for many years, the most common way of determining time standards was through the use of the stop watch. Although used less frequently today, it still is in common use for measuring certain jobs. Figure 8-1 shows a decimal minute stop watch of the type used extensively in industry. This watch has a sweep hand that makes one revolution per minute; therefore, each division on the large dial represents one one-hundredth of a minute.

---

[1] R. M. Barnes, *Motion and Time Study: Design and Measurement of Work* (New York: John Wiley & Sons, Inc., 1963), p. 15.

**Figure 8-1.** Decimal-minute stop watch.

Other timing devices that have been used to a lesser degree in industry are the motion-picture camera, the time-recording machine, and the Servis recorder. When the motion-picture camera is used, it is most frequently driven by a synchronous motor drive at a speed of 1000, 100, or 60 frames per minute (see Figure 7-6). This permits the measurement of time in either thousandths or hundredths of a minute or in seconds.

The time-recording machine (see Figure 8-2), which has had limited

**Figure 8-2.** Time-recording machine.

use in industry, consists of a small cabinet through which paper is drawn at a constant rate of speed. The tape has a printed scale in tenths of an inch, each division representing one one-hundredth of a minute. The machine has two keys, similar to those on a typewriter, and when these keys are depressed, marks are printed on the paper. By depressing one key at the end of each element and the other key at the end of the cycle, the time lapse for each element and for the cycle may be obtained.

A number of automatic recorders have been developed that may be attached to a machine to record working time or idle time. There are various ways of activating these recorders. They may be started by a control on a machine, by means of the vibration of a machine, or by other means.

## Work Measurement by Stop Watch

The steps usually performed in the making of a stop-watch time study are as follows:

1. Securing permission from the supervisor for making the study and explaining to the operator the purpose of the observations.

2. Checking the job method for improvements, standardizing the job method, and recording on the observation sheet complete information about the job and operator.

3. Breaking the job down into elements and recording these elements in detail on the observation sheet.

4. Determining and recording the times for each of the elements.

5. Rating or leveling the operator's performance.

6. Providing allowances for personal time, fatigue, machine delays, and so forth.

7. Calculating the standard or allowed time.

### Standardizing the Job Method

It is important that the work measurement analyst give consideration to the present job method prior to determining the time. Oftentimes, the methods being used are poor, and obvious improvements are in order. Whenever possible the job methods should be altered prior to the taking of the time study in order to insure that the analyst's efforts are not being wasted on a job that may soon undergo change.

The importance of standardized job conditions should not be under-estimated, since any variation in job conditions or methods will have a marked influence on the time required to perform the task. For this reason, it is difficult to set accurate time standards on those jobs that are undergoing frequent change, involve large fluctuations in materials, or contain other variables greatly influencing the production time.

Where there is a choice of operators of whose performance the study may be made, it is common practice to choose one who is neither the very best nor the poorest. Before approaching the operator, the analyst should secure the supervisor's permission and, where applicable, clear with the union. The supervisor should inform the operator in advance that a work measurement study is to be made, explaining the purpose of the study. At

## TIME STUDY SHEET

OPERATION _Drill oil hole in shaft_____ OPER. NO. _30_____

MACH.TYPE _Delta drill press_ MACH. NO. _214_____ DEPT. _A17___

PART NAME _Shaft_____ PART NO. _PL 138____ OPERATOR _B. Alden_

STUDY NO. _A-112-56_____ ANALYST _T.F. Jones___ DATE _____

**WRITTEN STANDARD PRACTICE**

| ELEM. NO. | LEFT HAND DESCRIPTION | RIGHT HAND DESCRIPTION | MACHINE ELEMENT | SPEED | FEED | STD. TIME |
|---|---|---|---|---|---|---|
| 1 | Get shaft from tote box and place in jig | Wait for left hand | | | | .111 |
| 2 | Grasp jig handle and close jig | Advance drill to part | | | | .203 |
| 3 | Hold jig closed while drilling | Advance drill 1¼" during drilling | Drill ⅝"×1¼ deep hole | 920 | | .747 |
| 4 | Open jig | Raise drill | | | | .058 |
| 5 | Remove shaft from jig and place in tote box | Wait for left hand | | | | .110 |
| 6 | Remove chips once every 20 pieces | Assist left hand | | | | .012 |

| STANDARD PRODUCTION — PCS./HR. 48.34 | STANDARD TIME — MINUTES / PC. 1.241 |
|---|---|

| SKETCH OF WORKPLACE | SET-UP, TOOLS, JIGS, FIXTURES, GAGES— |

Jig. No. DJ-532

⅝" high speed drill

Drill press

Unfinished parts

Finished parts

Operator

Scale: 1 square = 1'-0"

**Figure 8-3a.** Time study observation sheet (front).

no time should the study be made without the operator's knowledge—and never in secret.

The information on the observation sheet should be accurately recorded. It is important that all information that may be used to identify the operation and describe the conditions prevalent at the time of the study be put down carefully. Also, it is essential that a dimensioned sketch of the workplace showing all tools, machines, and materials be included on or attached to the observation sheet.

## Recording the Job Method

When an operation is being timed, the job should be broken down into separable parts and each of the parts timed. These parts are called *elements*

STUDY NO. *A-34-56*      STOP WATCH OBSERVATIONS      TIME BEGAN *9:10* TIME ENDED *9:33*  PRODUCTION DURING STUDY *20*

| ELEMENTS DESCRIPTION | 1 R | 1 T | 2 R | 2 T | 3 R | 3 T | 4 R | 4 T | 5 R | 5 T | 6 R | 6 T | 7 R | 7 T | 8 R | 8 T | 9 R | 9 T | 10 R | 10 T | AVE. ELEM. TIME | RATING | NORMAL TIME | ALLOW. | STD. TIME |
|---|---|---|---|---|---|---|---|---|---|---|---|---|---|---|---|---|---|---|---|---|---|---|---|---|---|
| Release shaft | 10 | 10 | 13 | 09 | 35 | 10 | 36 | 08 | 49 | 09 | 64 | 12 | 75 | 10 | 75 | 10 | 99 | 09 | 12 | 10 | .096 | 110 | .106 | 5% | .111 |
| Close jig | 19 | 09 | 31 | 18 | 42 | 17 | 52 | 16 | 67 | 18 | 81 | 17 | 91 | 16 | 04 | 19 | 15 | 16 | 30 | 18 | .176 | 110 | .193 | 5% | .203 |
| Back-off drill | 90 | 71 | 02 | 71 | 14 | 72 | 24 | 72 | 37 | 70 | 51 | 70 | 61 | 70 | 75 | 71 | 87 | 72 | 03 | 73 | .711 | 100 | .711 | 5% | .747 |
| Release jig | 95 | 05 | 06 | 04 | 18 | 04 | 29 | 05 | 43 | 06 | 56 | 05 | 65 | 04 | 80 | 05 | 92 | 05 | 07 | 04 | .046 | 110 | .051 | 5% | .058 |
| " shaft | 04 | 09 | 15 | 09 | 23 | 10 | 40 | 11 | 52 | 09 | 65 | 09 | 75 | 10 | 90 | 10 | 102 | 10 | 16 | 09 | .095 | 110 | .105 | 5% | .110 |
| | | | | | | | | | | | | | | | | | | | | | .010 | 105 | .011 | 5% | .012 |
| | 25 | 09 | 36 | 09 | 55 | 08 | 66 | 08 | 81 | 09 | 92 | 10 | 05 | 10 | 20 | 11 | 30 | 09 | 41 | 10 | | | | | |
| | 43 | 11 | 54 | 18 | 74 | 19 | 95 | 19 | 98 | 17 | 10 | 18 | 24 | 19 | 37 | 17 | 46 | 16 | 59 | 18 | | | | | |
| | 13 | 70 | 34 | 71 | 46 | 72 | 57 | 72 | 67 | 69 | 80 | 70 | 94 | 70 | 09 | 71 | 18 | 72 | 31 | 72 | | | | | |
| | 18 | 05 | 38 | 04 | 50 | 04 | 61 | 04 | 72 | 05 | 85 | 05 | 00 | 06 | 12 | 04 | 22 | 04 | 35 | 04 | | | | | |
| | 27 | 09 | 47 | 09 | 51 | 08 | 72 | 11 | 82 | 10 | 95 | 10 | 09 | 09 | 21 | 09 | 31 | 09 | 45 | 10 | | | | | |
| Remove chips | | | | | | | | | | | | | | | | | | | 65 | 20 | | | | | |

STANDARD TIME—MINUTES/PC *1.241*

FOREIGN ELEMENTS—

DETAILS OF ALLOWANCES—
*5% personal only*

**Figure 8-3b.** Time study observation sheet (back).

and contain a series of motions that can be identified, described, and recorded. (As an illustration, elements are listed on the observation sheet shown in Figure 8-3.) In separating an operation into elements, it is recommended that (1) the elements be as short as can be conveniently timed, (2) man-time be separated from machine-time, (3) constant elements be separated from variable elements, and (4) the elements have clear-cut beginning and end points.

Each element should be recorded in sufficient detail so that the job method is completely described and could be duplicated in identical fashion at a later date.

### Determining the Time

After the operation has been divided into elements the next step is to determine the time for each element. The two most commonly used methods of timing with the stop watch are known as the *continuous* and the *snapback* or repetitive. In continuous timing, the analyst starts the watch at the beginning of the first element and allows it to run for the duration of the study. At the end of each element, he observes the watch reading and records it in the proper place on the observation sheet. At the conclusion of the study, the time for each element is determined by subtracting the time for the beginning of the element from the time at the end.

In snapback or repetitive timing, the watch is started at the beginning of each element; at the end of the element, the watch is read, the watch is snapped back to zero, and the time is recorded on the observation sheet. This process is repeated for each element for as many cycles as desired in the study.

Each of the methods described above has obvious advantages over the other and in the hands of experienced work measurement analysts probably results in about the same degree of accuracy. However, the continuous method is generally considered best because it includes the overall time for the study, eliminates the possibility of leaving out delays, and eliminates the necessity for snapping the watch back to zero. The observation sheet shown in Figure 8-3 illustrates the use of the continuous method.

The time required to perform a job may be expected to vary slightly from cycle to cycle. Even if the operator works at a constant pace, some variation may be anticipated because of such things as the difference in exact position of materials or tools, difference in exact locations in which parts are disposed of, and variations in watch readings. Since work measurement is a sampling process, the analyst must insure that he times a sufficient number of cycles to give an adequate sample from the statistical population or universe from which the values have been drawn. It follows that the greater the number of cycles timed, the more nearly the results will be representative of the activity being measured. The greater the inconsistency of the time values for an element, the larger the number of observations that will have to be taken to assure a desired accuracy. To help in the determination of the number of observations required to provide the desired level of accuracy, Mundel[2] suggests the use of formulas such as the following:

$$N' = \left(\frac{40\sqrt{N \sum X^2 - (\sum X)^2}}{\sum X}\right)^2$$

where:  $N'$ = required number of observations to predict the true time within $\pm5\%$ precision and $95\%$ confidence level*

$N$ = actual number of observations of the element

$X$ = each stop watch reading

$\sum$ = sum of individual readings

If a $95\%$ confidence level and a precision of $\pm10\%$ were desired, then the formula becomes:

$$N' = \left(\frac{20\sqrt{N \sum X^2 - (\sum X)^2}}{\sum X}\right)^2$$

In addition to the formulas given above, Mundel and others have prepared tables and nomograms that may be used to determine the number of observations required to give the desired level of accuracy.

After securing the time values, the representative time for each element must be calculated. Most organizations use the arithmetic average, but some prefer to use the modal or most frequently occurring time. This representative time is then multiplied by a rating or leveling factor to get the normal time.

### Rating the Operator's Performance

In order to adjust the operator's performance to that of the normal or standard operator, most organizations rate or level each element of the time study. The Society for the Advancement of Management Committee on Rating of Time Studies has defined rating as follows:

> Rating is that process during which the time study man compares the performance of the operator under observation with the observer's own concept of normal performance.[3]

---

*This means that the probability is that $95\%$ of the time $N'$ will provide a sufficient number of readings to cover the chance variables and to provide a time value within $\pm5\%$ of the true mean time value.

[2]M.E. Mundel, *Motion and Time Study Principles and Practice* (Englewood Cliffs, N.J.: Prentice-Hall, Inc., 1960), p. 367.

[3]S.A.M. Committee on Rating of Time Studies, *Advanced Management*, VI, No. 3 (July-September 1941), p. 110.

A number of systems of rating have been devised in industry. Some organizations rate pace or tempo of movement only; others take into account skill and effort. No matter what system is used, the judgment of the work measurement analyst is required, and this allows room for possible error. The magnitude of this error, however, is surprisingly small for well-qualified analysts.

The majority of work measurement analysts rate each element of a time study, although many prefer to rate the overall study. The rating factor is most frequently expressed as a percentage of normal performance (normal performance = 100 per cent), and normal time for each element may be calculated as follows:

$$\text{Normal time} = \text{Average time} \times \frac{\text{Per cent rating}}{100}$$

The normal time is not the time allowed for the job, because it must be increased by any additional time allowed for interruptions, the operator's personal needs, and delays beyond his control.

### Determining Allowances

The normal time for an operation represents the amount of time the average operator would require when working at the normal pace and disregarding any additional time for personal needs, rest, and other delays beyond his control. Obviously, an operator cannot be expected to maintain this pace throughout the workday, and additional time in the form of allowances is usually provided to cover such items as personal needs, rest for overcoming fatigue, machine delays, materials delays, or other unavoidable delays.

The allowance for personal needs varies from about 2 per cent to 5 per cent for light work. For more rigorous work this allowance may be increased to as much as 50 per cent.

Inasmuch as modern industry has taken many steps to eliminate the causes of fatigue, and "fatigue" is a vague phenomenon that is difficult to measure, many companies do not make an allowance for it. Other companies have worked out satisfactory figures by trial and error. In many cases these figures are based upon the total weight lifted or moved by the worker and may amount to as much as 30 per cent or more.

Special allowances for machine delays, materials delays, materials variations, and similar events beyond the control of the operator, are usually determined by means of all-day time studies or delay studies. The *ratio-delay* or *work sampling* study is a particularly useful method of determining these allowances and will be discussed later. This method, which is a statistical sampling technique utilizing a large number of random observations by an analyst, may be used to determine the percentage of time a machine is down and the reasons why it isn't operating.

The standard or allowed time is determined by increasing the normal time by the total amount of the allowance as follows:

$$\text{Standard time} = \text{Normal time} \times \frac{(100 + \text{allowance in per cent})}{100}$$

## Work Sampling

In 1934 L. H. C. Tippett[4] described a statistical approach that he had used in the English textile industry to measure operator and machine delays. He found this method to be quite effective for determining the cause of loom stoppages in the factories he was studying.

R. L. Morrow[5], who was one of the first persons in this country to use Tippett's method, called it "ratio-delay." The ratio-delay method began to find gradual use in American industry and was given great impetus in 1952 when it was featured in an article by C. L. Brisley[6] in *Factory Magazine* and renamed "work sampling." Since 1952 work sampling has gained widespread usage in the following ways:

1. To measure the working and non-working time of men and of machines to use in estimating delay allowances.

2. To estimate the per cent of utilization time of machines and equipment, such as machine tools, fork-lift trucks, elevators, overhead cranes, and so forth.

3. To estimate the per cent of time devoted to each of the duties included in the jobs performed by such people as maintenance personnel, office workers, managers, and nurses.

4. To measure a task for the purpose of establishing a time standard on it.

Work sampling has become a popular tool for use in areas such as those listed because it is easy and convenient to use, possesses known reliability that can be established at the outset, and operates without the use of the stop watch or other timing devices.

Work sampling, as the name implies, is a sampling technique based

---

[4]L.H.C. Tippett, "Statistical Methods in Textile Research. Uses of the Binomial and Poisson Distributions. A Snap-Reading Method of Making Time Studies of Machines and Operatives in Factory Surveys," *Shirley Institute Memoirs*, Vol. 13 (November 1934) p. 35–93.

[5]R.L. Morrow, *Time Study and Motion Economy* (New York: Ronald Press Co., 1946).

[6]C.L. Brisley, "How You Can Put Work Sampling to Work," *Factory* (July 1952), p. 84–89.

upon the laws of probability. It is founded on the statistical premise that the occurrences in an adequate, random sample of observations of an activity will follow the same distribution pattern that might be found in a lengthy, continuous study of the same activity. This may be represented by the following proportion:

$$p = \frac{x}{N} = \frac{\text{Number of observations of the activity}}{\text{Total number of observations}}$$

Thus, the work sampling method consists of taking a number of intermittent, randomly spaced, instantaneous observations of the activity being studied and from this determining the per cent of time devoted to each aspect of the operation. To illustrate the manner in which this may be done, let us consider a man operating a fork-lift truck. By means of 50 instantaneous observations taken at randomly spaced times, the operator was observed and tally marks were noted to indicate whether he was working or idle (definitions have to be predetermined to establish what constitutes "working"), as indicated below:

| Operator's Status | Tally | Total |
|---|---|---|
| Working | 𝍤 𝍤 𝍤 𝍤 𝍤 𝍤 𝍤 𝍤 | 40 |
| Idle | 𝍤 𝍤 | 10 |
| | Total No. of Observations | 50* |

*It should be noted that the 50 observations used in this example is a much smaller number than normally would be required and in actual practice hundreds of observations may be necessary.

It follows then that (based upon the observations) the operator was working 40/50 of the total or 80 per cent of the time and was idle 10/50 of the total or 20 per cent of the time.

The simple approach given in the example just cited illustrates the manner in which work sampling may be used. The key to the accuracy of the technique is in the number of observations. A greater number of observations provides a higher degree of accuracy. The question of how many observations are necessary to insure a certain level of accuracy may be calculated through the use of standard formulas based on the binomial distribution.[7] Assuming a confidence level of 95 per cent and an accuracy of $\pm 5$ per cent are satisfactory, the number of observations required may be obtained by the following formula:[8]

---

[7] See I.W. Burr, *Engineering Statistics and Quality Control*, (New York: McGraw-Hill Book Company, 1953), p. 196.

[8] See R.M. Barnes, *op. cit.*, p. 520.

$$S_p = 2\sqrt{\frac{p(1-p)}{N}}$$

where $S$ = desired relative accuracy

$p$ = percentage expressed as a decimal

$N$ = number of random observations

At the time the study is initiated, it is common practice to estimate $p$ in order to get an estimate of $N$. Then as the study progresses, the values of $p$ can be calculated and $N$ redetermined.

The procedure for making a work sampling study consists of essentially the following steps:

1. Determine the objectives of the study, including definitions of the states of activity to be observed.
2. Plan the sampling procedure, including:
   a. An estimate of the percentage of time being devoted to each phase of the activity.
   b. The setting of the accuracy limits desired.
   c. An estimation of the number of observations required.
   d. The selection of the length of the study period and the programming of the number of readings over this period.
   e. The establishment of the mechanics of making the observations, the route to follow, and the recording of data.
3. Collect the data as planned.
4. Process the data and present the results.

As indicated earlier, work sampling has a number of advantages over conventional work measurement methods. Among these are the following:

1. It is economical to use and usually costs considerably less than a continuous time study.
2. It can be used to measure many activities that are impractical to measure by time study.
3. It isn't necessary to use a trained work measurement analyst to make the observations.
4. Work sampling measurements may be made with a pre-assigned degree of reliability.
5. Work sampling measures the utilization of people and equipment directly.
6. It eliminates the necessity of using the stop watch for measurements.
7. It provides observation over a sufficiently long period of time to decrease the chance of day-to-day variations affecting the results.

Even though work sampling is a valuable tool, it has limitations, namely:

1. Normally, it is not economical for studying work at a single location

or where work is highly standardized and can be studied by conventional work measurement methods.

2. It is of little value in helping to improve work methods and doesn't offer some of the opportunity for methods analysis that accompanies time study methods.

3. Management and the workers may not understand statistical work sampling.

4. Some of the observers may not adhere to the fundamental principles of sampling and may bias the results.

## Elemental-Motion Time Systems

Since the end of World War II there has been increasing usage of elemental- or basic-motion time systems for establishing time standards. These systems, which have been devised by several large companies and management consulting firms, are based upon the premise that the average time for a person to perform a basic motion or therblig should be relatively constant. Most of the systems ("methods time measurement," "work factor," "basic motion times," "method time analysis," "basic time survey," elemental time system," and so on) consist of tables of standard time values for performing various types of basic motions—move, reach, position, and so forth. The time values may be applied to any type of operation that may be resolved to the basic motions, eliminating the necessity for using the stop watch. Figure 8-4 illustrates the time values used in one system.

The procedure used in setting a time standard is to break the job method down into basic motions and then apply the appropriate time values for each motion. The sum of these time values becomes the standard time for the job. Additional time for allowances may have to be added in some cases depending upon the job being analyzed and the system being used.

The advocates of the elemental-motion time systems claim the following advantages for their use:

1. Time standards may be set in advance of the performance of the job.

2. It makes the analyst motion-conscious and facilitates obvious improvements in methods.

3. Production lines may be balanced in advance.

4. Cost estimates may be made in advance of making the product.

5. The use of standard data is facilitated.

6. It facilitates choosing between alternative methods.

7. It facilitates training supervisors to be methods-conscious.

# METHODS-TIME MEASUREMENT
# APPLICATION DATA IN T M U

## TABLE I—REACH—R

| Distance Moved Inches | Time TMU | | | | Hand In Motion | | CASE AND DESCRIPTION |
|---|---|---|---|---|---|---|---|
| | A | B | C or D | E | A | B | |
| ¾ or less | 2.0 | 2.0 | 2.0 | 2.0 | 1.6 | 1.6 | **A** Reach to object in fixed location, or to object in other hand or on which other hand rests. |
| 1 | 2.5 | 2.5 | 3.6 | 2.4 | 2.3 | 2.3 | |
| 2 | 4.0 | 4.0 | 5.9 | 3.8 | 3.5 | 2.7 | |
| 3 | 5.3 | 5.3 | 7.3 | 5.3 | 4.5 | 3.6 | **B** Reach to single object in location which may vary slightly from cycle to cycle. |
| 4 | 6.1 | 6.4 | 8.4 | 6.8 | 4.9 | 4.3 | |
| 5 | 6.5 | 7.8 | 9.4 | 7.4 | 5.3 | 5.0 | |
| 6 | 7.0 | 8.6 | 10.1 | 8.0 | 5.7 | 5.7 | |
| 7 | 7.4 | 9.3 | 10.8 | 8.7 | 6.1 | 6.5 | |
| 8 | 7.9 | 10.1 | 11.5 | 9.3 | 6.5 | 7.2 | **C** Reach to object jumbled with other objects in a group so that search and select occur. |
| 9 | 8.3 | 10.8 | 12.2 | 9.9 | 6.9 | 7.9 | |
| 10 | 8.7 | 11.5 | 12.9 | 10.5 | 7.3 | 8.6 | |
| 12 | 9.6 | 12.9 | 14.2 | 11.8 | 8.1 | 10.1 | |
| 14 | 10.5 | 14.4 | 15.6 | 13.0 | 8.9 | 11.5 | **D** Reach to a very small object or where accurate grasp is required. |
| 16 | 11.4 | 15.8 | 17.0 | 14.2 | 9.7 | 12.9 | |
| 18 | 12.3 | 17.2 | 18.4 | 15.5 | 10.5 | 14.4 | |
| 20 | 13.1 | 18.6 | 19.8 | 16.7 | 11.3 | 15.8 | |
| 22 | 14.0 | 20.1 | 21.2 | 18.0 | 12.1 | 17.3 | **E** Reach to indefinite location to get hand in position for body balance or next motion or out of way. |
| 24 | 14.9 | 21.5 | 22.5 | 19.2 | 12.9 | 18.8 | |
| 26 | 15.8 | 22.9 | 23.9 | 20.4 | 13.7 | 20.2 | |
| 28 | 16.7 | 24.4 | 25.3 | 21.7 | 14.5 | 21.7 | |
| 30 | 17.5 | 25.8 | 26.7 | 22.9 | 15.3 | 23.2 | |

## TABLE II—MOVE—M

| Distance Moved Inches | Time TMU | | | Hand In Motion B | Wt. Allowance | | | CASE AND DESCRIPTION |
|---|---|---|---|---|---|---|---|---|
| | A | B | C | | Wt. (lb.) Up to | Fac-tor | Con-stant TMU | |
| ¾ or less | 2.0 | 2.0 | 2.0 | 1.7 | 2.5 | 1.00 | 0 | |
| 1 | 2.5 | 2.9 | 3.4 | 2.3 | | | | |
| 2 | 3.6 | 4.6 | 5.2 | 2.9 | 7.5 | 1.06 | 2.2 | **A** Move object to other hand or against stop. |
| 3 | 4.9 | 5.7 | 6.7 | 3.6 | | | | |
| 4 | 6.1 | 6.9 | 8.0 | 4.3 | 12.5 | 1.11 | 3.9 | |
| 5 | 7.3 | 8.0 | 9.2 | 5.0 | | | | |
| 6 | 8.1 | 8.9 | 10.3 | 5.7 | 17.5 | 1.17 | 5.6 | |
| 7 | 8.9 | 9.7 | 11.1 | 6.5 | | | | |
| 8 | 9.7 | 10.6 | 11.8 | 7.2 | | | | |
| 9 | 10.5 | 11.5 | 12.7 | 7.9 | 22.5 | 1.22 | 7.4 | **B** Move object to approximate or indefinite location. |
| 10 | 11.3 | 12.2 | 13.5 | 8.6 | | | | |
| 12 | 12.9 | 13.4 | 15.2 | 10.0 | 27.5 | 1.28 | 9.1 | |
| 14 | 14.4 | 14.6 | 16.9 | 11.4 | | | | |
| 16 | 16.0 | 15.8 | 18.7 | 12.8 | 32.5 | 1.33 | 10.8 | |
| 18 | 17.6 | 17.0 | 20.4 | 14.2 | | | | |
| 20 | 19.2 | 18.2 | 22.1 | 15.6 | | | | |
| 22 | 20.8 | 19.4 | 23.8 | 17.0 | 37.5 | 1.39 | 12.5 | |
| 24 | 22.4 | 20.6 | 25.5 | 18.4 | | | | **C** Move object to exact location. |
| 26 | 24.0 | 21.8 | 27.3 | 19.8 | 42.5 | 1.44 | 14.3 | |
| 28 | 25.5 | 23.1 | 29.0 | 21.2 | | | | |
| 30 | 27.1 | 24.3 | 30.7 | 22.7 | 47.5 | 1.50 | 16.0 | |

## TABLE III—TURN AND APPLY PRESSURE—T AND AP

| Weight | Time TMU for Degrees Turned | | | | | | | | | | |
|---|---|---|---|---|---|---|---|---|---|---|---|
| | 30° | 45° | 60° | 75° | 90° | 105° | 120° | 135° | 150° | 165° | 180° |
| Small— 0 to 2 Pounds | 2.8 | 3.5 | 4.1 | 4.8 | 5.4 | 6.1 | 6.8 | 7.4 | 8.1 | 8.7 | 9.4 |
| Medium—2.1 to 10 Pounds | 4.4 | 5.5 | 6.5 | 7.5 | 8.5 | 9.6 | 10.6 | 11.6 | 12.7 | 13.7 | 14.8 |
| Large— 10.1 to 35 Pounds | 8.4 | 10.5 | 12.3 | 14.4 | 16.2 | 18.3 | 20.4 | 22.2 | 24.3 | 26.1 | 28.2 |

**APPLY PRESSURE CASE 1—16.2 TMU.    APPLY PRESSURE CASE 2—10.6 TMU.**

**Figure 8-4.** Elemental motion-time system (Courtesy MTM Association for Standards and Research.)

$$1 \text{ TMU} = .00001 \text{ hour}$$
$$= .0006 \text{ minute}$$
$$= .036 \text{ second}$$

## TABLE IV—GRASP—G

| Case | Time TMU | DESCRIPTION |
|------|----------|-------------|
| 1A | 2.0 | **Pick Up Grasp**—Small, medium or large object by itself, easily grasped. |
| 1B | 3.5 | Very small object or object lying close against a flat surface. |
| 1C1 | 7.3 | Interference with grasp on bottom and one side of nearly cylindrical object. Diameter larger than ½″. |
| 1C2 | 8.7 | Interference with grasp on bottom and one side of nearly cylindrical object. Diameter ¼″ to ½″. |
| 1C3 | 10.8 | Interference with grasp on bottom and one side of nearly cylindrical object. Diameter less than ¼″. |
| 2 | 5.6 | **Regrasp.** |
| 3 | 5.6 | **Transfer Grasp.** |
| 4A | 7.3 | Object jumbled with other objects so search and select occur. Larger than 1″ x 1″ x 1″. |
| 4B | 9.1 | Object jumbled with other objects so search and select occur. ¼″ x ¼″ x ⅛″ to 1″ x 1″ x 1″. |
| 4C | 12.9 | Object jumbled with other objects so search and select occur. Smaller than ¼″ x ¼″ x ⅛″. |
| 5 | 0 | Contact, sliding or hook grasp. |

## TABLE V—POSITION*—P

| CLASS OF FIT | | Symmetry | Easy To Handle | Difficult To Handle |
|--------------|--|----------|----------------|---------------------|
| 1—Loose | No pressure required | S | 5.6 | 11.2 |
| | | SS | 9.1 | 14.7 |
| | | NS | 10.4 | 16.0 |
| 2—Close | Light pressure required | S | 16.2 | 21.8 |
| | | SS | 19.7 | 25.3 |
| | | NS | 21.0 | 26.6 |
| 3—Exact | Heavy pressure required. | S | 43.0 | 48.6 |
| | | SS | 46.5 | 52.1 |
| | | NS | 47.8 | 53.4 |

*Distance moved to engage—1″ or less.

## TABLE VI—RELEASE—RL

| Case | Time TMU | DESCRIPTION |
|------|----------|-------------|
| 1 | 2.0 | Normal release performed by opening fingers as independent motion. |
| 2 | 0 | Contact Release. |

## TABLE VII—DISENGAGE—D

| CLASS OF FIT | Easy to Handle | Difficult to Handle |
|--------------|----------------|---------------------|
| 1—Loose—Very slight effort, blends with subsequent move. | 4.0 | 5.7 |
| 2—Close — Normal effort, slight recoil. | 7.5 | 11.8 |
| 3—Tight — Considerable effort, hand recoils markedly. | 22.9 | 34.7 |

## TABLE VIII—EYE TRAVEL TIME AND EYE FOCUS—ET AND EF

Eye Travel Time $= 15.2 \times \dfrac{T}{D}$ TMU, with a maximum value of 20 TMU.

where T = the distance between points from and to which the eye travels.
D = the perpendicular distance from the eye to the line of travel T.

Eye Focus Time = 7.3 TMU.

Figure 8-4. (Continued)

## TABLE IX—BODY, LEG AND FOOT MOTIONS

| DESCRIPTION | SYMBOL | DISTANCE | TIME TMU |
|---|---|---|---|
| Foot Motion—Hinged at Ankle. | FM | Up to 4″ | 8.5 |
|     With heavy pressure. | FMP | | 19.1 |
| Leg or Foreleg Motion. | LM — | Up to 6″ | 7.1 |
| | | Each add'l. inch | 1.2 |
| Sidestep—Case 1—Complete when leading leg contacts floor. | SS-C1 | Less than 12″ | Use REACH or MOVE Time |
| | | 12″ | 17.0 |
| | | Each add'l. inch | .6 |
|     Case 2—Lagging leg must contact floor before next motion can be made. | SS-C2 | 12″ | 34.1 |
| | | Each add'l. inch | 1.1 |
| Bend, Stoop, or Kneel on One Knee. | B,S,KOK | | 29.0 |
|     Arise. | AB,AS,AKOK | | 31.9 |
| Kneel on Floor—Both Knees. | KBK | | 69.4 |
|     Arise. | AKBK | | 76.7 |
| Sit. | SIT | | 34.7 |
| Stand from Sitting Position. | STD | | 43.4 |
| Turn Body 45 to 90 degrees— | | | |
|     Case 1—Complete when leading leg contacts floor. | TBC1 | | 18.6 |
|     Case 2—Lagging leg must contact floor before next motion can be made. | TBC2 | | 37.2 |
| Walk. | W-FT. | Per Foot | 5.3 |
| Walk. | W-P | Per Pace | 15.0 |

## TABLE X—SIMULTANEOUS MOTIONS

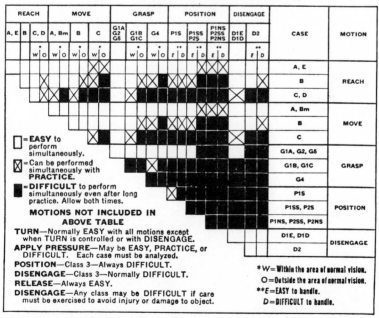

## MTM ASSOCIATION for STANDARDS AND RESEARCH
### Huron Towers, 2200 Fuller Road
### ANN ARBOR, MICHIGAN
© COPYRIGHT 1955

**Figure 8-4.** (Continued)

151

## Standard Data

Many organizations have adopted systems for synthesizing time standards from previously determined time values. These time values, which may be obtained from stop-watch time studies or from elemental-motion time systems, are accumulated in the form of times for elements that are common to many jobs and are frequently referred to as *standard data*. Through the use of these data, new time standards may be set on many kinds of jobs without the making of a time study. This makes it possible to set new standards in advance of performance of the operation, and to set them quicker, cheaper, and more consistently than by individual studies.

In establishing standard data, the following steps are commonly taken:

1. The range of items to be covered is determined.
2. A trial breakdown of elements common to all items is established.
3. Time studies are made of the entire range of items to be covered.
4. A master list of elements is prepared and listed on a master summary sheet.
5. The individual element times for each time study are posted on the master summary sheet.
6. The constant elements are separated from the variable elements and the results are shown in the form of curves, nomograms, tables, or formulas.

## Administration of Work Measurement

One of the major problems encountered in administering time standards is that of maintaining accurate standards. The work measurement department must provide a continuous check on the job method, materials, and tools to make sure there have been no changes that will affect the time values. This can be accomplished only by continuous review of job methods with complete cooperation of the supervisors.

Inasmuch as a great deal of judgment enters into the setting of a time standard, many work measurement analysts are subjected to frequent training sessions on rating and other phases of the time study procedure. This helps maintain reasonable consistency among the persons involved and provides uniform time standards throughout the plant.

Management has frequently been accused of "rate cutting" and "speed-up" and must guard against gaining this reputation. Most companies guarantee that unless there is a change in the job method the time standard will remain in effect no matter how high the incentive earnings of the workers may be. Oftentimes, this allows a worker, on whose job there is a "loose" standard, to work at a low pace and still get high incentive earnings. This presents a difficult problem and sometimes is solved only through collective bargaining.

### Criticisms of Work Measurement

The individual worker's reaction to work measurement is based largely upon how it affects him and his fellow workers. If he is working on a job where he can maintain a work pace that he doesn't consider too fast, and where he is able to receive sizable incentive earnings, then he is probably in favor of work measurement. On the other hand, if he feels he is forced to "speed up" and has difficulty in keeping up or in making a bonus, then he will probably be opposed to it. At the same time, his attitude will be greatly influenced by the attitude expressed by his union leaders.

As William Gomberg has so aptly stated, the attitude of unions toward time study will probably take one of the following forms:

1. Complete rejection of time study techniques as a guide to the setting of a fair day's work.

2. Consideration of the rate proposed by the time study engineers as an offer. The union reserves the right to determine whether or not it will accept the offer by any criterion, time study or otherwise, that it sees fit.

3. The joint acceptance of a time study system mutually satisfactory to union and management as a means of setting rates.

4. The development of a system of standard data that will serve as a basis for rate-setting.[9]

In recent years, a number of unions have attempted to provide a check on work measurement by establishing their own work measurement groups and by training their own analysts.

In spite of the progress made by many companies in improving their work measurement practices, innumerable companies maintain inadequate staffs of qualified analysts and may be condemned for faulty practice.

### QUESTIONS

1. How does work measurement contribute to the operation of a modern industrial concern?

2. How do you account for the fact that the stop watch has been the most commonly used timing device?

3. Comment on the suitability of work sampling to set time standards on maintenance operations.

---

[9]W. Grant Ireson and E. L. Grant, *Handbook of Industrial Engineering and Management* (Englewood Cliffs, N. J.: Prentice-Hall, Inc., 1955), p. 1148.

4. Why is it desirable always to secure permission before starting a stopwatch time study?
5. Why are job descriptions timed as a series of elements rather than as unit jobs?
6. Why is it desirable to rate or level a time study?
7. Is standard data a suitable substitute for an elemental-motion time system? Why?
8. How would you recommend training work measurement analysts to insure consistency of their rating ability?
9. Discuss any time study applications you may have encountered and evaluate the administration of the program.
10. Will the use of work measurement be eliminated in the factories of the future? Why?

## CASE PROBLEMS

### Keller Manufacturing Company

The Keller Manufacturing Company is a small company employing about 150 persons in the manufacture of aluminum windows. The company has made extensive use of time study for its wage incentive plan, production scheduling, and cost estimating for the past 10 years.

Last year Roger Bellows, a highly experienced time-study man, quit the company. This left the company without a trained time-study analyst. Mr. Davidson, the general manager, decided that the company could get along without replacing Roger Bellows and that Robert Musgrave, the timekeeper, could set time standards in addition to his other duties.

Robert Musgrave is a personable and conscientious employee, and he endeavored to do a good job of setting accurate standards. However, during the past year great inconsistency has crept into the time standards—some are much too "tight" and others too "loose." Several persons in the shop who appear to be loafing are able to make bonuses of 100% whereas others who are working hard are barely able to make a 10% bonus. Since the company has the policy of guaranteeing time standards against cutting, Mr. Davidson has stated that the standards that are too "loose" can't be altered. However, Mr. Davidson has decided that something must be done about the situation.

*Questions:*

1. Comment on the circumstances that led to the time-study predicament.
2. What can Mr. Davidson do to correct the situation existing in his company?
3. What stand will the union probably take in regard to any changes in the status quo?

### Remington Electric Company

Joe Robertson, who is responsible for the time standards in Department 38 of the Remington Electric Company, was asked by the foreman to set a new standard on a No. B-10-W bushing being turned on an engine lathe. Joe studied the operation and recorded the following data (using the continuous method of timing):

*Timed Cycles*

| No. | Description | 1 | | 2 | | 3 | | 4 | | 5 | | 6 | | 7 | | 8 | | 9 | | 10 | |
| | | R | T | R | T | R | T | R | T | R | T | R | T | R | T | R | T | R | T | R | T |
|---|---|---|---|---|---|---|---|---|---|---|---|---|---|---|---|---|---|---|---|---|---|
| 1 | RL Part | 09 | | 38 | | 67 | | 02 | | 34 | | 67 | | 98 | | 28 | | 61 | | 91 | |
| 2 | Engage Feed | 23 | | 52 | | 85 | | 17 | | 48 | | 81 | | 13 | | 44 | | 77 | | 05 | |
| 3 | Stop Lathe | 31 | | 59 | | 93 | | 26 | | 57 | | 88 | | 20 | | 52 | | 84 | | 13 | |

*Note:*  Readings are in hundredths of a minute.

| No. | Ave. Elem. Time | Rating | Normal Time | Allow. | Std. Time |
|---|---|---|---|---|---|
| 1 | | 120 | | | |
| 2 | | 110 | | | |
| 3 | | 110 | | | |

*Questions:*

1.  If Joe rated each element as indicated on the observation sheet, and the operator is allowed 5% allowance for personal time and fatigue, what should be the standard time for the operation?
2.  What should the standard be in hours per 1000 pieces?
3.  Did Joe time enough cycles? Why?

CHAPTER NINE

# Materials
# Handling

In order to manufacture any product, it is necessary that materials either move from one step of the manufacturing process to another or that operators move to the materials. The most common practice, of course, is to move the materials. This movement of materials from one processing area to another and from department to department necessitates the use of much manpower and the handling of tremendous tonnages of materials. It has been estimated[1] that: items are being worked on only 20 per cent of the time and in storage or undergoing handling 80 per cent of the time; 22 per cent of industries' manpower is used in handling materials; and throughout industry, 50 tons of product must be handled to produce one ton of finished products.

The handling of materials has always been an important factor in manufacturing. But only recently has attention been focused on this problem with a view toward the improvement of equipment and methods and the reduction of manufacturing costs. There has been growing realization of the magnitude of the problem and recognition of the high ratio of materials handling costs to other costs of manufacturing. For example, one survey showed an average of 22 per cent of the cost of manufacture was for the handling of materials; other estimates run as high as 60 per cent. This trend may increase as greater degrees of mechanization and automation appear in industry with the resultant decrease of the labor cost. It follows then that

---

[1]James M. Apple, *Plant Layout and Materials Handling* (New York: Ronald Press Co., 1963), p. 206.

**156**

materials handling presents one of the most potentially lucrative areas for the improvement of equipment and methods and the reduction of costs.

## Definition of Materials Handling

In a broad sense *materials handling* includes all movement of materials in a manufacturing situation. It has been defined by the American Material Handling Society as follows: "Materials Handling is the art and science involving the movement, packaging, and storing of substances in any form." This is an all-inclusive definition and can include fluids and semi-fluids, as well as discrete items. For the sake of simplicity, we shall limit our discussion in this chapter to the movement of discrete items, such as transistors, gears, tires, castings, and boxes. Likewise, we shall consider only the movement of materials within the plant or storage areas. Movement of materials between plants—particularly when common carriers are used—is generally considered a problem in *traffic* and is frequently handled by a separate traffic department.

Based on the somewhat restricted concept that we have established for discussing the subject of materials handling, we shall be concerned only with the storage and movement of goods that have been received by the manufacturer. This will include the handling of materials through various storages and operations from the raw materials state to the final completion stage and shipment of the product. Much of our discussion will revolve around the use of equipment, but we shall also take into consideration *man* as a materials handler.

Although the handling of materials as individual pieces or parts is common practice by the worker at the machine or bench, parts are usually assembled into unit loads for transport between work stations. *Unit load* refers to tote pans, boxes, pallets, or skids, which are designed to carry more than one part, package, or product at a time. Illustrations of unit loads are given in Figures 9-1 a, b, c.

Much has been done in the mechanization and automation of materials handling. As the automatic factory of the future is developed, the time may come when the handling of materials will be so closely integrated with the manufacturing process that the handling and processing of the product will be identified as one activity.

## Objectives of Materials Handling

The simplest solution to the materials handling problem—"No movement, no cost"—is hardly practicable for a complete manufacturing process. It is

**Figure 9-1a.** Baskets, which are collapsible when not in use, being handled by a fork truck. (Courtesy Clark Equipment Co.)

a basically sound approach when one is attempting to improve a complete production cycle, and when the number of handlings can be reduced. It is also a good solution in the making of heavy industrial equipment. In this latter situation it is often more feasible to bring the tools and workers to the product than to transport the product to the machine or work area.

In addition to the objective of reducing the overall costs of materials handling by reducing the number of handlings involved, the following may be considered as objectives of the engineer in his approach to this problem:

1. **Lower the unit materials handling costs.** It is obvious that the overall, or total, materials handling costs will be reduced if unit costs are reduced. This approach requires that costs of handling be allocated or identified to the units of product, or to its component parts that are moved. In many manufacturing situations this allocation is not too easy. For example, in a plant making many different products a shop truck may be used to move a load that has 12 tote pans, each pan containing different numbers of different parts. The breakdown of this cost of movement to the cost for each part handled (a unit handling cost) is not practicable. Considerable judgment is required to determine the detail into which materials

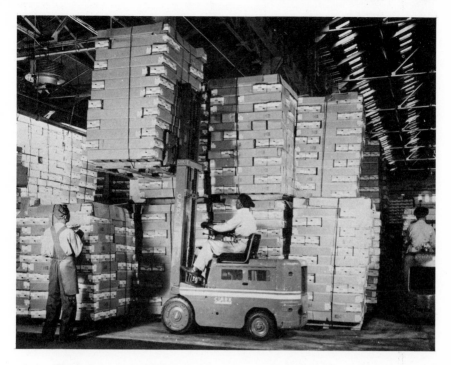

**Figure 9-1b.** A palletized load of boxes being handled by a fork truck. (Courtesy Clark Equipment Co.)

handling costs are to be analyzed. However, where feasible a unit-cost analysis may be very effective in determining which handlings involve excessive costs.

2. **Reduce the manufacturing-cycle time.** The total time required to make a product from the receipt of raw materials to the finished goods can be reduced through effective materials handling. Movement of materials can be speeded up or may be handled over shorter distances. Successful reduction of the manufacturing-cycle time will reduce inventory costs and other production costs incident thereto.

3. **Contribute towards a better control of the flow of goods.** A principal way in which good materials handling practice can effect savings is by making the control of goods easier—particularly in continuous manufacturing, where all operations are "tied together" by the materials handling plan. In this situation the problem of production control is reduced to control at the starting point of the process and to the watching of the rate of flow at selected control points throughout the process. On many assembly lines the conveyor actually controls the rate of output.

**Figure 9-1c.** A loaded skid being handled by a fork truck. (Courtesy Clark Equipment Co.)

4. **Provide for improved working conditions and greater safety in the movement of materials.** Safe handling of materials will be reflected in a better industrial accident record. This is both a tangible saving in reduced insurance rates and an intangible saving in improved employee morale resulting from safer working conditions.

5. **Provide for fewer rejects.** Care in the handling of the product will contribute to a better quality level of the goods produced. Products damaged by inefficient handling are all too often a major cost to manufacturers.

6. **Allow increased storage capacity.** Better movement and storage of materials should increase the utilization of storage space.

7. **Gain higher productivity at lower manufacturing cost.** Successful attainment of the above objectives contributes to this goal. Higher productivity can be gained for both machines and workers through better handling of materials. As higher productivity is attained, the overhead costs should eventually decline, and as a result more and better goods will be produced at lower costs.

## Principles of Materials Handling

Attainment of the objectives of good materials handling practice can be facilitated through the observance of a number of materials handling principles[2] such as are listed:

1. Eliminate wasteful methods by:
   (a) Reducing to a minimum the number of handlings of materials.
   (b) Eliminating unnecessary mixing and subsequent sorting.
   (c) Using mechanical aids to eliminate the use of hand labor in movement of materials.
   (d) Avoiding the unnecessary transfer of materials from floor to workplace or from container to container.
   (e) Utilizing containers and unit loads.
   (f) Utilizing gravity as a moving force wherever possible.
   (g) Introducing automaticity into the materials handling plan.
2. In laying out the plant:
   (a) Combine handling with processing wherever possible.
   (b) Provide for continuous or appropriate intermittent flow of materials.
   (c) Provide for the shortest transportation of materials between operations and with a minimum of retrograde movement.
   (d) Plan the layout of the work-station area for a minimum of handling of the product.
   (e) Coordinate the overall materials handling throughout the entire plant.
   (f) Plan for adequate receiving, storage, and shipping facilities.
   (g) Design adequate aisle and access areas.
3. In the selection and application of materials handling equipment:
   (a) Analyze equipment needs before considering the purchase of new equipment.
   (b) Insure that the existing equipment is being used effectively.
   (c) Use the simplest equipment that is adaptable to the problem; avoid the use of complicated mechanisms and controls.
   (d) Adopt standard equipment if possible; insure that if used, special equipment is economically justified.
   (e) Select equipment that is flexible in its application.
   (f) Determine comparative costs of equipment before purchasing.
   (g) Recognize the need for different equipment for different jobs.

---

[2]See Harry B. Stocker, *Materials Handling* (2d ed.; Englewood Cliffs, N. J.: Prentice-Hall, Inc., 1951); Gordon B. Carson (ed.), *Production Handbook* (New York: The Ronald Press Company, 1958); The Material Handling Institute, Inc., *Material Handling*, Booklet No. 2 (Pittsburgh: 1952).

(h) Recognize the need to provide suitable building conditions for the equipment.

(i) Provide for alternative methods for use in emergencies.

(j) Give consideration to the maintenance of the equipment.

Some general principles that can also be applied in the materials handling area are:

1. Use sound planning in the solving of materials handling problems. Keep the overall problem in mind, thoroughly analyze the problem and attempt to evaluate the results before taking final action.

2. Insure proper communications with all individuals concerned when installing a new method or piece of equipment. Many a sound solution to a materials handling problem has failed owing to lack of understanding by or improper instruction of the operators of the equipment.

3. Follow up the installation to insure its effectiveness and evaluate the results.

4. Do not hesitate to take such corrective action as is necessary—the best solution is not always attained on the first attempt. However, immediate corrective action may not be feasible in many instances, and the improvements may have to be tabled until another change in method or equipment can be justified economically.

Under certain circumstances the approach to the materials handling problem may be reduced to a checklist. In such cases care should be exercised to insure that the checklist does not become a crutch on which the materials handling personnel lean exclusively. Checklists, although very useful, may tend to limit the ingenuity and the creativeness of individuals which are so essential to industrial progress. The ability to approach any problem with an abstract and totally uninhibited attitude is invaluable to the engineer in materials handling, as it is in any other field of activity.

## Analysis of Materials Handling Problems

In the chapter on methods engineering, we discussed a systematic approach to the solution of methods problems. The same procedure will work equally well in solving materials handling problems. It necessitates the establishment of an objective, collecting as much factual data as possible, analyzing the data, applying known principles, and formulating a solution. In collecting the data, careful attention should be given to the effects of handling on the product, the present method, and cost factors.

Too often the materials handling engineer does a superficial job of analyzing the problem and thinks only, "What equipment can be purchased to do this job?" A better approach would be to analyze the problem thoroughly, formulate a solution, and only then give consideration to any equipment that may be required. An approach of this type led one company, a maker of collapsible wire containers, to discover that it could solve most of its materials handling problems by using its own product instead of purchasing outside equipment.

## General Types of Materials Handling Equipment

A detailed discussion of the many types of materials handling equipment and of the capabilities and characteristics of each is beyond the scope of this book. Such details, however, are important to the engineer developing the materials handling plan for a manufacturing plant. Extensive information covering specifications of various equipment is available, particularly from the materials handling equipment manufacturers.

There are so many different types of equipment developed or being developed for the handling of materials that classification may also be quite confusing.

According to the *Materials Handling Handbook*,[3] there are over 430 kinds of materials handling equipment divided into the following nine major categories:

1. Conveyors.
2. Cranes, elevators, and hoists.
3. Positioning, weighing, and control equipment.
4. Industrial vehicles.
5. Motor vehicles.
6. Railroad cars.
7. Marine carriers.
8. Aircraft.
9. Containers and supports.

The list contains a number of relatively specialized pieces of equipment that are not used within the typical manufacturing plant. Several of the more common items found in typical plants are illustrated in Figures 9-2 to 9-5. In selecting equipment, considerable attention should be given to the flexibility of the equipment. The greater the degree of flexibility designed into a piece of materials handling equipment, the easier it is for the planner to integrate the application of the equipment into the manufacturing situation.

---

[3]H.A. Bolz, and G.E. Hagemann, *Materials Handling Handbook* (New York: Ronald Press Co., 1958).

**Figure 9-2.** A 10-ton floor controlled overhead crane being used to move coils of steel. (Courtesy Harnischfeger.)

**Figure 9-3.** Chain-monorail conveyor used to deliver parts to work stations. (Courtesy Richards-Wilcox Manufacturing Company.)

Current trend is to consider more and more the entire production process as a complete materials handling problem and to so plan the equipment that total overall efficiency is attained. This naturally leads to the development of transfer devices and feedback controls—which in turn leads to automation.

## Factors Affecting the Selection of Materials Handling Equipment

The selection of materials handling equipment requires the attaining of proper balance between the production problem, the capabilities of the equipment available, and the human element involved. The ultimate aim is to arrive at the lowest cost per unit of material handled.

The production-problem factors that enter into this consideration are the volume of production to be attained (in terms of the rate of production),

Figure 9-4. Vacuum cleaners being placed on conveyor from the final assembly area. Note that the cleaners are plugged in while being moved. (Courtesy Mechanical Handling Systems Inc.)

the class of materials to be handled, and the layout of the plant and building facilities. The equipment that can be economically justified for the manufacture of 1000 television sets a day would be entirely different from the equipment used in a plant manufacturing 20 steam turbine generators a year; in this comparison both the production rate and the weight and class of the materials are different. Likewise, the equipment in a flour mill or food processing factory would present a quite different problem.

**Figure 9-5.** Operator-driven tractor train for intra-warehouse transfer of finished products. (Courtesy Procter & Gamble Company.)

It might well be assumed that in the designing of a new plant the layout and building facilities could be adapted to the best materials handling plan. However, in this most favorable situation some compromise may still have to be made owing to other factors, such as future plant expansion, flexibility of layout, or restrictions that may be placed on the type of building to be constructed. It is obvious that in the case of an existing plant the layout and building facilities affect the selection of materials handling equipment.

Equipment factors to be taken into consideration may well include the following:

1. *Adaptability.* The load-carrying and movement characteristics of the equipment should fit the materials handling problem.

2. *Flexibility.* Where possible the equipment should have flexibility so that more than one material, either as to class or size, can be handled.

3. *Load capacity.* Equipment selected should have great enough load-

carrying characteristics to do the job effectively, yet should not be too large and result in excessive operating costs.

4. *Power*. Enough power should be available to do the job.

5. *Speed*. Rapidity of movement of material, within the limits of the production process or plant safety, should be considered.

6. *Space requirements*. The space required to install or operate materials handling equipment is an important factor in its selection.

7. *Supervision required*. As applied to equipment selection this refers to the degree of automaticity designed into the equipment.

8. *Ease of maintenance*. Equipment selected should be easily maintained at reasonable cost.

9. *Cost*. The consideration of the cost of the equipment is an obvious factor in its selection.

Figure 9-6 shows an equipment-selection chart applying many of the above factors to specific items of equipment. There are other equipment factors that may enter a problem in materials handling equipment selection. These too may be important, even as the relative importance of the above is not indicated by the order in which they are listed.

The human element cannot be overlooked in the selection of materials handling equipment. The consideration of materials handling might bring to mind the laborer who is "all brawn and few brains," but modern materials handling equipment may in some instances require both intelligence and skill for its effective operation. Hence, the capabilities of the available manpower enter into the equipment selection.

Safety of personnel is an important human factor. The equipment selected must result in safe working conditions.

Finally, the equipment must be accepted by the workers. The eccentricities of labor in this respect must always be anticipated as closely as possible and steps taken to "sell" the new equipment to those who will operate or come into contact with it.

## Materials Handling Cost

General cost-accounting practice classifies the cost of handling materials as an indirect cost or overhead. This classification is based on the position that the movement of the materials does not contribute to their physical change or add value to them as a product or as a component part thereof. In some manufacturing situations, such as in a carbon black plant where the material is constantly moving during the production process, this contention of the cost accountants might be challenged. However, the problem of classification of unit handling costs in most situations is more of an academic than a practical problem. In many instances the clerical costs to deter-

MATERIALS HANDLING EQUIPMENT SELECTION CHART

| | Materials | | Movement | | | Supervision Required | | | Path | | | Speed | | | Power | | | | Load | | | | Space | | |
|---|---|---|---|---|---|---|---|---|---|---|---|---|---|---|---|---|---|---|---|---|---|---|---|---|---|
| | Bulk | Packaged | Vertical | Horizontal | Combination of Vert. & Horiz. | Close Supervision & Detailed Dispatch | Little Supervision & Detailed Dispatch | Automatic or Semi-Automatic | Completely Variable | Fixed Path | Fixed Area | Variable | Fixed | Either Fixed or Variable | Electricity - Line | Electricity - Bat. | Internal Combustion | Gravity | Unit Load with Limit | Continuous Loading | Max. Load per Unit | Fixed Units by Spacing of Carriers | Minimum Width Aisles | Constant Utilization of Fixed Area | No Floor Space |
| **Trucks - Industrial** | | | | | | | | | | | | | | | | | | | | | | | | | |
| **Manual** | | | | | | | | | | | | | | | | | | | | | | | | | |
| 4 wheeled platform | X | X | | X | | X | | | X | | | X | | | | manual power | | | X | | | | | X | |
| 4 wheeled platform | X | X | | X | | X | | | X | | | X | | | | manual power | | | X | | | | | X | |
| 2 wheeled platform | | X | | X | | X | | | X | | | X | | | | manual power | | | X | | | | | X | |
| 2 wheeled special (barrel, etc.) | | X | | X | | X | | | X | | | X | | | | | | | X | | | | | X | |
| Dollies | | X | | X | | X | | | X | | | X | | | | manual power | | | X | | | | | X | |
| Pallet Lift | | X | | X | | X | | | X | | | X | | | | manual power | | | X | | | | | X | |
| **Powered** | | | | | | | | | | | | | | | | | | | | | | | | | |
| **Driver-walk** | | | | | | | | | | | | | | | | | | | | | | | | | |
| Pallet Lift | | X | | X | | X | | | X | | | X | | | X | X | | | X | | | | | X | |
| Platform | | X | | X | | X | | | X | | | X | | | X | X | | | X | | | | | X | |
| High Lift Fork | X¹ | X | | X | X | X | | | X | | | X | | | X | X | | | X | | | | | X | |
| **Driver-ride** | | | | | | | | | | | | | | | | | | | | | | | | | |
| Pallet Lift | | X | | X | | X | | | X | | | X | | | X | X | | | X | | | | | X | |
| Platform | | X | | X | | X | | | X | | | X | | | X | X | | | X | | | | | X | |
| Low Lift Platform | X¹ | X | | X | | X | | | X | | | X | | | X | X | | | X | | | | | X | |
| High Lift Platform | X¹ | X | | X | X | X | | | X | | | X | | | X | X | | | X | | | | | X | |
| Telescoping Fork Lift | X¹ | X | | X | X | X | | | X | | | X | | | X | X | | | X | | | | | X | |
| **Tractors and Trailers** | | | | | | | | | | | | | | | | | | | | | | | | | |
| Industrial Tractor | | | | | | | | | | | | | | | | | | | | | | | | | |
| 3 wheeled | | | | | | | | | | | | | | | | | | | | | | | | | |
| 4 wheeled | | | | | | | | | | | | | | | | | | | | | | | | | |
| Industrial Trailer | | | | | | | | | | | | | | | | | | | | | | | | | |
| According to wheel arrangement | X¹ | X | | X | | X | | | X | | | X | | | X | X | | | | | | | X | X | |
| **Cranes, Hoists, and Monorails** | | | | | | | | | | | | | | | | | | | | | | | | | |
| **Crane** | | | | | | | | | | | | | | | | | | | | | | | | | |
| Overhead bridge, travelling | X¹ | X | | X | X | | | | | | | X | | | X | X | | | X | | | | | | X |
| Gantry | X¹ | X | | X | X | | | | | | | X | | | X | X | | | X | | | | | | X |
| Jib | | X | | X | X | | | | | | | X | | | X | X | | | X | | | | | | X |
| **Hoists** | | | | | | | | | | | | | | | | | | | | | | | | | |
| Chain, manual | X¹ | X | X | | | X | | | | | | X | X | | manual power | | | | X | | | | | | X |
| Elec. motor drive | X | X | X | X | | X | | | | | | X | X | | X | | | | X | | | | | | X |
| Pneumatic | X | X | X | | | X | | | | | | X | X | | X | | | | X | | | | | | X |
| **Monorail** | | | | | | | | | | | | | | | | | | | | | | | | | |
| Carrier | X¹ | | | X | X | | X | | X | | | | | | X | | | | X | | | | | | X |
| Trolley | | X | | X | X | | X | | X | | | | | | X | | | | | | | X | | | X |
| Chain Trolley | | X | | X | X | X | | | X | | | | | | X | | | | | | | X | | | X |
| **Conveyors** | | | | | | | | | | | | | | | | | | | | | | | | | |
| **Roller, Gravity** | | | | | | | | | | | | | | | | | | | | | | | | | |
| Spiral | X | X | | X | | | | | X | X | | X | | | | | | X | X | | | | | | X |
| Portable | X | | | X | X | | | | X | X | | X | | | | | | X | X | | | | | | X |
| Fixed | X | | | X | X | | | | X | X | | | | | | | | X | X | | | | | | X |
| **Roller, Live** | | | | | | | | | | | | | | | | | | | | | | | | | |
| Chain Drive | X | | | X | X | | | | X | X | | | | | X | X | | | X | | | | | | X |
| Belt Drive | X | | | X | X | | | | X | X | | | | | X | X | | | X | | | | | | X |
| **Wheel, Gravity** | | | | | | | | | | | | | | | | | | | | | | | | | |
| Portable | X | | | X | X | | | | X | X | | X | | | | | | X | X | | | | | | X |
| Fixed | X | | | X | X | | | | X | X | | | | | | | | X | X | | | | | | X |
| **Belt** | | | | | | | | | | | | | | | | | | | | | | | | | |
| Flat | X | X | X | X | X | | | | X | | | X | | | X | X | X | | X | | | | | | X |
| Troughed | X | | X | X | X | | | | X | | | X | | | X | X | X | | X | | | | | | X |
| Portable | X | X | X | X | X | | | | X | | | X | | | X | X | X | | X | | | | | | X |
| Fixed | X | X | X | X | X | | | | X | | | | | | X | X | X | | X | | | | | | X |
| **Drag** | | | | | | | | | | | | | | | | | | | | | | | | | |
| Pusher Bar | | X | | X | X | | | | X | | | X | | | X | | | | X | | | | | X | X |
| Screw | X | | | X | X | X | | | X | | | X | | | X | | | | X | | | X | X | | |
| Floor Chain | X¹ | | | X | X | | X | | X | | | X | | | X | | | | X | | | X | X | X | |
| Overhead Chain | X¹ | X | | X | X | | | X | X | | | X | | | X | | | | X | | | X | X | | |
| **Apron** | | | | | | | | | | | | | | | | | | | | | | | | | |
| Wood Slat | X | X | X | X | X | | | | X | | | X | X | | X | X | X | | | | | X | | | X |
| Steel Slat | X | X | X | X | X | | | | X | | | X | X | | X | X | X | | | | | | | | X |
| Ball Transfer | | X | X | | X | | | X | | | X | X | X | | manual power | | | | X | | | | | | X |
| Bucket Conveyor | X | X | | X | | | | | X | | | X | | | X | X | X | | X | | | | | | X |
| Continuous Chain Trolley | X¹ | X | | X | X | | | X | X | | | X | | | X | X | X | | | | | X | | | X |
| **Slides and Chutes** | | | | | | | | | | | | | | | | | | | | | | | | | |
| **Spiral or Straight** | | | | | | | | | | | | | | | | | | | | | | | | | |
| Wood | X | X | X | | X | | | | X | | | X | | | | | | X | X | | | | | | X |
| Steel | X | X | X | | X | | | | X | | | X | | | | | | X | X | | | | | | X |
| Vibrating | X | | X | | X | X | X | | X | | | X | | | X | | | | X | | | | | | X |
| **Pneumatic Systems** | | | | | | | | | | | | | | | | | | | | | | | | | |
| **Rigid Tube and Nozzle** | | | | | | | | | | | | | | | | | | | | | | | | | |
| Bulk loaders | X | | | | X | | | | X | | | X | | | X | | | | X | | | | | | X |
| Bulk unloaders | X | | | | X | | | | X | | | X | | | X | | | | X | | | | | | X |
| **Rigid Tube** | | | | | | | | | | | | | | | | | | | | | | | | | |
| Cylindrical Carrier | | X | | X | X | | | | X | | | X | | | X | | | | X | | | | | | X |
| Oval Carrier | | X | | X | X | | | | X | | | X | | | X | | | | X | | | | | | X |
| **Elevators** | | | | | | | | | | | | | | | | | | | | | | | | | |
| **Freight** | | | | | | | | | | | | | | | | | | | | | | | | | |
| Electric | X¹ | X | X | | | X | | | | | | X | X | | X | | | | X | | | | | X | |
| Hand | X¹ | X | X | | | X | | | | | | X | X | | manual power | | | | X | | | | | X | |
| Hydraulic | X¹ | X | X | | | X | | | | | X | | X | | X | | | | X | | | | | X | |
| Dumb waiter | | | X | | | | | | | | | | | | | | | | | | | | | | |
| **Continuous Lifts** | | | | | | | | | | | | | | | | | | | | | | | | | |
| Arm | | | X | X | | | | | X | X | | X | | | X | | | | | | | | X | X | |
| Tray | | | X | X | | | | | X | X | | X | | | X | | | | | | | | | X | |

(1) with scoop, bucket, etc.

**Figure 9-6.** Equipment selection chart. (From W. G. Ireson, *Factory Planning and Plant Layout*, Englewood Cliffs N.J. Prentice-Hall, Inc., 1952. Reprinted by permission.)

mine unit materials handling costs, either to apply them as a direct cost value or to use them as standard costs for the control of the operations, may exceed any savings that might be effected through such control or analysis.

Furthermore, as discussed above, the determination of a unit handling cost is at times quite difficult. But as the rate of production or flow of material is increased, and the different types or kinds of part and product are reduced, it becomes much easier to determine and allocate materials handling unit costs accurately. When feasible, costs should be determined on a unit cost basis for the proper evaluation of the materials handling problem. Such analyses will indicate those costs that are excessive, thus pointing out those areas where improvement of the materials handling system may pay the greatest dividends.

In any case, the expense of accumulating and determining unit costs must be justified through the use of such costs as a continuing control and guide for the reduction of the expense of handling materials.

It is evident that the current trend toward integrating materials handling with the actual operations required in the processing of the product will result in losing the identity of materials handling costs as such—these costs being included in the direct labor or machine costs for the manufacture of the goods.

## Economics of Materials Handling

Proper selection and use of materials handling equipment and methods is basically a problem in manufacturing economics. The ultimate objective is always the handling of goods at the optimum cost. This optimum cost must be evaluated on the total operation and may not be the lowest cost based upon a short-range computation. Both tangible and intangible values must be assessed and a balance of costs and savings arrived at that will prove most profitable to the enterprise in the long run.

Basically the cost of the equipment, as reflected in depreciation charges, and the cost of its operation must be balanced against the savings that can be effected through the use of the equipment and of the method that the equipment involves.

Tangible savings may be realized—or anticipated—on one or more of the following three bases:

1.  Lower total costs for the handling of materials.

2.  Lower unit costs for the handling of the product or assembly being manufactured.

3.  Lower unit costs for the handling of component parts, subassemblies, and assemblies.

These three bases call for a progressively greater breakdown of costs, the inherent problem being their determination. Generally speaking, the greater the degree to which costs are broken down, the more accurately they may be calculated. This is in itself a problem of economics; the value of such cost accuracy must be balanced against the expense involved in acquiring this accuracy.

Intangible savings that can be made through effective handling of materials are many. Some are:

1. Better control of production.
2. Better quality level of products produced.
3. Greater safety to personnel.
4. Improved morale of workers.

Other intangible savings may be realized. However, if a true economic picture of the materials handling problem is to be had, it becomes necessary to assign values to these savings. Determination of such values is one of the principal steps in the operations-research approach to this type of manufacturing problem.

The economic effect of the proper analysis and determination of unit loads should not be overlooked. Careful study of this phase of the materials handling problem—as well as that of packaging—will pay dividends in the form of reduced handling costs.

From this discussion it should not be assumed that mechanization and the elimination of hand labor will always result in the lowest cost. In many instances it may be found that the cost of equipment, and its operation, will more than offset any savings. In other words, manpower may still be the best when all factors are considered. Another case is where a visual inspection of the product is required; if the product has to be picked up and inspected, it does not stand to reason that a mechanical transfer device between conveyors (or between other materials handling means) is needed. The inspector can include such transfer as a part of his inspection operation.

## Relation of Materials Handling to Flow of Material and Plant Layout

The pattern of flow of materials in a plant definitely affects the materials handling costs. The production process should be so planned and the machines and benches so arranged that the handlings of materials are reduced to a minimum with as little backtracking of goods as possible. The type of manufacturing is a major factor in this respect.

In the layout of a plant for continuous manufacture the pattern of flow is planned well in advance; because of balanced machine and assembly lines, it lends itself to a well-planned flow of component parts, subassemblies, and assemblies. This makes it possible to plan the handling of materials in advance, procure and install the best equipment for the job, and design for a minimum materials handling cost. However, once installed the plan lacks flexibility—usually it cannot be changed without major expense.

The layout of a plant for intermittent manufacture may be much more flexible. Backtracking of materials should be minimized, but the nature of this type of layout makes this a more difficult problem to solve. Equipment selected will in most cases be more general purpose in nature, and as a result it may be changed for improved materials handling methods without incurring major expense.

The use of flow process charts is most helpful in planning processes and identifying the materials handling elements. This technique of methods analysis can be used not only as a designing tool but also for critical analysis of existing movements and handlings of materials. Instructional literature and forms are prepared by equipment manufacturers to assist their prospective customers in analyzing their materials handling problems.

In the same manner that good flow of materials should be planned for the plant layout as a whole, the layout of each work station—each machine location or workbench—should be carefully planned to insure the minimum of handling of materials by the most effective means. As has been previously pointed out this activity is really a part of operations analysis of the work to be done and the equipment to be used. Processing and materials handling must be closely coordinated for best results.

Another important materials handling factor in plant layout is the space required by the equipment to be used for moving goods. Factory trucks require certain turning radii, floor and overhead conveyors require space for installation, and cranes and hoists must be carefully laid out in the factory plan for maximum utilization. All this presents to the engineer a problem in compromising between building availability and the space requirements of the materials handling equipment to be used. It is seldom that the materials handling equipment can be planned first and the building planned around the equipment. Of course, the possible modification of building structure or layout must be considered when contemplating a change for the improvement of materials handling methods by the adoption of new equipment.

On assembly lines that involve manual labor the length of the line to be planned depends on attaining a proper balance between the work to be done by each assembler and the speed at which the line is to be operated. The work station for each man or woman on the line must be planned; the sum total of these stations affects both the floor space required and the design of the conveyor.

It is obvious that with the current trend towards automation the entire problem of space requirements for materials handling equipment will be gradually integrated with the processing-space requirements. As a matter of fact such integration exists today in large automobile factories and in plants producing large volumes of household appliances.

## Storage

Material in storage is generally thought to be stationary or idle. But the use of conveyors as storage devices is becoming quite popular. These conveyors may be overhead and constantly moving, yet utilizing ceiling-space storage. Such an installation is pictured in Figure 9-7. Other storage installations may be like the skate conveyors shown in Figure 9-8. In one midwestern furniture plant the complete floor of the finish drying room is covered by a large slat conveyor that moves very slowly; pieces placed on this "floor" at one side of the room are dry when they reach the other side.

Storage facilities and plans are also closely related to the unit loading plan for the product. Permanent racks and bins may be eliminated in a warehouse if goods are palletized in such a manner that the pallets can be stacked, or if the product is so packaged that the package can be used as

**Figure 9-7.** Overhead storage conveyors. (Courtesy General Electric Co.)

**Figure 9-8a.** View of control console in automatic warehouse. The operator at the console can determine the conditions at the truck dock by noting the light panel above the belt conveyor. To complete an order, he inserts a "begin order" punched card in a card reader on the console. (Courtesy The Alvey-Ferguson Company)

**Figure 9-8b.** View of automatic warehouse showing automatic pick racks. Cartons are released from these racks onto the belt conveyor. (Courtesy The Alvey-Ferguson Company)

**Figure of 9-8c.** View of automatic warehouse showing the merging point where the belt conveyors serving the automatic pick racks are brought together in a single line. (Courtesy The Alvey-Ferguson Company)

**Figure 9-8d.** View of automatic warehouse showing truck dock area. Five feeder lines convey assembled orders to preselected docks and each feeder line serves either of two adjacent docks. (Courtesy The Alvey-Ferguson Company)

a stacking unit (see Figure 9-9). Stackable tote boxes and bins also make the utilization of storage space quite flexible.

Increasing interest in the automation of storage warehouses is taking place (see Figures 9-8a, b, c, d). One such warehouse[4] constructed in the midwest handles cartons of toilet articles in a broad range of sizes and varieties. It can fill up to 800 average orders per day in a normal 8-hour shift. Up to 90 different items can be picked automatically from special racks and merged with previously hand-picked, low-demand items at speeds up

**Figure 9-9.** Palletless warehousing with unit loads handled with clamp truck. (Courtesy Procter & Gamble Company)

---

[4]See "Punched Cards Control Carton Order Picking," *Automation* (June 1963).

to 400 fpm. An order assembled in this manner can be routed automatically to any of five truck dock feeder lines in less than a minute. The five feeder lines can receive and/or accumulate orders simultaneously.

It is evident that materials handling and storage problems can be jointly solved to the mutual advantage of both. Likewise, the common solution directly affects the layout of the plant facilities, or is itself influenced by the existing floor plan and building construction.

## Packaging

Whether packaging is or is not a phase of materials handling is to some degree an academic question. The unit load is in itself a "package." Generally speaking, however, the term *packaging* is used to cover the preparation of the final product for shipment, particularly if the product is a consumer good.

From the viewpoint of a materials handling problem, packaging of the incoming materials as well as of the outgoing product directly affects materials handling methods and equipment—and the resultant materials handling costs. The designing of the package for a product, although usually identified as a separate activity or function, is closely interrelated with materials handling, methods of production, and marketing. Attractively packaged goods on the shelves and counters of the store, as well as the identification of large shipments on trucks and railroad cars, are effective advertising and sales promotion.

The package of today is a far cry from the crate and box used for shipment 10 or 15 years ago. Lumber may now be shipped in palletized loads instead of being piled in a boxcar so that each individual board must be handled when unloading. Furniture, which used to be carefully enclosed in wooden crates—the cost of which often equaled the value of the product being crated—is now boxed in fiberboard cartons. Delicate precision instruments that formerly required cushioned containers are now suspended in plastic envelopes in rigid boxes. These are just a few examples of the fairly recent improvements in the field of packaging.

Modern packages are also designed for efficient storage, not only from the standpoint of rigidity for stacking, but also for effective protection of the product from deterioration. The use of plastics, particularly in the packaging of foods, has contributed to the latter objective of sound packaging.

Mechanization has had important influence on the field of packaging. This is particularly true in the food processing industry, where special machinery has been developed that provides for the handling and packaging of the product without the use of the human hand. Looking into the future, a large manufacturer of electric refrigerators is now packaging the complete unit in a large fiberboard container on a completely automatic machine. In this case it is particularly interesting to note that the first step in this development was the redesign of the package. This first step was put into effect in the shipping room in advance of the availability of the special machine; and with the use of manual labor it still resulted in outstanding savings.

Thus, the package in which the material is handled, is an important part of the total materials handling problem in a manufacturing situation.

## Organization for Effective Materials Handling

Good materials handling practice is the responsibility of all members of the manufacturing team, from the top management down to the trucker working in the aisle of the plant. Very few other elements of manufacturing activity must be so carefully considered by each function in the manufacturing organization. Optimum effectiveness of materials handling procedures can only be attained if each individual recognizes and plays his part. Education and training in materials handling are prerequisite to minimum materials handling costs.

Although the responsibilities and duties involved in materials handling must of necessity become a part of each individual's job, the coordination of the total materials handling problem can be assigned to one individual or group. Large manufacturing organizations can well afford to organize specialists in materials handling into one of the staff or advisory groups reporting to the manager of manufacturing.

Responsibilities assigned such a staff group may well include:

1. Determine all new methods for the handling of new materials or products and select the equipment to be utilized.

2. Conduct research in materials handling methods and equipment.

3. Conduct education and training for all manufacturing personnel in good materials handling practices.

4. Establish controls of current materials handling costs by analysis of costs and comparison to budgets of either unit or total materials handling costs.

5. Initiate and conduct a continuing materials handling cost-reduction or cost-improvement program.

6. Determine measurements for effectiveness of materials handling that can become the yardsticks for progress in this activity.

7. Develop and conduct a preventive maintenance program for all materials handling equipment.

Each of the above activities will contribute to lower materials handling costs. In smaller plants these responsibilities must be assumed as part-time jobs by members of the manufacturing line organization. However, maximum effectiveness might be attained by assigning the principal coordinating responsibility for all materials handling activities to one individual or to a committee of several from the manufacturing group.

## QUESTIONS

1. Make a list of the materials handling devices that you might find in a modern home. Can any of these be improved? Are there any other new devices that might be feasible?

2. Make an analysis of the materials handling elements in the serving and eating of a meal. What proportion of the time is spent in materials handling?

3. Can the principles of materials handling be applied to your daily activity? How?

4. In what ways has the modern supermarket improved materials handling as compared to the small corner grocery?

5. A large manufacturer of bulbs for flashlights is now shipping them in bulk, that is, loose in cartons of 500 and 1000. Make a list of the cost factors that were considered in the adoption of this method of packaging and shipping.

6. Outline instances where product handling and processing either are combined or (as you see it) could be combined.

7. Should materials handling labor cost be a direct cost or an indirect one? Give reasons.

8. Do you see any particular role for the purchasing department to play in reducing materials handling costs?

9. To what extent does low materials handling cost depend upon efficient materials handling equipment?

10. Discuss the problem of setting up a suitable organization for materials handling in a factory.

## CASE PROBLEMS

**Grover Cotton Mills**

Grover Cotton Mills in Atlanta is a large producer of denim fabric. The company has long recognized that its handling and storing of baled denim is inefficient, but has found the problem difficult to solve.

The large steel-strapped bales of denim are hauled from the end of the production line to the finished goods warehouse by means of two-wheel hand trucks. Because of the weight of the bales they are usually placed on the floor or, at best, stacked two high. This has resulted in little usage of the cubage in the warehouse and excessive warehousing costs.

Grover's warehouse is a long (300 ft.), narrow (60 ft.) building with an archedtruss roof. The height is 22 feet in the center and about 12 feet along the walls. All material feeds into the warehouse from one side and out one end.

An increase in production has led to increased need for warehouse space, but the general manager refuses to authorize the building or renting of additional space. His contention is that adequate space is available if used efficiently. He has requested that the industrial engineering department analyze the warehouse situation and make recommendations for increasing its utilization.

*Questions:*

1. What recommendations should be made for improving the use of the warehouse?
2. Can manual handling be reduced? How?
3. Should new equipment be purchased? Why?
4. If new equipment is purchased, what is a reasonable time period in which to repay the investment?

## Acme Closure Company

The Acme Closure Company is one of the country's largest producers of metal closures for glass bottles.

The high-speed machines used by Acme enable it to meet its production demands, but have created a materials handling problem. This problem arises from the necessity to handle, move, and store the tremendous daily output of a battery of screw cap machines. Some of the machines turn out as many as 100,000 screw cap shells per hour. These must be moved either to a final manufacturing operation on a lower floor or to a storage area for future use.

James Elrod, the materials handling engineer, worked on the above problem for several weeks and has recommended that special box-type (30″ × 48″ × 36″) trucks be purchased These trucks come equipped with casters and can be easily moved by hand. A special feature of these trucks is a hinged door, which opens when the box is tilted forward. This would allow the caps to slide out and down a chute to the floor below, where final manufacturing is completed.

James Elrod has also recommended the purchase of storage racks on which the trucks can be stored in the storage area. By means of a fork-lift truck the box trucks can be stored three trucks high.

*Questions:*

1. Do you consider James Elrod's recommendation a good one? Why?
2. What other possibilities appear as feasible solutions to this problem?
3. In considering solutions to problems such as this, from where would you secure information?

# CHAPTER TEN

# Plant Layout

Plant layout is a plan of the most effective arrangement of the physical facilities and manpower for the manufacture of the product. It brings together and fully integrates all the work that has been done by the architect, the product engineer, the process engineer, the plant engineer, and the management in their careful planning for the production of goods in an optimum manner. Plant layout encompasses much more than the mere planning of the arrangement of the production equipment and should include a careful study[1] of the following:

1. External transportation facilities.
2. Receiving operations (unloading, inspection, stores).
3. Production activities.
4. Service and auxiliary operations.
5. Quality control and inspection areas.
6. Packaging operations.
7. Storage operations.
8. Shipping operations.

Plant layout is a valuable tool of management not only for the building of new plants but also in planning for changes in existing facilities. New products, new processes, or an increase or decrease in rates of production may require a rearrangement of production equipment. Of greatest importance is the adaptability of the plant layout to the forward planning of the company. The maintenance of the layout of a plant for historical purposes only is of little real value.

---

[1]See James M. Apple, *Plant Layout and Materials Handling* (New York: Ronald Press Co. 1963), p. 3–4.

We must not confuse plant layout with the design of industrial buildings. Obviously the two problems are closely related and in reality often require a compromise between the best design in each area. Seldom can a building be constructed around an "ideal" plant layout, and many times a layout must be changed to meet the requirements of the building.

*Plant layout* covers the planning of space requirements for all activities in an industrial firm—offices, warehouses, rest rooms, and all other facilities associated with the total manufacturing plant.

## Objectives of Plant Layout

The primary goal of plant layout is to maximize profits by the arrangement of all plant facilities to the best advantage of the total "manufacturing equation"—men, materials, machines, and money. If a finished layout is to fulfill this goal, it should be planned with the following objectives[2] clearly in mind:

1. Facilitate the manufacturing process.
2. Minimize materials handling.
3. Maintain flexibility of arrangement and of operation.
4. Maintain high turnover of work-in-process.
5. Hold down investment in equipment.
6. Make economical use of floor area.
7. Promote effective utilization of manpower.
8. Provide for employee convenience, safety, and comfort in doing the work.

All of these objectives might be summarized as *the planning of the plant for the best relationship between output, space, and manufacturing cost.* Output might be measured in dollar volume or in units of product. Space might be measured in square feet of floor or in cubic feet in the building structure. Manufacturing cost is obviously in money. In all manufacturing situations there is an optimum balance between these three, the attainment of which is made possible through effective plant layout.

## Factors Affecting Plant Layout

Many of the basic factors that affect the design of the product, the design of the manufacturing process, the selection of tools and equipment, and the planning for materials handling carry over to influence the plant layout. We shall discuss some of these in the following paragraphs.

---

[2]Apple, *ibid.*, p. 7.

**Product.** The type of product affects plant layout in many ways. Large and heavy equipment requires assembly bays. Also, in these cases it is often more economical to move the men and machines to the product than it is to move the product to the work area. Small and light products can be moved effectively, thus more attention can be given to machine locations and the handling of materials. Bulk products, such as cereals, gravel, or cement, more or less dictate a multi-story layout in order that the advantage of gravity can be utilized in the movement of the material.

**Volume or rate of production.** This is a key factor in all manufacturing planning. In plant layout it is reflected in the total size of the operation to be planned as well as being the principal factor in the determination of the type of manufacture to be employed.

**Quality.** The meeting of quality requirements in a product can be aided through effective plant layout. Soundproof rooms, "white" rooms, and air-conditioned factories are often needed to meet product specifications. In other cases the handling and storage of products—particularly if they may deteriorate—may contribute to the maintenance of the proper quality level.

**Equipment.** Adequate space must be provided for all equipment— manufacturing, materials handling, and service. Equipment specifications are of major importance to the plant-layout engineer.

**Type of manufacture.** It is obvious that a plant laid out for a continuous manufacturing process will be quite different from a factory operating as an intermittent plant. However, it should be pointed out that the advantages of continuous manufacture are such that it should be employed by the plant-layout engineer at every feasible opportunity. It is not uncommon in intermittent plants to set up temporary continuous lines whenever the rate of production warrants.

**Building.** Ideally, a building should be built to suit the best plant layout. This ideal is seldom attained. The adapting of a factory layout to an old building presents a real challenge to the plant-layout engineer. All proposals for modification of the existing structure must be economically justified. Even when a new building is to be constructed some compromise usually is required.

**Plant site.** The plant site is the connecting link between the factory and the surrounding community. Services such as railroad sidings, highways, and utilities may easily affect not only the positioning of the building on the plot but the internal arrangement of the departments as well.

**Personnel.** Comfort and safety of personnel must always be carefully considered when laying out a plant. A single operation, or work station, may within its own boundaries be safe yet endanger other workers in the general area. This calls for protective screens or possible relocation of the process. Comfort is considered in the location of rest rooms, drinking fountains, and other personnel services.

**Materials handling plan.** Basic to economical production is good materials flow and a soundly conceived materials handling system. Since materials handling is the skeleton on which the plant layout fits, it is inseparably tied in with the layout function. Thus, plant layout ties together the manufacturing plan and, in this way, dictates the specifications of the materials handling equipment. This plan also includes the providing of adequate aisles for movement of materials and the allocation of space for storage—not only in stock rooms but at the work stations.

Each and every one of the above factors presents a problem to the plant-layout engineer. We must realize that a solution that is completely favorable in all ways is seldom reached. As in most design situations a compromise must be made to attain an optimum solution.

## The Basic Plans for Plant Layout

Before discussing how plant layouts are made, we should identify the two basic plans for the arrangement of manufacturing equipment. These basic plans are the *process layout* and the *product layout*. Selection of the basic plan to be used depends upon many factors; however, of these, the type of product and the type of manufacture are of the greatest influence.

### Process Layout

In process layout the type and operational characteristics of the manufacturing equipment are the determining factors in the arrangement of the factory. This basic plan can be readily identified, as such plants will have machine departments, cleaning departments, finishing rooms, and assembly floors. Even within such departments machines of similar work characteristics are commonly grouped together (lathes, milling machines, drill presses, and so on).

### Product Layout

In product layout the work to be performed on the product is the determining factor in the positioning of manufacturing equipment. The aim is to arrange machines in the order of the operations that are performed on the many component parts, on subassemblies, and on the final assembly of the item being manufactured. Thus each work station—either machine or workbench —does whatever operation on the product that follows the work done at the preceding work station, then passes the product to the next work station in the line where the next operation is performed.

There are relative advantages for each of the basic types of layout. These advantages, together with comments as to when each type is to be used, are given in Figure 10-1.

Generally speaking, the *process layout* is characteristic of intermittent manufacturing, and the *product layout* is most common in continuous manufacturing. Process layout is probably the most common in industry today. However, with current trends towards automation the future may find more and more product layout in factories.

Both types present real challenges to the plant-layout engineer. In process layout he must so arrange departments—and subdepartments—that the material is moved with the least effort over minimum distances. This problem also holds true for product layout; however, it is complicated by the problem of "balancing out the line."

## Organization for Plant Layout

If the plant-layout activity in a manufacturing plant is to be effective there must be a well defined responsibility for its accomplishment. Large concerns have special plant-layout departments; smaller firms may designate the job as a part-time responsibility of one of the manufacturing staff or line. When a plant layout is required as a project—that is, to meet a particular need and not to be maintained on a continuing basis—a consulting firm may be engaged.

Some attempts have been made to determine on a quantitative basis the number of personnel in a manufacturing organization that should be engaged in this activity. These numbers generally are computed on the basis of the size of the plant, which is only one of many factors that might influence the need for plant-layout work. In reality, plant-layout departments must be measured by their contributions, both tangible and intangible, to the operation of the plant—and the funds and personnel for this activity should be allocated accordingly.

Plant layout is an *advance planning* activity. In determining the need for such an organization, management must consider the dynamic aspects of the manufacturing problem. If change is anticipated, owing to model changes, new products, technological improvements, or other causes, a plant-layout group will probably pay dividends.

A plant-layout organization is usually a part of the industrial engineering activity. However, it may report to the plant engineer, other department heads, or possibly direct to the plant management. In any event, in its activities the plant-layout group will have cooperative responsibility with practically every group engaged in manufacturing planning.

# PRODUCT VS. PROCESS LAYOUT

## Relative Advantages of Product and Process Layout

| PRODUCT LAYOUT | PROCESS LAYOUT |
|---|---|
| 1. Lower total materials handling cost | 1. Less duplication of equipment, hence lower total investment in equipment |
| 2. Lower total production time | 2. Greater flexibility of production |
| 3. Less work-in-process | 3. Better and more efficient supervision possible through specialization |
| 4. Greater incentive for groups of workers to raise level of performance (and greater possibility for group incentive pay plans with broader coverage) | 4. Greater incentive for individual workers to raise level of performance (and greater possibility for individual incentive pay plans) |
| 5. Less floor area required per unit of production | 5. Better control of complicated or precision processes, especially where much inspection is required |
| 6. Greater simplicity of production control — fewer controls and records needed, lower accounting cost | 6. Easier to handle breakdowns of equipment by transferring work to another machine or station |

## When to Use Product and Process Layouts

| PRODUCT LAYOUT | PROCESS LAYOUT |
|---|---|
| 1. One or few standard products | 1. Many types or styles of products, or emphasis on special orders |
| 2. Large volume of production of each item over a considerable period of time | 2. Relatively low volume of production on individual items (though total production may be high) |
| 3. Possibility of time and motion studies to determine rate of work | 3. Adequate time and motion studies difficult or impossible to make |
| 4. Possibility of good labor and equipment balance (each machine or work station producing equivalent number of units per hour) | 4. Difficult to achieve good labor and equipment balance |
| 5. Minimum of inspection required during sequence of operations | 5. Many inspections required during a sequence of operations |
| 6. Minimum of very heavy equipment or equipment requiring special facilities (isolation from general production areas, etc.) | 6. High proportion of very heavy equipment or equipment requiring special treatment |
| 7. Materials and products permit bulk or continuous handling by mechanical means | 7. Materials or products too large or too heavy to permit bulk or continuous handling by mechanical means (in extreme cases, process may have to be brought to work, instead of vice versa) |
| 8. Little or no occasion to use same machine or work station for more than one operation (minimum number of setups required) | 8. Frequent necessity to use same machine or work station for two or more different operations |

**Figure 10-1.** Product vs. process layout. (From W. G. Ireson: *Factory Planning and Plant Layout*, Englewood Cliffs, N.J.: Prentice-Hall, Inc., 1952. Reprinted by permission.)

There is one prime characteristic that should be considered in the selection of personnel for this activity. That characteristic is *creativeness!* For optimum effectiveness plant-layout engineers must be able to think creatively. They should not be bound by convention; they must be original in their planning. Only by such an approach can a plant-layout group pay maximum dividends to operating management.

## Plant-Layout Procedure

As in most industrial activities there is a sound approach to the plant-layout problem. First let us list the steps briefly, then discuss each in detail. In solving a plant-layout problem:

1. Accumulate all the basic data that will be needed.
2. Analyze and coordinate these basic data.
3. Determine a general flow pattern for the materials in process.
4. Design the individual work stations or production centers.
5. "Assemble" the individual layouts into the total layout in accordance with the general flow pattern and the building facilities.
6. Coordinate this plan with the plan for the handling of materials.
7. Complete the plant layout.
8. Prepare an appropriation request indicating the funds needed and justifying the expenditure of these funds.
9. Convert the plant layout into floor plans that can be used by the plant engineer in the location and installation of the equipment.

This is the general pattern of attack. But from time to time the sequence may be changed to advantage.

**Basic data.**    Basic data must be procured from practically every other function in the manufacturing organization. Standard process sheets from the process engineering group are needed to show how the product is to be made and the tools and equipment required. If the time standards are not already posted on this form, they will have to be obtained in order to determine the anticipated rates of production for each operation. In some companies this information is consolidated on a flow process chart, which coordinates all operations into the complete process required for the manufacture of the product. Equipment lists and the specifications of the equipment must be obtained to determine the space requirements and the productive capacity of the machines involved. The plant engineer is the source of information as to the building plans and specifications. From these plans the available space can be determined. From the production planning and control group information must be obtained regarding the required volume and rate of production. And, finally, from the product engineer complete specifications of the product and bills of materials should be procured.

**Analysis and coordination.** Careful analysis and coordination of the basic data by the plant-layout engineer is needed to determine:

1. The total number of employees that will be required.
2. The total number of work stations that must be planned for.
3. The kind, size, and number of every piece of equipment that must be accommodated in the layout.
4. Total space requirements for storage of inventories, including raw materials, work-in-process, and finished goods.

A more detailed and graphic description of the channels for this analysis is given in Figure 10-2.

Each part of the solution gained through this analysis should be questioned by the plant-layout engineer. All answers should be coordinated and carefully evaluated. When it is apparent that revisions in earlier planning can be made to good advantage, such changes should be recommended to the proper planning group. This is the initial compromise point in plant layout.

**Flow pattern.** Analysis and evaluation of the basic data will indicate the basic plan for the layout—process or product. After the selection of a basic plan, a general pattern of flow for the product should be determined. For a process layout this results in a tentative arrangement of the various functional departments involved in the manufacturing process. In the product layout it is a general plan for the location of the many processing and assembly lines. These general flow patterns are indicated in the block layouts shown in Figures 10-3 and 10-4. We should again remind ourselves that most industrial plants are actually a "mix" of these two basic types of layout plan.

**Work stations.** The individual work station or production center is the key in plant layout. Each station should be laid out for the most effective performance of the operation, taking into account space for storage of tools and materials, ease of maintenance of equipment, and worker safety and comfort. A typical work station layout is shown in Figure 10-5.

**Prepare plant layout.** Now the parts of the jigsaw puzzle must be fitted together within the frame of the picture. Work stations are arranged in accordance with the flow pattern and within the space limitations of the building structure. Also at this point allowances must be made for aisles, storage areas, cranes, offices, services, and all other such facilities. Again, each individual location should be evaluated and all possible solutions to the

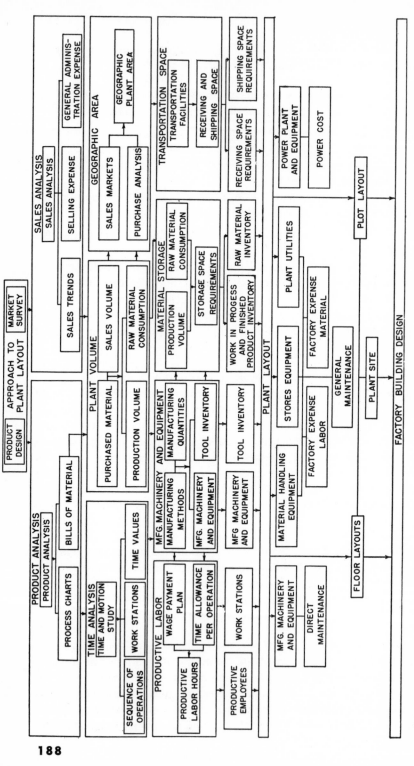

**Figure 10-2.** Evolution of information for a plant layout. The various separate sources from which this information is secured and the related sequence in which the data are integrated in process of development. (From R.W. Mallick and A.T. Gaudreau, *Plant Layout*, New York: John Wiley & Sons, Inc., 1951. Reprinted by permission.)

**Figure 10-3.** A two-dimensional block layout. (Courtesy General Electric Co.)

problem considered. This is another point for many compromises. However, every possibility must be considered and the best combination selected—it is much easier to move templates and models than it is to rearrange machines and equipment on the factory floor!

**Materials handling.**    The final solution of the materials handling problem is concurrent with the arrangement of the plant layout. A good plant layout makes for more efficient handling of materials. Likewise the selection of the most adaptable materials handling equipment contributes toward the arriving at the optimum layout of the manufacturing facilities.

**Appropriation request.**    The work of the plant-layout engineer seldom ends with the completion of the arrangement of the plant on paper. At every point in the making of the layout, cost must be considered. This cost is a total cost—it takes into consideration all factors involved. One of these

**Figure 10-4.** A three-dimensional block layout. Note that some of the buildings have five floors. (Courtesy General Electric Co.)

factors is the cost of installing and arranging the equipment in accordance with the layout plan. These installation costs must now be assembled in the form of an appropriation request for the money required to convert the plan into actuality. This proposal must be defended before management, and to do so effectively the plant-layout engineer must be thoroughly prepared with facts and figures. In any event the successful plant-layout engineer must at all times be cost-conscious.

**Floor plans.** After the plant layout has been approved, the final step is to arrange the physical facilities. In some instances this can be done directly from the layout, in others it is necessary to interpret the layout in the form of floor plans that can be used by the plant-engineering group, building contractor, and others. When such plans are required their preparation is generally the last step taken by the plant-layout group in completing their job. However, close liaison with all parties involved is usually necessary until the last machine or piece of equipment is installed and the plant is put into operation.

We might well ask if this completes the useful life of the plant layout. This is, of course, a question of the stability of the manufacturing process. If changes can be anticipated it is much easier to work them out by advance planning on an "active" plant layout. The maintenance of an up-to-date

**Figure 10-5.** A typical work station or production center, showing space allocation for machine, tool storage, materials, maintenance, and aisles. (From W. G. Ireson, *Factory Planning and Plant Layout*, Englewood Cliffs, N.J.: Prentice-Hall, Inc., 1952. Reprinted by permission.)

layout of a factory requires effective communications between the plant-layout group and all other manufacturing functions. Too often moves may be made in the shop without either consulting the plant-layout engineer or advising him of the change. If this condition is permitted to continue, the effectiveness of the keeping of the actual layout is lost.

## Plant-Layout Techniques

A detailed discussion of the exact methods whereby plant layouts are made is beyond the scope of this book. In recent years, however, rapid strides have been made in this field. Materials and procedures have been developed that not only result in better looking layouts but in a reduction of the time required for their preparation.

### Materials

The common base materials on which layouts are constructed consist of: (1) plastic sheets or boards on which grid lines have been printed or scribed, (2) metal-faced plywood with an appropriate finish on the metal, (3) sheet metal, plywood, or composition board with an appropriate finish, and (4) drawing paper or tracing paper. Many two- and three-dimensional templates are available commercially and can be procured. Self-adhering transparent tapes are available showing standard aisles, conveyors, arrows for indicating materials flow, walls and partitions, as well as other parts of the layout that used to be inked in by a draftsman. In many concerns standard templates and models are available, saving the time the plant-layout engineer would spend making measurements on the shop floor. Templates can be readily reproduced on foil either by photographic means or by Bruning or Ozalid processes. Double-coated self-adhering tape is used for mounting both templates and models, eliminating pins or adhesives previously used; with this new method moves can be made easily during the planning of the layout.

### Types of Layouts

Two principal types of plant layouts are in use in modern industry. These are:

1. Two-dimensional transparent template layouts.
2. Three-dimensional model layouts.

Prior to the preparation of either of these it is common practice to make a third type, a block layout.

**Block layouts.**    Block layouts are shown in Figures 10-3 and 10-4. This type of layout is usually prepared to a scale of $\frac{1}{8}$ inch equals one foot. It is a preliminary layout for study of materials flow patterns. By use of this technique a decision can be made as to the general arrangement of the plant before proceeding with the more detailed layout.

Block layouts may be either two- or three-dimensional. Figure 10-4 shows a three-dimensional block layout constructed with sheets of plexiglass.

**Template layouts.**    This is probably the most common type of plant layout. Modern techniques are characterized by the fact that the layouts are transparent and copies can be duplicated direct from these layouts for use in the plant or for record purposes. A template layout is commonly prepared to the scale of $\frac{1}{4}$ inch equals one foot. Figure 10-6 shows a transparent layout and Figure 10-7b shows a print duplicated from this transparency.

Some of the advantages of the two-dimensional layout are:

1. It is the least costly.
2. It can be readily interpreted by technical personnel.
3. Duplicate copies can be made.

On the other hand the disadvantages of the two-dimensional layout are:

Figure 10-6. Preparing a two-dimensional transparent layout. (Courtesy General Electric Co.)

1.   It is hard to visualize overhead equipment and check clearances for same.

2.   Interpretation by non-technical personnel is difficult.

**Model layouts.**   These layouts are not so common, probably owing to the expense involved. However, for the construction of new plants using any overhead equipment in the way of conveyors, cranes, or mezzanine installations, this type of layout should receive serious consideration. Model layouts are prepared to the same scale as template layouts—$\frac{1}{4}$ inch equals one foot. Model or three-dimensional layouts are shown in Figure 10-8. The relative advantages of this type of layout are:

1.   Helps "sell" the layout to management.

2.   Aids the visualization of the layout by non-technical personnel.

3.   Facilitates the work of the plant-layout engineer in making the layout; models can be shifted quickly for study of optional arrangements.

4.   Different arrangements can be photographed for comparative purposes.

5.   Provides means for checking overhead structures.

Disadvantages of the three-dimensional layout are:

1.   High cost.

2.   Requires storage area.

**Figure 10-7a.** Printing a duplicate of the plant layout directly from the layout shown in Figure 10-6. (Courtesy General Electric Co.)

3. Cannot be taken down to the shop floor for reference purposes.

4. For full effectiveness a two-dimensional layout has to be prepared from the model layout for informational purposes.

## Principles of Plant Layout

Over the years many principles have been developed for the guidance of the plant-layout engineer. In spite of this there is considerable art still involved in plant layout. Application of these principles is based more on a "cut-and-try" approach than on quantitative measurements. Considerable research has been conducted and is being continued to achieve a more scientific approach to the solution of plant-layout problems.

One example of such research is the attempt to balance assembly lines by mathematical models. Most assembly-line balancing has been done by trial and error methods. Recent research has resulted in several computer-oriented computational methods which are now being used in industry. These methods usually direct the computer to investigate all possible group-

**Figure 10-7b.** Print made from the layout in Figure 10-6. (Courtesy General Electric Co.)

ings of the assembly tasks and then to obtain the best grouping for a given set of conditions. New heuristic[3] methods have been developed that offer considerable promise for the future.

Some of the principles of plant layout that have proven sound are:

**1. Move materials minimum distances.**   This principle brings out the concept of "straight-line" production. However, in many instances it is more practical to take circular paths such as found in "merry-go-rounds" used in many production foundries.

**2. Avoid or minimize the back-tracking of materials.**   Backtracking will not only increase the distance of movement but can result in congestion of the channels of materials handling.

**3. Plan for a minimum of materials handling.**   The advantage here has been discussed earlier in this book. It is an overlapping principle, because

**Figure 10-8a.** Preparing a three-dimensional plant layout using models. (Courtesy General Electric Co.)

[3]See "Use Heuristic Production Line Balancing to Save on Material Handling," *Material Handling Engineering* (February 1963), p. 61.

**Figure 10-8b.** A completed three-dimensional layout. Note the facility for determining overhead clearances. (Courtesy General Electric Co.)

the effectiveness of the plant layout will make a major contribution to this end.

**4. Use manufacturing space economically.** This applies not only to the production areas but to the storage areas as well. In the past it has been common practice to regard this principle in terms of square feet of floor space only. Current trend is to consider the cubic space in the building. In many plants overhead conveyors are now being utilized as a storage device.

**5. Permit all flexibility possible.** The chance of change should always be considered and the equipment arranged so that changes can be made at a minimum of cost or disturbance of the manufacturing process. This is a problem of the automotive industry where model changes are involved.

**6. Allow for possible plant expansion.** The plant-layout engineer should always consider increase in production when planning the arrangement of a factory.

In many industries there are other "rules of thumb" that have been established by experience in plant layout. For example, it is not considered good practice to place large and expensive installations such as heat-treating equipment or drying ovens for finishes centrally—preferred practice is to locate them along an outer wall. However, such practices are not yet generally accepted as fundamentals of plant layout.

## Evaluation of Plant Layouts

Evaluation as to which—if any—plan represents the best plant layout is difficult. As we have noted, the objective is to get optimum output of product with a minimum of manufacturing space. There are, however, so many other factors that influence the productive efficiency of a plant that to measure the effectiveness of the layout by this alone can hardly be accepted as conclusive.

Analysis of the materials handling involved is another possible measure of layout effectiveness. It might well be assumed that the layout that results in the minimum of handling of materials is the best. On the other hand this layout might be much more costly in equipment and installation.

There is no doubt that currently developed techniques of plant layout and the continuing development of these techniques will contribute to the arriving at a good solution to a plant-layout problem. Nevertheless, good creative thinking and sound judgment on the part of the plant-layout engineer is prerequisite to a successful layout of a manufacturing plant.

## QUESTIONS

1. Discuss the application of the principles of plant layout to the kitchen in your home or place of residence.
2. Make a template layout of your own study room. Can you rearrange it to any advantage?
3. What plant-layout principles are applicable to the modern supermarket? Explain.
4. Make a sketch of the plant site of some local factory. Discuss the advantages and disadvantages of this site.
5. Make a template layout for a sewing machine, cookstove, or refrigerator. Indicate the additional space that you should allow beyond the actual dimensions of the equipment. Discuss how you arrived at these dimensions.
6. Discuss the placement of responsibility in an organization for an efficient plant layout.
7. List some appropriate criteria for use in determining whether a process layout or product layout should be employed in any layout problem.
8. What restrictions does the plant building place on the plant layout? Can any of these be modified or eliminated?
9. What type of layout materials do you suggest for use when laying out (a) a

machine shop, (b) an oil refinery, (c) a warehouse, (d) an office, (e) an aircraft carrier? State your reasons.

10. Of what value from a purely practical point of view are the principles of plant layout?

## CASE PROBLEMS

### Peerless Automotive Company

For many years the Peerless Automotive Company has made use of three-dimensional models for laying out its plant. These models are made by two craftsmen in the company's own model shop and are made as accurately as possible.

The plant layout section of the industrial engineering department is responsible for planning the layout of all machines and equipment prior to installing these items in the shop. Since the company has annual model changes that require changes in the production departments, six engineers are kept busy planning the layout for the new models of automobiles.

The three-dimensional layout is made on a number of large boards to the scale of $\frac{1}{4}$ inch = 1 foot. This layout is considered the master layout of the plant, and all changes on the board must be approved by the plant superintendent, the foreman, and the chief industrial engineer prior to making any changes in the factory.

Some persons have questioned the expense of building the models and maintaining the elaborate layout boards, but Alfred Smith, head of the industrial engineering department, contends that the expenditure for this type of layout is compensated for many times over by the savings realized. Further, he argues that this type of layout provides a degree of accuracy (plus or minus three inches on the plant floor) not afforded by other layout techniques.

*Questions:*

1. Do you agree with Alfred Smith? Why?
2. What benefits does Peerless Automotive gain from its system of plant layout which it probably wouldn't get from other systems?
3. What is your opinion of having all changes approved in writing?

### Shaw Company

The Shaw Company, which is located in a large eastern city, employs about 300 people in the manufacture of pharmaceutical products. The plant is located near the center of the city, and most of the employees either carry their lunch or eat in nearby restaurants. This has led to considerable dissatisfaction on the part of the employees, and they have repeatedly expressed the desire to have a company cafeteria.

The president of the company has decided that the employees' request is reasonable and that a cafeteria should be included in a new wing of a building that is being planned. He decides that Donald Jones, the chief industrial engineer, should be responsible for planning this cafeteria and that it should be capable of feeding at least a 300-person work force.

*Questions:*

1. In planning this cafeteria from whom can Donald Jones get the information he will need?
2. In what ways is the layout of a cafeteria similar to the layout of a production department?
3. What special problems may be encountered in laying out a cafeteria?

# Manufacturing Control

# CHAPTER ELEVEN

# Fundamentals
# of Control

Planned control of all activity is a basic characteristic of modern industry. Effective control of men, materials, machines, and money contributes towards the making of profits so essential to the free-enterprise system. In the next few chapters of Section III we shall discuss primarily the control of materials —their procurement and storage—and the processing of these materials by men and machines. First, however, let us study the fundamentals and principles that are common to all control procedures.

## Control Fundamentals

No matter which of the elements of manufacturing you plan to control, either singly or in combination, there must be four basic phases in the control system. All of these basic control steps are interdependent and dynamic in all manufacturing situations. The breaking down of any control problem into these four phases, and the determination of the effective operation of each step will materially assist in the attainment of a satisfactory solution. These four basic control phases are:

1. There must be a *plan.*
2. A record of *actual performance* must be maintained.
3. Actual performance must be continually *compared* to and *evaluated* with the plan.
4. Provisions must be made for *corrective action* in manufacturing operations when the results of the evaluation indicate the need for such action.

Let us briefly investigate why each of these steps is essential.

**Plan.**   A state of control can never exist unless some sort of a plan has been made.

One characteristic of today's industrial enterprise is the formulation of long-range plans, covering periods of from 5 to 15 years, or possibly longer. These plans involve all functions of the business—marketing, manufacturing, personnel, finance—and are based upon the policies and decisions of top management.

Manufacturing, on the other hand, is more often concerned with short-range plans that are made within the structure of the long-range plan. These short-range plans are made to cover that period of time during which the activities of manufacturing are fairly certain or "firm," for example, a 30-day production schedule showing daily output during that period. The establishment of a monthly or yearly budget—either in money or number of men—to be used for the maintenance of equipment is another short-range plan.

Day-to-day planning may be necessary for the effective implementation of the short-range plan. The planning of daily work assignments to meet the requirements of the 30-day schedule also may be necessary.

Plans can be identified with men, materials, machines, or money, or with any combination of these elements of manufacturing. However, in making a plan a "common yardstick" for measurement must be established. Any one of these elements may be used as a basis for measurement but the most common base for measurement—and as a result the foundation for most planning—is either money or time.

Time is the common denominator to which practically all manufacturing elements can be resolved.

**Actual performance.**   All effort used in making plans is a total loss unless attempts are made to follow these plans in the manufacturing activity. Keeping records of actual performance on the same basis of measurement as the plan is an activity that is prerequisite to any system of control.

**Comparison and evaluation.**   The comparison of the records of actual performance to the plan and the evaluation of the results tells us how well the plan was made and how well it is being followed. When the actual performance meets the planned performance the manufacturing situation is said to be "in control." When performance fails to meet the plan the situation is considered "out of control." It is possible to be "in control" and still not be operating at optimum efficiency; such a situation should be evident in the broad evaluation of performance.

Another aspect of evaluation is the prediction of possible failures in the manufacturing activity by a study of trends in performance. Anticipation of possible production bottlenecks or materials shortages by careful study of performance is one of the most valuable tools of management.

**Corrective action.**   Ideally, no corrective action should ever be necessary. Realistically, corrective action is the most important aspect in a control situation. Modern manufacturing is too complex to anticipate all possibilities of delays and failures when making the plan; and at the same time the allowance of too much time or money in anticipation of such problems is not good planning. As a result corrective action is often necessary and should be taken without hestitation.

There is a difference between *correction* and *replanning*. Corrective action does not recognize any change in the original plan, for the objective of the corrective action is to get operations back on the original schedule or budget. Generally speaking, schedules and budgets should not be changed to meet failures in performance. When such changes are made, the performance of the plant is the controlling element—not the plan. It is because of this that a state of control seldom exists except where effective corrective action is being taken.

**Replanning.**   Replanning has its place in modern control situations. However, it is most effective when used to improve the making of plans in the future. The key to successful manufacturing controls is the constant improvement of all plans for the manufacture and distribution of goods. The use of a "re-plan" to compensate for failure to meet an original plan should be made only when one is aware of all the circumstances involved.

## Common Characteristics of Good
## Control Procedures

For optimum results there must be a clearly defined  objective for every manufacturing control situation. This objective should state what is to be controlled and the degree of control that is to be maintained. Control is a tool of management that requires careful study and analysis in order to avoid the establishment of controls for the sake of control only. Too often many controls are planned that contribute little, if anything, to the efficient operation of the factory.

The objective of the control system must receive careful and continuing consideration when establishing the goals of plans. In a sense the objectives control the plans, which in turn are used for the control of manufacturing. In like manner any change in the ultimate plan—or replanning—automatically affects the objective. Replanning should be permitted only when the objectives of the control situation can be changed without excessive loss.

"Degree of control" means how close a control needs to be maintained. Is it necessary to record production every hour, day, or week? Must an accurate inventory count be made of all parts at all stages in their processing? It is obvious that there is a point of diminishing returns where the value of such records no longer justifies the cost of their accumulation. If possible, the desired degree of control should be clearly stated in terms of the objective of the system of control.

The design and installation of control systems presents a challenging problem to the industrial engineer. Some "bench marks" of good control procedures for the analysis or designing of control systems are discussed in the following paragraphs.

**Simplicity.**   Control systems should be made as simple as possible. The fewer the forms or records that must be maintained, the easier the system is to operate, and the fewer opportunities for error. Simple systems are also easily understood by the personnel involved.

**Low cost.**   This is an obvious "bench mark." As we shall see in later discussion of the many manufacturing controls, the savings that those controls make are often intangible. This makes the justification of high-cost systems difficult.

**Adequate and timely information.**   This is a principal characteristic of the second phase in a control system: the recording of actual performance. Determination of the *adequacy* of information the system will obtain requires considerable judgment. Enough information must be gathered for the making of decisions; however, in many cases the accumulation of all the information that might seem desirable is too costly. An economic balance must be struck between record costs and the value of the information obtained. Information must also be *timely*. If trouble spots are to be anticipated and corrective action taken, all records must be up to date. Learning of the failure to meet a production schedule a week or month ago does not permit taking steps to avoid such failure. Timely information predicts *before* the completion date that the schedule will not be met—this is the indication that corrective action is necessary.

**Flexibility.**   Although it is generally agreed that replanning should be held to a minimum, a certain amount is almost always necessary. This requires changes in plans with the resultant changes in the control records. In much the same manner corrective action will require adjustments in plans and schedules. A good control system permits the making of such changes without "upsetting the apple cart" and with a minimum of confusion and expense.

**Permit management by exception.**   The system of reporting actual performance and comparing and evaluating it with the control plan should be such that only situations that require corrective action are brought to the immediate attention of management or supervisory personnel. This is, of course, the basic principle of management by exception. However, procedures should be so established that corrective decisions can be made at the lowest level possible in the management structure.

**Force planning and corrective action.** A control system can be so designed that management and the personnel operating the system are continually forced to look ahead. Manufacturing control is dynamic in every aspect; it is not a static or "one-shot" affair. Good control plans should foster better planning for future operations. Also, good control plans force corrective action by signaling failures to the next higher level of management.

## Manufacturing Controls and People

One other area is common to all manufacturing control problems: people. In all cases people are involved—both management and labor. It makes little difference whether the industrial engineer is planning a new system of control or is concerned with the continuing effectiveness of an existing plan of control. At all times the personal factor must be considered. All personnel must first recognize the advantages of and the need for the effective control of the manufacturing activity. Next they must be "sold" on the system of control to be used, and finally they must be educated and trained for its effective operation.

**Recognition of need.** A definite recognition of the need for the control must be established. In many cases, as we shall see later, this is not too hard to do. Losses owing to ineffective controls can be identified and savings that will result from better controls predicted. The biggest obstacle here is the natural human tendency to resist change. It is often difficult to sell a new control plan to a management that is currently making good profits with the present system. The need for control must be clearly defined and kept constantly before all people involved.

**Selling the system.** A successful control procedure requires the full cooperation of all manufacturing personnel—from the operator on the machine or assembly line to the top management. Effective control is everybody's job. Many a plan has failed because not everyone involved believed in the need for the control or in the procedure planned for the system.

**Education and training.** A sound program of education and training will materially influence the success of any control program. This means the education and training of all, from the top management personnel on down to the worker. Of course, more detailed education and training is indicated for the personnel who will actually operate the system. Again, this also is not necessarily a one-time affair. Control systems maintain their optimum effectiveness only when a continuing program of education and training is conducted.

## Basic Causes of Control Failure

Many well-designed control systems fail to produce the anticipated results. It is not possible to enumerate all the factors contributing to such failures. However, we can briefly consider a few of the principal reasons why a control system or procedure does not function properly.

Any control system can be likened to a chain: it is as strong or effective as its weakest link. Most control procedures are in reality a system of industrial communications consisting of many steps. At each of these steps information is fed into the system, drawn from the system, or accumulated and compared with the goals of the plan. A failure at any point in the procedure "contaminates" all subsequent results that are recorded or observed by control personnel. All information up to the point of failure is valid; after the point of failure all information is inaccurate and may contribute to inefficient operation of the plant.

An entire system of control should not be condemned when in all probability failure can be isolated to only one—or at most a few—steps in the procedure. There are two basic sources of trouble: operating personnel and basic data.

**Operating personnel.**    It is obvious that incompetent personnel who continually make mistakes should be relieved of their assignments. This, however, may be only a short-range correction of the problem. The failure of a clerk may be due to lack of proper training. He did not understand the "what," "how," and "why" of his duties or their importance. In the preceding paragraphs we discussed the importance of education and training of personnel if the control procedure is to be effective. Also, we pointed out that personnel who are thoroughly competent must be "sold" on the system. Sometimes a system fails because a single person does not do his job.

**Basic data.**    The results obtained from any control procedure are no better than the accuracy of the information fed into the system. Inaccurate costs, standard times, inventory counts, or any one of the other items of basic data upon which the system operates will result in poor performance. One grossly inaccurate estimate either as to cost or production time for a large component part of a product may result in a poor plan for the control of production. The reporting of an inaccurate count of materials in a mass-production plant may result in a complete shutdown of the lines. Basic data must be as accurate as the degree of control demands.

Degree of control determines the degree of accuracy required in basic data. In a highly competitive market of consumer goods, costs must be controlled to tenths of one cent or possibly closer. For custom manufacture of heavy apparatus control need not be so close. In an inventory some items must be accurately accounted for; others may be counted in hundreds and this count made monthly or possibly only once a year. Basic data must be accurate within the units of measure that are dictated by the degree of control.

## Control as a Tool of Management

Any control procedure or system is a tool of management and not an end in itself. Maintenance of control communications and records must be justified by savings resulting either from their use in planning future operations or from the improved efficiency of day-to-day manufacture.

Every system of control has its limitations. Control procedures, for example, do not make decisions; they simply indicate when decisions are necessary and possibly what decision should be made. Effective use of manufacturing controls depends upon the considered judgment of the people involved. There must be a thorough understanding of the control system and of the extent and validity of the information resulting from the communication procedures in the system.

The objective of the system must be in evidence at all times. *The least control that accomplishes the objective is the best control.* The fewer the records, reports, and steps in the control procedure, the simpler and less costly the system. This is a simple principle; however, the realization of this overall objective is difficult.

## QUESTIONS

1. How would you apply the fundamentals of control to one of your own activities?
2. Prepare a plan covering your activities for the coming week.
3. What corrective actions might you take if you got behind in your own work schedule?
4. What units of measure might be used in setting up controls for:
   (a) The baking of bread in a bakery?
   (b) A community fund drive?
   (c) An insurance company?
5. By June 15 a gasoline service station has pumped 650,000 gallons. The sales

budget for June is 1,800,000 gallons. Is corrective action necessary? If so, what are some of the steps that should be taken?

6.  A print shop promised to deliver 5000 special envelopes to you last Friday. When you went for them they were not ready; you were asked to come back the following Tuesday. Make a list of the possible causes for this delay.

7.  Outline a scheme for controlling sales. What types of corrective action would be appropriate in this scheme?

8.  Apply the control fundamentals to a typical problem faced by a company president. Do the same for a department foreman. What basic differences are there between the two?

## CASE PROBLEMS

### Midwest Manufacturing Company

Upon his return from the management conference in New York City, William Brown, the vice president in charge of manufacturing for Midwest Manufacturing Company, called a meeting of some of his department heads. Those present included the managers of methods analysis, research, engineering, and time standards. Mr. Brown pointed out to the group that while in New York he had heard a very stirring talk regarding the fundamentals of control and their use in manufacturing, and he wanted to be certain that his organization was making full use of these fundamentals. He then distributed copies of the talk to those present and asked each to study it carefully. As soon as possible, each manager was to come back to Mr. Brown and discuss how his particular department was making use of these control fundamentals or how they were planning to make use of them in the future.

*Questions:*

1.  Explain how the fundamentals of control can be used in the departments represented at the meeting.

2.  Does Mr. Brown have any role to play in the carrying out of the control concept by the four department managers? In other words, how can he apply the control concept to his job?

3.  Comment on Mr. Brown's method of introducing and installing the control concept in his organization.

### Meldrum Manufacturing Co.

At a meeting with all his department heads Mr. Wilson Waterman, the factory manager of Meldrum Manufacturing Co., was discussing the use of automation in the plant. He expressed the opinion that the word had been overused and misused a great deal and that the true meaning related to a process that makes use of the fundamentals of control. He said a good example of automation is the temperature regulating system on home furnaces.

Mr. Balsa, the chief engineer, questioned this concept of automation and pointed out that a $100,000 machine recently installed by the company to produce plastic moldings automatically looked like automation to him. He emphasized the fact that this machine replaced a battery of 6 older machines and could be operated by one man while each of the older machines required 2 men.

*Questions:*

1.  Does automation include all four fundamentals of control? Explain.
2.  Does a temperature regulating device on a home furnace employ the four fundamentals of control? Explain.
3.  Outline Mr. Balsa's concept of automation in general terms.
4.  What general features would have to be included on the $100,000 machine to make it conform to Mr. Waterman's concept of automation?

# CHAPTER TWELVE

# Inventory Management
# and Control

For the next few chapters we shall be primarily interested in the control of material in manufacturing. Actually, we are concerned with the control of the "flow" of material from a "raw" state to a finished product. Most industries buy material, transport it to the plant, change the material into finished products, and sell and transport the product to the customer.

In our discussion of manufacturing controls, we will consider the planning for optimum quantities of material at all stages in the above-mentioned cycle, and the design and establishment of systems of control to attain this objective, as *inventory management*. The actual steps taken to maintain proper stock levels in "raw" material and finished goods we will refer to as *inventory control*. Control of the material as it is being processed will be covered in a later chapter on *production control*.

If we add to the above the activity of *purchasing*—or procurement—and *traffic*, which is generally considered to cover the movement of material to and from the plant, we complete our coverage of the entire flow cycle from the buying of raw materials to the delivery of the product to the customer.

With the continuous development of industry, the importance of this total field of activity in material is steadily increasing. Improved methods and mechanization have contributed to the trend of a greater material dollar content in each product and a reduced labor or machine dollar content. As a result in some concerns the functions of material control—inventory management, purchasing, inventory control, production control, and traffic—have been grouped under one function of *material management*.

## Inventory Classifications

Much as we identify the various functions in material management with the flow of goods, we can identify the different types of inventories or stocks of material maintained in a manufacturing plant. All plants use the same general classification of inventories, including raw material, purchased parts, work-in-process, finished goods, and supplies.

**Raw material.** A raw material inventory includes all items that after being received at the plant require additional processing before becoming an identifiable part of the finished product. It is obvious that the finished product of one plant—such as roll, bar, and sheet steel—may be the raw material for the next industrial purchaser.

**Purchased parts.** This classification of inventory is applied to component parts of a product that need no additional processing before being assembled into the finished product. In some cases this material may be classified as raw material inventory. More times than not, however, a separate classification is justified. The carburetor that is the finished product of one manufacturer becomes a purchased part to the automobile manufacturer.

**Work-in-process.** This classification of inventory is self-explanatory. All material that leaves either raw material stores or purchased parts stores enters the work-in-process inventory until the product is completed and placed in finished goods. This is the inventory of material the flow of which is controlled by production control procedures to be discussed later.

**Finished goods.** Again, this is self-explanatory—it is the stock of finished products. Generally speaking this classification applies to the quantities of finished goods that are held at the factory awaiting shipment. In many instances, however, it will include stocks held in warehouses owned and operated by the manufacturer, or stocks held on dealers' floors on consignment. In this latter case the value of the finished goods inventory is usually very high and a principal factor in the financial problem of the company. A typical example of this is the piston ring manufacturer who in addition to supplying the original car manufacturer also maintains large stocks of many different sizes of piston rings in automotive supply houses for quick service to the auto repairman. All of these stocks are on consignment; that is, the piston ring manufacturer does not receive any payment for the goods until they have been sold by the distributor.

**Supplies.** All the materials needed for the operation of the plant that are not used as parts of the finished product are classified as supplies.

The chapter on cost accounting identifies this inventory classification as "indirect material." On the other hand, the material that becomes part of the finished product is called "direct material." Lubricating oils, sweeping compound, light bulbs, and many other items fall into the supply category.

## Optimum Inventories

The complex relationship between modern industry and its market presents a real problem in the size of inventories that should be maintained. Large inventories in the face of declining sales mean lower profits. Small and inadequate inventories in the face of an increasing market demand may result in the loss of sales to competitors—and a decreased profit. Recognition of these conditions should indicate that the optimum inventory is not necessarily either the minimum or the maximum level of inventory; nor is it operation at a maximum inventory turnover.

**Inventory turnover.**   A very common index of inventory control is equal to the ratio of the value of the product shipped to the average investment in inventory for the same period.

$$\text{Inventory turnover} = \frac{\text{Value of product}}{\text{Value of average inventory}}$$

Obviously, the higher this index, the lower the inventory levels and the lower the cost of maintaining the inventories. Also it is obvious that a high index indicates a shorter manufacturing cycle with all the saving inherent therein.

Inventories represent a financial investment: the purchase price paid for the material, the cost of labor applied to goods that are in process or finished, and the cost of handling and storage. A determination of the proper ratio of this investment to operating profits can be used to establish optimum inventory levels for all classes of inventory. This may be done on a historical basis or by empirical means. On the other hand, it presents one of the most lucrative fields for investigation by use of the tools of operations research.

The planning of optimum inventory levels by inventory management requires close cooperation with the marketing function. Market trends must be predicted accurately and inventory levels adjusted—increased when increased sales are anticipated, and decreased when a lower sales volume can be foreseen. This is a problem in both marketing and manufacturing communications and again presents an opportunity for research and development of scientific means for determination of the proper solutions.

**Inventory models.**   In Chapter 5 we discussed the basic formula,

$$Q = \sqrt{\frac{2RS}{I}}$$

for determining an economic manufacturing lot size. This basic mathematical model also may be used to determine optimum inventory levels. However, it should be re-emphasized that this model does not take into account a number of factors (e.g., price discounts, warehousing costs, which may vary with maximum inventory rather than average inventory, budgetary limitations) and suitable mathematical models should be developed to fit specific situations.

In actual practice, the use of formulas is so time-consuming that they are not often used. Rather, tables, charts, and nomograms based upon suitable formulas, and more recently computers, are used to minimize computations.

## Factors Influencing Inventory
## Management and Control

Many factors influence inventory management and control. The principal effects of these factors are reflected most strongly in the levels of inventory and the degree of control planned in the inventory control system.

**Type of product.**    If the materials used in the manufacture of the product have a high unit value when purchased, a much closer control is usually in order. The jeweler is much more careful of his stock of diamonds than he is with a display case full of low-priced costume jewelry. This same principle holds in manufacturing.

If the raw material used in the product is available only in a short or controlled market, this may easily influence the purchase of this material and the level of inventories maintained. In the past this has been true in the tin can industry. Purchasing agents had to watch the world tin market very closely and buy large stocks of tin at the right time as controlled by the price rather than by the production demand of the factory producing the cans.

The manufacture of standard products as compared to production of custom items will influence the inventory problem. Standard products are usually made in greater quantities and at higher rates of production; also it is good practice to use raw material and purchased components that are standard items of the supplier. As a result, material is easier to obtain and the control of the inventory need not be so close. In addition, there is a greater chance of getting back the investment in the case of overages in stock.

Custom production is more of a "one-shot" affair. Close control is required to insure that special material and parts are not lost during manufacture. A special item worth only a few dollars may hold up the production of an order worth several thousands to the manufacturer. This situation occurs particularly when producing heavy equipment, such as special machine tools, large steam turbine generator sets, buildings, or ships. On the other hand expensive items, like motors and controls or other major components that represent a large investment, should not be received too far in advance of the date on which they are required. Inventory planning in such cases extends to include careful analysis of the delivery of material.

**Type of manufacture.** The close relationship between the type of product and the type of manufacture makes an analysis of the effect on inventory controls somewhat repetitious. Continuous manufacture is common to the manufacture of standard products. However, some standard products are made in batches. Where continuous manufacture is employed the rate of production is the key factor. Here, as a matter of fact, inventory control is of major importance and in reality controls the production of the product. The economic advantage of this type of manufacture is the uninterrupted operation of the machines and assembly lines in the plant. It is a major offense on the part of the inventory control personnel to have the plant shut down for the lack of material. Intermittent manufacture on the other hand permits greater flexibility in the control of material. Delays in the receipt of goods do not result in plant shutdowns, and steps can be taken to make up for lost time after the delayed items are received.

**Volume.** The volume of product to be made as represented by the rate of production may have little effect on the complexity of the inventory problem. Literally millions of brass bases for light bulbs are manufactured each month involving the control of only two principal items of raw material inventory. On the other hand the manufacture of a large locomotive involves the planning and control of thousands of items of inventory. Both the inventory problem and the difficulty of controlling production increase in difficulty with the number of component parts in the product, and not with the quantity of products to be made.

## Inventory Management

The planning of the control of inventory can be divided into two phases, *inventory management* and *inventory control*. Inventory management accomplishes the first phase, consisting of:

1.  Determination of optimum inventory levels and procedures for their review and adjustment.

2.  Determination of the degree of control that is required for the best results.

3.  Planning and design of the inventory control system.

4.  Planning of the inventory control organization.

The second phase of planning, which is the day-to-day planning required to meet production requirements, we shall discuss later as inventory control.

**Optimum inventory levels.**    Earlier, we discussed how inventory management is responsible for determining the inventory level that will result in the best profit. We have already pointed out that the trend of sales must be watched closely and inventories adjusted *in advance* of the change in rate of production as determined by actual sales. But this is not the only factor that must be considered by inventory management when determining inventory levels. The planning for the actual production of the product may involve problems of leveling production, that is, producing at a constant rate even though sales may fluctuate. In slack times products are built to stock; the finished goods inventory is increased to offset the demand anticipated when future sales surpass the production rate of the plant. The proper evaluation of this factor requires close cooperation with the manufacturing function.

The actual level of the inventory may also be improved by a close study of the manufacturing cycle. How long does it take a shipment of steel to pass from the raw material inventory to its appearance in the finished goods inventory as a part of the product? A study—in cooperation with the manufacturing function—of the ratio of actual processing time to waiting time may be most revealing; and when unnecessary delays are eliminated, the level of the work-in-process inventory may be materially reduced.

All these factors must be considered when inventory management seeks to establish the best inventory levels in all the different inventory classifications. It is easily recognized that this is a complex problem, which might be reduced to a mathematical model—as discussed in Chapter 5.

The interesting part of this problem is that it is not static. The picture is constantly changing; hence inventory management must plan for the review of the results as often as is necessary. Determination of what is "necessary" is in itself a problem. Some industries with consumer goods products such as food, soaps and detergents, and clothes have built up records such that reviews are needed only when major economic trends are apparent. There is considerably more risk in high inventory levels in industries manufacturing items such as the automobile or household appliances. In concerns with a multi-product line, trends of sales of each product must be watched; this is the case in furniture. Suffice it to say that once solved the problem of optimum inventory levels has just started!

**Degree of control.**    Inventory management must decide just how much control is needed to accomplish the objective. The least control—as evidenced by systems, records, and personnel—that is required to perform the function efficiently is the best control. This problem of the degree of control can be approached from the viewpoint of quantity, location, or time.

Economic purchase and manufacturing lot sizes are *quantity* considerations. These, however, are based largely on the economics of the supplier—the vendor in the first case and the manufacturing function in the second—and do not consider quantity from the viewpoint of the user. The user is concerned with the problem of optimum inventory quantities and the degree of control required for the maintenance of the planned inventory level. One approach that is gaining wide acceptance is the analysis of inventory requirements based upon the value of each item. Each item in the inventory is analyzed in relation to its yearly investment value. Almost inevitably it is found that a small percentage of the parts in the product represent a large portion of the inventory investment, while a large percentage of the parts actually require little investment of funds. For the "high-cost" items plans are made to keep close control of this inventory by accurate records of receipts and issues and by close coordination of incoming shipments with production requirements. On the other hand, the items that are "low-cost" may simply be ordered in larger quantities covering several months' need, no record being made of their issue to manufacturing. More stock is simply requested when the existing stock reaches a reorder point. The intermediate-value items may be established on a perpetual inventory but without the close control used for the high-value items.

From the standpoint of *location,* the degree of control is the number of controlled storages or control points that are to be established in the flow of the material. It has been generally recognized that inventories can be accurately controlled only if placed in locked storerooms and if written records are made for each change in the amount of each item. A full and strict compliance with such instructions often results in the inventory control being a burden instead of a tool to facilitate efficient production. One manufacturer of small radios has found that an accurate count of incoming material is the only control point needed in the operation of the plant until the assembled radios are accounted for in the shipping department. This, however, is an extreme case. How much inventory and of what classification requires controlled storage areas, and how often during the manufacturing cycle a record should be made of usage, is the problem of inventory management. The greater the number of controlled storages and control points, the greater are both the degree of control and the cost of maintaining it. (Again we should point out that the control of inventories in storerooms is referred to as *inventory control,* and the control of inventories during manufacturing processes is *production control.*)

The preceding paragraphs have to do with the adequacy of inventory control information. Frequency is another factor in degree of control. How often should inventory reports be made? One large plant makes a record of movement of all items in inventory every day, which through the use of machine records makes it possible to give management an accurate summary of the inventory each week or on a few hours' notice if requested. Is such control necessary? This is a problem of inventory management. In many large assembly plants movements of material through production control procedures are reported hourly in order that any possible delays on the assembly lines can be anticipated. Communications such as we have pointed out here are essential if a comparison of performance to plan—an essential step in any control procedure—is to be accomplished. The degree of timing planned for in any manufacturing situation must be justified by the prevention of losses that might be incurred if such communications were not in operation.

Having determined optimum inventory levels and the degree of control to be established to maintain such levels, it then is the problem of inventory management to design the required inventory control system and plan the organization for its effective operation. This team of system and personnel comprises the function of *inventory control* in a manufacturing organization.

## Inventory Control

The inventory control group puts the plans of inventory management into operation. These plans are seldom complete in every detail. The day-to-day planning required to meet production requirements—the second phase of planning for inventory control—is the responsibility of this group.

Another responsibility is the recording and reporting of transactions involving movement of material and of the effect on the different inventories. This is the picture of actual accomplishment by the plant of the flow of material. The comparison of this performance to the existing inventory plan, and the evaluation of the current material control situation, together comprise the next step in inventory control.

The most important step, however, is the initiation of corrective actions. As we have indicated before, modern manufacturing requires careful planning. When applied, these plans often go astray; manufacturing activities can be controlled only when such variations from the original plans are detected early enough to permit emergency measures that will bring production back into accord with the original schedule.

Later we shall discuss some of the techniques involved in inventory control. First, however, let us bring both inventory management and inventory control into better focus by restating and expanding the objectives of these functions.

### Objectives of Inventory
### Management and Control

The ultimate objective of all manufacturing controls is to realize a profit through the operation of the business. A more restricted objective of the control of material is to satisfy the customer by meeting the schedule for deliveries. Failure to deliver orders on time is one principal cause for loss of business and customers. Effective control of the material throughout the manufacturing cycle prevents this problem from arising.

Specific objectives of the inventory management and control group are to maintain optimum inventory levels and inventory turnover for operation of the business at maximum profit—also, through the control of inventories, to insure that the right material, in the right quantity and of the right quality, is made available at the right place at the right time. Let us discuss very briefly some of the ways in which this is done.

## Inventory Control Systems

Control of manufacturing inventories is basically a problem in industrial communications. Earlier we indicated that the complexity of these systems is directly proportional to the number of items in the inventories and to the number of transactions that have to be recorded to keep abreast of the movement of the material (thus maintaining the degree of control needed to meet the objectives).

When a close control of inventory items is needed, some form of perpetual inventory is usually employed. A sample perpetual inventory record is shown in Figure 12-1. This type of record is called a "perpetual" inventory because a new inventory figure is determined after each transaction, so that at any time the quantity in inventory can be determined. It is evident that the keeping of such records for low-cost items may often cost more than the stock of items is worth.

The basic information normally carried on perpetual inventory records includes:

1. *On order*. This part of the record shows the quantity of material ordered but not received. New orders are added in this column and receipts subtracted.

2. *Received*. All receipts are posted here; there is no balance quantity in this column.

3. *On hand*. This balance figure represents the quantity of the item that should be in the stock room. Receipts are added to this column and issues subtracted.

4. *Issued*. A record of all quantities issued to the factory is entered in this column.

5. *Allocated*. In this column are entered the quantities to be reserved for later issue for specific orders. Reserving of materials still in the stock room will insure their availability when they are needed on the manufacturing floor.

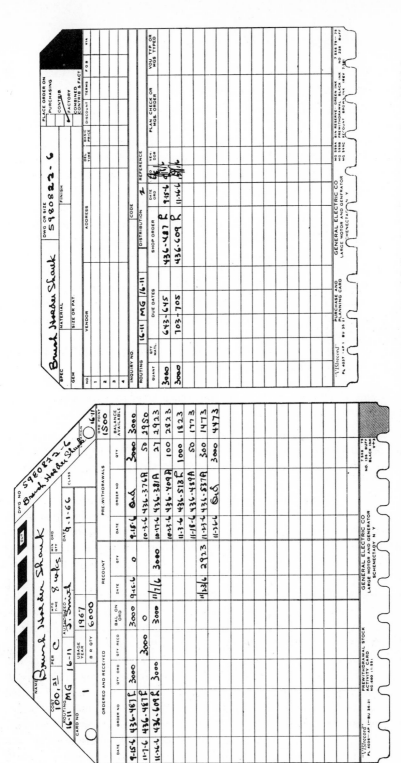

**Figure 12-1.** A typical perpetual inventory record. Note that it consists of a stock record card (left) and an accompanying order card (right); this latter card is forwarded to the order section to authorize the issuance of manufacturing orders. (Courtesy General Electric Co.)

6. *Available*. This is the quantity of material "on hand" that is still available for assignment to future orders.

The above is fundamentally the information that can be obtained from any perpetual inventory record. In essence it shows at any given time the quantity of material that can be assigned to incoming orders, the quantity that is being held for orders already received and in process, and the quantity of material that has been ordered from the vendor or the shop and has not yet been received by the stockroom.

Actual control of inventories is by the comparison of these levels of inventory to the planned level. Perpetual inventories are operated with a planned *minimum available* and generally with a *reorder quantity* that is greater than this value. When the availability reaches this reorder point a purchase requisition or shop order is originated and a record made in the "on order" column. Properly operated, a perpetual inventory system should never result in an oversupply of the item. However, a *maximum* is established, and if this should be approached by the availability quantity the situation should be investigated.

In some cases a value of the inventory is also recorded. This presents a problem in determining values.

**Pricing Inventories.** There are four basic ways to price inventories for accounting purposes:

1. *First in–First out* (FIFO). Under this procedure all issues are priced at the cost of the oldest lot until that lot is used up. Then the price of the next oldest lot is used, and so on. In other words, the first price into the inventory is the first price out of the inventory when issuing materials.

2. *Last in–First out* (LIFO). Under this procedure all issues are priced at the cost of the newest lot until that lot is used up. Then the price of the next to newest lot is used, and so on. If, in the meantime, another lot comes in, the price of this even newer lot is used when issuing material until the quantity involved is issued, at which time the price reverts to the next newest unused quantity.

3. *Average Value*. Under this system the values of issues are computed by using the weighted average cost of the material in stock. As new material is received at slightly different prices, a new computation must be made as to the weighted average cost of the total material on hand.

4. *Standard Costs*. A standard cost is established for each material and all disbursements are charged out at this standard value regardless of the price actually paid for the material. The standard cost is a calculation based upon possible replacement cost of the item, or an average of past purchase prices for that item. At any rate, the standard cost should be a good estimate of what the material in question should or will cost. As the price of new material varies from lot to lot, a difference between actual purchase price and disbursing price to the factory will be generated. This difference is

charged to an inventory variation account and is finally cleared out at the end of the year to the profit and loss account.

Two general points need to be made in connection with these pricing systems. The first point is that all systems deal with the problem of pricing and have nothing to do with the physical items themselves. A different set of policies will govern which items are being disbursed to the factory upon request. For example, if one is dealing with perishable items or with items that deteriorate with age, obviously one should issue these items on a first-in–first out basis. On the other hand, an inventory of lead slabs will undoubtedly be issued on the basis of last in–first out, from a practical point of view.

The second general point is the fact that these systems of pricing have only to do with the accurate costing of a manufacturing process. In the end, all such inventory accounts must balance out to zero, for one is not attempting to make or lose money at this point. Profit in a concern is made by charging a price for the final product over and above the cost of producing that product. In properly pricing inventories we are simply attempting to accurately determine the cost of production.

The FIFO and LIFO systems of pricing inventories have greatest application in businesses that deal with fairly large inventories of items held for long periods of time. Items where these systems come into use would include commodities such as corn, wheat, hides, and soybean oil; and perhaps steel bars and other units, more or less standard, which may be stockpiled over a period of time. In general, the preference is to use the LIFO system during a period of inflation and the FIFO system during a period of deflation. In following such a guide the business man is attempting to get rid of his highest-priced items first and thereby place himself in a more favorable position in the future. Shifting from one system to another, however, can only be done with the permission of the Internal Revenue Service.

For a great many inventory items the choice in pricing seems to be largely between the average system and the standard cost system. Many items are used up during an accounting period and so it becomes unnecessary to consider either a LIFO- or FIFO-type system. In addition, many items are not necessarily affected to any large extent by inflation or deflation, and any fluctuation in price that takes place is relatively minor. In these cases the average system is quite satisfactory although it has the drawback of repeated mathematical manipulations each time a new shipment is received. This is one of the reasons why many companies follow the standard cost system even though it results in a variation in inventory value that must be charged off at the end of the year.

**Basic communication forms.** The basic communication forms used in perpetual inventory control are:

1. *Purchase requisition.* This form is prepared by inventory control when new quantities of material should be ordered.

2. *Shop order.* This form is prepared by inventory control when quantities of material need to be made by the shop for stock.

3. *Receiving reports.* These are the record of material received by the stock room.

4. *Stores requisition.* This form authorizes the issuance of any class of inventory material from a controlled storage to the shop. These requisitions may be prepared by the production planner (as we will discuss under production control) or may be prepared by foremen, supervisors, or other authorized personnel.

These four forms are the principal sources of basic data in inventory control. Their names, although in common use, are not standardized. The name given to the form is not important; it is the function or purpose of the form that should be recognized at all times when evaluating its part in the inventory control procedure. Samples of these forms are shown in Figures 12-2 to 12-5.

**Figure 12-2.** A typical purchase requisition. (Courtesy Moore Business Forms, Inc.)

In many inventory control systems other forms may be used. One of these will be an inspection report. This report will record the quality of the material, which may be raw material received from a vendor, or else component parts, subassemblies, or assemblies produced by the factory. It is this form that ties inventory control with quality control. (The latter manufacturing control will be discussed in Chapter 15.)

One fundamental principle is that the *purchase requisition* is the *key to material control*. The careful study of the procedures originating this form, as well as of the personnel authorized to sign the requisition, will result in control of inventory at its very beginning. Inventory cannot exist in the plant unless raw material or purchased parts are ordered.

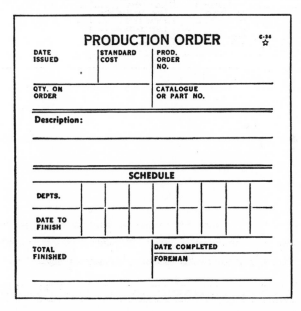

Figure 12-3. A typical shop order. (Courtesy McCaskey Register Co.)

**Inventory control records and procedures.**    A detailed discussion of the many records and procedures that are used for control of inventories is beyond the scope of this text. There are many commerical systems such as Ditto, McCaskey Register, Remington Rand, International Business Machines (IBM), and others too numerous to mention. Inventory records may be posted in ledgers or on cards with each entry made by hand. Basic data of inventory transactions may be punched on machine-records cards (see Figure 12-6) and the many calculations or reports prepared by mechanical or electronic interpreters and computers. The form of their reports are shown in Figure 12–7.

More recently, electronic computers with magnetic memory units are being used for perpetual inventory records. Large airlines maintain a record of available spaces on flights by such means. Large mail-order houses are using these new developments to advantage. Their use in manufacturing is also becoming more common.

The industrial engineer planning an inventory control system has many methods open for his consideration. He can also ask expert advice from the

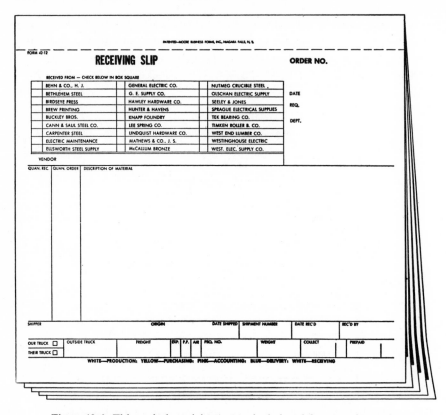

**Figure 12-4.** This typical receiving report is designed for reporting each receipt of goods. Listing of the common sources of supply simplifies the work of the receiving clerk. (Courtesy Moore Business Forms, Inc.)

systems engineers employed by the manufacturers of the equipment that we have discussed above. In the final analysis, however, whatever system or method is adopted, the economics of the situation must govern the choice— hand posting versus machine records, clerical payroll versus machine investment or rental.

**Bin control.** We have discussed perpetual inventories at length. Again, they are applicable to what we have previously designated as high- or intermediate-value inventory items. It is still evident that such procedures as we have touched on briefly are costly. For those items in which the cost of keeping such records cannot be justified a *bin control* is usually adopted.

In its simplest form the bin control is based on the minimum inventory quantity, reorder point, and maximum inventory quantity determined by the study of the numbers of items required to meet the production plans of the plant. When the material is stored in the bin, the quantity equal to the reorder

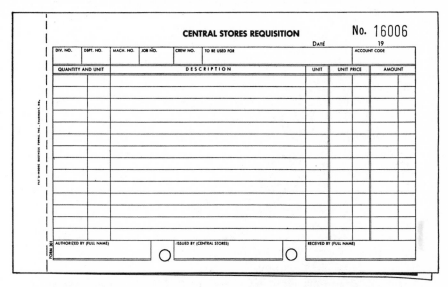

Figure 12-5. A typical stores requisition. Note the provision for the cost of the material withdrawn from the inventory. (Courtesy Moore Business Forms, Inc.)

quantity is boxed or sealed. Material is issued from the bin without any record being made of the quantities issued. At the point where the "reserve" stock is required to fill the stores requisition, a purchase requisition is prepared and forwarded to the purchasing department. Material will then be purchased to bring the quantity of stock up to the maximum. The minimum stock may also be sealed or boxed within the reserve or reorder quantity. If this second seal is broken it indicates that the material previously ordered should be expedited.

Bin control is a simple inventory control system. On the other hand, it should be realized that the minimums, as well as the reorder points, must be reviewed periodically in order that the stock of the item being controlled is maintained at an optimum level.

**Storerooms.**   Storerooms (or stock rooms) are areas in which material is held in controlled storage. All material received in the area is counted and recorded; none is issued without the proper stores requisition. Controlling materials in such a manner costs money in terms of space, personnel, and handling. These costs must be offset by better service to the factory and reduced loss of materials.

Proper location of storerooms must be related to the whole manufacturing process and considered when laying out the plant and deciding on the materials handling methods. Central storerooms require less personnel;

Figure 12-6. IBM Card. (Courtesy IBM.)

decentralized storerooms, located with material near its point of use in the factory, require more personnel but usually cost less in the handling of material.

Space allocated to storerooms is non-productive. As a result the general tendency is to reduce such space to a minimum, often crowding receiving and issuing areas until inefficiency results. There is a trend to evaluating storerooms on a cubic-foot basis rather than a square-foot basis—thus forcing the planner to utilize overhead space to a maximum.

In modern production plants storerooms are often replaced by overhead conveyors that are used for storage. This point was discussed in the chapter on plant layout. However, in again considering the entire situation, perhaps the problem in storerooms is whether or not they are needed at all. In many plants material is simply stored near the point of usage, without any controlled storage.

If storerooms are employed, the storekeeper should be held responsible for the material in his area. This can only be accomplished if the room is properly enclosed and locked and if only authorized personnel are permitted to handle the material being received or issued.

**Physical inventories.**   A physical inventory is used to verify the balances shown on the perpetual inventory records and to obtain a correct count on all items of inventory that may be on a bin control system. Physical inventories may be taken in two different ways.

Using the first method, plans may be made for a complete shutdown of manufacturing activity. During this period teams will count all material in storerooms and on the shop floor. Material in process must be identified as to the stage it has reached in the manufacturing process. After a complete physical count has been made, operation can be resumed. The effect of this procedure on production is self-evident.

The second method, a continuous physical inventory, offsets this problem. Under this system a certain number of items of inventory are counted

**Figure 12-7.** Machine printed IBM report. Note some of the cards used in the mechanical preparation of this report. (Courtesy IBM.)

each day or week and the perpetual inventory records adjusted accordingly. With careful planning the entire inventory can be checked with a minimum number of inventory teams and the entire job accomplished without disrupting production.

In addition to the adjustment of possible errors in the perpetual inventory the physical inventory is utilized to adjust the inventory accounts in the accounting department. This requires that the perpetual inventory be priced and extended. Again, the policy for this procedure must be established. First in–first out, last in–first out, average value, or some other procedure for pricing inventories must be decided upon. Once decided the policy must generally be adhered to—it cannot be changed from year to year.

## Inventory Control Organization

The number and the organization of the personnel required for the control of inventories in a manufacturing plant depend upon the system and procedure to be employed. It is only when the design of the inventory control system is completed that material management can plan the organization.

Sound organizational principles rather than any standard pattern should be followed in setting up an inventory management and control organization. Organization is a tool of management and not an end unto itself; it should be tailored to the circumstances and problems of the individual manufacturing enterprise.

Once the organization of the group is determined, the placement of the group in the overall manufacturing organization is a function of the importance of inventory management and control to the overall efficiency of the activity. We have already indicated how these functions may be grouped with production control, purchasing, and traffic under a manager of material. This still leaves the decision as to whether the materials manager should report to the manager of manufacturing or to the general manager. In Figures 12-8 and 12-9 we have shown two organizations, either of which may be effective.

**Figure 12-8.** A typical organization, with material management in the manufacturing functions.

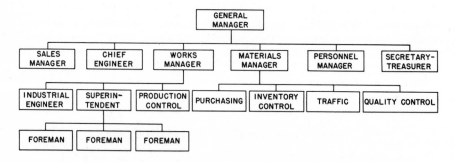

**Figure 12-9.** Another possible structuring of material management. A high material content of the ultimate sales dollar may justify this arrangement. Note the placing of control of the in-process inventory under the works manager.

## Future Trends in Inventory Management and Control

We have already mentioned some of the future trends in inventory management and control. Summarizing some of these and bringing them into focus, it is apparent that a more scientific approach to this problem is being developed.

First, the importance of establishing optimum inventories is becoming more evident. These values can be approached through the techniques of operations research.

Second, more attention is being given to the simplification of inventory control procedures. This in reality is simply another facet of work simplification.

Lastly, once work has been simplified, the elimination of hand labor by the use of machine records and electronic computers is gaining rapid acceptance.

## QUESTIONS

1. Under what circumstances might it be practicable to classify such items as nails, screws, paint, or glue as raw (direct) materials? As supplies (indirect materials)?
2. Assume that you are operating a corner popcorn stand. How would you go about deciding how much raw material (unpopped corn, popcorn oil, salt, and boxes) you should always have on hand—your optimum inventory of each item?
3. Select some product with which you are fairly familiar. Make a list of the parts or materials used in making this item and classify into:
   (a) High-value items.
   (b) Intermediate-value items.
   (c) Low-value items.
   What percentage of the total number of parts do you find in each classification?
4. What are the advantages of purchasing a week's supply of groceries at one time? In what way is this a form of inventory management and control? What factors affect the quantities that you purchase?
5. A manufacturer of small drill presses receives a rush order for two special machines. The base plate needed to build these machines is the standard base plate, K461. On checking the raw material of this item (K461) you find only 45 pieces in stock—all are allocated to stock order 4563. Explain what you would do.
6. You are setting up an inventory control system for a plant. One of the items is a small metal bracket purchased from a local source at $0.04 each. Your

annual requirements are for 10,000 parts. Explain whether or not you would put this item on a perpetual inventory. A bin control?

7. Does inventory control increase the profits of the business? Explain your answer.

8. Explain in general terms "when" an item on inventory should be reordered.

9. One company has eliminated all storerooms as such, and instead stores all material on the factory floor near the point of usage. Discuss the advantages and disadvantages of such a system.

## CASE PROBLEMS

### Curtis Heater Company

The Curtis Heater Company has been a manufacturer of water heaters for a number of years, and at present all operations are conducted in a number of small plants in the Chicago area. Recently a decision was made to build a new plant of sufficient size to house all manufacturing operations as well as company offices. Considerable time and effort has been put into the design of the new plant, in order to make it as efficient as possible.

One of the innovations under consideration for the new plant is elimination of all central storage area for incoming materials. Instead, at each work area, storage space will be provided for the incoming material needed for that particular operation. For example, sheet steel for heater shells is to be stored near the machine used for cutting the plates to the correct size. The same would be true for all other materials that are used in the product line. The only central storeroom would be used for maintenance supplies as well as for tools and dies.

Owing largely to differences of opinion among the executives as to the value of this system for storing materials, work has not started on construction of the new plant.

*Questions:*

1. What advantages can be claimed for this system?
2. What problems will be created by the installation of this system?
3. What approach should be used to resolve the problem?

### The Morrell Machinery Company

The Morrell Machinery Company is a producer of specialized pulverizing equipment. Almost all of its products are made to customers' special order, and vary from small units suitable for making face powder to huge machines used to pulverize rocks.

The company uses in its machines a number of bearings that are relatively expensive and that must be ordered from three to six months before the date they are needed. Because of the required lead time it has been the practice to keep a considerable inventory of bearings on hand. Under the circumstances it is almost impossible to predict future usage, but the general intent is to keep a six months' supply of bearings on hand at all times. Despite this considerable investment in bearings, however, it still has not prevented the delay of a number of orders as a result of an inadequate supply of the right kind of bearing for a specific job.

One difficulty seems to stem from the fact that frequently, when the storeroom clerk is busy with other work, the machine assemblers help themselves to the bearings needed. The assemblers, being more interested in machine assembly than in paper work, will seldom leave requisitions for the bearings they take.

*Questions:*

1. What steps can be taken to insure that bearings will be on hand when needed?
2. Is there any way the investment in bearing inventory can be reduced?

# CHAPTER THIRTEEN

# Purchasing

Purchasing is one of the key functions in the success of a modern manufacturing concern. As we indicated in the preceding chapter, no inventories are created until either raw material or purchased components are bought. This is true in most industrial enterprises, the exceptions being those primary industries that draw upon our natural resources such as coal, iron ore, and crude oil. Manufacturers' profits are affected by good purchasing practices based upon sound principles and effective purchasing procedures.

It has already been pointed out that the *purchase requisition* is the "key to material control" that initiates the purchasing activity. Later, we will discuss in greater detail how the judicious use of this form will contribute to better operating profits.

## Purchasing and the Control of Material

Purchasing is an important phase in the control of the flow of materials into the manufacturing plant from the vendor or supplier. The classes of inventory thus controlled are *purchased parts* and *raw material*. In addition, the inventory of *supplies* is controlled by the purchasing activity. We have already pointed out the importance of having material available when required for manufacturing operations, as well as the additional costs incurred if large quantities or expensive items are received too far in advance of the required date. Control of the flow of incoming material is an important responsibility of the purchasing group.

**234**

# Objectives of Good Purchasing

As a part of the overall material control activity, the statement of the objectives of the purchasing group will include most of the objectives of inventory management and control given in the preceding chapter. However, let us review them and then discuss these objectives from the viewpoint of the purchasing function.

The primary objective is to contribute towards the profits of the manufacturing activity. Another important objective is to insure the availability of materials so that delivery schedules can be maintained, thus keeping the customer satisfied. Specific objectives that support these goals are:

1.  Procurement of the right material, in the right quantity, and of the right quality.

2.  Receipt or delivery of this material at the right place and at the right time.

3.  Purchase of the material from the right source and at the right price.

In most organizations the purchasing department is not responsible for determining either what material is to be bought or its quantity and quality. Also, other manufacturing personnel may designate the time and place for delivery. However, for effective buying the purchasing group must be assigned the full responsibility and authority for the determination of the *sources of supply* and the *price to be paid*. Each of these factors will be covered in more detail when we discuss the purchasing procedure.

# Purchasing Procedure

The complete purchasing cycle consists of the following steps:

1.  Receipt and analysis of the *purchase requisition.*
2.  Selection of potential sources of supply.
3.  Issuance of *request for quotations.*
4.  Receipt and analysis of quotations.
5.  Selection of the right source.
6.  Determination of the right price.
7.  Issuance of the *purchase order.*
8.  Follow-up to insure scheduled delivery.
9.  Analysis of *receiving reports.*
10.  Analysis and approval of vendor's *invoice* for payment.

It will be evident as we discuss each of these steps that in many instances some of the steps will be bypassed. For example, when purchasing a standard item from an old and established source it is often assumed that the price and terms of purchase are right and the purchase order will be placed upon receipt of the purchase requisition. However, periodic review of such terms and prices is often warranted and may result in material savings in the cost of purchased material.

**Purchase requisition.** Purchase requisitions (see Figure 12-2, page 224) normally originate with the inventory control group. Regardless of the type of inventory—perpetual or bin—a reorder point is established. When existing stock reaches this level a purchase requisition is usually prepared and forwarded to the purchasing group. Minimum basic data that should be on a purchase requisition are:

1. *Material.* Specifications for this material are usually established by the product engineer. If they are not on file in the purchasing department, copies may have to be procured from engineering. In any event the purchase requisition must indicate clearly just what material is wanted and the required quality.

2. *Quantity.* The quantity is normally the amount that will bring the inventory back up to the maximum allowable as indicated on the inventory record. In the case of the purchase of raw material for processing, this maximum may or may not be the equivalent of the economic manufacturing lot size, Larger quantities may be purchased if the economic purchase lot is greater. We will discuss this a little later.

3. *Delivery date.* Sound inventory planning will usually result in the requesting of dates of delivery that can be readily met by the vendor. However, when the date cannot be met it is the responsibility of the purchasing group to notify the requisitioning group at once.

4. *Place.* Clear instructions as to the location for delivery are most essential, especially in larger plants where the receiving department may be decentralized. In any event the requisition is not "filled" until the material is actually placed in the inventory where the request was initiated.

Purchase requisitions should be carefully analyzed by the purchasing group to see that they are complete and understandable. In well-planned inventory control all material in purchased parts and raw material inventories will have been "accumulated" on the inventory record; thus the current total requirement for the item will be indicated by the purchase requisition. However, for miscellaneous supplies—particularly if not too well controlled —the purchasing group may accumulate requisitions until an economic purchase lot or quantity has been established.

**Sources of supply.** A purchasing group must constantly keep itself informed as to the best places to buy all items of material required. This is no small task. Effective purchasing cannot be accomplished on a status quo basis. It is true that in a going situation old established sources will in all probability be the best sources; however, new sources should be investigated from time to time and the performance of old sources evaluated periodically. If the purchase requisition is for a new item, then from the list of potential sources a selection should be made for inquiry by use of the *request for quotation.*

**Request for quotation.**   The title of this form is self-explanatory (see Figure 13-1). It is sent by the purchasing group to all the selected possible sources of supply. It should be as complete as a purchase order except for the statement of the price to be paid. It is up to the vendor to submit his price; this is his quotation. Because this form is so nearly like the purchase order form it is common practice to print in bold type across the form the statement: THIS IS NOT AN ORDER.

**Selection of the right source.**   Upon receipt of the many quotations from the vendors it then becomes the job of the purchasing group to select the right source. A comprehensive discussion of all the many factors that enter into this decision is beyond the scope of this book. Briefly, the purchasing group is interested in the reliability of the prospective source of supply. Questions such as these might well be posed: Will quality be maintained and shipments made on schedule? Does the vendor have adequate tools and equipment, trained personnel, and finances to handle the contract? What is the location of the vendor's plant in relation to the purchaser's plant; what means of transportation are available between these two points? These are just a few of the points that must be considered in the selection of the right source. Obviously, another major consideration is the price quoted. However, the lowest bid may not be from the best source in light of the factors mentioned above.

**Determination of the right price.**   This is a major responsibility of the purchasing group. Many factors influence what is a "right price" and again a comprehensive discussion is hardly possible. In a broad sense a right price is one that is "right" for all concerned—the purchaser, the vendor, the buyer's customer, and the public. Obviously, the purchaser must be able to buy material at a price that will enable him to sell his product at a profit—but profits are also essential to the vendor. Modern industry is too complex and interrelated to permit sharp buying tactics that drive prices to a level at which the supplier cannot make a profit. Profits are essential to our economic system, and as such essential to the public. In addition, the buyer must consider the reliability of the vendor and in some instances be willing to pay a little more for better service in quality and delivery. The final agreed price

Figure 13-1. A typical request for quotation. (Courtesy Moore Business Forms, Inc.)

may or may not be the quoted price; in some instances when all factors are considered it is conceivable that it may be higher. In any event, when the price is agreed upon the purchase order is issued.

**Purchase order.** A purchase order (see Figure 13-2), once accepted by the vendor, constitutes a contract for the delivery of the goods in accordance

**Figure 13-2.** On a typical purchase order such as this, detailed terms of the purchase contract may be printed on the reverse side of the original copy that is sent to the vendor. (Courtesy Moore Business Forms, Inc.)

with the terms of the purchase agreement. This constitutes a legal document, and it usually contains many other terms of agreement in addition to the quantity, quality, delivery, and price. Both state and federal laws influence purchase contracts, and as a consequence most firms have printed purchase order forms that comply with the laws under which they operate. Once the purchase order has been placed, it is usually the practice to notify the requisitioning source so that they can enter the quantity in the "on order" column of the inventory record.

**Follow-up and delivery.** The plan for the flow of material into a manufacturing plant is established by the purchasing procedure. Determination of the actual performance and comparison and evaluation of this performance can only be accomplished by effective follow-up of purchase orders.

The actual production and shipment of the purchased material and component parts are, of course, the responsibility of the vendor. It is in turn the responsibility of the purchasing group to make sure that the vendor is fulfilling these responsibilities. This assurance must be had far enough in advance of the actual specified delivery date so that corrective action can be taken when necessary to get materials into the plant as originally planned. This is usually accomplished by periodic follow-up of all purchase orders requesting the vendor to reconfirm his ability to ship the goods on schedule.

For a "tight schedule" it may also be necessary to follow the shipment or, if it is delayed, have the carrier—that is, the railroad, trucking line, or air freight service—trace the shipment and expedite its handling. This action is one of the most common tools of "corrective action." However, it should be realized that increased delivery costs are often involved. Other ways in which a purchasing group can take corrective action include transferring some of the orders to other sources of supply and assisting the vendor in his production problems. Docile acceptance of delayed delivery of material shifts control from the purchaser to the vendor. Corrective action—the final element in control—is often necessary to avoid this condition.

**Receiving reports.** Careful inspection of all incoming material and parts is essential to effective material control. The purchase order is the basic source of reference. Of course, it is often supplemented by engineering specifications and blueprints. The receiving report (see Figure 12-4 page 226) is a record of what is actually received; by comparing it to the purchase order variations in quantity can be determined. In passing it might be well to note that a variation in quantity is often agreed upon in the purchase contract; that is, in large quantity production plus or minus 5 per cent is often acceptable. If the shipment is "short" it simply means that the reorder point will be reached sooner. "Over" shipments delay the placing of the next order with the vendor. Shortages in excess of the allowed limit are usually placed on a *back order* by the supplier. Accumulations of back orders must be watched carefully by the purchasing group. Too often they are forgotten and all of a sudden stocks start building up beyond the planned maximum.

Inspection reports may be a component part of the receiving report, or they may supplement it. In any event a report on the quality of the purchased goods is necessary. Discrepancies either in quantity or quality should be called promptly to the vendor's attention. This is normally a function of the purchasing group, but it may be a joint activity of purchasing and inspection. It is an important function of purchasing because, in addition to providing purchasing with a valid measure of vendor capabilities, it insures that proper shipments are received. Control is effective only if quantity and quality of incoming goods are maintained.

**Payment of invoices.** Invoices received from vendors for goods shipped should receive the approval of the purchasing group. This is the final control step in the purchasing procedure. Invoices should be checked to insure that quantities billed conform with the quantities accepted by the receiving and inspection departments. It is also good practice to check the unit prices on the invoice and the extension of these prices to the total bill. Finally all discounts and other terms of the original purchase contract should be checked against the invoice. By this final control step payment is made only for the value of goods received.

Although the above description of the purchasing procedure is brief, we want to point out again that all the steps are not followed in every purchasing situation. However, purchasing procedures should be reviewed often to insure that the correct steps are being included.

**Purchasing work simplification.** The size and complexity of modern industry makes the job of purchasing correspondingly difficult. Like any other procedure, purchasing work can be analyzed, simplified, and improved by work simplification techniques. Study and the reduction of the number of forms used, as well as use of flow charts of the purchasing procedure, will not only increase the efficiency of the system but should reduce the cost of the purchasing operation. As with inventory control, the magnitude of the purchasing job and of all of the records involved is determined by the number of parts or items for which records have to be maintained. In a large company manufacturing a multi-product line of goods many thousands of separate purchase records must be maintained. Current trends are toward mechanization of these records by the use of electronic computers and similar devices.

## Value Analysis

Although value analysis has been discussed in the methods engineering chapter, it requires further amplification here inasmuch as the value analysis function is commonly thought of as a part of the purchasing activity. The basic idea of value analysis is simply that of a cost-reduction technique, and as such it might logically be treated as a part of methods engineering and of purchasing simplification as discussed in the previous section. However, as it is frequently used, purchasing people have a very definite role to play; so perhaps it is logical for value analysis to be under their general direction.

The objective of value analysis is to get more value from an item in terms of function. This can and should be done whether the item is manufactured within the plant or purchased from the outside. Outside purchases make it relatively easy to evaluate savings since there is often a difference in quoted prices for the items, and the difference is a real savings to the company. The General Electric Company pioneered value analysis work, and we cite one or two of their experiences to illustrate what is meant by this process.

One of their parts was a push button that had been made as a screw machine part. Investigation among suppliers resulted in a push button that could be cold-headed from aluminum wire. Cost of the item dropped from nineteen cents to two cents. Another part was a steel "J" bolt with threads on the long end. The drawing simply said, "cut thread." A rolled thread specialist studied the part and suggested that the words "cut thread" be removed from the drawing, thereby making it possible to roll the thread. This was done and the part could then be purchased at 1.5 cents as compared to 11.7 cents formerly. The company saved eighty thousand dollars.

In both of the cases cited the function of the part remained the same, and the new part could perform this function as well as the old. The difference was the tremendous savings in cost of purchase; hence value of the parts increased enormously.

## Value Analysis Approaches

A number of approaches have been suggested and used to facilitate the development of value analysis, and many of these approaches have been used in methods work for years. The reader is reminded, however, that any special techniques developed for value analysis should be applied to parts produced *by* the plant as well as to those purchased *for* the plant.

Asking questions is probably the simplest and most effective approach. The General Electric Company has worked out ten particular questions they feel are of value in analysis work, and they submit each part to the ten questions. Typical questions are: Does it contribute value? Does it need all of its features? Can a standard product be found that will be usable? If a part fails any of these questions the analyst makes a more detailed investigation. However, much depends upon the knowledge and ability of the analyst, and a part may not fail one of the test questions until after the analyst has thought of another possible solution to the function being performed by the part in question.

Frequently, a lucrative source of cost reduction can be found by asking questions of designers and others who may indicate specifications on blueprints and on bills of material. Designers who specify tolerances for a part much closer than those actually required in the application will obviously cost the company more money in either obtaining the quality specified or in purchasing that quality. The "J" bolt example mentioned earlier is a case in point. The designer most likely indicated "cut thread" for this part because he was unaware of any other way to produce the thread.

Making a comparative analysis is another approach used by value analysts. Investigation of all similar type parts purchased by the company might reveal some opportunities to cut costs of some of those parts. One analyst reviewed all the die castings purchased by his company and obtained clues as to how expensive features might be eliminated on some of the castings. Some analysts plot the weight of similar parts purchased against their cost per pound. If most parts seem to fall on a smooth line, but a few parts fall away from the line, these few might present opportunities for special investigation.

Supplier contacts are a technique of value analysis that may be of considerable value to the purchasing department. Any alert purchasing group is constantly looking for improvement and cost-reduction ideas from the various suppliers with whom they deal, and, likewise, suppliers are normally quick to make suggestions to their customers as to how they can save money. Some companies, however, have arranged supplier seminars to which they invite representatives from all their main suppliers and show special product displays in which every detailed part of their product is spread out on a table or attached to a display board. Suggestions for improvements are solicited from the supplier even if the supplier does not make the part in question. The point is that undoubtedly the supplier knows more about his particular specialty than any of his customers do, and therefore would constitute a valuable source of cost-reduction ideas.

Standardization is another approach of value analysis although standardization, as such, has been employed by industry for many years. To the extent that a value analysis of various parts and components suggests the possibility of standardization when it has been overlooked previously, value analysis must be given credit. One company reviewed 1447 items in its stock and found it could eliminate 794 of them through standardization. The savings were estimated at $102,000 over a two-year period. Value analysis programs are designed to reduce the cost of an item, but standardization programs may eliminate the item entirely. Certainly, costs cannot be reduced any lower than that!

## Factors Affecting Purchasing

In the following sections we will attempt to list the many factors that influence both purchasing practices and the results of the work of the purchasing group.

**Requisitioning authority.**   No purchases should be made without a properly signed purchase requisition. The first and most important step in the control of material is control of the authority to sign purchase requisitions. If "every Tom, Dick, and Harry" can requisition material, then the control of material is to all practical purposes lost before it starts. Authority to sign purchase requisitions should be limited to as few individuals as possible. In turn, within this group there may be limitations as to the type or value of the requisition that can be signed. In an office one of the stenographers might be authorized to requisition all office supplies to a monthly limit of $250 total. On the other hand the requisition for a $10,000 machine probably would require the signature of a member of top management.

**Type of manufacture.**   The type of manufacture influences the purchasing activity. Continuous manufacturing industries such as those that produce radios and automobiles normally operate extensive assembly lines. Material is scheduled to these lines with a minimum of stock inventory, and the majority of the control of material becomes the responsibility of the purchasing group. Also in this case there is a tendency to have a higher dollar content of purchased parts in the product. On the other hand, in an intermittent custom building situation the dollar content of purchased parts may be low; thus raw materials are the principal problem of the purchasing group. There is more flexibility in schedules for incoming material. However, for large machine tools and heavy apparatus delivery of major items is scheduled closely.

**Subcontracting.**   Items purchased on subcontracts are actually purchased parts or components. However, subcontracting generally takes place when it is not possible to produce the parts in the local plant. In the placing of this type of purchase order the vendor is in competition with the purchaser. Care must be exercised to insure that a valid comparison is made between the price quoted and the local manufacturing cost. Close cooperation between product engineering, manufacturing, and purchasing is prerequisite to a successful subcontracting program.

**Standardization of product.**   In the chapter on manufacturing processes we discussed the advantages of the standardization of products and their component parts. Often it is overlooked that suppliers also attempt to standardize the items that they sell. One of the principal activities of the purchasing group is to encourage the inclusion of vendors' standards in the product design of the purchaser's product. Material and labor costs can often be reduced by the purchase of standard sizes of items such as cold rolled bar steel, if the product designer accepts the finished surfaces and dimensions of the raw material as the finished specifications of the product that he is designing. This is only one example of the type of savings that can be effected through standardization. Another approach to standardization for the purchasing group is to analyze the standard stock items (such as screws, bolts, and nails) and request a reduction in the number of sizes required. Minor product-design changes can often be made to accomplish this end.

**Economic purchase lot.** Earlier, we mentioned the economic purchase lot. It is similar to the economic manufacturing lot that has been discussed in the chapter on manufacturing processes; only the cost factors are different. Larger quantities of goods can usually be purchased for lower unit costs. These savings must be balanced against the increased costs for the carrying charges, the same as in the manufacturing lot. In manufacturing we saved in setup costs; here we save in the cost of preparing the purchase order and on all the other steps in the purchasing procedure. Owing to the cost factors involved, it is easier to calculate economic purchase lot quantities.

**Short and controlled markets.** We have already said that purchasing people have to know where to buy the required items of material. Even if we know the purchasing source, it is not always easy to buy. Some markets are "short"; that is, there is not enough material to meet the demand. Other markets are "controlled"; material is available but total sales are restricted. This is particularly true in times of war; material is allocated to industries, and many items are virtually non-available for the production of civilian goods. Both of these situations present real problems to purchasing.

**Cancellations.** Cancellation of purchase orders cannot be totally avoided. If work has been started by the vendor, or he has made other commitments on the strength of the order, he may lose considerable money. It is the problem of the purchasing group to keep this loss at a minimum. Most purchase orders have standard clauses covering the liability of the purchaser as well as the supplier. Close cooperation between marketing, engineering, manufacturing, and purchasing is required to anticipate a situation that may result in order cancellations. The sooner purchasing knows of such a possibility, the better are the chances for making the cancellation with a minimum cost to all involved.

**Trade relations.** Modern industry is so specialized and extensive that many purchases are made from vendors who in turn buy back their material in the form of the purchaser's product. This is termed *reciprocal buying*. Too often this presents a real problem to the purchasing group. Vendors who are also customers may expect advantages in price, terms, or by other means. This detracts from the possibility of arriving at a "right" price. The maintenance of good trade relations under these situations is a real test of a good purchasing group. To be able to give the business to another source and still retain the goodwill of the customer-supplier is the objective of trade relations.

## Purchasing Organization

**The law of agency.** Purchase orders and contracts are signed by individuals each of whom acts as an agent of the company or corporation. As *agents* they have been given either *specific* or *implied authority* to act for their employer in the purchase of material, supplies, and services, or in any other type of agreement constituting a purchase. As a consequence the individual is known as a *purchasing agent*. If the purchasing agent is an officer of the company or corporation, the authority is probably specific; however, as the position is usually appointive, most purchasing agents have implied authority. In either event they act for the concern in the procurement of the necessary material and services.

**Organization structure.** There is no set pattern of purchasing organization. The same sound principles of organization apply to purchasing as to all the other functions in the manufacturing enterprise. The position of the purchasing group in the overall organization is largely dependent on the importance of the function. As we have already indicated, in cases where a large portion of the manufacturing dollar is represented by purchased material the senior purchasing agent may have vice-presidential status—and a large purchasing organization to perform the purchasing activities. In a small operation, on the other hand, we may find a single purchasing agent handling all the duties and reporting to anyone from the shop superintendent to the owner of the enterprise.

**Centralization and decentralization.** In large organizations—particularly in multi-plant industries—there is a problem of centralization or decentralization of purchasing activities. A full discussion of the advantages and disadvantages of each is beyond the scope of this book. However, decentralized operations are more flexible, and the trend toward increased decentralization of large corporations indicates that this method of organization is currently the most popular. Major purchase contracts for principal materials may be retained on a centralized basis to gain bargaining advantage.

**Purchasing group.** The purchasing group in larger organizations usually consists of several purchasing agents, buyers, expediters, and the necessary clerical and stenographic personnel. Organization of this group may be on the basis of product line or purchased material. If the latter, one agent may specialize in the purchase of steel, another in plastics, another in supplies, and so on, the entire organization being developed along these lines. In a multi-product manufacturing plant the purchasing organization may be divided so that certain groups do all the buying for a specific product and other groups for the other products.

Regardless of the basis of the organization pattern, its success will lie in the application of sound organizational procedure and in clear-cut understanding by all personnel of their duties and responsibilities.

## Purchasing Practices

It might be well to discuss a few of the many practices of modern purchasing.

**Salesmen relations.** Both purchasing and selling are rapidly gaining professional recognition. The continuing technological advance in both materials and processes requires that purchasing and sales personnel be more than "glad-hand artists"—they have to know what they are selling and what they are buying. "Sharp trading" is no longer accepted practice. As we indicated earlier in the chapter, purchases should be made at the *right price;* this can be done only if the buyer and the seller each respect the knowledge and integrity of the other. Courteous treatment of the salesman is prerequisite to modern purchasing practice. Unnecessary waiting can be avoided by giving appointments. It should always be remembered by the buyer that the salesman is one of his principal sources of current information as to markets, products, processes, and all developments in the field in which they are both interested.

**Discounts.** Industrial purchases are usually subject to cash, trade, and quantity discounts. Purchasing agents and buyers must be thoroughly acquainted with these discounts as they apply to the purchases that they are making—and with the legal aspects of same. To promote fair trade, free from restraint and undue favoritism, laws such as the Robinson-Patman Act, Sherman Act, and Clayton Act must be common knowledge of purchasing personnel, and their regulations must be observed. However, by the use of discounts within the legal limitations the buyer can effect substantial savings in money expended for material and services. Quantity discounts are allowed for the purchase of increased quantities of goods and are the determining factor in the establishment of economic purchase lots. Cash discounts are made for prompt payment of invoices; of late, however, it is often the practice to make an additional charge for lack of prompt payment. Trade discounts are applied to material that has a fixed list price, the discount being allowed to the trade or related activity of the purchaser.

**Multiple sources.** It seldom is advisable to "put all your eggs in one basket." Where large quantities are involved, a good purchasing practice is to develop more than one source of supply and divide requirements between these sources. This takes considerable tact on the part of the buyer but insures against the loss of delivery that may result from fire, flood, labor troubles, or other causes that may interfere with the production of a single source of supply.

**Forward buying.** Although quantities to be purchased are normally determined by inventory management and control, it is often advantageous to purchase quantities in excess of the normal operating requirements of the manufacturing plant. If operational considerations or supply conditions indicate the need for such an inventory reserve, these purchases are termed *forward buying*. Forward buying is done to build up a reserve stock and thereby avoid possible shutdowns, to increase purchase quantities and thereby take advantage of quantity discounts, to purchase in economical transportation units such as a carload or shipload, to protect against risk of material shortages, and in a short market to insure the procurement of material of the proper quality. Successful forward buying requires good judgment on the part of the purchasing agent and management.

**Speculative buying.** This is not forward buying. In speculative buying materials are bought and held for resale, the hope being to gain the advantage of a rise in prices.

**Gifts.** A real problem to the purchasing organization is the practice of vendors of making gifts to purchasing personnel, particularly at Christmas. Although such gifts are not intended as bribes, it is hardly realistic to assume that they will not influence the considerations of the buyer. Many concerns now prohibit their buyers from accepting such gifts. Good purchasing practice, of course, would not consider the acceptance of favors a valid reason for deciding where to buy.

## Purchasing Research

Purchasing research can be in three areas. We have already mentioned the accumulation of purchasing records by the purchasing group. Study of these records, catalogues, trade directories, and journals, and attendance at trade shows and conventions will yield extensive knowledge both as to material available and the best sources for the material and other services. Thus the object of the first two areas of purchasing research is to make available current and complete information as to (1) sources of supply, and (2) latest developments in material, equipment, and services. Full utilization of this information requires close communication with all the other functions in the organization; the product engineer is interested in material, the manufacturing engineer in processes and equipment, and others in material, equipment, and services as they affect their operations.

The third area of purchasing research involves procedures for more effective purchasing: better records and systems, better communications— not only with vendors but within the local organization—and other ways to do a better job of buying at less cost including the development of value analysis.

## Evaluation of Purchasing

As an overall activity it is difficult to make a valid evaluation of the purchasing activity. General measures such as the ratio of the cost of purchasing to the value of material purchased, or to the value of sales, may provide a useful index within a given organization. It is easier to set up measures related to the more specific objectives of the purchasing group: is the right material of the right quality and in the right quantity being procured from the right source at the right price and delivered at the right place and at the right time? Continuous rating of the accomplishment of these objectives will indicate the success of the function if not the total efficiency. Insofar as these objectives might be accomplished at excessive cost by the purchasing organization it might be well to consider the ratio of purchasing costs to the profits of the concern—but again so many other factors affect these profits that a valid measurement is highly doubtful. Continued research in the field of purchasing will no doubt result in effective ways of measuring this principal activity in the control of material in manufacturing.

## Traffic

Because it is normally the prerogative of the purchaser to designate the route and method of shipment of material, in smaller manufacturing operations the function of traffic management is included in the purchasing operation. However, in larger companies traffic departments are charged with traffic responsibilities.

Traffic functions include:

1.   The planning of routes for incoming material, including the selection of the method of transportation.

2.   Preparation of rate charts for delivery of material.

3.   Tracing of shipments to insure prompt delivery.

4.   Auditing and approval of incoming freight and other transportation bills.

5. Coordinating the receipt of large shipments to avoid demurrage charges.

6. Handling the adjustment of claims for goods damaged or lost in transit.

Traffic functions need not be restricted to incoming material. In many instances manufacturers accept the responsibility for delivery of their product to the customer. It is interesting to note that one of the first steps in the design of a large steam turbine generator unit is careful planning of the route of shipment. Traffic restrictions along the route, such as the dimensions of an underpass, often must be taken into consideration in the initial design stages. In such cases as these, traffic works closely with sales, engineering, and any other functions of the organization concerned with the delivery of the product to the customer.

## QUESTIONS

1. What are the advantages and disadvantages to the housewife in purchasing a whole side of beef and keeping it in a storage locker? Discuss in relation to the principles of purchasing.
2. Assume you are the salesman for a lumber mill. Prepare a brief statement to justify the price you are asking for your lumber.
3. What is the "right price" for an automobile? Outline all considerations involved.
4. Look at the pen or pencil that you are using. If you were buying this item in large quantities for the school or an office what would you want to know before placing your order?
5. The advantages and disadvantages of centralized and decentralized purchasing were not covered in the text of the chapter. However, prepare such a list, basing it on your own judgment. Justify each advantage and disadvantage.
6. As a purchasing agent you are considering placing an order for 5000 waste-baskets. One quotation is $1.07; another is $1.18; and a third is $1.56—these quotations being for each basket. What additional information do you want before placing your order? Explain your answer.
7. On what basis could a purchasing agent justify purchasing a standard item from one vendor at a higher price than he could purchase the identical item from another vendor?
8. Discuss the importance of the purchase requisition.
9. Using normal procedures, how does the inventory control department know that an item has been ordered? That it has been received?
10. Is it always good practice to have more than one source of supply? Explain.

## CASE PROBLEMS

### Midway Products, Inc.

The maintenance department of Midway Products sent a purchase requisition to the purchasing department for 75 heavy-duty push brooms. The purchasing department asked for quotations from three distributors and received the following bids:

Distributor A: $2.00 each list, less discount of 30%
Distributor B: $2.15 each list
   Discount schedule:
      10 or more–20%
      50 or more–30%
      100 or more–35%
   Terms: 2%—10: net 30
Distributor C: $2.00 each list, less 20% and 10%

*Questions:*

1. Assuming the quality is the same for all three, with which distributor should the purchasing department place the order?
2. Would your answer have been the same if the item had been bearings for a special production order, rather than brooms? Explain.

### Bassett Soap Company

The Bassett Soap Company manufactures and sells soap powders for both household and industrial uses. During the production and packing processes a quantity of fine dust is created; this dust is removed by means of a vacuum dust collecting system. Inserted in the air stream for the purpose of trapping the fine dust particles are filters composed of several hundred cotton bags. If any of the filter bags break, dust is blown into the atmosphere; the result is a loss of soap as well as an annoyance to the community surrounding the plant.

Over the years, plant personnel have learned that the bags last for a little over a year, after which small holes begin to appear. It has therefore been the regular practice of the plant to install a complete new set of filter bags each year during the two-week vacation shutdown.

The plant regularly placed a purchase requisition for the replacement bags about 3 months ahead of the scheduled shutdown, and the same quality of bag from the same supplier had been ordered and used for a number of years. To fill the last requisition, however, the purchasing department placed the order with another supplier. It did this on the claim of the second supplier that their bag possessed the same quality characteristics but cost 22 cents less per bag.

The new bags were installed as usual during the last shutdown. Two weeks later some of the new bags began leaking dust as the result of holes that had developed. Four weeks later an emergency order was placed with the former supplier for a whole new set of bags, and a crew of six men was brought in on a week end at overtime rates to install the new set of filter bags.

*Questions:*

1. What was wrong with the procedure followed by the purchasing department? What should they have done?
2. Should the plant personnel have accepted the substitute bags since they were not what had been specified on the requisition?
3. What are the extra costs involved as a result of the incident?
4. Who should be charged with these extra costs?

# CHAPTER FOURTEEN

# Production Planning
# and Control

In the preceding chapters we have discussed the control of static inventories —raw material, purchased parts, finished goods, and supplies—by the use of inventory management and control. The control of the flow of materials into the plant was covered in the chapter on purchasing. *Production planning and control* is concerned with the control of the work-in-process.

Inventory management and control, as well as purchasing, are controls of material. The scope of production planning and control is broader. To control work-in-process effectively it becomes necessary to control not only the flow of material but also the utilization of men and machines.

## Production Planning and
## Control Functions

All of the four basic phases of control of manufacture are easily indentified in production planning and control. The *plan* for the processing of materials through the plant is established by the functions of *routing*, *loading*, and *scheduling*. The function of *dispatching* puts the plan into effect; that is, operations are started in accordance with the plan. *Actual performance* is observed and recorded by the function of *reporting* or *follow-up*. Actual performance is then compared to the planned performance and, when required, *corrective action* is taken. In some instances *replanning* is necessary to insure the effective utilization of the manufacturing facilities and personnel. Let us examine more closely each of these functions.

**Routing.** The determination of *where* each operation on a component part, subassembly, or assembly is to be performed results in a *route* for the movement of a manufacturing lot through the factory. Prior determination of these routes is the job of the routing function.

Routing may be generalized or detailed. In a large manufacturing works area a general route may be established by buildings. More commonly it is established by departments, such as machine shop, assembly, finishing, inspection, or others. *Detailed routing* would indicate the specific work station or machine to be used for each operation. Regardless of the detail in which the routing is initially planned, a precisely detailed route eventually has to be determined. For example, if a lot of parts is routed to the machine shop for processing, and there are three separate operations to be performed in that department, the decision by the foreman or dispatcher as to the three machines to be used for the job determines the detailed route of this lot of goods through the machine shop. However, this is too often a last-minute decision, depending only on the availability of the machines instead of being guided to an effective degree by planning. On the other hand, in continuous manufacturing when a processing line of machines is used, or an assembly line is installed, the route of the materials must conform to the line; the routing function was incorporated in and accomplished by the original layout of the plant. The source of basic information for the routing function is the standard process sheet, which indicates the type of machine or work station required for each operation in the process.

**Loading.** Once the route has been established, the work required can be *loaded* against the selected machine or work station. The total time required to perform the operation is computed by multiplying the unit operation times given on the standard process sheet by the number of parts to be processed. This total time is then added to the work already planned for the work station. This is the function of *loading* and results in a tabulated list or chart showing the planned utilization of the machines or work stations in the plant.

One of the problems in loading is the amount of utilization that can be planned for a given workshift, such as an 8-hour day. For example, owing to factors such as maintenance, repair, setup, and others, 85 per cent utilization is considered a good average for machine tools. Under these conditions only 6.8 hours of productive work should be loaded for an 8-hour shift. But if workers can be expected to earn an average of 20 per cent bonus—and the 6.8 hours is based on standard times—a total of 8.16 standard hours can be loaded against an 8-hour shift.

Thus far we have indicated that loading is by work station or machine. This is *detailed loading*. Loading may be generalized, like routing; that is, groups of machines or departments may be loaded as a single unit. For example, all lathe work may be loaded against the lathe department, or all milling to be done simply charged to the group of milling machines in the plant. The objective of the loading function is to maintain an up-to-date picture of the available capacity in the plant. If a general type of loading is adequate this should be used and no further breakdown of loads made. Often it is sufficient to keep load charts on only the critical productive units or departments and assume that all other departments have adequate capacity to keep abreast of the production rate.

Obviously load charts would be referred to when determining routes of orders through an intermittent manufacturing plant. In this case the route is influenced by the availability of a department, machine group, or work-station capacity.

**Scheduling.** Scheduling is the last of the planning functions. This function determines *when* an operation is to be performed, or *when* work is to be completed; the difference lies in the detail of the scheduling procedure. In a centralized control situation—where all routing, loading, and scheduling for the plant is done in a central office—the detail of the schedule may specify the starting and finishing time for an operation. On the other hand, the central schedule may simply give a completion time for the work in a given department (as in the machine-department situation mentioned above). Here the foreman would be held responsible for having all three operations completed by a given date. The detailed schedule for the completion of each of the three operations in the machine department would have to be determined by the foreman or the dispatcher. Again, this is more than likely to be an after-the-fact determination rather than sound planning. However, as with routing, all general schedules eventually become detailed schedules.

Prior determination of *when* work is to be done is the function of scheduling.

**Combining functions.** While it is easy to define "where" as *routing*, "how much work" as *loading*, and "when" as *scheduling*, in actual operations these three functions are often combined and performed concurrently. How far in advance routes, loads, and schedules should be established always presents an interesting problem. Obviously, it is desirable that a minimum of changes be made after schedules are established. This objective can be approached if the amount of work scheduled for the factory or department is equal to or slightly greater than the manufacturing cycle. For optimum control it should never be less than the manufacturing cycle.

If it normally takes three days for work to pass through a department, the work load should never be scheduled less than three days in advance. The total work load ahead of the department might be three or six months. Obviously, scheduling all of the work load in advance would not be necessary for the effective day-to-day operation and would present a problem if changes in schedule were necessary.

Scheduling too far in advance of operating requirements introduces a degree of inflexibility in the control of production. Load charts may be maintained in addition to the schedule charts showing the total load ahead. This is justified only if it is necessary to identify critical shortages of productive capacity in advance of the normal scheduling procedure. Work can be loaded against a work station or department without being scheduled—but it cannot be scheduled without being loaded.

**Dispatching.** Authorizing the start of an operation on the shop floor is the function of dispatching. This function may be centralized or decentralized. Again using our machine-shop example, the departmental dispatcher would authorize the start of each of the three machine operations—three dispatch actions based upon the foreman's routing and scheduling of the work through his department. This is decentralized dispatching. Another case of decentralized dispatching would be where the departmental dispatcher dispatched work based upon plans of a central control office, advising them only when the work had been started. In a centralized dispatch situation, when a job had been completed on a machine or at a work station the departmental dispatcher would call a central dispatcher and ask what job should now be started; the actual assignment of work thus would remain at a central point.

**Reporting or follow-up.** The manufacturing activity of a plant is said to be "in control" when the actual performance is within the objectives of the planned performance. When jobs are started and completed on schedule there should be very little, if any, concern about the meeting of commitments. Optimum operation of the plant, however, is attained only if the original plan has been carefully prepared to utilize the manufacturing facilities fully and effectively.

The effectiveness of any production control system is dependent upon timely and adequate information regarding actual performance. This basic information normally originates with the dispatcher. Although the reporting of jobs completed is important, it is of even greater importance that delays in production be anticipated and work that is lagging behind the anticipated production rate be reported promptly to the production planning and control function. A good production control procedure makes this reporting, and a system of counter-checks by follow-up, automatic. The system by its very procedures will call attention immediately to danger points in the manufacturing activity.

Effective corrective action is based upon these reports. Realistically, some jobs will always be running behind schedule—others may be ahead of schedule. Careful analysis of the situation may indicate how a few changes can bring the late work back on schedule by using productive capacity made available by the jobs that are running ahead of schedule.

**Corrective action.** This is the keystone of any production planning and control activity. A plant in which all manufacturing activity runs on schedule in all probability is not being scheduled to its optimum productive capacity. With an optimum schedule, manufacturing delays are the rule, not the exception. However, if these delays are accepted without concern and schedules revised, then the actual output of the plant, not the management, is controlling the production. It is by corrective action that management maintains full control. Means are found to get the work back on the original schedule. Jobs are shifted to other machines or work stations, overtime is authorized, and extra help is put on the job. There are many ways in which production emergencies can be met.

**Replanning.** Replanning is not corrective action. Replanning revises routes, loads, and schedules; a new plan is developed. In manufacturing this is often required. Changes in market conditions, manufacturing methods, or many other factors affecting the plant will often indicate that a new manufacturing plan is needed.

In summation: Production planning and control plans, in advance, the route of work through the plant, determines the amount of productive capacity required to do the work, and—based upon the availability of this capacity—schedules all phases of the work so that the plant will be effectively utilized. Once these plans are established, production control provides the means to keep track of manufacturing activity and when necessary take corrective action or replan. It is simple: "Make your plan, then work your plan!"

We have discussed each of the production planning and control functions, emphasizing that their application in manufacturing is not uniform. However, it should be remembered that at no time can any function be eliminated. Routing, loading, scheduling, dispatching, reporting, and corrective action are component parts of any effectively managed manufacturing operation. This is just as true of a streetcorner popcorn stand operated by one man as it is of a large concern employing many thousands and producing a wide line of products. Production planning and control of itself is a simple procedure; it becomes complex only in its application to a manufacturing situation. Decisions must be made as to the degree of control necessary, centralization or decentralization of the production control procedures, and when the various functions are to be performed.

Let us now discuss some of the factors that affect the application of production planning and control procedures and techniques.

# Factors Affecting Production Planning and Control

The factors that affect the application of production planning and control to manufacturing are the same as the factors we have already discussed as affecting inventory management and control. Let us briefly review these in relation to production planning and control.

**Type of product.** Again, it is the complexity of the product that is important, not what the product is, except as this may in turn relate to the market being served. Production control procedures are much more complex and involve many more records when manufacturing large steam turbine generator sets or locomotives to customer orders than when producing large quantities of a standard product involving only a few component parts, such as electric blankets, steam irons, or similar small appliances. Of secondary importance is the type of market being served. A seasonal market may require careful planning of production for maximum output during a limited period of time (this is particularly true in the canning industry). On the other hand, a seasonal market in rubbers and overshoes may be offest by planning to manufacture to stock during the slack seasons. Manufacturing to stock, as opposed to producing only to the customer order, presents an entirely different situation.

**Type of manufacturing.** This is probably the most important influencing factor in the control situation. For a large continuous manufacturing plant producing a standard product we have already indicated that the routing was included in the planning of the plant layout. Also the detailed scheduling of work between operations was accomplished when the many production lines were balanced. As a result, about all that is left for the function of production planning and control in the operation of the plant is to set up key control points in the lines and, once manufacturing is started, to make sure that all the many feeder lines are producing adequate stock so that no shutdown occurs owing to lack of partially completed component parts or subassemblies. As we have mentioned previously, this situation is for all practical purposes a control of materials at the start of the lines.

Intermittent manufacture of multi-product lines presents a quite different problem. Optimum operation of the factory is dependent upon the effective use of all of the functions of production planning and control. All production planning and control functions occur after the manufacturing order is approved; this cannot be avoided. Depending upon the degree of control desired, the length of the manufacturing cycle, and the decentralization or centralization of control wanted, a production planning and control system must be developed that will result in the optimum operation of the intermittent plant.

Once more, the volume produced, or the size of the factory, is not a factor directly affecting the problem of the design of the control system.

# Objectives of Production Planning and Control

The ultimate objective of production planning and control, like that of all other manufacturing controls, is to contribute to the profits of the enterprise. As with inventory management and control this is accomplished by keeping the customers satisfied through the meeting of delivery schedules. Specific objectives of production planning and control are to establish routes and schedules for work that will insure the optimum utilization of materials, men, and machines and to provide the means for insuring the operation of the plant in accordance with these plans.

# Production Planning and Control Procedures

A detailed discussion of all the techniques and procedures of production planning and control is beyond the scope of this text. We have already indicated that these practices will vary widely from plant to plant. Further, the many ways in which each of the functions might be carried out in practice were indicated earlier in this chapter.

It might be well, however, to point out again that any production planning and control procedure should meet the bench marks of good control practice that were outlined in Chapter 11 on manufacturing controls. Though no production control function can be entirely eliminated, the least control that results in effective operation of the factory is the best control. It must be remembered that production planning and control systems should be tools of management. The objective is not an elaborate and detailed system of controls and records; the objective is the optimum operation of the plant for maximum profits.

## Production Planning and Control Systems

Because production planning and control is the control of the work-in-process, the system will in effect tie together all previous records and forms developed in all planning for the manufacture of the product. In like manner this activity brings together all the other functions of the enterprise—marketing, engineering, personnel administration, finance, and manufacturing. Later in our brief discussion of organization we will point out that the production planning and control group is most generally a subgroup of the manufacturing function.

Basically, production planning and control systems are industrial communications established to insure proper relationship between market forecasts, customers' orders, manufacturing capacity and rates of production, and shipments.

Let us take a quick look at some of the records or forms that enter into the consideration of the production planning and control group in the performance of their duties. Those records and forms prepared by other functions are said to be sources of basic data—of information that is needed by production planning and control for the effective use of its own records and forms.

**Market forecast.**    The market forecast will be discussed in the chapter on marketing. Its value to production planning and control is that it will indicate future trends in manufacturing requirements. Workshift policies, plans for increase or decrease of manufacturing activity, or possible plant expansions may often be based upon the market forecasts, and in turn affect the planning of the production planning and control group.

**Customer order.**    These are received initially by the sales department. This is the *first* of five types of orders involved in a manufacturing situation. Although there is no uniform terminology for all five of these classes of orders, each can be readily identified by what is ordered or authorized by the form. By a *customer's order* we mean an agreement to purchase the product; this becomes a legal contract once the order is accepted by the manufacturer. It is really the customer's purchase order (see Figure 13-2). Such orders are usually forwarded to production planning for confirmation of the delivery date requested by the customer. This delivery date—or shipping date—must be carefully considered and agreed upon, often without an analysis of the order and its integration into load or schedule charts. If the request for delivery cannot be met, the matter should be promptly referred back to the sales group for further discussion with the customer before accepting the order.

**Sales order.**    This is the *second* of the five classes of orders. It is a rewrite of the customer's order specifying what he has purchased—product and quantity—and authorizing shipment of the goods to the customer. Multiple copies are prepared and all interested functions are furnished a copy. Sales orders may be written by marketing, inventory control, or production control. In any event they are processed through the finished goods inventory (if one is maintained). In a custom manufacturing situation these orders are the base upon which all activity in preparation for manufacture is made. If items are to be shipped from stock, the shipping department will use this order as a requisition to draw the products from finished goods and to package and ship the order. In other cases these orders are accumulated until economical manufacturing lots are on order and a stock order placed with the plant to manufacture the goods, shipment then being made as the material is received in the shipping department. In all cases, however, the production planning and control group must use these orders as the basic data for the shipping promises to which they are committed.

**Stock order.**   This *third* class of order is not always used. In the preceding paragraph we indicated how it may be used after sales orders accumulate to an economical manufacturing lot. It is, of course, the principal order when manufacturing to stock. It will authorize production in anticipation of future sales. It may be issued by inventory control, or by marketing, but should always be confirmed by the marketing function to insure that surpluses of products are not made that will result in loss owing to obsolescence. As with the sales order, the production planning and control group will determine a completion date for stock orders and from this file will keep track of the dates for which they have commitments.

**Shop order.**   This *fourth* class of order deals with the manufacture of component parts. Customer orders, sales orders, and stock orders are for the finished product. In the preceding chapters we discussed how by product explosion the requirements are established for component parts to build assembled products. Based upon the shortages that appear in the component parts inventory, shop orders are prepared by inventory control. This order (see Figure 12-3, page 225), when passed on to the production planning and control group, becomes the basis for the majority of routing, loading, and scheduling.

**Standard process sheet.**   This form, which is prepared by process engineering, has been discussed in detail in Chapter 5. Also, in discussing the function of routing we pointed out that this is the source of basic data as to the type of machine to be used, the time required for processing, and the sequence of operations in the manufacture of the product. Routing and scheduling of shop orders, as well as loading of work stations in advance of scheduling, depend upon up-to-date standard process sheets being available to the production planning and control group.

**Engineering specifications.**   Blueprints and bills of materials are used by production planning and control when they become a component part of the packaged instructions issued to the shop through the control office.

One good planning procedure is to accumulate all necessary data for a shop order in a single package—the standard process sheet, the blueprint, the bill of material (if an assembly operation is involved), the route sheet, and possibly the schedule for the production of the order. This complete package is then held pending the dispatching of the work to the shop.

This completes a brief review of the basic-data forms used by production planning and control. The following forms and records are prepared by the production planning and control group.

**Route sheet.** This is the form upon which the route of a shop order is indicated. In practice this form is generally combined with one of the other forms in the system. For example, the shop order, the standard process sheet, and the route sheet are often one piece of paper—and usually called the *shop order* or the *manufacturing order* (see Figure 14-1).

| SPECIAL MFG. CO. | PRODUCTION AND MACHINE TOOL ROUTING | | | | | | | | | | | MIDWEST, IND. |

PART NAME __Cover - Gear Housing__ _____ PART NO. __728L5__

MATERIAL __Cast Iron__ ____ROUGH SIZE __As Cast__ ROUGH WEIGHT __3 pounds__ DATE EFFECTIVE __8/15/66__

MODEL __E-33__ _____QUANTITY PER ASSEMBLY ____1____ SHEET NO. __1__ OF __1__

| OP. NO. | DEPT. NO. | OPERATION NAME | MACHINE NAME | MACH NO. | TOOLS & GAGES | TOOL NO. | GROUP NO. | REQ. NO. | STD. TIME | | CAP EACH MACH. PER HOUR |
|---|---|---|---|---|---|---|---|---|---|---|---|
| | | | | | | | | | MINS. | HRS. | |
| | 307 | Receive | Receiving Dept. | | (1) Foundry Insp. Fixture | 728L5-T-1 | | | | | |
| | | | | | (1) Cutter Driver | 728L5-T-2 | | | | | |
| | 327 | Laboratory test | Laboratory | | (2) Cutter | 728L5-T-3 | | | | | |
| | 317 | Inspection | Bench | | (1) Receiving Insp.Fixture | 728L5-T-4 | | | | | |
| | 338 | Stock | Stock Room | | (1) Tool | | | | | | |
| 5 | 355 | Locate-from (3) Foundry pads on edge of flange and on (3) foundry pads on back side of flange. | 12" x 5' Leblond Engine Lathe. | 777 | Layout (1)Face Plate Fixture | 728L5-T-5 | | | 3.60 | .06 | 13.89 |
| | | Face end of casting to 1.3915 ± .005 from foundry pads on back side of flange. | | | (1) Tool Bit #DSF-2-NF | 728L5-T-6 Std. | | | | | |
| | | Finish face joint face of bolt flange to .829 ± .003 dim. from end of casting. | | | (1) Flush Pin Gage to Check 1.3915 ± .005 dim. | 728L5-T-7 | | | | | |
| | | Leave 1/32 rad. in corner. Finish turn pilot to 3.998 ± .001 dia. Leave 1/32 radius in corner. | | | (1) Flush Pin Gage to check .829 ± .003 dim. | 728L5-T-8 | | | | | |
| | | Break edges. | | | (1) 3.998 ±.001 Snap Gage. | Std. | | | | | |
| 10 | 366 | Final Inspection. | Bench | | (1) Flush pin gage to check 1.3915 ± .005 dim. | 728L5-T-7 | | | | | |
| | | | | | (1) Flush pin gage to check .829 ± .003 dim. | 728L5-T-8 | | | | | |
| | | | | | (1) 3.998 _.001 snap gage. | Std. | | | | | |

| REMARKS: | | | ENGR. GROUP INDEX | ASSEMBLY NO. 93724 | WRITTEN BY C.E.M. | TOTALS PER PC. | | .06 | |
| | | | | | | PER JOB | | | |

Figure 14-1. A typical Standard route chart. (From L. E. Doyle, *Tool Engineering Analysis and Procedure*, Englewood Cliffs, N. J.: Prentice-Hall, Inc., 1950. Reprinted by permission.)

**Load charts.** These are prepared to show the productive capacity that has been "sold"—and at the same time the available productive capacity (see Figure 14-2). As we pointed out when discussing the function of loading, these charts may be prepared for each workstation or machine in the plant;

or they may be for groups of machines or departments. One large manufacturer of heavy apparatus actually loads the entire plant, using as his scale the kilowatt capacity of the equipment he is producing. Load charts, as such, are not too common. This function is usually combined with scheduling, and only one set of charts is maintained: the schedule charts.

| MACHINES | DAILY MACHINE CAPACITY (HRS.) | ASSIGNED ORDERS (HRS.) AUGUST | | | | | | |
|---|---|---|---|---|---|---|---|---|
| | | *1* | *2* | *3* | *4* | *5* | | |
| *TURRET LATHES* | *160* | *160* | *152* | *136* | *160* | *92* | | |
| *SHAPERS* | *24* | *24* | *24* | *24* | *0* | *0* | | |
| *PLANERS* | *8* | *8* | *6* | *6* | *6* | *6* | | |
| | | | | | | | | |

Figure 14-2. A portion of a machine load chart. (From P. O'Donnell, *Production Control*, Englewood Cliffs, N. J.: Prentice-Hall, Inc., 1952. Reprinted by permission.)

**Schedule charts.** Schedule charts are prepared to show the planned utilization of departments, groups of machines, work stations, or machines in the plant. These charts not only show what work is ahead of each productive unit, but also when it is planned that the work shall be done. They are usually a graphical representation—such as the Gantt charts shown in Figures 14-3 to 14-6.

In discussing scheduling we pointed out that "firm" schedules (schedules not subject to change) should never be less than the manufacturing cycle, and for flexibility should not be too much greater than this period of time. A usual solution is to prepare these schedule charts for a three-months period, the first month on the chart being a firm schedule, the last two months being tentative.

In a large shop it becomes quite a problem to transmit schedule information to the many departments involved. We have indicated that it might be included in the shop order package. This solution has the disadvantage that if changes in schedules have to be made there is a lot of paper floating around the shop that has to be located and changed. Another solution is to furnish each department with the portion of the schedule chart that applies to that manufacturing unit. Finally, the schedule clerk might draw off the chart a job priority list for each unit or work station and furnish only these lists to the shop; this has the disadvantage that the departmental dispatcher will not be as apt to anticipate work running behind schedule.

Another problem in schedule charts is the matter of keeping them up to date. At least, it is often believed to be a problem. But if we accept the concept that schedules once firm should not be changed, then the incomplete work indicated on the chart will show us a *true* "late" condition of our manu

**Figure 14-3.** A load planning chart. Shows for each machine the work available each week (light lines) and the total backlog (Heavy line.) (From W. Grant Ireson and Eugene L. Grant, *Handbook of Industrial Engineering and Management*, Englewood Cliffs, N. J.: Prentice-Hall, Inc., 1955. Reprinted by permission.)

DEPT: *Assembly*    PRODUCT GROUP: *Type Totals*

| MONTH | *November* | | | | | *December* | |
|---|---|---|---|---|---|---|---|
| WEEK | *1-5* | *8-12* | *15-19* | *22-26* | *29-3* | *6-10* | *13-17* |
| DAYS ELAPSED | | | | | | | |
| *Type R* (std. hours) | 715 | 700 | 675 | 550 | 710 | 710 | |
| | 604 | 553 | 577 | | | | |
| | 715 | 1415 | 2090 | 2640 | 3350 | 4060 | |
| *Type J* (std. hours) | 420 | 400 | 400 | 320 | 380 | 360 | 360 |
| | 416 | 529 | 565 | | | | |
| | 420 | 820 | 1220 | 1540 | 1920 | 2280 | 2640 |
| *Type P* (std. hours) | 1800 | 1760 | 1760 | 1310 | 1640 | 1600 | 1620 |
| | 1622 | 1685 | 1520 | | | | |
| | 1800 | 3560 | 5320 | 6630 | 8270 | 9870 | 11490 |

**Figure 14-4.** A progress control chart for a continuing activity (Departmental production by product groups). Weekly numbers indicate work scheduled, actual work accomplished, and cumulative work scheduled. Bars indicate cumulative progress against schedule to date. (From W. Grant Ireson and Eugene L. Grant, *Handbook of Industrial Engineering and Management*, Englewood Cliffs, N.J.: Prentice-Hall, Inc., 1955. Reprinted by permission.)

**Figure 14-5.** A machine scheduling chart. Shows planned starting and completion time for each job scheduled to each machine. Also indicates work assignment of (key punch) operators. (From W. Grant Ireson and Eugene L. Grant, *Handbook of Industrial Engineering and Management*, Englewood Cliffs, N.J.: Prentice-Hall, Inc., 1955. Reprinted by permission.)

**Figure 14-6.** A job scheduling and progress control chart illustrating application of Gantt "layout" chart to complex tasks. This type of chart is commonly used for following progress of jobs scheduled to machines. (From W. Grant Ireson and Eugene L. Grant, *Handbook of Industrial Engineering and Management*, Englewood Cliffs, N.J.: Prentice-Hall, Inc., 1955. Reprinted by permission.)

facturing activity. By so doing this chart will be most valuable in the planning for corrective action. Once an order is late it should remain late until brought back to the original planned schedule.

**Job tickets.** This is the *fifth* and last type of order in a manufacturing situation. Job tickets (see Figure 14-7) authorize the performance of individual operations in the manufacturing process. Whether they should be

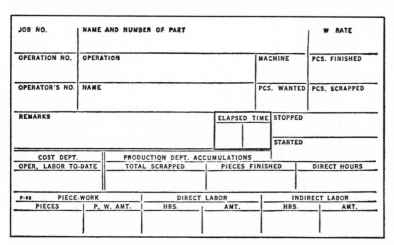

| JOB NO. | NAME AND NUMBER OF PART | | W RATE |
|---|---|---|---|
| OPERATION NO. | OPERATION | MACHINE | PCS. FINISHED |
| OPERATOR'S NO. | NAME | PCS. WANTED | PCS. SCRAPPED |
| REMARKS | | ELAPSED TIME | STOPPED |
| | | | STARTED |

| COST DEPT. | PRODUCTION DEPT. ACCUMULATIONS | | |
|---|---|---|---|
| OPER. LABOR TO-DATE | TOTAL SCRAPPED | PIECES FINISHED | DIRECT HOURS |

| P-48 PIECE-WORK | | DIRECT LABOR | | INDIRECT LABOR | |
|---|---|---|---|---|---|
| PIECES | P. W. AMT. | HRS. | AMT. | HRS. | AMT. |
| | | | | | |

**Figure 14-7.** A typical job ticket. (Courtesy McCaskey Register Co.)

pre-written by the production control group or made out by the departmental dispatcher when needed is not of great importance. However, this is probably one of the most important forms in the production control system. Initially it simply authorizes that a particular operation is to be performed. However, when finally filled out upon the completion of the operation it becomes the "feedback" form that shows not only that the job is complete but also the number of parts processed and the actual time required. This is the principal form in the reporting and follow-up steps in the control of production.

Again, let us remember that there is no uniform terminology for the forms we have just discussed. However, if we get a clear understanding of what each form is being used for in the control situation, we can readily identify these forms in a manufacturing plant regardless of what title appears at the top of the sheet or card.

### Project Planning Methods

Although the Gantt chart, as shown in Figures 14-3 to 14-6, has been used for many years as a project planning, scheduling, and control device, weaknesses developed when it came to the planning of long-term complex projects.

Through investigating an area known as network analysis appropriate methods were discovered that would permit optimal or near optimal sequencing and utilization of resources.

The best-known methods that have been developed are CPM (for critical path methods) and PERT (for Program Evaluation and Review Technique). The original PERT technique is now considered, more accurately, PERT TIME, whereas a later development is known as PERT COST.

PERT was developed in 1958 by the U.S. Navy Special Projects Office in conjunction with the consulting firm of Booz, Allen, and Hamilton. The Navy's interest at the time was to accelerate the Polaris missile and submarine project, and through the use of the PERT technique they were able to complete the project two years ahead of schedule with a savings of millions of dollars. PERT and PERT COST are becoming almost standard procedures for companies dealing with large development projects, particularly those that have contracts with the Department of Defense and/or the National Aeronautics and Space Administration.

CPM was developed by the DuPont Company and Remington Rand at about the same time as PERT. Its purpose at the time was to plan the construction of a plant, and CPM is used extensively by construction people today although it lends itself very well to other types of projects also.

The use of these tools requires first of all that all elements, steps, activities, jobs, and so forth, that are required for a project be completely identified and detailed. Further, a sequencing order must be determined, which is based upon any technological or administrative dependencies of one part of the project upon another. Finally, the time and cost to perform each task or activity must also be estimated. At this point one is prepared to construct a network or an arrow diagram that illustrates the information collected. Figure 14-8 illustrates such a diagram for a simple project. On the diagram each arrow represents a single activity, and each circle represents an event. An event is the completion of one or more activities. Arrows originating at

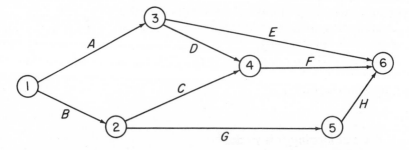

**Figure 14-8.** A critical path network diagram. Numbers correspond to events, and letters correspond to activities and the time taken to complete the activity.

a circle (event) indicate activities that can begin only after all activities (arrows) terminating at that circle have been completed. In this way precedents for the various activities are indicated.

Events are differentiated by numbers within the event circles, and each event should have a higher number than the immediately preceding event, and no two events should have the same number. Figure 14-8 makes use of letters to identify the arrows. In practice the letters would be replaced by word descriptions of the particular activities involved. This would be true particularly when initially setting up the project and identifying all of the various steps and their precedents. After all activities have been identified and time estimates made for the completion of these activities, a new diagram is constructed in which the letters, shown in Figure 14-8, are replaced by the time estimates for completion. With this information it becomes clear that there would be one path through the network that would be longer than all of the other paths. Such a path is called a "critical path" because if any job or activity in that path is delayed, there will be a corresponding delay in the completion time for the entire project.

In many situations, of course, it is difficult to estimate the time required to complete an activity; also, it is often possible to complete an activity in less than normal time, at greater cost. CPM is designed to consider any additional data that may help in the comprehensive analysis of any project. In addition to normal times for these various activities the method can also consider crash time for these activities as well as the cost figures associated with these times. CPM, then, can provide management with a number of alternate schedules, each having a total project time somewhere within and including the limits of the all-crash and all-normal solutions. For each alternate plan there is a corresponding total project cost. For all but the smallest project, the computations necessary to produce this kind of information would be quite formidable. As a result, computers become a necessary tool in CPM work, and computer manufacturers can provide the necessary programs to make possible the calculations required.

As referred to earlier, the original PERT concept is one that deals with time only. In PERT the planner is asked to supply three estimates of time for each activity: (1) an optimistic estimate, (2) a pessimistic estimate, and (3) the most realistic estimate. These three estimates are then used to give us not only an expected lapsed time for the entire project, but to give us a measure of the probability of meeting that expected completion date.

Time estimates are usually expressed in calendar weeks although any unit of time could be used. The *optimistic* time estimate would be the least amount of time that an activity can take. This estimate would be made on the assumption that everything works the first time, and the estimate can be expected to be met in only one out of a hundred cases. The *pessimistic* estimate would be the maximum amount of time that an activity can take.

It would be the expected time if unusually bad luck were experienced and would include the possibility of initial failure followed by a fresh start. The most realistic estimate, or *most likely* time, would be the time used if only one time estimate is required. It is the expected time for an activity if that activity were repeated many times under identical conditions or, it would be the estimate given most often if many qualified persons were asked to provide such a time estimate.

From the optimistic, most likely, and pessimistic times, the Expected Elapsed Time ($t_e$) can be obtained by statistical techniques. The relationship of the three estimates to the Expected Elapsed Time is given by the formula:

$$t_e = \frac{a + 4m + b}{6}$$

where  $a$ = optimistic time
       $b$ = pessimistic time
       $m$ = most likely time

It can be seen from the formula that the most likely time estimate is given four times as much weight as the optimistic and pessimistic estimates when computing the expected time.

The following table depicts two activities in a PERT network having identical most likely times, but different optimistic and pessimistic times:

| Activity | a | m | b |
|----------|---|---|---|
| R | 1 | 4 | 7 |
| S | 3 | 4 | 5 |

Utilizing the formula given for the Expected Elapsed Time one can show that $t_e$ for both of these activities would be identical or 4.00.

Just casual inspection of the data, however, shows that there is considerably more uncertainty associated with the expected time for the activity $R$ than there is for the activity $S$. In PERT analysis work it is desirable to know the degree of uncertainty, or variance, associated with each expected time for such activity. This variance is calculated using the following formula:

$$\sigma^2(\text{variance}) = \left[\frac{b - a}{6}\right]^2$$

In other words, we are saying that $1/6$ of the range between the optimistic time and the pessimistic time is the estimate of the standard deviation. This figure when squared equals the variance. We now have a single best estimate of the time we expect an activity to take ($t_e$) and an estimate of the degree of certainty associated with that expected time.

If we turn our attention from activities to events, we see that $T_E$ of an event is defined as the expected time for that event to be reached, given the expected activity times in a network. Two other definitions may be helpful. $T_S$ is called the scheduled time and is the contractual obligation date for the whole project, or the schedule completion time for certain major events within the project. $T_L$, on the other hand, is the latest allowable completion time for an event, so that an entire project is kept on schedule. The $T_L$ for each event must be defined in such a way that if every event in a network is completed by this time, the scheduled time for the entire project, $T_S$, will be met. The slack of an event is a measurement of the excess time available to reach that event. It is the number of time units by which the latest allowable completion time exceeds the expected time for an event, or it would be $T_L - T_E$.

The PERT COST system differs from PERT TIME inasmuch as two different estimates are required for each activity. These are (1) a minimum time estimate and its cost; and (2) a minimum cost estimate and its time. The minimum cost estimate for all activities is used and the critical path determined for these data. The result would then be a completion date that is based upon minimum cost requirements for completing the project. This completion date and the length of time required under these minimum cost conditions may be too great, and alternative times, requiring greater cost, can then be substituted for chosen minimum cost activities along the critical path. In this way, the critical path would be shortened until such time that either another branch becomes critical or a suitable compromise has been worked out along the original critical path. Obviously, compromises between cost and time are necessary for activities along the critical path, and this technique is designed to provide a logical approach to these trade-offs between cost and time. As with CPM, the computation for any project of appreciable size would be possible only with the assistance of a computer.

### Procedure Analysis and Work Simplification

As with other manufacturing control systems and procedures, production planning and control lends itself to modern mechanization techniques such as machine accounting and use of electronic computers. Careful study of the control system through procedure analysis will indicate the savings that may be effected by the utilization of modern equipment. These savings may be in the clerical help required in the administration of the system or in the advantages of quick compilation of data, which in turn results in up-to-date control data.

Many mechanical aids have been in use for some time. These are, in effect, mechanical Gantt charts, or adaptations thereof. Some of these devices are shown in Figures 14-9 and 14-10.

All control systems should be reviewed periodically to insure that all steps in the procedure are necessary to the effective operation of the plant. The maintenance of any record or form can only be justified if it actually contributes to the current and future planning and control of the manufacturing activity.

**Figure 14-9.** Demonstration setup of a visible margin leaf schedule board. (Courtesy Remington Rand, Inc.)

**Figure 14-10.** A 100-item "Produc-Trol" peg board. (Courtesy The Wassel Organization, Inc.)

## Production Planning and Control
## Organization

It should be obvious that there is no single pattern for the organization of the production planning and control activity. In many small plants the routing, loading, and scheduling functions may well be included in the duties of the operating line: the shop manager, superintendent, and foremen. But it is difficult to combine day-to-day work with adequate planning, and as a result it is more often feasible to break away the production planning and control functions and assign them to qualified specialists. These groups should be organized as staff sections and normally report to the top manufacturing executive.

### Centralized Production Planning
### and Control

Centralization or decentralization of duties of the production control staff depends upon the design of the production planning and control system. In a completely centralized setup, determination of shipping promises; analysis of sales, stock, and shop orders; preparation of routes, load charts, and schedule charts; dispatching of work to the shop complete with job tickets and all other necessary paper, would be accomplished by a central production planning and control unit. In addition, as work is completed a careful analysis of the actual performance would be made and if corrective action were required, it would be initiated by this group.

Fully centralized production planning and control presents a real problem in industrial communications. Often some portions of the job are decentralized to the various departments in the plant. The most common practice is to assign a departmental dispatcher to each foreman. In this situation the central office will dispatch work by the day, week, or some longer period. The final dispatch is then made by the dispatcher in each department.

### Decentralized Production Planning
### and Control

We have discussed at great length that no matter how general the planning may be in a central office, the plan must eventually be developed into a detailed plan on the shop floor. Some companies are now endeavoring to make each foreman a manager of his own departmental operation. In these cases the foreman is furnished with a complete staff for the production planning and control of the activities in his department.

Regardless of the degree of centralization or decentralization of these duties, the activities can be readily divided into the *planning phase* and the *control phase*. Also, there can seldom be complete decentralization. Some general production planning and control will have to be retained in a central office in order that the efforts of the various departments be coordinated in the whole.

**Planning phase.** We have already indicated in some detail the duties involved in the production planning phase. Working from the basic data mentioned earlier in this chapter, the personnel in this part of the activity prepare routes, load charts, and schedule charts.

**Control phase.** The completed job ticket is the key to this phase of the production planning and control system. This is the vehicle of report back from the shop floor that indicates that a job is completed; or if daily job tickets are turned in the daily progress of a job can be determined. These tickets should be compared to the shedule chart and the progress of work indicated. The schedule chart is the point at which the status of the work in the shop should be presented in concise and readable form. Again, however, all of the record-keeping in the world will not control a shop. Production control records are a tool only. Alert personnel must see where orders are running late and have the initiative to take corrective action.

### Relation to Other Functions

Good relationships with all the other functions in the enterprise are essential to effective production planning and control. Full cooperation with the marketing group is necessary, particularly in view of the importance of market conditions and of the goodwill of customers. Both product engineering and process engineering must keep production planning and control informed as to their plans to avoid the manufacture of goods either to incorrect specifications or by an improper method. Cost control depends upon production control for essential cost information: the actual time that was required to process the material. This is just another effective use of the completed job ticket.

## Measurements of Effectiveness

In determining the effectiveness of a production planning and control system there are quite a few problems.

The key criterion might well be whether or not shipping promises are being kept—the percentage of the orders shipped on time. This, however, would not be a true criterion if excessive overtime or expediting costs were involved in getting any of these orders shipped.

The cost of the control system in relation to the value of goods shipped is another possibility. Again this may not be sound; if markets slump a bad ratio will develop. Many good production planning and control systems have been discontinued because of "high costs" under these conditions—and never revived after business picked up.

## Use of Operations Research

The problems of measuring effectiveness, as previously mentioned, are often complicated by our inability to make adequate production planning and control decisions at the outset. It is true that decisions must be made and are made in every case, but they are often made without adequate facts or information. The growing use of operations research has done much to alleviate both of these problems—making for better decisions and better measurement of effectiveness.

In our introduction to operations research in Chapter 1, several possibilities for its use were listed. An examination of the list (as well as any such list) will show that much of the work of operations research has been in the areas of production control, inventory control, manufacturing processes, quality control, and purchasing. In other words, production work generally lends itself to the methods and techniques of operations research. Although operations research as such is beyond the scope of this book, it might be helpful to discuss briefly the general method used.

Operations researchers first secure all available information concerning the problem presented to them, identifying both constant and variable factors. From this information, a model is set up, usually a mathematical equation or formula, which accurately describes the relationships that exist among the factors identified. The model can usually be tested for accuracy by inserting data that are known to produce a certain result. If no such data are available, the model remains as a theory until it is sufficiently tested under operating conditions. Management can use the model as a guide in making production decisions, for from it the outcome of various decisions can be predicted. Solving mathematical equations to predict the probable outcome of managerial decisions can be a time-consuming and laborious process, but the introduction and use of electronic computers has done much to alleviate this problem.

One of the more useful tools of operations research, particularly in production work, is that of linear programming. Linear programming is a mathematical method for selecting the most effective of many possible solutions. A practical problem would be one of scheduling many orders to many machines for least machining time or one of determining from which warehouse to ship to which customer. The approach used under linear programming follows the general scheme that was outlined earlier. First, all variables are quantified, and one is selected to be minimized or optimized. Then it is examined in relation to the others. The quantitative information is arranged in a matrix or table of the horizontal and vertical columnar form, which is basic to all linear programming problems. There may be restrictions or special conditions that apply, but from this point on the problem is solved by means of advanced mathematical techniques. However, once the technique has been developed, often it can be simplified to the extent that clerical employees can be taught enough of the mechanics of it to solve routine types of problems.

There are other methods and techniques that fall under the general heading of operations research and that have application in production work. Game theory, symbolic logic, queuing theory, information theory, and research theory are some that are discussed quite extensively[1] in the literature. Much of the work is currently of a theoretical nature, but more practical applications come forth every day, and the rate can be expected to increase.

## QUESTIONS

1. During World War II a West Coast plant constantly failed to get its product to its customers when they needed the material. An investigation of the plant's production control charts indicated that all work was progressing according to schedule. What was wrong? What would you do to correct this situation?

2. In what way are the principles of production planning and control applicable to the:
   (a) home?
   (b) supermarket?
   (c) school?

3. Prepare a detailed schedule chart for your own activities next week. How could you use this chart to advantage?

4. Discuss in greater detail why the volume to be produced has little effect on the design and operation of a system of production planning and control.

5. Assume you are organizing a small plant for the manufacture of cigarette lighters. How many of the different types of orders would you use? Explain your use of each type.

6. Compare the advantages of centralized dispatching with those of decentralized dispatching.

7. How does production planning and control contribute to the profits of the business?

8. Outline how a production foreman makes use of production planning and control concepts even though there is no such department in his plant.

---

[1]In particular, see *Operations Research*, published by the Operations Research Society of America, and *Management Science*, published by the Institute of Management Sciences.

9. What are some work simplification opportunities that present themselves in production planning and control?
10. Distinguish between production planning and production control. Should these be organized separately within a plant?

## CASE PROBLEMS

### Atwater Pen Company

The Atwater Pen Company manufactures a line of fountain pens, which it sells through its salesmen directly to dealers located in cities throughout the United States. In addition to its standard line, it has always been the company's policy to try to furnish special items a customer might want. For example, it has furnished gold pens containing a one-half carat diamond in the clip, platinum pens, and white pens for nurses.

In an attempt to give the foremen as much responsibility as possible, the company uses a system of decentralized production control. Production orders, containing the routing and scheduling for each part, are submitted to the production departments once each week. The foremen are given considerable leeway on the production schedule, and the only requirement is that the operation must be completed by the date scheduled. Thus, if a foreman wants to dispatch a lot of parts to a machine two days before the deadline scheduled for that lot, he is free to do so.

Recently, the production control department has been plagued with frequent rush orders for special pens. This has necessitated sending a number of special manufacturing orders to Department 32 where the caps and barrels are made. Clifford White, foreman of Department 32, has been complaining about all of the rush orders and maintains that he can no longer plan the work in his department so as to operate most efficiently. Bert Akers, head of the production planning and control department, is sympathetic with Mr. White's problem, but states that it is beyond his control.

*Questions:*

1. Should a company manufacturing products to stock also try to produce "special items" for its customers?
2. Under circumstances such as this, what effect do "special items" have on scheduling?
3. Would this situation be improved by centralizing all production control? Why?
4. What benefits can be gained from giving some of the production control responsibility to foremen such as Clifford White?

### Taylor Engine Company

Wilbur Armstrong, the vice president in charge of manufacturing for Taylor Engine Company, has decided that something must be done to correct the appalling production and materials control system that exists in his company. Recent reports have disclosed that approximately 25% of all engines coming off the final assembly line are minus a manifold, fuel injection system, or some other item.

These engines are then stored for as long as one to two weeks awaiting completion.

During a conference with the plant superintendent, the head of production control, and the chief inspector, Mr. Armstrong found that some parts failed to get to the final assembly line at the right time because they weren't scheduled in time, others were held up because of supply problems, and still others were delayed because of production problems.

Since Taylor Engine is growing very rapidly and will probably double its dollar volume of business within the next year, Mr. Armstrong has resolved that something must be done to bring about better coordination between the production control, purchasing, and manufacturing departments. After much consideration he decided to call in a management consulting firm to advise him. They analyzed the situation and recommended that Taylor Engine revamp its control system and install complete data processing equipment to integrate materials and production control and manufacturing departments.

*Questions:*

1. Comment on the proposed installation of data processing equipment.
2. What is the nature of and what can be accomplished with this equipment?
3. Could Taylor Engine afford to continue operating with its old system of production control? Why?
4. How do you account for the fact that a highly progressive company like Taylor Engine could have let a situation such as this develop?

# CHAPTER FIFTEEN

# Quality
# Control

Quality control refers to all of those functions or activities that must be performed to fulfill the company's quality objectives. These functions are very broad in some companies and encompass many employees, whereas they are limited only to inspection and a few employees in other companies.

Quality begins with the design of a product in accordance with the customer's specifications. Further, it involves the establishment of measurement standards, the selection of a suitable manufacturing process and the necessary tooling to make the product, the performance of the necessary manufacturing operations, and the inspection of the product to check on conformance with the specifications. All of this is followed by use of the product by the customer, and the feedback of information from the customer to use in any necessary redesign of the product. It is evident that control of quality is the responsibility of many people.

Before going further, let us discuss the term *quality*. Confusion arises in the use of this term because it is used indiscriminately to refer to three different things: (1) quality of design, (2) quality of conformance with specifications, and (3) quality of performance.

We commonly associate quality with cost and think that a Rolls Royce is superior to a Ford; that a hammer purchased at Woolworths for 98c is inferior to a $2.98 hammer from the neighborhood hardware store. It is obvious that this conception of higher quality begins on the drawing board and with the establishment of rigid design specifications. As a rule, high quality of design results in high cost of manufacture and usually results in high performance value. Recognizing this, the manufacturer usually thinks of the quality of his product in a different sense than does the layman. He is concerned with how his product meets the customer's specifications and how it compares with his competitor's in the same price class. To the manufacturer then, quality is not absolute but is relative to other factors such as the selling price of the item, the use for which it is intended, and the adherence to measurable quality standards.

Quality control is concerned with the prevention of defects in manufacturing so that the item may be made right and not have to be rejected. An important component of quality control is the inspection function, which provides a means of checking the conformance of the item with the measurement standard. In many organizations quality control consists merely of inspection and does not contain the many facets of the complete control function. Still other companies think only in terms of statistical quality control when they refer to quality control.

## Organization for Quality Control

The administrative responsibility for quality control is frequently vested in a chief inspector or quality manager. The position of this person in the organization structure will depend to a considerable extent upon the nature of the business. In those companies manufacturing products requiring a high degree of precision, the quality control function is very important, and the person responsible for it will commonly occupy a position on the same level as the person in charge of manufacturing. It is generally accepted that it is not good policy to assign responsibility for quality control to the manager who is responsible for getting out production, the reason being that he may slight quality in order to meet production demands.

In considering the organization for quality control, it becomes readily apparent that quality control is a responsibility shared by many members of the enterprise. It involves the members of management who set the quality policies, the salesmen who contract to sell products of a certain quality, the design engineers who set the product specifications, the buyers who purchase raw materials of the right quality, and the manufacturing personnel who are responsible for making the product according to prescribed specifications. It is only through the wholehearted cooperation of all these persons that a sound quality control program can be maintained.

## Quality Standards

In the final analysis the quality standards for a product are established by the customer. His decision to buy or not to buy for a given price will be based upon his satisfaction with the product. Of course, in order to secure the customer's business the vendor must give consideration to ways of maintaining quality levels that will meet or exceed his needs. Thus, it becomes necessary for management to decide what characteristics the product shall possess and then design and produce a product that embodies all the pre-selected characteristics.

Many companies have established long-standing reputations for manu-facturing high-quality products, and their customers rely upon them always to exceed the minimum specifications established. To illustrate this point, a large manufacturer of diesel truck engines has established a reputation for producing high-quality engines guaranteed for at least 100,000 miles of operation. The manufacturer is proud of this reputation and maintains an extensive quality control program in order to insure the fulfillment of the quality standards.

## Responsibility for Quality

The product engineers, working with the sales department, are responsible for initiating the standards to be maintained in manufacturing the product. In designing the product the engineers determine the degree of precision to be adhered to in manufacturing the component parts and set forth the necessary materials, dimensions, and other specifications on the design drawings. In considering the standards of quality to be adhered to, the design engineers should take into account: (1) the end use of the item, (2) the value of the item, (3) the relationship of the item to other components, (4) the establishment of design standards that can be attained and main-tained by the shop, and (5) the chance and assignable variables that may enter into the manufacture of the item. It is important that the design engineers be familiar with the manufacturing processes so that realistic standards can be established. If the standards (tolerances) established for the product are beyond the capabilities of the manufacturing equipment, then the item cannot meet the minimum acceptance level and will have to be rejected.

Recognizing the importance of designing for economic and high-quality production, some companies now have the process engineers and quality control engineers work closely with the design engineers to facilitate the design of products of attainable standards and to insure economical produc-tion.

As pointed out previously, the engineering department in consultation with the sales department and manufacturing engineers is responsible for setting the standards to be maintained in producing the product. For items such as producer goods, the sales engineer will be instrumental in conveying the customer's requirements to the engineering department. Obviously, if the product is being purchased by the customer to meet certain performance standards, it is imperative that it meet or exceed his needs.

All persons associated with production play a vital role in maintaining quality. The process engineer is responsible for planning the necessary steps in the manufacturing process that will allow the product to be made according to the specifications. Failure to route the product through the right machines or other production centers may result in a rejected item.

The individual workers performing the various operations on the product are also key persons in maintaining high-quality standards. There are varying levels of acceptability on the product; if the operator just barely meets the acceptance standards, the product may tend to be a borderline product. On the other hand, if the workers try always to exceed the minimum level of acceptability then there is strong likelihood that the level of quality will be high. In order to insure that the caliber of workmanship is kept at acceptable levels, some companies have established quality incentives. For example, it is not uncommon in the meat-packing industry to pay the "skinners" (operators who cut the hide off the beef) a bonus for each hide that is free of cuts. Also, it is accepted practice to pay operators working on incentive-wage plans only for the good parts they produce. Thus, they must correct any reject before they will be paid for producing the part.

There is an old saying that *you can't inspect quality into the product*, and wise management recognizes the wisdom of this statement. To illustrate the logic of this axiom, let us consider a situation witnessed by the authors in a small plant. This plant was experiencing a high percentage of rejects on its product, and the customer was returning them by the truckload. The president of the company witnessed the return of one truckload of the items and commented, "We just have to hire another inspector." However, after further consideration he became aware of the fact that the company didn't need another inspector; it simply needed greater adherence to the quality standards by the manufacturing departments. The supervisors and workers lacked a spirit of quality-mindedness, and the company was suffering from their failure to worry about anything but production quotas.

In recent years, industry has given a great deal of thought to the establishment of more effective quality control programs to help prevent needless waste of labor and materials. This has led to the development of sound quality control plans and the application of statistical techniques and other means to control processes. These tools of quality control will be discussed later in this chapter.

## Inspection

Inspection is the component of the quality control program that is concerned with checking on the conformance of the item to the specifications set for it. It may be likened to the policing action necessary to force compliance with our laws. In the same way that communities need policemen, companies also need inspectors. Naturally, if everyone is doing his job of meeting the quality standards, then the need for inspection is reduced. However, even in the best-managed companies there are still many needs for inspection. Men are not infallible and make mistakes, materials may be faulty, and machines and tools are subject to wear and tend to get out of adjustment. Because of the many variables that enter into manufacturing, inspection is a never-ending function.

The inspection department fulfills four primary responsibilities: (1) it checks the quality of incoming materials, (2) it checks on all finished goods to insure that only acceptable products reach the customer, (3) it aids in maintaining process control and attempts to locate the flaws in manufacturing that would cause subsequent difficulties, and (4) it serves in an advisory capacity in attempting to correct or prevent quality control problems.

Inspection includes all types of activities, such as testing, gaging, and so forth, that are required to determine whether the product meets the prescribed standards. For the most part, our discussion of inspection will refer to that performed by qualified inspectors who are members of the inspection department and whose responsibility is to check on the attainment of the minimum standards of quality.

### Items That Need Inspection

In general, we may say that purchased materials, goods in process, and finished products should be inspected. This very general statement needs amplification. It will be discussed in greater detail in the sections that follow.

**Purchased materials inspection.** Purchased materials should be inspected at the time they are received and before they are stocked or sent to assembly. The receiving department personnel should make at least an identifying inspection of all incoming items and note obvious damage. In some cases they may need to do more extensive checking or route the material to qualified inspectors for checking. Faulty parts, of course, should be returned.

It is not uncommon to find inspectors working in or adjacent to the receiving department. For example, in one large aircraft engine plant there is a sizeable inspection department next to the receiving department. Owing to the critical nature of all purchased parts, most of them are inspected in this department as soon as received. Following this inspection, the parts are then sent either to the stock room or assembly lines. Through this procedure the company is assured that operations will not be performed on faulty materials.

Receiving inspection should always be located in such a place that all incoming materials must pass through the receiving and inspection room. The nature of the inspection will vary with the nature of the items being purchased. The inspection may be very complex using many measuring devices, or it may be little more than a visual inspection. It may be performed on 100 per cent of the items or it may be merely a sampling inspection on each lot received. In some cases operational tests may be run on purchased items such as electric motors, pumps, and similar items.

In recent years, some companies have established quality certification programs with some of their vendors that have eliminated the necessity of inspecting that vendor's products.

**In-process inspection.** Because of the many variables that permeate every phase of manufacturing, it is essential that in-process materials be given an optimum amount of inspection. The term "optimum" is used because it is possible either to over-inspect or under-inspect an item. Either practice will prove to be costly.

In nearly every manufacturing process two types of inspection will prevail. A considerable amount of *informal* inspection will be performed by the production workers. The *formal* inspection will be performed by qualified inspectors from the inspection department. As a part of the informal inspection, the workers will usually subject the piecepart to visual inspection. In addition they may do some gaging, and they will reject parts containing faulty materials.

A number of general principles apply to the determination of what, when, and where to inspect. When a new operation such as a stamping operation is being set up, the first parts produced on the machine should be inspected to insure that they meet the specifications. When a piecepart will be subjected to several successive operations, it is usually uneconomical to inspect after each operation. For the most part only a patrol-type inspection (to be discussed later in this chapter) can be justified. In some cases the operator may be equipped with the necessary gages or measuring devices to provide a running check on the item.

It is frequently desirable to inspect a piecepart just before moving on to a very expensive operation. By rejecting the part before the expensive operation, the additional cost increment is not added to an item that will probably have to be scrapped.

It is common to inspect items after a series of manufacturing operations has been performed. Also, it is sound practice to inspect parts or assemblies when they have been completed in one department and are to be moved to another department. In general, an item that will become a component part of an assembly and will be difficult to replace or may result in damage to other parts should be thoroughly inspected before assembly. Items should be inspected before going to an operation in which the defects might be covered up, as in painting or plating.

In the highly mechanized processing that exists today, the designers of automatic machines frequently design automatic gaging devices into the machines. These devices check the critical dimensions or other characteristics and either reject the faulty items or signal the operator that satisfactory items are not being produced. In some cases a feedback system automatically resets the machine to correct for the error.

In-process inspection may be performed in several locations: on the line or at the machine by a full-time inspector, by a roving or patrol inspector who calls periodically at the machine for parts to inspect, in an inspection crib or an air-conditioned room, or at centralized inspection points.

**Finished goods inspection.**    Finished goods inspection should be made by qualified inspectors. The items should be checked by measurements, operating tests, or other means to insure compliance with the specifications. Failure to provide a thorough check at this point may allow a faulty product to be sent to the customer.

## Inspection Responsibility and Practices

The inspection department possesses the authority to reject those items that fail to meet the standards. Thus, as pointed out previously, it must pass on purchased materials, the processing of materials, and finished products. Also, it may be responsible for the inspection of all jigs, fixtures, dies, gages, and measuring devices used by both the inspectors and production workers. Supervision of the procedure for the disposal or rework of rejected items may be another responsibility assigned to the inspection department.

To carry out its responsibilities, the inspection department will need to establish a number of policies and procedures. It must decide what to inspect, where to inspect, how to inspect, and many other pertinent matters. Some of these have already been discussed in the preceding section; still others will be treated in the sections that follow.

**Location for inspection.**    In most cases the operator himself will inspect his work as he performs it. He should catch most of the obvious errors. However, his informal inspection is not sufficient. Even if he is conscientious his checks will not be infallible and may allow faulty parts to be forwarded to the next operation. Then, too, the production worker, particularly if working on a piecework incentive plan, is primarily concerned with getting out production; he places less emphasis on quality. It therefore becomes necessary to provide an additional check by inspectors.

Inspection points should be planned carefully and should be located where they will produce the most economical end results. In locating the inspection points, consideration must be given to whether the materials are to be inspected at a machine or work station or checked at a centralized inspection point. If the inspection is made at the work station, it is called "floor" inspection. Some floor inspection is done by inspectors who go from machine to machine and perform sampling inspection of the parts produced. This type of inspection is frequently referred to as "patrolling" or "traveling" inspection. In contrast to floor inspection is "centralized" inspection. This type of inspection takes place in a centralized location and necessitates taking the items to be inspected to the inspection station.

Each of the above types of inspection has advantages and disadvantages. Floor inspection allows a minimum of material handling, reduced storage and reduced delay of material in process, close contact between the inspector and work station, and prompt communications and correction of processing difficulties. On the other hand, it may not occupy the full time of the inspector; he may be idle part of the time. Then, too, some items require special inspection devices that may be available only in a central inspection or test station.

Centralized inspection allows the items to be inspected where the various inspection devices may be located. In addition, it facilitates the full use of the inspectors' time and is conducive to increased output per inspector. Supervision of the inspectors and adherence to standard inspection procedures is also improved.

**Amount to inspect.** One of the important phases of any quality control program is the determination of the frequency of inspection and of the percentage of items to inspect. It is neither practical nor economical to expect that every item should be inspected for every specification. Therefore, it is essential that the most critical specifications be determined and that maximum concentration be placed upon adherence to these standards. We should never lose sight of the fact that inspection costs money and that *the amount of inspection should be reduced to the minimum required to maintain the degree of control desired.*

In some cases 100 per cent inspection of each of the items may be necessary to attain the control desired. For example, a company that manufactures automobile horns or headlight-dimming switches will probably subject each of these items to performance tests before shipping them to the customer. On the other hand, a company manufacturing sheet steel will not subject each sheet to chemical and tensile tests before shipping to the customer.

Reference is frequently made to "100 per cent" inspection or to "sampling" inspection. In 100 per cent inspection all of the items are checked for the characteristic being measured. Sampling inspection, on the other hand, does not involve a check of each item. It is based upon the statistical probability (to be discussed later in this chapter) that the characteristics of a sample will be the same as those of all items in the lot. We should not assume that 100 per cent inspection is necessarily more exacting than sampling inspection. It doesn't guarantee that all faulty items will be detected. Inspectors are subject to all the frailties of the human being and may fail to catch many items that should be rejected.

Many factors will influence the decision on the amount of inspection to be used—for example, the type of product being made, the variability of the manufacturing process, and the variability of the materials. Items made on automatic machines (such as an automatic screw machine) are usually subject to much less variability than the same items made on a manually operated engine lathe. For this reason, these parts would usually be subjected to only a sampling inspection.

**Inspection procedures and records.** It is essential that each item be analyzed to determine its inspection needs and that an adequate inspection procedure be planned for it. Likewise, each inspector should be thoroughly acquainted with the procedure to be followed and the characteristics to be measured. He should be equipped with adequate inspection devices and know exactly what to do about items that fail to meet the standards.

An important component of a quality control program is the maintenance of a sound system of records. The inspection plan for each part or assembly should be specified on a suitable form, and the nature of the inspection, the equipment required, and the inspection procedure should be stipulated. Also, each of the inspection points for each item should be indicated as one of the routing steps on the standard process sheet. Suitable inspection and quality control records and reports should be maintained. These may consist of scrap and rework tags, receiving inspections forms, sampling inspection records, patrol inspection logs, final inspection reports, and similar items. Through the maintenance and analysis of these records it is possible to accomplish the third step of our control procedure—to detect those points in the manufacturing process where control is falling down. This then provides the basis for accomplishing the final step: corrective action. As will be pointed out later in this chapter, statistical quality control procedures provide a means of keeping quality in bounds and do not require the same degree of "after-the-fact" correction.

### Inspection Devices

The specification sets forth certain characteristics that are to be attained in manufacturing the product. In many cases it is impossible to judge these characteristics by human senses. For example, to determine the diameter of a shaft to the dimension of $2.00000 \pm .00005$ without the aid of some measuring device would be virtually impossible. Thus, inspection must be accomplished by means of devices capable of measuring the characteristics desired. These characteristics may involve dimensions, surface finish, hardness, ductility, color, shrinkage, plasticity, viscosity, efficiency, operating characteristics, and many others. Inspection procedures must include equipment that gives the inspector an answer on the acceptability of the item. A few of the common inspection devices will be discussed in the paragraphs that follow.

Many of the inspection devices are referred to as *gages*. These may be used for checking the actual dimensions against the standard. Among the most common of these are the *fixed gages* (such as go-no-go gages, ring gages, plug gages) and the *indicating gages* (such as micrometers, dial indicators). (See Figure 6-8.) The fixed gages merely tell whether a part is under-size, within limits, or oversize. The indicating gages give a measure of the actual state of affairs and how much variation is occurring. With the increasing trend toward process control and the avoidance of defects, the indicating gage is becoming increasingly important.

A device frequently used to check on profiles or contours of objects is the contour projector or comparator (see Figure 15-1). This instrument casts an enlarged shadow of the profile being checked onto a screen on which the specified contour has been marked. Failure to get coincidence of the shadow with the fixed model will reveal a defect. This device is particularly good for inspecting items such as threads and the small gears in a watch.

Great advances have been made in the development of instruments for checking surface finish, color, internal structure, and similar measurements. The surface analyzer and profilometer are two instruments widely used for measuring surface smoothness. The spectrophotometer is finding extensive use in the paint and other industries concerned with close matching of colors. Industrial radiography, ultrasonics, and magnetic particle suspension are all recent developments that have found extensive applications in the inspection of defects in the interior or surface of metals.

In order to attain in-process control of quality and to keep pace with the automating of industry, instruments must be designed that may be integrated with the manufacturing process. Examples of the numerous automatic inspection devices that have been developed include the continuous monitoring of sheet steel thickness by means of beta rays and the monitoring of enamel thickness by means of a magnetic circuit. Still another example is a fully automatic, mechanical-electric tester that checks the compressibility of golf balls and classifies them into four categories of compressibility: two good, one over standard, and one below standard.

Modern manufacturing makes use of many other tests to measure physical or chemical characteristics. Sizable laboratories are maintained to accomplish these tests. Also, extensive use is made of performance testing to insure the attainment of the desired standards.

**Figure 15-1.** Contour measuring projector used to measure the angle of a thread (Courtesy Bausch & Lomb Optical Co.)

## Gage Inspection and Control

As pointed out previously, gages are frequently under the supervision of the inspection department. It is essential then that a system be established for controlling the issue, accuracy, and maintenance of all inspection devices.

Gages should be subjected to the same inventory control procedures as other devices. For the more complex instruments, suitable maintenance records should be established. Most instruments are subject to wear and should be calibrated periodically against master gages. This checking should be done under carefully controlled conditions and as often as is necessary to maintain the degree of accuracy desired. In many cases gages may have to be checked daily.

## Statistical Quality Control

Statistical quality control is one of the scientific tools that modern management is using to an increasing extent in the maintenance of quality standards. It is based upon the laws of probability and may be described as a system for controlling the quality of production within specified limits by means of a sampling procedure and continuing analysis of inspection results.

When used in key points, statistical quality control makes it possible to determine whether or not a given manufacturing process is capable of turning out products with prescribed specifications. It not only provides this information but also provides control limits at which an operation can be stopped before poor work is produced. Thus, statistical quality control makes it possible to determine the capabilities of a manufacturing process at the outset and it establishes the necessary controls so that the operations may be corrected for excessive tool wear, excessive variations in raw materials, and similar variations.

### Advantages of Statistical Quality Control

The proper application of statistical quality control should result in the following benefits:

1. More uniform quality of product.
2. Provides a means of catching errors at inception.
3. Reduces inspection costs.
4. Reduces the number of rejects and saves the cost of material.
5. Promotes the understanding and appreciation of quality control.
6. Improves the relationship with the customer.
7. Points out trouble spots.
8. Provides a basis for attainable specifications.
9. Provides a means of determining the capability of the manufacturing process.

## Tools of Statistical Quality Control

Statistical quality control starts with the idea that variability is to be expected in manufacturing. It recognizes that the dimension of a part produced on a machine or process is not a constant but a variable. Thus, if we were accurately to measure the diameter of cylindrical parts coming off an automatic screw machine, we would find that these parts would vary somewhat in their dimensions. A typical distribution of one hundred of these parts might be as illustrated in Figure 15-2. In this or any other manufacturing situation we can expect to find a certain amount of variation that is due to *chance*. This

**Figure 15-2.** Frequency distribution of the diameters of 100 bushings.

chance variation is inherent in the manufacturing process and is the result of many small and more or less independent influences that affect each of the pieces. So long as no other, or *assignable*, causes are operating in the system it is said to be in *statistical control*. When the minute assignable causes, such as tool wear or faulty materials, begin to influence the system, then it gets out of statistical control.

In using statistical quality control, information about the variability of a manufacturing process comes from a sampling procedure. Rarely does the quality control engineer know what the true distribution of the variables in a process is. Thus, he tends to establish control limits on the basis of sampling the distribution of the measurable variables. This will be discussed in somewhat greater detail later in this chapter.

One of the advantages of statistical quality control is that it deals with samples and doesn't necessitate 100 per cent inspection. In using samples, there is no guarantee that the sample will necessarily have the same characteristics as the entire lot; however, through proper *random* sampling[1] it is possible to determine the probability of the accuracy of the samples and to know what risks are being taken.

Sampling inspection is of two kinds: lot-by-lot sampling inspection and continuous sampling inspection. In *lot-by-lot sampling inspection*, the sample is drawn from the lot, and the lot is either accepted or rejected on the basis of the number of rejects in the sample. This is referred to as *acceptance* sampling and will be discussed in detail later. In *continuous sampling inspection*, the current sampling results are used to determine whether sampling inspection or 100 per cent inspection is to be used for the next items inspected. A further classification of sampling plans is whether the sampling is for the purpose of determining a measurement expressed in numbers, i.e., *variables* inspection; or whether the sampling is for the purpose of determining whether the articles are defective or non-defective, i.e., *attribute* inspection.

The tools of statistical quality control include the following statistical devices: (1) frequency distribution, (2) control charts, and (3) acceptance sampling. These will be discussed briefly in the sections that follow.

*Frequency distribution.* One of the basic tools used by the statistician is the frequency distribution. The frequency distribution is essentially a list of the magnitudes of a variable and the number of times these magnitudes occur. It may be represented in a number of ways. One such distribution is presented in the form of a histogram in Figure 15-2. As pointed out previously, statistical quality control is based upon the assumption that there is inherent chance variability in the manufacture of items and that these items will fall into a frequency pattern. This was illustrated in Figure 15-2. If a curve is fitted to the frequency distribution illustrated in Figure 15-2, a bell-shaped curve called a *probability curve* will result (see Figure 15-3). If sufficient items were manufactured and measured this curve would probably assume the shape of a symmetrical bell-shaped curve. This curve would then resemble the *normal distribution curve* about which we have considerable knowledge.

The *normal distribution curve* has a specific mathematical function and is the most important of all frequency distributions. Many data in real life

---

[1]Random sampling refers to the getting of a representative sample; i.e., selecting the sample so that every item has an equal chance of being selected.

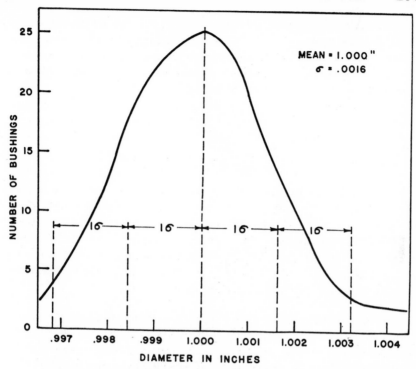

**Figure 15-3.** Probability curve for the bushings' diameters illustrated in Fig. 15-2.

(e.g., heights of men, lengths of life of electric light bulbs, intelligence test scores) appear to follow the normal curve closely. There are statistical tests that can be used to determine how closely a distribution of values approximates normality. An examination of the normal curve will reveal several apparent characteristics: (1) the curve has only a single peak or *node;* (2) the values tend to cluster around the center of the distribution; (3) there are several measures of central tendency (*mean* or arithmetic average, the *median* or midpoint value, the *mode* or most frequently occurring value) that fall at the same value; and (4) the curve is symmetrical around the center and the distances from the central value to the extreme values on each side are equal. In addition to the normal distribution, there are a number of other important distributions that are useful in quality control, namely: binomial, hypergeometric, and poisson.[2]

Two measures of variability that can be obtained from the frequency distribution are of great importance in statistical quality control. These are

---

[2]See Albert H. Bowker and Gerald J. Lieberman, *Engineering Statistics*, (Englewood Cliffs, N.J.: Prentice-Hall, Inc., 1959), p. 70–92.

the range and the standard deviation. The range is the simplest measure of variability and is the difference between the highest and lowest values in the distribution. The standard deviation ($\sigma$) is the most frequently used measure of variability in statistics and may be defined as the square root of the average squared deviation from the mean; i.e.,

$$\sigma = \sqrt{\frac{\sum (x - \bar{x})^2}{N}}$$

Also

$$\sigma = \frac{1}{N} \sqrt{N \sum x^2 - (\sum x)^2}$$

where $N$ equals the number of items and $x$ represents each measurement. For a normal distribution curve, we know that the mean (average) plus or minus one standard deviation will encompass 68.3 per cent of the area or probability. In the same way, the mean plus or minus two standard deviations will include 95.5 per cent; and three standard deviations will include 99.7 per cent of the cases (see Figure 15-3). These mathematical relationships provide the basis for statistical quality control.

**Control charts.** Earlier in this chapter, it was pointed out that no manufacturing process is completely consistent and that variability enters into the output of every product. Process control is one way to keep this variability in check by separating the variability that is due to "chance," or normal causes in the process, from those that are due to "assignable" causes. Assignable causes are those that might arise from such factors as faulty tools, differences in materials, faulty machines, operator errors, and so forth. Process control is usually accomplished through control charts, and a process is said to be in control if all of the observed variations in performance are from chance causes only.

A control chart is a statistical tool that may be used to disclose those variations in the quality of output that are due to both chance and assignable causes. Control charts are valuable devices in that they tell the appropriate parties when to and when not to take action on a process. The commonly used charts are the Mean ($\bar{X}$) Chart, Range ($R$) Chart, Defective ($p$) Chart, and Defects-per-Unit ($c$) Chart.

Control charts may be used whether the inspection is for attributes or variables. In using control charts for variables, the most commonly used charts are the $\bar{X}$ and $R$ charts. Examples of these charts are illustrated in Figure 15-4. Examination of these two charts reveals several interesting features, namely: (1) the $\bar{X}$ values that are plotted are the mean values obtained from samples of 5 measurements; (2) the $R$ values are the differences between the maximum and minimum values for each sample; (3) the control limits have been established well inside the product specification limits; (4) the trend of the points indicates when the process begins to get out of control.

**Figure 15-4.** $\bar{X}$, $R$ chart with conventional ($3\sigma$) and modified (based upon the specifications) limits. The cross-hatched areas are outside of the modified limits. (From W. G. Ireson and E. L. Grant, *Handbook of Industrial Engineering and Management*, Englewood Cliffs, N.J.: Prentice-Hall, Inc., 1955, p. 992. Reprinted by permission.)

Before proceeding farther, let us consider the manner in which the upper and lower control limits may be established. Based on our previous discussion of the normal distribution, it is only natural to expect that we would use the standard deviation of the samples as the basis for establishing the control limits. This could be done. However, it is common practice to use a short-cut method, which is based on the range, for calculating the control limits. The procedure used is to calculate the range for each of the subsamples and then to determine the mean ($\bar{R}$) of the ranges. The three sigma control limits[3] are then determined by $\bar{\bar{X}} \pm 3\bar{R}/\sqrt{nd_2}$. Values of

$$\frac{3}{\sqrt{nd_2}} = A_2$$

are given in Appendix B, Table A-5. Just as for the $\bar{X}$ chart, a table of factors (See Table A-5, Appendix) is available for calculating the upper and lower control limits for the $R$ chart. These three sigma control limits may be determined from:

$$\text{UCL}_R = D_4\bar{R} \quad \text{and} \quad \text{LCL}_R = D_3\bar{R}$$

It is common that control charts for variables are based on averages for small samples rather than for individual measurements. The principal reason for this is that even though the population may differ somewhat from a normal distribution, the distribution of the means of random samples can be treated as approximately normal because of the control limit theorem.

Attribute control charts must necessarily be somewhat different than those for variables, but the same statistical basis applies. If you will recall, attribute inspection is an absolute type of inspection for the purpose of determining whether the item should be accepted or rejected. Control charts for attributes then are based upon the percentage of rejections. The $p$ chart and the $c$ chart are frequently used for controlling attributes.

The basic statistic that we are concerned with in fraction defective charts is:

$$p = \frac{d}{n}$$

where $p$ is a fraction and $d$ is the number of defective parts found in a sample of $n$ pieces inspected. Since the characteristic being plotted is $p$, the chart is frequently referred to as a $p$ chart. The probability distribution that is applicable in this type of situation is the binomial distribution. For the binomial distribution, the standard deviation ($\sigma_p$) is

$$\sigma_p = \sqrt{\frac{p(1-p)}{n}}$$

where $n =$ the size of the sample. In setting up control limits, industrial engineers have concluded that $\pm 3\sigma$ limits around the mean ($\bar{p}$) work very well. Thus, it is common practice to set the control limits on a $p$ chart with the upper control limit (UCL) $= \bar{p} + 3\sigma_p$ and lower control limit (LCL) $= \bar{p} - 3\sigma_p$. The use of a $p$ chart is illustrated in Figure 15-5. This

---

[3]Albert H. Bowker and Gerald J. Lieberman, *ibid.*, p. 383.

**Figure 15-5.** p-chart for transistors. (Reproduced by permission from Irwin Miller and John Freund *Probability and Statistics for Engineers.* (Englewood Cliffs, N.J.: Prentice-Hall, Inc.)).

chart is based on checking 100 transistors daily against the electrical specifications and determining the per cent of defective parts. Note that there is only 1 point out of control on the high side but 7 out of control on the low side. Since in this case, it was the aim of the production line to turn out at least 60 per cent of satisfactory transistors, it appears as though the process is potentially capable of doing better than that if it can be properly stabilized.

There are situations where it is essential that the number of defects in a product be controlled, such as the number of defects per hundred yards of wallpaper or the number of paint defects per automobile. A $c$ chart may be used to control this type of process. If $c$ may be taken as the number of defects per manufactured unit, it is taken as the value of a random variable having the poisson distribution. If $K$ is the number of units of product available for checking the defects,

$$\bar{c} = \frac{1}{K} \sum_{i=1}^{k} c_i$$

**Figure 15-6.** c-chart for number of rivets missing. (Reproduced by permission from Irwin Miller and John Freund *Probability and Statistics for Engineers* (Englewood Cliffs, N.J.: Prentice Hall, Inc.)).

and the control-chart limits for the $c$ chart are

$$UCL = \bar{c} + \sqrt{3\bar{c}}$$
$$LCL = \bar{c} - \sqrt{3\bar{c}}$$

As an illustration of the use of this chart, examine Figure 15-6, which pertains to the number of rivets missing from an aircraft.

Control charts are often set up at the machine where they may be maintained either by the operator or a roving inspector. By having the chart in this location, emphasis on quality is ever-present and the opportunity for corrective action is facilitated.

**Acceptance sampling.** Acceptance sampling is a widely used sampling technique used for attribute inspection. In using this system, samples of a lot are inspected; the number of rejects in the sample determines whether the lot is to be accepted or rejected. When rejected, the balance of the lot is usually screened to separate the defective parts from the acceptable.

Acceptance-sampling plans are of most value when the nature of the process used to manufacture the product remains relatively homogeneous. Under such circumstances, it has been common for purchaser and supplier to enter into an agreement whereby the lot will be accepted or rejected according to the proportion of rejects found in the sample inspected. It is obvious that both buyer and seller assume some risk in using this procedure. However, the savings in inspection cost will usually more than offset the risk involved.

The acceptance-sampling plans in common usage are the single, double, and sequential. Among the best-known and most generally applicable plans are those based upon the Dodge and Romig[4] Single and Double Sampling Inspection Tables and those based upon Mil-Std-105.[5] In using these plans it is necessary first to decide the acceptable quality level (AQL) to be used. This value is usually expressed in terms of per cent defective.

The Dodge and Romig Tables may be used for providing specified consumer protection at a minimum total inspection cost for a fixed-incoming quality level. Thus if we know the per cent defective for a process for a previous run of parts, we can pick out of the Tables a plan that gives this assurance on a minimum amount of inspection. The type of quality protection may be either for lot tolerance per cent defective (LTPD) or for average-outgoing quality limit (AOQL).

---

[4] H. F. Dodge and H.G. Romig, *Sampling Inspection Tables* (New York: John Wiley and Sons; Inc., 1944), pp. 70–71.

[5] Military Standard 105C, "Sampling Procedures and Tables for Inspection by Attributes," Superintendent of Documents (Washington, D.C.: U.S. Government Printing Office, July 18, 1961).

The Military Standard 105 Tables place primary emphasis on the maintenance of a specified AQL. The Tables provide a choice of single, double, or multiple sampling plans and a choice of inspection levels. These tables are the most popular in use and have become the standard for this type of inspection for all of industry.

Following are examples[6] taken from Table VI-K of Mil-Std-105 that illustrate the use of each type of sampling using an AQL of 1.0 and normal inspection for per cent defective:

Single sampling plan. Select and examine 110 units. If three or fewer defectives are found, accept the lot. If four or more are found, reject the lot.

Double sampling plan. Select and examine 75 units. If no more than one defective is found, accept the lot. If six or more defectives are found, reject the lot. If two, three, four, or five defectives are found, select and examine 150 additional units. If in the combined sample (225 units), five or fewer defectives are found, accept the lot. If six or more defectives are found, reject the lot.

Multiple sampling plan. Select and examine 30 units. If three or more are defective, reject the lot. Acceptance is not possible with first sample. If two or fewer are found defective, select and examine 30 additional units. If, in the two samples (60 units), none are defective, accept the lot. If three or more are defective, reject the lot. If one or two are defective, take a third sample and so on. The process is continued until a decision to accept or reject the lot is complete. A final decision on acceptance or rejection must be made after the seventh sample has been taken.

Whereas single sampling bases the acceptance or rejection of a lot on a single sample, and double sampling may use two samples, sequential sampling may use one, two, three, or more samples.

## Reliability

One of the outgrowths of the electronic and space ages has been the tremendous emphasis placed on the capability of a product not to break down in operation. This has led to a new concept referred to as reliability. Reliability has been defined as "the probability of performing without failure a specified function under given conditions for a specified period of time."[7] In contrasting it to quality control, reliability is associated with quality

---

[6]Adapted from Bertrand L. Hansen, *Quality Control: Theory and Applications* (Englewood Cliffs, N.J.: Prentice-Hall, Inc., 1963), pp. 133–135. Reprinted with permission.

[7]AGREE Report, *Reliability of Military Electronic Equipment* (Washington, D.C.: U.S. Government Printing Office, June 1957).

over a length of time, whereas quality control is primarily concerned with the relatively short time required to manufacture the product.

Reliability has come into great prominence because of the increasing complexity of aircraft, space vehicles, and electronic equipment. Whereas the designer used to be able to use a high safety factor and redundancy to offset possible breakdowns, weight and space limitations on many products have tended to make this impossible. The causes of unreliability are great, and one of the major causes is the sizeable number of components contained in many products. The difficulty of successfully combining many parts is clearly illustrated by the multiplication law of probability which Pieruschka[8] states as follows:

"The reliability of an item of equipment equals the product of the individual reliabilities of all its components when they are connected in series."

If $P$ represents the product reliability, the $i$th component is represented by $p_i$, and the total series of connected components is represented by $n$, then the above definition becomes:

$$P = p_1 p_2 p_3 \cdots p_n$$

Based on this formula, given an assembly of 10 parts each of which has a reliability of 0.99, the reliability of the equipment would be only about 0.90. A unit of equipment with 100 components, each with 0.99 reliability, would have the surprisingly low reliability of only about 0.368. It does not take too much imagination to realize the level of reliability that components must have on a complex assembly (such as a missile with about 40,000 parts) in order to function satisfactorily.

In order to turn out a reliable product, there are five key areas that must be given consideration, namely: design of the product, production, measurement and testing, maintenance, and field operation. A number of companies have established reliability engineering groups to plan, to coordinate, and to integrate all phases of a complete reliability program.

## QUESTIONS

1. A nationally advertised shirt sells at department stores for $5.00 whereas a comparable shirt sold by a mail-order house sells for $3.98. How would the relative quality of these two shirts be determined?
2. Are the quality standards for products always established by the customer? Explain.
3. Are chance variables always prevalent in a process? Why?
4. If a quality control program were operating perfectly would it be necessary to have inspectors in a plant? Why?

---

[8]See Erich Pieruschka, *Principles of Reliability* (Englewood Cliffs, N.J.: Prentice-Hall, Inc., 1963), pp. 45–47.

5. Would it be desirable to place inspectors on some kind of incentive plan to increase their output? Why?
6. Is it necessary for a company to inspect all incoming materials? Discuss.
7. Under what conditions would patrol inspection be particularly desirable?
8. Discuss a manufacturing situation in which centralized inspection would be particularly desirable.
9. Under what circumstances would sampling inspection be a requisite?
10. In what way can statistical quality control aid in promoting the understanding and appreciation of quality control?
11. If a company maintains a good quality control program, will this insure high reliability of their products? Why?

## CASE PROBLEMS

### Hoffman Company

The Hoffman Company manufactures road graders and other heavy equipment. Six months ago Cecil Watterson was brought into the company as factory manager. During the short time since he joined the company he has noticed the high percentage of rejects that appears on the inspection reports. Also, he has found that the company employs what seems to be an excessively large number of inspectors.

In conferring with Alex Richardson, the chief inspector, about this problem, Mr. Watterson learned that the large number of inspectors had been hired in an attempt to catch faulty parts from being assembled into the products. The company had always had a reputation for turning out high-quality products, and the former general manager had been a great believer in maintaining a large inspection staff.

Cecil Watterson recognized that much of the quality control problem was vested in the hands of the employees but that they had apparently not been made "quality minded." He called his staff together and proposed the following plan:

1. Immediately initiate actions to make all employees aware of the importance of quality.
2. Henceforth, perform most inspection by a reduced number of roving inspectors.
3. If a defect is found in any lot of parts, return that lot to the last operator responsible for working on it; he will be required to check every piece in the lot.
4. Award operators incentive earnings on only those parts that meet the quality standards. Time spent in checking returned lots will be at the operator's expense and will detract from his bonus for that day.

*Questions:*

1. To what do you attribute the high number of rejects that existed in the Hoffman Company?
2. Comment on Mr. Watterson's plan for improving quality.
3. How do you think the employees will react to such a plan?

## Robertson Bearing Company

The Robertson Bearing Company is a large manufacturer of precision ball bearings. It has experienced difficulty in maintaining the quality standards on some operations, and its executives have become interested in using statistical quality control. To assist them in establishing this program, they have retained Professor C. G. Scitamehtam from the local university.

Professor Scitamehtam decided to illustrate some of the tools of statistical quality control by using actual data from one of the company's operations. A grinding operation, used to finish the outside diameter of a No. 2-1-26 bearing, was selected for securing samples. Ten samples, with 5 bearings in each sample, were taken at 30-minute intervals, and the results were as indicated on the following table:

Measurements on Each of
Five Items in Sample

| Series No. | A | B | C | D | E | $\bar{X}$ or Ave. | R or Range |
|---|---|---|---|---|---|---|---|
| 1 | 1.849 | 1.842 | 1.844 | 1.845 | 1.843 | 1.845 | .007 |
| 2 | 1.845 | 1.846 | 1.841 | 1.845 | 1.843 | 1.844 | .005 |
| 3 | 1.846 | 1.849 | 1.847 | 1.841 | 1.847 | 1.846 | .008 |
| 4 | 1.847 | 1.850 | 1.848 | 1.850 | 1.850 | 1.849 | .003 |
| 5 | 1.844 | 1.846 | 1.844 | 1.845 | 1.846 | 1.845 | .002 |
| 6 | 1.840 | 1.842 | 1.840 | 1.839 | 1.842 | 1.841 | .003 |
| 7 | 1.845 | 1.844 | 1.843 | 1.844 | 1.844 | 1.844 | .002 |
| 8 | 1.848 | 1.844 | 1.847 | 1.846 | 1.845 | 1.846 | .004 |
| 9 | 1.846 | 1.846 | 1.847 | 1.846 | 1.845 | 1.846 | .002 |
| 10 | 1.844 | 1.845 | 1.847 | 1.848 | 1.846 | 1.846 | .004 |

Note: $\bar{\bar{X}} = 1.8450$
$\bar{R} = 0.0040$

*Questions:*

1. Show the measurements in the table on a "frequency" or "histogram" type chart.
   (a) Sketch a normal curve on the chart.
   (b) Estimate $3\sigma$ limits—(99.7% of all cases).
   (c) Indicate mean ($\bar{\bar{X}}$).
   (d) Show specification tolerances (1.845 $\pm$ .005).
2. Using the data in the table construct an $\bar{X}$ chart. Show on the chart:
   (a) A line for the average of all samples ($\bar{\bar{X}}$).
   (b) A point for the average of each sample.
   (c) UCL and LCL.
3. Construct range chart and locate it directly beneath above $\bar{X}$ chart. Show control limit.
4. Can this process be used for producing the part? Why?

# CHAPTER SIXTEEN

# Maintenance
# Engineering

Anyone that has been delayed on a trip because of a breakdown in an airplane, a train, or a bus can vouch for the inconvenience and frustration that it caused him. Although it is doubtful if most people give it much thought, this same breakdown may have indicated a weakness in the transportation company's maintenance program. It is on this general subject of keeping equipment in operating condition that we shall be dwelling in this chapter.

Maintenance engineering is that function of manufacturing management that is concerned with the day-to-day problem of keeping the physical plant in good operating condition. It is an essential activity in every manufacturing establishment, because it is necessary to insure the availability of the machines, buildings, and services needed by other parts of the organization for the performance of their functions at an optimum return on the investment, whether this investment is in machinery, materials, or employees.

The widespread mechanization of industry is adding to the complexity of industrial maintenance programs and is making it increasingly important that equipment be kept operating and production rolling. Industry keeps its wheels turning at a sizable maintenance cost estimated to be in excess of $14 billion per year. This tremendous cost is becoming an increasing part of the total cost of manufacturing.

As we discuss the various phases of maintenance engineering in the sections that follow, it should be evident that it is closely related to many of the other functions that have been discussed previously. We have chosen to discuss maintenance engineering along with other areas of control because many of the phases of a well-conceived maintenance engineering program are an essential part of manufacturing control.

## Scope of Maintenance

Maintenance is necessary in all manufacturing establishments because machines break down, parts wear out, and buildings deteriorate. All of the many segments that comprise the industrial enterprise require attention, including: the buildings, grounds, machinery, equipment, materials handling equipment, heating and generating equipment, waste disposal systems, air-conditioning equipment, washrooms, cafeterias, and so forth.

The *Maintenance Engineering Handbook*[1] classifies maintenance engineering into the following primary and secondary functions:

*Primary functions*:

1. Maintenance of existing plant equipment.
2. Maintenance of existing plant buildings and grounds.
3. Equipment inspection and lubrication.
4. Utilities generation and distribution.
5. Alterations to existing equipment and buildings.
6. New installations of equipment and buildings.

*Secondary functions*:

1. Storekeeping.
2. Plant protection, including fire.
3. Waste disposal.
4. Salvage.
5. Insurance administration.
6. Janitorial service.
7. Property accounting.
8. Pollution and noise abatement.
9. Any other service delegated to maintenance engineering by plant management.

Many activities are of such a specialized nature that they frequently can be done cheaper by outside contractors. Thus, many companies contract with outside firms to maintain their elevators, power plants, burnt out motors, and their computers and office equipment. The washing of windows and care of grounds are two other activities that are commonly performed by outside companies.

Much of the housekeeping is commonly assigned to the individual production departments. Each workman may be given the responsibility for keeping his work area clean and free from chips, shavings, oil, or other such items. It is the departmental foreman's responsibility to insure that tidy conditions are maintained in his department.

---

[1]L.C. Morrow (ed.) *Maintenance Engineering Handbook*, (New York: McGraw-Hill Book Company, 1957), pp. 1–4.

## Organization for Maintenance

There is no one best maintenance organization that can be used in all cases. The organization should be tailored to fit the particular technical, geographical, and personnel situations involved. In establishing the maintenance organization it should be recognized that the basic necessity is to maintain a plant at a level consistent with low cost and high productivity.

Considerable debate takes place among maintenance engineers as to the level to which they should report. Some are of the opinion that they should be under production whereas others think that they should be on equal footing with the production people. In general, it is probably sound practice to have the director of the maintenance function report to the level that is responsible for most of the other plant groups that the maintenance engineers serve.

The nature of the industry, that is whether it is primarily electrical, chemical, or mechanical, will have considerable influence on the maintenance organization. Also, the size of the plant and the scope of activities to be performed are significant factors that will affect the organization. In a small plant utilizing a minimum of mechanical equipment, the maintenance

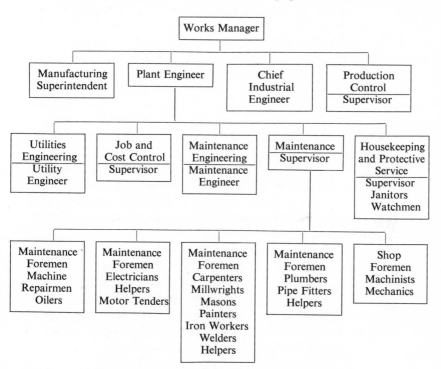

**Figure 16-1.** Structure of a maintenance organization.

department might consist of an all-round mechanic and a helper or two. In larger companies the maintenance group would be much more lavish and contain a variety of craftsmen. A typical organization chart for a medium-size plant is illustrated in Figure 16-1. Close scrutiny of this chart will reveal a number of features worthy of discussion.

The person in charge of the maintenance engineering activities is usually an engineer and most frequently carries the title of *plant engineer*. Other titles in use include maintenance superintendent, superintendent of maintenance, and manager of maintenance. Engineers may be used elsewhere in the maintenance organization to perform such functions as the supervision of the power plant operation, the design of special pieces of equipment, the checking of installation specifications, and the planning and scheduling of major projects.

One of the noteworthy features of most maintenance organizations is the large number of crafts represented in the group. This number will vary considerably depending on the variety of manufacturing processes present and the amount of work involved. Another factor that will influence the number of craftsmen required is the availability of skilled outside contractors and management's policy regarding the use of outside maintenance organizations. It is difficult to present any basis for determining exactly how many people are necessary in each craft in the maintenance organization. The ratio of maintenance to production employees will vary with the level of machinery and capital investment per operating employee and the efficiency of the maintenance organization.

An important part of the organization structure, as is illustrated in Figure 16-1, is the job and cost control section. This section is responsible for scheduling work for the maintenance personnel and for maintaining cost figures on all jobs. It makes possible the efficient utilization of the craftsmen anywhere in the plant but, at the same time, does not prevent localized routine daily assignments.

Machine and repair shops and storerooms provide essential supporting sections within many maintenance organizations. The shops commonly contain machinists and mechanics capable of repairing equipment, making new parts (otherwise not available), and rebuilding equipment. The storerooms maintain a supply of spare parts (bearings, shafts, electric motors, pumps) and general maintenance materials (pipe fittings, standard hardware, light bulbs, switches, lubricants) needed by the maintenance force.

Other service groups that are commonly under the supervision of the plant engineer are the utilities engineering section and the housekeeping and protective service groups. The former is responsible for the operation of the power and heating plant, and the other group is responsible for keeping the plant clean and protecting the premises.

## Economics of Maintenance

As pointed out earlier in this chapter, maintenance is a costly activity. It is one of the sizable indirect costs that enters into manufacturing, and, for this reason, it should be given considerable attention by management. Although maintenance methods are being improved constantly, the costs of maintaining equipment keep going up because the level and pay of the maintenance personnel keeps improving and there is more equipment to service—and most plants are willing to pay a high price to get stalled machinery back on line. Then too, industry tends to spend too little for replacement of obsolete production equipment, and old equipment poses many maintenance problems.

Since maintenance is such a costly undertaking, management should give consideration to all of the pertinent economic factors in establishing the company's maintenance policy. Much thought must be given to answering such questions as: (1) How much maintenance is needed? (2) What size maintenance crews should be used? (3) Is centralized maintenance desirable? (4) Should maintenance be done by outside contractors? (5) Should a preventive maintenance system be established? (6) Should maintenance work be scheduled? (7) Should maintenance jobs be covered by a suitable work measurement system? (8) Should maintenance workers be covered by a wage-incentive system? (9) Is adequate use being made of work simplification, work sampling, waiting line theory, monte carlo simulation, critical path method and other techniques in analyzing work methods and crew sizes?

**Maintenance policies.** Fundamentally, maintenance policy must answer the question of the size and extent of the maintenance facilities. Foremen and manufacturing people will naturally want maintenance crews large enough so that every job can be done on a moment's notice. What mechanics do when they are not working on a maintenance job is not the concern of a production foreman. Management must look at the long-range picture and establish policies that will make possible the completion of necessary maintenance work and at the same time keep costs at a reasonable level. Skilled mechanics are not easy to come by, and of course they are expensive to employ and train. Management therefore wants the "right" number on hand.

Points worthy of consideration in establishing maintenance policy are:

1. Contract out some work during peak periods to avoid getting too far behind and also avoid hiring temporary extra help.

2. Defer some maintenance work until slack periods so as to keep

the work force intact during such periods. Overhaul work and painting projects are often handled on this basis.

3. Replace machines and equipment at the optimum time. This time is difficult to determine, but many machine tool manufacturers stand willing and able to assist in such determination. The point is to replace machines before they get too old and require too much repair work. (See Chapter 6 on equipment replacement.)

## Maintenance Work Assignments and Procedures

All too often maintenance work is initiated by a frenzied call from a production foreman informing the maintenance department that a machine has broken down, a conveyor has stopped, or something has happened to stop production. Such calls usually result in immediate action in order to get production rolling again. Not all maintenance work will be this urgent, and most companies utilize a maintenance work order form to initiate the maintenance work. This form may be as elaborate or as simple as the company's accounting system demands.

If control is to be maintained on maintenance activities (as will be discussed later), no work should be done by any members of the maintenance department without a work order authorized by a responsible supervisor. The work order (see Figure 16-2) authorizes the maintenance craftsman to perform the work. Also, it provides a record of what was done, the date on which it was done, the cost of the job, the department to which it is to be charged, the materials and parts used, and similar information. Work orders may originate in the following ways:

1. Operating departments may request work to be done.
2. Regular inspections performed by the maintenance department may disclose work to be done.
3. Changes may be initiated by engineering, management, or production departments.

Such maintenance work as lubrication and inspections that are done on a regularly scheduled basis are usually covered by a patrol or blanket work order. Large maintenance jobs involving new machine or equipment installations or major machine or building repairs generally require the approval of some higher level of management before the work order can be initiated. One of the first steps on large jobs, such as installing a new conveyor, is to secure a cost estimate from the maintenance department. If the cost is such that the departmental foreman does not have the authority to approve the work, then he has to submit a proposal to the proper level

| Received | | **Maintenance Repair Order** |
|---|---|---|
| | Completed | |

| | | CLASSIFICATION | MRO # |
|---|---|---|---|
| IN | MAN | Emergency _____ | Account # |
| OUT | TIME | Machine Down _____ | Time Paid |
| IN | MAN | Preventative _____ | Mat'l Cost |
| OUT | TIME | Start On _____ | Ordered By |
| IN | MAN | Complete By _____ | Date |
| OUT | TIME | | |

Mach. _____ No. _____ Inv. No. _____

**PRELIMINARY ESTIMATE OF TROUBLE**

| IN | MAN |
|---|---|
| OUT | TIME |
| IN | MAN |
| OUT | TIME |

**ESTIMATE OF WORK AND ALLOWED TIME**

| IN | MAN |
|---|---|
| OUT | TIME |
| IN | MAN |
| OUT | TIME |
| IN | MAN |
| OUT | TIME |
| IN | MAN |
| OUT | TIME |
| IN | MAN |
| OUT | TIME |

**MATERIAL AND COST**

| IN | MAN |
|---|---|
| OUT | TIME |
| IN | MAN |
| OUT | TIME |
| IN | MAN |
| OUT | TIME |
| IN | MAN |
| OUT | TIME |
| | Total Time |

Form 788

TOTAL COST _____

**Figure 16-2.** Maintenance work order (Courtesy Fairfield Manufacturing Company).

of management requesting approval of the project. On large projects considerable time may elapse between the time the estimate is received and the actual performance of the work because of the necessity to plan the work, to make any necessary blueprints, to secure materials and parts, and to plan work schedules.

The manner in which work assignments are made to the maintenance men will vary with the craftsman involved and whether he is performing emergency or routine duties. Many small jobs are rush jobs that are initiated by a telephone call from the production supervisor. The maintenance clerk will record the request and, if the job is small, may be authorized to contact an appropriate craftsman to do the job. If the job is a large one, he probably will contact a maintenance foreman and ask him to check on the work to be done. The maintenance foreman, in turn, may pull his men off lower priority jobs to do the necessary work.

Since maintenance men are used all over the plant, and the foreman must travel throughout the plant to check on jobs and to inspect work in progress, communications presents a big problem. As an example of the magnitude of this problem, consider an automobile assembly plant in California where there are 13.6 miles of conveyors and hundreds of process units and service equipment to keep running. To facilitate the maintenance communications in this plant, the company uses seven citizen band radios and coded light panels located at strategic locations. When there is an equipment failure, the correct panel section will flash on indicating by code, correct location of the stoppage. Contact with the appropriate maintenance group can then be made by means of radio or telephone.

**Control of maintenance.** Maintenance control necessarily involves paper work and records. Adequate records are necessary to a successful maintenance program almost regardless of the size of the plant. Even in our own homes more successful operation of our many gadgets could be achieved if we set up a simple schedule of inspection for obvious defects, recorded dates and findings, and took appropriate action before breakdowns occurred.

Some of the control measures used and forms that assist are as follows:

1. *Work authorization.* As indicated previously, a work authorization or work order is usually required before any maintenance work can be started. The form is made out by the operating foreman concerned or by someone who has direct responsibility for operation of equipment. The order includes information concerning location of work, the work that is to be done, and the date work should or could start. Approval by others in authority is usually required, not only as a control measure to be sure the work is necessary, but also to be certain that materials and labor are available, to work the order into the overall schedule, and to be sure that this order doesn't call for a violation of company policy, safety rules, or building codes.

2. *Work schedule.* One of the more difficult phases of maintenance control is the working out of a satisfactory schedule when a group of authorized work orders are on hand. As a first step the maintenance foreman or job control supervisor must estimate the number of men and the time required for each work order. Then, knowing the number of men available

on the crews, he can derive some kind of a schedule estimate. Emphasis needs to be placed on the word "estimate," for any maintenance schedule is just that. Even in the best plant an emergency call will frequently come in that disturbs the carefully worked out schedule.

3. *Material costs.* Costs of maintenance jobs are usually figured by keeping track of the materials used and the labor hours expended on any one job. Material costs are determined by the use of storeroom requisitions. A mechanic needing a new bearing to repair a machine checks the bearing out of the storeroom, indicating on the requisition that it is to be used on a machine on Work Order No. 246. All charges to Work Order No. 246 can then be accumulated to show a total material cost for that particular job.

4. *Labor costs.* Labor hours spent on any one job may be recorded in various ways. Some companies have each mechanic turn in a special card at the end of each day indicating how long he spent on each job assigned him.

The dollars charged to any hour of a mechanic's time spent on a maintenance job may be the actual dollars paid that mechanic, an average wage figure for all mechanics, or a figure representing not only average wage dollars but also the overhead of the maintenance department itself. This latter charge would include such things as maintenance foreman's salary, storeroom upkeep, and power used in the shop.

5. *Budgets.* Although maintenance costs fluctuate some estimates must be made for budget purposes. Here experience is the best guide. Next year's maintenance costs will not vary too much from last year's, assuming that the production schedule is about the same and that the management does not permit (or is planning not to permit) the general level of maintenance to go up or down. Budgets are frequently set up on a percentage basis or on the basis of so many dollars of maintenance for so many units of production output. Again, experience is the guide. If actual maintenance required over the past several years worked out this way, then it is feasible to plan that way for future budgets.

In budgets a distinction is usually made between repair jobs and improvements. Repair jobs simply put the equipment back into its original condition. Improvement jobs, on the other hand, make the equipment more useful or valuable to the company than it was originally. The repair job is charged as an operating expense while the improvement job must be capitalized and shown on the books as an asset. The income tax situation, then, makes it attractive to some of the more unscrupulous companies to designate improvement jobs as repair jobs.

6. *Equipment records.* Records of equipment such as shown in Figure 16-3 are a necessary part of every good maintenance program. Such records include all the pertinent data concerning the equipment itself, such as serial

| 13-21-12 | | Drill Press | | | 39-2120 | | 1762521 | |
|---|---|---|---|---|---|---|---|---|
| MACHINE NO. | | TYPE MACHINE | | | CAT. NO. | | SERIAL NO. | |

VENDOR: **Perfect Machine Co.**

PURCHASE COST: **$1500.**  INSTALLATION COST: **$150.**  TOTAL COST **$1650.**

DATE PURCHASED **9-15-62**  DATE INSTALLED **11-30-62**  DEPRECIATION: **10** YEAR **$150.** PER YEAR

## MECHANICAL EQUIPMENT

### DEPRECIATION SCHEDULE

| YEAR | DEPRECI-ATION | ADDED TO VALUE | TO BE AMORTIZED | MAINTENANCE COST |
|---|---|---|---|---|
| 19 63 | | | | |
| 19 | | | | |
| 19 | | | | |
| 19 | | | | |
| 19 | | | | |
| 19 | | | | |
| 19 | | | | |
| 19 | | | | |
| 19 | | | | |
| 19 | | | | |
| 19 | | | | |
| 19 | | | | |
| 19 | | | | |
| 19 | | | | |
| 19 | | | | |
| 19 | | | | |
| 19 | | | | |

### ELECTRICAL EQUIPMENT

| | |
|---|---|
| EQUIPMENT | *Motor* |
| MAKE | 20 C L |
| SERIAL NO. | 425322 |
| TYPE FRAME | CD-67 |
| VOLTAGE | 230 |
| PHASE | — |
| AMPERES | 10 |
| HORSE POWER | 5 |
| R. P. M. | 850/170 |
| DRIVE | |
| CIRCUIT | |
| DATE INSTALLED | 11-30-62 |

CAT. NO. 1-9151   REMINGTON RAND INC.   KP-26044

## MAINTENANCE RECORD

MACHINE NO.   TYPE MACHINE

### MECHANICAL AND ELECTRICAL INSPECTIONS SCHEDULE

| YEAR | 1 | 2 | 3 | 4 | 5 | 6 | 7 | 8 | 9 | 10 | 11 | 12 | 13 | 14 | 15 | 16 | 17 | 18 | 19 | 20 | 21 | 22 | 23 | 24 | 25 | 26 | 27 | 28 | 29 | 30 | 31 | 32 | 33 | 34 | 35 | 36 | 37 | 38 | 39 | 40 | 41 | 42 | 43 | 44 | 45 | 46 | 47 | 48 | 49 | 50 | 51 | 52 |
|---|---|---|---|---|---|---|---|---|---|---|---|---|---|---|---|---|---|---|---|---|---|---|---|---|---|---|---|---|---|---|---|---|---|---|---|---|---|---|---|---|---|---|---|---|---|---|---|---|---|---|---|---|
| 19 63 | X | | | | X | | | | X | | | | X | | | | X | | | | X | | | | X | | | | X | | | | X | | | | X | | | | X | | | | X | | | | X | | | |
| 19 | | | | | | | | | | | | | | | | | | | | | | | | | | | | | | | | | | | | | | | | | | | | | | | | | | | | |
| 19 | | | | | | | | | | | | | | | | | | | | | | | | | | | | | | | | | | | | | | | | | | | | | | | | | | | | |

### OIL CHANGE AND LUBRICATION SCHEDULE

| YEAR | 1 | 2 | 3 | 4 | 5 | 6 | 7 | 8 | 9 | 10 | 11 | 12 | 13 | 14 | 15 | 16 | 17 | 18 | 19 | 20 | 21 | 22 | 23 | 24 | 25 | 26 | 27 | 28 | 29 | 30 | 31 | 32 | 33 | 34 | 35 | 36 | 37 | 38 | 39 | 40 | 41 | 42 | 43 | 44 | 45 | 46 | 47 | 48 | 49 | 50 | 51 | 52 |
|---|---|---|---|---|---|---|---|---|---|---|---|---|---|---|---|---|---|---|---|---|---|---|---|---|---|---|---|---|---|---|---|---|---|---|---|---|---|---|---|---|---|---|---|---|---|---|---|---|---|---|---|---|
| 19 63 | X | X | X | X | X | X | X | X | X | X | X | X | X | X | X | X | X | X | X | X | X | X | X | X | X | X | | | | | | | | | | | | | | | | | | | | | | | | | | |
| 19 | | | | | | | | | | | | | | | | | | | | | | | | | | | | | | | | | | | | | | | | | | | | | | | | | | | | |
| 19 | | | | | | | | | | | | | | | | | | | | | | | | | | | | | | | | | | | | | | | | | | | | | | | | | | | | |

### MAINTENANCE COST SUMMARY

KP-26043

| YEAR | | JAN | FEB | MAR | APR | MAY | JUN | JUL | AUG | SEP | OCT | NOV | DEC |
|---|---|---|---|---|---|---|---|---|---|---|---|---|---|
| **1 9 5 3** | LAB | — | — | — | 14.00 | — | | | | | | | |
| | MAT | — | — | — | 11.35 | — | | | | | | | |
| | TOT. | — | — | — | 25.35 | — | | | | | | | |
| | Y TO D | — | — | — | 25.35 | — | | | | | | | |
| **1 9 5** | LAB | | | | | | | | | | | | |
| | MAT | | | | | | | | | | | | |
| | TOT. | | | | | | | | | | | | |
| | Y TO D | | | | | | | | | | | | |
| **1 9 5** | LAB | | | | | | | | | | | | |
| | MAT | | | | | | | | | | | | |
| | TOT. | | | | | | | | | | | | |
| | Y TO D | | | | | | | | | | | | |

MACHINE NO.   MAKE   MODEL   LOCATION

KP-26043

| 27 | 28 | 29 | 30 | 31 | 32 | 33 | 34 | 35 | 36 | 37 | 38 | 39 | 40 | 41 | 42 | 43 | 44 | 45 | 46 | 47 | 48 | 49 | 50 | 51 | 52 |
|---|---|---|---|---|---|---|---|---|---|---|---|---|---|---|---|---|---|---|---|---|---|---|---|---|---|
| 1 | 2 | 3 | 4 | 5 | 6 | 7 | 8 | 9 | 10 | 11 | 12 | 13 | 14 | 15 | 16 | 17 | 18 | 19 | 20 | 21 | 22 | 23 | 24 | 25 | 26 |

| 13-21-12 | Drill Press | 39-2120 | 4-11 |
|---|---|---|---|

**Figure 16-3.** Equipment record that incorporates both a preventive maintenance schedule and a maintenance cost summary in one record. (Courtesy Remington Rand, Inc.)

number, supplier, and initial cost. Such information is of course necessary when ordering parts or when seeking information about that equipment from the supplier. A record card might also contain a record of repair work performed, the schedule for inspections, and the costs of inspection and repair. Repair cost information is especially valuable, for with such information one can determine when costs are running much higher than normal —possibly calling for replacement.

Some companies are now making excellent use of data processing equipment and digital computers to assist in maintaining maintenance records. One aircraft company utilizes punched cards to feed data into the system and can get almost immediate answers to such questions as: who received service, when and where did they receive service, what kind of service was performed, how much time did the maintenance man spend, what was accomplished, how much did it cost, and where are excessive maintenace costs being incurred. Also, this system is of tremendous assistance in making decisions on what to do when, to forecast equipment-replacement schedules, and so forth.

## Planning and Scheduling Maintenance Activities

It has been said that the tools of good maintenance are planning, scheduling, and cost accounting. The planning and scheduling section of the maintenance department has the basic responsibility for establishing job priorities, for insuring that necessary tools and materials are available, and for preparing and issuing written schedules of jobs to be done.

The size and organization of the planning and scheduling group will depend on the size and complexity of the maintenance organization. In a small company, all of the planning and scheduling may be performed by the maintenance supervisor. Under such circumstances the planning and scheduling will probably be handled on quite an informal basis. Larger companies, as indicated in Figure 16-1, utilize a special group to plan and schedule jobs. Although much of the work done in this section is clerical in nature, the supervisor of the group should be a person with broad experience in maintenance methods. Such knowledge frequently is necessary to coordinate the scheduling of the various craftsmen in the maintenance department.

In order to do the necessary day-to-day and long-range planning required to make most effective utilization of the maintenance personnel, suitable routines are necessary. These will involve: (1) the securing of necessary approval from the plant engineer for any projects that are of sufficient magnitude to require his attention; (2) the securing of information from equipment records, work orders, work measurement data, craft and shops work force reports, storekeeper's procurement reports, the plant production schedule, and other pertinent sources; and (3) reference to existing master schedules. As is true of all scheduling activities, basic to maintenance scheduling and control is an estimate of the time required for each work order prior to doing the work.

The scheduling of maintenance work involves essentially two steps—a master plan of all jobs that can be predicted in advance and a daily adjustment of this plan necessitated by emergencies. In most plants there are a number of machines and other items of equipment that need to be taken out of service periodically for inspection and overhaul. The frequency of these occurrences will vary with the equipment, but experience figures subjected to suitable mathematical and statistical analysis will indicate the optimum time for the minimum overall costs. After these times have been established, they can be incorporated into the master maintenance schedule.

The master maintenance schedules may be broken down into weekly or daily maintenance schedules. If used, the weekly work schedule will provide information to each craft and shop concerning the work to be done on each job for each day in the following week. This schedule would normally be issued every Thursday or Friday and would be the basis for each maintenance foreman to issue daily work assignments to his men. Some maintenance departments prefer to centralize this function and have daily work assignments issued directly by a dispatcher in the job control section. Whatever system is used, it is sound practice to issue work assignments for the next day to each craftsman prior to the end of his workday.

Accurate information on the number of hours of labor spent on each job and any materials used are essential items for cost-accounting purposes. These charges are made against the pertinent departments and become one of the costs of manufacturing. Further, the costs provide a check on the operating effectiveness of the departments concerned.

## Types of Maintenance

Maintenance may be classified into three general categories: corrective, preventive, and predictive. Brief descriptions of each of these will be discussed in the sections that follow.

**Corrective maintenance.**    Corrective maintenance is the fix-it variety, the kind most of us think of when the word "maintenance" is mentioned. In this sense maintenance becomes repair work. Repairs are made after the equipment is out of order—an electric motor will not start, a conveyor belt is ripped, or a shaft has broken. In cases such as these the maintenance department checks into the difficulty and makes the necessary repairs. If the maintenance department does only corrective work, theoretically it is idle except when equipment has broken down and repairs are required.

**Preventive Maintenance.**    In marked contrast to corrective maintenance is preventive maintenance, which is undertaken before the need arises and aims to minimize the possibility of unanticipated production interruptions or major breakdowns. Preventive maintenance consists of: (1) proper design and installation of equipment, (2) periodic inspection of plant and equipment to prevent breakdowns before they occur, (3) repetitive servicing, upkeep and overhaul of equipment, and (4) adequate lubrication, cleaning, and painting of buildings and equipment.

Preventive maintenance starts on the drawing board with those design features included in a product to minimize maintenance. As an example, one of the large rubber companies had considerable difficulty with a metal-lined pump that was used to pump liquid latex. The metal pump curdled the latex and kept clogging the line. They installed glass-lined centrifugal pumps that decreased the friction of flow and reduced their maintenance cost by 75 per cent. Not only did they reduce the maintenance cost, but the new pumps were cheaper.

Even though preventive maintenance is practiced to some extent in about 75 per cent of all manufacturing companies, every preventive mainte-nance program has to be tailored to an individual plant. The key to all good preventive maintenance programs, however, is inspection. This inspec-tion should cover virtually everything, including: production machinery, motors, controls, materials handling equipment, process equipment, light-ing, buildings, and plant services. Some plants inspect only items costing $500 or more, but others go as low as $50. As a general rule, if a failure in upkeep may harm an employee, stop production, or waste plant assets, then consideration should be given to including it in the preventive mainte-nance program. Suitable statistical techniques have been developed for determining how often to inspect. Suffice it to say that too much inspection is false economy.

A well-conceived preventive maintenance program should contain the following features:

1.   Proper identification of all items to be included in the program.

2.   Adequate records covering: volume of work, cost, and so forth.

3.   Inspections on a definite schedule—with standing orders on specific assignments.

4.   Use of checklists by inspectors.

5.   An inspection frequency schedule—may vary from as often as once every 6 hours to as little as once a year.

6.   Well-qualified inspectors—have craftsmen familiar with items being inspected and capable of making simple repairs at time trouble is observed.

7.   Use of repair budgets for major items of equipment.

8.   Administrative procedures that provide necessary fulfilment and follow-up on program.

There are many returns to the users of preventive maintenance programs: greater safety for workers, decreased production down time, fewer large-scale and repetitive repairs, less cost for simple repairs made before break-down, less standby equipment required, better spare parts control, identification of items with high maintenance costs, and lower unit cost of manufacture. As industry becomes more highly mechanized, it becomes more in need of the advantages of preventive maintenance. The costs of modern equipment are high and so are the costs of production breakdowns. Down time in excess of one per cent is considered critical in one highly mechanized auto plant and is justification for their elaborate preventive maintenance program.

**Predictive maintenance.** One of the newer types of maintenance that may be anticipated to gain increasing attention is called predictive maintenance. It is a preventive type of maintenance that involves the use of sensitive instruments (e.g., vibration analyzers, amplitude meters, audio gauges, optical tooling, pressure, temperature, and resistance gages) to predict trouble. Conditions can be measured periodically or on a continuous basis, and this enables the maintenance people to establish the imminence of need for overhaul. This will allow an extension to the service life without fear of failure. In an example cited by Quinn,[2] "some large turbo-generators were being dismantled for inspection every year, and more recently every three years. Now under predictive maintenance they have been operating continuously—and satisfactorily—without dismantling for over five years."

## Housekeeping and Protection Service

Many of the housekeeping chores in a plant start in each employee's work area. As pointed out previously, this has led many companies to hold each worker responsible for keeping his machine or work area free from chips, shavings, excess oil, and similar items. Some equipment and areas are not in direct personal use by individual workers, and no one is directly responsible for them. Thus, the aisles, the washrooms, the windows, and the warehouses need to be tended by someone else. The plant engineering and maintenance department, by its very nature, is called on to maintain so much of the plant that it is quite logical to make all housekeeping a part of its duties.

It is common practice to divide the plant and offices into cleaning zones and to assign a janitor to each zone. The janitors sweep and scrub the floors, clean lavatories, clean drinking fountains, and perform similar duties. Power sweepers have replaced manual sweeping in many plants and are used to patrol the entire plant area.

---

[2]James D. Quinn, "The Real Goal of Maintenance Engineering," *Factory*, June 1963, pp 90–93.

Plant security and fire protection pose continuous problems in every manufacturing plant, and these two functions are frequently included as a part of the plant engineer's responsibility. It is common to use guards at all of the plant entrances to insure that only authorized persons are allowed on the company's property. Watchmen are also needed to patrol the plant during non-working hours to guard against theft and fire. Some companies that are confronted with considerable fire hazard employ full-time firemen and maintain their own fire fighting equipment.

## Trends in Maintenance Engineering

Several significant trends are taking place in maintenance engineering. Increasing attention is being given to the design of buildings, facilities, and processes to eliminate as much maintenance as possible. There is increasing emphasis on manufacturing system reliability and procurement of equipment with a prescribed level of quality assurance. From an operational point of view, the maintenance engineers will be making more effective use of statistical tools to analyze the service life of the components of a manufacturing system and will be able to pinpoint problem areas and provide justification for improvement of component reliability or for periodic replacement to maintain system availability.

The increasing complexity of manufacturing processes will necessitate the continuous upgrading of maintenance personnel. One plant engineer, in response to a query about the problem of maintaining a highly automated production line, stated that he virtually needed maintenance men with the technical knowledge of electrical engineers to cope with all of the controls on the line. His statement may not be too farfetched, and some maintenance experts have predicted the need for a diagnostic engineer who would trouble-shoot the complex equipment and instruct less skilled mechanics in repair.

Predictive maintenance will get increasing attention as better instrumentation is developed to detect flaws in operating conditions.

## QUESTIONS

1. Make up a preventive maintenance checklist for your house, car, or some appliance with which you are familiar. Would your list be practical to put into use? Explain your answer.
2. Outline at least three types of situations in a manufacturing plant that would justify a program of preventive maintenance.
3. Through what procedure does a company keep track of the cost of a repair job?

4. What advantages does the use of a work authorization form have over the simple use of person-to-person communication concerning repair work? What disadvantages?

5. What is the distinction between a "repair job" and an "improvement"? Is this distinction important?

6. Outline cases both for and against the keeping of equipment records.

7. What role in safety work is played by maintenance engineering?

8. Some maintenance engineers contend that preventive maintenance on many items is absolutely unnecessary. Comment on this opinion.

9. How can the effectiveness of a maintenance department be evaluated?

## CASE PROBLEM

**Akron Forgings Company**

Bill Barnes had reason to be proud of the Akron Forgings Company's maintenance record for the past six months. Not once during that time had there been production holdup because of machinery breakdowns. As maintenance supervisor, Bill had been striving for six years to achieve this goal. He knew the record probably couldn't hold for another six months; but nevertheless he appreciated that the plant manager, Stephen Cross, was predicting that it would. Mr. Cross had made this prediction when he made it a point to come out to the shop and commend Bill.

A few days later the cost records for the past six months reached Mr. Cross's desk and he noticed that maintenance costs for the period were considerably higher than they had been for similar periods during the past two years. Production levels for all three years were roughly the same.

*Questions:*

1. How do you account for the high maintenance costs?

2. Was Bill's record really a good one?

3. What action should Mr. Cross take?

# CHAPTER SEVENTEEN

# Cost Control

In a manufacturing concern accounting activities are usually divided into two parts: namely, financial accounting and cost accounting. Financial accounting deals with the business as a whole, and at the end of a designated accounting period produces information about the current financial status of the business, as well as the amount of profit or loss incurred during the period in question. This information is in the form of balance sheets and profit and loss statements, both of which are discussed in some detail in Chapter 24. Cost accounting, on the other hand, may be thought of as that part of the accounting procedure that deals with the determination and analysis of the costs of particular processes, jobs, or departments, within the company. Such cost accounting becomes the basis of cost-control systems and budgetary control plans. Cost control and budgetary control are both essential in the operation of a modern industrial enterprise, for they permit management to plan ahead and to know when to make changes in order to fulfill the plan.

## Role of Cost Accounting

Balance sheets and profit and loss statements do not reveal how profitable one product is versus another, or whether one plant produces more efficiently than another. Although the stockholder or investment analyst may care little about details of efficiency and cost, since to him the overall profit of the business is sufficient, management must take a different point of view. Naturally management is interested in maintaining the overall position of the company, but in order to insure the overall position it must have some indication of costs and profits as the accounting period goes along. In today's industrial world a company cannot afford to wait and see how profits turn out at the end of the year. Management must know at any point during the year the approximate position of costs and profits so that it may take corrective action before it is too late. This function is called cost control, and to achieve it cost accounting is necessary.

In cost accounting the total expenditures in operating a business are broken down on a per item or per unit basis, as for example the cost of producing a gallon of gasoline, a ton of coal, a dozen shirts, or a refrigerator. The same idea can be extended to cost per production order, as when a special product is made for a customer, or further extended to cost per activity or operation, such as the cost of drilling half-inch holes, or plating sheet metal of a certain size and quality. In other words, cost accounting is the job of taking overall business costs and separating them into greater detail according to unit of product produced, operation performed, or orders. For a company that manufactures only one product and only one size and style, cost accounting is no special problem, for the cost per unit can easily be determined by dividing the total cost figure by the number of units produced. In a more typical situation, however, a company may manufacture more than one product, and each product may be of a varying size and style. In that case the company must know how much of the total production cost was due to the manufacture of one product, and how much was due to another. Even in the company that manufactures only one product in one size and style, there would be a need to know the cost of one operation versus another for purposes of controlling these costs as time goes on.

Specifically, cost accounting provides information for the following purposes:

1. *Cost determination.* The costs and expenses of a business are recorded, classified, and allocated to various jobs, departments, products, or services.

2. *Costs for pricing.* Once costs are determined this information also serves as a guide regarding prices to be quoted to customers. Even though selling prices are only partly governed by the costs of production, in the long run the selling price must at least equal the cost of production, or there will be serious consequences to the profit and loss statement.

3. *Cost for managerial decision.* In a sense both the above items of cost determination and cost for pricing provide bases for managerial decisions. Although managerial decision-making actually becomes much more complex than the above statement implies, cost information may be helpful in making decisions that have to do with (a) whether to add a new product, or to drop one that is now being produced, (b) whether to manufacture a certain unit, or buy it on the outside, and (c) whether to add certain sales territories and to drop others.

4. *Cost control.* One of the more essential purposes of cost accounting is control of expenditures. Such control leads to efficiency in use of labor, materials, machines, and plants. Although to a large extent selling prices are determined by competition, the profit-making capacity of a business is guided by the efficiency with which costs are controlled.

## Basic Cost Elements

There are three basic cost elements with which we shall deal in this section. They are direct material cost, direct labor cost, and overhead. Overhead will be further subdivided as to whether it results from factory operation, sales effort, or general administration. Figure 17-1 shows in chart form the derivation of basic cost elements.

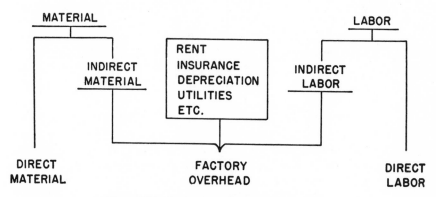

**Figure 17-1.** Derivation of basic cost elements.

*Direct material cost* is the cost of the material that can be directly iden- tified with the product and is delivered to the customer. In practice any scrap or waste of material is still charged as direct material even though it is not delivered to the customer. Also, one must take a practical point of view when applying this strict definition of direct material and arriving at direct material costs. Some direct material may cost so little that it is not worth-while to identify and charge it as direct material. Paint is a good example. Each unit of product may be delivered carrying a coat of paint, but the dollar value of the cost of paint is usually so small compared to the value of the product that it would be more reasonable to charge the paint simply as indirect material or overhead.

Indirect material in general may be thought of as those items used in the manufacture of a product that do not become an integral part of it. Costs of these materials become overhead costs. Good examples of indirect material would be light bulbs to light the area, cleaning rags, sandpaper, and hand tools.

The concept of *direct labor cost* is very similar to that just described for direct material cost. The direct labor costs are the costs of labor that can be identified directly with the manufacture of the product or the direct results of which are delivered to the customer. As before, if an item of direct labor becomes so small as to have little dollar value, it may be more feasible to consider it as indirect labor and treat it as overhead. Good examples of indirect labor in manufacturing operations are maintenance work, cleaning operations, and clerical work.

The direct material and direct labor costs when added together for any one product are called *prime cost*. Prime cost then represents the total *direct* cost of producing a product and is usually a figure relatively easy to determine and to determine with reasonable accuracy. Overhead costs present a different kind of problem.

*Overhead* costs are often defined as all manufacturing costs other than direct material and direct labor or other than prime costs. This may seem like a backward definition, but it turns out to be as useful a definition as one can devise. In practice, overhead costs are arrived at in essentially this manner. If a cost item isn't either direct labor or direct material, it must be overhead.

We have mentioned two common types of overhead: indirect material and indirect labor. Other items that usually fall into the overhead category are heat, light, power, insurance, rent, depreciation, taxes, and telephone. Often it is possible to identify overhead expense with a particular product, as when a special lubricant is used only in the manufacture of one product. In such a case one may be tempted to charge the entire cost of the lubricant to that product, instead of putting it in overhead to be later apportioned among all products; but this is seldom done because the additional accuracy obtained would not be worth the cost of the extra bookkeeping. Exceptions might be in cases where expensive dies or tools are required for one product or where readily identifiable and separable departments or buildings are used on only one product.

We have been discussing overhead costs that are incurred by the factory. These overhead costs when added to prime cost yield what is commonly known as *factory cost*. Factory cost can be thought of as the total unit cost of manufacture. There are other costs of the business, however, and these are generally thought of as additional overhead costs, namely, the cost of selling and the cost of general administration.

The idea of separating factory, sales, and administrative costs in a company can best be grasped by visualizing separate physical locations for each of the three functions (not an uncommon situation in modern industry). When viewed in this light one can see that sales expenses would include salaries and commissions of salesmen, advertising, traveling expenses, rent on sales offices, clerical help, and general supplies. General administration expenses would be the costs of supporting the "front office," including such items as salaries of executives, clerical assistance, legal and other professional fees, and office rent. As before, it will be possible at times to identify certain sales and administrative expenses with certain specific products, but such handling of these expenses is rare. Instead, they are totaled and apportioned among the various products in a manner to be discussed in the next section.

## Obtaining Unit Costs

The previous section has been largely concerned with defining cost elements. Let us consider how these cost figures are obtained, particularly on a per-unit or a per-product basis.

Direct material and direct labor present little difficulty. One can generally measure the amount of direct material used, and total cost is available from invoices. Product yields being known, the direct material dollars per unit can be easily obtained. Most factories require their employees to keep time records, and from these records can be determined the number of direct labor hours spent on any product or order. Knowing hourly rates and units of output, one can easily compute direct labor dollar cost per unit.

Getting overhead costs on a per-unit basis presents a different kind of problem. We have a total dollar figure for overhead for perhaps a month's operation. Part of this money was spent just in keeping the building and equipment intact, part was spent on providing supervisory, clerical, maintenance, and cleanup help for all departments and products, and part was spent on each of the various products produced or orders filled during that month. The question is, how much of the total should one charge to each product produced during that month?

This question can never be answered to the complete satisfaction of all, and it usually becomes necessary to compromise in some respect. In theory, overhead costs should be allocated to the various products manufactured on the basis of each product's responsibility for that cost. In practice, however, this is either impossible or too costly; so the theoretical ideal is approached as closely as possible by selecting that one of the commonly used systems of allocation that best fits the situation. Common bases for the allocation of overhead costs are:[1]

---

[1]This treatment oversimplifies the problem of overhead distribution as faced in most companies. Overhead usually is distributed to *all* departments first before being distributed to those departments that produce products. For example, the personnel department would be allocated its share of costs (heat, light, wages, and so on). Total personnel department costs would then be allocated to producing departments on some basis. This two-step process is necessary since the personnel department (like many others in a factory) has no "product" to which its services can be charged.

1. Number of employees.
2. Direct labor costs.
3. Direct labor hours.
4. Direct material costs.
5. Machine hours.
6. Floor area.
7. Prime costs.

A simple example of a company making but two products will serve to illustrate the allocation procedure. Let us assume this company wished to allocate factory overhead on the basis of direct labor hours, for it appears that there is a close relationship between direct labor hours and factory overhead incurred. If overhead to be allocated for the month is $20,000 and Product A required 400 direct labor hours and Product B 600 direct labor hours, the total overhead chargeable to each product would be as follows:

$$\text{Product A} \quad \frac{400}{1000} \times \$20,000 = \$8,000$$

$$\text{Product B} \quad \frac{600}{1000} \times \$20,000 = \$12,000$$

Knowing the number of units of each product produced during the month one could determine the overhead cost per unit.

The same type of allocation will be necessary for sales expense and administration expense, except that the basis of distribution will generally be even more arbitrary than that used for factory overhead. When sales and administrative expenses on a unit basis are added to unit factory cost, the result is total cost. This is summarized in Figure 17-2.

The concept of *contributed value* is one to be mentioned at this point.

Figure 17-2. Development of the total cost of a product.

Contributed value is factory cost minus direct material cost and is commonly used as a measure of the effectiveness of a manufacturing operation. In a sense a company has no control over the cost of direct materials it purchases, but does have control of all of the costs after the purchase of that direct material, and so may find it useful to know what these contributed costs are and how much they vary from time to time.

## Past Versus Future Costs

We have been speaking of cost determination and cost allocation strictly in the historical sense. In other words, our discussion so far has looked at costs *after* the accounting period is over and products have been stored in the warehouse; and we have then tried to determine costs on a per-unit basis. Such figures are interesting and helpful to some extent, but they are not completely adequate. In managing operations we need sufficient information about what future costs should be so that bids may be placed on jobs, selling prices may be estimated ahead of time, and a basis for corrective action may be provided. The use of standard costs is helpful both in predictive work as well as in control.

Standard costs are carefully worked out estimates of what the various costs elements should be. Such estimates can usually be made only after much study and considerable experience. Even then it may become necessary to alter them because some factors were overlooked or changed considerably. Nevertheless, actual historical costs can be compared with standard costs from time to time and thereby indicate to management where cost-reduction efforts would be most fruitful. This is the heart of cost-control work as it is in any control system: comparison of actual with standard.

In a standard cost system the comparison of actual with standard is facilitated by setting up a number of variance accounts. Typical variance accounts are material price variance, material usage variance, labor cost variance, and burden variance. At the end of any accounting period, usually a month, the variance accounts indicate the amount of money that actual costs exceeded or were less than standard costs. In the case of purchased materials, differences between actual costs and standard costs could occur either because more or less material was used than should have been used; or because the price paid for the material was more or less than standard. This accounts for the two material variance accounts mentioned earlier.

The determination of the standard costs for a product is a complex operation, but is similar in nature to the process of obtaining unit costs, which was discussed earlier in this chapter. As before, the determination of a direct material cost can be made in a fairly straightforward manner by studying blueprints and bills for material, and by having knowledge of yields from the various processes or machines used. Scrap factors may also have to be taken into account, but if one has had very much experience in producing the product whose cost is being standardized, the determination of direct material cost will be relatively easy and relatively accurate. Direct labor cost also will prove to be straightforward if one has had experience in manufacturing the product and has accurate time records for the employees involved. Direct labor cost determination on a standard basis is made considerably easier if the company makes use of time standards as discussed in Chapter 8. If time standards are available for all jobs, the data for any particular product need only be added in order to determine the standard labor cost for that product.

As with the allocation of overhead discussed earlier, the determination of standard overhead rates is a rather arbitrary procedure. To determine estimated overhead rate, one divides the estimated overhead for the period by the estimated production for the period in units, hours, or dollars, depending upon the previously determined base. Estimated overhead for the period may be developed from an actual study of costs to be expected, or may be based on past costs at a similar level of production and similar product mix. A typical overhead rate would be 225 per cent of prime cost. To estimate overhead cost per unit, then, one simply takes 225 per cent of the prime cost per unit. Of course, as with standard costs in general, overhead rates should be computed and used only after thorough study and experience.

It should be recognized that the differences or variances that occur between standard costs and actual costs will not have any real effect on the profit or loss of the business for the period in question. Variances are charged out to the profit and loss account so that the actual profit for the period turns out to be the same as though books had been kept on a purely historical basis. On the other hand, incorrect standard costs may have an influence on the business, if one uses them as a basis of bidding on new business. For example, if a standard cost for a product is quite high in comparison to actual historical cost, and one uses the standard cost as the basis of a bid, the bid may be lost because of its high price. Likewise, a "low" standard used as a basis of a bid may serve to secure the job, but cause the company to lose money on the job. The point is to make as certain as possible that standard costs are correct costs and that operations are controlled so that actual costs then coincide as closely as possible with the standard.

## Job Order Costs and Process Costs

Whether one is developing standard costs or historical costs, the problems involved will vary depending on whether one follows the job-order cost method or the process-cost method. Sometimes it is necessary to combine the two methods, but for the most part the method one uses depends upon the type of manufacture.

The job-order cost method collects the cost of jobs that are kept separate during the manufacture or construction period. The cost unit is the job, the order, or the contract; and the accounts show the cost of each order. This method assumes that the jobs can be physically identified and separated from each other. A variation of the job-order cost method is the costing of orders by lots. In many shops it is much more convenient and economical to consider a product in lots of a dozen or one hundred rather than individually.

The process-cost method consists of computing an average unit cost by dividing the total manufacturing cost by the total number of units produced in the factory over a given period of time. In particular this would apply in those plants where the product could not be physically separated in units and would be applicable to industries such as flour mills, chemical plants, textile factories, and breweries. Because of the multiple output, it is necessary to compute a unit cost at the end of each process. Furthermore, the plan is used to cost production when the product of one process becomes the material of the next and when different products or by-products are produced by the same process.

A variation of the process-cost method is the method of costing by operations. Operations constitute the labor or the machine performances that are necessary in the manufacture of a commodity. Several different products may go through the same process and the cost of that process would have to be divided among the various products going through it.

## Cost Reduction and Cost Control

At some time or other almost every company has had some kind of program of cost reduction. The precise reason for any particular program of cost reduction may vary considerably from time to time and from company to company, but all such programs have in common the basic need to reduce costs of operations below their present level. Specific reasons could be the softening of the economy generally, particularly rough competition in a specific product line, or a wish to reduce the selling price of a particular product and thereby broaden its market.

We have been emphasizing throughout this chapter and indeed throughout this section of the book the desirability of planning and controlling operations. Specifically, in regard to costs, this means it is necessary to establish what costs should be for operations, and then to make certain that these cost goals are met by careful follow-up and control of all aspects of the production process. If this plan were followed religiously, the need for cost-reduction programs would be considerably reduced. Unfortunately, however, many companies do not follow such a plan of standardizing and controlling costs, and other companies may have such a plan but are not strict in adhering to it. In other words, their variances may always be on the high side, and in time they have a tendency to increase their standard costs rather than to decrease their actual costs. There follows a gradual upcreep in costs of operation, and one wonders why the company should have the standard cost system in the first place if it does not really make it work. This upcreep in costs is most likely to happen during periods of prosperity when profits are relatively easy to come by, and managers see no particular harm in overspending their standard costs or overspending their budget. The facts of economic life often catch up with such attitudes, however, with the result that cost-reduction programs must then be instituted and are often of the variety of an arbitrary percentage cut of all costs across the board.

It should be noted that even with good and tight control of costs many companies find "fat" creeping into their costs of operation. This "fat" may not be any one person's fault but may simply follow in the wake of a gradual introduction of new processes or new systems without a corresponding reduction in other costs. Sometimes the elimination of old products and old systems is not done thoroughly enough to eliminate all the costs involved with that old product or system. This means that even in the very well-run company, a cost-reduction program of a relatively short duration may be desirable from time to time. If for no other reason, the program could serve to re-educate everyone in the necessity to hold costs down and also provide an opportunity to trim off the "fat," which may have been developing over the months.

Finally, we must mention the regular and continuing cost reduction efforts that should be a routine part of every manufacturing activity. Some parts of engineering departments essentially have a full-time job devoted to cost reduction although they may not always regard it in that light. Methods engineers, process engineers, and product engineers almost always measure their accomplishments in terms of cost reductions they are able to bring about. All of the control functions mentioned earlier in this section should have as a part of their regular duties the reduction of the cost of carrying out that particular function. As an example, the quality control function not only attempts to reduce the cost of manufacture by improving the quality level produced, but should also attempt to reduce the cost of performing the quality control function. In other words, it should attempt to find better and cheaper methods for controlling the quality of the product.

## Budgetary Control

The previous sections outlined the use of cost standards as a device for controlling manufacturing operations. Cost accounting, although not a control device itself, provided the necessary information for setting up cost standards. Budgets are also used for cost-control purposes and will be discussed in that role in the pages that follow.

## Budgets and Their Use

We normally think of budgets in terms of a number of dollars and a list of items on which those dollars will be spent. A business budget differs somewhat from this common concept inasmuch as it must be more detailed. It will specify units to be produced, broken down into sizes and styles, as well as costs of production. In fact, a considerable part of the budget comes from the use of the estimated cost breakdown figures discussed earlier. The budget can then be thought of as an overall plan for the operation of the business in terms of sales, production, and expenditures. One can see that it thereby acts as a coordinating device among the various functions of the business. If the overall budget is to have any meaning or any usefulness, executives in charge of the various functions are going to have to work together in developing their plans for the year ahead.

Another useful purpose of the budget is to facilitate planning within the company. A budget prepared without adequate planning is hardly worth the paper it is written on. Executives must have a good idea of what lies ahead before they can develop adequate budget estimates.

A third purpose of budgets has already been mentioned, namely, that of control. After having made plans for the year ahead and coordinated all plans in a consolidated company budget, we can then use the budget figures to control operations during the year. "Control" here is used in the usual sense of noting when expenditures fall outside the budget estimates, tracing down the cause of such variation, and taking corrective action as necessary.

## Fixed and Flexible Budgets

The preparation of a budget begins with an estimate of sales for the year ahead. Techniques for making such forecasts are discussed in Chapter 25. From sales forecasts can be determined production requirements, taking into account the inventory situation. The production estimate then becomes the basis for determining material, personnel, plant, and equipment requirements and the costs allied with each (see Chapter 24).

A budget made up in this manner based on one level of production output is called a *fixed budget*. There is one budget figure for each item of cost, and this figure becomes a ceiling on the cost of that item. Fixed budgets are very satisfactory for stable businesses, but should a business be subject to fluctuating sales or varying rates of output, the rigidity of a fixed budget imposes hardship. To overcome this some companies make use of *flexible budgets* or budgets made up for different levels of production. For example, budgets might be made up for 80 per cent, 100 per cent, and 120 per cent of production capacity. If the plant is operating one month at 120 per cent of rated capacity, it will be expected to adhere to the 120 per cent budget. Next month, operation may be at 100 per cent capacity. In this manner smooth, continuous budgetary control is assured even during times of varying production. See Figure 17-3 for an example of a flexible budget for manufacturing expenses.

|  | *Operating Capacity* | | | | |
| :--- | :---: | :---: | :---: | :---: | :---: |
| *Account* | *80%* | *90%* | *100%* | *110%* | *120%* |
| Clerical | $7,000 | $7,200 | $8,000 | $8,200 | $9,000 |
| Watchmen | 3,200 | 3,200 | 3,200 | 3,200 | 3,200 |
| Maintenance | 7,000 | 7,500 | 8,000 | 8,500 | 9,000 |
| Power, light & heat | 3,700 | 3,900 | 4,100 | 4,300 | 4,500 |
| Gas | 210 | 220 | 220 | 220 | 220 |
| Water | 1,100 | 1,150 | 1,200 | 1,250 | 1,300 |
| Rent | 12,000 | 12,000 | 12,000 | 12,000 | 12,000 |
| Depreciation | 12,900 | 12,900 | 12,900 | 12,900 | 12,900 |
| Compensation insurance | 2,800 | 3,300 | 3,800 | 4,300 | 4,800 |
| Fire insurance | 1,200 | 1,200 | 1,200 | 1,200 | 1,200 |
| Property taxes | 5,200 | 5,200 | 5,200 | 5,200 | 5,200 |
| Supervision | 14,500 | 19,800 | 19,800 | 19,800 | 22,300 |
| *Total* | $70,810 | $77,570 | $79,620 | $81,070 | $85,620 |

**Figure 17-3.** Flexible budget for manufacturing expenses.

## Breakeven Charts

Examining the breakdown of costs that appears on a flexible budget, one finds certain costs such as rent, taxes, and insurance that are constant even as production varies. Other cost items such as wages and materials vary as production varies. These differences in the basic nature of production costs suggest the construction and use of breakeven charts. A breakeven chart shows the cost of production at various levels of output as well as the income from sales at the same output levels. It must necessarily be assumed that all goods produced are sold, or else the chart has little meaning. With this assumption a typical chart will show total income at various output levels (see Figure 17-4). Where the two lines cross is the breakeven point, for if the plant produces at that level it won't lose any money, but on the other hand it won't make any money either. Output above the breakeven

**Figure 17-4.** Simplified version of breakeven chart.

point will result in a profit and output below will result in a loss—the amounts of which can be determined by reading the appropriate points on the graph.

The breakeven chart in Figure 17-4 is designed largely for illustrative purposes; it is doubtful whether any firm has a breakeven chart as simple as this one. Instead, practical breakeven charts are much more complex and as a result are much more difficult to construct. The main difficulty is that costs never break out as simply as this chart would imply. Fixed costs turn out to be straightforward but variable costs have differing degrees of variability. The breakeven chart of Figure 17-4 shows all variable costs as being *directly* variable with production, and this is seldom the case. Some may be directly variable like direct labor and direct material, but many costs like supervision will vary in a manner other than directly. This has given rise to a classification of *semivariable costs*, which would include all costs that are not fixed and are not directly variable. Under this concept it is possible to have more than one breakeven point, and a company might choose to produce at a point so as to maximize profit or to minimize loss. A feeling for this type of possibility comes by visualizing a production situation where expanded output would necessitate the opening of another wing of the plant but would not allow full utilization of all the additional area. Figure 17-5 shows a more realistic version of a breakeven chart although it too is simplified.

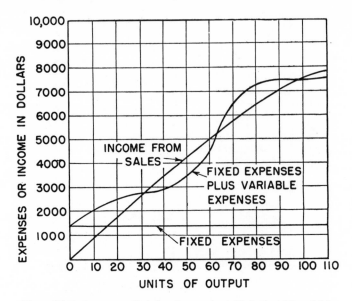

**Figure 17-5.** A more realistic breakeven chart. Note that (1) variable expenses are not all directly variable with production, and (2) for this particular plant there is more than one area of unprofitable operation.

The reader should not get the impression that breakeven charts are easy to construct or that every company knows precisely what its breakeven point is. Companies attempt to determine their breakeven points in two ways. One is to build up basic cost and sales data much in the manner we have discussed in this chapter. The other is to accumulate historical cost and sales data for each accounting period and plot these on a set of axes. Of course, several accounting periods will be required before a coherent chart is developed, but at least the company will have the satisfaction of knowing that the points represent actual operation rather than planned or hoped-for operation.

### Profit Centers

Attempts are often made to apply the breakeven-chart technique to the company as a whole. If the company produces and sells but one product, such an attempt will be relatively successful. On the other hand, if a number of products are produced and sold, summary figures of sales and costs may not have too much meaning. Variations in product mix will cause variations in summary figures, which might in turn lead to erroneous conclusions. It makes much better sense to divide the organization into units or centers and to compute costs and profits for each unit.

A center could be a department, a machine, a group of machines, or a process. The only requirement is that the various activities or parts of the unit have a common interest so far as producing the product is concerned. Although many such centers are thought of strictly on a cost basis, certain centers such as departments can often be thought of as profit centers, for they produce a product or perform a service that is sold and thereby produces income.

Interpreting any center or unit as a profit center rather than a cost center has great value—psychological and otherwise. We have discussed earlier how standard costs are computed and actual costs compared with standard, with the result that everyone attempts to "control" actual costs to keep them in line with the standard. Such a system will work very well, but in many cases much more interest and enthusiasm is generated on the part of all concerned if profit rather than cost is used as a criterion of performance. To determine that costs have risen by 15 per cent seems to have less meaning than to determine that profits have fallen by the same per cent. Apparently "profits" sound closer to home than do "costs." This device will be especially useful if "income" to a department or unit can be easily determined. A more obvious extension of the profit-center idea is the evaluation of branch plants of a multi-plant company based upon profit produced. This would necessarily entail separate financial statements for each branch plant.

## Accounting and Management

In this chapter we have discussed the use of accounting, especially cost accounting, in the management of a manufacturing enterprise. Before ending the chapter it may be well to emphasize that cost accounting is a means to an end and not an end in itself. This familiar and overused phrase is particularly applicable in this case, for often we become overawed with the apparent accuracy of cost figures, with the possible result that the company is being operated for the convenience of the cost-accounting department. Cost accounting is a tool or an aid to good management the same as many other functions are aids. All must be kept within the proper framework so that the company as a whole may prosper.

This is easier said than done, for it is desirable to have everyone who works in a staff capacity develop great enthusiasm for his particular activity. But in encouraging enthusiasm for staff activity we may overshoot to the point where concern for the company is in second place rather than first.

In accounting work people sometimes get the mistaken impression that the accounting staff "makes" the profits and that the cost accounting staff "determines" the costs. Both costs and profits are *determined* by the way management conducts the business. Accounting people simply keep records and compute results according to best accounting practices. By looking at past results and making use of engineering estimates, accountants can set budgets, standard costs, and other control devices—which again are designed to assist management in running the business. Of course, as accounting practices change it may appear that accountants are manipulating costs and profits; but although some manipulation of accounts undoubtedly takes place in the business world, it is only the manipulation of figures and not the manipulation of the manner in which the business is operated. After operating results are reported by the accountants, whether they be short term or long term, some modification in the operation of the business may be called for. This is the true function of accounting and cost accounting, for in this way they assist in the management of the business.

## QUESTIONS

1. What is the difference between cost accounting and cost control?
2. Explain the use of the four fundamental steps in control (see Chapter 11) in terms of the cost-control situation.
3. Why is the cost of producing a product only a guide in establishing selling price? What other factors enter in?
4. Select some common product such as a desk, table, or chair and list all direct and indirect materials that were probably used in its manufacture. Do the same for direct and indirect labor.
5. If a company has "low overhead," will this mean lower prices to purchasers? Explain your answer.
6. What are some logical bases that could be used to apportion (1) sales expenses and (2) administrative expenses?
7. Explain how it is possible to predict overhead costs ahead of time.
8. List and briefly explain the three uses for budgets in manufacturing.
9. Why are flexible budgets used in industry?
10. The breakeven chart of Figure 17-4 suggests that this manufacturer should expand his operations, for the more he expands the greater the spread between the cost and sales lines and hence the greater his profit. Would this be true in an actual situation? Explain your line of reasoning.
11. Distinguish between a cost center and a profit center. Explain the usefulness of each.

## CASE PROBLEMS

**Wimmert Machine Company**

The Wimmert Machine Company operates a small but successful machine shop in northern Indiana. Two reasons for its success are the careful attention paid to cost information and the accurate estimating that precedes the acceptance of every order.

The general estimating procedure followed is to study the blueprints submitted and ascertain the amount of material required. The cost of this material is then determined with the aid of vendor's catalogs. Direct labor dollar cost is obtained by multiplying the estimated direct labor hours by the appropriate hourly rates. For all small jobs, overhead is charged at the rate of 110% of direct labor cost.

Last week the estimating department was told that the company could secure an order for 600 special pump parts from the Mattoon Refrigerator Company if the factory cost were no more than $8.50 per unit. If factory cost can be kept at or below this figure, the selling price will not only cover administrative and selling expenses but will yield a good profit. A study of the job revealed the following cost data per unit:

> Estimated direct material cost: $3.18 each
> Direct labor cost:
> > 10 minutes @ $1.80 per hour
> > 30 minutes @ $2.40 per hour
> > 50 minutes @ $2.00 per hour

Since this job would tie up the entire shop facilities for one month, last year's average monthly factory overhead of $1374 was selected to be used as a guide, instead of the usual rate of 110%.

Soon after the above cost estimates were completed, it was learned that an order for 600 units of the pump part per month for the next twelve months might be secured if the factory cost were no more than $5.50 each.

To undertake such an order new equipment would be required, and the tool designers found that there were three possible tooling programs. Tooling A would cost $5760, tooling B would cost $3600, and tooling C would cost $1440. In addition, the following was determined:

> Tooling A production rate:   2 units/labor hr. @ $1.80/hr. labor rate
> Tooling B production rate:   2 units/labor hr. @ $2.00/hr. labor rate
> Tooling C production rate: 1.5 units/labor hr. @ $2.00/hr. labor rate

Since a large quantity of material was to be purchased, a 10% reduction in direct material costs could be obtained from the vendor. Overhead could be computed in the usual manner of 110% of direct labor cost, since the special tooling would release equipment for other orders.

*Questions:*
1. Should the Wimmert Machine Company accept the initial order for 600 pump parts?
2. Should the company accept the order for 600 pump parts per month?
3. Which tooling program do you recommend and why?
4. Evaluate the method of estimating overhead in the two cases.
5. If a 20% gross profit on sales is required, what would be the selling price of the initial order? (Use your computed factory cost.)

## Lane-Patton, Inc.

Mr. John Willard, the general manager of Lane-Patton, Inc., was not convinced that the company was using the proper costing methods when it placed bids on jobs. Since the company operated strictly as a job shop producing machined steel parts, it was particularly important that each job be priced properly. Seldom did any order run over 100 or 200 pieces. Recently the company had lost some jobs because their prices were "out of line," and Mr. Willard wondered if these "out-of-line" prices might be due to improper allocation of overhead. Overhead for the entire shop was high and its improper allocation to jobs could easily cause a price to be too high or too low.

In order to study the situation more closely Mr. Willard asked the chief accountant to supply him with a series of data. The data are presented below and represent average monthly figures based on operations during the past year.

| | |
|---|---|
| Direct material dollars: | $ 46,000 per month |
| Direct labor dollars: | $125,000 per month |
| Direct labor hours: | 50,000 per month |
| Machine hours: | 35,000 per month |
| Total factory cost: | $585,000 per month |
| Total factory area: | 260,000 square feet |

Mr. Willard soon realized that additional investigation would be necessary before he could establish proper overhead rates.

*Questions:*

1. With the information given, compute as many different overhead rates as feasible.
2. What would be the general requirements of any method of allocating overhead in this company?
3. What additional information could Mr. Willard use before making up his mind concerning overhead allocation?
4. Of the methods you used in Question 1, which would be easiest and least costly to put into use? Which would be most costly?

# Manufacturing
# Relationships

# CHAPTER EIGHTEEN

# Personnel
# Management

In spite of modern technology and all the systems and controls coming into widespread use, *people* remain the most important factor in modern manufacturing. None of these techniques or management methods are effective unless they are administered and carried out by competent employees. Dynamic leadership must be applied at the top of an organization, and capable employees must exist throughout the organization in order for a company to operate, grow, and prosper.

## The Role of People

The role of people in industry has been recognized to some extent since earliest recorded history, but its degree of importance seems to vary with the times. The history of early industrial development in the United States reveals there was little concern for workers as human beings. They seem to have been regarded as simply other machines. This attitude resulted in great dissatisfaction on the part of employees, which no doubt led to more rapid growth of unionism. Between World War I and World War II, however, there was increasing emphasis upon the importance of the human being and a great growth of personnel departments as well as interest in "human relations." In fact, attention to human relations became so fashionable that it was almost a cult. In some instances it might seem that the human relations angle may have overpowered the employee angle to the point that companies are more concerned with their employees' happiness than they are with their employees' output.

In recent years, with the introduction of data processing, computers, and automation generally, some fresh employee dissatisfaction seems to have been generated. Management has installed these devices without proper indoctrination of the employees involved, with the result that once again employees have begun to think of themselves as merely machines, and not very important machines at that. The fact that all employees in their daily lives, whether in or out of the company, seem to receive more and more types of identification numbers for various reasons may contribute to this attitude.

Although there are many things we do not know and understand about employees, we do know that employees like to be treated as individuals. On the other hand, a company planning and outlining a personnel program must set up fair policies and administer them consistently so as to avoid accusations of favoritism. Whether or not a company can successfully follow a path between individual treatment on the one hand, and consistent policy on the other, is seriously open to question. Obviously, some companies are better than others at this delicate balancing game, and all companies consistently attempt to improve their performance.

Although personnel and industrial relations departments are given the responsibility for administering much of a company's personnel program, personnel work as such goes on everywhere in the organization. Personnel relations are personal relations, and they affect all the people whose work must be directed and coordinated. In this sense, then, every supervisor and officer of the company is a personnel man and must act accordingly. The central personnel department acts as adviser and overall coordinator in addition to maintaining records and providing certain services. The areas generally administered by such a department are: (1) employment, (2) training, (3) health, (4) safety, (5) benefits, (6) services, (7) labor relations, and (8) wage administration. The first six of these items are discussed in the pages that follow in this chapter. The next chapter covers the subject of labor relations, and Chapters 20 and 21 cover wage administration. Figure 18-1 outlines the duties usually assigned many industrial relations jobs.

## Employment

The fundamental purpose of the employment section of the industrial relations department is to maintain an adequate supply of qualified workers. This is done by (1) maintaining adequate sources of recruits and (2) careful selection from those recruited.

The recruitment of potential employees refers to the contacting of qualified people who may be interested in working for the concern. A company wouldn't normally offer jobs to all those recruited, but the more people

# Industrial Relations Jobs in Business Organizations

*(This is a partial list to be augmented through further study)*

**Figure 18-1.** Jobs in industrial relations. (Courtesy Industrial Relations Center, University of Minnesota. Kriedt and Bendston, "Jobs in Industrial Relations.")

it recruits the more selective it can be in filling jobs. Sources of new employees to fill any particular job openings may be categorized as either inside the organization or outside the organization. The sources within the organization include transfers from some other department or job and promotions within the company. Some companies make it a policy to fill all jobs requiring any degree of skill from within the organization. Such a policy usually means better morale on the part of present employees, for they feel they will have an opportunity to get ahead.

Of particular interest in connection with filling job openings inside the organization are the practices of "job bidding" and "bumping." The details of either practice vary according to company policy and union agreement. In general, however, job bidding or posting refers to the practice of posting a notice on company bulletin boards to the effect that a specific job is open and anyone interested in being placed on this job should so indicate within a certain time limit. The duties and pay connected with the job are also indicated. At the end of the designated time period the employment manager lists the names of those employees who have submitted their applications, and the final selection is then made by the supervisor of the department involved who selects the employee who best qualifies for the job on the basis of ability and seniority. Bumping practice varies tremendously, but the main idea is that one employee may claim or "bump" another employee from his job, usually only on the basis of seniority. Rules are usually established having to do with the skills involved, whether or not one can bump jobs in other departments in the plant, and whether one can bump up hill as well as down hill. Bumping usually gets started during periods of layoffs and obviously can create a great disruption in jobs and personnel. Both bumping and job bidding may become headaches to the employment manager, since both practices create delays in getting people placed on their final job and in making clear what type of person or skill is needed from outside sources.

Outside sources of recruits cover a wide variety of possibilities. Among the more popular sources are the following: (1) employment agencies—both private and public, (2) schools, including specialized trade schools as well as the public schools, (3) casual applicants who come to the employment office directly, (4) miscellaneous organizations such as churches, lodges, and veterans' groups, (5) special arrangements with other businesses whereby employees laid off in one company may be hired by another, and (6) recommendations from present employees. The alert employment manager will develop these sources to a fine degree so that he can in a relatively short time supply to his company employees possessing the needed skills and abilities.

## Employment Policies

Before an employment manager can begin hiring, he must be familiar with both written and unwritten employment policies imposed upon his department by the company. These policies not only influence the sources he might pursue for recruits, but also are a basis for his preliminary screening and final selection of employees. Detailed analyses of employment policies are beyond the scope of this book; however, increasing public attention is being given to the discriminatory practices of many organizations, and it is clear that it is important to a company that it have well considered and defensible employment policies. Companies that have discriminated against applicants in the past owing to their religion, race, sex, physical handicaps, or other characteristics, would do well to reconsider the background and reasons for such policies. This is true, not only because of enlightened social pressures, but because the broadening of one's point of view might uncover some heretofore untapped sources of employees.

Unfortunately, many companies appear to hire employees under the principle of "survival"; i.e., the person hired is one who survives the many hurdles placed in his path. These hurdles include not only various tests and interviews that are administered but also certain employment policies, which may in effect really discriminate against certain people. No one condemns an employment manager for attempting to protect the best interests of his company; however, it is proposed that his "best interest" might be served if he takes a positive approach to recruiting and hiring. Such an approach would be to carefully determine the skills and abilities required upon a particular job and then to hire a person who best meets these requirements. By thus avoiding artificial barriers, the employer discriminates in favor of ability and against incompetency, instead of unrelated factors such as race and religion.

## Steps of Selection Procedure

Recruitment was described as the process of getting potential employees willing to apply for a job with the company. If recruitment is successful, several will apply, and from these the more desirable applicants must be selected. The basis of selection will normally be outlined on a job specification form which will list the qualifications a person must possess before being assigned to any particular job. For an applicant to be selected, he usually will have to pass satisfactorily several steps in the selection procedure.

Companies will often include preliminary steps of either a preliminary interview or a preliminary application blank in their selection procedure. Such steps are designed to eliminate the applicant who is obviously unfit for the type of work offered. Lack of certain requirements in education or experience might determine unfitness.

A preliminary step offers advantages not only to the company but to the applicant as well. If an applicant is eliminated in the early part of the selection procedure, the company is saved the expense of processing him through the remaining steps of the procedure. The applicant is also saved the time and trouble of going through the same procedure.

Whether or not a preliminary application blank is used, there is almost always a step in the selection procedure calling for the applicant to supply detailed information about himself on a complete application black. A typical example is shown in Figure 18-2. The application blank should call for information that has a bearing on the fitness of the applicant for the job, but, on the other hand, it should be as simple as possible. Questions having no bearing on suitability for the job should be eliminated and other questions calling for long or complex answers might better be asked and answered during an interview.

Employment tests are becoming an accepted step in selection procedures. However, they should be considered simply a step and not a replacement for the other phases of the procedure. The real value of tests frequently lies more in eliminating those applicants who have very little chance of job success than in selecting those applicants who will definitely be successful on a job.

There are several types of tests that are used in selection procedures, among which are performance tests, aptitude tests, intelligence tests, dexterity tests, interest tests, and personality tests.

Performance tests are designed to measure what an individual knows about a particular job or his degree of proficiency in performing certain tests. They are probably most useful in hiring employees at the lower levels for one can easily discover the ability of a prospective typist or welder by simply having him perform the task involved.

Aptitude tests attempt to measure a person's capacity to learn the skills required in a particular area. Examples would be a clerical aptitude test or a mechanical-relationships test. These tests usually determine specific aptitudes, although tests have been designed for measuring a whole group of aptitudes at the same time.

Intelligence tests are designed to measure the individual's ability to deal with abstract symbols, ideas, words, numbers, and so forth. The intelligence test was the first type of test to be used in personnel work, and probably it is still the most popular. Although the majority of questions asked are practical and job-oriented, there are many that are abstract.

## APPLICATION FOR EMPLOYMENT

Print your
name in full:_____
First       Middle (Married women use       Last
            maiden name here)

Street
Address _____        Nearest
                               telephone_____

                               Social
                               Security
City_____  State_____      Number_____

How long at this address_____

        Date of
Age_____Birth_____  _____  Height_____  Weight_____
        (Mo.)  (Day)   (Year)

Married?
Single?
Widowed?            Sports;
Divorced?_____ Sex_____  Hobbies?_____

Number of    List other        Have you any physical
children _____dependents_____  defects? What?_____

Were you ever employed    Names of relatives or
by this Company?_____   friends working here_____

Trade or
occupation? _____

Other work
you can do: (1)_____

"          (2)_____

Wages expected?_____

How many days have you lost
by illness in past 2 years?_____

| EDUCATION | Name of school | Location | Years attended | Years completed | Graduated? |
|---|---|---|---|---|---|
| Grammar School | | | 19___to 19___ | | |
| High school | | | 19___to 19___ | | |
| Other education or special training | | | 19___to 19___ | | |

I declare and warrant that the answers made herein are correct and true and that I am willing to undergo a physical examination and be fingerprinted.

**THE PROCTER & GAMBLE COMPANY**
**THE PROCTER & GAMBLE MANUFACTURING COMPANY**    (Signed)_____ (Date)_____
(SEE OVER)

**RECORD OF EMPLOYMENT:** Are you now employed?_____If not, how long have you been unemployed?_____
Beginning with your present or last position, record below complete details of your experience.

| From | To | Employer | Address | Wage | Duties | Reason for leaving |
|---|---|---|---|---|---|---|
| | | | | | | |
| | | | | | | |
| | | | | | | |
| | | | | | | |
| | | | | | | |
| | | | | | | |

What is the best job
you have ever had? Employer:_____ Address:_____ Occupation:_____

Service in
U. S. Armed Forces?   Branch of Service_____  Rate or  Date  Type of
                                                Rank____ from_____ 19___ to_____ 19___ Discharge_____

APPLICATION WILL NOT USE THIS SPACE          FORM

Remarks:_____                                          Selec.
                                                         Form 1
_____
                                                         Cler.

_____                                                  C

Date_____ Signed_____

**Figure 18-2.** Application blank for factory workers. (Courtesy Procter & Gamble Co.)

The whole point of any question used on such a test is whether or not it consistently helps to select the employee who will be successful in the future.

Dexterity tests are used to discover a person's cleverness with his hands. Many jobs require the skilful use of one's hands and body, and standardized dexterity tests can simplify the selection of persons to fill these jobs.

Interest tests are designed to measure an individual's preferences for certain activities of either a vocational or avocational nature. These tests usually have been used for vocational counseling, although they have some application in personnel selection, especially for sales jobs or other jobs requiring contact with other people.

Personality tests are undoubtedly the least useful of all those mentioned simply because of their lack of validity. Many personality tests have been devised for the purpose of measuring such characteristics as emotional adjustment, self-confidence, originality, and other "traits." But until more is known about personality, it is doubtful if most of these tests can be of much value in the selection process. There are a number of this type of test available on the market today. Although many may possess high validity and reliability under certain conditions, these same results cannot always be duplicated under different conditions. For this reason the generally preferred procedure is to have industrial psychologists develop tests that take into account the particular needs of the company. Even then the tests should not be considered a cure-all. They might be expected to improve the percentage of successful employees selected, but they can't be expected to raise that percentage to 100.

Application blanks and tests provide much valuable information about the applicant, but normally not enough to decide whether or not to hire him. Additional information that can be learned only through personal contact is required. An interview gives the company an opportunity to learn of special abilities, interests, and desires or personal characteristics possessed by the applicant, which might not otherwise be revealed. The interview also gives the applicant a chance to ask questions about the company, job, and future prospects. In other words, a more complete understanding should result from the interview.

The success of the employment interview will depend to a large extent on the conditions surrounding it and on the abilities of the interviewer. Some good principles of interviewing are as follows: (1) conduct the interview in private, (2) make the applicant feel at ease, (3) give the applicant your full attention, (4) discount your own personal prejudice, (5) keep control of the interview, and (6) arrive at a conclusion—not necessarily about offering or not offering a job, but about what comes next in the procedure or what action needs to be taken.

Many persons do not regard references as an important determinant in employment procedures, because information received from previous employers of the applicant or from his personal acquaintances may not reveal enough—one way or another. This has been true particularly when the reference check was carried on by mail. Personal interviews or telephone calls are more helpful and are used when checking on applicants for higher-bracket jobs. Some companies still use reference checks on hourly employees

# EASTMAN KODAK COMPANY
## ROCHESTER 4, NEW YORK

*Applicant Appraisal Form*

**AND ASSOCIATED DIVISIONS**

— *including* —

**Kodak**

TENNESSEE EASTMAN COMPANY
TEXAS EASTMAN COMPANY
EASTMAN CHEMICAL PRODUCTS, INC.
RECORDAK CORPORATION
DISTILLATION PRODUCTS INDUSTRIES

To:

Applicant:

An application has been received from the individual whose name is given. We should appreciate your evaluation of this person's characteristics, ability, and potential by completing this form. In particular, we should appreciate any comments you can provide on the back of this form, as such information is especially valuable. Your evaluation and comments will be held confidential.

It is important that the completed form be returned promptly so we may proceed with our consideration. A self-addressed envelope is enclosed for this purpose. Your co-operation will be most helpful and very much appreciated.

*Please use as a basis for rating, the comparison of this individual with all of the students with whom you have come in contact in your teaching (or working) career.*

Yours very truly

Business & Technical Personnel Department

| | NO BASIS FOR RATING | POOR | FAIR | AVERAGE | GOOD | SUPERIOR |
|---|---|---|---|---|---|---|
| 1. GENERAL APPEARANCE<br>Neatness, grooming, posture, dress, physical appearance. | | | | | | |
| 2. SOCIAL IMPRESSION<br>Social ease, speech and expression, mannerisms. | | | | | | |
| 3. ABILITY TO GET ALONG WITH OTHERS<br>Patience, open-mindedness, adaptability, respect for others. | | | | | | |
| 4. COMPETENCY<br>Ability to learn easily, ability to apply knowledge and ideas readily, creativeness, ability to analyze and plan, accuracy, reliability. | | | | | | |
| 5. ABILITY IN MAJOR FIELD<br>Comprehension of material studied, depth of interest. | | | | | | |
| 6. DRIVE TO ACCOMPLISH<br>Perseverance, thoroughness, initiative, enthusiasm. | | | | | | |
| 7. MATURITY<br>Common sense, stability, self-confidence, realistic outlook. | | | | | | |
| 8. LEADERSHIP<br>Ability to inspire confidence, organizational ability, desire and capacity for responsibility, ability to initiate, ability to make decisions. | | | | | | |

KO 1537  KP₆ 41845D                              (OVER)

**Figure 18-3.** Appraisal form for business and technical applicants. (Courtesy Eastman Kodak Company) simply to verify the facts concerning previous employment. Such facts would include time employed and jobs held. Figure 18-3 illustrates one type of reference form.

The use of physical examinations as a step in an employment procedure serves three purposes. First, it is a genuine selection device. A company generally wishes to hire only people who are in good physical condition and are free of communicable diseases. The company may have health standards as well as intelligence test standards or skill standards. Secondly, the physical examination assists in placing employees on specific jobs. An applicant may pass general health standards but be better qualified to work on certain jobs from a physical point of view. Thirdly, the company's general health program is facilitated by this initial physical examination. Later physical checkups will indicate whether the employees' general health is improving or deteriorating.

On the basis of these selection steps the employment department can arrive at a decision as to which applicants should be offered jobs. Inasmuch as the employment department is a staff department, it is clear that this selection is not a final one but instead is a recommended or preliminary one. The foreman or supervisor in the department where the job opening exists will usually make the final selection. Another way to look at this procedure is to say that the employment department selects for the company and the foreman selects for his department.

## Training

The first task of the training department so far as the new employee is concerned is to introduce him to his job and to the plant environment. Such introduction shouldn't be on a casual "he'll pick it up in time" basis, but instead, a planned, well-thought-out program. He must learn locations of lockers, washrooms, and cafeteria and must meet the people for and with whom he is to work. He must learn company policies on matters of immediate concern to him, and finally he will have many questions that must be answered as completely and accurately as possible. His future success on the job will depend to a large extent on the manner in which he is introduced to the job and company.

The orientation of the new employee actually begins when he first hears about the company and begins to make inquiries for a job. The employment interview that follows covers many aspects of the company's operations such as products, pay, working conditions, and other items of interest. However, once the person is hired these facts need to be covered again so as to be certain that no misunderstanding has developed. Three approaches are usually followed: the first is a group meeting of all new employees conducted by a representative of the personnel department. The meeting may have speakers from other departments such as medical services, and the safety committee, whose presentations are directed toward getting the new employees started off on the right foot. Although questions may be answered during the group meeting probably the best place for the new employee to get his questions answered is during an individual conference with his immediate supervisor. This conference is the second step of orientation, and on a man-to-man basis is probably the best opportunity for complete and thorough indoctrination. Thirdly, written orientation aids are used to contribute to the learning process. In general, these are handbooks or leaflets that contain facts, regulations, and policies of all types of interest to the new employee. It is unlikely that the new employee takes time to read and understand all the information presented in such a handbook, but at least he has it available for future reference.

New employees with some past experience may be able to take over certain jobs with little or no training, but in spite of experience, some training is usually necessary for anyone beginning a new job. Training of hourly workers generally takes one of the following forms: on the job, classroom, cooperative, apprentice, or vestibule school.

### On-the-job Training

Training factory workers on the job that they will eventually take over is a universal practice in industry. It is simple and inexpensive, and the actual training is performed by the employee's supervisor or by an experienced worker already familiar with the job. This method of training is entirely satisfactory under many conditions; however, it will not produce skilled workers in a short time nor will it produce workers uniformly skilled. Since on-the-job training tends to be administered and coordinated on a somewhat haphazard basis, these limitations are not surprising.

Nevertheless, on-the-job training is still one of the most effective and popular means of training in industry. Its flexibility allows a program to be started and stopped at will and to be adjusted to the individual concerned. The employee has firsthand experience with the job and learns by doing. With adequate supervision and guidance, his correct performance can be immediately applauded, and his wrong performance can be immediately corrected. Perhaps this direct contact with the job helps compensate for the lack of organization of material presented and the possibility that certain factors may be omitted.

### Classroom Training

Classroom training is conducted in a room set aside for the purpose and makes use of procedures similar to those used in regular group discussions. Classroom training makes it possible to handle a maximum number of trainees with a minimum number of instructors and so is suitable for carrying out large-scale instruction. On the other hand, unless the groups are limited in size, there may be some hesitancy on the part of the individual participant to ask questions and the effectiveness of this method of instruction may be limited.

A common failing of classroom instruction is for the instructor to depend entirely upon lectures as his medium of training. The lecture method by itself is seldom completely satisfactory, but its value can be enhanced by the use of audio-visual aids and by the use of some of the participative methods, such as role-playing and discussion sessions. Figure 18-4 shows a role-playing training session in progress.

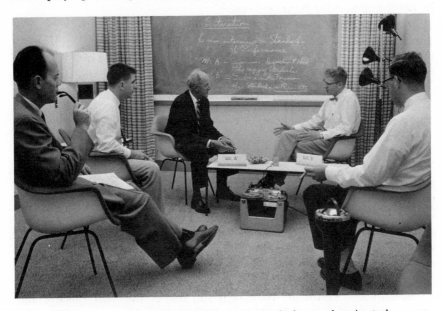

**Figure 18-4.** A training class makes use of role-playing as a learning technique. Note the tape recorder. (Courtesy the Eastman Kodak Company)

## Apprentice Training

Apprentice training is really a variation of on-the-job training, but it has a different goal. In on-the-job training, the objective is to qualify the trainee to take over the job calling for a specific set of work patterns. In apprentice training, the trainee is being trained to take over a job requiring highly skilled work applied to varying work patterns. The training provided prospective machinists, electricians, or tool makers is commonly handled by means of an apprentice program.

As companies add more automatic equipment, apprentice programs are being directed toward the development of skilled mechanics who maintain such equipment. Mechanics to handle this type of job require a much broader type of apprentice-type training than has normally been provided in the past.

An apprentice program will usually last for a number of years, and during that time the trainees will carry out a planned sequence of jobs as well as spend a prescribed number of hours in the classroom. Pay will normally start at a relatively low rate and increase as the apprentice completes definite steps in the program. When he completes the entire program, he is considered qualified to receive the minimum of the regular pay range for a journeyman of his particular craft.

In recent years apprenticeship training programs have been influenced by federal and state legislation. Laws regulate such factors as the pay, number of hours worked, and amount of time devoted to schooling. Apprenticeship training usually entails arrangements involving the trainee, the employer, the union, and perhaps a vocational trades school.

### Cooperative Training

Cooperative training is now made available by many high schools and colleges and trade schools. In such training programs the student spends part of his time in a practical job experience and part of his time as a student in school. This division of time may be made each day, or perhaps during different parts of a school year. In any case, the student is compensated for the time he spends at work, and his job experience is related to his academic work in the classroom. A student not only secures some income but has some experience to indicate on his application blank when he seeks permanent employment following the completion of his educational goal. The cooperating companies usually benefit from such an arrangement because they have made contact with prospective employees to be hired upon graduation.

### Vestibule Schools

When large numbers of workers are to be trained in similar skills, and when it is desirable to have them trained quickly and uniformly, vestibule schools are usually the answer. Such a school is set up on the company property, and the equipment actually used on the production floor is duplicated as closely as possible. The trainees' slowness in learning or the mistakes they make while learning naturally have no effect on actual production. When the trainees become proficient in the school, they are transferred to the production floor where they can take over a regular job with a minimum of delay. If the simulated work setup in the vestibule school is not exactly like the actual work setup, some on-the-job training still will be necessary; however, the time and effort required will be much reduced.

Vestibule schools are not without certain disadvantages. The cost of setting up such a school is such that not every company can afford it, and any company will need to study its long-run training needs very carefully before launching such a school. The school also has maintentance costs that sometimes constitute a disadvantage. The space and the skilled instructors needed may also work a hardship on the organization.

### Teaching Machines

The use of teaching machines in industrial training was inevitable despite the differences of opinion regarding learning theory and educational technique. Although training typically teaches a student only "what" to do, and education attempts to explain "why," developers of teaching machines claim that they are able to impart some of both to the student with the use of these devices.

Most teaching machines work on the principle that the learner is presented certain factual material after which he is to indicate a response. Immediately upon making his response he is informed whether or not this response was correct. A correct response allows him to go on to the next point, whereas an incorrect one forces him to go back and review what he has missed. This procedure reinforces his learning process and allows him to progress at his own rate.

Some electronic manufacturers are making use of combined tape recordings and slide projections to train workers in the assembly of electronic panels. Pre-recorded tapes tell the operator what to do step by step, and the projected slide lets the operator compare the appearance of what he has done with the correct appearance. Both the slide projection and the tape recording are under the control of the operator and may be repeated as often as he finds it necessary. See Figure 18-5.

Some manufacturers have made use of the device described above in such a way as to eliminate training altogether for the assembly of certain panels. In other words, the operator is not expected to learn how to wire the panel, but instead is led through the wiring program step by step and repeats the program on the tape recording and slides for each panel he wires. In such a case a set of slides and a tape recording is checked out together with the raw materials necessary to do a job. Such a procedure seems highly desirable in a setup where only a few panels of any one type are made at any one time. In some cases the instructions on the tape recordings also

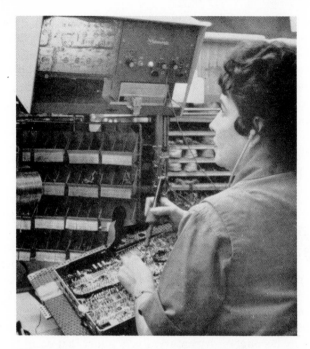

**Figure 18-5.** An audio-visual instruction system in use. (Courtesy Videosenic Systems Division, Hughes Aircraft Company)

serve to pace the operator through the job. In between instructions background music is heard, and in at least one instance, the girls on the job reported that they would prefer to listen to the background music on the tape recorder than to be free to talk with their neighbors.

## Health

Maintaining the good health of employees is certainly a factor in having an effective work force. Workers who do not feel good physically will not work at their top level of efficiency; so it behooves management to take an interest in any deterioration of employee health, whether the cause be inside or outside the plant.

### Physical Examination

The role of the physical examination as a part of the selection procedure and as a part of the general health program has already been mentioned. At this point let us re-emphasize the importance of maintaining adequate records of the physical deterioration of employees, particularly when such deterioration may be caused by the conditions under which the employee works. The effect of harsh chemicals, dust, fumes, oils, and excessively loud noise must be watched, for the company may be held responsible for any physical deterioration that occurs. Any effect on employee health from these conditions may be slow in manifesting itself, and careful records of periodic examinations may be the only way it can be detected.

### General Treatment

It is not common practice for the company doctor or nurse to treat employees for their general ailments unless the condition has resulted from their jobs. The main service the company doctor renders in this connection is in early detection and in recommending that the employee consult his own family physician. Of course, there is no hard-and-fast-line between those ailments the company doctor will treat and those that he won't treat. Treatment of minor colds and general first aid are usually handled by the company hospital staff regardless of the origin of the ailment.

Treatment of all injuries that occur within the plant is the main purpose of the company hospital or dispensary. Every injury that occurs in the plant is a potential "accident" in the technical sense and must be given close attention. The problem in this connection is to get the injured employee to report to the hospital for treatment. One employee ignored a piece of rope fiber that became lodged in his finger. A week later he spent three days in the hospital with an infected finger, and a lost-time accident was chalked up against him and his department.

Being equipped and able to handle the more serious and emergency injuries is also one of the important phases of the work of the company hospital. Factories working around the clock have a special problem in this respect. If such a company has enough employees to warrant it, a nurse is kept on duty all night. Otherwise, a doctor or nurse is always on call. Training supervisory people and other employees in first aid will facilitate the handling of the emergency cases when they arise.

## Safety

A consistently good safety record doesn't come about through chance alone. Companies that enjoy good safety records have had to spend much time and effort working toward that goal. This time and effort is coordinated by the safety director. Sometimes the coordinated effort is called a "safety program" and will be referred to by that name here. The name "program," however, should not imply that it has a beginning and an end. Safety programs never end. More or less emphasis may be placed on the program but it must be continuous if a good safety record is to be achieved or maintained. Analysis of most successful safety programs will disclose that they contain the four "E's"—Engineering, Education, Enlistment, and Enforcement.

Mention has already been made of the importance of coordinating safety and "engineering" when it comes to the design and installation of new machines or equipment. If jobs can be *designed* so they are safe, a big forward step will have been made in any safety program.

The "education" of employees in safe practices and in being alert to hazardous conditions is another important part of the safety program. Normally workers do not instinctively follow methods that will protect them from injury. Instead, correct and safe methods must be taught thoroughly enough to become habitual.

The next "E" of a good safety program is "enlistment" and concerns the attitude of workers and management toward the program and its purposes. In spite of hazards that may exist on the job, it becomes necessary from time to time to inject into the minds of all concerned a greater interest in accident prevention and a certain safety-consciousness. This need is emphasized through safety meetings, safety posters, safety contests, safety films, safety committees, and numerous other devices.

"Enforcement" is the last "E" and in many respects can be the most important. A safety program must have the support of management, from the top levels on down to the foreman. However, management must not only observe safe practices and participate in the program, but must be willing to enforce adherence to safety rules and safe practices generally. A management that gives lip service to safety but winks at violations of sound, safe practices cannot expect a safety program to yield beneficial results beyond a bare minimum.

### Costs of Accidents

There are definite costs associated with accidents. Some are direct and measurable; others are indirect and somewhat intangible but nevertheless real. Companies pay for the costs of accidents in three ways: (1) medical and hospital care that may be required by the injured employee, (2) weekly payments to the injured employee computed as a percentage of his regular weekly wages and continuing for as long as the employee is unable to work, and (3) increased rates of compensation insurance.

There are other costs connected with accidents. An accident may mean damage to tools, equipment, or materials, the cost of which can be computed. Some production time will be lost by the injured worker. Other workers will cease work in order to assist or investigate at the time of the accident. Even if they don't cease work altogether, a slackening of pace is almost sure to take place. Time will be spent by foremen, safety engineers, and company executives in investigating the accident. This time, however, cannot be considered entirely wasted if it is fruitful in preventing another accident. Of course, morale of employees throughout the plant will sag, and if a plant becomes known as one having frequent accidents, its reputation throughout the community suffers. This may have an effect on employee and public relations in general.

### Evaluation of the Safety Program

The first problem in evaluation is the definition of an "accident." In general an accident is any unforeseen event that causes personal injury or property damage. Although this definition covers both the cut finger and the broken leg, there may be a need to separate them statistically. A common way to categorize accidents is as follows:

*Minor injuries:* all injuries that can be adequately treated in the company hospital or dispensary. This would usually include the cut fingers, the splinters, and the sprained ankles.

*Compensable injuries:* those injuries that require treatment beyond routine first aid and that do *not* result in the employee's losing time from his job. Injuries of this nature would be covered under the workmen's compensation laws; a typical example would be a broken finger, which would require an X-ray and setting.

*Lost-time accident:* an injury that causes the employee to lose time from his job either immediately or sometime later. This requires interpretation, for all injuries result in some lost time for treatment if nothing else. If an employee is injured one day and as a result is off the rest of that day *but* returns to work the next day, the injury is not considered lost time. The accident becomes lost time if the worker fails to return the next day or some subsequent day.

The evaluations and comparisons of most safety records are based upon lost-time accidents. Obviously these are the really serious ones and so warrant maximum attention. Studies of minor and compensable injuries are nevertheless worth-while, for the record of these injuries may indicate trends or show opportunities to eliminate hazards. Contests or safety record comparisons based on minor injuries are to be avoided, for if employees become too worked up over the record, they may become reluctant to report their injuries. The same could be true of compensable injuries, although to a lesser degree.

Frequency rates are determined from the number of lost-time accidents per million man-hours worked. This ratio relates the number of lost-time accidents to the exposure to possible injury. For any particular time period it can be computed using the following formula:

$$\text{Frequency rate} = \frac{\text{Number of lost-time accidents} \times 1,000,000}{\text{Number of man-hours worked}}$$

Obviously this ratio will not tell the whole story, for some lost-time accidents are more serious than others. The severity rate takes this into account, and it measures the total time lost in days per million man-hours of exposure. For any given time period the formula would look like this:

$$\text{Severity rate} = \frac{\text{Total time lost in days} \times 1,000,000}{\text{Number of man-hours worked}}$$

It can be seen from these two formulas that a good safety record would call for both a low frequency rate and a low severity rate, and "low" can be considered only in a relative manner. One company's frequency rate may be low compared to the rest of the industry, or lower this year than last. So long as all computations are made on the same basis the results are comparable.

It is customary for companies to compute frequency and severity rates both monthly and yearly. In addition, they will keep track of the number of man-hours worked since the last lost-time accident. A desirable goal for a plant to work toward is one million man-hours worked without a lost-time accident. It is not too uncommon for plants to reach this goal, and a few have managed to go considerably beyond it.

### Accident Causes and Prevention

There is no single cause of accidents nor is there any sure way to prevent them. Many people are quick to point out that accidents don't just happen but instead are caused by either an unsafe act or an unsafe condition.

The majority of accidents happen because of an unsafe act by the person concerned. Such an act may occur because of the employee's ignorance or forgetfulness or because he deliberately took a chance. Experience shows that he may "get away with it" for awhile, but eventually he'll have to pay the price. Operating a fork truck too fast, tying down safety switches, and failure to use personal safety devices are all examples of unsafe acts.

Unsafe conditions are those situations in our physical environment that *could* cause accidents. The broken safety guard, the leaking acid valve, and the protruding packing-case nail are all examples of unsafe conditions. Eliminating unsafe conditions is relatively easy—once they are identified.

### Environmental Factors

In addition to providing facilities for training employees, an employer is responsible for providing a work environment that is reasonably free of conditions that might be detrimental to the physical well being of the employee. Besides correcting unsafe conditions that might cause an accident and providing hospital facilities for aid in treatment, companies must also attend to various environmental factors that may influence employee's health and safety.

Lighting has probably received more attention than any other factor of work environment. Management has long realized that illumination affects not only health and safety, but also efficiency and morale as well. In planning for good illumination consideration must be given to distribution, intensity, and color of light.

Noise has been a controversial factor of work environment largely because studies of the effect of noise have been inconclusive. People have different reactions to noise. Some find any type of noise distracting; others seem indifferent to it, and still others claim that noise facilitates their work. In spite of these contradictions, in recent years management has given increasing attention to the problems of noise, particularly since the courts have granted some compensation to employees based upon the claim of loss of hearing resulting from high noise level.

Individual differences make it difficult to determine precise safe limits of noise. However, the possibility of permanent auditory damage exists at about 90 decibels, and at 120 decibels the probability of permanent damage to the hearing after long exposure is very high. Noise containing high frequencies is more damaging than that composed largely of low frequencies, and explosive noise is more damaging than continuous noise. Companies should make periodic surveys of noise levels in various parts of their plants and should also establish a hearing-testing program in order to detect any trend that may develop in loss of hearing owing to the work environment. A hearing-testing program would also help to protect the company in case of possible claims for workman's compensation.

Proper ventilation has received greater emphasis during recent years and in many companies is considered to be as important as lighting in its effect upon employee's health and safety as well as upon employee efficiency and morale.

Almost every manufacturing concern has some type of health hazard that should receive special attention as part of a health and safety program. Departments working with chemicals, radioactive materials, and similar toxic items should get special treatment. Excessive amounts of dust and odors from processes may constitute specific health hazards as well as detriments to employee efficiency and morale.

In addition to the environmental factors already mentioned, it is also important that work surroundings be attractive in physical appearance. Neatness and cleanliness in both plant and office areas are conducive to safe and efficient operation. Serving the personal needs of employees by providing clean washrooms and well-ventilated locker rooms as well as attractive eating facilities is an important part of an effective health and safety program.

## Benefits

There is no clear-cut distinction between *benefits* and *services* that are offered employees by companies, but we have chosen to consider benefits as the "extras" that result in financial gain to the employee. The employee may or may not contribute to their support, but even if he does contribute he receives a gain financially because he is an employee. Group insurance plans would be an example. Most benefits could show up in the pay check but for various reasons do not, and the word "fringe" is often applied to benefits because they are outside the pay check.

Services are considered to be all those other extras that do not consist of a financial gain to the employee but do fulfill social, recreational, or cultural needs of the employees and at the same time make life easier because of sheer convenience. These will be discussed in the next section.

### Pay for not Working

In spite of the insistence of some employers that they will never pay a man for not working, almost every company does; and the tendency, if anything, seems to be increasing. It shows up usually in three forms: rest periods, paid holidays, and paid vacations.

The rest period is usually divided into two parts for the two halves of a shift, each period being from 10-20 minutes in length. Each period usually provides for the employees an opportunity to smoke or procure food and drink. Although some research indicates that workers maintain their efficiency better throughout the day if allowed rest periods, for many plants this is not the determining factor. It is simply a matter of having time off. In very heavy and hot jobs rest periods are a necessity and may total several hours in a day. An extension of the rest-period idea exists in some plants in the form of allowance for lunching on company time. This practice is prevalent where continuous operations take place.

Six paid holidays a year are common in industry, and every indication is that the number may soon be 8 or 10. Employees are given straight-time pay for the holiday not worked. Should it be necessary for an employee to work on a paid holiday, he may receive double or triple pay, depending on the union agreement or company policy.

The length of paid vacations offered to employees usually varies with the length of service and nature of position. A typical pattern would be one week of vacation for less than five years' service, two weeks for five to 15 years' service, and three weeks for service over 15 years. Some companies have gone to 4 weeks' vacation for 20 or 25 years of service. Pay will usually be either at a straight-time rate or at an average rate if the employee has been working on incentive-pay jobs during the year.

With so many employees getting vacations, some companies have found it economical to shut down during the vacation period instead of trying to operate all summer long with many people missing. The shut-down period also offers an opportunity to perform large maintenance jobs on buildings and equipment.

### Suggestion Systems

Suggestion systems are designed to tap the tremendous store of ideas that rest in the minds of employees. Some employees will volunteer ideas for improvements simply because of the satisfaction that comes from having made a suggestion. For the most part, however, employees will be reluctant to volunteer suggestions without some kind of system that makes it easy for them to do so and offers some reward. Two methods for computing remuneration are prevalent. One is a flat rate system such as $25–$50 per accepted suggestion. The other is a certain percentage of the first year's savings that result from application of the idea. Awards under the latter system have run into several thousand dollars.

A certain amount of "ballyhoo" seems to be necessary in order to make a suggestion system fully successful. The recipient should be given non-financial recognition as well as the cash award. Presentation dinners, newspaper stories and pictures, and appropriate notations on the employee's record card can all be made a part of the promotion campaign so as to encourage other employees to turn in their ideas too.

### Health Benefits

Health benefits in general were discussed earlier. To the extent that the plant hospital will treat the employees' ailments not directly connected with their jobs, this would be a true health benefit. Conceivably much of the treatment received would have to be paid for on the outside if it were not available within the plant.

### Insurance Plans

Workmen's compensation is certainly a benefit offered by the employer, even though the employer is forced by law to provide it. Workmen's compensation, however, gives no coverage for illness or injury that occurs outside the plant. To handle this contingency companies provide disability, hospitalization, and surgical insurance for their employees. In some cases the employee pays the entire cost of coverage, in others the company pays the premiums, and in still others the cost is shared. In any case the cost of coverage is usually less than private individual coverage, because the coverage in the company plan is on a group basis.

Individual plans vary considerably in details, but the intent is usually the same and that is our main interest here. Disability coverage is intended to provide some income to the employee during the time that illness prevents him from working. The income may be a flat amount or computed as a percentage of his average earnings. Most disability plans will contain provisions stating that the employee must be under a physician's care during the period—as evidenced by a signed certificate—and that payment will be made only if his absence lasts a certain minimum length of time, usually a week. These provisions minimize the effect of one- or two-day absences caused by colds or by the fact that someone just didn't "feel" like coming to work. Hospitalization insurance pays specified amounts toward board and room charges and also toward any X-ray, operating-room, or other hospital charges. Limits are usually placed on the total number of days per year a person can collect for the same ailment. Surgical insurance pays specified amounts toward the doctor's fee for performing surgery.

Group life insurance coverage for employees is probably the most common type of insurance in industry today. The cost of coverage is small because of the group feature, and although the face value is usually not large (commonly $1,000 to $5,000) some protection is provided for the employees' families.

### Retirement and Pension Plans

With the population becoming older and the trend being toward early retirement, it seems natural that employers would be offering pension plans either of their own volition, through pressure from unions, or by law. Under the Social Security Act both employers and employees are required to make contributions toward a federal fund that provides benefits on retirement. Many companies supplement Social Security benefits by setting up a pension plan of their own, and the combination might provide a total monthly pension to a retired employee of $300-$500. Some companies tie their profit-sharing and pension plans together. Profits, instead of being distributed in cash, are held in a trust fund until retirement at which time an annuity would be purchased for the employee. In cases like this, if profits have been good, the total pension might approach the employee's former monthly wages.

The most important aspect of any company's retirement plan is that it provides sufficient retirement income to insure that the employee suffers no fear for his security. However, a good retirement program should do two other things, namely, prepare the employee for retirement, and continue a relationship with the employee after his employment is terminated. Preparation for retirement should preferably start two or three years before the actual retirement date. In this manner the employee is helped to make the necessary social and psychological adjustments, and is encouraged to develop ideas concerning hobbies, additional jobs, community services, or business pursuits in which he would like to engage sometime in the future. Many employees are reluctant to think of these things ahead of time, for on their own initiative they are unable to visualize a future life in which the pressures, worries, and companionships of their current jobs are no longer present. A preparation for retirement program need not be elaborate. Many successful programs are maintained by companies in which employees about ready to retire are provided an opportunity to meet together and discuss the problems they share.

An equally important part of any retirement program is its role in maintaining contact between the company and the employee after he is retired. Employees who have worked many years for a company have developed a loyalty and feeling of attachment toward the organization, which, wisely, should be fostered and continued as insurance of security and goodwill in the minds of the retirees. Many companies make certain that the names of the retirees are kept on the mailing list to receive the company's newsletter and other literature. Retired employees are also invited to company social activities and given certain other privileges and services entitled to by active employees. A retired employees' club is another way to allow the retiree to keep in touch with the company as well as his former associates.

### Other Benefits

Guaranteed wages, guaranteed employment, profit-sharing, and stock-purchase plans are all commonly found in industry today. These will be discussed in the chapters on wage administration.

# Services

All the items just discussed as benefits were included because they provide some element of financial return to employees. *Services*, on the other hand, are provided by the company in order to fill some particular need of some or all of the employee group. Some services may be more necessary than others in any particular situation; some are simply conveniences and may not be "necessary" at all. Companies provide services in order to instill a feeling of group solidarity and general loyalty to the company. Pleasant "off-job" relationships probably make for more efficient "on-job" relationships. It is not our purpose to cover all possible services that a company might offer. Instead, some of the more common and more important ones will be discussed with emphasis being placed on how they fit into the total industrial relations picture.

## Communications

The general problem of communications in a manufacturing concern is much too complex to attempt to cover here, but one of the aspects of this problem is getting information to employees. Two common methods of accomplishing this are the bulletin board and the company magazine or newspaper. Both of these usually come under the jurisdiction of the personnel department, which accounts for their inclusion under employee services.

The bulletin board is usually reserved for official notices on company or union affairs. Some companies provide a true employees' bulletin board where anyone can post a notice signifying his desire to sell a car, buy a boat, or give away a spare kitten. The company newspaper or magazine may contain some official information, but it is more apt to include material of general interest to employees. General news items concerning fellow employees, standings of the company softball team, and a feature article concerning Joe's vacation trip to Alaska will all be of interest.

The use of "rack service" has been growing in industry during recent years. At convenient points throughout the plant will be located racks of booklets on various subjects that might be of interest to employees. All are free, informational, and void of what might be called propaganda. Typical topics of such booklets would be "Vacation Auto Trips," "The Atom at Work," and "History of the Automobile." Employees seem to appreciate this source of unbiased information.

## Social Programs

Social programs vary in extent all the way from the annual company picnic to the employees' social club offering all varieties of social activities throughout the year. Parties, dances, and general get-togethers are designed in such a manner that every employee will find some feature enjoyable. Games and contests are arranged for all ages with appropriate prizes being awarded the winners. Families become an important part of these affairs as well as the employees themselves.

An overall employees' social and recreational club may oversee the entire social program or there may be small clubs appealing to people with specialized interests. Garden clubs, stamp clubs, rifle clubs, and drama clubs are only a few of the possibilities. Such clubs would be separately organized, each carrying on its own program in its own field of interest. The nature of the club to which any one employee belongs would usually be determined by his hobby interests.

Musical activities are receiving increasing attention as part of social programs. Choral groups and orchestra groups provide enjoyment not only for the actual participants but also for other employees who enjoy listening.

## Athletic Programs

For those who desire active physical exertion, athletic programs are offered by many companies. Bowling and softball are the two more popular sports since they do not require the specialized skill of basketball or football. Competition is maintained between departments within a plant and also between plants. Industrial leagues for both bowling and softball are quite active in many communities.

Although the major sports may receive most of the attention and publicity, there is still a lot of room in the industrial recreation program for minor sports. Some, such as tennis, horseshoes, ping pong, and badminton have a special appeal, for often they can be enjoyed during the noon hour and do not require after-hours arrangements. Other sports such as swimming, hockey, and golf have their appeal to those interested, but they require facilities and are definitely after-hours or weekend activities.

## Eating Facilities

Companies situated in isolated areas or operating around the clock find it almost mandatory to offer restaurant or cafeteria services to their employees. To expect everyone to carry his lunch is too much in these days of emphasis on hot meals and good nutrition. Even without any special set of circumstances companies provide eating facilities simply as a convenience. Less time is consumed in obtaining and eating the meal, and often-times the prices are less than in commercial establishments since the cafeteria is operated on a non-profit basis. There is never any compulsion to buy food in the company cafeteria although all are invited to eat there even though they bring their lunches from home.

A variation of the company cafeteria is the lunch wagon that circulates throughout the plant as a convenience to those employees who must eat on the job. Such wagons also provide the coffee and doughnuts for the daily rest period. This service eliminates the necessity of employees' rushing to the neighborhood coffee shop and back.

The vending machine has had a phenomenal growth as a factor in food service and may soon replace both the lunch wagon and the cafeteria. Vending machines are now able to provide both hot and cold foods, and to the extent that their operators can provide good food at reasonable prices, and keep the machines from breaking down, the vending machine may be the answer to the in-plant eating facility problem.

### Professional Services

Of course, the medical service discussed earlier is a professional service, but there are a few others commonly provided. Legal advice is one of these and can be a real service, since employees seldom know what to do when faced with legal difficulties. Company legal departments do not carry out court actions but simply make recommendations and perhaps help in selecting competent legal counsel to carry out the court action.

Another professional service sometimes offered is personnel counseling. The counselor might be anyone from a white-haired grandfather to a trained psychologist or ordained minister. The point is that someone is available to hear the employee's story and maybe offer a little advice. Experience has shown that a good listener can often be of more value to an employee who has a personal problem than an expert who gives freely of advice.

### Credit Union

It can hardly be said that a company offers a credit union to its employees, although a company may permit and cooperate in the formation of a credit union by the employees themselves. The credit union is really a small bank, licensed by the state, and operated by employees for their own benefit. Employees can deposit money in the credit union and receive interest on it. In addition, loans can be obtained at rates far less than those charged by private loan companies. Companies cooperate with the credit union and will make deductions from pay checks for the purpose of deposits or to pay off a loan. In this way much of the bookwork is eliminated.

## Policies Regarding Benefits and Services

Companies that adopt many of the benefits and services discussed in this chapter do so to gain certain returns—be they tangible or intangible. The maximum return will be obtained only if proper policies are followed in the installation and operation of the various benefits and services. There is no set of policies that will meet every situation; however, the following principles will be worthy of consideration in any situation.

### No Substitute for Wages

There is *no substitute* for a sound wage structure, and this structure should stand on its own feet without help from any benefit and service program. Employees who feel they are not paid fair wages, that their hours are too long, or that working conditions are inadequate, will not respond to the fringe offerings of the employer. Any doubts concerning employee reaction to wages, hours, and working conditions should be removed before benefit and service plans are seriously considered.

### Fulfilling Need

Employers in their more philanthropic moments sometimes decide that their employees need a particular benefit or service. The decision may be correct in some cases, but, in general, such a method of determining need is unsound. Such an approach was used many years ago only to fail miserably and to be labeled "paternalism." The label continues to be applied in certain instances even against the employer with the purest of intentions.

A more successful approach is to fulfill a request from employees for certain benefits or services. A recreation club will be much more successful if set up at the request of a group of employees than if set up because the employer feels his employees "need" it. Of course, an employer can and perhaps should do what he can to stimulate interest and in that way assist in the creation of a need. Hints dropped at the right time and place may grow to such an extent that everyone becomes convinced that the idea came from the employees themselves.

### Competing Services

Closely related to the establishment of a need is the point that company benefits and services should not be set up in competition with benefits and services already adequately established in the community. There is no need to start a new hospitalization plan if coverage is already adequately provided by some community plan. By the same token, if the union has an active social program under way, there may be little need for a similar program sponsored by the company.

### Financial Support

By their very nature, *benefits* will tend to have the complete financial support of the company. Employees may contribute to a certain extent, such as in contributory pension plans or in profit-sharing or stock-purchase plans that are tied in with employee savings. Following the collective bargaining history of any one company, however, one usually finds that year by year the employer pays a larger percentage of the benefit bill.

Services are a little different. These in particular should be established after employee request, and employees should be made to demonstrate their interest by contributing time, effort, and even money. Such contributions will make people work harder for the success of the endeavor and, of course, make employees feel that it is really *their* organization or activity.

A satisfactory way for service organizations to obtain financial support is through the proceeds of vending machines. Vending machines appear to be quite necessary in our plants today, and since companies never want to "make money" from their employees, contributing the profits to employee service organizations works out fine for all concerned.

### Complete Coverage

One of the knotty problems concerning the establishment of service activities in a plant is the danger that the activities will serve only a few. Each clique or group satisfies its particular desire and worries little about the others. Coverage of service activities should be broad enough that everyone finds something of interest, even if only as a spectator. This is easier said than done, but it deserves consideration.

### Sincerity

Our last and probably most important point is that the employer should enter into each benefit or service with complete sincerity and with a genuine desire to see it benefit his employees. If he regards a plan as a "gimmick" to "keep 'em happy for awhile" or to "keep out the union," the plan as well as employer-employee relationships are doomed to failure. There is more to good industrial relations than a recreational building, a profit-sharing program, or a softball club. The substitute for a genuine interest in one's fellow man—whether he be an employee or a neighbor—has yet to be found.

## QUESTIONS

1. List several specific sources of employees in a community with which you are familiar. Briefly discuss the worth of each source.
2. Comment on the role of each of the selection steps when hiring a floor sweeper. Do the same for the hiring of a welder.
3. Distinguish between on-the-job training and apprentice training.
4. Outline a training situation in a company where the use of a vestibule school would definitely pay off.
5. Why should a company concern itself with the general health of its employees?
6. List and explain the four "E's" of a good safety program.
7. Discuss the necessity of some arbitrary definitions of accidents.
8. For what reasons would employees demand and employers grant fringe benefits such as insurance, pensions, and health programs instead of simply increasing wage rates?
9. Some companies have been accused of hiring new employees based on their ability to play basketball, bowl, or perform in other sports so as to strengthen the company team. Would you call this a good or a poor practice? Give your reasons.
10. Should a company store or cafeteria be operated on a profit basis? State your reasons either way.
11. How can an employer be certain that a new benefit or service fulfills a need?

### Case Problems

**Lucas Products, Inc.**

For the past ten years Mr. Paul Millis, the industrial relations director of Lucas Products, Inc., has been computing employee turnover according to the following formula:

$$\frac{\text{Number of replacements}}{\text{Average number on payroll}} \times 100$$

The computation was made on a monthly basis, and the average number of employees on the payroll was determined by averaging the number on the payroll the first day of the month with the number on the payroll the last day of the month.

Mr. Millis felt that this formula for employee turnover gave him a reliable indication of the overall efficiency and performance of industrial relations in the Lucas organization. He took pride each month in showing the general manager the current employee turnover figure and comparing it with the results of the last several years. And the record did look good. During the ten year period employee turnover had never exceeded 10% and in recent months had been running about 5%. Mr. Millis was careful to point out each month that he claimed no personal credit for this record but that the efforts of everyone, in particular the foremen and supervisors, made the record possible.

Yesterday a clerk gave Mr. Millis the turnover figure for last month and it showed a sharp rise to 9.6% from 4.3% for the previous month. Needless to say Mr. Millis was shocked and immediately went to work to determine the causes. He knew he would have to do a lot of explaining when he next saw the general manager.

*Questions:*

1. In searching for causes for the sharp rise, what types of things should Mr. Millis look for?
2. Should Mr. Millis feel on the defensive concerning the sharp rise in employee turnover? Explain.
3. Was Mr. Millis correct in placing so much faith in this computation of employee turnover as a measure of overall efficiency and performance of industrial relations? Explain.
4. Can you think of any improvements in the calculation so it would more closely accomplish what Mr. Millis expected?
5. Would you agree that the turnover record of Lucas Products as described was a good one? Explain.

## The Sieber Pen Company

The Sieber Pen Company has a plant located in a city of 10,000 population in eastern Kansas. For the past 25 years the company has been the principal employer in the community, and at present employs about 1500 people. Approximately one-half of these are women, many of whom are under 21 years of age.

Sieber Pen Company has a reputation in the community as being a good place to work. The relations between the employees and the employer have always been congenial, and to date no serious attempt has been made to unionize the plant.

In an attempt to provide sound recreational facilities for its employees, the company built a $300,000 employee recreation club in 1948. This club contains a gym, squash courts, bowling alleys, billiard tables, shower rooms, a dining room and guest rooms as well as a number of other facilities. All of the facilities, except the dining room and guest rooms, may be used by any employee without any dues or other charge.

When the recreation club was first built, a considerable number of employees made use of its facilities; however, very few people have availed themselves of this privilege during recent years. The management has in part justified the existence of the club by using it as headquarters for dealers attending company training schools.

Within the past few months, word has reached top management that a number of workers have expressed a desire for an increase in the number of bowling alleys in the club so that an intra-plant bowling league may be organized. Also, inasmuch as the plant does not have a cafeteria, several employees have asked to have a cafeteria installed in the club so they can eat their lunch there. Employees can eat lunch in the dining room of the club, but the general feeling is that the dining room is too elegant for employees to use when attired in work clothes.

*Questions:*

1. Should the Sieber Pen Co. go ahead and install the requested extra facilities? How should they go about arriving at their decision?
2. What can be done to stimulate greater usage of the club's facilities?
3. How can the company evaluate the value of the club to the company and to the employees?
4. What recommendations can you make regarding the company's policies in regard to employee services?

CHAPTER NINETEEN

# Labor Relations

The total personnel program of any company contains many facets. This chapter deals with the area generally known as labor relations, and is concerned with the conditions of employment as arranged between the employer and groups of employees. The process of arranging for these conditions of employment is generally referred to as "collective bargaining," as contrasted to "individual bargaining." We usually think of collective bargaining taking place when a union is present. However, companies without a union representing their employees must still give considerable attention to the collective reactions of employees to the work conditions established.

## Influence of Unions

Strangely enough, unions do not represent the bulk of workers. In 1960 it was estimated that only a quarter of the total labor force in the United States were members of trade unions. If agricultural workers are eliminated, organized labor consists of about one third of the work force. Furthermore, the labor unions have experienced some difficulty in recent years in increasing their membership on a percentage basis. Organized labor has consisted of approximately one third of the non-agricultural work force for about the past ten years.

There are a number of reasons for this leveling off in the growth of labor union membership, but one particularly important reason is the changing nature of the American work force. With the advent of automation and the growth of service industries generally, the work force has tended to become more of the white collar type rather than blue collar, and white collar workers generally tend to resist the organization drives of labor unions. This historical fact may change in the future as labor unions change their organizing tactics. On the other hand, companies may become more successful in persuading their employees to identify themselves more with the company than with a trade union, and thereby reduce the role played by the union. The improvement of personnel programs by management has undoubtedly had its effect on the slowing down of the labor union movement; nonetheless the presence of a union or the threat of a proposed union has made companies extremely interested in the subject of labor relations. Since all companies must abide by the law, whether or not a union is present, the law in connection with the work force is of particular interest.

Certainly a company's success is dependent to a large extent upon the mutual understanding that can be developed between the management and workers as represented by their union. It is important, therefore, that management have some familiarity with union objectives, policies, and organization, as well as with the problems confronting the leaders of these unions. The following topics considered in this chapter will provide background information concerning unions, their operations, and the law that applies to both the company and the union:

1. The union movement.
2. The history of American unions.
3. Independent unions.
4. Union organization and operation.
5. Union security.
6. Economic weapons of the union.
7. Labor law.
8. Relations with the union.

## The Union Movement

Attempts have been made to trace the lineal descent of the trade-union movement of the nineteenth and twentieth centuries from the guilds of the Middle Ages; but trade unionism as we know it was clearly the creation of modern industrial conditions. It owes its birth to the capital system, and, viewed after more than a century of growth, it is seen as a sort of self-protection of workers against the complex economic changes that they fail to understand. Labor unions were and are a defensive and offensive method for maintaining and improving working conditions. In recent years, however, they have become much more than simply that, for they are now an integral part of the machinery of industrial life. In addition, labor unions have become a significant part of our social and political lives as well.

The attitude of American law toward unions has been derived naturally from the English common law. There was a time when, by common law of England, combinations of work people were, with minor exceptions, regarded as illegal. They were considered to be contrary to public policy and fell into the category of "conspiracies in restraint of trade." Membership in such a body was punishable by fine and imprisonment, and although the common law applied to combinations of both masters and workers, it was against the workers that the law was later developed and directed. From the time of Edward I to the end of the first quarter of the nineteenth century there were more than thirty legal enactments that enforced and extended the common law in connection with labor unions, and all of these measures were designed to prohibit and prevent labor organizations.

Although unionism in America can be traced to colonial days, developments in the movement were generally several years behind English developments. American courts tended to hold the same view of unions as did English courts and ruled that unions were conspiracies until 1842. The decision of the Supreme Court in the *Commonwealth* v. *Hunt* case removed the conspiracy label from labor unions and opened the way to the growth of such bodies. Changes in public attitudes regarding unionism began to follow, and during the quarter century until the Civil War unionism grew gradually, together with many radical and utopian offshoots.

One such offshoot organization, called Knights of Labor, was organized in 1869 as a secret group. It appeared in the open in 1880 as a union of all workers, skilled and unskilled, manual, clerical, and professional, and even of the small businessman. By 1886 the Knights had a membership close to one million and an influence far exceeding its size. But it had neither the financial resources nor the staff to carry out its basic objective, the organization of all workers.

Support for the Knights of Labor came largely from a spontaneous uprising of workers, and when strikes ended in failures, and strikers lost their jobs, the inability of the Knights to provide assistance made it exceedingly difficult to arouse enthusiasm for the organization. Much of the attention and energy of the officers of the organization was dissipated in carrying out the various economic programs of the Knights, which dealt with everything from central trade union action to schemes for the reorganization of the currency and banking system of the country. The Knights ran into further trouble when they attempted to take over the jurisdiction of the various craft unions that existed in the country at that time.

Probably the main contribution of the Knights of Labor to the union movement in this country was that their mistakes later served as guidelines to the founders of the American Federation of Labor.

## The History of American Unions

The direct forerunner of the American Federation of Labor (hereafter referred to as AFL) was the Federation of Organized Trades and Labor Unions, begun in 1881. The AFL appeared on the scene in 1886 under the leadership of Samuel Gompers and his associates. Mr. Gompers was elected its first president and is considered the "father of the American labor movement."

Previously, the Knights of Labor sought to absorb the existing craft unions, to remove their autonomy, and to involve them in industrial disputes in which their own interests were apparently not at stake. The AFL benefited from the mistakes of the Knights and organized a loose federation of the various craft unions, which remained for a half century the sole unifying agency of the American labor movement. The AFL followed a policy of "business unionism", and made it a point to keep out of political entanglements other than using votes for "rewarding friends." Union leaders devoted their efforts to improving wages, hours, and working conditions.

The national and international unions within the AFL were originally composed mainly of skilled crafts workers. Furthermore, most of these unions were opposed to the addition of industrial workers or unskilled workers into the AFL ranks. Much of this opposition was due to the fear of the crafts groups that their status would be weakened by bringing in the less skilled workers from the mass production industries. Nevertheless, there was considerable interest in the many thousands of workers in the mass production industries, which were then unorganized, and in 1935 John L. Lewis, president of the mineworkers, together with the presidents of seven other unions, formed a Committee for Industrial Organizations within the AFL structure.

The Committee was organized as a protest against the failure of the AFL organizing campaign, and its unwillingness to grant full jurisdictional rights to the new unions in mass production industries. It hoped to demonstrate the feasibility of organizing non-union industries and to protect the young industrial unions from attacks from the older craft unions. There was no intent to do this outside the AFL, but later events indicated otherwise.

A few months after its formation the CIO undertook its first campaign and met with great success. The AFL still refused to recognize the organization of the CIO despite its organizing success and declared that its activities were outside the lawful rights of its constituent unions. The Committee was ordered to disband under the threat of suspension and eventual expulsion if it failed to comply. When the CIO unions defied this order in 1938 they were all expelled. Shortly thereafter expelled unions along with some other unions set up a rival federation of labor and challenged the jurisdiction of the AFL in all industries and occupations. In November 1938, it held its first constitutional convention and changed its name to the Congress of Industrial Organizations. By 1939 the CIO claimed at least fifty affiliated national unions and more than four million members.

During the ensuing years competition for members caused bitter jurisdictional clashes between the AFL and CIO union groups. By tradition the

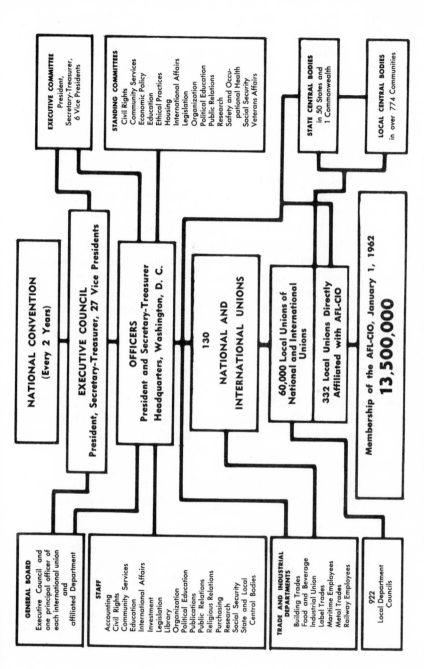

**EXECUTIVE COMMITTEE**
President,
Secretary-Treasurer,
6 Vice Presidents

**STANDING COMMITTEES**
Civil Rights
Community Services
Economic Policy
Education
Ethical Practices
Housing
International Affairs
Legislation
Organization
Political Education
Public Relations
Research
Safety and Occu-
pational Health
Social Security
Veterans Affairs

**STATE CENTRAL BODIES**
in 50 States and
1 Commonwealth

**LOCAL CENTRAL BODIES**
in over 774 Communities

**NATIONAL CONVENTION**
(Every 2 Years)

**EXECUTIVE COUNCIL**
President, Secretary-Treasurer, 27 Vice Presidents

**OFFICERS**
President and Secretary-Treasurer
Headquarters, Washington, D. C.

130
**NATIONAL AND
INTERNATIONAL UNIONS**

60,000 Local Unions of
National and International
Unions

332 Local Unions Directly
Affiliated with AFL-CIO

Membership of the AFL-CIO, January 1, 1962
**13,500,000**

**GENERAL BOARD**
Executive Council and
one principal officer of
each international union
and
affiliated Department

**STAFF**
Accounting
Civil Rights
Community Services
Education
International Affairs
Investment
Legislation
Library
Organization
Political Education
Publications
Public Relations
Religious Relations
Purchasing
Research
Social Security
State and Local
Central Bodies

**TRADE AND INDUSTRIAL
DEPARTMENTS**
Building Trades
Food and Beverage
Industrial Union
Label Trades
Maritime Employees
Metal Trades
Railway Employees

922
Local Department
Councils

Figure 19-1. AFL-CIO organization chart. (Courtesy AFL-CIO Speaker's Bureau)

373

AFL was thought of as a craft union organization, and the CIO as an industrial union organization, but their organizational clashes soon broke down these traditional barriers, since the main concern of each was to gain additional members. The CIO made a particular effort to gain the support of minority groups by trying to avoid racial and religious discrimination. It also encouraged political activity by unions at all levels. Although political activity on the part of unions was curbed somewhat by the Taft-Hartley Act in 1947, unions still participated in political campaigns by endorsing candidates sympathetic to labor and attempting to persuade their members to vote for these candidates.

Rivalries between AFL and CIO did much to mar the public image of the American labor movement, and there was considerable public pressure to merge the two groups. After a number of faltering efforts the two groups were reunited in 1955 into a single AFL-CIO organization. The merger at the top, however, did not solve all the problems throughout the organization. Competition between unions and individual labor leaders created many problems, and some of these remain to this day in spite of the settlement of the jurisdictional and "no raiding" disputes among the affiliates. Figure 19-1 shows the current structural organization of the AFL-CIO organization.

## Independent Unions

Although the majority of national labor unions are affiliated with the AFL-CIO organization, a number of them representing an estimated three million members, remain independent and unaffiliated. The most outstanding examples are the Railway Brotherhoods. Other unions go in and out of the AFL-CIO organization owing to differences in policies, accusations of being Communist-dominated, and various other reasons. This makes it difficult to keep an accurate count as to the number of affiliated and unaffiliated unions.

Another type of independent union is commonly referred to as a "company" union. In past years the term company union referred to one accused of being a company-dominated union. The domination of a union by a company is now illegal under federal labor law, and so a company union is now, technically, a union whose membership is limited to the employees of a particular company. Many such unions exist and are just as vigorous in representing their members as any other union. Needless to say an AFL-CIO organizer would disagree with this statement, for he would argue that affiliation with the larger labor organization brings considerably more pressure to bear upon the employer concerned. On the other hand, many members of such company unions like their present arrangement inasmuch as they do not have to contribute dues to the national organization, and they can pursue their particular interests and local concerns without interference from a national representative.

## Union Organization and Operation

Except for those unions that are local in scope, a union organization typically consists of a parent organization known as the national or international union and a group of affiliated unions. Groups having locals in Canada refer to themselves as international unions. Local unions are the basic units within the national unions and have considerable strength by virtue of the united efforts that they can exert through the national union.

The national union is the primary source of authority and control within the union organization, and its constitution provides the rules and conditions which must be met before the local unions can be admitted to the national organization. Further regulations are often imposed upon the local in regard to the collection of dues, the admission of members, and the need to bargain with employers for standard provisions in the labor contract. National unions also provide many services and forms of assistance to the locals. This may be in the form of technical assistance and contract negotiation and administration, financial assistance during periods of organizing drives or strikes, and education and publicity guidance.

The local union is the organizational unit that has direct contact with employers and with workers, and to both groups is probably "the union." The officers of the local union are workers within the company or plant involved and are well known to the company management. Management and the union bargaining committee negotiate the labor contract although the union may receive outside help from representatives of the national union. The local union has its own charter, and its bylaws must be written in accordance with the national organization's constitution. In smaller unions the officers hold full-time jobs and often perform their duties without pay. In larger unions the major officers may be full-time employees of the union.

Two union officials worthy of special mention are the business agent and the union steward. These are the union officials with whom employers have the most frequent and direct contact, and their attitude and behavior can be an important factor in the degree of cooperation and harmony between the company and the union. The business agent is elected by the members of the local and is employed full time to administer the business affairs of the local union. Usually he has worked his way up within the local organization and has held other offices. He may exercise a stronger influence within the local than any of the other officers because of his experience and background. His duties include not only seeing that the labor contract is followed by the employer but helping to prepare for and conduct negotiations for new contracts. He processes members' grievances in many cases and serves as general administrator for the union office. In other words, he frequently serves as "all things to all persons" within the union.

The union steward or "shop steward" is technically a union representative rather than an officer of the union. He represents the union in his designated area of the plant and becomes the union counterpart of his foreman in that particular area. He is responsible for seeing that the rights of the members whom he represents are protected, and that the grievances of these members are processed properly. In so doing, most of his relationships are with the foremen of the departments involved. The steward is generally elected by the members within the area that he represents, and this area may vary depending upon the number of members working in a plant. Many plants have a number of stewards, in which case a chief steward is usually designated to coordinate the activities of the various shop stewards. Obviously, the steward has a key role to play in the union organization. However, some unions have found it difficult to get capable members to accept the added responsibility and problems of this position. Shop stewards usually serve without pay, although most labor contracts allow them time to handle union business at company expense.

## Union Security

Every union wishes to gain maximum recognition and security in its relation with employers. The degree of recognition and security achieved by unions is an important factor in determining their ability to bargain for further concessions from an employer and to enforce demands when these bargaining efforts fail. The degree of security also affects a union's ability to withstand similar bargaining and economic pressures that the employer may exert.

Below are listed and briefly discussed the many forms of union security that are in existence today. The following discussions are general, and many contracts may introduce a great number of variations in any particular form of union security. Also, we refer to security for the union as an organization only, and security for the individual worker or union member is a different matter. The nine items are listed roughly in the order of increasing degree of union security.

**1. Closed non-union shop.** Strictly speaking, this item does not belong in this list since it offers no union security and is, in fact, just the reverse of union security. In this situation the employer runs the shop in such a manner that anyone belonging to a union is either not hired, or is fired if he should join a union after he is employed. The employer, thus, clearly discriminates against union members. This employment situation has been illegal since 1935. Obviously, if union discrimination is a violation of the law, unions are in a stronger position to press for one of the true forms of union security.

**2. Open shop.** The open shop is an employment situation wherein employees of the company are able to join or not to join a union as they wish. The company does not discriminate against union members, and by the same token individual members can bargain directly with the employer. Several states have passed what is known as "right to work" laws, which forbid any employee from being forced to join a union in order to hold his job. In those states, therefore, a form of open shop is mandatory.

**3. Dues checkoff.** The dues checkoff is an arrangement whereby an employee authorizes the company to deduct union dues from his paycheck and turn it over to the union directly. Under the Taft-Hartley Act a union cannot compel its members to pay its dues in this manner. However, most members usually authorize the employer to make the deduction if such an arrangement is available. The checkoff is a considerable advantage to the union inasmuch as it assures the union of an income and reduces the work of collecting dues individually from each member. Employers are generally cooperative in making these dues deductions for they benefit by eliminating the need for soliciting dues by union members, frequently done on company time, and by eliminating the need to discharge any employee because he has failed to pay his dues. Such a discharge requirement would exist only if one of the other higher forms of union security were in effect. The dues checkoff usually occurs fairly early in union-management relationships and remains throughout such relationships. In other words, although the dues checkoff is listed as number three in the order of increasing union security, it continues to exist throughout the remaining other forms in most instances.

**4. Bargaining for members only.** This type of shop arrangement involves only limited recognition for a union, for the presence of the union is simply acknowledged by the management. Although technically the union has a right to bargain for those employees who are members only, it is difficult to visualize a concession being made to union members and being withheld from non-union members in today's industrial environment.

**5. Exclusive bargaining shop.** As the name implies, this arrangement is such that the union is not only recognized as the bargaining agent for its members, but acts as the bargaining agent for all employees whether or not they are members of the union. This arrangement does not force employees to join the union, nor does it force the employer to give union members any special treatment. It does require the employer to bargain exclusively with the union in regard to all employment conditions.

**6. Maintenance of membership shop.** Under this arrangement an employer may hire whomever he wishes, and employees are not required to join the union as a condition of employment. However, a cutoff date is provided after which those employees who are union members must retain their membership in the union during the life of the contract or suffer loss of their jobs. Such a provision protects the union against having employees drop their membership while the contract is in effect.

**7. Agency shop.** The agency shop does not require employees to be members of the union as a condition of employment, but it does require them to pay equivalent dues to the union. The reasoning behind such an arrangement is that the union, acting as bargaining agent for all employees, has been able to secure certain benefits that are enjoyed by non-union members as well as union members. The cost of securing these benefits, therefore, should not be borne alone by the union members, but by the non-union employees as well. Payment of equivalent dues to the union then provides support for the bargaining efforts without forcing the employee to become a member of the union. Agency shop has come into use only during recent years and is undoubtedly the union's answer to the view that no employee should be forced to join a union as a condition of employment.

**8. Union shop.** A union shop clause in a contract would specify that all employees in a bargaining unit must become members within a certain period of time after employment. According to the Taft-Hartley Act this can be no less than thirty days. Under today's federal law the union shop arrangement gives a union the highest degree of union security that is legal. Certainly, in a situation where all employees must become members of the union eventually, the union has considerable strength and is able to maintain control and discipline among its members. True, in this situation employees have been required to join a union as a condition of employment and to many people such an arrangement not only gives the union too much power, but is not consistent with concepts of American freedom. On the other hand, many employers prefer a union shop arrangement, since it eliminates certain difficulties that otherwise exist when a union is forced to fight for its status.

**9. Closed shop.** Under a closed shop arrangement an employer can hire only union members for his employees. Although made illegal by the passage of the Taft-Hartley Act in 1947, in actuality many closed shop arrangements still exist throughout the country today. While probably no union contract exists that specifically enumerates a closed shop arrangement, the practical workings between union and management result in a closed shop. This is particularly true in what may be called the "casual trades," or those situations where employees do not enjoy any form of tenure for long periods of time. The employer finds it much easier to call the union and ask it to send over the number of workers desired than to recruit workers from the general market. Both the employer and the union benefit from the arrangement, so there are few complaints. The persons who suffer from the arrangement are workers who would like to get good jobs in a trade but are unable to do so inasmuch as the union will not admit them as members.

Another illegal arrangement sometimes occurring is referred to as a "preferential shop." This is an arrangement whereby union members are given preferential treatment in various phases of their employment. This might occur in the hiring of new personnel, promotions, or priority in layoffs and rehirings. Such an arrangement provides a certain degree of security for the union involved and might appropriately be listed in our hierarchy of types of security between numbers four and five. As mentioned, the arrangement is illegal, since under the law an employer cannot discriminate in favor of a union member any more than he can discriminate against a union member.

## Economic Weapons of the Union

On the whole, employers and unions settle their differences through peaceful and voluntary means. However, in certain circumstances one side or the other may bring economic pressure to bear in an attempt to force the other to concede. Unions bring economic pressure upon an employer by (1) striking against him, (2) picketing him, or (3) boycotting his product and encouraging others to do so. These forms of union economic pressure are discussed briefly in the following paragraphs. Employers can bring economic pressure by shutting down their operations and laying off their employees. This is commonly termed a "lockout" and is rarely used, although the threat of a lockout perhaps is always present. It has been used most commonly by employers within an association to support one of its members that has been struck by a union.

A strike is, simply, the refusal of employees to perform their jobs and may be done by any group of employees or in a more organized fashion as indicated by a union. Success of the strike depends upon the ability of the strikers to keep the employer from continuing to operate. If the employer continues to operate through the use of supervisory personnel or by hiring other employees, obviously much of the impact of the strike is lost.

Picketing is almost a standard practice when a union strikes an employer. Persons are placed at the entrances of the employer's plant to give notice of the dispute and to discourage others from entering or leaving the premises. Many times the striking employees represent only a small portion of the total employees of the plant, but the non-striking employees will often refuse to cross the picket line, thereby helping to exert pressure upon the employer. Even more pressure is brought to bear upon the employer when the employees of other companies refuse to cross the picket line as they make deliveries or pick up goods from the struck employer. Obviously, refusal to cross the picket line is a basic tenet of the union movement, and most union members are generally receptive to the practice of supporting other unions. This is not always the case, however, when rival unions are involved, or when individuals are involved who consider it more important to work than to simply respect a union principle.

Peaceful picketing is generally regarded by the courts as a form of free speech, but sometimes it is not peaceful. Employees who attempt to cross the line may be subjected to insults or even physical violence. Mass picketing has been employed, whereby the pickets become so numerous that the path of anyone attempting to enter the plant is blocked physically. Pickets are usually union members, but sometimes unions employ outsiders to picket for them and are known to select them particularly for their physical attributes of size and strength. Such practices usually result in court action and also do much to arouse unfavorable public opinion against the union and its activities.

Boycotting is another economic weapon employed by unions that may adversely affect an employer, although it seems to have lost its importance in recent years. A manufacturer who is able to continue operating during a strike by hiring non-union workers might find his market considerably reduced if the striking union members were to refuse to buy the product of the manufacturer and were successful in influencing other union members to do the same. Such a practice on the part of unions is technically termed a primary boycott and is considered legal. Should the union go further, however, and boycott other employers with whom it does not have a labor dispute in an effort to force them not to patronize a second employer with whom the union does have a dispute, the appropriate term would be a secondary boycott, and this is declared illegal under the Taft-Hartley Act.

## Labor Law

Labor law, like other forms of jurisprudence in this country, developed through the common law or that body of law that came through custom or through the precedence of previous court decisions. Our early common law in turn derived largely from the English common law, and in the case of labor unions tended to favor employers and not unions. The efforts of employees to form unions to bargain collectively with employers were interpreted as being criminal acts of conspiracy until the *Commonwealth* v. *Hunt* decision in 1842. That decision, along with growing union strength and an apparent change in public attitude, meant the beginning of a body of statutory law that tended to give recognition to unions and establish their right to bargain collectively with employers. For the most part, the federal government led the way in the field of labor legislation, with the states playing a secondary role. The federal government has exercised control over labor relations by virtue of two authorities: the first is the regulation of interstate commerce, and the second is its control over public contracts.

Perhaps the most important legal victory for the union movement came in 1887 when the Interstate Commerce Act was passed. This gave the federal government the right to settle labor disputes in the railroads. Specific railway legislation was passed later which will be discussed in the next section. As time went on, however, the Supreme Court interpreted the federal government's authority in interstate commerce to cover a broader and broader area, and it is undoubtedly these interpretations which allow the federal government to be predominant in the labor legislation area.

The second method by which the federal government influences labor relations is through its control over the conditions of employment in public contracts. These are contracts with the federal government to supply materials or to perform construction work. It is logical that the federal government should have the right to specify the terms of these contracts and the employment conditions to be observed by the successful bidder. The conditions of employment covered by these contracts are generally more restrictive than those specified in the broader federal labor laws. A contractor must therefore choose between keeping his work on the public contract separate from his other work, or simply meeting the stricter conditions for all of his employees, regardless of what contract they are fulfilling. An example would be overtime pay for a workday longer than eight hours. The general labor law on wages and hours specifies that overtime will be paid for work longer than 40 hours per week, but the public contract acts specify that overtime pay shall be paid for work over 40 hours per week, or 8 hours per day. Obviously, most employers follow the more restrictive public contract proviso. The various acts dealing with public contracts are discussed in Chapter 20.

### Railway Labor Legislation

The Arbitration Act of 1888 was the first federal labor legislation and provided that disputes in railway and other transportation industries be resolved by submitting them to an arbitration board, provided that such action was agreeable to both parties. If the voluntary arbitration was not agreeable, the law gave the President the power to appoint a commission to investigate the dispute. The arbitration provisions were never exercised, but a commission was appointed in 1894 to investigate the Pullman strike, and that commission report led to the replacement of the Arbitration Act with the Erdman Act of 1898. The Erdman Act set up a permanent mediation and conciliation commission to handle the voluntary arbitration of railway labor disputes. It provided for a cooling off period in the event of a dispute and permitted court enforcement of the arbitration awards. It also had a provision forbidding the use of yellow dog contracts, which employees were sometimes required to sign, whereby they agreed not to join the labor union. This clause was later declared unconstitutional by the Supreme Court, but its inclusion in the Erdman Act is significant in the development of labor law.

A number of laws dealing with railway labor problems were enacted in 1913 and 1916, but these were all finally consolidated into the Railway Labor Act of 1926. As well as providing for the peaceful settlement of disputes, this act also included specific provisions guaranteeing railway employees the right to organize and bargain collectively through their representatives. Railroads were forbidden to interfere with union organizations or to require their employees to sign yellow dog contracts. The act was therefore an important piece of labor legislation, for it was the first to provide for the protection of employee bargaining rights. It was amended in 1934, after which the protection of bargaining rights was assigned to a new national mediation board, and a national railway adjustment board was created to handle grievances and labor disputes. For many years the Railway Labor Act was cited as a model act for maintaining labor peace. However, the nationwide railway strike in 1946 revealed that this act was not the panacea for solving union-management difficulties as had been thought previously.

## Background of Federal Labor Law

The current law governing union-management relations is the outgrowth of both earlier antitrust legislation as well as labor legislation. Some of the more important legislative acts that provide this background are: (1) Sherman Antitrust Act of 1890, (2) Clayton Act of 1914, (3) Norris-LaGuardia Act of 1932, and (4) National Industrial Recovery Act of 1933. It is ironical that one of the first laws to affect the activities of labor unions was one aimed primarily at controlling business monopolies. There is some controversy as to whether Congress intended the Sherman Antitrust Act of 1890 to apply to labor unions. However, in 1908 the Supreme Court ruled that labor unions were subject to its provisions. The Court's historic decision in the Danbury Hatters case gave the company $252,000 in compensation for losses suffered as the result of a boycott undertaken by the union. This decision naturally reduced the bargaining power of labor unions by nullifying one of their economic weapons, the boycott.

After these developments unions waged a vigorous campaign to be exempted from the provisions of the Sherman Antitrust Act, and their efforts were rewarded by the inclusion of certain key sections in the passage of the Clayton Act of 1914. These sections exempted labor from antitrust protection, curbed the power of the federal courts to issue injunctions against unions, and granted the right of a jury trial to persons who were charged with contempt of court for violating a court injunction. While the passage of the Clayton Act was first hailed as an outstanding victory for labor, later Supreme Court decisions ruled that the act did not give labor unions complete exemption from antitrust prosecution. The Supreme Court ruled that certain activities of the unions such as the boycott, which were proved to be in restraint of trade, were still subject to both injunctions and prosecution. It was not until 1932 that organized labor obtained the protection from injunctions that it had hoped to gain from the Clayton Act.

## The Norris-LaGuardia Act

The Norris-LaGuardia Act of 1932 was the first of a number of legislative enactments that improved considerably the status of unions during the thirties. The passage of this act, and the fact that it was later upheld by the Supreme Court finally gave the unions the protection from the injunction they had long sought. During earlier years, the injunction was the main device used by employers to fight unions, for they were easily obtained from judges who were prone to protect property rights, and who felt that strikes and boycotts interfered with these rights. The Norris-LaGuardia Act does not prohibit federal courts from issuing injunctions, but it did establish such rigid requirements in regard to their use that the injunction ceased to be a threat.

The Norris-LaGuardia Act also contained a clause long sought by labor unions, namely, the banning of the yellow dog contract. The Supreme Court, when it upheld this provision of the act, reversed itself from earlier decisions.

## The National Industrial Recovery Act

The National Industrial Recovery Act of 1933 was one of the first pieces of legislation passed in the Roosevelt Administration and was an attempt by the federal government to promote economic recovery by permitting industries to establish regulatory codes concerning their operation. Organized labor was recognized in the famous Section 7-A of the act. This section endorsed the concept of collective bargaining and the right of employees to join organizations without employer interference. It established a national labor board to help settle disputes and to handle employee representation problems as well as violation cases under the act. The National Industrial Recovery Act was later declared unconstitutional in its entirety, but in 1935 the section dealing with labor was lifted and passed as the Wagner Act, which remains the law of the land today. The Wagner Act goes considerably beyond the NIRA provision, but the basic philosophy is the same.

### The Wagner Act

The primary aim of the Wagner Act was to place the support of the federal government behind the efforts of workers to organize and bargain collectively. In addition the act was designed to curtail some of the weapons employers used to resist the efforts of their employees to form unions and bargain collectively. The one-sided nature of the act simply reflected the sympathetic attitudes toward organized labor at the time.

The most important feature of the act was the guarantee that it gave to employees in exercising their right of collective bargaining. The following quotation is taken from Section 7 of the act: "Employees shall have the right to self organization, to form, join, or assist labor organizations to bargain collectively through representatives of their own choosing, and to engage in concerted activities, for the purpose of collective bargaining or other mutual aid or protection . . ."

Section 8 of the act attempted to make this guarantee more specific and listed five employer activities, which were considered to be in violation of the bargaining rights of employees. These were defined as unfair labor practices and include the following: (1) to interfere with, restrain, or coerce employees in the exercise of the rights guaranteed in Section 7; (2) to dominate or interfere with the formation or administration of any labor organization or contribute financial or other support to it; (3) by discrimination in regard to hire or tenure of employment or any term or condition of employment to encourage or discourage membership in any labor organization; (4) to discharge or otherwise discriminate against an employee because he has filed charges or given testimony under this act; (5) to refuse to bargain collectively with the duly chosen representatives of his employees.

The Wagner Act also established a national labor relations board whose functions remain about the same under the Taft-Hartley Act as they were with the Wagner Act, namely; (1) determination of bargaining units, (2) representation elections, (3) unfair labor practices.

### Taft-Hartley Act

The Wagner Act and its interpretations by the National Labor Relations Board were so one-sided in favor of labor that by 1947 it was amended by the Labor-Management Relations Act, more commonly referred to as the

Taft-Hartley Act, in an attempt to make the labor law of the land fair to both sides. All of the provisions of the Wagner Act remained in effect under the Taft-Hartley Act, but certain provisions have been added that give additional rights to employees, employers, unions, and protection for the public. Brief statements of some of these provisions are listed below:

Provisions giving employees rights in addition to above:

1. Closed shop is outlawed.
2. Checkoff permissible only after authorization from employee.
3. Excessive union initiation fees prohibited.
4. Employee can process grievances by himself or through union.
5. Employee can be dismissed in a union shop only after nonpayment of initiation fees and dues.
6. Union members entitled to annual union financial reports.
7. Employee welfare funds must be administered through joint employer union board.

Rights of employer:

1. Can express himself on union matters as long as no threat or coercion to union members is implied.
2. Can discharge employees who engage in illegal strikes.
3. Can ask N.L.R.B. for vote to determine bargaining agent.
4. Can insist that unions also bargain in good faith.
5. Can sue unions in federal courts.
6. Is free from rules requiring that pay be given for work not done.
7. May refuse to bargain with unions representing supervisors.

Rights to unions under proper conditions:

1. Can ask N.L.R.B. for recognition election.
2. Can require employer to bargain in good faith.
3. Represents all employees eligible to vote.
4. Maintains its status for one year without fear of jurisdictional dispute.
5. Represents employees in processing grievances.
6. Files charges with N.L.R.B. against unfair labor practices.
7. Calls strikes.

Protection provided for the public:

Strikes affecting public health and safety can be delayed for 80 days while a special board investigates and reports.

Figure 19-2 outlines the processing of unfair labor changes through the National Labor Relations Board.

## Labor Reform Act

The only significant addition to labor law since passage of the Taft-Hartley Act in 1947 has been passage of the Labor Management Reporting and Disclosure Act of 1959, more commonly known as the Labor Reform Act. This act resulted from the findings of congressional investigations regarding the activities of union leaders. Many instances of theft or embezzlement of union funds were uncovered, and it was felt that union members needed protection from their own leaders. The main provisions of the law govern

# BASIC PROCEDURES IN CASES INVOLVING
# CHARGES OF UNFAIR LABOR PRACTICES

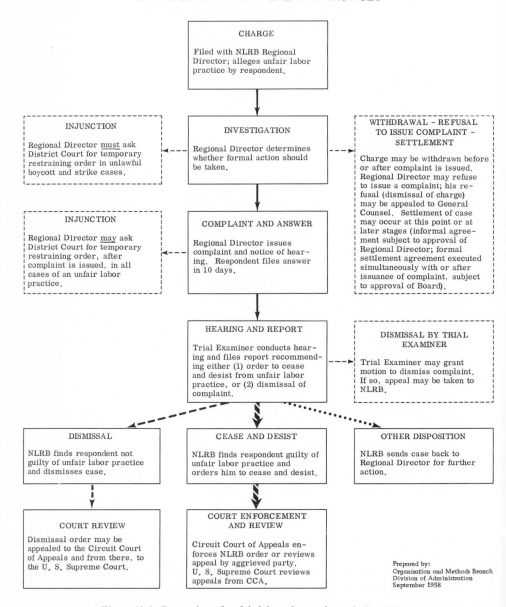

**Figure 19-2.** Processing of unfair labor charge through the NLRB.

the handling of union funds and regulate the activities of union officers in position of trust. The principal technique employed is disclosure. Every union must file annually with the Secretary of Labor a detailed financial report. In addition, it must make the information contained in the report available to each of its members. Another proviso is that union officers and employees must file annual reports of all conflict of interest transactions in which they or their wives or children have engaged. Theft or embezzlement of union funds is expressly made a crime, punishable by fine and imprisonment.

## Relations With the Union

Normal relations with the unions usually entail the following: (1) negotiating labor contracts, (2) processing grievances, (3) day-to-day relations with employees and union officials.

In some companies negotiation of labor union contracts can be a full-time job in itself. No sooner is a contract signed than it is time to begin thinking about the next bargaining session. In fact, in companies having very successful union-management relationships, bargaining is essentially a continuous operation with the formal signing of a contract taking place at periodic intervals. Figure 19-3 contains the table of contents from a typical union contract. From this list one can see the range of matters that are considered bargainable under modern labor relations, and the list expands yearly.

*Table of Contents*

Article I. Bargaining Unit, Recognition and Union Membership
    Section 1—Bargaining Unit
    Section 2—Recognition
    Section 3—Union membership

Article II. Employees' *Definitions*
    Section 1—"Employee" *defined*
    Section 2—"Regular employee" *defined*
    Section 3—"Temporary employee" *defined*

Article III. Wages
    Section 1—Wage scales
    Section 2—Incentive pay
    Section 3—Off-standard work, down time, and waiting time
    Section 4—Rates for new machines
    Section 5—Report-in pay
    Section 6—Pay on temporarily assigned jobs
    Section 7—Shift differentials
    Section 8—Rest periods
    Section 9—Holiday pay

Article IV. Check-Off

Article V. Hours of Work
    Section 1—Normal workday
    Section 2—Normal work week
    Section 3—Scheduling and division of overtime

**Figure 19-3.** Table of contents of typical union contract. (Continued on page 388)

**Figure 19-3.** Continued.

One section of most labor contracts usually deals with the matter of grievances. A "grievance" is an official complaint filed by an employee or by the union in regard to an action taken by management or to an interpretation of the labor contract. Basically a grievance can be considered as a difference of opinion between the company and union on some matter. Of course such differences occur all the time, but when they become "official" differences of opinion a grievance procedure is specified in order to settle the issue. Figure 19-4 outlines a typical grievance procedure. Final settlement

| Step Number | Union Representative | Employer Representative |
|:---:|:---|:---|
| 1. | Employee or steward, or both | Foreman |
| 2. | Chief plant steward | Superintendent of department |
| 3. | Plant grievance committee | Plant manager |
| 4. | National union representative | President of company |
| 5. | Arbitration | |

**Figure 19-4.** Steps of a grievance procedure.

will take place under a procedure such as this, since in the last step the issue is placed before an impartial arbitrator who must make a decision. If the parties do not like the arbitrator's decision, they are free to negotiate over the item at the next contract-signing time. In the meantime, however, both parties are committed to abide by the arbitrator's decision. Both parties are usually anxious to settle any issue before it reaches the arbitration step and will spend a great deal of time investigating and discussing the issues during each of the preceding steps in the grievance procedure. If there are many grievances active at any one time, one can see that union officials and company officials alike will be spending considerable time processing them and attempting to get them settled.

There is indeed more to labor relations than negotiating for signed labor contracts and processing grievances. In addition to these rather formal aspects, day-to-day matters arise that must be handled with labor union officials or with employees directly. This type of work usually entails interpreting the labor contract, or arriving at a mutually agreeable solution to a problem in the absence of a clear-cut method for handling it in the contract. The way in which these daily contacts and daily compromises are handled makes the difference between strictly formal labor relations conducted at "arm's length" and the sincere, informal "let's get our problem solved" type. Examples of both types appear in the news practically every day. Some companies and unions always seem to be at odds with one another, with strikes, shutdowns, and controversy being the usual thing. Other relationships seem to go on year after year without these outward evidences of internal strife. There is no known sure answer for the achievement of "labor peace," but experience seems to indicate that a genuine and sincere attempt, day by day, to work with department stewards and union officials in the handling of mutual problems will do much to achieve that nebulous goal.

This is not to imply that a company *must* have its employees represented by a labor union in order that good relations may exist between management and workers. Many companies have been and still are operating with no labor union involved—and doing so successfully as far as good relations are concerned. Some large companies with scattered plants will have some plants organized by labor unions and others not—again with apparent success. Why unions get started in one plant and not in another is beyond the scope of this treatment. Let us simply point out that successful management-worker relations do not seem to hinge solely on whether or not unions are present but on the kind of treatment given workers by the management. Unions may serve as protective agencies in some cases; apparently in many plants and companies no protection is necessary.

## QUESTIONS

1. How does a typical grievance procedure operate?

2. Differentiate between a "grievance" and a "complaint."

3. From an employer's point of view, what are the advantages of dealing with a union representing employees?

4. Under the law, are foremen and supervisors prohibited from joining a union? Explain.

5. On what basis did Congress pass a law prohibiting closed shop employment agreements?

6. What authority is possessed by the National Labor Relations Board when it comes to handling charges of unfair labor practices?

7. Does industry-wide bargaining appear to be in violation of the antitrust laws?

8. Distinguish between mediation, conciliation, and arbitration.

9. Why do some employees object to and even refuse to join unions?

10. What influence will the use of computers and automation generally have on labor unions and their growth?

11. What would happen to the collective bargaining process if *all* workers were members of one huge union?

12. How is the general public protected in labor disputes?

## CASE PROBLEMS

### Munson Mills

Munson Mills had been a textile plant in a large Vermont city for as long as anyone could remember. It had been started by "Jep" Munson who ran the company with an iron hand, but who had a reputation of taking good care of all his employees. The tradition was carried on by his son, by his grandson, and by his great grandson. In other words, for four generations the company was run by members of the same family all of whom followed the same patterns and traditions.

Generally speaking, the Munsons had all been very progressive and very aggressive. As a result, the business had grown and prospered. The company possessed one of the more modern textile mills in the country and was able to compete with all the other mills that had moved South, while at the same time paying the relatively high wages of the North.

There was one difficulty, however, and that was that the Munsons were violently opposed to unions in any form and to any degree. Over the years there had been many attempts to organize the employees, gain union recognition, throw up picket lines, and call strikes. These had been only partially successful, for the Munson in power had always held firm. The Federal Government tried to nudge the company toward union recognition during World War II, and there were some court battles; but the war ended and with it the power of the government agencies causing the trouble.

A month ago the last Munson, Charlie, died suddenly in his sleep of a heart attack. Since he was only 55 and thought he had many more years of control ahead of him, he had failed to make any provision for his successor in the company. He had no sons and only one daughter, who had married a very competent super-intendent in one of the mills named John Spencer.

John has just been informed that the family has decided to place him in charge of the company as president. He is pleased and flattered. However, he stipulates that he will do so only on condition that he be allowed to cooperate with unions rather than fight them. He feels that the battle with unions was responsible for his father-in-law's premature death.

*Questions:*

1. Can an employer such as Munson Mills be forced to bargain with a union?

2. Can John Spencer legally decide to recognize a union of his choice and have them represent his employees?

3. What would be the result of any attempt of Spencer's to kill the union with kindness rather than with threats?

4. Why would well paid employees like Munson's wish a union to represent them?

## The Tower Corporation

Ben Been and Charlie Walters got along together very well—so well, in fact, that they often fished together, in addition to bowling on the same team. The relationship seemed unusual to many inasmuch as Ben was the plant manager of Tower's midwestern plant of 1200 employees, and Charlie Walters was the president of the union representing those employees.

Charlie had been elected for a two-year term, and from the beginning the two men hit it off. There were some heated discussions at bargaining sessions, but two contracts had been signed during Charlie's term, which added substantially to employee benefits. At the same time, Charlie demonstrated his concern for company success and prosperity, saying that without a prosperous company there would be no jobs and no union. Naturally, this attitude endeared him to Ben Been, particularly as contrasted to that of earlier union presidents.

Since things were going so well, Charlie assumed that his re-election would be almost automatic. A month before the election, however, a rival for his job began a vigorous campaign asserting that Charlie was a tool of management and did not really have the welfare of the union and its members at heart. Charlie lost the election by a small margin. Although this was a blow to Charlie's pride, both he and Ben Been feared what would happen to labor relations at the plant in the future.

*Questions:*

1. Comment on Charlie Walter's attitude and approach toward labor relations.

2. Why did Charlie Walters lose the election?

3. Would it have helped the situation if the friendship between the two men had been less obvious?

4. What difference would there be in such a situation as this between an independent union and one affiliated with the AFL-CIO?

5. What was Charlie Walter's responsibility to the union as compared to his responsibility to the employees? Did he fail one or the other?

# CHAPTER TWENTY

# Wage and Salary Administration— Policy Considerations

One of the major problems that confronts the management of every company is the determination of a satisfactory wage structure. This problem is doubly difficult in industry today because of the many forms of indirect remuneration that have become commonplace and because of the social and psychological implications associated with a man's wage. It has become accepted practice for the business to provide its employees with group insurance, retirement, recreational, and other benefits—all of which become forms of indirect wage payment. But the present concept of "wages" involves other factors. In our society, a man's wage determines his standard of living and his social position. Consequently, for the individual, there are tremendous psychological implications associated with his wage.

*Wage and salary administration* is that function of management that is concerned with the determination of how much the employees are to be paid, based upon thorough analysis of all factors affecting such remuneration. The many factors entering into this determination make it a very complex problem. It is confused by internal as well as external considerations, many of which we shall discuss in later sections of this chapter and in a chapter on job evaluation and merit rating.

## Wages vs. Salaries

"Wages" as construed in the broad sense covers all forms of compensation paid to the employees of a business. This includes salaries, bonuses, com-

**393**

missions, or any other form of monetary payment. Based upon popular usage, the term "wages" is frequently used to refer to the cash compensation given to hourly-paid employees who are employed on nonsupervisory jobs. On the other hand, "salaries" are sometimes distinguished from "wages" and are considered the sums paid non-hourly-rated employees. This distinction has become a widely accepted one as a result of a wage and hour regulation contained in the Fair Labor Standards Act, which exempts certain employees including supervisors, managers, and salesmen from premium pay for overtime.

## Take-Home Pay and Real Wages

Over the years, the term "take-home pay" has come into common usage. This has come about largely because of the payroll withholding for such items as Social Security, union dues, hospitalization, group insurance, and bond purchases. Because of these withholdings, the worker tends to think of his pay as that which he takes home in his weekly check.

As a result of "annual improvement" clauses contained in several employer-union agreements, the worker's pay has been increased each year to provide him with an improved standard of living. This has probably led to an increasing awareness on the part of employees of the difference between "monetary wages" and "real wages." "Real wages" refers to the purchasing power of his earnings and his "real wage" may be determined by dividing his "monetary wages" by an appropriate cost-of-living index.[1]

In spite of the creeping inflation in the United States, the "real wage" of the employee has been rising. As a result, his purchasing power and his standard of living have continued to rise and all predictions point to a continuation of these trends.

## Wages—a Motivating Factor

If an organization is willing to pay high wages, it can usually attract well qualified employees. There are many motivating factors—security, job status, opportunities for advancement, recognition, and good working conditions—that influence a person's feelings about his job, but his pay is still one of the foremost considerations. If his earnings are at an acceptable level, based upon his evaluation of his worth, the other factors will become less important. If his earnings are inadequate, then there is strong possibility he will become dissatisfied.

---

[1]The cost-of-living index most frequently used is that issued periodically by the Bureau of Labor Statistics, United States Department of Labor.

## Basis for Paying for Jobs

At the outset of considering an equitable basis for paying employees, management is confronted with a number of questions:

1. Should pay be on a basis of worker needs, or on the value of the job to the company?

2. How can the conflicting interests of the owners, the worker, and the customer best be reconciled?

3. How can the worth of jobs be determined?

4. What are the economic elements in wages?

In this country, most employers have assumed that the worker should be paid on the basis of what his job is worth and not on the basis of his personal needs. Thus, a single man and a married man of equal competence and years of service would usually receive the same pay.

The conflicting interests of the owners, workers, and customers are sometimes difficult to reconcile because they tend to oppose each other. The workers are anxious to receive high wages because their wages are their livelihood; the owners are anxious to receive a good return on their investment and may frown on the payment of exorbitant wages; and the customer will buy from the company only if the price and quality are right. It is management's problem to keep each of these groups happy by (1) paying the workers a fair wage so that they will remain a satisfied, productive group; (2) operating the business at a profit so that adequate dividends can be declared for the stockholders; and (3) maintaining costs and quality at such a level that the company will be in a good competitive position.

One of the difficult aspects of wage and salary administration is that of determining the worth of jobs. In considering this problem management must recognize that (1) its salary structure should be at the level required to attract the type of workers it wants to hire and retain, (2) the variances in wages and salaries paid for the different jobs within the company are just as important as the level of wages, (3) an employee's feelings about his wages are relative to what others receive, and (4) employees expect wages to increase as the degree of responsibility and authority increases. At its best, the basis for paying for jobs is quite arbitrary. But in recent years industry has attempted to bring about a more systematic approach to this problem through the use of job evaluation, which will be discussed in detail in Chapter 21.

There are no economic laws that stipulate exactly how much a company should pay in wages. Many theories have been offered but, to date, there are no formulas that can be used in determining wages, and it is probable that the variables are so great that no stipulation in purely economic terms is possible. Hence, the company is subjected to the realistic situation of paying the wage that the various economic factors in the labor market force it to pay.

In competing for workers' services the company is confronted with much the same problem that is encountered in a commodity market. If there is a shortage of a particular skill, it becomes possible for the workers in that field to demand and get a higher wage; if there is an oversupply of labor, the result may be lower wages, unemployment, or both. In any one labor market, however, the wages paid the employees will reflect the wage policies of the employers. For the most part, the most profitable firms will pay the highest wages and less successful firms the lowest. Obviously, those companies that are able to pay the highest wages find themselves in a highly advantageous position in attracting good employees.

## Organization for Wage and Salary Administration

The position of wage and salary administration in the organization varies from company to company. In the larger companies there is usually a staff department of wage and salary administration, which is responsible for advising and aiding the entire organization on wage problems. Because the setting of wages and salaries plays such an important role in manpower management, this department is most commonly found in the industrial relations or personnel department.

In smaller organizations, the wage and salary function may be assigned to the controller, treasurer, or some other administrator whose responsibilities include other fields. Where this is done, it is important that the attention given this function not be subordinated to the other duties of the administrator.

Whatever the position of wage and salary administration in the organization, top management should insure that it be given adequate attention and should adhere to sound wage policy. Although it is difficult to state a wage policy that will have universal application to all companies, the following factors are usually considered important:

1. The company's wage policy should be consistent with its stated personnel policy. The company's wage level should be at least equal to the prevailing wages for similar jobs in the labor market.

2. A consistent basis for determining the relative worth of the jobs within the company should be established and adhered to. As a part of this, the job content should be reviewed periodically.

3. Provision should be made for periodic review of wages and a sound basis for merit increases established.

4. Consideration should be given to the establishment of individual or group incentives wherever applicable in order to reward additional effort of the workers.

5. Standards of performance should be established at reasonable levels consistent with the policy of a "fair day's pay for a fair day's work," and these standards should be maintained at this level.

6. Complaints arising from any phase of wage administration should be given prompt attention and settled in accordance with the facts of the case.

7. Complete information on all phases of the wage program should be expressed in writing and disseminated to all employees, and management should be willing to discuss any phase of it whenever requested.

## Factors Influencing Wages

In considering the proper compensation for the employees of a company, many complex factors enter. It isn't as simple as determining that each employee should be paid at the rate of so much per hour or per piece. Workers also receive paid sick leave, paid vacations and holidays, and premium pay for overtime and holidays. These and other forms of indirect remunerations are commonly referred to as "fringe benefits."[2] In addition, a few companies have profit-sharing arrangements in which the employees receive some of their compensation through participation in the profits of the company. Closely related to profit-sharing plans are stock-ownership plans designed to encourage employees to purchase company stock.

As a part of the wage determination process, management must take all of the influencing factors into account. A number of these deserve special attention.

**Labor legislation.** Several federal laws have had a marked influence on minimum wages, working hours, and payroll withholding. Chief among these are the Davis-Bacon Act of 1931, the Social Security Act of 1935, the Walsh-Healey Public Contracts Act of 1936, and the Fair Labor Standards Act of 1938. The principal provisions of these four laws are presented in summary form in Figure 20-1.

**Collective bargaining.** For those employees who are members of unions, one of the major factors influencing their wages will be the union scale, which results from collective bargaining. The labor agreement usually

---

[2]The term "fringe benefits" is commonly used to refer to group life insurance, unemployment compensation, retirement programs, Social Security benefits, paid vacations, paid holidays, severance pay, and similar employer expenses that compose indirect forms of remuneration (see Chapter 18).

| *Name of Law* | *Provisions Pertaining to Wages and Hours* |
| --- | --- |
| Davis-Bacon Act of 1931 | Provided for payment of prevailing wage rates (for similar job classifications on similar projects) on Federal construction projects in excess of $2000 and established an eight-hour working day, except for certain emergency contracts. |
| Social Security Act of 1935 | Provided for payroll withholding from employees and for employer contributions to cover a system of old-age and survivors insurance and unemployment insurance. |
| Walsh-Healey Public Contracts Act of 1936 | Established certain standards of work done on U. S. Government contracts exceeding $10,000, specifically, payment of time and one-half for all hours worked in excess of eight in one day or 40 in one week. It also permitted the fixing of prevailing minimum wages in those industries performing contracts. |
| Fair Labor Standards Act (Wage and Hour Law) of 1938 | Provided for minimum hourly wages and time and one-half the employee's regular rate for overtime over 40 hours per week for employees engaged in interstate commerce, including those in any closely related process or occupation directly essential to such production. The statute set forth what was meant by minimum wages, stated conditions under which overtime provisions might be exceeded, exempted certain employees—executives, administrators, professionals, and outside salesmen—from coverage, and prohibited the employment of children under 16 (18 for hazardous occupations) in commerce or in the production of goods for commerce. The Act has been amended several times, and the minimum rate has steadily increased. |

**Figure 20-1.** Principal provisions of federal labor legislation affecting wages and salaries.

provides a pay scale for various job classes which will be in effect during the life of the agreement. It may also stipulate the minimum earning potential available under incentive systems.

The effect of collective bargaining in a labor market will be felt even by non-unionized companies. Some employers may desire to equal or exceed the union scale in order to avoid the unionization of their employees.

In recent years, the collective bargaining in several major industries, has had considerable influence on other companies. There has been a tendency to use one large company as a lever against another company, and this has had tremendous impact on the wage picture in both large and small firms. Also, the union's demands for some type of guaranteed employment plan and other fringe benefits have added considerable indirect payment to the workers.

**The labor market.** In a labor market the supply and demand for a particular type of labor will tend to seek a balance. Seldom, however, will it attain an absolute balance, and wide differences will usually prevail in the hourly rates paid by various employers for equivalent labor on similar jobs. Owing to the immobility of labor, surpluses of some skills may exist in one area while shortages exist in others.

The shortage of qualified workers for certain jobs may have considerable influence on the wages demanded by persons possessing those skills. This has been the prevailing situation for engineers during recent years. The shortage of engineers has had tremendous influence on the starting pay offered young engineers.

**Geographic location.** Wage differentials have always existed among different geographical areas. Some jobs are rated higher in a large city than in a smaller community, or higher in the North than in the South. The common explanation for this difference is that the cost of living is less in one area than in another.

**Cost of living.** During periods of rising prices, the cost of living becomes an item of major importance in wage determination. It frequently may be one of the foremost items posed by the unions in collective bargaining sessions and has led to "escalator" clauses being incorporated into a number of union agreements. Based upon the provisions of these clauses, the wages of the employees are adjusted upward or downward periodically, depending upon the rise or fall of a cost-of-living index (the one prepared by the Bureau of Labor Statistics).

Tying wages into the cost of living may prove to be a troublesome consideration for management, because sales, income, and profits may not coincide with the retail prices used in calculating the cost-of-living index.

**Ability to pay.** "Ability to pay" has been used frequently by employers to counter a demand for wages that they feel are excessive. One of the best illustrations of this usage arose in the General Motors negotiations several years ago where both the company and union (UAW-CIO) made claims and counter-claims as to the company's breakeven point, costs, and profit picture. In other cases the employer has used this argument to request a reduction in wages on the grounds that the present wage level would jeopardize the future of the company. For the most part, however, employers have argued that ability to pay has nothing to do with wages.

Over the long run, a company's wage policy must reflect its ability to pay. The company cannot afford to pay wages at an exorbitant level at the expense of its customers or owners. At the same time it must pay wages at the level necessary to maintain the caliber of the workforce. If wages were cut because the company was operating at a loss, some of the employees would leave to work elsewhere.

**Wage level.** The wage level maintained in a company is influenced by the company's wage policy and by the "going rates" for jobs in the labor market. If the policy of the company is to pay at least as well as other industries in that area, then its pay scale will be based upon the community wage level as determined from wage surveys. This will be discussed in greater detail in Chapter 21.

## Compensation of Supervisors and Executives

The compensation of supervisors and executives presents a special problem. There are few if any good bench marks to use as a guide in paying these employees. Wage surveys usually do not include these jobs, and there are no "going rates" for the positions of president, vice president, plant superintendent, or foreman. Moreover, even with the data that are available from community or other wage surveys, the duties and responsibilities inherent in the different positions vary so much that such rates are of little value.

Determining equitable compensation for a supervisor presents a difficult problem because of the relationship between his pay and that of persons he supervises. It is generally assumed that the supervisor should earn 10 to 20 per cent more than those he supervises. But this differential, which is usually based upon the worker's normal weekly earnings, will be eliminated when the workers put in overtime and receive 50 per cent more pay or when some of the employees working on incentive plans are able to make a 10 to 50 per cent bonus. As a counter to this problem, some companies have placed their supervisors on a bonus plan making it possible for them to receive increased pay for increased productivity.

The pay scale for executives is determined on a basis that is even more arbitrary than that used for the production workers. Although a number of executive surveys have been undertaken by the National Industrial Conference Board and other agencies, these surveys are difficult to make because of the many variations in compensation of executives. Consequently, the determination of an executive's pay tends to be based upon what his subordinates and superiors receive and on the amount required to hire and keep him. Some companies have attempted to do something about this situation and have attempted to evaluate the worth of executives' jobs and to affix salary boundaries for the various position classifications. For example, in an eastern candy company everyone who is a division director gets the the same salary.

## Methods of Compensation

One of the policy decisions that every company must make is that of determining the method of compensating its employees. In general, the methods of wage payment may be grouped into two major classes: those based upon some unit of time, and those based upon some unit of output or accomplishment. Each of these will be discussed in detail in later sections of this chapter.

In selecting an appropriate method of wage payment, we must keep in mind that it should adhere to the company's overall wage policy and be appropriate for the type of work being performed. For example, it is unheard of to pay the chief engineer of a company on an hourly basis. He is usually paid an annual salary at so much per month and accepts this as being a satisfactory method of wage payment. In the same way, a worker on an assembly line would consider an hourly rate of so much per hour and payable once a week as an acceptable form of wage payment.

Among the considerations that must be taken into account in selecting a suitable method of compensation are:

1. Does it provide proper incentive to get the job done?
2. Does it facilitate managerial controls?
3. Is it easy to administer?
4. Does it keep the employees satisfied?
5. Is it appropriate for the type of work being performed?
6. Is it based upon a sound system of job evaluation?

### Wage Payment Based on Time

The most common form of wage payment is that based on some unit of time, for example: $3.00 per hour for a worker in the plant, $100 per week for a clerk in an office, $750 per month for a foreman in a plant, or $6000 per academic year for a schoolteacher. In the case of hourly wages, the employees receiving them are usually paid at weekly or biweekly intervals. Persons receiving higher salaries are usually paid on a monthly basis.

A number of advantages may be cited for the time wage-payment plan. It is simple to compute and to understand, it requires no time standards or production records, the payroll remains fairly stable and payroll accounting is simplified, it is favored by many unions, and quality is not sacrificed because there is no attempt to stimulate high production.

On the other side, there are a number of disadvantages of this form of wage payment. There is no strong motivation to maintain high production, no monetary recognition is given for increased worker effort and performance, and unit costs are more difficult to compute than under systems requiring time standards.

The adoption of a time wage-payment plan is generally advisable under the following conditions:

1.  Time standards for the job are very difficult to set and maintain.
2.  Output is beyond the control of the individual and subject to considerable fluctuation.
3.  The worker is paced by a machine or other item of equipment such as a conveyor.
4.  The job requires concentration, creative thought, or decision-making (e.g., engineering design, research, supervision).
5.  Employees and union insist upon its use.
6.  Quality of workmanship is more important than quantity.

### Wage Payment Based on Output

Wage-payment plans based upon output or accomplishment vary a great deal in complexity but are commonplace for a variety of jobs. Salesmen frequently receive their compensation in the form of commissions on sales; executives may be paid bonuses based upon the earnings of the company; and production workers may be paid an amount for each unit they produce. The method of compensating workers for goods produced is commonly referred to as an "incentive system" of wage payment and it is to this system that we shall devote most of the discussion in this section.

Many incentive systems of wage payment have been devised; some of these are illustrated in Figure 20-2.

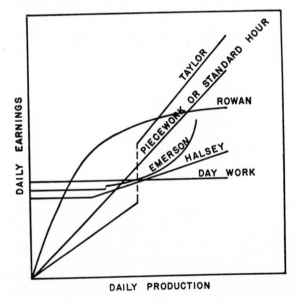

**Figure 20-2.** Earnings from typical wage incentive plans.

The most widely used incentive plan has been piecework, in which the individual is paid a fixed rate for each part produced. These rates are usually determined by time study and are usually designed to provide the average worker with a fairly large bonus (20 to 30 per cent above the regular hourly rate is common). The formula for the computation of the wage under this plan is as follows:

$$W = N \times R_p$$
where $\quad N =$ Number of pieces produced
$\quad R_p =$ Rate per piece in dollars
$\quad W =$ Wages earned

Many companies have preferred to establish an incentive system known as a "standard hour" plan instead of using piecework. As may be seen in Figure 20-2, the earnings for these two are the same but the "standard hour" plan has a decided administrative advantage in that a change in the worker's hourly rate doesn't necessitate other changes, whereas when using the piece-rate plan it would require changing the price per piece. The formula for this plan is illustrated below:

$$W = H_s R$$
where $\quad W =$ Wage
$\quad H_s =$ Standard hours of work produced
$\quad R =$ Rate of pay per hour

The scope of this chapter doesn't permit discussing the many plans that have been adopted by industry, but Figure 20-2 illustrates some of the prevailing characteristics of typical plans. As may be seen, some plans offer a constant incentive, others a high initial incentive and then diminishing returns, and still others an ever increasing incentive as the worker's output increases.

Among the advantages that are commonly associated with wage incentive plans are the following: they provide strong monetary motivation and are a means to maintaining high production; they reward the individual for increased effort and performance; they reduce the degree of supervision required; and they provide a useful basis for cost control purposes. On the other hand, the disadvantages commonly cited include the following: earnings may be difficult to calculate; they require additional administrative overhead in the form of time-study men and clerks; they are frowned upon by many unions; quality may be sacrificed in an effort to get high production; and malpractice has led to "speeding up" the workers.

A number of characteristics are usually associated with a good wage incentive system, expressed in the following rules:

1. The plan should be simple and easily understood by the employees.
2. The plan should reward employees in direct proportion to increased output.

3.   Hourly base rates should be established by job evaluation.

4.   The task imposed for the incentive plan should allow sufficient earning potential so that the worker can make at least 20 per cent above his hourly base rate.

5.   Time standards should be established by a sound system of work measurement and should be guaranteed against any change except where there has been a definite change in methods, tools, equipment, specifications, or materials.

6.   Shop procedures involving production control, materials control, and other items should be standardized.

7.   Time standards should be based on definite quality standards.

8.   Provision should be made for handling production and other delays that are beyond the control of the operator.

9.   The plan should be applied to as many direct and indirect workers as possible.

10.   The plan should be rigidly maintained.


### Profit-Sharing

One of the methods used to augment the compensation of employees is through the sharing of the profits of the enterprise. Profit sharing has had a long history. Although there has been no pronounced trend toward the adoption of profit-sharing plans, the movement is growing. A nationwide Council of Profit Sharing Industries was established several years ago, and this council has urged many companies to develop programs. Evidence of the interest in the profit-sharing movement is indicated by the inclusion of profit sharing in the agreement between American Motors and the United Automobile Workers in 1961.

Profit-sharing plans differ markedly in coverage and in their methods of distributing the profits. In some companies they are limited to executives, whereas in others they have universal coverage. In general, they provide a system of distributing net profits, after dividends have been set aside, on some predetermined basis at the end of an annual or other stipulated period. These payments have recently been ruled by federal courts as being part of the operating costs of running the business and not subject to the profit tax.

The method of distributing the profits to the employees differs from firm to firm. Some organizations apportion the payments among the employees on the basis of their years of service with the firm; others pay them a fixed percentage of their total wages during a stipulated period; and still others prefer to pay on the basis of the merit ratings of the individuals. In companies having excellent records of earnings, the payments may be sizable and, in such notable companies as the Lincoln Electric Company in Cleveland, may actually equal or exceed the individual's annual wage.

The proponents of profit sharing claim a number of benefits from their programs. Among these are increased productivity, reduced labor turnover and greater loyalty on the part of the workers, better cooperation among the employees, and improved attitudes toward their jobs and the company. But profits cannot be shared unless the business has a successful record of earnings, and this poses one of the problems associated with such programs. The workers come to expect some form of profit distribution and if the sum is lower than anticipated, they may be disappointed and disgruntled. The long-term nature of the profit-sharing period provides little day-to-day motivation, and many of the most successful programs have been accompanied by direct wage incentive systems. Also, the most successful programs appear to have been in those companies that stressed sound managerial practice and placed considerable emphasis on maintaining an excellent personnel management program.

### Guaranteed Annual Wage

The guarantee of an annual wage or annual employment has long been the desire of the worker, but it has only been in recent years that this subject has created national interest. The successful attempt of the United Auto Workers Union to secure a partial wage guarantee from the major automotive companies lent great strength to this movement.

A number of firms, including the Procter and Gamble Company, Nunn-Bush Company, Hormel Company, Armstrong Cork Company, and Sears, Roebuck and Company, are widely recognized for their contributions to wage stabilization, and have had a long history of successful operation of their programs. Although the plan in each of these companies differs somewhat from the others, the net effect is to guarantee the employees a minimum number of weeks of work each year. In some of the more recent programs, the employment guarantee has been tied in with the unemployment compensation benefits provided through Social Security.

For the most part, companies that have established wage stabilization programs have been in the consumer-good industries. The employees usually become eligible after a fixed period of service and may be guaranteed all or a stipulated proportion of weekly wages for a certain number of weeks. The costs of operating such a program vary widely and have been estimated at as high as 20 per cent of the annual payroll. It is obvious that it is not easy to stabilize employment in businesses subject to seasonal fluctuations in sales, and this poses a real problem for management. Extensive consideration must be given to market research, business forecasting, diversification of the product, new markets, and manpower control in order to maintain production at a stable level.

## QUESTIONS

1. A worker is employed on a job in a plant that pays him $20 a week less than his best friend receives for similar work in a different company. What psychological implications may this have for him?

2. The supervisor of Department A in a company works about 45 to 50 hours per week with no overtime pay because he is exempted by the Wage and Hour Law. On the other hand, the workers in his department get overtime pay for all hours worked in excess of 40. Is this a good situation? Why?

3. The ABC Company makes it a policy always to pay at least the prevailing wage for all its jobs. Is this a good policy? Why?

4. What influence do fringe benefits have on a company's ability to pay wages?

5. To what extent has labor legislation influenced the wages paid by industry?

6. To what extent has collective bargaining influenced the wages paid by industry?

7. Are geographic wage differentials as large as they used to be? Why?

8. Do you think that company presidents are worth as much as they get paid? Why?

9. The Peerless Products Company employs 150 production workers on a large number of precision machining operations. The company's costs have been rising and it has been suggested that they install a wage incentive plan. What problems might the company encounter in such an installation?

10. Would a profit-sharing plan be a desirable program to install in a company that is trying to increase the productivity of its workers? Why?

## CASE PROBLEMS

**Steelcraft Metal Products Company**

The Steelcraft Metal Products Company is a small metal stamping company located in an industrial city of about 600,000 population. The company has been operating for 40 years, and now employs about 400 non-union men and women production workers. During the past few months the company has received numerous complaints on its wage system, and the president has asked the chief industrial engineer to submit a report on the company's wage program and to make recommendations for improving it. The principal provisions of the wage program were found to be as follows:

1. No employees working on incentive are allowed to earn more than 20% in excess of their day rate.

2. Time standards are subject to change at management's discretion.
3. Time study sheets and time standards are not available to employees.
4. Women receive 10¢/hour less than men employed on the same job.
5. The Halsey 50-50 wage incentive plan is used on nearly all production jobs. The day rate is guaranteed by management.
6. Indirect workers are not on incentive.
7. Employees on incentive are paid their day rate during all non-productive periods, e.g., down time, vacations, and holidays.
8. All employees participate semiannually in the profits of the company. All shop employees receive the same amount of bonus. Executives' bonuses are based upon a different system determined by the president.
9. Wages and salaries are adjusted as management deems desirable. Management attempts to keep all wage rates on a par with similar jobs performed in the community.
10. Wage increases are granted individuals based upon merit, and all wages are reviewed at least once each year.

*Questions:*

1. Based upon the above information, analyze each of the ten items included in the wage policy and give your reasons for retaining, discarding, or correcting it.

2. In order to analyze the wage program completely, what additional information should be obtained?

3. What additional policies should be adhered to?

### Kessler Corporation

The Kessler Corporation employs about 350 production employees in the manufacture of packaging machinery. Since the corporation is located in the same community as a large automotive plant, its employees are represented by the United Automobile Workers. It was only natural that when the local auto parts company agreed to a special type of guaranteed annual wage plan, the union demanded that Kessler Corporation agree to the same plan.

Ned Fish, president of Kessler Corporation, refused to grant any kind of guaranteed wage plan. His arguments were that his company was too small and its business too uncertain to be pinned down by such a program. In addition he contended that if his company agreed to guarantee wages, it would be the smallest company in the state burdened by such a plan and that its security would be jeopardized.

The union agreement was finally signed without any guaranteed wage plan provision. Following the signing of the agreement, Mr. Fish confided to the personnel manager that he thought they would probably not be so fortunate in their next negotiation (three years hence) and that they might have to agree to some kind of guaranteed wage plan.

*Questions:*

1. Comment on this situation.

2. What problems would a guaranteed wage plan pose to the company?

# CHAPTER TWENTY-ONE

# Wage and Salary Administration— Job Evaluation and Merit Rating

In the preceding chapter, we noted many of the problems that arise in the field of wage and salary administration. Few of these are more complex than that of determining the worth of jobs. This is particularly difficult because employees have their own methods of evaluating jobs. It behooves the employer, then, to use a systematic approach to job evaluation rather than "hit-or-miss," "rule-of-thumb" techniques.

Closely related to the problem of determining the worth of a job is that of determining the worth of the employees performing that job. If a wage rate range exists for the job there should be some way of determining whether Joe is worth more than Bill. It is for the purpose of answering this question that industry has established formal systems of merit or employee rating.

This chapter will be devoted to a discussion of the above two areas.

## Job Evaluation

Examination of any organization will reveal it to contain a number of jobs, and someone will have established a wage rate for each of these jobs. Some companies' wage rates will have been established by managerial intuition, others by "rule-of-thumb" techniques, and still others by a formal system of job evaluation. It is with the formal system of job evaluation that we shall be concerned in this chapter.

Job evaluation is a systematic procedure for determining the relative worth of jobs within an organization and for establishing an adequate wage structure. This function has been commonly performed by the wage and salary administration department or by the industrial engineering department.

The usual objectives of a job evaluation program are as follows:

1. To eliminate wage inequities.
2. To establish sound wage differentials among the jobs.
3. To provide a sound wage base for incentive and bonus plans.
4. To establish a sound wage structure.
5. To facilitate the maintenance of a consistent wage policy.

The methods used in evaluating jobs will frequently consist of the following major steps:

1. Determining the jobs to be evaluated.
2. Analyzing each job.
3. Evaluating each job.
4. Fitting the jobs into the wage structure.

### Range of Jobs to Be Evaluated

Before a suitable method is selected for evaluating the jobs in an organization, the scope of the program will have to be decided. Very few companies have included all jobs in their job evaluation program. For the most part, the program has been limited to the jobs in the shop or in the office.

At the outset it will be wise for us to differentiate between the commonly used terms "task," "position," and "job." A *task* exists whenever human effort must be exerted for a specific purpose. A *position is an aggregation of duties, tasks, and responsibilities assigned to and requiring the services of one individual.*[1] From this definition it may be seen that in any organization there are as many positions as there are workers.

A job may be defined as a position or a group of positions involving substantially the same duties, skills, knowledge, and responsibilities; or as a number of positions, or groups of tasks, which are somewhat similar in nature and worker requirements, and which are performed by a number of workers who customarily change about from one position to another.

---

[1]War Manpower Commission, Division of Occupational Analysis, *Training and Reference Manual for Job Analysis* (Washington, D.C.: U. S. Government Printing Office, 1944), p. 7.

## Job Analysis

The basis for job evaluation, as well as for certain other personnel department activities, is provided by job analysis. The purpose of job analysis is to collect complete information on all requirements of the job. Among the items of information collected will be: (1) complete identification of the job, (2) the duties performed on the job, (3) the responsibilities required by the job, (4) the working conditions under which the job is performed, and (5) the personal qualifications required by the job. The job analyst may secure this information by questioning the person working on the job, from the worker's supervisor, from others familiar with the job, or from actual observation.

It is common practice to use one or more forms in performing the job analysis, but the most frequently used form is the *job description*. Such forms are usually similar to that illustrated in Figure 21-1.

## Evaluating the Jobs

Following the analysis of the jobs, the next step will be to evaluate them in non-financial terms. This evaluation assumes that the jobs can be weighed objectively by means of factors or definitions arbitrarily assigned. The most frequently used methods for performing this evaluation are the (1) ranking method, (2) job classification method, (3) point method, and (4) factor comparison method. Each of these will be described briefly in the sections that follow.

**Ranking method.**    The ranking method is the simplest of the job evaluation methods. It consists of having supervisors or other persons compare the overall job contents (usually without the aid of a job description) of the various jobs and then arrange them in a job hierarchy. Oftentimes the names of the jobs are placed on cards and the persons doing the evaluating arrange the cards in the order of importance in which they feel the jobs should be evaluated. A common method of accomplishing this is to pick out the most important and least important jobs first and then several other key jobs somewhere in between. The other jobs to be evaluated are then placed in the proper place among the jobs first selected. When the persons doing the evaluating have come to agreement as to the location of the jobs, then the jobs may be grouped into job classes for affixing the wage rate.

The "paired comparison"[2] method of ranking jobs has been devised in

---

[2]For a detailed discussion of this method, see David W. Belcher, *Wage and Salary Administration*, (Englewood Cliffs, N. J.: Prentice-Hall, Inc., 1962) p. 242.

## JOB DESCRIPTION

Department ....................................    Standard Code .............................

Subdivision ....................................    Standard Title ..............................

Branch of Plant ............................    Plant Title ...................................

Date ............................................    Plant Code ...................................

*Summary of Duties*

*Detailed Statement of Work Performed*

*Source of Supervision*

*Tools and Equipment*

*Materials*

*Responsibility* (For safety of others, company funds or property, for performance of work without supervision, etc.)

*Qualifications Required:*

Special Knowledge:

Previous Experience:

Physical:

*Working Conditions:*

Surroundings:

Hazards:

*Relation to Other Jobs*

Promotion from:

Promotion to:

Job Analyst........................................

Approved By ............................................... Date ..........................

**Figure 21-1.** Job description form.

an attempt to improve the reliability of ratings and is a better method of ranking jobs. It consists of comparing every job with every other job by pairs. The jobs are randomly paired, and the job most often considered most valuable is rated as the top job, the one picked next most often becomes the second job, and so forth. A convenient device for performing this comparison is a table such as that illustrated in Figure 21-2. Using such a table, the rater is asked to check the higher of the two jobs indicated by each of the cells of the table. The job receiving the most checks is ranked first, the next highest is ranked second, and so forth.

| | Stenographer | Clerk Typist | Secretary | Mail Clerk | Typist |
|---|---|---|---|---|---|
| Stenographer | | | | | |
| Clerk typist | | | | | |
| Secretary | | | | | |
| Mail clerk | | | | | |
| Typist | | | | | |

**Figure 21-2.** Paired comparison table.

The ranking method of job evaluation has several obvious disadvantages: (1) it is difficult to use except where the number of jobs is small; (2) it requires several raters who are familiar with the jobs and it may be difficult to find qualified raters; (3) the biases of the raters will tend to influence their evaluations of the jobs; (4) it is difficult to defend the individual ratings; and (5) it assumes equal spacing between ranks. On the other hand, it is simple and may prove to be a very satisfactory method in small plants having a small number of jobs.

**Job classification method.**    The job classification method has become well known through extensive use for evaluating United States Civil Service jobs. Although it has been in common use in governmental circles for many years, it has found little use in industry.

The job classification method consists of setting forth broad definitions or descriptions describing the content of several job classes, which are arranged in order of importance. An example of such descriptions is illustrated in Figure 21-3. New jobs to be evaluated are then compared to these descriptions, and the jobs are placed in those classes most closely indentifying them. A class, then, includes all jobs considered to be of the same grade without any detailed analysis of the job.

*Grade 1.* Performs simple routine tasks under close supervision and following standard or established procedures. Work is light manual, requiring only minor degree of mental alertness such as sorting or arranging in alphabetical, numerical, or chronological order—counting, stamping, delivering messages, and mailing.

*Grade 2.* Performs routine tasks under close supervision involving minor degrees of skill and easily learned, elemental business and office procedures such as posting, filing, and simple calculations and limited use of typewriter, addressograph, duplicating machine, and other office equipment. Has no business contact with others and any errors in workmanship and judgment have little consequence.

*Grade 3.* Performs, with normal degree of supervision, semi-routine tasks involving good working knowledge and understanding of business and office procedures, the ability to think out simple problems, and the expanded use of office equipment. Independent action permitted within prescribed limits with irregularities referred to supervisor. Has business contacts only with employees in related fields and exercises limited supervision over personnel in lower grades.

*Grade 4.* Performs non-routine work with limited supervision, involving considerable knowledge of a specific area of work, the ability to handle special calculations and problems in the specific area, and an understanding of the operations of office equipment. Has the ability to investigate irregularities and ordinary discrepancies; takes responsibility for monies and confidential matters. Has considerable contacts with public and fellow employees, exercising supervision over employees in lower grades.

*Grade 5.* Performs, with little or no supervision, tasks of high-grade clerical nature, requiring an intimate knowledge of the operational functions of the organization, with ability to assemble designated information and to prepare a comprehensive report. Maintains and advises superior on daily schedules, planned activities, and reports. Supervises employees in lower grades. Makes both employee and public contacts.

**Figure 21-3.** Grade descriptions of clerical positions. Source: Charles W. Brennan, *Wage Administration* (Richard D. Irwin, Homeward, Ill., 1963), p. 123, reprinted by permission.

The principal disadvantages that arise in using this method are the problem of writing grade descriptions in terms such that jobs can be compared to them and the difficulty of placing a borderline job in the correct class.

**Point method.** The point method of evaluating jobs is by far the most widely used in industry. It consists of a "yardstick" containing various factors such as skill, education, responsibility, and so forth, that are inherent in the jobs and that vary in importance. The degree of importance of each factor is determined by arbitrary decision, and a suitable point value is specified for each. As an aid, each factor is described by a suitable definition and appropriate benchmark jobs may be selected for comparison purposes. One of the most widely used plans of this type is that put out by the National Electrical Manufacturers Association whose evaluation form is illustrated in Figure 21-4.

| *Factors* | *Degrees and Points* | | | | |
|---|---|---|---|---|---|
| | *1st degree* | *2nd degree* | *3rd degree* | *4th degree* | *5th degree* |
| **SKILL** | | | | | |
| 1. Education ......................... | 14 | 28 | 42 | 56 | 70 |
| 2. Experience ......................... | 22 | 44 | 66 | 88 | 110 |
| 3. Initiative and ingenuity ......... | 14 | 28 | 42 | 56 | 70 |
| **EFFORT** | | | | | |
| 4. Physical demand ................. | 10 | 20 | 30 | 40 | 50 |
| 5. Mental and/or visual demand ... | 5 | 10 | 15 | 20 | 25 |
| **RESPONSIBILITY** | | | | | |
| 6. Equipment or process ........... | 5 | 10 | 15 | 20 | 25 |
| 7. Material or product .............. | 5 | 10 | 15 | 20 | 25 |
| 8. Safety of others .................... | 5 | 10 | 15 | 20 | 25 |
| 9. Work of others .................... | 5 | 10 | 15 | 20 | 25 |
| **JOB CONDITIONS** | | | | | |
| 10. Working conditions .............. | 10 | 20 | 30 | 40 | 50 |
| 11. Hazards ........................... | 5 | 10 | 15 | 20 | 25 |

**Figure 21-4.** Degrees and points assigned to job factors. (Courtesy National Electric Manufacturers Association).

## Education or Trade Knowledge

This factor measures the job requirements in terms of the mental development needed to think in terms of, and understand, the work being performed. Such mental development or technical knowledge may be acquired either by formal schooling, night school, or through equivalent experience.

Trades or vocational training is considered as a form of education and should be evaluated under this factor.

1ST DEGREE
Requires the ability to read and write, add and subtract whole numbers.

2ND DEGREE
Requires the use of simple arithmetic such as addition and subtraction of decimals and fractions, together with simple drawings and some measuring instruments such as caliper, scale.

3RD DEGREE
Requires the use of fairly complicated drawings, advanced shop mathematics, handbook formulas, variety of precision measuring instruments; some trade knowledge in a specialized field or process.

4TH DEGREE
Requires the use of complicated drawings and specifications, advanced shop mathematics, wide variety of precision measuring instruments, broad shop trade knowledge.

5TH DEGREE
Requires a basic technical knowledge sufficient to deal with complicated and involved mechanical, electrical, or other engineering problems.

**Figure 21-5.** Definition of education factor. (Courtesy National Electric Manufacturers Association).

An idea of the content of the definitions for each of factors used in this plan may be obtained from the definition for the Education Factor contained in Figure 21-5.

In the evaluation of any particular job, its description is compared to the job factors on the evaluation form and those degrees most appropriate are assigned. The total points for all the factors then determine the relative position of that job among other jobs. Of course, the point values must be converted into money values; we shall discuss this in a later section of this chapter.

The point system has become the most popular method of job evaluation because it possesses a number of advantages over the non-quantitative methods. By using graphic or other rating scales, it is possible to attain consistency among the raters. The factors and point values may be agreed upon in advance by the employer and the union. The raters do not have to be thoroughly familiar with the jobs in order to do an accurate job of rating. Also, it tends to minimize the effects of personal bias of the raters. The total point values that arise from the use of this method make it easy to group the point values into job classes.

One of the disadvantages of this system is the problem of constructing it so that proper factors are selected and proper weightings are assigned them. In addition, the system is difficult to explain to the employees and is time-consuming and costly.

**The factor comparison method.** The factor comparison method is favored by many wage and salary administrators because it is tailored to fit each company. It is like the point system in that it makes use of arbitrarily selected factors, but it differs by making use of key or benchmark jobs as the basic yardstick. These key jobs are selected by a committee as being representative of the job hierarchy of the company both in their content and in the wage rate being paid for them. The committee arbitrarily selects several factors—such as skill, physical requirements, responsibility, working conditions, and mental requirements—for which they feel the company should pay. Then they rank each key job in order for each of the factors as is illustrated in Figure 21-6.

Using these ranks as a guide, the next step is for the committee members to divide the present hourly rate being paid each key job among the five factors in accordance with their judgments as to how the money should be distributed among the factors. When they have agreed on this distribution, a table such as that illustrated in Figure 21-7 may be prepared.

After the job-rating scale has been established as indicated in Figure 21-7, all other jobs can be evaluated against this yardstick. Each job is broken down into the five factors and compared factor by factor against the rating scale. Thus if the job contains approximately the same degree of skill as

*Average Rank*

| Job | Mental Require-ments | Physical Require-ments | Skill Require-ments | Responsi-bility | Working Con-ditions |
|---|---|---|---|---|---|
| Gager | 2 | 13 | 2 | 3 | 15 |
| Pattern maker | 1 | 12 | 1 | 1 | 16 |
| Common laborer | 16 | 1 | 16 | 16 | 1 |
| Power shear opr. | 11 | 11 | 9 | 5 | 4 |
| Plater | 10 | 6 | 6 | 12 | 9 |
| Riveter | 12 | 3 | 12 | 14 | 8 |
| Blacksmith | 13 | 2 | 8 | 13 | 7 |
| Punch press opr. | 14 | 4 | 13 | 15 | 5 |
| Automatic screw machine opr. | 4 | 8 | 3 | 2 | 13 |
| Casting inspector | 3 | 7 | 4 | 4 | 10 |
| Millwright | 9 | 10 | 5 | 6 | 11 |
| Tool crib attendant | 7 | 16 | 14 | 10 | 14 |
| Arc welder | 8 | 9 | 7 | 9 | 3 |
| Electric truck operator | 6 | 15 | 11 | 8 | 12 |
| Crane operator | 5 | 14 | 10 | 7 | 6 |
| Watchman | 15 | 5 | 15 | 11 | 2 |

**Figure 21-6.** Average ranks of 16 tentative key jobs as assigned by committee. Source: David W. Belcher, *Wage and Salary Administration* (Englewood Cliffs, N.J.: Prentice-Hall, Inc., 1962), p. 264. Reprinted by permission.

*Average Cents per Hour Assigned*

| Job | Mental | Physi-cal | Skill | Re-sponsi-bility | Work-ing Con-ditions | Present Rate |
|---|---|---|---|---|---|---|
| Gager | .72 | .38 | 1.02 | .51 | .45 | 3.08 |
| Pattern maker | .90 | .39 | 1.13 | .60 | .23 | 3.25 |
| Common laborer | .18 | .60 | .21 | .14 | .50 | 1.63 |
| Power shear opr. | .41 | .42 | .51 | .48 | .42 | 2.24 |
| Plater | .44 | .51 | .59 | .30 | .33 | 2.17 |
| Riveter | .39 | .56 | .41 | .26 | .33 | 1.95 |
| Blacksmith | .33 | .59 | .68 | .27 | .48 | 2.35 |
| Punch press opr. | .30 | .54 | .30 | .23 | .38 | 1.75 |
| Automatic screw machine opr. | .62 | .48 | .98 | .57 | .24 | 2.89 |
| Casting inspector | .63 | .50 | .62 | .50 | .29 | 2.54 |
| Millwright | .48 | .45 | .90 | .47 | .27 | 2.57 |
| Tool crib attendant | .53 | .26 | .29 | .35 | .24 | 1.67 |
| Arc welder | .50 | .47 | .53 | .36 | .44 | 2.00 |
| Electric truck opr. | .57 | .32 | .44 | .38 | .26 | 1.97 |
| Crane operator | .60 | .36 | .50 | .45 | .36 | 2.27 |
| Watchman | .20 | .53 | .23 | .32 | .45 | 1.73 |

**Figure 21-7.** Average distribution of present wages. Sources: David W. Belcher, Ibid, p. 265. Reprinted by permission.

a punch press operator, it would be assigned that amount for that factor. The total of the five values assigned the job becomes its evaluated rate.

The factor comparison method possesses a number of advantages not found in other methods of job evaluation. It is not difficult to set up a job comparison scale, and this scale is tailored to fit the company's jobs. In using the scale to evaluate jobs, the jobs are compared to other jobs, they are evaluated in terms of their monetary worth, and it is unnecessary to convert from points or job classes into money.

The major disadvantage of the factor comparison method involves the design of the rating scale. If the going rates of the key jobs, and the monetary values assigned each factor for each key job are incorrect, then new jobs will be evaluated at incorrect rates. An additional disadvantage is its complexity and the difficulty of explaining it to the employees.

## Evaluation of Office, Professional, and Executive Positions

Much of the material previously covered will apply equally well to clerical and other office positions. The principal difference between job evaluation in the office and in the shop is that direct classification of whole jobs is still commonly used in the office.

Many companies have adopted job evaluation plans for use in their offices, and there appears to be a definite trend in this direction. Of the plans in effect, there is much more widespread usage of the ranking and job classification methods than in the shop. Also, where the point or factor comparison methods are employed, separate plans will be used and will include factors more pertinent to office jobs.

Owing to the nature of many scientific-professional positions in industry, limited application of job evaluation has taken place for these positions. In attempting to evaluate engineering positions, for example, it is difficult to measure the creativity that may enter into a designer's or researcher's work. However, this has not prevented some plans from being designed and put into effect with a high degree of success. The Engineers' Society of Milwaukee has designed a point plan applicable to engineering positions that is thorough in coverage and should give excellent results.

Limited but growing use has been made of job evaluation for supervisory and executive positions. The principal reason for this limited use is that it is difficult to analyze the complex and varied characteristics that compose supervisory and executive positions. We need but think about the many activities performed by supervisors and executives to realize the problem of isolating and evaluating the activities that are required on these jobs. However, this has not prevented some companies from installing salary evaluation plans that apply to their supervisors and middle executives. Among the companies that have installed such plans are Westinghouse Electric Company, S. C. Johnson Company, General Foods Corporation, General Aniline and Film Corporation, and the General Electric Company.

### Pricing the Jobs

Inasmuch as it would be far too unwieldly to try to fit every job separately into the wage structure, it is common practice to categorize the jobs by job classes and to pay jobs of equal or approximately equal difficulty the same rate or in the same rate range. The wage structure that results from pricing the job classes is most frequently shown graphically in the form of a wage curve.

**Wage curve.** The wage curve is merely a graphical method of showing the relationship between wage rates (present, community, and collective bargaining) and number of points, job classes, or evaluated rates. Most employers are interested in knowing how their wage rates compare with similar jobs in other companies in their community, and this information is usually obtained from a community wage survey. The manner in which this survey is conducted will vary from area to area. It may be performed by telephone calls, questionnaires, or by other means. The data may be used for establishing community wage curves for the jobs with which the company is concerned.

The position of the company wage curve with regard to the community level will depend upon management policy and upon the demands of the union. If it is the policy of the company to pay wages above the going rate for the community, then its wage curve must be above the community curve.

**Establishing the wage structure.** A number of decisions must be made before a company can establish its wage structure. Among the questions that must be answered are: (1) Is provision to be made for merit increases? (2) Are jobs to be grouped into job classes? (3) Are the wage rates for job classes to overlap? If so, how much? (4) How should borderline jobs be treated?

According to Otis and Leukart, "Most companies today use a wage range in pricing jobs and job classes. The wage range usually consists of a minimum or starting rate and a maximum rate and enough money spread between the two to make it possible to grant several wage increases."[3]

---

[3]By permission from *Job Evaluation* (Englewood Cliffs, N.J.: Prentice-Hall, Inc., 1954), p. 436.

**Figure 21-8.** Wage structure with overlapping rate ranges.

Figure 21-8 illustrates the wage structure for a point method of job evaluation in which the hourly rate is plotted against point values. Note that in this curve each job class has a range of 50 points and that job classes overlap.

The procedure for pricing the job structure will vary somewhat depending upon the method of job evaluation used. When the point plan is used, the rates for certain key jobs can be plotted against their point values and a best-fitting line determined. This line will represent the average wage paid by the company and may be compared with the "going rates" for the community. When the company's wage curve has been determined and necessary adjustments made in it, then the rates for job classes will be established. Also, a decision will have to be made as to how the rates above and below the wage curve are to be handled.

For the other methods of job evaluation, the company's wage curve may be compared with the "going rates" for the community for key jobs and then any necessary adjustments made in the wage curve. Following this, the present rates may be compared to the evaluated rates and necessary adjustments made in the job rates. After the wage rates have been assigned, jobs are usually grouped into classes or grades. The purpose of this is to reduce the administrative problem associated with many different wage rates.

## Administration of Job Evaluation

In administering the job evaluation program, the wage and salary administrators are confronted with many problems and issues. In those companies having unions, one of the foremost of these is the relationship with the unions. As Gomberg[4] has pointed out, the attitudes of the unions fall into three different groups:

"1.  Complete rejection.
2.  Coyness.
3.  Full joint participation in the installation and administration of the technique by both the union and the management."

It is necessary for management to decide at the outset, then, the extent to which the union is to be involved in the program. Another far-reaching decision that must be made pertains to the job evaluation committee. Considerable thought should be given to insure that this committee contains persons sufficiently high in the company to be able to accomplish its objectives.

During the process of designing the method of job evaluation to be used, many questions arise that must be answered. For example, if a point plan is to be used, how many factors should be used in the plan, and what weighting should be assigned to these factors? Many point plans are subject to criticism because they involve too many factors[5] and improper weightings of factors. Another question that must be resolved is, How are the employees to be informed of the system in such a way that they will understand it?

Many day-to-day problems will arise to confront the administrators. Some of these are:

1.  How can job descriptions be kept current?
2.  How should out-of-line jobs be treated?
3.  How should borderline jobs be evaluated?
4.  At what rate should transferees be paid?
5.  How can the influence of supply and demand be taken into account?

In the paragraphs that follow, we shall discuss briefly preferable practice on each of these issues.

It is very difficult to keep job descriptions current unless the complete cooperation of the supervisors and others familiar with job content can be secured. A plan should be devised for having them report all job changes and, in addition, periodic reviews should be initiated to provide a check on all jobs.

One of the touchiest aspects of job evaluation is that of establishing a policy on the method of pricing out-of-line jobs. For example, based on the wage structure illustrated in Figure 21-8, what should be done about those

---

[4]See discussion by William Gomberg in *Handbook of Industrial Engineering and Management*, edited by W. Grant Ireson and Eugene L. Grant (Englewood Cliffs, N. J.: Prentice-Hall, Inc., 1955), p. 1135.

[5]For a discussion of this area, see Otis and Leukart, *op. cit*, p. 123.

jobs that fall above or below the rate range in any job class? It is usual practice to guarantee the employees that their wage rates will not be reduced because of the job evaluation program, and yet, the aim of job evaluation should be to get the wage rates in line with the evaluated rates. The jobs priced too low present no real problem and are merely raised on the evaluated rate. Some authorities are of the opinion that this should be done over a period of time in small increments, such as a 5-cent-per-hour increase every three or six months. The jobs priced too high can not be handled this easily, and it is common practice to let the present job holders retain their old rates permanently or for some fixed period. On the other hand, new persons hired on these jobs are paid at the evaluated rate.

It is difficult to devise a sound approach to the treatment of "borderline" jobs. These are the jobs on the fringe area between two adjacent job classes, and there is little choice but to make an arbitrary decision as to the class in which each one best fits. The use of overlapping point values for adjacent grades is one technique that has been used as a means of minimizing friction, but even this does not solve the problem.

Employees transferred from one job to another present no problem if their new job pays the same or higher wage rate than their old job. However, they will resent taking a pay cut if demoted to a lower-paid job. If the worker has had experience on the new job to which he is being demoted, it is common to pay him at the maximum rate for the new job. Other companies will pay him the maximum on the new job if it is anticipated that he is capable of performing the job even if he has had no previous experience on it. In still other cases where the individual has had no previous experience and his performance may be questionable, he may be started at the midpoint of the range.

The influence of supply and demand is one of the complex problems encountered in job evaluation programs. In a number of cases, a shortage of qualified persons may make it necessary for a company to exceed the evaluated rate in order to hire the employee needed. Where this happens, immediate consideration should be given to alleviating the situation by initiating a training program or by adding additional responsibilities to the job to upgrade it to a higher job class. Certainly, deviation from the wage structure should not be considered the only solution.

Based upon our previous discussion of the many aspects of job evaluation, it should be self-evident that job evaluation is not a scientific method of determining job rates but is merely a systematic approach to a difficult problem. It is subject to the forces of collective bargaining, supply and demand, and other external factors. Like all programs involving human judgment, it is not infallible. However, its many virtues so completely outweigh its shortcomings as to make it a *must* in well-managed companies.

# Merit Rating

In contrast to the impersonal nature of job evaluation, *merit rating*[6] is concerned with employee evaluation. It is a systematic and (so far as possible) impartial procedure for determining the excellence with which an individual is performing his job. Merit rating programs are usually installed in an attempt to eliminate the many different approaches to employee rating that may be exercised by the supervisors in a business. As a result, employees are evaluated by means of a standardized system, and the ratings are more consistent, fair, and impartial.

Merit rating programs should be tailored for the employees they are to cover and should take into account those factors that are important in performing the jobs on which the individuals are employed. The rating should cover those items for which the company is willing to pay and may include such factors as experience, skill, judgment, dependability, adaptability, and other matters that have a bearing on job performance. It is common practice to use one rating scale or method for production workers, another for office workers, and still another for salesmen, engineers, or other groups.

## Purpose of Merit Rating

The information obtained from merit rating may be used for a number of purposes, including the following:

1. As a basis for pay increases.
2. As a basis for promotions, transfers, or layoffs.
3. To determine the proportion of profit-sharing bonuses to be paid employees.
4. As a basis for counseling employees.
5. To provide information for employee placement.
6. As a criterion for the evaluation of personnel programs such as personnel testing.
7. As a means of uncovering special talents and abilities.

In addition, merit rating probably forces closer and better supervision, in that the supervisors must observe the employees closely if they are to rate them accurately.

---

[6]Other names used to refer to employee rating are "efficiency" rating, "progress" rating, "performance" rating, "personnel" rating, and "service" rating.

FCA 7-6

## EMPLOYEE APPRAISAL

Employee's Name _____    Classification _____

Bank _____ Department _____ Division _____

Rating Supervisor _____    Section _____

This form is designed to help you appraise accurately the value of employees to the organization. You are asked to rate the employee on each of the several traits or qualities listed here. After each trait there is a line representing various degrees of the trait. The descriptive phrases beneath the line indicate the amounts or degrees of the trait represented by five points along the line. They are guide-posts. You rate the employee by checking at any place along the line that represents your judgement of him.

In view of the importance of these ratings, you are asked to study and observe the rules printed on the other side of the sheet.

**QUALITY OF WORK**

| Doubtful that quality is satisfactory. | While not unsatisfactory, quality is not quite up to standard. | Quality is quite satisfactory. | Quality of work is superior to that of general run of empoyees. | Exceptionally high quality. | No chance to observe. |

**VOLUME OF WORK**

| Unusually high output. | Turns out more work than general run of comparable employees. | Average, satisfactory output. | Inclined to be slow. | Insufficient output. | No chance to observe. |

**CAPACITY TO DEVELOP**

| Future growth doubtful. | Moderate development ahead. | Shows promise. | Very promising promotional material. | Great future growth probable; should go far | No chance to observe. |

**Figure 21-9.** Portion of a simple personnel rating scale using descriptive phrases. (From W. G. Ireson and E. L. Grant, *Handbook of Industrial Engineering and Management*, Englewood Cliffs, N.J.: Prentice-Hall, Inc. 1955. Reprinted by permission.)

423

## Methods of Rating

The rating of employees is one of the oldest and most universal practices of management, but it is only in recent years that systematic merit rating programs have been installed in industry. In establishing these programs, a great variety of methods have been devised for rating the employees. Among these are: man to man, paired comparison, forced choice, checklists, critical incident, and graphical scales.[7] The use of a graphical scale such as is illustrated in Figure 21-9 has proved to be one of the most popular methods of rating. Considerable care must be taken in designing these scales to insure that they contain suitable traits, a limited number of degrees of each factor, adequate descriptions of factors, and sound weightings of factors.

## Administration of Program

Anything that may influence an employee's pay is of utmost importance to him and may lead to considerable friction if not properly administered. Therefore, management should give a great deal of attention to the design, installation, and maintenance of the merit rating program. Many of the problems that might otherwise be encountered in a merit rating program can be prevented through proper planning and installation. A suitable plan must be selected, the employees must be thoroughly acquainted with the program, competent raters must be selected, and the raters must be trained in the use of the system. It is common practice to perform the rating either every six months or annually, and then to discuss the ratings with the employees. This provides an effective basis for counseling employees and lets them know "how they stand" in the eyes of their boss.

For the most part the rating is done by the employee's immediate supervisor, but it is not uncommon to have a general foreman, plant superintendent, or other executive rate the individual. Whenever possible it is desirable to have more than one person rate the ratee, taking care that every rater has sufficient opportunity to observe the ratee and is competent to perform this important function.

In any rating system a number of deficiencies will appear that must be taken into account. The administrators of the program must provide a continuous check on the system's validity (does it measure what it is supposed to?) and reliability (does it measure consistently?). Also, they must guard against the common rating errors of: (1) *halo effect*—the tendency of the rater to rate the ratee too high or too low on every trait because of some bias,

---

[7]For a detailed discussion of these methods, see John Mee, *Personnel Handbook* (New York: Ronald Press Co., 1951).

(2) *leniency effect*—the tendency to rate the individual higher than he should be, and (3) *central tendency*—the tendency to avoid the extremes of the scale in rating the employees. By and large, these rating errors can be reduced to a minimum through proper design of the rating scale (or other method) to be used, and then by thoroughly training the raters in its use.

Like job evaluation, merit rating is subject to the shortcomings of any program involving human judgment. However, employees must be rated, and merit rating provides a means for placing employee evaluation on a systematic basis. Thus it, too, has come to be accepted as an indispensable tool of well-managed companies.

## QUESTIONS

1. Will a job evaluation program remove all wage inequities? Why?

2. The Jackson Manufacturing Company, which employs about 350 production workers in the manufacture of metal office desks, is considering the installation of a job evaluation system. It has been proposed that all employees of the company (workers, clerks, supervisors, and others) be covered by the same plan. Would this be desirable? Why?

3. What is the relationship between job evaluation and wage incentive plans?

4. Why is it desirable to analyze jobs before attempting to evaluate them?

5. Would the job classification method of evaluating jobs be a good method for evaluating factory jobs? Why?

6. In the point system of job evaluation, how important is it that proper weightings be given to each of the factors?

7. Would the factor comparison method of job evaluation be a desirable method to use in a company having only 40 jobs? Why?

8. What factors would be particularly important in a point system for evaluating executive jobs?

9. What problems might be encountered in trying to secure data to establish a community wage curve?

10. Some companies have used the practice of bringing out-of-line jobs that are above the wage curve back into line by keeping such jobs at their present levels and then letting the wage curve catch up to them through subsequent across-the-board wage increases. Comment on this practice.

## CASE PROBLEMS

### Autotune Radio Company

The Autotune Radio Company is a progressive midwestern company employing 500 union and nonunion employees in the manufacture of radio transmitters. The company, which is about 20 years old, has never had a job evaluation program. Recently, Joseph Richards, the personnel manager, approached top management with the suggestion that a job evaluation program be installed for the purpose of eliminating wage inequities and providing a sound wage structure. Michael Harris, the president of the company, thought this an excellent idea and has advised Joe Richards to draw up recommendations for a program which would fit the company's needs.

In checking on the present employees of the company, Joe Richards found them classified as follows:

| Type of Employee | No. Employed |
|---|---|
| Sheet metal workers | 20 |
| Cabinet painters & finishers | 5 |
| Platers | 5 |
| Machinists | 10 |
| Machine operators | 30 |
| Crystal makers | 15 |
| Tool & die makers | 3 |
| Maintenance men | 10 |
| Inspectors | 17 |
| Wiring operators, coil winders, etc. | 137 |
| Chassis assemblers | 55 |
| Final assemblers | 25 |
| Wiring testers | 20 |
| Chassis aligners | 13 |
| Final testers | 10 |
| Packers & shippers | 8 |
| Stock, receiving, & shipping clerks | 8 |
| Tool crib attendants | 2 |
| Stock replenishers | 6 |
| Janitors | 4 |
| Watchmen | 9 |
| Truck drivers | 3 |
| Foremen and other supervisors | 25 |
| Draftsmen | 6 |
| Engineers (research, development, testing, etc.) | 12 |
| Office clerks, stenographers, & secretaries | 30 |
| Executives | 12 |

*Questions:*

1. What recommendations should Joe Richards make? Why?

2. Who should be included in the program and which evaluation method would probably be most suitable? Why?

## Blodgett Company

The Blodgett Company has been in the woodworking business for 8 years and during that time has experienced rapid growth. It now employs 400 employees on one shift.

Wage rates have developed in a rather haphazard manner over the years and Roger Smith, the general manager, now realizes the need for a more scientific method of wage determination.

As a result, a point system of evaluation has been developed by the industrial engineering department and all jobs have been evaluated under this system. A comparison of the points assigned each job and base rates *presently* paid on each job follows:

| Job # | Points | Present Rate | Job # | Points | Present Rate | Job # | Points | Present Rate |
|-------|--------|--------------|-------|--------|--------------|-------|--------|--------------|
| 1 | 150 | $1.50 | 11 | 700 | $1.78 | 21 | 800 | $2.25 |
| 2 | 120 | 1.45 | 12 | 400 | 1.80 | 22 | 740 | 2.32 |
| 3 | 180 | 1.48 | 13 | 305 | 1.98 | 23 | 710 | 2.10 |
| 4 | 290 | 1.58 | 14 | 450 | 1.82 | 24 | 760 | 2.25 |
| 5 | 220 | 1.68 | 15 | 480 | 1.90 | 25 | 725 | 2.15 |
| 6 | 220 | 1.58 | 16 | 450 | 1.78 | 26 | 750 | 2.15 |
| 7 | 120 | 1.38 | 17 | 650 | 1.98 | 27 | 900 | 2.30 |
| 8 | 250 | 1.42 | 18 | 525 | 1.95 | 28 | 880 | 2.40 |
| 9 | 200 | 1.48 | 19 | 600 | 2.10 | 29 | 905 | 2.40 |
| 10 | 510 | 1.85 | 20 | 575 | 2.10 | 30 | 930 | 2.45 |

*Questions:*

1. Assume that you are the industrial engineer and you decide to plot a scatter diagram of the above data using evaluation points as the abscissa. Draw the straight line of best fit (by eye).

2. After viewing the chart drawn above, Roger Smith feels the general level of wages drawn by your line is about right. However, some jobs are out of line. He decides that about 10 pay grades should be set up with all jobs in the same pay grade being paid on the same basis. Draw appropriate pay grade division lines on your diagram.

3. List the rate ranges and the point ranges that go with each pay grade. (No overlapping rate ranges.)

4. Do you advise the use of a rate range for each pay grade, or the adoption of a single rate for each pay grade? Briefly state your reasons.

5. What steps do you suggest to get those jobs that are out of line back into line?

# CHAPTER TWENTY-TWO

# Research, Development, and Engineering

This chapter is concerned with the development of new products and processes and the improvement of old products and processes. For a company to prosper and grow it must do more than keep up with its competitors—it must get ahead of them wherever possible. "Getting ahead" almost invariably hinges upon research, development, and engineering activities. In considering the subjects of research, development, and engineering, this chapter will attempt to give meanings to these terms individually, but of more importance, it will attempt to show the interrelationships and need for coordination among these functions within a manufacturing concern.

Research seeks to make basic discoveries and uncover new principles. Some of this work is "pure," i.e., it has no foreseeable practical application; and other work is "applied," meaning that it is directed toward the solution of some particular practical problem. These concepts will be developed later, but we should bear in mind that both types of research make use of the basic sciences, the distinction between them usually being that of motivation.

Development usually follows applied research and often is concerned with the construction of pilot plants to show that a process is feasible, or with the construction of models, to demonstrate the basic ideas incorporated in the new product.

The work of the research and development groups must next be transformed into commercial benefit. This means achieving a workable process on a production basis, or a product capable of economical manufacture, or both. Such transformation is the work of engineering.

Undoubtedly many successful companies spend little effort or money on the three functions just mentioned. Many such companies depend on the designs of their customers and simply supply materials, parts, and components for use in the products of their customers. Other companies make it a practice to appropriate the designs and ideas of their competitors. Although this does not enable them to get ahead of their competitors, it does reduce their cost of research, development, and engineering.

To some degree, engineering will be required even in these last two categories of companies mentioned. Engineering processes probably have a higher priority than engineering of products. However, some companies even avoid much of their process engineering work by using the services of equipment suppliers. There are many small concerns with only one engineer on the payroll, and this man may perform many duties other than strict engineering work.

Our concern here is primarily with the company that does perform an appreciable amount of research, development, and engineering work. Such a company is aware that tomorrow's profit depends to a large extent upon today's research, but it is also aware that dollars invested now in research and development probably will produce no income for a number of years to come. Without the research and development effort, however, there may not be a future for the company.

## Types of Research

In the general sense, "research" is simply a systematic search for as-yet-unknown facts and principles. However, "research" is such a popular word in the present age that its use has been extended to cover many varied types of activities. For example, some companies have research departments that are largely concerned with uncovering knowledge of a type that is known by someone, although not by this particular company. Research of this sort consists largely of searching the literature and various reports published by institutions of one type or another. Although such activity is necessary in any company, it does not constitute a true research activity in the strict sense.

In this section we are going to identify and briefly discuss some of the commonest areas of research as broadly defined. It must be remembered that companies frequently identify subdivisions of research activity, largely for the purpose of more clearly organizing and controlling their total research effort.

### Pure Research

Pure research, sometimes referred to as "fundamental research," refers to investigations undertaken primarily for the sake of knowledge itself. In this type of research activity there is no consideration of commercial possibilities, and the effort is directed primarily toward learning nature's laws simply for the sake of knowing nature's laws. A study of why grass is green is often cited as a classic example of pure research. The direction of any pure research activity is usually not specified in advance, but is determined as the work progresses and promising avenues for further investigation identify themselves.

With a few outstanding exceptions, pure research is normally not indulged in by the industrial concern. Instead, such work is usually performed by universities or by special projects financed by the federal government or by independent research agencies. The expense is too great and the return too small and nebulous for most industrial concerns to get very far into pure research. Nonetheless, some of the larger concerns that maintain elaborate research facilities have made real contributions to the scientific knowledge of the country. And certain projects started on a pure research basis have turned out to have very practical applications. An example is the development of nylon by du Pont. Other companies conducting pure research are Eastman Kodak, General Motors, Bell Laboratories of A.T.&T., and General Electric.

### Applied Research

As its name implies, applied research is normally directed toward solving some specific problem, or has a definite practical purpose. Applied research frequently finds uses for the results of pure research. In any case, a vast store of pure research findings or a vast store of knowledge concerning nature's laws must be available in order for applied research efforts to be successful. It is possible to succeed in solving a practical problem simply by chance alone, but in research effort, whether it is pure or applied, there is emphasis upon a systematic search for solutions.

Applied research has more appeal to the industrial concern, for it can see the prospects for quicker return for the investment made. In this type of research the basic sciences are adapted to industrial processes, materials, or products. The hope is to improve the present product by making it cheaper using a better material, improving the container, adding a new customer appeal, or improving its appearance. In addition the company might hope to improve the operating efficiency of the plant or even develop a totally new product. It follows that most industrial research is applied research, for in most industrial projects the goals are rather specific, and practical applications are expected from the results.

### Product Research

Probably all types of research could be classified as either pure or applied, but it is common and also helpful to further break down and identify the research areas. One common category is product research, and as the name suggests, it attempts to insure continued prosperity of the company by uncovering new product ideas that will meet the requirements of customers and prospective customers.

In expanding product research, particular effort may be directed toward altogether new and different products, new and original uses for present products, or the utilization of a by-product. It is obvious that the stimulation for product research could come from many sources including the results of some pure research effort, some ideas from customers, the need to utilize some particular technical skills possessed by the company, or simply the desire to expand the product line in whatever direction seems most feasible. In any case, emphasis is placed upon discovering a useful and saleable product.

## Manufacturing Research

The discovery of new products is one path toward improved prosperity of a company, but the improvement of manufacturing processes and the resultant reduction in costs is another equally good path. For this reason more and more companies are performing research effort in the manufacturing area and with good results. Tape controlled machines are a case in point, as are a number of developments of machines made by the Western Electric Company that assemble parts and solder connections. In fact, the Western Electric Company operates a special manufacturing research division in Princeton, New Jersey.

Manufacturing research is usually directed toward the development of tools and equipment, handling devices, and methods of manufacture all of which tend to reduce costs and increase productivity. In many cases, however, manufacturing research must be carried on at the same time as product research, for a product research idea may be feasible only if a feasible manufacturing method can be devised. In other words, product research and manufacturing research can be carried on as separate and distinct activities, but in some cases they may have to join forces in order to achieve the best overall results.

## Materials Research

Materials research is basically linked with both product research and manufacturing research, for the discovery and improvement of materials often makes possible new products or new processes that were impossible prior to that time. The jet and missile age has placed great emphasis upon materials research, and the success of many of the space programs was made possible only after the development of materials that could withstand the stresses imposed. In recent years, materials research has brought about significant improvements in almost any material one can name.

## Market Research

Market research is more thoroughly discussed in Chapter 25, but needs to be mentioned here as another type of research activity. The principal aim of market research is to learn the needs and desires of customers. With this information a company can carry out the technical phases of a research project with greater assurance of customer acceptance later on, and the company is also in a better position to plan its sales promotion campaign, pricing schedules, and sales effort generally. Undoubtedly, many manufacturers have produced products and placed them on the market with no idea in advance as to the possible customer acceptance of that product. The prudent manufacturer in today's world of high costs and high risks, however, attempts by means of market research effort to learn the reaction of his customers to the product before tooling up to produce that product.

## Operations Research

Operations research has been referred to and discussed in many places throughout this book, but perhaps this is the one place where we should attempt to give it a definition. This is extremely difficult to do, for there appear to be as many definitions of operations research as there are operations researchers. It seems safe to say, however, that operations research is the organized application of the methods and techniques of science to the study of operating problems in business, government, or military activities. In practice, the word "science" in the sentence above turns out to be essentially mathematics. In other words, generally speaking, operations research usually involves quantifying a problem and developing mathematical models that help explain actual events in an enterprise and that will permit experiments of a theoretical nature. This results in a number of factual data that are used as an aid in arriving at management decisions.

Although operations research has been very helpful to many companies and has reportedly enabled these companies to save considerable sums of money, it should not be considered a cure-all for poor management. Perhaps its greatest difficulty is the need to quantify all of the facts relating to a particular situation under study. This necessarily requires some assumptions to be made in most cases, which in turn casts some doubts upon the validity of results. The results of any operations research effort can only be as good as the input data, which causes us to emphasize once again that operations research is simply an aid to decision-making. The executive responsible for the ultimate decision must consider not only the evidence produced by the operations research work but must have knowledge of the input data and arrive at his decision after taking into consideration many other factors, which perhaps were not included in the model used. Some of these factors might be the financial position of the company, long-range goals of the company, special public relations considerations, and varying human factors. These as well as many others defy quantification but are highly important in any managerial decision.

## Development

The distinction between research and development sometimes becomes rather fine. *Research*, whether pure or applied, attempts to discover or uncover facts or principles heretofore unknown or unrecognized. *Development* concerns the most economically feasible method for applying the facts or principles identified. It follows that development work many times is carried on after the applied research has been completed, and that applied research many times follows the completion of pure research.

The chemical industry presents an outstanding example of the use of development work as well as research work. Chemical research for the most part is conducted in laboratories making use of the test tubes and other equipment of small size, which can be easily handled on a bench or table. With such arrangements many new facts, principles, and reactions are discovered. And these discoveries, if properly exploited, may have great use and application for industry if they can be adapted to large-scale manufacture. This is where the development people come into the picture with the construction of a pilot plant.

A discovery that was made in a laboratory using small equipment may be perfectly valid. But will the discovery prove valid with large-scale production equipment? The pilot plant is an intermediate step between the laboratory and the plant production equipment and is designed to provide at least a partial answer without too much expense. The pilot plant uses relatively small equipment for the purpose of studying and perfecting the chemical engineering aspects of the discovery. If the pilot plant proves successful, a full-scale plant can be constructed with some assurance that it too will work out satisfactorily.

### Process Development

Development is generally concerned with putting new scientific discoveries into practice. Some of these discoveries may be incorporated into products and others into manufacturing processes. For the most part, development work is the work of engineers rather than researchers, although in many cases both groups must work together.

Process development has to do with machines, tooling, methods, plant layout, and the design of any special device or combination of devices needed to manufacture products. Although basic process discoveries have been made in an earlier research effort, it is the job of the development engineers to reduce the discoveries to practice and to make certain the ultimate designs will hold up under repeated use and possible abuse. Process development as just described becomes very close to manufacturing engineering which is discussed in a later section of this chapter, and not every company separates one function from the other. When separated, however, process development would probably concern itself most with the development and design of individual components, whereas manufacturing engineering would be more concerned with the installation and integration of the various components.

### Product Development

Like process development, product development is a bridge between research work and engineering work. Typically, the work of product development groups consists of making several product designs and then testing and evaluating these designs. Through testing such designs not only in the market but in terms of performance in the laboratory or on the customer's premises, the group hopes eventually to come up with one best design.

Another possible activity of a product development group, usually carried on in cooperation with process development, would be the making of one or more pilot runs of the new product. Such runs would provide some actual products for testing as mentioned above as well as give an opportunity to examine the process being used and to work out any flaws that might turn up. In addition to revealing the need for minor changes in product design, tooling, and methods of work, such runs also reveal some cost information that would be useful in price setting.

## Organization for Research
## and Development

Ideally the director of research and development should report directly to the president. In this way the research activity will receive the attention it requires, and coordination with the other activities will be facilitated. The importance of coordination of research effort needs to be emphasized.

The research director is frequently in a position where he must ask for continually increasing appropriations while being able to show only prospective gains to balance the department budget. His requests must be adequately supported and explained to those who are responsible for budgets and financing. The role of the engineering department must also be worked out, clearly defined, and coordinated. The engineers may be responsible for development as previously defined, or they may come into the picture only when production equipment is ready to be installed and maintained. In any case close liaison is a prime requirement.

Coordinating research with sales and production is another point worthy of consideration. Such coordination is a prime necessity when research is of the applied variety, for the goal is the discovery of practical applications. In this case research people must have a keen understanding of and appreciation for the requirements of the markets. In addition they must keep in mind the present production facilities and the adaptability of the facilities to new uses or new products. Coordination of this type is usually obtained by the use of a new-products committee, which committee is composed of representatives of all the interested groups of the organization.

The internal organization of a research department varies in the same way that companies vary one from another. In a small concern it is no particular problem, for the director heads up whatever technicians and research workers there are. In a large company with a large research department the problem of internal organization becomes acute, for one must make certain that the researchers are divided into effective and efficient units. There are three common methods of division.

One way research activities may be divided is according to *plants or manufacturing departments*. Each plant or department in such a case would be engaged in making a product more or less distinct from that of the other plants, so research problems would also be distinct. Of course, if there is no valid distinction, then this method of dividing research activities would have its drawbacks because it would mean a duplication of men, effort, and equipment at each of the plants.

The second common division of research activities is made on the basis of *specific purposes*. Under this arrangement one research laboratory serves all plants in the company, but this laboratory is broken down into groups of specialists for each problem or process on which the company is working. For example, one unit may specialize in "pumping" problems and another may specialize in "power plant" work.

The third method of division is according to *research techniques*. Thus, there might be a group of organic chemists as one unit, nuclear physicists as another, and so on. This may seem the most natural division of activities, but it places a great premium on collaboration among the groups.

Very large companies make use of a combination of these methods, at the same time maintaining flexibility in their organization structure. Should a particularly urgent project come along the organization structure of research may be rearranged so as to get the right people with just the right skills to work on the project. When that project is complete some other type of organization structure is set up to handle the next project.

It was mentioned earlier that small companies have no particular problems with the internal organization of their research departments. But they do have a problem in carrying out research, because their funds usually are limited. One company has solved this problem by setting up a "research advisory committee" as part of its external organization structure for research. The committee is made up of outside scientists who are employed elsewhere full time (most at universities) and who consult with this company on research projects. In this way the company receives the advice of experts in the field without the expense of a large full-time research staff or elaborate facilities. Other companies have made extensive use of private research facilities such as Battelle Memorial Institute, Midwest Research Institute, Armour Research Institute, and so forth. Still other companies have financed continuing research projects in the universities.

## Engineering

In considering the role of engineering in an industrial concern we should keep in mind that this discussion refers to functions to be performed, and not to people or departments that may be responsible in any one company for performing the function. Figure 22-1 shows the functional relationship between research and development and the normal engineering activities carried on in a plant.

Although engineering skill and practice enters almost all phases of manufacturing activity, in general, engineering functions are considered to fall into three categories: product engineering, manufacturing engineering, and plant engineering. Engineers with various kinds of professional training, such as in electrical engineering, industrial engineering, or mechanical engineering, may receive various assignments to perform any of the three functions.

## Product Engineering

Product engineering as a function is mainly concerned with product design, that is, design of the product for manufacturing. Research and development have also been concerned with design, but at that step design is largely of the laboratory type. Product engineering will design for commercial usefulness or application.

Figure 22-1. Three groupings of the engineering functions in manufacturing.

PRODUCT IDEA → PRODUCT DESIGN → PRODUCT MANUFACTURE → CONTINUED PRODUCTION

**RESEARCH AND DEVELOPMENT**
1. PURE RESEARCH
2. APPLIED RESEARCH
3. PILOT PLANT

**PRODUCT ENGINEERING**
1. DESIGN OF COMPONENTS
2. PREPARATION OF SPECIFICATIONS
3. PRODUCT STANDARDS
4. PRODUCT TESTING
5. ENGINEERING SERVICE

**MANUFACTURING ENGINEERING**
1. DESIGN OF PROCESSES
2. TOOLING AND EQUIPMENT
3. METHODS
4. LAYOUT AND MATERIALS HANDLING
5. QUALITY CONTROL
6. ECONOMIC EVALUATION

**PLANT ENGINEERING**
1. INSTALLATIONS
2. PLANT SERVICES
3. MAINTENANCE
4. SAFETY

**Design of components.**  The ideas or models conceived through research and development must be further developed into specific practical designs. This will entail considerable sketching and drafting work and must be performed in close liaison with the research and development people, assuming that different persons are involved. Those responsible for design of the various components must have specialized training, background, and experience. Knowledge of basic principles, manufacturing methods, and market demands can result in a product design that will make a sizable contribution to the success of the business.

**Preparation of specifications.**  Once the product design has been settled the next step is to prepare product specifications for production departments. Such specifications will outline in some detail the finishes required and to some extent the processes to be used. Bills of material, which list all the materials and parts needed and in what quantities, must also be prepared. These will be used by the purchasing department to order from suppliers as well as by the production departments. Engineering drawings will naturally be supplied all interested departments together with any other production details essential for the desired result.

**Product standards.**  Quality of materials going into the product as well as standards of performance of the completed product are the concern of product engineering. Materials going into the product must be of sufficiently high quality to insure successful product performance, but not so high as to increase costs unreasonably. By the same token product performance must meet customer requirements, but need not do more than this. To provide a product design and specifications that will meet these requirements is a big order. However, every product engineering activity is constantly striving to do just that.

Product engineering has another opportunity to keep costs down, and this is by standardizing as much as possible on parts and components. Close coordination among design personnel will do much to achieve this desirable goal.

**Product testing.**  Specifying design and standards is oftentimes not good enough, for product engineering will also be concerned with final product performance. This is particularly true in the manufacture of large units such as steam turbines or jet engines. Each unit must be thoroughly tested to be certain it meets the specifications of performance and has no defects. With complex equipment the testing operations are more than routine; so the work is assigned to qualified test engineers.

**Engineering service.**  In many cases product engineering may be called upon to perform service activities for both the manufacturing and sales departments. To aid sales, product engineers may confer with customers about complex problems, particularly if the company isn't large enough to have sales engineers, In addition, product engineers may be called in on certain manufacturing problems, particularly when there is some discrepancy between product specifications and the capabilities of the machine being used.

## Manufacturing Engineering

Figure 22-1 shows the next step after product design to be product manufacture. Actual manufacture will be performed by production departments; however, engineering plays a considerable role in getting efficient manufacturing processes set up and operating properly. This function is frequently called *manufacturing engineering* and much of the work is done by industrial engineers.

**Design of processes.** As the name implies, product engineering is mainly concerned with the *product* and getting it ready for production. Manufacturing engineering as a function will be more concerned with the *process*, with the means and methods used to produce the product. Design of a suitable process is the main subdivision of manufacturing engineering activity. Frequently this work must be closely coordinated with product engineering, since the design of a suitable product may depend to a large extent on the design of a suitable process. Chapter 5 covered in some detail the design of manufacturing processes.

**Tooling and equipment.** Basic production equipment (such as milling machines or draw presses) may be available for the manufacture of a new product but must be tooled or adapted for the new job to be done. New dies may have to be designed, new inspection devices worked out, or automatic controls rearranged. All this is included in manufacturing engineering and was covered more completely in the chapter on industrial equipment (Chapter 6).

**Methods.** Another problem for manufacturing engineering is the analysis of methods of using processes, machines, and equipment. The study of methods may entail modification or addition of equipment, but the main emphasis will be on the work pattern to be followed by the workers as they use the machines and equipment (Chapter 7).

**Layout and material handling.** Closely allied with methods will be the layout of machines and equipment and the means of transporting materials between the machines. These two considerations go together; the layout used determines to a large extent the type of materials handling problems that must be met. These topics were discussed in Chapters 9 and 10.

**Quality control.** Setting product standards, one of the phases of product engineering discussed earlier, includes both quality limits and performance standards. A problem in production is the maintenance of certain quality limits throughout the manufacturing process, and it is the function of manufacturing engineering to set up controls for doing just that. Usually manufacturing engineering will work closely with product engineering in setting the original quality specifications. This is necessary so that quality limits will not be called for that are beyond the basic capabilities of the machines and processes available. Quality control was discussed in Chapter 15.

**Economic evaluation.** Manufacturing engineering must be cost-conscious throughout the fulfilment of all its functions; so economic evaluation is performed by almost everyone involved at every step. A manufactured product must be satisfactory not only in quantity, quality, delivery, and function but also in cost. Manufacturing engineering makes one of its greatest contributions by constantly devising ways and means to reduce costs. The control of costs was treated in more detail in Chapter 17.

## Plant Engineering

The final engineering function in manufacturing shown by Figure 22-1 is plant engineering. For the most part plant engineering will be responsible for continued production after the facilities are designed and laid out. Other activities such as plant services and safety are in many cases also made the responsibility of plant engineering because of the close tie with maintenance work generally.

### Installation

With manufacturing engineering having accomplished the design and layout of processes, it is usually the lot of plant engineering to perform the installation work. This comes about quite naturally. Plant engineering departments usually have the skilled mechanics under their direction, and these mechanics may do maintenance work as well as installation work. In the large plant there may be two sets of mechanics—one set working exclusively on new installations and another set working exclusively on repair and maintenance.

## Plant Services

Plant engineering departments traditionally operate all central services in a factory—for example, the power plant and the supplying of power, steam, air, and water. Elevators also fall into this category so far as direct responsibility for maintenance is concerned. If services are purchased from outside suppliers, the plant engineering department arranges for such purchases, checks equipment, checks usages, and generally coordinates the activities of the operating departments with the outside suppliers.

The care of buildings and grounds can be included too. This work is of such broad nature that it is best handled by plant engineering. Some plant engineering departments are also responsible for the company fleet of cars and trucks.

## Maintenance

Probably the most important responsibility of plant engineering is that of maintaining the plant facilities and equipment. Only if equipment is adequately maintained can it be expected to operate properly and thereby yield a product of high quality at reasonable cost. Maintenance as a manufacturing activity was discussed in considerable detail in Chapter 16.

## Safety

Safety as a function that gives concern to management is more completely covered in the chapter on personnel management (Chapter 18). However, since engineering departments frequently have some responsibility for safety work in a plant, it is well to discuss some aspects here.

Although this section is included under plant engineering, the engineering aspects of safety are just as applicable to manufacturing engineering. Safety begins on the drawing board and continues through every step of the design and construction of a machine, workplace, or plant. A safety-minded designer or engineer should be certain that every possible precaution is taken to prevent human injury. Many times it is just as easy to design a machine safe to operate as it is to ignore the problem. The only difference is whether or not the designer is safety-conscious.

Plant engineering may be given a sort of overall responsibility for plant housekeeping. They would not be required to take any direct action, but more probably they would inspect for poor housekeeping conditions and make appropriate reports. Housekeeping has a direct effect on equipment maintenance, on safety and health, and on fire hazards. Since plant engineering is directly concerned with these things, it thereby becomes concerned with good housekeeping throughout the plant.

## Product Development Cycle

The development of a new product or the improvement of an old one commonly goes through seven steps before the new product is ready for the customer to purchase. These steps are:

1. Obtaining ideas.
2. Screening ideas.
3. Technical evaluation.
4. Market evaluation.
5. Final decision.
6. Getting into production.
7. Introduction to the market.

These steps aren't always separate and distinct, for in many cases it is desirable to carry on two or more steps at the same time. The point is that all are carried out—either knowingly or unknowingly—in the development of any new product.

**Obtaining ideas.** Any new product comes from someone's idea. A company wanting to develop and introduce new products must provide some means to obtain new product ideas. There are many possibilities. The job of some research people is to dream up new ideas. Employees, customers, and suppliers often have ideas worthy of consideration. Some companies even advertise for people to send in their ideas for new products. The aggressive concern should assure that all sources are investigated so that any possible ideas will not be overlooked.

**Screening ideas.** After having collected a series of new product ideas, a company must screen them to separate the foolish ideas from those having real merit. This is naturally much easier said than done. There are any number of cases on record where a company thought it was rejecting a foolish idea only to have someone else accept it and achieve considerable success with it.

Preliminary screening is usually handled by the director of research and development or by someone under his direction whose task is to consider new ideas. Those ideas having any merit at all are passed along to a committee made up usually of the research director, the sales manager, the production manager, and the president plus others who may be concerned with the new idea. This committee has final say as to whether the idea is to be investigated further or else forgotten. The members of the committee by virtue of their position, their experience, and their knowledge of the business and its policies are supposedly qualified to make such a decision.

**Technical evaluation.** Should the committee decide to investigate the new idea further, one aspect of such an investigation would be a technical evaluation. Such an evaluation might attempt to answer such questions as method of manufacture, cost of manufacture, performance characteristics, and labor and machine requirements. Even before these questions are answered, some applied research may be necessary. In this or some other way an investigation might get out of hand in spending time and money. To forestall this possibility the committee may authorize the expenditure of a fixed number of dollars in time and equipment to investigate any one idea. When the money is spent the research director must report back to the committee stating results to date and making his recommendations. More money may be authorized or the idea may be dropped completely. One company spent $500,000 investigating an idea only to drop it at last, but during the process of technical investigation complete control was maintained by the simple expedient of regulating the money to be spent.

**Market evaluation.** Concurrent with the technical evaluation there is also the need for a market evaluation. Again some controls over the evaluation must be established and this is also done in terms of money allotted. Perhaps the first evaluation will be simply a cursory survey by salesmen. If the idea still looks promising, later on enough money might be appropriated to make a nationwide scientific survey of the market.

**Final decision.** Suppose we have gathered all the information possible (within reason) on both the technical aspects and the marketing aspects of a new product idea. A final decision is now necessary. Are we going to go ahead and make the product, or shall we shelve the whole idea as did the company mentioned earlier who had already poured in $500,000? This decision will undoubtedly be made by the executive committee of the company or by the board of directors, based upon the recommendations of the new-products committee.

**Getting into production.** Assuming we have decided to go ahead, the next step is to transform the idea into a saleable product. From our technical evaluation we know pretty much the steps required in terms of design work, machines to be ordered or constructed, workers to be trained, materials to be ordered, and control systems to be established. If the product is to be mass produced, the problems of getting into production are greater than if the product is to be made on a job-lot basis. In any case there are many decisions to be made and problems to be solved—many of which are discussed throughout this book.

**Introduction to the market.**   Perhaps even while we are getting into production, plans are being considered for introducing the product to the market. From the market evaluation the size, location, and characteristics of the market are known, and now ways and means must be devised to impress this market favorably with the new product. This is normally the work of the sales and advertising departments. Problems dealing with packaging, channels of distribution, prices, discounts, guarantees, and service must all be worked out as part of this step.

## Product Protection

To conduct a great deal of research and development work and introduce a new product only to have some competitor start making the same product soon thereafter is, to say the least, heartbreaking. Not only that, it may be financially disastrous. If this happened often, few companies would be interested in performing research and development work. Our federal laws are designed to prevent this situation, for they provide that inventors may patent their inventions, thereby keeping others from using them without permission. Patents are issued by the Patent Office in Washington, D.C., and may be secured either for new products or processes or for improvements on old products or processes.

In applying for and securing a patent a full description of the product or process must be made. The wording of the patent itself must be very carefully devised or else the patent's value may be restricted because its coverage is restricted. Of course, the Patent Office will not grant the patent unless they feel it does not infringe on some other patent, and this again places great importance on wording and description. A company will want to have on hand copies of all patents relating to its field (available from the Patent Office) not only to avoid applying for a patent that infringes on someone else's, but to be certain that its own patents are not being infringed on.

Patents run for seventeen years and are not renewable. After that time they are in the public domain and anyone who wishes to is free to use the ideas. The government has simply granted seventeen years of protection in return for the inventor's divulging the idea so that after seventeen years all can use it. Sometimes the effective life of a patent can be extended by patenting improvements. In such a case competitors may use the basic patent but may not use the improvement patent without permission.

A patent in itself is no *absolute* guarantee of exclusive right for seventeen years. In spite of the best patent attorneys a company may hire, and despite the fact that the Patent Office won't issue a patent unless the officials feel it does not infringe on any other patent, the holder of a patent may have to fight for his rights and get them established in a court of law. If Company A starts to make a product covered by a patent held by Company B, then it is up to B to sue and establish in the courts the validity of the patent. The Patent Office in this case is an innocent bystander.

Frequently products will appear with "Patent Applied For" or "Patent Pending" imprinted on them. These are simply used in an attempt to prevent prospective competitors from entering the field.

Since patents give protection for only seventeen years, and since they sometimes have to be fought for in the courts, some companies attempt to keep their ideas secret rather than apply for patents. In this case the protection lasts indefinitely so long as someone doesn't discover the secret. If the secret is discovered, there is nothing the company can do to prevent its use. Keeping a secret is very difficult, particularly with *products*, that is, if the products are sold to customers. *Processes* are easier to keep secret, for the people who come in contact with the process can be carefully selected and their number restricted. In one company where the process is a secret only a handful of people are permitted access to the process room. The finished product comes out of the room through a slot in the wall.

## Simplification, Diversification, and Standardization

The process of adding new products to a line or adding more varieties and sizes of product is known as *diversification*. We have emphasized the need for a company to add new products to a line in order to prosper and grow. Sales departments in particular are anxious to have a diversified product line so that they can meet almost any objection or requirement that a customer might pose.

Of course, the idea of diversification can be carried too far. There can become so many types, styles, colors, and varieties of products that many are sold at a loss rather than a profit. It then becomes necessary to reduce or eliminate many of the marginal lines of products; this process is called *simplification*. Companies sometimes have to adopt elaborate programs of simplification because over the years their product line has been gradually expanded in order to supply the various needs of customers. The process has been so gradual that it is not noticed until someone thinks to raise the question. One company making electrical equipment found they were offering over 9000 different varieties of products. By redesigning products, talking with customers about their needs, and simply dropping some products, the company was able to reduce the line to about 300 varieties with no appreciable loss in business.

A third term frequently used is *standardization*. In a narrow and somewhat technical sense standardization refers to the setting up of exact specifications or precise measurements. For example, there is the standardization of light sockets or the standardization of the lengths of measure.

There is undoubtedly a use for this narrow concept of standardization, but for the most part and for our purposes in this book there is little practical difference between standardization and simplification. Companies like to standardize on certain parts that are used in their products. This reduces the inventory problem and simplifies maintenance and repair. But this standardizing of the line, if it involves reducing variety, is equivalent to simplification.

Much standardization (simplification) has been accomplished on an industry-wide basis under the guidance of the Department of Commerce, the Bureau of Standards, the American Standards Association, the A.S.M.E., and others. Light sockets have been mentioned, but much standardization has also been carried out in bottles, nuts and bolts, flashlights, and hundreds of other items ranging from adhesive plaster to yarn. Such standardization works very well until competition becomes keen, and then someone comes out with something different in spite of standardization.

The optimum point between diversification and standardization has to be worked out for each company. There is much to be said for the application of standardization in the strict sense when applied to parts and small components. But when considering the product itself, even Henry Ford had to give in and offer cars in colors other than black. To go too far in varieties, however, may mean a considerable inventory and manufacturing problem with no gain in net profit. Every new product or variety of product should fill a need and justify its existence.

A company considering the question of diversification or expansion of its product line should ask the following questions: (1) Can some proprietary right be established for the new product? In other words, if a patent is secured on the product, or if a part of the process could be kept a secret, would the new product have a greater chance of payoff? (2) Will the new product complete a line of products, or make possible some sales that have heretofore been lost? (3) Can the product be marketed through our present sales organization and sales contacts? If the present sales staff does not possess the necessary know-how about the new product, or if another sales organization and distribution channel must be established, a company is essentially launching a new business rather than expanding a present one. (4) Are the research, development, and engineering technologies involved in the new product similar to those we already possess? (5) Is the manufacturing technology required by the new product in line with those technologies we already possess? Having to learn new technologies is not undesirable, but one should recognize the time, cost, and risks involved if such learning is necessary in order to diversify a product line. (6) Can raw materials for the new product be purchased at some particular advantage to us? (7) Can some by-product be utilized in the new product development?

## QUESTIONS

1. Outline a suitable management philosophy in regard to research and development—assuming the company wishes to prosper and grow.

2. General Motors at one time conducted research into why grass is green. Would this be pure or applied research? Explain.

3. What role could a pilot plant play in a company that manufactures products made from plastic?

4. Make a clear distinction between the technical evaluation of a new product idea and the market evaluation of that idea.

5. How could the work of a research advisory committee, made up of people outside the company, be coordinated with the work of a new-products committee, made up of people inside the company?

6. What "rights" does a patent give the owner of that patent?

7. Through what process is the validity of a patent fully established?

8. Suggest some bases that might be used to determine when to eliminate an item in a product line.

9. Describe the functional relationships between the various engineering activities carried on in a manufacturing plant.

10. What contributions could a trained engineer make in a research and development department?

11. Distinguish between product design and process design. In what types of situations would they be closely allied?

12. What role in safety work is played by product engineering? By manufacturing engineering? By plant engineering?

## CASE PROBLEMS

### Tudor Electric Company

The complete line of the Tudor Electric Company included over 900 items, all of which were manufactured in the company's Milwaukee plant. The company could supply any need in the way of small electrical equipment with the exception of wire, which it did not make. Its heaviest sales were in relays, switches, and sockets, which were produced in a variety of types of sizes.

An active and aggressive research and development department had been responsible to a great extent for the expansion of the company's line of products. During the past year 17 new products had been developed and turned over to the engineering department.

Getting the new products into production proved to be a long and difficult process in almost every case. Ed Belcher, the manufacturing manager, had experienced so much trouble along this line that he learned to dread any new product developments. He was increasingly confronted with recurring complaints from foremen that "designs don't work" or that "Engineering expects us to do the impossible." When Mr. Belcher investigated specific complaints, however, he found that few were really justified. Unfortunately, there had been two instances during the past year when the R & D department had actually requested the "impossible," and the engineering department, in working out the specifications, had not caught the error. In talking over these two cases with the director of research and the chief engineer, Mr. Belcher emphasized the general need for closer coordination. Both men assured him of their willingness to cooperate in any scheme that would reduce friction and eliminate such costly errors.

*Questions:*

1. What coordination plan can you suggest for this company?

2. Would you say that coordination is the only problem facing Mr. Belcher?

## Atlantic Chain Company

The Atlantic Chain Company manufactures millions of feet of roller bearing chain annually. Until recently, 130 different chains were made, stored, and sold. The differences among the chains were minute and resulted from slight variations in dimensions and in other minor respects. Since the volume of sales on 50 of the styles was very low, a start at simplification was made by eliminating the 50 low-volume styles. Inasmuch as the company had been losing money on the 50 styles eliminated, profits were expected to increase, even if the customers who had purchased one or more of these 50 styles should fail to switch to one of the remaining 80 styles.

An analysis of costs and sales seemed to indicate that the company was making money on each of the remaining styles, but common sense told the management that there was no reason why 80 styles were needed.

*Questions:*

1. What steps could the company take so that further simplification of the chain styles could be effected?

2. Would there be any objections to simply eliminating those styles that contribute the least profit? Why?

# CHAPTER TWENTY-THREE

# Forms of Ownership

Basically, every industrial enterprise is in business to make a profit. It does this by producing goods or services for sale in a market. There appear to be many other purposes of modern business—for example, to provide income and security for employees, aid the government in defense, aid in the performance of certain public services, or even bring entertainment such as television shows to viewers. Regardless of how worthy each of these purposes may seem, we must return in the end to the realization that the enterprise would not be possible if someone were not willing to invest his money in it. Being human, such an investor does so only because he hopes or expects to receive some profit.

In return for this investment, the owners enjoy certain rights and privileges. They decide what goods or services are to be offered to the market. They set basic policies on how the business will be managed. They decide how much money is needed, how it will be obtained, and how it will be spent. They reserve the right to change the general nature of the business or even dissolve it if it suits their pleasure. These rights and many others that could be enumerated go automatically to those who by virtue of investing their money have become owners.

The owners use various frameworks of business organization in exercising their rights and accomplishing their objectives. Several forms of ownership are available, and the owners will select the one that best meets their needs. Among these are (1) the individual proprietorship, (2) the general partnership, (3) the limited partnership, (4) the cooperative, and (5) the corporation.

**449**

## Individual Proprietorship

A business owned by one person is an *individual proprietorship.* This is the oldest and simplest form of ownership, and although in many types of business it is outmoded, it still plays an important role in the present-day economic structure. Individual proprietorships are particularly important in agriculture, retail trade, and service industries. In manufacturing, the individual proprietorship seems over the years to have decreased in importance. This has come about because of the capital required in many kinds of manufacturing; however, manufacturing that can be conducted on a small scale is adaptable to the individual proprietorship form. Examples are the clothing and canning industries.

The greatest advantage of the individual proprietorship is its ease of formation. Another advantage is the complete control the owner can exercise in operating the business. He may change at will the type of business in which he engages, and, with the possible exception of special licenses, he pays no special organization or franchise taxes. Any profits made by the business belong to him, and he doesn't have to share any special trade or business secrets with others unless he chooses to do so. But all is not ideal with the proprietorship. There are some disadvantages too.

It was stated above that the proprietor can keep the profits for himself. Unfortunately, the same goes for losses. And his right to run the business as he sees fit, which seems to be an advantage, can work as a disadvantage. Not every proprietor is qualified to handle all the many problems of finance, production, and sales. He may hire assistants, but then he has to know how to pick men, or losses may result.

A further disadvantage of the average individual proprietorship is the difficulty in raising large amounts of capital. The reason is the unstable nature of such a form of ownership. Should anything happen to the proprietor, the business as such no longer exists. So the proprietor has nothing but his personal credit position to aid him in securing loans.

The owner is liable for all the debts of the business even though those debts may exceed the amount of his investment. This means that in the event the business should fail, the creditors could take his personal property as well as his business property in order to settle their claims. The owner of an individual proprietorship thus enjoys his unlimited rights to profits and to the control of the business at the price of unlimited liability for debts and losses.

## General Partnership

The *general partnership* overcomes some of the disadvantages of the individual proprietorship and has an important place in our economic system.

A general partnership is an association of two *or more* persons to carry on a legal business as co-owners for profit. Sometimes there is confusion about how many persons can be partners in a partnership; strictly speaking, there can be any number, despite the common impression that the limit is two.

A partnership may be formed by means of a written agreement, or it may be simply an oral understanding among the people concerned. In either case a partnership exists in the eyes of the law. In a general partnership each partner has full agency powers and may bind the partnership by any act. In a sense, each partner may act as though he were an individual proprietor—the difference being that his actions affect not only himself but his partners as well.

The general partnership keeps many of the advantages of the individual proprietorship. It is, in the first place, easy and inexpensive to form. There are no organization taxes, and two or more people can form a partnership by nothing more than a verbal agreement. The partners then have direct control of the business and, of course, have full rights to all profits.

Two additional advantages, however, distinguish the general partnership from the individual proprietorship. First, since there are more owners, there may be more capital available. There are, at any rate, more people to be held responsible for the business, and more credit will be available to the firm. The second advantage is that more talent is available for running the business. It was mentioned earlier that rarely does one man possess all the abilities needed to operate a business successfully. A number of men, each with different skills and abilities, might form a partnership and as a group operate a very successful business, whereas any one of them going it alone might be likely to end up in bankruptcy.

There are certain disadvantages to the general partnership. The most serious is the fact that *each* partner has unlimited liability for the debts of the firm. If one partner commits the firm to the payment of large sums of money, the other partners are also held responsible and can be made to pay even to the extent of having their personal property attached.

The second disadvantage to a partnership, almost as important as the first, is the premium it places on the partners' ability to get along with one another. Since all partners can act as general agents, there is a great need for complete agreement as to who will do what. Usually these things are worked out thoroughly ahead of time—preferably by means of a written agreement. But even with a written agreement there can be times of misunderstanding, disagreement, or mistrust that may lead to catastrophe for the enterprise.

There are other disadvantages to the partnership. Like the individual proprietorship, it lacks permanence and stability. Should a partner die or go insane, the partnership as such no longer exists; all activity of the business is stopped, books are closed, and the deceased's estate is allotted its share of the assets. Then, if desirable, a new business is started, which may or may not be another partnership.

And, although the partnership enjoys a better credit rating and better access to capital than the individual proprietorship, there are still serious limitations on both. Many investors hesitate to invest money in a firm when they must take on personal liability for the firm's debts. Lenders hesitate to lend money because of the firm's lack of stability. Further, a partnership compares unfavorably with an individual proprietorship in that profits must be shared, keeping business affairs secret is more difficult, and there is a risk of choosing incompetent or dishonest partners.

## Limited Partnership

In order to overcome the main disadvantage of the general partnership, namely, the unlimited liability of each partner, many states have statutes that permit the formation of a limited partnership. The limited partnership is an association of one or more general partners who manage the business and one or more limited partners whose liability is limited to the capital they have invested in the business. The limited partners must be genuine part owners rather than moneylenders, and they receive a share of the profits rather than interest on their invested money. The limited partner has limited liability only so long as he does not share in the control or the management of the business or attempt to interfere with the general partner in his management of the business. In other words, the limited partner, in order to protect his limited liability status, must be a "silent" partner.

It must be borne in mind that under this arrangement there must be at least one general partner who manages the business and therefore is subject to unlimited liability. The limited partnership is applicable only in the state in which it is organized and will probably be treated as a general partnership in any other state unless it is also organized under the laws of that state. Obviously, its chief advantage is its ability to attract risk capital from those persons who would not enter a general partnership because of its unlimited liability features.

## Cooperative

Strictly speaking, the cooperative can hardly be considered a form of ownership available to an individual who wishes to start a business. However, it is a form of private ownership, and it contains features of the partnership as well as some features of the corporation. The principal intent of the cooperative is to eliminate profit and thereby provide goods and services to the members of the cooperative at cost. Special laws deal with the formation and taxation of cooperative associations; so they enjoy separate and distinct status as a form of ownership.

There are shareholders in the cooperatives in addition to a board of directors and elected officers, similar to the corporation. Members buy shares and pay fees to the association, and profits, or rebates, are distributed to its members periodically. The concentration of control in a few members is avoided by the stipulation that each member has only one vote.

For the most part cooperatives exist in two forms, namely: the consumers' cooperatives, which deal in retail trade and services, and producer cooperatives, which are organized for group buying and selling of items such as fruits, grain, or livestock. Cooperatives are a much more popular form of organization in Europe than they are in the United States and do not appear to be particularly active in manufacturing operations. This has changed somewhat in recent years and gives promise of changing more in the future, as the line of demarcation between agriculture and business becomes less distinct. "Agri-business" is becoming a popular concept, and even now some consumers' cooperatives manufacture some of the products that they sell to their members.

## Corporation

There are many reasons for the popularity of the *corporation* as a form of ownership. One is the recognition of its creation by the state in which it is organized. The laws surrounding the formation and operation of a corporation are fairly clear-cut, and the owners have a good idea of how they stand. Of course this works a hardship too, for it means that the corporation is subject to many controls, regulations, and taxes.

Another reason for the popularity of the corporation is the limited liability of the owners or stockholders. Usually the liability of the stockholder is limited to the amount of his investment, although there have been exceptions to this in cases where workers had been unpaid for their services.

The corporation is recognized by the state as an "artificial person." This artificial person can hold property, sue, and be sued. The shares of stock that are evidence of ownership can be transferred without affecting the company; this means that the corporation can enjoy stability and long life.

The owners or stockholders of the corporation elect a board of directors who are charged with the responsibility of running the business. The board of directors then elects the officers who make the day-to-day decisions necessary for successful operations. The profits of the business are paid out to the stockholders from time to time in the form of dividends as the board of directors sees fit.

Stability, long life, legal sanction, transferability of shares, and limited liability all mean that the investor can invest without fear of jeopardizing his other holdings and with some assurance that the worth of his investment will increase as the years go by. This has made it possible for the corporation to raise capital with relative ease.

There are some disadvantages to the corporation. Its being subject to various taxes, controls, and reports has already been mentioned. Another objection is the usual lack of interest on the part of the stockholders. A great many stockholders look only for their yearly dividend and take little or no interest in the affairs of the business.

A final objection is that the corporation's income is taxed twice. It is taxed first as income to the corporation. Then, as profits are paid out, they are taxed as personal income to the individual stockholders. This has led some corporations to hold back on dividend payments until those years when income tax rates are low.

### Where to Incorporate

On first thought one might assume that a corporation would incorporate in the state where it anticipated doing the major portion of its business. Closer examination will show that this is not necessarily so. Many considerations may make it desirable to incorporate in one state and do business in another.

The general corporation laws of the states vary considerably. Some are considered more liberal than others; some states have a reputation for being tough on corporations; others enjoy a reputation of being fair and equitable. When a state's incorporation laws *are* liberal, it doesn't necessarily follow, from the point of view of the stockholder, that it would be desirable to incorporate in that state. Liberal laws may not sufficiently restrict operations to protect the investors' interests. States sometimes both liberalize their laws and lower their tax rates in order to attract businesses into locating there as well as incorporating there.

To incorporate in one state is not automatically to gain license to do business in other states. The incorporating state can give its own permission to the corporation to do business in other states; but to the other states the corporation is a "foreign" corporation, and they are not required to admit it. As a matter of practice the states do admit "foreign" corporations, but the "foreign" corporation must meet certain requirements. These requirements may be the payment of certain taxes and fees and the filing of annual reports. The reports are usually more or less routine, but the taxes and fees might be a real burden. Penalties for failure to comply with the laws pertaining to "foreign" corporations may be even more burdensome. Such penalties may be fines or perhaps the refusal of the state courts to enforce the contracts of the corporation.

### Small and Large Corporations

It is difficult to draw a sharp line between small and large corporations because there is no clear agreement on their definitions. However, some distinction between the two should be made in order to clarify previous points and to introduce a few new ones in regard to the corporate organization.

It should be kept in mind that the corporation is first and foremost a form of ownership, and there is no requirement that a company must be of a certain size before it qualifies for the corporate form. It therefore follows that many very small businesses are organized as corporations and may perhaps have only one or a few stockholders. On the other hand, there is no reason why a proprietorship or partnership should not become a very large company in terms of number of employees or dollars of assets, although this seems highly unlikely because of the unlimited liability feature of these forms of ownership. If a business having only one or two owners should reach such large size, the owners would undoubtedly incorporate in order to protect their personal holdings. For many years the Ford Motor Corporation was owned entirely by the Ford family even though it was one of our country's largest manufacturing concerns.

Of course, most of our very large corporations have large numbers of stockholders, sometimes up into the hundreds of thousands. In many of these corporations, no one person owns as much as one per cent of the stock, and such situations lend credibility to the observation that stockholders sometimes lack interest in the affairs of the corporation. In many cases it has been demonstrated that stockholders do not even know the products of the corporation in which they own an interest or know the kind of business involved. This is because of the ease with which shares of stock can be traded and the fact that many people buy and sell shares of stock in the hope of making a profit rather than with the intent of becoming part owner of a business concern.

When one person owns all or at least 51 per cent of the stock in a corporation, control of a corporation is obviously no problem. This person undoubtedly selects a board of directors of his choice who in turn can be expected to elect officers of the choice of the major stockholders. It follows that in a very small corporation the owner of the stock is also a member of the board of directors and probably president of the corporation. In some states there is specified a minimum number of members of the board of directors; in such a case the sole owner of the stock may have to get one or two of his close friends or members of his family to serve on the board of directors with him. He nevertheless wields complete control of the corporation as he sees fit.

Control of a corporation becomes a different matter when no one person or group of persons owns 51 per cent or more of the stock. Particularly interesting is the problem of control in the corporation mentioned earlier whereby no one person owns as much as one per cent of the outstanding shares. In cases such as this, current management of the corporation sends out to the stockholders proxy solicitations. The proxy is simply a form on which the stockholder may, by signing and returning, it, authorize the management of the corporation to vote his stock as it sees fit at the forthcoming stockholders' meeting. If there are important issues to be discussed at the meeting the proxy solicitation may offer the stockholder an opportunity to indicate how he wishes his stock voted on these particular issues. On specified issues the management is obligated to vote the stock as indicated by the stockholder. On other issues the management is free to vote the stock as it sees fit if the stockholder signs and returns his proxy in time.

Thus, through the proxy system, the management of many large corporations perpetuate themselves in office even though they personally own a very small fraction of the outstanding shares. So long as they conduct the business in a manner satisfactory to the stockholders, the stockholders almost automatically sign and return the proxies without question. There have been a number of outstanding cases, however, when stockholders became unhappy with the way the corporation was being run and managed successfully to overthrow the current management and vote in another management more acceptable to them. It is possible for others to solicit proxies in the manner described above, and there have been a number of very interesting proxy fights in a few companies during recent years. The very threat of such action may be a potent factor in keeping the management of a corporation on its toes. It is well for everyone to keep in mind that management personnel are employees just as are other personnel in the corporation and serve at the pleasure of the owners of the corporation.

### Charter and Bylaws

The activities of a corporation are controlled by three things: (1) the statutes in the state where formed, (2) the corporation charter or articles of incorporation, and (3) the corporation bylaws. The statutes vary somewhat from state to state, but in every state the incorporators are required to draw up a petition outlining certain facts about the proposed corporation. This petition is called the charter, or the articles of incorporation, and is addressed to the proper state official, usually the secretary of state or a commissioner of corporations; and when the appropriate state official approves it, it becomes the corporate charter or articles of incorporation. The official at the time of his approval will ordinarily issue another certificate, which signifies his approval of the application, and the corporation automatically comes into being. Approval of the charter by the state official usually has the additional meaning that the law of the state is considered part of the charter. This has the effect of notifying the corporate officers that they should become familiar with the state law and comply with it.

Since the incorporators make out the charter, they can place anything in it they wish so long as it meets the requirements of the state law. As a result, charters or articles of incorporation often confer very broad powers on the corporation, for certainly it is better to have powers unused than to lack powers later necessary.

Although the charter gives many details about the general nature and administration of the corporation, it does not give all of them. The by-laws are for the purpose of guiding the officers of the corporation in the management of the company, and for the sake of completeness the bylaws will often contain the same information given in the charter. Some common provisions of corporate bylaws are as follows:

1. Date and place of annual stockholders' meeting.
2. Date and place of meetings of board of directors.
3. List of officers of corporation, including their duties, terms of office, and method of appointment.
4. The number, term of office, powers, and compensation of directors.
5. The method of amending the bylaws.
6. Types of proposals that must be submitted to the stockholders for approval.

The stockholders have the power to make and amend the bylaws, although they may delegate this power to the board of directors. Practically speaking, the stockholders have very little control over the activities of the corporation officers or the board of directors. They must exercise control by the broad measures or controls set up in the bylaws. The bylaws outline the fundamental policies of the corporation, and it is up to the board of directors to see that they are carried out.

### Stock and Stockholders

There are many varieties of stock in existence, but for the most part all varieties can be classed in two groups: *preferred* and *common*. In either case, the holder of a share is a part owner of the corporation. He does not hold title to the assets of the corporation, for title is held by the corporation itself; but the share of stock does represent a pro rata interest in the assets.

Preferred stock, as the name implies, is a stock that in some manner is preferred over common stock—usually in terms of dividends or assets or both. Preference as to assets means that in case the corporation is dissolved the preferred stockholder has claim to the assets ahead of the common stockholder. Of course, all creditors and bond holders must be paid off before even the preferred stockholder has any claim. The amount paid the preferred stockholder in such a case is the par value of the stock, or, if the stock has no par value, an amount either stated on the stock certificate or in the charter.

Preferred stock may also take precedence in dividends. The percentage dividend paid to preferred stockholders is usually fixed at the time of issue —for example, at 5 per cent. The 5 per cent dividend to preferred stockholders would have to be paid before any dividend could be paid the common stockholders, and the 5 per cent would be computed based on original selling price, usually $100. If the preferred stock is cumulative, dividends not paid in any year cumulate and the total must be paid the preferred stockholder before any are paid the common stockholder. If the preferred stock is non-cumulative, a dividend skipped in any one year is not made up in any subsequent year.

The attraction of preferred stock can be seen from the above discussion. It confers certain privileges as to dividends and assets, and its rate of return is usually constant. However, if the corporation should have very high profits, the preferred stockholder might receive no more than the usual fixed return. In such a case the stock is called *non-participating*. If the stock is *participating*, the preferred stock is paid its dividend first; then the common stock is paid its dividend up to a rate equalling that paid the preferred stock; finally, both participate at equal rates in any further dividend.

Preferred stock may also be made redeemable, which means that such stock may be purchased by and at the option of the company under the conditions and terms specified in the certificate. The stock may also be made convertible at the option of the holder into other securities as specified in the certificate. In some instances the preferred stockholder is denied the right to vote except, perhaps, on certain issues or under certain conditions such as the skipping of his dividend. In one company the preferred shareholder has one and one-half votes per share as compared to one vote per share of common stock. Obviously, preferred stock issues vary considerably, and the corporation that issues them offers enough features to make the stock attractive to the market at the time.

Common stock is the simplest form of corporate ownership. The holders of such stock enjoy all the rights of stockholders but without any of the special privileges discussed above. Corporations normally prefer to have their ownership entirely in the hands of common stockholders, not wishing to grant special privileges to the preferred stockholder. The pattern in issuing stock is oftentimes one of issuing common stock when the corporation is first formed; then, sometime later, when times become a little difficult and the company needs more capital, it may issue preferred stock. In difficult times common stock may not sell well, so in order to raise capital, some special attraction is necessary.

Although common stock does not offer the security of preferred stock, it does have speculative value. If profits are high, the common stockholder may receive high returns. On the other hand, if profits are low, he may receive nothing. Common stock in some of the so-called blue chip companies has paid regular dividends for a number of years and so has become almost as secure as preferred stock. This status is made possible by good management of both the financial and the productive aspects of the business.

Not all stock carries voting rights at the stockholders' meetings. Although the practice of issuing non-voting stock is frowned upon, some nevertheless is current. Non-voting stock is sometimes issued to raise capital while leaving control in the hands of the original incorporators. Some preferred stock has no voting right unless dividends are skipped.

Reference has been made to the *par value* of stock. This is usually a somewhat arbitrary original value assigned to a share of stock. The actual selling price may be more or less than this amount. Selling price will usually reflect the earning power of and the assets behind the stock, and so the par value of a share is often meaningless. Therefore, it is common practice to issue common stock with no par value.

Stockholders are the true owners of the corporation, and as such they have certain rights both individually and collectively. As an individual the stockholder has a right to his dividend when declared, a right to vote in stockholders' meetings, to share in the assets in case of dissolution, to sell his stock, to inspect the records of the corporation, and to participate in additional issues of stock. Collectively the rights of stockholders are much broader and include the power to:

1. Adopt and amend the bylaws.
2. Elect the directors.
3. Sell the assets of the corporation.
4. Amend the charter with the consent of the state.
5. Dissolve the corporation.

### Bonds and Bondholders

Bonds are quite different from stocks. Stocks represent shares in the ownership of a corporation, and money invested in them becomes a permanent part of the capitalization. Bonds, on the other hand, are corporate credit obligations, and the holders of the bonds are creditors. It is expected that the money received from the sale of bonds will be returned on the date of maturity. Throughout the bond's life the corporation must pay interest on it, just as if it had borrowed from a bank.

Bonds are bought and sold just like stocks, and the interest is paid to whoever holds the bond on the day of payment. The investment risk in a bond is less than that in either preferred or common stock. The interest rate on bonds is fixed; the money paid out as interest is a cost of doing business. In case of liquidation, the bondholders have prior right to assets ahead of all stockholders.

So long as the corporation pays the interest due on the bonds and can pay them off at maturity, the bondholder has nothing to worry about. Should the corporation default in its payments, then the bondholder can exercise certain rights as set forth in the charter, bylaws, and trust indenture. Basically, the rights of bondholders in such a case are similar to those of any creditor—the right to take over the property concerned. Since bonds, like stocks, are usually widely held, it would be extremely difficult for the bondholders to be sure the corporation was always living up to its obligations. Consequently, at the time of issue a *trustee* is appointed to look out for the rights of the bondholders, and the trust indenture will specify the action to be taken in case of interest default. In the end the trustee may foreclose, take possession, and sell the property for the benefit of the bondholders—a procedure similar to the one followed in case of default by individuals on car or house payments.

A corporation may retire an outstanding bond issue in a number of ways. First, it can pay off the bonds at maturity, usually 20 years or more after issue. Secondly, it can call in its bonds for payment prior to maturity if it has reserved that right. Thirdly, it can purchase its own bonds in the securities market. Finally, at the option of the bondholder the bond may be converted into preferred or common stock. Sometimes too, bonds are paid off at maturity by the process of "refunding." In this case, a new issue of bonds is sold in order to raise money to pay off the old issue. A corporation might use this procedure if it continued to need the capital.

### Board of Directors

Except in those matters that are reserved for the consideration of the stockholders, the board of directors has final authority in all corporate matters. The number of directors varies, but state laws usually set a minimum. Variations from three to 20 are not uncommon. The term of office is usually one to three years, but it is common for directors to be re-elected, with the result that many serve for long periods.

Specific powers usually exercised by the board of directors are:

1. Election of officers.
2. Making contracts in the name of the corporation.
3. Declaring dividends.

4. Issuing corporate stock.
5. Determining corporate policies.

Of the specific duties listed above, the more important ones are the decisions on company policies and the making of contracts in the name of the corporation. In carrying out these duties the board exercises control over the expenditure of large sums of money; and it gives its approval to plans to exploit new markets. It is common for the corporate officers to formulate policies and plans for the board's approval, for usually the officers are more familiar with details than are the directors; but the officers must "sell" the plan to the directors. Should the plan fail, the directors will no doubt be more careful in approving the next plan and may even start looking for new officers.

Directors acting as a group may make serious mistakes that cost the corporation dearly. If they have acted in good faith and have exercised reasonable caution, they are not held liable. However, should they have been negligent in the conduct of corporation affairs, they may be held personally liable for the resultant losses. If any one director feels that the action taken by the board as a whole is not to the best interests of the corporation, he can protect himself against liability by stating his disapproval and having his statement duly recorded in the minutes of the meeting at which the action was taken.

The makeup of the board of directors varies considerably among American corporations. One school of thought holds that members of the board for the most part should *not* be employees of the company, and many corporations, following this practice, make certain that a majority of the board members are not employees. In such cases, the only employees who are board members probably are the duly elected officers of the corporation. A second school of thought believes that board members *should* be employees, and although such an arrangement is quite common in a very small organization with only a few members on the board, it is also followed by a few of our very large corporations. The advantage of having directors who are also employees is that they are more familiar with the affairs of the company and perhaps would be in a better position to make decisions or contribute to the making of important decisions. On the other hand, one of the more significant functions of a director is to ask discerning questions, an activity that does not depend upon an extensive knowledge of the affairs of a business. The ability to ask perceptive questions comes from experience in decision-making in a variety of business situations, and such persons often develop an intuitive feeling about business problems and considerations and are almost instinctively able to ask the kinds of questions that should be asked before a new venture is launched. The purpose of the questions is not to place the management on the spot but to be certain that all facts are considered, that all facets of the problem have been explored, and that the alternative courses of action have been properly rejected. It seems reasonable to assume that if management had to present their proposals to a board made up of persons able to ask this discerning type of question they would do their utmost to anticipate the questions and to exercise considerable care in preparing and presenting any proposal. By such a process, both board and management contribute toward the future growth and success of the organization.

### Corporate Officers

The bylaws of a corporation usually provide for the election of four officers, though there may be more. The four are president, vice president, secretary, and treasurer.

The *president* is usually the chief executive officer and has responsibility and authority to carry out the policies adopted by the board of directors. He provides guidance to the other executives and keeps the board of directors informed on the progress of the various phases of the business. Although the office of *vice president* was created originally in order to have someone to take over should the office of president become vacant, it currently denotes the head of an executive function such as sales or manufacturing. The person designated to take over in the absence of the president is frequently called the *executive vice president*.

The *secretary* has a number of legal duties to perform, such as filing reports with state officials, maintaining stockholder lists, handling stock

**Figure 23-1.** Basic organization of a corporation.

transfers, and sending out notices of stockholder and director meetings. The *treasurer* has charge of the receipt and disbursement of all corporate funds and will render reports from time to time accounting for the money entrusted to his care. Figure 23-1 shows the basic organization of a corporation, with the officers indicated.

## Government Regulation

The corporation, having been created with the authority of the state, finds itself very much regulated by the laws of the state. Laws requiring corporations to file various forms and reports have already been mentioned.

There are state laws that tax the corporation's income and that regulate the sale of its securities. The federal government likewise has laws that control many phases of the corporation's work if it is engaged in interstate commerce. And, of course, whether or not the corporation is doing business across state lines, it is subject to the federal tax on income.

Each of the states has its own laws that attempt to protect the public from buying fraudulent securities. Usually such laws require the corporation to file a statement qualifying it to sell the proposed securities. The corporation can then proceed only after approval by the state authorities. In the meantime, investigations can be made as to the truth of statements and claims. In general, statements are approved if there is no untruth stated or implied in them. The government doesn't assume the responsibility of saying whether or not a security is a good buy; but it does want the whole truth put before the investor before he buys.

The depression of the early thirties, when many people lost millions of dollars in worthless securities, led to the passage of federal laws regulating the issuance and sale of securities. The main laws were the Securities Act of 1933, the Securities Exchange Act of 1934, the Public Utility Holding Company Act of 1935, and the Investment Company Act of 1939.

The Securities Act of 1933 followed the principle of getting all the facts about the issue before the public. A registration statement giving all the essential facts must be filed with the Securities and Exchange Commission if the issue is to be offered publicly in interstate commerce. A waiting period is provided between the filing of the statement and the issuing of the securities, so that the stated facts may be investigated. The commission is given effective powers to force observance of the law.

The Securities Exchange Act of 1934 provided for supervision of the stock exchanges and of the activities of the security markets. The Holding Company Act of 1935 gave the Securities and Exchange Commission powers over the financing of public utilities and broke up some of the holding companies in the public utility field. Investment companies and investment advisers were placed under control by the Investment Company Act of 1939.

## Ownership Combinations

The combining of businesses is a continuous process taking place in order to effect operating economies or increase profits. In the early days companies combined in an effort to increase profits through monopoly and restraint of trade. Today, companies combine in one manner or another to increase profits through diversification or to provide an outlet for some technical skill or marketing ability.

In 1890, all business combinations designed to restrain trade were prohibited by the passage of the Sherman Antitrust Act. This act applies to all businesses engaged in interstate commerce. It may be of historical interest to indicate what a trust was prior to 1890, since this is what the Sherman Antitrust Act specifically prohibited. Strictly speaking, the trust was a "voting trust," which was an arrangement whereby the holders of stock in competing companies turned their shares over to trustees, who would then vote all of the stock and thus control the policies of the several corporations. Trust certificates were issued in place of the shares turned over to the trustees. There were leading trusts formed in the oil, whiskey, sugar, lead, and cotton oil industries.

The Sherman Antitrust Act made the above form of business combination illegal and was the first of a series of federal acts designed to protect trade and commerce against unlawful restraints of trade and monopolies. The Clayton Act was passed in 1914 to correct some abuses that had not been affected by the Sherman Act, and in the same year the Federal Trade Commission Act, which prohibited unfair methods of competition, was passed. In 1936, the Clayton Act was amended by the Robinson-Patman Anti-price Discrimination Act; the Tydings-Miller Act was passed in 1937, amending the Sherman Act; and in 1938 the Federal Trade Commission Act was amended by the Wheeler-Lea Act. Whereas the Sherman Act made illegal the existence of monopolies, the later acts and amendments were generally designed to prevent tendencies toward monopolies. In spite of all such legislation, one only has to read current reports of antitrust suits to recognize there is a certain amount of inconsistency in public policy regarding the definition of monopolies and tendencies toward them.

A consolidation of two or more corporations takes place when the existing corporations are fused into a single new one. The plan of consolidation must necessarily meet the legal requirements of the state in which it is formed, but generally speaking, upon the approval of the specified percentage of the outstanding shares and the filing of the contract of agreement as to the fusion of the various corporations, the actual exchange of the stock certificates of the old companies for that of the new can take place, and the original companies no longer exist.

The merger is slightly different from a consolidation inasmuch as one or more corporations is absorbed into another corporation. Again, agreements are worked out whereby the stock of the corporation that is to remain active is exchanged in some ratio for the stock of the corporation that is to be absorbed. When approved by the required number of stockholders, the exchange is made, and the merger takes place with the result that the absorbed company ceases to exist.

Effective combination of corporations can take place through the sale of assets or the lease of assets. One corporation could sell its assets to another and continue to exist as a corporation, although if it ceased to exist the combination would simply be a merger. The leasing of assets is also commonly practiced, and some of these leases endure for a hundred years, thereby having about the same effect as a sale.

We commonly think of a holding company as one that holds stock in other corporations but performs no operations itself. This may be true in the strict sense, although many corporations today conduct operations of their own as well as hold stock in other corporations. In some cases the stock held constitutes a large proportion of the outstanding shares and the "held" company may be operated as a separate division. In such a case, one company is usually referred to as the parent company and the other as the subsidiary.

## QUESTIONS

1. Compare the means by which owners exercise their rights in a partnership with the means to this end in a corporation.

2. Some thought has been given to putting government-operated business on a profit basis. Is this a desirable step? Explain your answer.

3. Distinguish between the words "company" and "corporation." Are they ever interchangeable?

4. Corporations have often been called "monsters with no soul." Explain the justification for such a statement.

5. Explain the double taxation of a corporation's income.

6. What is the distinction between the corporation charter and the corporation bylaws.

7. Distinguish between "par value" and "market value" of a share of stock.

8. An issue of preferred stock is cumulative and participating and also takes precedence in dividends and distribution of assets. Explain in some detail the basic features of this issue.

9. How can someone own less than 51 per cent of the shares of a corporation and still control it?

10. What are the rights of bondholders in a corporation?

11. What is the source of the authority of the board of directors?

12. Would it be possible in a corporation for the officers, the board of directors, and the stockholders to be the same group of people? Explain.

13. If the Securities and Exchange Commission approves an issue of stock, does this mean that the stock is a good buy? Explain.

## CASE PROBLEMS

### Seitz and Johns

Eight years ago Bob Seitz and Ed Johns, residents in a Chicago suburb, saw an opportunity to pick up some extra cash by manufacturing picture frames in their spare time. Ed had developed a unique design for picture frames and Bob had a couple of power driven woodworking tools; so the two men went to work. In two years their market had grown large enough to justify hiring a man to spend full time on the manufacturing end of the business. Both Bob and Ed continued to devote only odd hours on weekends and evenings to the business, sharing all expenses and profits on a fifty-fifty basis.

The business gradually expanded, but the installation of better machines made it unnecessary to hire more people.

The arrangement proved very satisfactory for a period of six years, until Ed Johns was promoted by his company to a job in a branch plant in California that paid more than double his former salary.

Ed couldn't think of turning down the promotion, but neither did he want to sell out his share of the picture-frame business. He had invested considerable time and money in it and regarded it as a sound long-term investment. He realized, however, that some new ownership arrangement would be necessary if he moved to the West Coast.

*Questions:*

1. What would be the best ownership arrangement from Ed Johns' point of view?

2. What would be the best ownership arrangement from Bob Seitz's point of view?

### J.J. McCormick, Inc.

The board of directors of J. J. McCormick, Inc., has given final approval of a plan to expand production facilities over 100%. The approval was voted with the proviso that a satisfactory proposal for raising the necessary capital be submitted by the treasurer of the company. The money to be raised would more than double the company's present capitalization of $200,000.

In appraising the various possibilities for raising capital the treasurer notes that the company is in good financial position and has paid regular dividends on the common stock since incorporation 25 years ago. He also notes that the present board of directors as a group owns over 50% of the common stock.

*Questions:*

1. List factors both for and against a recommendation that the expansion be financed by the sale of
   (a) common stock.
   (b) preferred stock.
   (c) bonds.

2. Based on your listings in Question 1, what method would you recommend? Outline any assumptions made.

3. Would a decision be easier to reach if the board as a group owned only 5% of the common stock?

# CHAPTER TWENTY-FOUR

# Financial Management

Someone has said, "It takes money to make money." Though not always true, this statement does contain a large element of truth when applied to a business or industrial establishment.

Capital is the lifeblood of a business. Regardless of how good an idea one has, money will be required to turn that idea into profits. There must be sufficient capital to organize the business, to provide necessary buildings, machines, and equipment, to buy raw materials, to meet advertising and sales expenses, to meet payrolls, and to take care of a host of other expenses incurred in getting established. Enough capital must be available also to carry the business until it shows more income than outgo.

## Kinds of Capital

In using the word "capital" the businessman usually lumps together all of the elements he will need to start an enterprise, namely: land, buildings, machinery, tools, and materials. In the technical sense land should be distinguished from the other means of production because the latter are reproducible, and land is not. However, this distinction is rarely made. Furthermore, capital is most often thought of in money terms, for promoting a new enterprise or expanding a present one is largely a financial operation. Money and credit are the chief means for acquiring the elements of production just mentioned, including the land, so it seems logical to employ the word capital in this purely financial sense. For our purposes, then, capital will mean the cash money and credit required to start and operate a business. Money and credit should not be regarded as simply that, however,

**468**

but should be considered with a special view to their source, time needed, and use intended. Failure to make these distinctions has led many businesses, large and small, into financial difficulties.

### Equity Capital and Borrowed Capital

Equity capital is that money put into the business by the owners of the business and may be in the form of land, buildings, machinery, or materials, as well as cash itself. Borrowed capital, obviously, is that money obtained from some outside source with a promise to repay at some future date. This is almost always in the form of cash. The difference between these two kinds of capital is highly significant for the beginning or expanding business. Of necessity, the borrowed capital contains a commitment to repay at some specific future time, as well as an obligation to pay interest during the intervening time. The equity capital contains no such firm promise, although there is naturally an expectation and a moral obligation to pay dividends if profits should be forthcoming. The difference between these two types of obligation is particularly significant during a period of depressed business conditions. A company highly dependent upon borrowed capital may find itself forced out of business by its creditors, whereas a company more dependent upon equity capital could delay dividends to its stockholders until a time that profits would justify such payments. Lack of profits does not cancel a company's obligations to its creditors, or to its sources of borrowed funds.

### Short-Term, Intermediate-Term, and Long-Term Capital

In capital funds that are borrowed another important distinction is made according to the time period for which the loans are made. Business loans are usually made by banks, although insurance companies do sometimes make the longer-term loans to manufacturing concerns. Short term capital refers to loans made for periods of one year or less. Thirty-day loans are not uncommon and are generally made for the purpose of paying for material, labor, or other items for the production of goods, which will be completed and sold in the very near future. Money borrowed as intermediate capital would be for a period of a few years, rarely exceeding five, and would be for the purpose of purchasing tools, machinery, and other equipment having a life of several years and therefore likely to have an appreciable effect upon costs and profits during that time. Long-term capital would be that money borrowed for repayment in ten, twenty, or even fifty years. This money would normally be for the purpose of financing the purchase of land, erection of buildings, and purchase of basic machinery having a long life. Since pay-off of this kind of investment could not be expected for a number of years, one would logically arrange long-term capital rather than short-term or intermediate-term capital.

The distinctions regarding the time periods of borrowed capital are not always clear and simple, and there is likely to be much overlapping. For example, the borrower of intermediate capital may obtain the benefit of long-term capital through successive renewals of his loan. Likewise, the borrower of long-term capital may gain some of the advantages of intermediate-term capital by having the privilege of paying off the loan before it matures. The three classes, however, do represent three different types of capital funds and become important, not only because they show the different financial needs of a business, but because they identify different sources of funds.

### Fixed and Working Capital

This final classification of capital refers to the use made of the money. The typical industrial enterprise has land, buildings, machinery, tools, and equipment. Assets of this type are intended for use over and over again for a long period of time and are commonly called fixed capital. In addition, an enterprise needs funds to cover its cost of operating. This includes purchase of materials, payment of wages, storage costs, advertising, maintenance, and shipping. Moreover, there is a need for money to carry the enterprise during the time lag between the sale of its products and the payment for them. Funds to cover these costs are commonly called working capital.

The relationship between the needs of capital and its sources should be fairly obvious. Money for basic facilities such as land and buildings should normally and preferably come from equity sources, but if borrowed capital must be used it should be of the long-term variety. Short-term loans could supply some of the working capital with the possibility of intermediate capital being used for the same purpose. Clearly, sound financial management depends upon the proper balance of the following factors: sources of capital, methods of raising capital, the time elements involved, and the uses that are to be made of the capital.

## Sources of Capital

Where does one get money to start a business or to breathe new life into it after it is started? The main sources of capital are savings, loans, sale of securities, trade credits, and profit plowback. Which source one taps will depend upon many factors. Some are appropriate when the business is getting started, some are more appropriate later on, and some are appropriate at any time. We will discuss each in turn, indicating desirable and undesirable features.

## Savings

Fundamentally, all capital for investment in business and industry comes from savings. People, rich or poor, save their money, or, more explicitly, save what money they have left over after paying their bills. With this money they buy shares in building and loan concerns, they purchase life insurance, they buy stocks and bonds; or they put cash in the bank for a "rainy day." In any of these events the money is made available for further use and investment. If people did not save or did not have some money left over after their bills were paid, much of the money used for capital expansion would no longer be available.

Although this general concept is important to the future growth and expansion of our economy, it is the problem of financing an individual business we wish to pursue here. If we think in these narrower terms, we might ask where Joe Jones gets the money to start a machine shop in his basement. Chances are he gets the money from savings—his own personal savings, for this is the way that many such businesses get their start. The great advantage of the use of personal savings is the freedom from outside interference it gives the founder. In addition, the founder is probably more careful since he is risking *his* money and not someone else's. Personal savings may not be enough, and other sources may have to be tapped, but excepting a few clever promoters, most founders of businesses must make some personal contribution toward the initial capitalization.

With the introduction of the progressive income tax in our country, the savings of individuals cannot play the role that they once did in financing and making possible industrial expansion. It is extremely difficult for a man to accumulate a fortune by savings alone. In spite of this, people do save, and they do invest either in their own businesses or the businesses of others. Even high taxation cannot kill the American spirit of competition. Everyone hopes that his mouse trap or his can opener is the one that will revolutionize the industry.

## Loans

To consider loans as a source of capital is to see a multitude of possibilities open. The first possibility is to borrow from friends or relatives. These personal loans are frequently made to get small businesses started, and although they can be handled as formally as a bank loan, they oftentimes are not. There may not be any definite rate of interest or time for repayment. Under such circumstances they are more favors than loans.

Of course, there are many institutions in the country that are strictly in the lending business. They are not just doing a businessman a favor by lending him money; they are in business to lend money, and they make money doing it.

Banks come to mind first when lending institutions are mentioned. Commercial banks and savings banks collect the savings of individuals and in turn make them available for financing. In addition, we have building and loan associations, insurance companies, finance companies, foundations, and other institutions that have funds they wish to invest for a good return.

These lending institutions are all privately owned and controlled, although they must abide by certain government regulations. The federal government has been and is in the lending business also. For many years the Reconstruction Finance Corporation made loans to private businesses either to get them started or later to refinance them. The RFC was abolished in 1953 and replaced by the Small Business Administration, whose main purpose is still to lend money to businesses in need—but supposedly only to those small businesses that cannot obtain funds from some private source.

Borrowing money to start or finance a business saddles the business with a fixed obligation that must be met. Interest must be paid on time and the loan itself must be paid back at the agreed-upon date. Such repayment may not be possible or desirable, and further borrowing or refinancing may be necessary.

On the other hand, borrowing allows the founder or owner to retain his ownership rights in the business and thereby his control. Many founders have lost control of their enterprises when financial interests have manipulated the voting stock. If financing can be performed adequately and successfully by loans, avoiding the sale of stock, then the founder need not fear loss of control.

## Sale of Securities

Financing a business by the sale of securities necessarily means that the founders have decided upon the corporate form of ownership. Of course, using the sale of securities as a method of financing could be a strong reason for forming a corporation in the first place, or it could be a reason for changing from one of the other forms of ownership to a corporate form.

A corporation just starting will finance itself through the sale of common stock. Later on, should extra funds be required and the market for common stock appear not too favorable, the corporation might issue and sell preferred stock. By so doing, it may find money available that otherwise would not be forthcoming. Another way of obtaining additional funds after a corporation has begun operation is by the sale of bonds. This is usually possible only after the corporation is old enough to have established its credit and earning power. Since the sale of bonds is essentially the borrowing of money, the lender will require security for his loan. This security may be in the form of a mortgage on some of the assets of the corporation, but in addition the bondholder, or the trustee acting for him, will want to be certain the business is stable enough and strong enough to make the interest payments when they are due.

If complete freedom of choice is theirs, many businessmen will normally finance their corporations entirely by means of common stock—both in the initial financing and in the financing of expansion. By so doing they avoid assuming the burden of the fixed charge of interest that bonds impose. Preferred stock commits the corporation to a stipulated dividend and of course means that the corporation has granted certain special privileges to the owners of these certificates. The use of only common stock puts all stockholders on the same basis. On the other hand, financing through the sale of more and more common stock in many cases dilutes the ownership. In closely held corporations, this may mean that the orginal owner loses control. In addition, the owner may expect large profits from his operations and may wish to retain them for himself. A stated dividend on preferred stock or stated interest rates on bonds permits the owner (common stockholders) to retain the extra profits.

Obviously, each businessman must weigh all methods of financing and decide which one is best for him. Experience shows that most business concerns have their profitable years and their lean years. And so the selection among methods of financing through the sale of securities often becomes a matter of expediency: the corporation *must* sell the kind of securities that the public will buy.

### Security Exchanges

Contrary to the belief of many, the various security exchanges do not buy and sell stocks and bonds, and they are not lending institutions. Instead, they fufill the function of providing a market or trading place for those people who wish to buy and sell stocks and bonds. Various brokerage firms are members of the exchanges, and the representatives of these firms do the actual buying and selling for their clients. For example, an individual who wishes to buy ABC Corporation stock, which is listed on one of the exchanges, contacts his broker. The broker's representative on the exchange floor offers to buy ABC Corporation stock, and after so doing, he learns that some other broker's representative has some ABC Corporation stock to sell. Assuming that the two representatives can agree on price, the deal is closed. In this manner a man in New York could easily sell his stock to another man in California without either knowing it—and this could all be done in a matter of minutes!

The security exchange also provides a certain amount of protection for investors. An exchange won't "list" a security until the company meets certain requirements. For example, to be listed on the New York Stock Exchange a company must have demonstrated an earning power, under competitive conditions, of one million dollars annually, after all expenses including federal income and excess profits taxes. Net tangible assets should be at least eight million dollars, and in the case of common stock issued there should be a broad distribution of at least four hundred thousand shares among not less than fifteen hundred holders. This is exclusive of concentrated or family holdings and of stockholders holding less than one hundred shares. The New York Stock Exchange also refuses to list any common stock of a non-voting variety. These requirements provide the investor with a higher degree of confidence in any "listed" security that he might purchase as compared to an "unlisted" issue. It is possible for a corporation to sell a stock or bond issue worth several million dollars all over the United States in a matter of days. The exchanges and their member brokers, who in turn have contacts with thousands of investing individuals and institutions, provide a market. Strange as it may seem, there is always someone willing to buy a "good" security at a "good" price. If there can be agreement on the definition of the word "good," then a corporation can easily raise capital through the sale of securities.

### Profit Plowback

Obviously, at the outset, a new business cannot be financed through the plowback of profits; nevertheless, profit plowback is a method of financing commonly used by established companies. This means that instead of all the profits being paid out to the stockholders or owners as dividends, they are retained in the business and used to finance expansion. By so doing the present stockholders finance the expansion, whether they want to or not. Of course, they can always sell their stock or voice their objections at the stockholders' meetings. But theoretically they haven't lost anything by the plowback, because the value of their stock is supposed to have gone up. If the expansion is successful, the value of a share of stock will increase beyond the value of the dividends that were originally retained.

Some companies make it a practice to finance expansion in this manner. They avoid any long-term debt and do not dilute the ownership by the sale of voting stock. Here is what happened when one company financed expansion in this manner:

A share of stock sold for one hundred dollars when the company was first incorporated. A person buying one share at that time and holding it over the years would have had to invest another $890 in order to exercise the various rights that were issued and buy up odd shares of stock that resulted from stock splits. So our hypothetical person would have had to make a total investment of $990 over a period of 70 years. However, at the end of the 70 years he would own 1680 shares of common stock worth a market value of $134,400. In the meantime, he would have received approximately $40,980 in dividends. This illustrates the growth that is possible through the wise plowing back of profits to expand a business. Of course, profit plowback was not the only contributing factor. Certainly the management was of high caliber, for otherwise the profits would not have been there to plow back.

## Trade Credits

We normally don't think of trade credits as a method of financing a business enterprise. But when one stops to consider, trade credits are one of our main methods of financing—particularly in the small enterprise. Some businesses during their early life or during difficult periods depend upon trade credits to finance machinery, materials, and miscellaneous equipment. Just as a farmer borrows on a future wheat crop, through trade credits a manufacturer borrows on a future "crop" of production.

Of course, one cannot recommend this method of financing as the one for a business to be entirely dependent upon. Trade credit has a way of disappearing sometimes when it is needed most. But it is a source that can be useful and one that plays an important role in short-term financing.

## Financial Statements

The preparation of financial statements is a necessary part of every business, no matter what the form of ownership or the type of business activity. Because these statements show the financial status and progress of the company, they are of interest to the managers, the owners, the lenders, the employees, the creditors, and almost anyone who has any interest in or concern for the business. In most businesses, two financial statements are prepared. These are the *balance sheet* and the *profit and loss statement.* Manufacturing enterprises have need for a third statement, the *manufacturing cost statement.*

These three statements are usually made up by the controller or by the division of the business which deals with financial matters. It is not our purpose to delve into the techniques and problems of accounting, but we do feel it necessary for the reader to achieve a basic understanding of these financial reports. Many business decisions are made only after consulting balance sheets and profit and loss statements or after *financially* justifying the move.

The preparation of the balance sheet and of the profit and loss statement is normally referred to as a job of "financial accounting." The manufacturing cost statement is usually the work of "cost accounting." Cost accounting and cost control work in general have been treated in Chapter 17. The manufacturing cost statement is included at this point simply to complete the financial status picture.

## The Balance Sheet

The balance sheet is a statement showing the financial status of the company at any given time. The statement itself is divided into three parts: (1) *assets*, which are what the company owns; (2) *liabilities* which are what the company owes; and (3) *net worth*, or capital, which is the amount by which the assets exceed the liabilities. In formula form this would be: ASSETS = LIABILITIES + NET WORTH. Note that this relationship holds true on the sample balance sheet shown in Figure 24-1.

Assets have been defined as what the company owns. There is considerable variation in the manner in which assets are listed on balance sheets, but common practice would include the following groups:

CURRENT ASSETS
INVESTMENTS
FIXED ASSETS
INTANGIBLE ASSETS
DEFERRED CHARGES

**Current assets**   include those items that the company expects to "turn over" during the following accounting period, or else those items that can be quickly turned into cash. Typical items would be cash (naturally), accounts receivable, notes receivable, and inventories.

**Investments**   include stocks and bonds of other companies, or other property that the company has purchased with the expectation of a financial return. United States government bonds and United States Treasury notes are also common investments of industrial concerns.

**Fixed assets**   are those items that are more or less permanently used in the business and are not for sale. Such items would include buildings,

## THE ABC COMPANY, INC.
### Balance Sheet, December 31, 19......

*Assets*

Current assets:
| | |
|---|---:|
| Cash | $ 42,650 |
| Accounts receivable | 44,931 |
| Notes receivable | 10,744 |
| Inventories | 160,734 |
| Total current assets | $259,059 |

Investments:
| | |
|---|---:|
| U. S. Government bonds | $ 4,717 |
| Other marketable securities | 16,360 |
| Total investments | $ 21,077 |

Fixed assets:
| | |
|---|---:|
| Land | $ 11,638 |
| Buildings and equipment | 391,382 |
| Total | $403,020 |
| Less accumulated depreciation | 138,589 |
| Fixed assets, net | $264,431 |
| Goodwill, patents, and licenses | 2,519 |
| Deferred charges | 7,026 |
| Total | $554,112 |

*Liabilities*

Current liabilities:
| | |
|---|---:|
| Bank loans | $ 9,000 |
| Accounts payable | 69,002 |
| Accrued taxes | 20,984 |
| Total current liabilities | $ 98,986 |
| Long-term debt | 31,525 |
| Total liabilities | $130,511 |

*Net Worth*

| | |
|---|---:|
| Preferred shares | $ 2,250 |
| Common shares | 48,844 |
| Earned surplus | 372,507 |
| Total net worth | $423,601 |
| Total liabilities and net worth | $554,112 |

**Figure 24-1.** Balance sheet of a corporation.

land on which the plant buildings are situated, machinery, tools, and other production and office equipment.

**Intangible assets** include such items as copyrights, patents, goodwill and franchises. As the name implies, it is difficult to attach a fair value to these items. We know, for example, that the General Foods Company enjoys a large amount of goodwill throughout the country, but how much stated in dollars? The same line of reasoning holds for the other items. The result is that most companies follow the conservative practice of listing these items at a very low valuation—unless the items have been purchased from some other company, in which case they would be listed at the purchase price.

**Deferred charges** are sometimes referred to as "prepaid expenses" and include those items that have been paid for in advance. An unexpired insurance premium or taxes paid in advance would be good examples.

The method of listing liabilities also varies, but commonly liabilities are shown as "current" and "other." "Current" liabilities include those items that must be paid within the next accounting period. These would typically be accounts payable, notes payable, and expense items such as taxes and wages. "Other" liabilities for the most part include only long-term debts, such as a long-term loan from a bank or an outstanding bond issue.

While net worth is the difference between total assets and total liabilities, it also represents the worth of the ownership of the company. In the case of the proprietorship or the partnership the net worth represents the amount of money the owners have invested in the business. As profits are made they are either removed by the owners or allowed to stay in the business, in which case the net worth is increased just as if the owners had invested more money.

In the case of the corporation, the net worth account is divided into two parts. One is the *capital stock* account, which indicates what the original shares of stock were sold for. The second part is called *surplus*. As profits are earned they are placed in the surplus account and are then available to be distributed to the stockholders in the form of dividends, or to be used to finance expansion of the business, or to be kept for that inevitable "rainy day"—as the board of directors sees fit.

The preparation of a balance sheet can be likened to the snapping of a photograph. Both the photograph and the balance sheet give you a picture that represents a single instant; the next instant the view may be different. In order to appraise a business properly, one needs to take a financial picture from time to time. After the picture is taken, oftentimes certain ratios are computed to aid in financial appraisal. For example:

$$\text{Current ratio} = \frac{\text{Total current assets}}{\text{Total current liabilities}}$$

A desirable current ratio is usually considered to be 2:1. This means that every dollar of current liabilities is covered by two dollars of current assets.

$$\text{Proprietary ratio} = \frac{\text{Total net worth}}{\text{Total liabilities and net worth}}$$

Proprietary ratio indicates the degree of dependency of a company on its creditors for capital funds.

One must keep in mind that these ratios, as well as others that can be computed, do not show much by themselves. They are of value only when compared with other ratios—either ratios computed for the same company from year to year or similar ratios computed for other companies. An analysis of trends is of great importance when it comes to studying the financial status of a company.


## Profit and Loss Statement

While the balance sheet shows the financial status of the company at one instant of time, the profit and loss statement summarizes the operations of the company for a period of time. This is done in terms of a profit realized or a loss suffered during the period. To show this effect the statement starts with a report of the income for the period, from which are deducted all the costs incurred as a result of operations. The net figure is the profit or loss for the period. In the case of a corporation it is customary to divide the

THE ABC COMPANY, INC.

Profit and Loss Statement
Year Ended December 31, 19......

| | |
|---|---:|
| Net sales | $1,038,290 |
| Cost of goods sold | 663,096 |
| Gross profit | $ 375,194 |
| Marketing and administrative expense | 254,092 |
| Profit from operations | 121,102 |
| Interest on investments | 1,462 |
| Other income | 310 |
| Other expense (deducted) | 1,944 |
| Profit before income taxes | 120,930 |
| Federal income taxes | 54,240 |
| Other income taxes | 7,372 |
| Total taxes on income | 61,612 |
| Net profit | $ 59,318 |
| Profit per share of common stock outstanding | 3.05 |

**Figure 24-2.** Profit and loss statement for a corporation.

profit for the period by the total number of shares outstanding so as to arrive at the earnings per share of stock.

As is shown in Figure 24-2, companies often have income from sources other than the sale of manufactured goods. There might be income from stocks or other investments. By the same token a company might have expenses other than those connected with the manufacture of goods. There might, for example, be interest charges on debts or notes. Both these items of "other" income and "other" expenses are usually shown separately on the profit and loss statement, enabling the reader to appraise the results of the manufacturing operations apart from "other" operations.

The main point of interest in the profit and loss statement on the part of stockholders—or of anyone interested in the business—is naturally the amount of profit made. However, just as with the balance sheet, it is possible to work out some ratios that will allow a better financial evaluation. Using figures from both the balance sheet and the profit and loss statement, typical ratios would be:

$$\text{Net profit ratio} = \frac{\text{Net profit}}{\text{Net sales}}$$

This shows percentage of profit for each dollar of sales.

$$\text{Rate of return on investment} = \frac{\text{Net profit}}{\text{Net worth}}$$

This shows the earnings rate of the company for each dollar invested by the stockholders.

$$\text{Rate of earnings on total capital employed}$$
$$= \frac{\text{Net profit}}{\text{Total liabilities and net worth}}$$

This shows the percentage return for every dollar of liabilities and net worth employed.

Many other ratios might be computed, but we have illustrated the principle. Again, we must keep in mind that the ratio has meaning only if it is computed the same way for a number of years and therefore shows trends. Bankers considering a loan of money to industrial concerns will be very interested in many of these ratios and in their trends over the years. In this way a better appraisal of the financial position of the company can be made.

### Manufacturing Cost Statement

In examining the profit and loss statement in Figure 24-2, one will notice the listing of income followed by a list of expenses, as is typical. The first item of expense listed, however, is the cost of goods sold; and in this case this one item alone accounts for about 64 per cent of the net sales. Since this percentage is so large, it seems desirable to break down the cost of goods sold into greater detail. Sometimes this is done right on the profit and loss statement, but it is probably more common to submit a separate statement called the *manufacturing cost statement.*

The statement in Figure 24-3 is a typical manufacturing cost statement. In general, it will show the dollars spent for direct labor, materials, and manufacturing expenses. "Manufacturing expenses" include all the miscellaneous items necessary for the manufacturing operation, such as repairs, heat, light, and taxes.

To summarize the manufacturing cost statement, it lists and outlines all the costs of manufacturing products during the period covered by the profit and loss statement. The methods used to arrive at and control these manufacturing costs were explained in the chapter on cost control (Chapter 17.)

### THE ABC COMPANY, INC.

Manufacturing Cost Statement
Year Ended December 31, 19......

| | | |
|---|---:|---:|
| Materials consumed: | | |
| Inventory raw materials Jan. 1, 19 ............ | $ 9,645 | |
| Add purchases of raw materials ............. | 326,148 | |
| Total raw materials handled ............... | $ 335,793 | |
| Less inventory raw materials December 31, 19.. | 13,954 | |
| Material consumed ......................................... | | $ 321,839 |
| Direct labor ................................................ | | 248,031 |
| Manufacturing expenses: | | |
| Indirect labor ........................... | $ 45,328 | |
| Indirect materials ......................... | 8,967 | |
| Power and light .......................... | 5,627 | |
| Repairs ................................. | 11,411 | |
| Miscellaneous expenses .................... | 3,018 | |
| Property taxes .......................... | 14,842 | |
| Depreciation of buildings and equipment ...... | 23,618 | |
| Insurance .............................. | 2,180 | |
| Total manufacturing expenses .......................... | | $ 114,991 |
| Manufacturing charges for the period ............................. | | $ 684,861 |
| Add inventory goods in process, January 1, 19 ..................... | | 81,131 |
| Total goods in process handled ......................... | | $ 765,992 |
| Deduct inventory goods in process, December 31, 19................ | | 94,320 |
| Cost of goods manufactured ..................................... | | $ 671,672 |
| Add inventory finished goods, January 1, 19 ....................... | | 43,884 |
| Total cost finished goods available for sale ......................... | | $ 715,556 |
| Deduct inventory finished goods, December 31, 19 ................. | | 52,460 |
| Cost of goods sold ........................................... | | $ 663,096 |

**Figure 24-3.** Manufacturing cost statement for a corporation.

## Risk and Insurance

Practically everything we do involves a certain amount of risk. When we carry on economic activities, however, it is a special problem to be *aware* of all the risks involved. The farmer is well aware of his risks and of what might happen to his crops because of weather, insects, diseases, or even market price. He does all that he can to avoid these hazards or at least minimize their effects. The manufacturer is no different from the farmer in this respect. He must recognize his risks and do all that he can to avoid them or minimize their effects.

First, the manufacturer must contend with economic variations. The business cycle may take a dip just when he can least afford it. Or perhaps there is a long-term trend taking place wherein people are changing their habits and needs. Both of these economic fluctuations might cause loss, and both are extremely difficult to guard against. But the astute businessman can watch economic trends and business forecasts, thereby minimizing the guesswork about the future. Over and above being familiar with general business and market conditions, the manufacturer can reduce his own economic risk by being in close touch with his own particular market. This he does by studying his customers, their needs, and their desires. In this way he can be more nearly certain that what he produces will meet his customers' needs, and that his customers will buy his products. This is the job of *marketing research*, which is treated in more detail in the next chapter.

The manufacturer also faces property risk. There are possibilities of fire, flood, storm, or earthquake. This type of risk can best be minimized by proper plant location and by proper selection and installation of equipment, both of the productive type and of the protective type. Productive equipment must be non-hazardous; the protective equipment, such as sprinklers and fire extinguishers, must be able to do the job when called upon. A certain amount of property risk can be shifted to others by the purchase of insurance. But this is never completely satisfactory in case of a loss. For example, even if the plant were fully insured, a fire might cause the additional loss of several months of production.

A company places a great deal of confidence and trust in its top executives. But what if one or more of these executives makes poor decisions, embezzles the company's money, or dies? What happens to the business then? This is an administrative risk that must be borne. Such risks are usually minimized by proper organization, making for the best decisions and minimizing the possibility of collusion. Independent auditors hired by the board of directors keep tab on the financial status. By good organizational planning companies provide for replacements in case something should happen to one of their top men. Finally, many companies take out life insurance on their top executives. Although the company may have a replacement being groomed for the job, some disruption still is likely when a new man takes over, and the life insurance policy will protect the profit account during that period.

Risks other than those discussed above exist for the manufacturer. Manufacturers run risks that their employees will be injured while on the job. This risk is partially covered by workman's compensation. People coming into the plant may fall or otherwise injure themselves. This possibility can be covered by liability insurance. Finally, the manufacturer runs the risk that someone else will develop and market a better product or will develop an improved and cheaper method of manufacturing the present one. Either might have a very serious effect on the future welfare of the business. The manufacturer, then, must be certain that he keeps up to date on new developments and techniques.

## Budgets and Financial Control

Budgets and their use in control have been discussed briefly in the chapter on cost control (see Chapter 17). We bring up the topic again at this point to indicate the role of budgets in the overall financial control of the business enterprise.

A complete budget is a coordinated financial plan for a business enterprise including estimates of sales, production, purchases, labor costs, miscellaneous expenses, and financial operations. Its purpose is to facilitate the planning, coordinating, and controlling of the various departments, divisions, and activities of the business. The total budget will be broken down into various departmental budgets, which will show the requirements for the departments for the period ahead. Most budget estimates are naturally stated in dollars and cents; however, in some cases supplementary estimates must be prepared in other terms. Estimates of sales and production are usually made in terms of units of product, which in turn may be broken down into various styles and sizes. Purchases must be estimated not only in dollars but in units of material required. The labor budget should indicate not only the dollars of cost but the number of workers involved and possibly the skill level of those workers required.

Costs of operation and production are naturally an important aspect of the total budgeting problem. However, the complete budget must provide for the possible expansion of plant facilities and the procurement of funds through bank loans or other sources in order to make the expansion plans possible. In addition, cash may be required to finance research activities and to finance operations until such time that payment is received for the goods produced and sold during the budget period. There is need, therefore, for a strictly financial budget, which usually comes under the jurisdiction of the treasurer or comptroller, and which is concerned largely with the flow of cash during the budget period and with the possible need to raise additional cash on the outside to meet requirements.

### Budget Preparation

One person is usually designated as chief budget officer and is responsible for the preparation of the complete budget. This person is likely to be the comptroller or someone connected with the accounting office because of his knowledge of the activities of the company and of the dollar figures of income and expenses that are associated with those activities. The chief budget officer usually does not have power to approve or disapprove a requested budget item but serves only as coordinator and adviser to the other executives and department heads as they put together their financial requirements for the budget period ahead.

The submission of any budget figures must be preceded by a study of past performance combined with an analysis of the prospects and plans for the following year. A department head must have this information at his finger tips before he can adequately prepare his proposals. The chief budget officer will probably transmit to him information from the sales forecast and production budget as his department is influenced by these items, and this information, in addition to his own knowledge of past costs, allows him to make plans for future operations. These plans are then transmitted to the chief budget officer, who then compares them with the plans and budget estimates of all the other department heads. Obviously, the various estimates must dovetail with each other, and this is the primary responsibility of the budget officer. Performance in one department may depend completely upon the performance of another department, and both must be allowed for in the budget plans. It is likely that the original budget proposals submitted by the department heads will need to be revised and resubmitted, perhaps a number of times, before a complete and coordinated plan of operation for the following year is evolved. If a company genuinely considers the budget to be an operating and controlling device, the preparation of the budget becomes a very careful operation and may require a great deal of time on the part of department heads and their staffs.

The most common budget period is one year in advance. Financial budgets including plans for the financing of plant expansion are usually made for a much longer period, perhaps ten years or more. Operational budgets, while projected for the year ahead, are usually broken down further into quarters and perhaps even months. Some companies project their budgets twelve months in advance on a continuous basis. At the end of each month the current month is dropped from the estimates and the corresponding month of the following year is added. This enables each department to make plans and commitments on a continuous basis rather than in steps. The step approach is one used by companies that set up a budget for one year or six months at a time and provide little or no opportunity to change the plans during the period in question. Smooth operation is somewhat inhibited under such a system, unless the budget is a flexible one rather than one that is fixed. A flexible budget allows for different levels of output and provides a better control over expenditures for the manufacturing operation in those plants where frequent variations in volume of production occur.

While the budget is a considerable aid in planning, coordination, and control, it should not be regarded as a strait jacket, as it might limit the exercise of good business judgment during the budget period. On the other hand, if the budget has too much "flexibility" in it, control can be easily lost. The point is simply this: in these days of professional management, no manager can afford to sit back and simply wait to see how things come out at the end of the year. Instead, he must make certain that they will come out in the manner desired, and the budget is a way of achieving this. A budget, however, is simply a plan, an estimate, and a prediction, which may not allow for all eventualities; so, realizing this, the astute manager provides all the flexibility he can in the design of the budget without losing control.

### Subsidiary Budgets

Figure 24-4 is an abridged breakdown of the total budget showing how it would be built from a sales forecast and would end in an estimated profit and loss statement and estimated balance sheet. Although this is an abbreviated picture of the budgeting process, it is designed to indicate the division of production costs into the components of labor, material, and overhead. These headings are much too broad to be meaningful in an actual budget preparation, and it should be obvious that much more detailed breakdowns are normally necessary. For example, the use of a purchases budget is common, and such a budget would estimate the purchases to be made during the coming year, taking into account the inventories of materials on hand and the established reorder points. In addition, certain purchases may have to be made in order to handle the maintenance budget, which would normally be considered a part of the overhead budget. So the maintenance budget not only has in it material requirements but a certain amount of labor requirements for various categories of repair work and

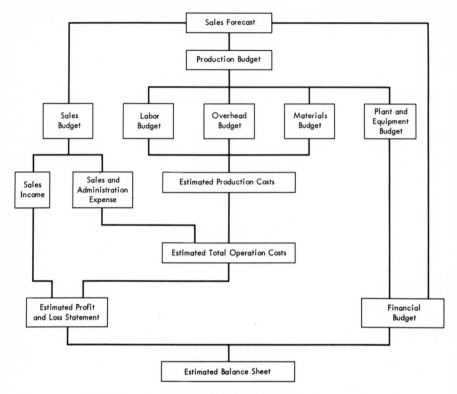

**Figure 24-4.** Development of total budget from sales forecast.

preventive maintenance. These examples should illustrate the complexity possible in budget preparation, and the need for a coordinator of this work if the budget is to have any meaning.

The plant and equipment budget shows projected changes in the investment in fixed or capital assets. Such changes would be dependent upon the requirements of the production budget and would include both the scrapping of obsolete equipment as well as the purchase of new equipment. The role of the financial budget is that of providing the necessary cash to operate the plant during the period in question as well as providing the necessary new equipment. Research expenditures would also be considered a part of the financial budget inasmuch as they relate to long-term investments rather than short-term operating expenses.

### Budget Operation

The preparation of the budget is only the first step in the total program, for the success of budgeting requires follow-up and control. The accounting department should prepare monthly or periodic reports, which show the budgeted amount for each item of income or expense, and which compare this amount to the actual amount of income and expense to date. Variations will be evident, and operating people should be asked to explain significant variations. The purpose is not to put anyone "on the spot" but to improve operations. In the long run, an operating official should be able to outline accurately his plans for the future and then be able to carry out those plans as outlined.

## Capital Budgeting

The previous discussion has dealt largely with the matter of budgeting of operating expenses, although some mention was made of the necessity to have plant and equipment items shown in the operating budget because of their close relationship. In general, however, operating budgets are considered separately from capital budgets because of the differences in the sources of funds as indicated in the first part of this chapter. Since funds for the investment in capital assets are usually limited in any given period of time, many companies are turning to the concept of capital budgeting or capital rationing in dealing with their expansion programs. Let us assume, for example, that the XYZ Company has a hundred thousand dollars available next year for investment in capital assets. It is likely that this company has a number of proposals for capital expenditures during the year to follow, and it is also likely that the total cost of these proposals is probably several times more than the hundred thousand dollars available. The capital rationing concept would then have the company list these proposed projects in order of decreasing prospective rate of return on the investment. One would then simply go down the list as far as the hundred thousand dollars available would permit and install those projects that had the highest prospective rate of return. The process is more simply said than done, but the principle is sound inasmuch as one should be certain that money is invested in projects having relatively high rates of return.

## QUESTIONS

1. Outline the various channels through which the personal savings of the people living in your community might eventually be used to finance the expansion of one of your local industries.

2. List the advantages to a corporation of financing expansion (1) by borrowing, and (2) by sale of stock.

3. Could a stockholder have any particular reasons for desiring the corporation to expand by plowing back profit?

4. What is the essential difference between the balance sheet and the profit and loss statement in connection with the date shown on each?

5. What is the main method of financing expansion employed by the ABC Company? (See Figure 24-1.)

6. What makes intangible assets intangible?

7. Someone mentions that a particular company made 12 per profit last year based on sales. Would you say this was high or low? What would you need to know in order to give a completely adequate answer?

8. What is the need for a manufacturing cost statement if you already have a profit and loss statement for the period in question?

9. Make a list of all the possible risks that a manufacturer takes and after each indicate how he can minimize that risk.

10. Does the corporate form of ownership involve fewer risks than the proprietorship and the partnership? Explain.

## CASE PROBLEMS

### The ABC Company
Financial statements for the ABC Company are shown in this chapter (see Figures 24-1 and 24-2). Referring to the information on these statements, answer the questions indicated below:

*Questions:*

1. What is the current ratio?

2. What is the proprietary ratio?

3. What is the net profit based on sales?

4. What is the net profit based on total capital employed?

5. What is the net profit based on total investment of stockholders?

6. Would you say the profit percentages computed in Questions 3, 4, and 5 are high or low? Explain your answer.

7. What is the book value of a share of common stock?

8. What factors will influence the market value of a share of this stock?

### Walker Metal Parts Company
The issue was clear to the management of the Walker Metal Parts Co.: unless new and improved machinery could be installed within the next two years, competition would drive them into bankruptcy. Slow and inefficient equipment simply cost too much to operate and maintain. Unfortunately, however, the company did not have the $100,000 necessary to make the needed purchases.

The company was considered to be in good financial condition. It had never missed paying a dividend since incorporation, some 40 years before this crisis.

Total capitalization was $500,000 when the company was formed and consisted entirely of common stock. There is currently less than $5,000 surplus shown on the company's books as a result of a rather liberal dividend policy over the years.

*Questions:*

1.  What would be the best method of raising the $100,000?

2.  Would you suggest any modification in future dividend policy? In equipment replacement policy?

# CHAPTER TWENTY-FIVE

# Marketing Management

Most of this book is about manufacturing a product. Certain chapters deal with setting up, financing, and organizing the business. Others deal with the physical facilities that a company must provide and maintain. Another group is concerned with control of the various manufacturing functions, and still others consider the employees who actually produce the product. All of these activities are necessary and worth-while, but it must be emphasized that they would all be useless without the ultimate sale of the product to a customer. The customer may be a consumer who enjoys and ultimately "consumes" the product, or the customer may be another manufacturer who makes use of the product to make still another product. Basically, all of these manufacturing activities are carried out only because the company assumes that someone has need for its product and therefore will buy it. This belief or hope that someone will buy a product cannot be left to chance. Too much is at stake for a business enterprise to concentrate entirely on manufacturing and not to concern itself with marketing. Hence the growth of the field of marketing.

We shall consider this problem of marketing particularly as applied to manufacturing. In so doing, we shall begin by noting the general nature of markets and the common channels of distribution. Following this, we will examine the five basic marketing functions performed by most manufacturing concerns.

## Classification of Goods to Be Sold

Goods that must be marketed by manufacturers can be classed into two groups: consumer goods and industrial goods. Consumer goods are those items that will be used ultimately by the household consumer. Examples are cigarettes, refrigerators, and rugs. Industrial goods, on the other hand, are those items that are used to produce other goods. Examples are machine tools, steam turbines, and overhead cranes.

Such a classification helps us to understand marketing patterns and to appreciate the different marketing techniques used. For example, one could hardly conceive of advertising machine tools, an industrial good, by means of television. On the other hand, television may be a very appropriate means of advertising soft drinks, a consumer good.

### Consumer Goods Market

The consumer goods market can be further broken down into classifications of durable goods and non-durable goods. As the name implies, non-durable goods are those that last a short length of time or that are destroyed by use or after use. Examples would be food, facial tissues, and soap. Durable goods are those items that last for some time or wear out slowly. Examples would be automobiles, household appliances, and furniture. Drawing the line between these two is often difficult. Inability to draw a definite line often leads to a classification called semi-durable goods. A typical example is clothing.

These various classifications of consumer goods create some inconsistencies when it comes to describing the characteristics of the market, but the characteristics are so decidedly different from the industrial goods market that confusion seldom results. Some of the important characteristics of a consumer goods market are as follows:

1.  It is a nationwide or worldwide market, although a company can concentrate on the market in a particular area or region. It exists wherever people live and can be no greater than the demands of these people. Certain differences in the needs and desires of people depend on the section of the country or world in which they live (snow skis do not sell well in Florida). For consumer goods markets one must look to where people live, work, or play.

2.  Most consumer goods are produced before orders are placed, rather than after, as is often the case with industrial goods. Bathing suits are made during the winter in anticipation of a summer demand. There is obviously a certain element of risk in producing goods ahead of the demand; however, this risk can be minimized by thorough knowledge of the market.

3.  The ultimate buyers of consumer goods are generally not very skilled at buying. Consumers are influenced by a clever presentation, a "fast talker," the extra services provided by the store or outlet, or the recommendations of a friend. Less thought is given to efficiency, economic values, or long-run costs in most consumer goods purchases at the user level.

4.  Most consumer goods have a small dollar value attached to them.

This, of course, doesn't hold true for durable goods; however, for non-durable goods the average item costs very little. This may account for the consumers' lack of skill in buying. Development of buying skill seems to some to be hardly worth the trouble when so few dollars are involved.

5. The final characteristic of the consumer goods market is that many items are sold through mass-distribution channels. Such items as food and drugs are well adapted to this type of distribution, as our supermarkets have discovered. In the past many specialty items have not been mass-distributed, but more and more we see consumer items, both durable and nondurable, marketed in this fashion. The growth of "discount houses" in recent years has disturbed classical distribution methods, with the result that distribution costs and prices to consumers are generally lower. As an example of the changing methods of distributing consumer goods, we note that one department store has offered for sale "his" and "hers" airplanes. (We have no information, however, concerning the number of sales!)

## Industrial Goods Market

Like consumer goods, industrial goods can also be classified as either durable or non-durable; however, it turns out that our general concept of industrial goods leaves little that is non-durable. "Supplies" are about the only industrial goods in the non-durable category. Other items such as equipment, both major and accessory, parts, tools, and materials used in production, are certainly durable.

Some characteristics of the industrial market are as follows:

1. The demand tends to fluctuate widely as business conditions fluctuate. When times are bad, users of machine tools, for example, make the old machine last a while longer instead of buying a new one. When times are good, machines are replaced and the demand is often more than the manufacturer can supply.

2. The number of prospective customers is limited, depending somewhat on the type of product. A particular machine will probably have application in a limited number of plants, although some machines or industrial items (for example, conveyors) can be adapted to many plants. Certainly the industrial market is smaller than the consumer market in number of customers, although not necessarily in number of dollars.

3. Buyers of industrial goods are generally skilled at their work. Purchasing agents enjoy a certain amount of professional stature and are tending more and more to leave personal prejudice or emotion behind when buying industrial goods. Instead they are carefully studying costs of operation, effect on safety, and productivity before signing a purchase order.

They usually ask the advice of many people within their companies before deciding on purchases.

4. Although some industrial items are produced in anticipation of demand (lubricants and standard cutting tools, for example), many are made to order. The specialized or the very large machine may have many "standard" parts, but it is usually built to meet the customer's specifications. This generally means production after the order is signed.

5. The last characteristic of the industrial market we shall mention here is the role of the engineer or technical specialist in this field. Because so many items in the industrial field are special or must be engineered to meet technical requirements, the engineer plays an important role. As a sales engineer he not only sells the product to the customer but also renders engineering service before, during, and after installation. To be only a salesman is often not enough in industrial sales work.

## Distribution Channels

Getting his product into the hands of the ultimate consumer is one of the manufacturer's problems. It is not so much a physical problem as it is organizational. The physical movement of products is a concern of the traffic department and is not to be considered here. To speak of a "channel of distribution" is to refer to the exchange of ownership of the product until it finally reaches its user. Manufacturers commonly make use of the following channels of distribution:

1. Direct to user, who may be an individual, a company, or another manufacturer.

2. Through wholesalers or jobbers, who in turn sell to retailers or to other manufacturers.

3. Through agent middlemen to other manufacturers or users.

Selling direct to users is a popular method in the marketing of industrial goods. The more specialized or technical the product, the more chance there is of selling it directly. By so doing, the manufacturer can be certain that he understands the customer's problem and is delivering what he desires. Another factor is that many industrial items require follow-up and service that can be better provided by the manufacturer than by a middleman. Without doubt direct selling gives the manufacturer maximum control over selling practices and policies, while the use of other channels tends to reduce his control.

Some consumer goods are sold direct, but with consumer markets being so broad and with many items being small in value, this method of distribution becomes rather inefficient. Industrial purchases in many cases run into the tens of thousands of dollars each, while consumer purchases average no more than a dollar or two per item. Although we often try to "eliminate the middleman," it becomes obvious that such elimination won't always bring reduced prices.

The classic distribution channel for consumer goods is through wholesalers or jobbers to retailers and then to consumers. Some industrial goods such as supplies are handled this way, particularly when no one customer purchases very much at a time. This becomes an efficient channel for consumer goods because one jobber or wholesaler can handle and deliver the products of many manufacturers to one retailer in the small quantities required. A toothpaste manufacturer could hardly sell one case of toothpaste to the local drugstore at any kind of a reasonable price. A wholesaler, on the other hand, can afford to buy toothpaste by the truckload and deliver one case to the local drugstore if at the same time he can deliver small quantities of candy, cosmetics, first aid supplies, and other items.

*Agent middlemen* are of three types: brokers, manufacturer's agents, and selling agents. One of the distinctions between the agent middleman and the wholesaler or jobber is in the matter of title to the products handled. Wholesalers and jobbers usually buy the products handled and store them until sold to their customers. Agent middlemen, on the other hand, seldom purchase the products they handle. Instead, they arrange the sale of the product and then collect a commission based on the amount of the sale.

Fundamentally, *brokers* find buyers and/or sellers for their clients and negotiate with them on price and terms of sale. Their greatest use is in the marketing of standardized goods where price is the predominant factor in determining a sale. Hides, cotton, and steel are typical products marketed through brokers.

A *manufacturer's agent* sells the products of a number of non-competing manufacturers in his particular territory of operations. He will usually handle industrial goods of fairly standard types. By selling non-competing lines for several manufacturers he can offer more complete lines to his customers and more closely meet his customers' needs. Such an agent might offer a complete line of materials handling equipment by representing a company making fork trucks, another making conveyors, a third making cranes.

The *selling agent*, also sometimes known as a selling house or commission house, assumes full responsibility for the sale of the manufacturer's product in a territory or in all markets. In a sense the selling agent is a sales department not under the control of the manufacturer. This, of course, can become a bad feature of the selling-agent method of distribution as the manufacturer may find himself with little control over selling policies and practices. On the other hand, a small manufacturer who has limited financial resources but requires wide distribution may find the selling agent the best answer to his marketing problem.

Manufacturers who are particularly concerned about having control over the price, terms, and method of sale of their products will practice *consignment selling*. Under this arrangement, title to the goods remains with the manufacturer until the goods are resold to consumers, and the retailer will make payment to the manufacturer or wholesaler after the sale is made. Many retailers and wholesalers favor consignment selling because they have no capital invested in the merchandise and are able to handle it without responsibility for the goods. The manufacturer, on the other hand, can prevent price cutting, which is often thought to be destructive to product prestige.

## Cost of Distribution

Several possible channels of distribution and their application have been discussed. Obviously, a manufacturer considers many different angles in selecting the channel of distribution that is best for him. One factor, however, that he must always consider is the matter of cost. In the long run a manufacturer will usually employ the channel that allows distribution of the product at the least cost to him. If he doesn't do this, eventually he may be out of business.

The determination of distribution costs is not an easy matter, and it is for this reason that cost analysts have tended to concentrate on manufacturing costs and bypass distribution costs. Changes are taking place, for companies more and more are realizing the need for analyzing distribution costs. Figure 25-1 shows an analysis of distribution costs of two products. Such analysis has been very enlightening to companies who thought they were making a profit on a product only to find they were actually suffering a loss.

| | Product A | Product B |
|---|---|---|
| Warehousing and handling | .63% | 8.20% |
| Delivery | .06 | .87 |
| Office | .93 | 2.33 |
| Selling | 2.50 | 2.50 |
| Administrative | 2.00 | 2.00 |
| | 6.12% | 15.90% |

**Figure 25-1.** Distribution costs for two products.

## Marketing Functions

The broad functions of marketing management consist of the following: (1) marketing research, (2) product planning, (3) advertising, (4) sales, and (5) product service. Although these operations constitute the main areas

Figure 25-2. The General Electric planning process. (Courtesy The General Electric Company.)

of marketing management and serve as units of discussion to follow, we must recognize that there are a number of other miscellaneous operations— dealing with the total marketing problem—that must be performed and that are often assigned to a marketing department. Most of these activities are discussed in other chapters of this book, as appropriate; however, when applicable to marketing situations, they are simply adapted to meet the requirements of marketing problems. They include, for example, such functions as warehousing the product, control of finished goods inventory, coordination with production scheduling, order servicing, organization of the total marketing function including the various sales units and the

**496**

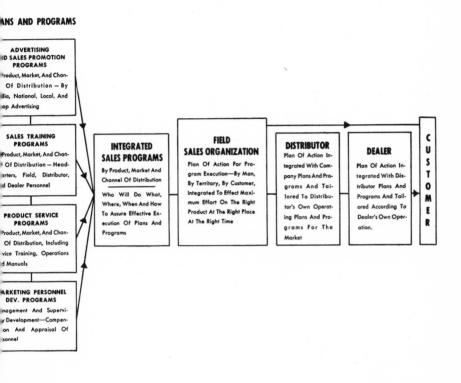

ADVERTISING
AND SALES PROMOTION
PROGRAMS
By Product, Market, And Chan-
nel Of Distribution — By
Media, National, Local, And
Coop Advertising

SALES TRAINING
PROGRAMS
By Product, Market, And Chan-
nel Of Distribution — Head-
quarters, Field, Distributor,
And Dealer Personnel

PRODUCT SERVICE
PROGRAMS
By Product, Market, And Chan-
nel Of Distribution, Including
Service Training, Operations
And Manuals

MARKETING PERSONNEL
DEV. PROGRAMS
Management And Supervi-
sory Development—Compen-
sation And Appraisal Of
Personnel

INTEGRATED
SALES PROGRAMS
By Product, Market And
Channel Of Distribution

Who Will Do What,
Where, When And How
To Assure Effective Ex-
ecution Of Plans And
Programs

FIELD
SALES ORGANIZATION
Plan Of Action For Pro-
gram Execution—By Man,
By Territory, By Customer,
Integrated To Effect Maxi-
mum Effort On The Right
Product At The Right Place
At The Right Time

DISTRIBUTOR
Plan Of Action In-
tegrated With Com-
pany Plans And Pro-
grams And Tai-
lored To Distribu-
tor's Own Operat-
ing Plans And Pro-
grams For The
Market

DEALER
Plan Of Action In-
tegrated With Dis-
tributor Plans And
Programs And Tail-
ored According To
Dealer's Own Oper-
ation.

CUSTOMER

MARKETING SERVICES DIVISION
GENERAL ELECTRIC
570 LEXINGTON AVE., N. Y. 17, N. Y.

recruiting, selection, training, placement, and development of personnel throughout the marketing department.

The General Electric marketing-planning process shown in Figure 25-2 illustrates the role of many of the marketing functions mentioned above.

## Marketing Research

The purpose of marketing research is to determine who and where the customer is; what he needs, wants, and will buy; where and how he will buy; and how much he will pay. We apply the scientific method in learning answers to these questions so as to maximize the service rendered and the net profits earned.

Some years ago manufacturers considered hunches and trial-and-error experience to be completely adequate in managing the marketing phase of their businesses. If manufacturers carried on research activities at all, they were of the technical variety such as are discussed in Chapter 22 under the heading of Research, Development, and Engineering. This early philosophy ruled out the possibility of research in the marketing field.

Today, the picture is different. Marketing research has come to be a very important part of the marketing function. Marketing research, when properly conducted, is just as valuable to the manufacturer as is technical research. However, we must quickly point out that the state of the art is not as advanced. Management will seldom know as much about the performance of the marketing function as about the manufacturing phases of the business.

Tremendous progress has been made during recent years in developing marketing research techniques and we have every reason to believe that such progress will continue. But one can appreciate the difficulties of marketing research when the intangible factors become evident. Determining how many times a refrigerator door can be opened and closed before it falls off is relatively easy, but determining why a housewife buys one kind of refrigerator in preference to another is a different kind of problem.

## Types of Marketing Research Activity

Essentially, all marketing research activity consists of the gathering, analyzing, and interpreting of facts and opinions that concern marketing, and doing so early enough to insure sound decisions in all aspects of the marketing process. Actually, it would be easy for a company to determine the success of a particular product by producing and selling it and then measuring the number of units that were sold. If very few were sold, it could be concluded that the product was a failure; if a great number were sold, it could be assumed that the product was a success. This is an expensive process, however, and few companies can afford it. A more prudent practice would be to make some studies regarding the proposed product ahead of time in order to form a basis of prediction as to its probable success, and its influence upon the company's profit and loss position.

Marketing research personnel, for this reason, conduct a number of various types of studies in order to provide the type of answers needed by all of the various marketing functions. These studies can generally be grouped into four areas outlined below, although one should realize that in an actual research program there might be considerable overlap among the four areas, depending upon the nature of the problem.

**Research relating to product or service.** This area of research is concerned with customer reaction to a product. In other words, what does he think or feel about the product? In durability tests a certain brand of refrigerator may be the best one on the market, but if potential purchasers for some reason don't like it and therefore won't buy it, then it matters little how long the refrigerator will last. Product research in marketing attempts to uncover customer likes and dislikes for products and to do so before the product is placed on the market. Typical studies under this heading might concern the following: new product development (non-engineering), improvement of present products, new uses for old products, competitive position of company's products, packaging, pre-testing of new products, customer preferences, product elimination or simplification of lines, and naming of products.

**Research relating to markets.** This type of research attempts to learn all aspects of the market for a product. In general, it will attempt to measure the size of a market, its location, and any peculiarities concerning it that may be helpful in planning a sales program. More specific types of studies would include the following: analysis of consumer markets (including industrial), analysis of wholesale markets, relative profitableness of markets, analysis and interpretation of general market data, estimate of potential sales, estimate of demand for new products, market analysis by customer, market analysis by areas, establishment of sales territories, establishment of sales quotas, competitive conditions in markets, general business forecasting, analysis of potential new market areas, and analysis of potential of old market areas.

**Research relating to sales methods.** Studies of sales methods relate largely to the problems of distribution and advertising. In the study of distribution we are attempting to select a method of distribution that will result in the lowest cost. In advertising studies we are attempting to determine the value and influence of advertising. The two main concerns in advertising research are (1) what advertising messages have greatest appeal? (copy research), and (2) where should messages be placed? (media research). More specific studies include the following: advertising practices in relation to competitors, distribution costs, sales devices, choice of advertising copy, choice of advertising media, selection of distributive channels, sales performance tests, and sales training.

**Research relating to policy.** This area of research is concerned with general company policies and not specific policies regarding new products. Success of a marketing activity may depend to a large extent on how problems are handled when they involve the following: price structure, sales methods, advertising policy, cancellations, returned goods, credit, discounts, public relations, dealer relations, transportation, sales compensation, whole-sale and dealer margins, premiums, raw materials, price changes, and in-ventory.

## The Methods of Marketing Research

There are three different kinds of basic research data, namely: (1) historical data, (2) survey data, and (3) experimental data.

The routine operations of the business enterprise frequently are recorded, and these records, often extending back through the years, provide a valuable source of information. Sales data classified by territory, product, class of customer, salesman, and so on, are frequently available from routine records without any special research effort. Also, it is possible to get from other sources a great deal of information concerning the characteristics of the various groups that constitute the consumers and potential consumers of any product. Various government bodies have such data available, and many local chambers of commerce and trade associations may have data concerning special segments of the population. The statistical analysis of the sales data of an individual enterprise and of the relationship of these data to other variables such as income or population is known as "sales analysis." Such analysis is probably more widely used than any other method of research as a basis for marketing decisions, inasmuch as the data are usually available without any large expenditure of energy or money and can be made to yield suggestive hypotheses concerning the consequences of alter-native marketing decisions.

The second major source of information for marketing research work is the survey. The survey attempts to reach a representative group of the population under study, (for example, consumers or dealers), in order to learn directly from them particular information of interest. Such information might include a reaction to a product, or an intention to buy the product within the next year.

There are two types of survey, one being a single communication with a segment of the population under study, and the other being a repeated contact, or panel-type survey. The one-time communication is usually made through a personal interview, a telephone interview, or a mailed question-naire. The interview, whether in person or by telephone, solicits answers from the respondent concerning his reaction to a product. This may refer to its design, package, or usefulness, depending upon the purpose of the study. The questionnaire does the same thing by mail but places an extra premium on careful construction of the questions, since a confusing question may bring confusing answers. The panel is simply a group of cooperative respondents who agree to give repeated reactions to new products, new designs, or new packages. The people or family chosen for the panel are necessarily supposed to be "representative" of the buying public.

The third major type of data that can be used as evidence of the probable effects of alternative marketing decisions are data arising from experiments. In this context, an experiment is a process created or conditioned by an investigator so that observations can be made that will yield meaningful conclusions concerning the relationships between the observed variables. For example, different methods of shelf display may be instituted in a number of self-service retail stores in order to observe the sales resulting from each method. Such experiments are frequently called sales tests. Manufacturers often make other sales tests on a new product by producing it in limited quantities and offering it for sale in selected outlets under rather carefully controlled conditions. Such experiments provide useful data in predicting customer acceptance of the product.

## What Marketing Reseach Does for a Business

Generally speaking, marketing research contributes in four ways:

1.  It keeps the business in touch with its markets.
2.  It uncovers new product ideas.
3.  It assists in sales management.
4.  It measures market potential.

Keeping in touch with the market reveals such things as overall market size for any specific product and the portion of the market *our* company has or can secure. Learning the likes and dislikes of the market is important and must be done on a continuing basis, for customers, whether industrial or consumer, from time to time change their tastes.

Uncovering new product ideas includes ideas for the improvement of old products as well as ideas for totally new products. A company anxious to grow and maintain its position in the market must have many good sources of new product ideas. Marketing research provides one of the better sources.

Sales management is frequently faced with problems of setting up territories, measuring territorial potential, and setting standards for salesmen's performance. Marketing research can provide a basis for answers to these problems as well as help in the making of overall sales forecasts for the company.

## Product Planning

Product planning is the function that makes certain that new products are added, old ones are discontinued, and questionable ones changed at the right time. It involves setting up clear-cut objectives for the complete line of products and adopting policies in line with these objectives. Furthermore, it is usually charged with developing the sales forecast for each product and for each territory for specific periods of time in the future. Obviously, then, the operations of product planning may be aided considerably by the results of various marketing research studies.

During periods of prosperity when industrial goods are in demand, a manufacturer tends to neglect thinking of the future. When he receives more orders than he can fill, his attention is directed almost entirely to the problems of production, but when the cycle of business reverses and he awakens to the fact that orders are no longer running his plant to capacity, he turns his attention to the cultivation of old customers and the development of new ones. By then, however, he may be too late. The wise manufacturer does not wait for a period of recession or depression before taking corrective action. Through a combination of marketing research and product planning he is in touch with the market, and he has planned his product line so as to meet the needs of his customers and thus maintain a higher level of manufacturing activity.

Product planning is a necessary activity for the long-run success of the business and must be carried out regardless of whether a buyer's market exists or a seller's market exists. Constant attention must be paid to the various product lines to be certain they are meeting the requirements of the customer in regard to performance, appearance, pricing, and service. Product simplification and component standardization are also important aspects of meeting customer needs as well as reducing costs of manufacture.

The sales forecast has an important role in the operation of a business and must be made with the greatest care. Production schedules will be set up based upon the forecast, and errors on either the high side or the low side could be very costly to operations in general. Usually, the forecast is projected for a year and then is broken down into quarters, months, or even weeks. The forecast represents a commitment on the part of the sales department and each of its divisions and becomes a goal against which the effectiveness of the department will be measured. It becomes clearer, therefore, that the sales force should actively participate in the determination of the sales forecast so that they will be motivated to put forth their best efforts.

## Advertising

A good argument can be started at almost any kind of a gathering by asking, "Why do companies spend so much money on advertising?" The argument occurs because some people regard all advertising as a waste of money and others look upon it as an absolute buying guide. Probably neither view is correct. Instead, advertising plays a role somewhere between these two extremes.

Consumers and buyers, in general, regard advertising as an informative device. Through advertising one learns of bargains at the local department store, or of the introduction of a new-model automobile. Often the potential buyer gains all of the following information:

1. The fact that a product exists.
2. Where it can be procured.
3. What it will do.
4. The price.
5. How to care for it.
6. How to use it.
7. Probable length of life.

The seller on the other hand looks at advertising as a means of reducing selling costs. Any product can be sold to a degree through the use of personal selling or salesmen. But can you imagine getting wide distribution of cigarettes solely by means of salesmen and with no advertising? It undoubtedly could be done, but the costs would be tremendous. The cigarettes would be so expensive that few of us could afford to smoke them. The same line of reasoning can be applied to almost any product. Mass production can be supported only by mass distribution, which is made possible by mass advertising. A manufacturer may use personal selling, but he will usually depend upon advertising to reduce the selling job required of his salesmen.

### Types of Advertising

Advertising can be divided into two principal types:

1. Advertising that promotes a product.
2. Advertising that promotes an idea or the name of a company.

The first type is perhaps the more common, the one that first enters our minds when someone mentions advertising. Newspapers and magazines are full of advertisements of this type—all designed to get the customers to come and buy a particular item. The approach is direct with the hope of obtaining immediate action.

Advertising that promotes an idea is a little more subtle in its approach. This type is also commonly known as goodwill or institutional advertising and is usually employed by a company in order to keep the company's name before the eyes of the public. Companies sponsoring symphony broadcasts or running special "art" paintings in magazines under the company name are using this type of advertising.

### Advertising Media

The advertising medium may be thought of as the carrier of the advertising message. Basically the problem is one of communications, for in some way the manufacturer must communicate with his customers or his potential customers. Common media used by manufacturers are:

1. Newspapers.
2. Magazines.
   (a) General magazines.
   (b) Trade journals.
   (c) Sports and hobby magazines.
   (d) Farm magazines.
   (e) Technical and professional journals.
   (f) Men's or women's magazines.
3. Radio and television.
4. Direct mail.
5. Outdoor transportation.
6. Exhibits and displays.
7. Merchandising aids.
8. Motion pictures.

Probably no one manufacturer uses all of these but instead will select those most likely to reach the market for his product. This means a careful analysis of markets so that advertising dollars can be most efficiently utilized.

Producers of consumer goods will usually employ media giving wide contact with the buying public. Popular magazines, radio, and television are widely used for this purpose. Manufacturers of producer goods, on the other hand, will be much more selective in deciding upon media. A manufacturer of machine tools, for example, will probably use direct mail, trade journals, and exhibits. Even these he will use on a restricted basis after careful analysis of what constitutes his market.

### The Advertising Agency

From the above one can see that the selection of media for advertisements is a specialized problem that can be answered only after careful research. To aid them in doing this work manufacturers frequently employ advertising agencies. These agencies, in addition to rendering advice on media, present ideas and themes for advertising programs and prepare the separate advertisements. This means that the advertising agency is simply an outside consultant; but it does not mean that the manufacturer can regard it the same as other outside consultants, because the advertising agent is paid for his services in a unique way.

The usual charge for the services rendered by the advertising agency is 15 per cent of the media cost. The advertiser is billed for the full rate, and the agency takes out its 15 per cent and remits the balance to the media. In other words the 15 per cent is not an additional charge; it is deducted from the money the media would normally receive. The manufacturer pays no more for his advertising whether or not he uses the services of an advertising agency. By using the agent he saves the expense of employing a staff of advertising specialists. In addition, if the manufacturer should become dissatisfied with the work of his agency, it is much easier to change to another agency than it is to reorganize an advertising department.

Just because the advertising agency offers so many advantages to a manufacturer doesn't mean that he will not have an advertising department as part of his organization. Such a department, however, will usually act largely as a coordinating group between the company and the agency. The advertising department will supply necessary information, product samples, and records and give approval to the campaigns laid out by the agency.

## Coordination of Sales and Advertising

We have been speaking of sales and advertising largely as separate and distinct functions in a business enterprise. Although they may be organized in this manner and shown thus on the organization chart, special emphasis needs to be placed on the need for close coordination between the two. Neither can go its own separate way without causing ultimate harm to the business.

Some companies have one man heading up both the sales and advertising functions. On paper this appears to insure close coordination, but it doesn't necessarily follow. Instead, true coordination comes through close contact among the people concerned with the two functions. For example, here are some kinds of coordination that benefit a business:

1. Advertising should pave the way for salesmen's calls. First calling the customer's attention to a new product through advertising will make a sale easier.

2. Securing leads for salesmen. Inquiries that result from advertising should be passed on to salesmen for follow-up.

3. Advertising should "contact" buyers between the salesmen's calls. This will tend to maintain interest.

4. Advertising can be used to relieve salesmen of unprofitable accounts. Rather than lose small accounts altogether, advertising could solicit what business there is.

5. Salesmen should report on customer reaction to advertising copy. In this way copy can be improved constantly.

6. Salesmen can lend assistance in planning advertising campaigns. Their knowledge of customers and territories will be of considerable aid.

## Selling

In one sense all activities of the marketing department may be considered selling; however, in this case we refer in particular to the work of the salesmen. Salesmen and sales offices are often required to perform many of the other activities mentioned under the various headings of marketing, and certainly the sales force should participate in many of these activities—sales forecasts, for example—although they may not be given direct responsibility for these areas. We are choosing to regard selling as a separate and distinct function because of its extreme importance to the success of the whole manufacturing activity.

Once the plans and policies for the manufacture and distribution of products have been established and the advertising material has been distributed through various media, it becomes the responsibility of salesmen and the various branch sales offices to make personal contact with the customers and to secure the orders. This personal approach seems to have no substitute that is fully adequate, for many customers make their choice of products in terms of their likes and dislikes of the salesman. This is particularly true in those market areas that have many competing products available. Maintaining personal contact with customers presents quite a challenge to a selling activity, particularly if the sales area involved covers a large geographical area. For this reason many companies restrict their overall marketing area in order to give better contact and service to those territories that they do attempt to cover.

There are some special considerations to be borne in mind when setting up and administering the selling function. The problems involved are different from those of a typical manufacturing department, and it is important that these differences be clearly recognized.

1. The importance of the salesman and the fact that he represents the culmination of all prior planning and effort in the entire manufacturing enterprise should be recognized. If he should fail on his job, the entire effort has been for nothing.

2. The salesman represents the company and speaks for the company. Whatever he says or does will reflect on the company in some manner and perhaps have a definite influence on present or future business relationships.

3. The salesman as he performs his duties is alone. He must often make spot decisions whether or not he is qualified, or has the knowledge to do so. Unlike someone performing a job in the plant, he cannot go ask his boss what to do about a particular situation or problem.

4. The performance of selling is a costly one and one in which it is extremely difficult to measure the benefits of money expended. One should make every effort to keep these costs low; however, the influence of personal contact with customers may be considerable, and one must guard against cutting costs to the point where accounts are not properly serviced.

It is difficult to overemphasize the importance of proper selection, training, and development of the sales force.

## Product Service

Product service is the function that makes certain that all moral and legal responsibilities connected with product performance are properly fulfilled so that customer satisfaction and repeat business are obtained. More and more, such service is becoming an essential part of the sale itself. A manufacturer of production machinery finds it essential to see that his products are properly installed. He does this not only as a service to his customers but as protection against possible complaint or general dissatisfaction. Once the equipment is installed, the manufacturer may instruct the maintenance crew of the customer in its proper care. Of course he may charge a fee for maintenance service, but this presents an additional problem inasmuch as he must then be able to provide complete and rapid service through a network of branch offices.

Sometimes the salesman is also responsible for product service, and, depending upon the complexity of the product involved, the salesman may have to be a trained engineer in order to provide the service required. Some companies employ engineers as salesmen, not only to render service after the sale, but to facilitate the sale in the first place. This practice is common in companies that produce specialized items that are highly technical in nature and require close cooperation with the customer's engineers before specifications are drawn up and the item ordered. There are many fine opportunities in industry for trained engineers who enjoy contact with customers and the challenge of solving customer problems.

Whether the manufacturer employs a combined salesman and product service man, or sets up his product service group separately from his selling group is of no particular importance for our discussion. He will follow one method or the other, depending upon the problems he faces and his ability to work out solutions. The important thing for our purposes is that the concept of product service must not be overlooked if the long-run success of the business is to be assured.

## QUESTIONS

1. Discuss the role of marketing in a manufacturing organization.

2. How would the sales organization of a manufacturer of consumer goods differ from that of a manufacturer of industrial goods?

3. From the basic characteristics of consumer and industrial markets outline desirable qualifications of salesmen for each of these markets.

4. What features distinguish the three basic channels of distribution?

5. How could a distribution cost analysis cause a manufacturer to change the basic price structure of the products he sells?

6. Describe the role of advertising in today's economy.

7. The advertising agency performs what functions for the manufacturer?

8. What are some important factors to be considered in the selection of a suitable advertising medium?

9. Make a clear distinction between product research and market research.

10. Describe the function of marketing research in a manufacturing concern.

## CASE PROBLEMS

### Canary Appliance Corporation

At its plant in Cleveland, Ohio, the Canary Appliance Corporation manufactures a complete line of small electrical appliances, including an electric iron, broiler, fry pan, blender, toaster, coffee maker, deep fat fryer, mixer, and roaster. An annual volume of sixty million dollars is sold through a variety of outlets such as appliance wholesalers, chain stores, mail-order houses, hardware jobbers, variety stores, and auto-accessory distributors. Sales to these various outlets are handled by a group of 25 salesmen who have been assigned territories throughout the country.

The manufacture of small appliances created some painting problems, and Mr. Lester Frey, who was chief engineer for the company, had spent considerable time on these problems. Two years ago he and some of his assistants developed a new paint-spraying process that cut the cost of painting in half and reduced scrap caused by poor painting to almost nothing. In addition the process was adaptable to the use of different colors, which is in line with current trends away from the traditional white.

At the time the process first showed promise of success the company applied for a patent on it in Mr. Frey's name. After the patent was issued Mr. Frey suggested that the company manufacture the various key parts of the spray-painting system and sell them to other manufacturers. He visualized a tremendous market and predicted there would be several thousands of dollars added to net profit the first year. He argued that the patent protection would minimize competition and that the company's experience in developing and using the process would enable them to manufacture it for sale to others with very little extra trouble.

*Questions:*

1. Should Canary Appliance Corp. put their spray-painting process on the market?

2. If they do, what channels of distribution should be used?

3. What problems do you visualize if the new process is marketed?

4. Outline how the company could determine the size of the market for the new paint-spraying process.

## Ace Tool Co.

For many years the Ace Tool Co. has been manufacturing and selling a line of hand tools for use by the mechanic in the shop as well as by the home craftsman. For the most part the tools were sold through hardware jobbers, although special lines were sold to mail-order houses under private labels. Total volume last year was just under $8,000,000.

Recently the company decided to develop a line of special, extremely quiet pneumatic tools for industrial use. In addition it will take on production tooling jobs on a contract basis from other manufacturers. With this expansion program the intent is to be able to supply all tooling needs of its customers.

In connection with the expansion program the sales manager was faced with two perplexing problems. One dealt with the type of salesmen that could be used in the new line of work and the other with the appropriate advertising program. He was uncertain as to the advisability of using present salesmen and present advertising methods with the new industrial sales program.

*Questions:*

1. What would be the qualifications for salesmen of the new product line?

2. Should the same salesmen be used for both lines of business?

3. What advertising media would be appropriate for the new line of business?

# Appraisal of
# Manufacturing Results

# CHAPTER TWENTY-SIX

# Management Requirements

For the most part the earlier chapters of this book have dealt with the various aspects of manufacturing and related activities that are necessary to the success of manufacturing and the manufacturing establishment. Throughout our discussion of these functions reference has been made to the managerial aspects, and in particular to the organizational problems involved. In this chapter we wish to devote more specific attention to the general problem of management. In other words, consideration will be given to the process of management itself with the contention that the process is applicable to all of the various components of a manufacturing enterprise. This does not minimize the importance of technical competence in the particular area in which a manager works, for any person in charge of a particular activity must bring to his job a high degree of technical competence as well as managerial competence.

## Management Defined

Management has often been defined as "the accomplishment of goals through others." This may be an oversimplified definition but it leads us to some points that need to be made at the outset. The first point relates to the "accomplishment of goals." Management in the true sense involves the accomplishment of goals or objectives and is not simply a position within a business. Many people have the word "manager" in their titles, but in actuality they merely preside over an activity rather than manage it toward the accomplishment of a certain objective.

The second point in relation to our definition deals with the "through others" aspect. Management as an activity is concerned with the work of other people, namely, subordinates; and it is concerned with the direction and coordination of the effort of those people. Although every manager may have a few specific duties, which only he can perform, his role as a manager, strictly speaking, is based on the fact that he must coordinate and direct the activities of his subordinates. In this sense a manager may be more concerned with the accomplishments of his subordinates than he is with his own, for their accomplishments mean the meeting of the overall goal or objective set.

Finally, in relation to our definition, we must recognize that it applies to all levels of the organization. The lowest-level supervisor is a manager in the same way as the high-level executive. Job content varies, authority varies, and the types of problems faced vary, but nonetheless all levels of an organization hierarchy are composed of managers if they have goals set as a measure of performance, and if they have subordinates who assist in the carrying out of the objectives specified.

## Management in Manufacturing

The general concept of management had its beginning in manufacturing activities, as will be recalled from our discussion in Chapter 2. Frederick Taylor's experience as an apprentice and as a worker in the factory led him to conclude that much could be gained by "managing" the operations in the factory rather than just allowing them to take place as the various workers involved thought fit. Certainly he was concerned about the practice of "soldiering," which he knew to take place, but he was also concerned by the fact that each worker was allowed to perform his task as he liked without having to conform to any standardized method or procedure. This led to his many studies in an attempt to improve operating efficiency, and these studies were of a technical and operational nature as well as of a managerial nature. However, it was his studies regarding management that essentially ushered in the general concept.

Although Taylor's background was largely in the factory, both he and his contemporaries saw the value of applying the new concepts to all phases of business life. It has been repeatedly demonstrated that success in a business activity can be insured and enhanced through the application of management principles and concepts. Admittedly, some businesses succeed *in spite* of what the management does; however, we are directing our attention toward the business that succeeds *because* of what the management does.

## Management and Ownership

To sharpen our understanding of the subject at hand we must recognize the separation of management and ownership that exists in most large manufacturing concerns today. During the hundred years prior to Taylor's time it was common for the "manager" of a concern to also be its owner. As businesses grew in size, not only with increased trade but with increased mechanization, and as more risk was involved, ownership gradually moved to the corporate form with its many owners and the spreading of risk. Of course people invest their money and accept risk only with some hope of return, and this hope manifested itself in a demand for improved performance of the organization as a whole. Heads of corporations were almost forced to introduce new methods and concepts that were being developed and publicized, if for no other reason than to satisfy the demands of the many stockholders.

The net result of all of this was and is that there are many managers throughout industry who hold little or none of the stock of the company for whom they work, but they accept a large portion of the responsibility for achieving the results desired by the corporation. True, many modern-day managers own some shares of stock in a corporation and may even have options to buy more. In most cases, however, the amount held is not sufficient to have any direct influence on the votes taken at the stockholder's meetings. Their influence is much greater in their role as an employee or manager of the corporation.

Of course many corporations are owned, and all their stock is owned by one man or a few men, who in turn manage the concern. But for our purposes these people are simply wearing two hats, one as an owner, and one as a manager. Our attention will be directed toward the role of the manager without regard to his ownership status.

### Management as a Profession

With many persons becoming interested in management as a separate and identifiable field of activity and with many persons making their living as managers, it was inevitable that there would be some tendency toward a professionalization of management. Since, indeed, this trend continues today, we must give some attention to the possibility of management becoming a true profession.

Definitions vary as to what constitutes a profession, but in general a true profession has the following characteristics:

1.  It is a specialized body of principles, skills, and techniques.
2.  It has formalized methods of achieving training and experience in the field.
3.  There is an organization composed of persons in the field with professionalization as its goal.
4.  Its conduct is guided by a set of ethical codes.
5.  Charging of fees is based on services rendered, but with due emphasis given to service rather than to monetary reward.

Although the field of management appears to be making progress in many of the areas stated above, it seems clear that management is still not fully a profession. The requirements would seem to indicate that licensing of managers would be in order, much as doctors and lawyers are licensed; however, such licensing is non-existent and there is no large movement underway to promote it. There is an abundance of literature in the field filled with principles, techniques, and specialized knowledge. However, one cannot help but feel that in many cases quantity has been used to compensate for a lack of quality. Furthermore, the direct relationship between a knowledge of this literature and success in a managerial position has yet to be fully established. In the literature increasing attention is being given to the importance of ethics, so there is evidence of improvement in this regard. There is an abundance of management consulting firms throughout the United States, so it would appear that if the charging for services rendered is a criterion for a profession, management would qualify as such in that area, at least.

Instead of just one organization whose aim is the professionalization of management, there are a number of management associations and associations of specialists all with slightly different goals and attitudes toward the idea of professionalization. Some organizations, such as the American Management Association and the Society for the Advancement of Management, deal with the subject generally and essentially act as information exchange groups. Many other associations are organized around a particular type of function or activity within an enterprise and are more concerned with the professionalization of that activity than they are with management in the broader sense. Typical of such organizations would be those of engineers (or a branch of engineering), purchasing agents, quality control people, and personnel specialists. These groups do also have an interest in management since each specialty or function must be managed, but their greater interest seems to be directed toward the speciality involved.

Management has become such a popular word in recent years, and the number of people interested in management has so increased, that it is a rare educational institution that does not offer some kind of a program to develop one's managerial skills or prepare one to enter this field. Perhaps the interest in this field of management stems more from an image of status and privilege connected with anyone holding such a position, rather than with the performance requirements attached to that position.

It is not unusual for a freshman entering college to state his preferred field of interest to his counselor as one of "management." It is questionable whether a student can devote his college years to a study of pure management as such and thereby qualify himself to perform any kind of managerial activity upon graduation. Such an attitude of the student indicates his failure to understand the technical competence that must be associated with any managerial position. It is better that he achieve technical competence in some specialized field such as accounting, engineering, or law, with the study of some managerial concepts on the side. After he has proved his worth in this technical area he can then perhaps move into a position where he can combine technical skills and managerial skills.

## Universality of Management

Though management may lack truly professional status, the principles, skills, and techniques involved enjoy considerable amount of transferability from one industry to another. Many examples can be cited of persons leaving high-level positions in one type industry and going to similar high-level positions in very diverse types of industries. No doubt there are limitations to such transferability, for it seems improbable that a successful baseball manager would be equally successful in managing the open hearth department of a steel mill.

The point is, that to the extent a second job requires the analytical, human, and managerial skills used on the first job, a person might be successful in transferring from one to another at the managerial level. To the extent, however, that the second job involves a large number of technical skills not present in the first job, nor present in the background and training of the man involved, a successful transfer could not be made until those technical skills are achieved in some manner. To illustrate, in one instance, a high-level military officer resigned and took on the position of president of a manufacturing concern. Before taking over the direction of the concern he spent almost a year touring all of its facilities and learning the many technical phases of that business. Certainly he must have been a highly capable individual to be able to do even this, and certainly he brought to the job many managerial skills he had learned firsthand in the military. However, he must be credited for recognizing that pure management ability was inadequate in an organization where he lacked knowledge of the technical factors involved.

## Responsibilities of Management

Managements of today's industrial concerns are considered to have responsibilities toward four groups: stockholders, employees, customers, and the general public.

To stockholders management has the traditional responsibility of protection of investment plus the earning of a return on that investment. This responsibility hasn't changed over the years except in the concept of return on investment. Managers today look more at long-run return on investment than at short-run return. This comes about because of the growing responsibilities to the other groups.

To employees, management today has a variety of responsibilities. Management must provide steady jobs at good pay, hours, and working conditions, besides providing for physical security during and after working hours and economic security after retirement.

To customers management must provide a quality product at a competitive price and render satisfactory service as required. This means keeping up to date with progress in the field so that customers always have available the latest improvements.

To the general public management has the responsibility of always being a good citizen. This means taking an interest in the affairs of the community, complying with the spirit as well as the letter of the law, being particularly careful about nuisances such as waste disposal, noise, or odors, and in every way appearing as an asset to the community rather than as an eyesore.

It is within the framework of these four broad responsibilities that management must operate; and operation might as well take place in a goldfish bowl, for all groups and subdivisions of each group will be watching closely for evidence of failure to live up to the responsibilities prescribed. Criticism might follow and could manifest itself in proxy fights, labor unrest, loss of sales, or restrictive ordinances. Any or all of these might result in financial loss to the company, which in turn might ultimately cause bankruptcy. No doubt the trend could be stopped before it reached the bankruptcy stage; the point here is the necessity for a balanced viewpoint toward responsibilities in place of the old saw that management's responsibility is to make a profit. Profits are necessary—so necessary that they can hardly be called a responsibility. Instead profits are an *obligation*. They *must* be obtained before management can even approach the fulfillment of responsibilities. Profits may be obtained in the short run by following a short-sighted policy in regard to the responsibilities outlined. But for long-run profits and growth of the company, management must seriously consider responsibilities to all groups rather than just to stockholders.

### Role of Objectives

Mention has been made earlier of the fact that some people head businesses and in so doing simply preside over them instead of managing them in the true sense. A significant feature of true management is the establishment of objectives and their use as guidelines in the direction of the enterprise. One can possibly argue that certainly every person in a managerial position has objectives toward which he is attempting to direct the enterprise; however, one can also just as forcefully argue that many such objectives so stated are not really driving forces throughout the enterprise but something fabricated on the spur of the moment to answer the question raised. It is relatively easy for managers to ignore objectives, for they often become so involved in performing tasks that they forget what it is that they are attempting to achieve. Also, many of us adopt the attitude of "let's see how it turns out," rather than "let's make it turn out the way we want it to."

To have meaning, an objective must have definiteness. It is not uncommon for companies to publish a list of objectives designed for popular consumption; and these objectives tend to read a little bit like the list of responsibilities mentioned in the previous section. Such a list may be desirable as general objectives, but they do not assist to any great extent in the operation of the business, for they are not sufficiently definite. Definiteness usually involves quantification. If an objective cannot be quantified, its interpretation is then open to question and no one can say whether or not it is accomplished. If one desires as an objective the establishment of a certain sales goal, it should be clearly established ahead of time how sales are to be measured, (dollars or units, for example), where we stand currently so far as these sales measures are concerned, and what we expect to achieve or where we expect to be in relation to sales at a certain definite period in the future. Some objectives defy quantification, but nonetheless many objectives now stated in rather general and nebulous form could probably be quantified if additional effort were made to do so.

The establishment of objectives should be carried out throughout an organization. In other words, one can visualize a hierarchy of objectives the same as a hierarchy of managerial levels. There would be a set of objectives for the company as a whole—in particular objectives to be met during a certain measured period in the future such as six months or one year. There would be another set of objectives for each of the main subdivisions of the business. These subdivisions of course would contribute to the attainment of the overall company objectives. A similar line of reasoning would be applied to all of the other levels within the organization, including the very lowest ranking supervisor in either the line or staff departments. Every person in a managerial capacity should have a complete understanding at all times exactly as to the objectives he and his own unit within the business are attempting to achieve. If each supervisor has such a clear understanding of his objectives, he will be less apt to get lost in the performance of tasks to the detriment of the achievement of results.

## The Functions of the Manager

The managerial functions are generally agreed to be planning, organizing, staffing, directing, and controlling. Although authors may differ slightly in their use of these terms or the order in which they are listed, there is general agreement as to the content of each function. This section discusses each of these functions and devotes some attention to the problem of coordination.

Although coordination is not generally regarded as one of the basic management functions, it is extremely important to the success of any organization.

The reader must appreciate that we are discussing these functions as having almost universal application. In other words the various activities of a manufacturing concern such as selling, production, engineering, or purchasing, all require management, and the functions we describe here all have applicability to the management of each of these activities.

### Planning

Planning in the managerial sense is the determination of what to do and how to do it. Planning, therefore, becomes a matter of making decisions from among many alternatives. Obviously, the manager must have knowledge of the many opportunities that present themselves and must have ability to create and develop opportunities, but in the long run he must be able to analyze the opportunities and to select the best one for the conditions that exist. Decisions must be made, for example as to what product lines to offer for sale, the prices to be charged, the method of production to be used, wage levels to be paid, and the amount of research to be carried on.

It is apparent that there are two kinds of planning: long-range planning and short-range planning. Long-range planning obviously stems from the company's long-range objectives and involves steps to be taken toward meeting these objectives. For example, to get a desired foothold in a certain market it may be necessary to introduce one product this year, another product next year, and to build a new plant the third year. In the short run, however, the manager must work out precisely the steps to be taken to develop and introduce the new product. In the very short run this involves the placing of orders for certain materials and the hiring and training of workers. The shorter the time period involved, the more specific the plans must be.

Much of the planning activity of the manager may be handled by various staff groups. Earlier we discussed process planning, production planning, and product planning, and although these may be the responsibility of certain designated managers, the managers may make use of staff assistants to help them work out possible alternatives and make recommendations as to the best alternatives. In recent years many of the mathematical techniques such as linear programming, PERT, and operations research generally have been used by these various staff groups to aid them in making analyses of alternatives and, later, recommendations for decisions. Let us not forget, however, that these techniques do not make decisions but only indicate guidelines for decision making. Decisions are always made by managers.

Evidence of planning in a manufacturing concern may be found in the statement of objectives and in the outline of plans to achieve those objectives. Further evidence of planning is revealed by production schedules and shipping schedules, books or statements of company policies, manuals of paperwork procedures, books of manufacturing or operating procedures, and rule books. Not all companies have all of these books, and some companies may have many more, but these are typical of printed matter found in a company that is evidence that the managerial function of planning is being carried out.

## Organizing

Organization has been discussed separately (see Chapter 3), but organization is not something that can be done once and for all and then forgotten about, for organizing becomes a basic function of every manager and one to which he must give constant attention if he is to achieve the objectives set. Basically, organizing involves the determination of the activities required to achieve the objectives established, grouping these activities in a logical basis for handling by a subordinate manager, and finally, assigning a person to the job designed. In carrying out these steps it is assumed that the manager will delegate the necessary authority to the person or persons involved as subordinates, and that these subordinates will assume the responsibility necessary.

As stated in our earlier discussion on organization, the organization structure should not be regarded as an end in itself, but as a tool for accomplishing the objectives of the enterprise or department within the enterprise. One type of organization is better than another only because it enables a better job to be done in accomplishing these objectives, not because it "looks better" or because it is one used by some other company. Every manager must perform the function of organizing, but he must also keep in mind that it is a dynamic thing and that it is a means to an end and not an end in itself.

## Staffing

Staffing as a managerial function involves the developing and placing of qualified people in the various jobs in the organization previously designed. Like organizing, this function is not performed once and for all, but must be constantly worked at in order to have qualified people available in the future to move into vacated positions or to allow the company to expand its activities. This function, therefore, includes such things as the development of manpower requirements for all the various existing jobs, the appraisal and selection of candidates for positions, and the training and development of both candidates and present incumbents on jobs in order to improve their capability and potentiality. Personnel departments and training departments frequently exist as an aid in carrying out this managerial function; however, the basic responsibility for managerial development and for staffing in general rests with each individual manager, and he cannot sidestep this responsibility by assuming that the training department will handle it for him. Good managers develop managers.

### Direction

Direction, or supervision as it is frequently called, involves the motivation and guidance of subordinates toward the objectives. The concept is a simple one and one with which we are all familiar, for throughout our lives we are constantly being guided by or are attempting to guide others. However, it is also evident in our everyday lives that the guidance of some is more effective than others. The superior manager should have knowledge of the more effective techniques of supervision and use them in order to improve the performance of his subordinates.

A detailed discussion of the methods of supervision is beyond the scope of this book, but mention should be made of a few principles of direction. In general, workers perform better on a job when they know what is expected of them and are well trained in performing that job. Furthermore, workers appreciate having knowledge concerning the job to be performed and how that job fits into the total picture. To be told to do a job simply because the boss says to do it does not usually lead to maximum performance on that job. Subordinates appreciate having some authority delegated to them and will normally develop within themselves a comparable amount of responsibility to go with the authority delegated. Every supervisor would do well to make a study of the psychological needs of people and appeal to these needs in his subordinates as he attempts to motivate them toward improved overall performance.

### Controlling

Chapter 11 was devoted to a discussion of the fundamentals of control, and many of our manufacturing activities have as their role in life the control of manufacturing performance. Control compels events to conform to plans. Compelling events to conform to plans invariably means determining what person or persons are responsible for the deviation from plans and taking the steps necessary to see that these persons modify their performance. Although we have many aids and tools for this process, basically things are controlled by controlling people.

### Coordination

Coordination is not generally regarded as a separate function of the manager, but it is so essential to the successful performance of any manager that we wish to devote some attention to it. Basically, it is the achievement of harmony of individual effort toward the accomplishment of organizational goals. In this sense it becomes particularly important as an aspect of the function of direction.

Communications play an extremely important role in coordination, for many breakdowns in coordinating efforts occur because people simply do not have the information or knowledge they need in order to bring about coordination. Coordination is also facilitated if the persons involved have had some part to play in the planning and policy-making phases of the management process. This does not mean that the manager should abdicate his planning role, but simply that he might facilitate his own task of direction and of coordination by allowing his subordinates to assist him in the developing of plans. The plans themselves thereby become much more important to the subordinates, and they normally put forth greater effort to be certain that these plans are carried out successfully. Informal relationships within a company also tend to facilitate coordination, for workers who know each other well outside the job will normally work together better on the job.

## Principles of Management

Frederick Taylor developed what he called principles of management, which were intended for rather broad application; however, his emphasis was not upon general management but upon management at the shop level. He was mainly concerned with the efficiency of workers and managers in actual production. As it happens, a French industrialist by the name of Henri Fayol was also interested in management and was writing on the subject at about the same time as did Taylor. Fayol was primarily interested in the other end of the managerial hierarchy, for he held the managing directorship of a coal company in France for a number of years before his retirement in 1918.

Fayol's book, *General and Industrial Management*, first appeared in France in 1916; however, an English version of his book was not available in the United States on a general basis until 1949. His work has had a profound influence upon the development of management thought throughout the world, and we cite his work as being important in the development of managerial principles and as having a great deal of application today.

Fayol warned that principles of management must be flexible and not absolute—must be usable regardless of changing conditions. He listed fourteen such principles that grew out of his experience, and these are summarized as follows:

1.  Division of work. Fayol applies this principle to all kinds of work, managerial as well as technical and factory work.
2.  Authority and responsibility must be related.
3.  Discipline.
4.  Unity of command—meaning that employees should receive orders from one superior only.
5.  Unity of direction. This means that each group of activities having the same objective must have one plan and one head. This is a broader concept than the unity of command mentioned above.
6.  Subordination of individual to general interest.
7.  Remuneration must be fair and bring the maximum satisfaction to employees and employer.
8.  Authority should be centralized to the degree that it will give the best overall performance.
9.  Scalar chain. Fayol thinks of managers as a "chain of superiors", from the highest to the lowest ranks. Though one should not depart from the chain needlessly, the chain should be short-circuited when its strict following would be detrimental to performance.
10.  Order. By this Fayol refers to the idea that everything and everyone has his place or role in the organization.
11.  Equity. Managers should deal with subordinates with kindness and justice.
12.  Stability of tenure.
13.  Initiative. Fayol advised his managers to sacrifice their personal vanity in order to permit subordinates to exercise their own initiative.
14.  *Esprit de corps.* Here, Fayol emphasizes the need for teamwork and the importance of communications in obtaining such teamwork.

Fayol was careful to point out that his list was not an exhaustive one but was simply a list of those principles he had had the most occasion to use. We offer the list with the hope that the reader will appreciate the need for some general concepts or principles to apply in any managerial situation that may arise. Principles are not meant as cut-and-dried answers to managerial problems, but simply as guides to the decision-making process necessary to solving problems.

## Schools of Management Thought

With all the interest shown in management on the part of students, teachers, researchers, and practitioners, it was inevitable that different schools of management thought would evolve, and that the proponents of each school would advocate that their approach was the best. In actuality there are probably as many schools as there are persons who study the subject, but the major schools are discussed in the following paragraphs:

### Management as a Process

The process school of management regards it as the performance of certain activities or functions by a management member of an organization as compared to a non-management member. The performance of these functions is considered a process, and the school analyzes the process establishing a conceptual framework and identifying the principles involved. Fundamentally, this school is the one followed by Taylor and Fayol as discussed herein.

### Experience

The experience or empirical school emphasizes the study of managers—successful and unsuccessful ones. Typical of this school are those that study cases, and these persons expect the student to draw general conclusions from the study of a number of individual situations. In this way a student is expected to achieve a type of "experience" as he makes a detailed study of one company or one situation. Precedent would play a large role in any later managerial action that might take place, and there are those who feel that precedent cannot always be relied upon to solve the problems of a dynamic age.

### Human Behavior

The human behavior school of management thought simply recognizes that management is a series of relations with people. Hence, it concentrates on the understanding of people and why they do what they do. This school results from the application of the behavioral sciences, especially psychology and social psychology to the management problem. Certainly one cannot minimize the influence of human relations, motivation, communications, training, or leadership in the management process.

### Social System

The social system school of management uses management as a system of cultural interrelationships. This school of thought comes from the behavioral sciences and is sometimes confused with the human relations school. This school is sociologically oriented and seems most concerned with the identification of various social groups and therefore considers management and, in fact, a company as a whole as social groups interacting with other social groups in a given community. One cannot deny that an analysis of social behavior and a study of group behavior in the social system has great value in the field of management, but one can question whether this aspect should be allowed to dominate management thought.

### Mathematics

The mathematics or quantitative school of management regards management as a logical process that can be expressed in terms of mathematical symbols and relationships. Perhaps the most widely known persons of this school are the operations researchers or operations analysts, who frequently call themselves "management scientists." Although this school is a relatively recent one, it has grown rapidly and has been very useful in many areas of management.

Many of these concepts have been discussed earlier in this book; however, it must be remembered that the success of this approach depends entirely upon the ability to define and quantify all of the variables involved in a particular problem and then work out mathematical relationships, which can identify possible solutions. This means that the most useful areas for these techniques have been those that relate to physical problems of management such as production control and inventory control. Problems dealing with human behavior seem to defy this approach at the present state of the art.

Again, the schools of management thought referred to above should not be considered an exhaustive list of those that exist. Indeed, two other schools are often mentioned, namely: the decision theory school and the economic analysis and accounting school. The decision theory school concentrates on the achievement of a rational decision and the selection from among a number of possible alternatives. The adherents to this school would concentrate upon the evaluation of alternatives, and in recent years they have depended more and more upon mathematics and statistics as a means of evaluation so that it becomes difficult to discern this school from the mathematics school. The economic analysis and accounting school concentrates upon the role that costs play in managerial problems. To this way of thinking all managerial decisions are cost decisions. Unfortunately, this school must get the bulk of its data from past performance or from past costs; so this method may tend to perpetuate past practices rather than allow for the innovation necessary for managerial process.

In summary, it is safe to say that all of these various schools of management thought have a role to play in management performance. It is difficult to defend one school of management thought to the exclusion of all the rest. Furthermore, it would be unwise to apply one school of thought to the exclusion of others in an actual managerial situation. All schools of thought should be encouraged to grow and develop so long as they have anything of value to contribute to the improvement of managerial performance. However, in the final analysis, managerial performance should be judged against the criteria applied rather than whether or not the manager happens to have followed any particular school of thought. The last chapter deals with the general subject of the appraisal of management performance.

## QUESTIONS

1. Describe the coordinating role of management.

2. Select some company with which you are familiar and develop a series of statements outlining the responsibilities of the management of that company.

3. Do profits come to a company after responsibilities have been met, or must a company make a profit before it can meet its responsibilities?

4. Compare and contrast "scientific management" with "management science."

5. Managerial positions are held by many people who are not managers in fact. Explain how this can be.

6. Compare the job of a plant foreman with that of a vice president of manufacturing as far as the five basic functions of management are concerned. To what extent does each apply to the two jobs?

7. Does engineering qualify as a profession according to the criteria stated?

8. How successful could a department store manager expect to be as a baseball team manager?

9. Outline a reasonable set of objectives for each of the various levels in a manufacturing concern of your acquaintance.

10. Can you defend one school of management thought over the others? What is the basis of your argument?

# CASE PROBLEMS

## Welsh Manufacturing Co.

From its beginning the Welsh Manufacturing Co. has been known as a progressive concern, both in its products and in its management. All members of the board of directors are active in the management of the company and are constantly pressing for progress, improvement, and innovation.

For the past several months the board has been considering new management tools that have been discussed in management literature—operations research, linear programming, and data processing. In line with their usual philosophy the board members are anxious to employ these tools as soon as possible. In this case, however, they are not certain exactly what is meant by the words that express these new management concepts, nor are they sure how they differ from the tools the company has used in the past.

To assist in their analysis they asked Mr. David Kern, a management consultant, to meet with them and discuss these new tools. Mr. Kern has been in the consulting business a number of years and is highly respected by the Welsh board of directors.

*Questions:*

1. Does the board of directors of Welsh Manufacturing Co. seem to belong to any particular school of management?

2. Outline some feasible approaches Mr. Kern could take in answering the questions raised concerning these new management tools.

3. Outline a program for this company to follow in taking advantage of these new management tools.

4. How should Mr. Kern conduct himself in this situation, if he is to be a true professional?

## Turbo-Trucks, Inc.

The growth of Turbo-Trucks, Inc., over the past 10 years has been phenomenal. Although having started with little more than an idea for a new type fork-lift truck, Walter Lapp is now president of a concern that has over 800 employees and does about ten million dollars worth of business a year in fork-lift trucks. In spite of his past success Mr. Lapp felt that his turbo-truck market could not last forever and that certainly within five years the company would be in serious difficulty unless it diversified its product line or at least developed some improved versions of its fork-lift truck line.

To this end Mr. Lapp was considering setting up a research and development department and was prepared to spend a considerable sum of money to get the department organized and some research projects launched. He was not interested in spending money on research and development for its own sake or simply because everyone else in the industry was doing so. He did want to go slow in getting organized and be fairly certain of success before getting into any expensive projects.

In discussing the problem with a management consultant, Mr. Lapp learned that many companies regularly spend 3% of every sales dollar on research and development and that frequently it takes ten years or more before a new research and development department can produce enough results to pay its own way. Mr. Lapp was surprised by these predictions but still thought that under proper guidance a research and development department could get by on a smaller budget and could produce fruitful results sooner.

*Questions:*

1. Outline how Mr. Lapp could apply the basic managerial functions in establishing his new department.

2. Is Mr. Lapp correct in his feeling that his company must diversify in the future?

3. How can Mr. Lapp keep "control" of the new department so as to reap benefits at minimum cost?

4. What peculiarities do you see in the *planning* or research and development as a new activity as compared to any of the activities discussed in other chapters?

# CHAPTER TWENTY-SEVEN

# Appraisal
# of Results

This book has had for its purpose the familiarization of the reader with the many activities and functions that make up the modern industrial enterprise. For the most part the various functions discussed would be handled by staff groups and would be designed and set up in a manner that would aid the operating people in performing their work. Operating people, or the line, are usually charged with carrying out the specific objectives of the business, namely, manufacturing a quality product to sell at a competitive price.

These simple statements outline generally the assignments of staff departments (perhaps more appropriately called "service departments") and operating departments, but how does one determine whether any department is performing the job assigned to it? How can results be measured? Indeed, how can it be determined whether or not the management of the entire company has been successful in carrying out its mission? Answers to these questions are not simple, but in this last chapter we would like to discuss the appraisal problem.

## Objectives as a Basis for Appraisal

Throughout this volume much has been said about goals, objectives, and purposes, not only as related to the business as a whole but as related to all the various divisions, departments, or functions carried on within the business. In other words, we have emphasized that any and all activities in a manufacturing concern should be carried on for a particular purpose or with a view toward the contribution which that activity can make to the business, and should not be carried on simply for the sake of that activity. Much has been said about control and the fundamentals of control; and the reader will recall that the first step of control was that of developing a plan or purpose. Our point here is that appraisal of results is not to be regarded as a separate type of problem, but is to be considered in relation to the results that were initially desired.

The use of objectives will not solve all of the problems of appraisal, and in many cases, may simply transfer the problems of appraisal to the problems of setting objectives. However, this is a desirable transfer, for it will concentrate attention upon those factors that should contribute to the success of the enterprise. More will be said on the setting of objectives later.

## Coordination of Functions

It was stated above that operating or line departments are charged with carrying out the direct objective of the company, and staff departments exist for the purpose of assisting or servicing the operating departments. There will be very little argument about the fundamental principle covered by this statement, but there will be arguments concerning the details of carrying out this principle in any industrial situation. Operating departments often back away from their responsibilities while staff departments overstep their authority and encroach on the "rights" of other departments or functions. This is where coordination by management plays its important role. Instead of allowing each department to go its separate way, management must see that the efforts and activities of each department, whether operating or staff, contribute to the good of the business as a whole. The building of individual empires within the organization structure must not be permitted unless such empires fit into the overall company picture and can make a worthwhile contribution. Departments must not be allowed to assume a minor role just because they are headed by an unimaginative person, if it is decided that for the long-run good of the business these departments should play a major role.

This, then, is the coordinating job of management—captain of a team of specialists. Each specialist (department) knows more about his own field than any other and may become so engrossed in that field that he loses perspective. It will be easy for him to forget that what he does in his department must be integrated with the activities of other departments. Management must serve as the integrator, the coordinator, and, in extreme cases, the arbitrator of conflicting interests.

## Appraising Functions

Appraising the results of the efforts of operating or line departments is relatively easy. The outputs of such departments are measured in units produced and such output can be compared with schedules or with outputs during previous periods as well as with total budget figures. Using cost-control figures, the cost of this production, broken down into various categories such as wages and materials, can be compared with costs from previous periods or with ideal costs. Quality control records will indicate quality levels of production, and other figures may be available showing machine efficiencies or yields. It can be seen, therefore, that the operating departments represent the basic reason for the existence of the manufacturing enterprise, and appraisal of the results of the efforts of operating departments is facilitated by the many control techniques available to management.

Staff departments, such as personnel, engineering, or purchasing, present different kinds of problems. Their mission is to do everything possible to assist the line or the operating departments, and if they perform their mission properly, the operating department has an even better record. But how much of the improved record is due to the efforts of the staff department? If the work of the staff department were expanded, would even better operating performance be obtained? What would be the effect on operating performance if staff activities were somewhat curtailed?

Any attempt to answer questions such as these runs directly into a characteristic of human nature, for seldom will anyone in a staff capacity suggest that his work should be curtailed, that he is not making a sizeable contribution to the company's welfare, or that he couldn't increase his contribution by an expansion of his activities. With such an attitude on the part of staffs, efforts toward appraisal may be directed more at justification of existence rather than at an evaluation of efficiency. For example, training departments often report the number of employees trained or number of hours spent in training during any month or year. There is no doubt that such figures represent *activity* but do they represent *contribution*? Similar examples could be cited for other staff groups.

This is not to condemn staff departments or their attempts to justify their existence; instead, the hope is to distinguish between the reporting of activity and the appraisal of results. Almost by definition staff departments are in a difficult position on this score and so must devise ways to measure results. Returning to the training department: a measure of knowledge obtained or of skills acquired by employees would be much more revealing than the number of hours spent in training periods. This would not only show that the department had been busy but would also demonstrate to top management that results had been obtained and that the position of the company had been strengthened.

Even if such a technique as this were readily available to training departments, management would still be faced with a problem of coordination and control. From an overall company point of view, what knowledge should be imparted to employees? What skills should they be trained in? What skills are apt to be needed five to ten years from now? Is it easier and cheaper to hire people with these skills than to use training programs? Do we train for the sake of training—or because we see a need for that training in the company?

These questions must be answered by management in all cases. Management must define both short-range and long-range objectives and goals for the company and then interpret these for each department or function within the company's organization. In our example this would mean outlining precisely the role of the training department within the framework of overall goals and objectives. With such a clear statement of objectives, it becomes easier for accomplishments to be appraised later on, for the task reduces itself to one of simply comparing standards with results. Training directors, as well as the heads of other staff departments, would do well to secure a clear-cut agreement with their superiors about goals and objectives both for the long run and for each six-month or annual budget period in the future. When the budget period is complete, the staff department head compares the record with the objectives. He will need to be on the defensive only if he hasn't live up to his stated objective.

Top management will be faced with setting objectives for each department and with being certain that objectives for all departments dovetail together. This usually can be facilitated by obtaining the active participation of all department heads in the preparation of plans and in periodic conferences at which progress is discussed. The preparation of budgets also serves as a coordinating device, for price tags must be placed on all projected activities, which gives a common denominator to all plans. Participation of all concerned in preparing plans, setting up budgets, and periodically appraising progress will do much to get department heads to adopt a broad point of view—to put company goals first and department goals second.

## Appraising Managers

It is probably a moot point whether one can distinguish between the appraisal of a particular function and the appraisal of the manager who happens to be in charge of that particular function. After all, if the record of performance for a particular function is commendable, does it not follow that one should commend the man in charge of that function? The answer is "yes." Generally speaking, the criterion for judging managers should be performance; i.e., to the extent that performance can be meaningfully determined. It is true as we have pointed out before that in some cases companies have been lucky enough to succeed in spite of their management, and not because of it. But conversely, it is not true that some companies fail, despite having "good men" in charge. When companies do poorly in the market place and in profits, and their managers have the authority to match their responsibility, then quite simply these managers are not "good men" at their jobs, despite any other virtues they may have. When appraising managers, "the proof is in the pudding."

Let us not overplay the point, however, for there are some instances when it is not only desirable but necessary to try to appraise an individual and his performance separately from the performance of the activity in which he is engaged. Such an instance is when we are dealing with trainees. We are expecting a trainee to comprehend new material daily and to qualify himself to undertake certain duties and responsibilities in the future. In the classroom, tests can be administered to measure progress, and such a procedure is sometimes used in the training situation in industry. More often, however, the trainees' supervisor is forced to rely on his own personal judgment as to the progress of the trainee and his readiness to move on to the next position. Even in the training situation, however, it is often possible to assign specific and short-range tasks to the trainee and then measure his performance on this task in terms of objective results.

Also, in approaching the problem of appraising managers, the differences among staff-type activities must be kept in mind. Many staff assignments are of a purely consultative or advisory nature, whereas others are more accurately described as service-type functions. Consider the quality control function as an example. Without attempting to completely identify the nature of quality control in industry, it can be recognized that quality control might have several facets. One function might be to study and recommend control plans to management. A measure of performance for this role might be related to the outgoing quality of the product shipped. On the other hand, one function of quality control might simply be that of making periodic checks on the actual quality of product being produced and posting the results of these checks on control charts. Whereas this activity contributes to quality of the final product, it really becomes a kind of routine service activity, and performance is probably measured in terms of postings on charts, time taken to make a round of checks, or cost of the overall activity. These two measures of performance are of decidedly different characteristics, the first dealing with study and creativity and the second more with observance of strict routine. It would seem desirable, therefore, to take this difference into account when appraising the men in charge of these respective activities and look for other characteristics in the nature and behavior of these men that might make them more valuable to the company in some other assignment. In many cases a manager can only do as well as he is offered the opportunity to do. Another assignment might provide that opportunity; so one must make some evaluation as to the potential of the person involved, even though there are few opportunities to measure that potential on the present assignment.

## Tools for Appraisal

Appraisal tools have been mentioned throughout a number of the previous chapters. However, since we are attempting to summarize the problems of appraisal, at this point it is appropriate to summarize some of the tools available. A very common type of tool is the computation of some ratio, index, or percentage in connection with an activity or department. Seldom do ratios have meaning in and of themselves, but they are useful when comparing one time period with another, or comparing one department with another. Following are some examples:

$$\text{Labor turnover} = \frac{\text{Number of separations}}{\text{Average payroll}}$$

$$\text{Machine efficiency} = \frac{\text{Quantity of production} \times 100}{\text{Theoretical production capacity}}$$

$$\text{Materials yield} = \frac{\text{Materials in the product} \times 100}{\text{Materials used in producing the product}}$$

$$\text{Labor efficiency} = \frac{\text{Standard times} \times 100}{\text{Actual time}}$$

$$\text{Departmental performance} = \frac{\text{Products produced}}{\text{Products scheduled}}$$

Many more examples could be cited, but this should be sufficient to illustrate the prossibilities of arriving at some formulas or ratios that would aid the appraisal process. Interest in appraisal falls into three categories, namely, outputs, time, and costs. Outputs are ordinarily subdivided into quantity of output and quality of output. Formulas as an aid in appraisal usually involve one or more of the above categories. The Gantt chart, PERT, and the critical path method (discussed in Chapter 14) are all examples of appraisal techniques, although they are planning techniques as well. The combination of planning and appraisal in the same system is an advantage of these techniques. The Gantt chart method is the oldest and probably the most widely used, inasmuch as it is easy to apply and requires no special forms, tools, or computations. True, it does not lend itself to more complex scheduling and production problems, but it does provide an inexpensive method for planning and appraising performance as far as time schedules and production schedules are concerned.

Control charts were discussed in Chapter 15 in connection with quality control. These charts constitute a means of both planning and appraisal so far as quality is concerned. It is common for us to think of these control charts in connection with quality work, but there is no reason why these same basic statistical concepts cannot be applied to other types of activities as well. Why not control employee turnover in the same manner that we control quality of product? Looking at past records we could compute three sigma limits based upon the array of data we have available, and then be in a position to appraise our employee turnover in the future more adequately. Such action would allow us to appraise our turnover as to whether it was significantly higher or significantly lower than past performance.

Budgets are also useful tools of appraisal—as well as planning devices. If all plans for each product, department, or activity contain realistic and meaningful budget figures, their appraisal is facilitated. A comparison between planned expenditures and actual expenditures permits management to appraise past performance and to provide for improved performance in the future. Caution must be exercised, however, in requiring that all expenditures coincide exactly with the plans in all categories. Such procedure may place unnecessary burdens upon supervisors and detract from their carrying out other important duties. Although in general costs should be as low as possible, this may not be true in all categories of cost; and this possibility must be borne in mind. In maintenance, for example, a reduction in current expenditures may mean a major breakdown in the future. Similarly, curtailing salesmens' travel expenses under budgeted figures may mean that they are not sufficiently servicing their customers, and as a result orders may fall off in the future. In other words, in using budgets as an appraisal tool management must ascertain that a savings in cost in one category will not result in a future larger expenditure in another category.

## Management Appraisal

Appraising the achievements of operating and staff departments presents some problems as discussed above, but let us now consider the question of appraising the management itself. How well has the company been managed? What measures are available to indicate good or poor management? How can opportunities for improvement be brought to the foreground?

Appraising the performance of management is of considerable importance because of the prevalence of hired managements over owner-management in industry today. Managers who are also owners can operate their business almost any way they see fit. Hired managers, on the other hand, are forced to please not only owners but other groups as well, as we have seen in the last chapter.

Each group will appraise using its own particular sets of standards, but we will want to examine the problem without regard to satisfying the desires of any one group. Instead our goal will be to achieve that delicate balance point where all groups are reasonably well satisfied. This is practically an impossible task, but hired management in today's world is forced to try.

### Approaches to Management Appraisal

Managements have been appraised for years by simply looking at the balance sheet and profit and loss statement for a particular period. From these statements certain ratios and indices are computed that give indication of management efficiency. Such a method of appraisal is at least partially satisfactory. It won't tell the whole story of how good an overall job management has done, but it tells some of it—provided that some standards of financial performance have been established.

Certain inadequacies of appraisal by financial statement are evident. For example, in looking at financial statements we are tempted to conclude that so much profit was made per dollar of sales. This may be true on the average, but it doesn't represent the true situation for all sales. This was shown in our earlier discussion of breakeven charts (see Chapter 17), which clearly indicate losses on sales up to the breakeven point and profits on sales above that point. This comes about because of certain fixed costs that exist in a manufacturing business whether or not any products are made and sold. Knowing a company's breakeven point assists in appraisal, for it serves as a sensitive barometer in indicating the need for a change in operations to insure profits.

Another difficulty with the use of financial analyses as a sole means of management appraisal is that seldom can one obtain from such analyses any indication of future strength or prospects for a company. Financial strength can easily be ascertained from a balance sheet, but at no place on the balance sheet is there an indication of new product development that might be necessary for the future of the business, nor is there a place to indicate what is being done to train and develop managers for the future operation of the business. Almost by definition, financial analyses must simply be analyses of the past. Other methods of appraisal are usually necessary in order to measure the company's position in relation to its preparation for the future. A discussion of some of these methods follows.

An approach to management appraisal is the *management audit*. A management audit is usually a subjective comparison of a rather detailed breakdown of the responsibilities of management with actual performance or with company policy in regard to each item. In this way the auditor can arrive at a general conclusion as to how well management has fulfilled its responsibilities. Management audits are not conducted usually for the purpose of arriving at a numerical answer pertaining to performance, but instead to uncover opportunities for improvement. For example, should the audit reveal a policy of giving employees only two paid holidays per year when the national average is nearer six, management has had pointed out an opportunity to improve. Without a periodic audit covering specific points of importance, management will often become lax and make inaccurate or wrong assumptions concerning its performance. The audit forces a fresh look from time to time.

Some companies attempt to audit themselves, and this procedure is satisfactory to the extent that the internal auditors can be objective in their phrasing of questions and acceptance of answers. Many companies, however, bring in outside consultants to conduct audits, feeling that these outsiders have had wider experience at the audit type of work and, also, will bring a fresh outside point of view to the whole procedure. In either case the audit should be regarded as a "fresh look" at the company's position and should attempt to evaluate where it is, where it is heading under present programming, and whether its present objectives and plans to meet those objectives are still valid in the light of any changes in the social, technical, or political environment. It is relatively easy for managers at all levels to become so engrossed in day-to-day activities that they overlook an evaluation of overall performance in relation to long-range objectives. The management audit, if made annually, or perhaps every two or three years, might serve to force managers at all levels to stop and consider both current goals and future ones. Frequently, even day-to-day decisions will be simplified by a clear picture of where the business is headed.

The American Institute of Management has done considerable work on the problem of management appraisal and has devised a system that is fundamentally an extension of the audit idea mentioned above. When appraising the management of a particular company, the institute employs a list of 301 questions, which are asked of corporate officers, as well as many other sources inside and outside of the company. Answers to these questions allow the institute personnel to assign ratings to each of ten categories that are considered important areas of management performance. The ten factors are:

ECONOMIC FUNCTION.
CORPORATE STRUCTURE.
HEALTH OF EARNINGS.
SERVICE OF STOCKHOLDERS.
RESEARCH AND DEVELOPMENT.

DIRECTORATE ANALYSIS.
FISCAL POLICIES.
PRODUCTION EFFICIENCY.
SALES VIGOR.
EXECUTIVE EVALUATION.

The maximum number of points possible is ten thousand, although there are different weightings given to each of the ten categories. For example, 500 points is the maximum number possible for corporate structure, and 2200 the maximum for executive evaluation. The minimum number of points necessary for a company to be considered excellently managed, in the eyes of the AIM, is 7500, and each year the AIM publishes a list of companies that have been rated by them and have achieved a minimum number of points for an "excellence" rating.

The AIM system of management evaluation leaves much to be desired, for among other things it is difficult to understand how the answers to 301 general questions can be translated into point values. However, the effort should be commended for its attempt to stress excellence in management and to develop some kind of quantitative measure of that excellence. Certainly, if the same system and criteria are applied to a company from time to time the answers will have meaning from a comparative standpoint and will indicate management's opportunity for improvement. It should be noted, in all fairness to AIM, that in publishing the system they are careful to note that the system was developed as a comparative guide and that the values derived should not be regarded as statistical measures.

## Management Decentralization

For many years the du Pont Company and the General Motors Corporation have not only decentralized their manufacturing operations but have decentralized their management as well. Each division head is held directly accountable for the operation of his division in all respects and can operate his division more or less as a separate company. In du Pont the appraisal of each division head is based largely on "return on investment" computed as is illustrated in Figure 27-1. The influence of intangible factors is recognized, but this method of decentralized management puts the division manager in "business for himself," and under these circumstances return on investment must be satisfactory in the long run.

The success of this philosophy of operation has been so great that many other large companies have adopted it (Ford and General Electric among others). Smaller companies that do not have large separable divisions can still use the same basic idea by setting up profit centers. A department, group

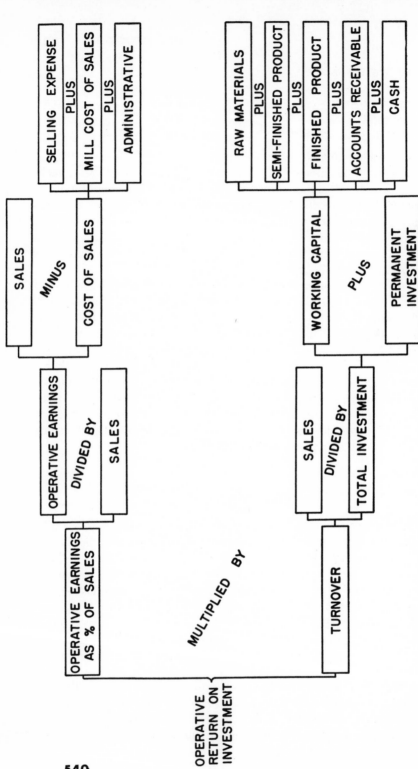

**Figure 27-1.** Return on investment computation as used by the du Pont Company. Read from right to left. (Courtesy the du Pont Co.)

of departments, or product can be set up on a profit-or-loss basis. Monthly reports as to profit or loss for that particular operation will have more meaning to all concerned than efficiency or labor turnover figures. Efficiency and labor turnover figures are important, but they do not have quite the impact and meaning of a report showing that on the X line of products the company lost $5000 last month. The manager of the X line can readily see that prompt action on his part is needed, for in the final analysis the success of a business is determined by whether or not it makes money.

## Management—an Art, or a Science?

In this chapter we have seen the great difficulty experienced in attempting to appraise adequately the efforts of management. One may well ask if the appraisal task is an art or a science—in fact, is management itself an art or a science?

It is has been over half a century since Frederick Taylor pointed out such a job classification as "management." Taylor called his concept "scientific" management, but how far have we come during this time toward a *real* science of management? We wonder how anyone in a managerial position conducts himself from day to day and arrives at the many decisions necessary. Are intuition and experience his only guides, or is there some science connected with his work, a science he can expect to learn and to apply in the fashion that he learns and applies the law of gravity?

Throughout this book the reader will see numerous instances where the management of a particular function has become more a science and less an art. The development of quality control techniques is an outstanding example. In recent years the efforts of a great number of individuals and groups have been directed toward making management even more a science. In general, this work involves the application of mathematics and statistics in the solution of managerial problems. Much of the work has yielded very beneficial results, and there is little doubt that even more benefits will be forthcoming as its use increases.

In spite of the development of the management sciences, it seems unlikely that the "art" of management will become extinct in the near future any more than the factory worker will in the near future be made extinct by automation. The application of management sciences and computers may enable some decisions to be made automatically, but as long as the human being is a factor in production and consumption, the "automatic decision" will have to be tempered with good judgment. The application of management sciences, however, should improve the performance of management in general and make the task of appraising performance much easier.

## QUESTIONS

1. Outline how one might appraise the work of a production control department, including any "measures" that you can think of.

2. In the measures you developed in answer to the above question, can you distinguish between those that represent "activity" and those that represent "contribution"? Which are more important?

3. Explain how top management should "control" the work of the training department.

4. How does decentralization assist in solving the appraisal problem?

5. Cite some examples of management problems and possible answers that show the difference between management as an art and management as a science.

6. To what do you attribute the success of General Motor's use of the managerial decentralization concept? Why aren't other companies rushing to take advantage of this idea?

7. List as many devices or techniques as you can that would assist the coordination of activities and functions within a company.

8. How can computers be used to aid the appraisal task?

9. Discuss the appraisal problem as it applies to you and your schoolwork. Can you differentiate between "performance" and "activity"?

10. In what ways can the management audit idea be improved so it will be more meaningful and therefore more helpful to management?

## CASE PROBLEMS

### National Products Co.

There are sixteen separate divisions of the National Products Co., each having its own headquarters and officers. The divisions are not separate in a corporate sense but are divisions of National Products operating under a plan of decentralization—both in physical location and in management. Each division manufactures a line of products unrelated to the others. For example, one makes oil drilling equipment, another makes special metals, and a third has a line of chemicals. Total employment of National Products is over 9000, but there are no more than 225 employees at any one location, since each division has from 2 to 8 manufacturing plants. The small size of manufacturing plants occurred largely through the parent company's acquisition of small companies over the years.

The general offices of National Products are located in New York City and in addition to corporate offices comprise a number of staff departments, which act strictly in an advisory capacity to the divisions.

For many years the president of National Products has been concerned about the problem of developing and maintaining adequate managerial personnel throughout the company. It has been common practice to transfer managerial personnel from one division to another, but the president could never be certain that the proper choices were being made.

Recently the president hired Mr. Lewis Gilbert to study the problem and gave him the title of assistant to the president. Mr. Gilbert had worked a number of years for a management consulting firm and had specialized in management appraisal problems. The president made clear to Mr. Gilbert that his first assignment was to develop some methods for appraising the worth of persons in managerial positions from foreman on up. Later on Mr. Gilbert was to study the problem of identifying people with managerial potential and to recommend management development programs.

*Questions:*

1. What are some approaches Mr. Gilbert might take to handle his first assignment?

2. Can the worth of a division president be determined simply by how much profit the division makes in a year? In ten years?

3. How can Mr. Gilbert expect to identify people with managerial potential?

4. What would constitute a good management development program for National Products?

### Stanley Holt Corporation

The following is an excerpt from a letter received by Mr. Edward Cole, president of the Stanley Holt Corporation, a few days after the company's annual report had been mailed to stockholders:

". . . On page six of the report you mention the responsibilities the company has to four groups: stockholders, customers, employees, and the community. You go on to explain how the company is meeting these responsibilities. The implication of your description is that the company's responsibilities to the four groups are *equal* or that if one group suffers, all must suffer.

"If this is the correct interpretation of the words in the report, I wish to express my disagreement with the philosophy. I feel that the company has a prime responsibility to stockholders and that this responsibility must come *first*—in all cases. I am quite satisfied with the company's dividend performance in the past, but I am afraid that if the above philosophy is carried out, the excellent dividend record may soon come to a halt."

Signed, Edward Johnson

Mr. Cole checked the stockholder records and found that Mr. Johnson owned less than 1% of the stock of the company. There was no indication that he was one of the stockholder hecklers who frequently write companies.

*Questions:*

1. Formulate a letter in reply to Mr. Johnson's letter, expressing a sound philosophy of management responsibilities.

2. Should company responsibilities be on an "equal" or "unequal" basis?

3. What changes would you make in your reply if Mr. Johnson owned 62% of the stock of the company?

APPENDIX A

# Interest Tables[1]

[1]The Tables in this Appendix have been reproduced by permission from H. G. Thuesen and W. J. Fabrycky, *Engineering Economy* (Englewood Cliffs, N.J.: Prentice-Hall, Inc., 1964), pp. 492–498.

**Table A-1.** 4% interest factors for annual compounding interest.

| n | Single Payment | | Equal-Payment Series | | | |
|---|---|---|---|---|---|---|
| | Compound-amount factor | Present-worth factor | Compound-amount factor | Sinking-fund factor | Present-worth factor | Capital-recovery factor |
| | SP *i-n* ( ) | PS *i-n* ( ) | SR *i-n* ( ) | RS *i-n* ( ) | PR *i-n* ( ) | RP *i-n* ( ) |
| 1 | 1.040 | 0.96154 | 1.000 | 1.00000 | 0.96154 | 1.04000 |
| 2 | 1.082 | 0.92456 | 2.040 | 0.49020 | 1.88609 | 0.53020 |
| 3 | 1.125 | 0.88900 | 3.122 | 0.32035 | 2.77509 | 0.36035 |
| 4 | 1.170 | 0.85480 | 4.246 | 0.23549 | 3.62990 | 0.27549 |
| 5 | 1.217 | 0.82193 | 5.416 | 0.18463 | 4.45182 | 0.22463 |
| 6 | 1.265 | 0.79031 | 6.633 | 0.15076 | 5.24214 | 0.19076 |
| 7 | 1.316 | 0.75992 | 7.898 | 0.12661 | 6.00205 | 0.16661 |
| 8 | 1.369 | 0.73069 | 9.214 | 0.10853 | 6.73275 | 0.14853 |
| 9 | 1.423 | 0.70259 | 10.583 | 0.09449 | 7.43533 | 0.13449 |
| 10 | 1.480 | 0.67556 | 12.006 | 0.08329 | 8.11090 | 0.12329 |
| 11 | 1.539 | 0.64958 | 13.486 | 0.07415 | 8.76048 | 0.11415 |
| 12 | 1.601 | 0.62460 | 15.026 | 0.06655 | 9.38507 | 0.10655 |
| 13 | 1.665 | 0.60057 | 16.627 | 0.06014 | 9.98565 | 0.10014 |
| 14 | 1.732 | 0.57748 | 18.292 | 0.05467 | 10.56312 | 0.09467 |
| 15 | 1.801 | 0.55526 | 20.024 | 0.04994 | 11.11839 | 0.08994 |
| 16 | 1.873 | 0.53391 | 21.825 | 0.04582 | 11.65230 | 0.08582 |
| 17 | 1.948 | 0.51337 | 23.698 | 0.04220 | 12.16567 | 0.08220 |
| 18 | 2.026 | 0.49363 | 25.645 | 0.03899 | 12.65930 | 0.07899 |
| 19 | 2.107 | 0.47464 | 27.671 | 0.03614 | 13.13394 | 0.07614 |
| 20 | 2.191 | 0.45639 | 29.778 | 0.03358 | 13.59033 | 0.07358 |
| 21 | 2.279 | 0.43883 | 31.969 | 0.03128 | 14.02916 | 0.07128 |
| 22 | 2.370 | 0.42196 | 34.248 | 0.02920 | 14.45112 | 0.06920 |
| 23 | 2.465 | 0.40573 | 36.618 | 0.02731 | 14.85684 | 0.06731 |
| 24 | 2.563 | 0.39012 | 39.083 | 0.02559 | 15.24696 | 0.06559 |
| 25 | 2.666 | 0.37512 | 41.646 | 0.02401 | 15.62208 | 0.06401 |
| 26 | 2.772 | 0.36069 | 44.312 | 0.02257 | 15.98277 | 0.06257 |
| 27 | 2.883 | 0.34682 | 47.084 | 0.02124 | 16.32959 | 0.06124 |
| 28 | 2.999 | 0.33348 | 49.968 | 0.02001 | 16.66306 | 0.06001 |
| 29 | 3.119 | 0.32065 | 52.966 | 0.01888 | 16.98372 | 0.05888 |
| 30 | 3.243 | 0.30832 | 56.085 | 0.01783 | 17.29203 | 0.05783 |
| 35 | 3.946 | 0.25342 | 73.652 | 0.01358 | 18.66461 | 0.05358 |
| 40 | 4.801 | 0.20829 | 95.026 | 0.01052 | 19.79277 | 0.05052 |
| 45 | 5.841 | 0.17120 | 121.029 | 0.00826 | 20.72004 | 0.04826 |
| 50 | 7.107 | 0.14071 | 152.667 | 0.00655 | 21.48218 | 0.04655 |
| 55 | 8.646 | 0.11566 | 191.159 | 0.00523 | 22.10861 | 0.04523 |
| 60 | 10.520 | 0.09506 | 237.991 | 0.00420 | 22.62349 | 0.04420 |
| 70 | 15.572 | 0.06422 | 364.291 | 0.00275 | 23.39452 | 0.04275 |
| 80 | 23.050 | 0.04338 | 551.245 | 0.00181 | 23.91539 | 0.04181 |
| 90 | 34.119 | 0.02931 | 827.984 | 0.00121 | 24.26728 | 0.04121 |
| 100 | 50.505 | 0.01980 | 1237.624 | 0.00081 | 24.50500 | 0.04081 |

**Table A-2.** 5% interest factors for annual compounding interest.

| $n$ | Single Payment | | Equal-Payment Series | | | |
|---|---|---|---|---|---|---|
| | Compound-amount factor | Present-worth factor | Compound-amount factor | Sinking-fund factor | Present-worth factor | Capital-recovery factor |
| | SP $i$-$n$ ( ) | PS $i$-$n$ ( ) | SR $i$-$n$ ( ) | RS $i$-$n$ ( ) | PR $i$-$n$ ( ) | RP $i$-$n$ ( ) |
| 1 | 1.050 | 0.95238 | 1.000 | 1.00000 | 0.95238 | 1.05000 |
| 2 | 1.103 | 0.90703 | 2.050 | 0.48780 | 1.85941 | 0.53780 |
| 3 | 1.158 | 0.86384 | 3.153 | 0.31721 | 2.72325 | 0.36721 |
| 4 | 1.216 | 0.82270 | 4.310 | 0.23201 | 3.54595 | 0.28201 |
| 5 | 1.276 | 0.78353 | 5.526 | 0.18097 | 4.32948 | 0.23097 |
| 6 | 1.340 | 0.74622 | 6.802 | 0.14702 | 5.07569 | 0.19702 |
| 7 | 1.407 | 0.71068 | 8.142 | 0.12282 | 5.78637 | 0.17282 |
| 8 | 1.477 | 0.67684 | 9.549 | 0.10742 | 6.46321 | 0.15472 |
| 9 | 1.551 | 0.64461 | 11.027 | 0.09069 | 7.10782 | 0.14069 |
| 10 | 1.629 | 0.61391 | 12.578 | 0.07950 | 7.72174 | 0.12950 |
| 11 | 1.710 | 0.58468 | 14.207 | 0.07039 | 8.30641 | 0.12039 |
| 12 | 1.796 | 0.55684 | 15.917 | 0.06283 | 8.86325 | 0.11283 |
| 13 | 1.886 | 0.53032 | 17.713 | 0.05646 | 9.39357 | 0.10646 |
| 14 | 1.980 | 0.50507 | 19.599 | 0.05102 | 9.89864 | 0.10102 |
| 15 | 2.079 | 0.48102 | 21.579 | 0.04634 | 10.37966 | 0.09634 |
| 16 | 2.183 | 0.45811 | 23.657 | 0.04227 | 10.83777 | 0.09227 |
| 17 | 2.292 | 0.43630 | 25.840 | 0.03870 | 11.27407 | 0.08870 |
| 18 | 2.407 | 0.41552 | 28.132 | 0.03555 | 11.68959 | 0.08555 |
| 19 | 2.527 | 0.39573 | 30.539 | 0.03275 | 12.08532 | 0.08275 |
| 20 | 2.653 | 0.37689 | 33.066 | 0.03024 | 12.46221 | 0.08024 |
| 21 | 2.786 | 0.35894 | 35.719 | 0.02800 | 12.82115 | 0.07800 |
| 22 | 2.925 | 0.34185 | 38.505 | 0.02597 | 13.16300 | 0.07597 |
| 23 | 3.072 | 0.32557 | 41.430 | 0.02414 | 13.48857 | 0.07414 |
| 24 | 3.225 | 0.31007 | 44.502 | 0.02247 | 13.79864 | 0.07247 |
| 25 | 3.386 | 0.29530 | 47.727 | 0.02095 | 14.09394 | 0.07095 |
| 26 | 3.556 | 0.28124 | 51.113 | 0.01956 | 14.37519 | 0.06956 |
| 27 | 3.733 | 0.26785 | 54.669 | 0.01829 | 14.64303 | 0.06829 |
| 28 | 3.920 | 0.25509 | 58.403 | 0.01712 | 14.89813 | 0.06712 |
| 29 | 4.116 | 0.24295 | 62.323 | 0.01605 | 15.14107 | 0.06605 |
| 30 | 4.322 | 0.23138 | 66.439 | 0.01505 | 15.37245 | 0.06505 |
| 35 | 5.516 | 0.18129 | 90.320 | 0.01107 | 16.37419 | 0.06107 |
| 40 | 7.040 | 0.14205 | 120.800 | 0.00828 | 17.15909 | 0.05828 |
| 45 | 8.985 | 0.11130 | 159.700 | 0.00626 | 17.77407 | 0.05626 |
| 50 | 11.467 | 0.08720 | 209.348 | 0.00478 | 18.25593 | 0.05478 |
| 55 | 14.636 | 0.06833 | 272.713 | 0.00367 | 18.63347 | 0.05367 |
| 60 | 18.679 | 0.05354 | 353.584 | 0.00283 | 18.92929 | 0.05283 |
| 70 | 30.426 | 0.03287 | 588.529 | 0.00170 | 19.34268 | 0.05170 |
| 80 | 49.561 | 0.02018 | 971.229 | 0.00103 | 19.59646 | 0.05103 |
| 90 | 80.730 | 0.01239 | 1594.608 | 0.00063 | 19.75226 | 0.05063 |
| 100 | 131.501 | 0.00760 | 2610.026 | 0.00038 | 19.84791 | 0.05038 |

**Table A-3.** 6% interest factors for annual compounding interest.

| | Single Payment | | Equal-Payment Series | | | |
|---|---|---|---|---|---|---|
| | Compound-amount factor | Present-worth factor | Compound-amount factor | Sinking-fund factor | Present-worth factor | Capital-recovery factor |
| $n$ | SP $i$-$n$ ( ) | PS $i$-$n$ ( ) | SR $i$-$n$ ( ) | RS $i$-$n$ ( ) | PR $i$-$n$ ( ) | RP $i$-$n$ ( ) |
| 1 | 1.060 | 0.94340 | 1.000 | 1.00000 | 0.94340 | 1.06000 |
| 2 | 1.124 | 0.89000 | 2.060 | 0.48544 | 1.83339 | 0.54544 |
| 3 | 1.191 | 0.83962 | 3.184 | 0.31411 | 2.67301 | 0.37411 |
| 4 | 1.262 | 0.79209 | 4.375 | 0.22859 | 3.46510 | 0.28859 |
| 5 | 1.338 | 0.74726 | 5.637 | 0.17740 | 4.21236 | 0.23740 |
| 6 | 1.419 | 0.70496 | 6.975 | 0.14336 | 4.91732 | 0.20336 |
| 7 | 1.504 | 0.66506 | 8.394 | 0.11914 | 5.58238 | 0.17914 |
| 8 | 1.594 | 0.62741 | 9.897 | 0.10104 | 6.20979 | 0.16104 |
| 9 | 1.689 | 0.59190 | 11.491 | 0.08702 | 6.80169 | 0.14702 |
| 10 | 1.791 | 0.55839 | 13.181 | 0.07587 | 7.36009 | 0.13587 |
| 11 | 1.898 | 0.52679 | 14.972 | 0.06679 | 7.88687 | 0.12679 |
| 12 | 2.012 | 0.49697 | 16.870 | 0.05928 | 8.38384 | 0.11928 |
| 13 | 2.133 | 0.46884 | 18.882 | 0.05296 | 8.85268 | 0.11296 |
| 14 | 2.261 | 0.44230 | 21.015 | 0.04758 | 9.29498 | 0.10758 |
| 15 | 2.397 | 0.41727 | 23.276 | 0.04296 | 9.71225 | 0.10296 |
| 16 | 2.540 | 0.39365 | 25.673 | 0.03895 | 10.10590 | 0.09895 |
| 17 | 2.693 | 0.37136 | 28.213 | 0.03544 | 10.47726 | 0.09544 |
| 18 | 2.854 | 0.35034 | 30.906 | 0.03236 | 10.82760 | 0.09236 |
| 19 | 3.026 | 0.33051 | 33.760 | 0.02962 | 11.15812 | 0.08962 |
| 20 | 3.207 | 0.31180 | 36.786 | 0.02718 | 11.46992 | 0.08718 |
| 21 | 3.400 | 0.29416 | 39.993 | 0.02500 | 11.76408 | 0.08500 |
| 22 | 3.604 | 0.27751 | 43.392 | 0.02305 | 12.04158 | 0.08305 |
| 23 | 3.820 | 0.26180 | 46.996 | 0.02128 | 12.30338 | 0.08128 |
| 24 | 4.049 | 0.24698 | 50.816 | 0.01968 | 12.55036 | 0.07968 |
| 25 | 4.292 | 0.23300 | 54.865 | 0.01823 | 12.78336 | 0.07823 |
| 26 | 4.549 | 0.21981 | 59.156 | 0.01690 | 13.00317 | 0.07690 |
| 27 | 4.822 | 0.20737 | 63.706 | 0.01570 | 13.21053 | 0.07570 |
| 28 | 5.112 | 0.19563 | 68.528 | 0.01459 | 13.40616 | 0.07459 |
| 29 | 5.418 | 0.18456 | 73.640 | 0.01358 | 13.59072 | 0.07358 |
| 30 | 5.743 | 0.17411 | 79.058 | 0.01265 | 13.76483 | 0.07265 |
| 35 | 7.686 | 0.13011 | 111.435 | 0.00897 | 14.49825 | 0.06897 |
| 40 | 10.286 | 0.09722 | 154.762 | 0.00646 | 15.04630 | 0.06646 |
| 45 | 13.765 | 0.07265 | 212.744 | 0.00470 | 15.45583 | 0.06470 |
| 50 | 18.420 | 0.05429 | 290.336 | 0.00344 | 15.76186 | 0.06344 |
| 55 | 24.650 | 0.04057 | 394.172 | 0.00254 | 15.99054 | 0.06254 |
| 60 | 32.988 | 0.03031 | 533.128 | 0.00188 | 16.16143 | 0.06188 |
| 70 | 59.076 | 0.01693 | 967.932 | 0.00103 | 16.38454 | 0.06103 |
| 80 | 105.796 | 0.00945 | 1746.600 | 0.00057 | 16.50913 | 0.06057 |
| 90 | 189.465 | 0.00528 | 3141.075 | 0.00032 | 16.57870 | 0.06032 |
| 100 | 339.302 | 0.00295 | 5638.369 | 0.00018 | 16.61755 | 0.06018 |

**548**

**Table A-4.** 10% interest factors for annual compounding interest.

| n | Single Payment | | Equal-Payment Series | | | |
|---|---|---|---|---|---|---|
| | Compound-amount factor | Present-worth factor | Compound-amount factor | Sinking-fund factor | Present-worth factor | Capital-recovery factor |
| | SP $i$-$n$ ( ) | PS $i$-$n$ ( ) | SR $i$-$n$ ( ) | RS $i$-$n$ ( ) | PR $i$-$n$ ( ) | RP $i$-$n$ ( ) |
| 1 | 1.100 | 0.90909 | 1.000 | 1.00000 | 0.90909 | 1.10000 |
| 2 | 1.210 | 0.82645 | 2.100 | 0.47619 | 1.73554 | 0.57619 |
| 3 | 1.331 | 0.75131 | 3.310 | 0.30211 | 2.48685 | 0.40211 |
| 4 | 1.464 | 0.68301 | 4.641 | 0.21547 | 3.16987 | 0.31547 |
| 5 | 1.611 | 0.62092 | 6.105 | 0.16380 | 3.79079 | 0.26380 |
| 6 | 1.772 | 0.56447 | 7.716 | 0.12961 | 4.35526 | 0.22961 |
| 7 | 1.949 | 0.51316 | 9.487 | 0.10541 | 4.86842 | 0.20541 |
| 8 | 2.144 | 0.46651 | 11.436 | 0.08744 | 5.33493 | 0.18744 |
| 9 | 2.358 | 0.42410 | 13.579 | 0.07364 | 5.75902 | 0.17364 |
| 10 | 2.594 | 0.38554 | 15.937 | 0.06275 | 6.14457 | 0.16275 |
| 11 | 2.853 | 0.35049 | 18.531 | 0.05396 | 6.49506 | 0.15396 |
| 12 | 3.138 | 0.31863 | 21.384 | 0.04676 | 6.81369 | 0.14676 |
| 13 | 3.452 | 0.28966 | 24.523 | 0.04078 | 7.10336 | 0.14078 |
| 14 | 3.797 | 0.26333 | 27.975 | 0.03575 | 7.36669 | 0.13575 |
| 15 | 4.177 | 0.23939 | 31.772 | 0.03147 | 7.60608 | 0.13147 |
| 16 | 4.595 | 0.21763 | 35.950 | 0.02782 | 7.82371 | 0.12782 |
| 17 | 5.054 | 0.19784 | 40.545 | 0.02466 | 8.02155 | 0.12466 |
| 18 | 5.560 | 0.17986 | 45.599 | 0.02193 | 8.20141 | 0.12193 |
| 19 | 6.116 | 0.16351 | 51.159 | 0.01955 | 8.36492 | 0.11955 |
| 20 | 6.727 | 0.14864 | 57.275 | 0.01746 | 8.51356 | 0.11746 |
| 21 | 7.400 | 0.13513 | 64.002 | 0.01562 | 8.64869 | 0.11562 |
| 22 | 8.140 | 0.12285 | 71.403 | 0.01401 | 8.77154 | 0.11401 |
| 23 | 8.954 | 0.11168 | 79.543 | 0.01257 | 8.88322 | 0.11257 |
| 24 | 9.850 | 0.10153 | 88.497 | 0.01130 | 8.98474 | 0.11130 |
| 25 | 10.835 | 0.09230 | 98.347 | 0.01017 | 9.07704 | 0.11017 |
| 26 | 11.918 | 0.08391 | 109.182 | 0.00916 | 9.16095 | 0.10916 |
| 27 | 13.110 | 0.07628 | 121.100 | 0.00826 | 9.23722 | 0.10826 |
| 28 | 14.421 | 0.06934 | 134.210 | 0.00745 | 9.30657 | 0.10745 |
| 29 | 15.863 | 0.06304 | 148.631 | 0.00673 | 9.36961 | 0.10673 |
| 30 | 17.449 | 0.05731 | 164.494 | 0.00608 | 9.42691 | 0.10608 |
| 35 | 28.102 | 0.03558 | 271.024 | 0.00369 | 9.64416 | 0.10369 |
| 40 | 45.259 | 0.02209 | 442.593 | 0.00226 | 9.77905 | 0.10226 |
| 45 | 72.890 | 0.01372 | 718.905 | 0.00139 | 9.86281 | 0.10139 |
| 50 | 117.391 | 0.00852 | 1163.908 | 0.00086 | 9.91481 | 0.10086 |
| 55 | 189.059 | 0.00529 | 1880.591 | 0.00053 | 9.94711 | 0.10053 |
| 60 | 304.482 | 0.00328 | 3034.816 | 0.00033 | 9.96716 | 0.10033 |
| 70 | 789.747 | 0.00127 | 7887.469 | 0.00013 | 9.98734 | 0.10013 |
| 80 | 2048.400 | 0.00049 | 20474.000 | 0.00005 | 9.99512 | 0.10005 |
| 90 | 5313.022 | 0.00019 | 53120.222 | 0.00002 | 9.99812 | 0.10002 |
| 100 | 13780.611 | 0.00007 | 137796.110 | 0.00001 | 9.99927 | 0.10001 |

# Factors for
# Computing Control
# Chart Lines

## Table A-5. Factors for computing control line charts [1]

| Number of observations in sample, $n$ | Chart for averages | | | Chart for standard deviations | | | | | | Chart for ranges | | | | | | |
| | Factors for control limits | | | Factors for central line | | Factors for control limits | | | | Factors for central line | | Factors for control limits | | | | |
| | $A$ | $A_1$ | $A_2$ | $c_2$ | $1/c_2$ | $B_1$ | $B_2$ | $B_3$ | $B_4$ | $d_2$ | $1/d_2$ | $d_3$ | $D_1$ | $D_2$ | $D_3$ | $D_4$ |
|---|---|---|---|---|---|---|---|---|---|---|---|---|---|---|---|---|
| 2 | 2.121 | 3.760 | 1.880 | 0.5642 | 1.7725 | 0 | 1.843 | 0 | 3.267 | 1.128 | 0.8865 | 0.853 | 0 | 3.686 | 0 | 3.267 |
| 3 | 1.732 | 2.394 | 1.023 | 0.7236 | 1.3820 | 0 | 1.858 | 0 | 2.568 | 1.693 | 0.5907 | 0.888 | 0 | 4.358 | 0 | 2.575 |
| 4 | 1.500 | 1.880 | 0.729 | 0.7979 | 1.2533 | 0 | 1.808 | 0 | 2.266 | 2.059 | 0.4857 | 0.880 | 0 | 4.698 | 0 | 2.282 |
| 5 | 1.342 | 1.596 | 0.577 | 0.8407 | 1.1894 | 0 | 1.756 | 0 | 2.089 | 2.326 | 0.4299 | 0.864 | 0 | 4.918 | 0 | 2.115 |
| 6 | 1.225 | 1.410 | 0.483 | 0.8686 | 1.1512 | 0.026 | 1.711 | 0.030 | 1.970 | 2.534 | 0.3946 | 0.848 | 0 | 5.078 | 0 | 2.004 |
| 7 | 1.134 | 1.277 | 0.419 | 0.8882 | 1.1259 | 0.105 | 1.672 | 0.118 | 1.882 | 2.704 | 0.3698 | 0.833 | 0.205 | 5.203 | 0.076 | 1.924 |
| 8 | 1.061 | 1.175 | 0.373 | 0.9027 | 1.1078 | 0.167 | 1.638 | 0.185 | 1.815 | 2.847 | 0.3512 | 0.820 | 0.387 | 5.307 | 0.136 | 1.864 |
| 9 | 1.000 | 1.094 | 0.337 | 0.9139 | 1.0942 | 0.219 | 1.609 | 0.239 | 1.761 | 2.970 | 0.3367 | 0.808 | 0.546 | 5.394 | 0.184 | 1.816 |
| 10 | 0.949 | 1.028 | 0.308 | 0.9227 | 1.0837 | 0.262 | 1.584 | 0.284 | 1.716 | 3.078 | 0.3249 | 0.797 | 0.687 | 5.469 | 0.223 | 1.777 |
| 11 | 0.905 | 0.973 | 0.285 | 0.9300 | 1.0753 | 0.299 | 1.561 | 0.321 | 1.679 | 3.173 | 0.3152 | 0.787 | 0.812 | 5.534 | 0.256 | 1.744 |
| 12 | 0.866 | 0.925 | 0.266 | 0.9359 | 1.0684 | 0.331 | 1.541 | 0.354 | 1.646 | 3.258 | 0.3069 | 0.778 | 0.924 | 5.592 | 0.284 | 1.716 |
| 13 | 0.832 | 0.884 | 0.249 | 0.9410 | 1.0627 | 0.359 | 1.523 | 0.382 | 1.618 | 3.336 | 0.2998 | 0.770 | 1.026 | 5.646 | 0.308 | 1.692 |
| 14 | 0.802 | 0.848 | 0.235 | 0.9453 | 1.0579 | 0.384 | 1.507 | 0.406 | 1.594 | 3.407 | 0.2935 | 0.762 | 1.121 | 5.693 | 0.329 | 1.671 |
| 15 | 0.775 | 0.816 | 0.223 | 0.9490 | 1.0537 | 0.406 | 1.492 | 0.428 | 1.572 | 3.472 | 0.2880 | 0.755 | 1.207 | 5.737 | 0.348 | 1.652 |
| 16 | 0.750 | 0.788 | 0.212 | 0.9523 | 1.0501 | 0.427 | 1.478 | 0.448 | 1.552 | 3.532 | 0.2831 | 0.749 | 1.285 | 5.779 | 0.364 | 1.636 |
| 17 | 0.728 | 0.762 | 0.203 | 0.9551 | 1.0470 | 0.445 | 1.465 | 0.466 | 1.534 | 3.588 | 0.2787 | 0.743 | 1.359 | 5.817 | 0.379 | 1.621 |
| 18 | 0.707 | 0.738 | 0.194 | 0.9576 | 1.0442 | 0.461 | 1.454 | 0.482 | 1.518 | 3.640 | 0.2747 | 0.738 | 1.426 | 5.854 | 0.392 | 1.608 |
| 19 | 0.688 | 0.717 | 0.187 | 0.9599 | 1.0418 | 0.477 | 1.443 | 0.497 | 1.503 | 3.689 | 0.2711 | 0.733 | 1.490 | 5.888 | 0.404 | 1.596 |
| 20 | 0.671 | 0.697 | 0.180 | 0.9619 | 1.0396 | 0.491 | 1.433 | 0.510 | 1.490 | 3.735 | 0.2677 | 0.729 | 1.548 | 5.922 | 0.414 | 1.586 |
| 21 | 0.655 | 0.679 | 0.173 | 0.9638 | 1.0376 | 0.504 | 1.424 | 0.523 | 1.477 | 3.778 | 0.2647 | 0.724 | 1.606 | 5.950 | 0.425 | 1.575 |
| 22 | 0.640 | 0.662 | 0.167 | 0.9655 | 1.0358 | 0.516 | 1.415 | 0.534 | 1.466 | 3.819 | 0.2618 | 0.720 | 1.659 | 5.979 | 0.434 | 1.566 |
| 23 | 0.626 | 0.647 | 0.162 | 0.9670 | 1.0342 | 0.527 | 1.407 | 0.545 | 1.455 | 3.858 | 0.2592 | 0.716 | 1.710 | 6.006 | 0.443 | 1.557 |
| 24 | 0.612 | 0.632 | 0.157 | 0.9684 | 1.0327 | 0.538 | 1.399 | 0.555 | 1.445 | 3.895 | 0.2567 | 0.712 | 1.759 | 6.031 | 0.452 | 1.548 |
| 25 | 0.600 | 0.619 | 0.153 | 0.9696 | 1.0313 | 0.548 | 1.392 | 0.565 | 1.435 | 3.931 | 0.2544 | 0.709 | 1.804 | 6.058 | 0.459 | 1.541 |
| Over 25 | $\dfrac{3}{\sqrt{n}}$ | $\dfrac{3}{\sqrt{n}}$ | ...... | ...... | ...... | * | ** | * | ** | ...... | ...... | ...... | ...... | ...... | ...... | ...... |

$$*1 - \frac{3}{\sqrt{2n}} \qquad **1 + \frac{3}{\sqrt{2n}}$$

[1] This Table has been reproduced by permission from Albert H. Bowker and Gerald J. Lieberman, *Engineering Statistics* (Englewood Cliffs, N.J.: Prentice-Hall, Inc., 1959), p.382.

**552**

# Index